IFIP Advances in Information and Communication Technology 572

IFIP – The International Federation for Information Processing

IFIP was founded in 1960 under the auspices of UNESCO, following the first World Computer Congress held in Paris the previous year. A federation for societies working in information processing, IFIP's aim is two-fold: to support information processing in the countries of its members and to encourage technology transfer to developing nations. As its mission statement clearly states:

IFIP is the global non-profit federation of societies of ICT professionals that aims at achieving a worldwide professional and socially responsible development and application of information and communication technologies.

IFIP is a non-profit-making organization, run almost solely by 2500 volunteers. It operates through a number of technical committees and working groups, which organize events and publications. IFIP's events range from large international open conferences to working conferences and local seminars.

The flagship event is the IFIP World Computer Congress, at which both invited and contributed papers are presented. Contributed papers are rigorously refereed and the rejection rate is high.

As with the Congress, participation in the open conferences is open to all and papers may be invited or submitted. Again, submitted papers are stringently refereed.

The working conferences are structured differently. They are usually run by a working group and attendance is generally smaller and occasionally by invitation only. Their purpose is to create an atmosphere conducive to innovation and development. Refereeing is also rigorous and papers are subjected to extensive group discussion.

Publications arising from IFIP events vary. The papers presented at the IFIP World Computer Congress and at open conferences are published as conference proceedings, while the results of the working conferences are often published as collections of selected and edited papers.

IFIP distinguishes three types of institutional membership: Country Representative Members, Members at Large, and Associate Members. The type of organization that can apply for membership is a wide variety and includes national or international societies of individual computer scientists/ICT professionals, associations or federations of such societies, government institutions/government related organizations, national or international research institutes or consortia, universities, academies of sciences, companies, national or international associations or federations of companies.

More information about this series at http://www.springer.com/series/6102

Rachid Benmoussa · Roland De Guio ·
Sébastien Dubois · Sebastian Koziołek (Eds.)

New Opportunities for Innovation Breakthroughs for Developing Countries and Emerging Economies

19th International TRIZ Future Conference, TFC 2019
Marrakesh, Morocco, October 9–11, 2019
Proceedings

Springer

Editors
Rachid Benmoussa
Cadi Ayyad University
Marrakesh, Morocco

Sébastien Dubois
INSA Strasbourg
Strasbourg, France

Roland De Guio
INSA Strasbourg
Strasbourg, France

Sebastian Koziołek
Wrocław University of Technology
Wrocław, Poland

ISSN 1868-4238 ISSN 1868-422X (electronic)
IFIP Advances in Information and Communication Technology
ISBN 978-3-030-32499-5 ISBN 978-3-030-32497-1 (eBook)
https://doi.org/10.1007/978-3-030-32497-1

This Springer imprint is published by the registered company Springer Nature Switzerland AG
The registered company address is: Gewerbestrasse 11, 6330 Cham, Switzerland

Preface

The high performance and innovation requirements resulting from the emerging countries striving to modernize the industrial and services sector, give rise to a deep impact on research and development activities being implemented. These requirements push companies to adopt customized tools to be attentive to market demand and to optimally mobilize limited material, technical, and human resources. It also requires reviewing the scientific methods solving invention problems as well as the innovation management procedures used by companies and organizations as part of their research and development process.

TRIZ is a theory of inventive problem solving that can indeed support companies to improve their research and development process. TRIZ was developed by Genrich Altshuller as a problem-solving, analysis, and forecasting theory derived from the study of patterns of invention in the patent literature. TRIZ was developed to assist engineers in systematically solving product design problems and develop next-generation technologies and products with less risk. Altshuller stated that TRIZ can be used to minimize energy requirements as well as complexity of engineering products. TRIZ is an organized theory for problem solving which can be applied to different areas.

ETRIA (European TRIZ Association) has been working for two decades towards the advancement of TRIZ and its impregnation in academic, scientific, educational, and industrial circles. Each year, ETRIA organizes, through one of its members, an annual conference in a different city and country – TRIZ Future Conference (TFC). TFC aims globally to promote TRIZ knowledge, tools, and methods worldwide. It brings together industrials and academics to share experiences, achievements, and progress on the subject of how to use and develop TRIZ.

The 19th International TRIZ Future Conference (TFC 2019) took place at ENSA Marrakesh, Cadi Ayyad University, Morocco, during October 9–11, 2019, under the theme 'New opportunities for innovation breakthroughs for developing countries and emerging economies.' The TFC conference series encourages research and feedback that deals with TRIZ theory and its applications in all areas. It also encourages professionals who are unfamiliar with TRIZ to submit their experiences with research development as well as the difficulties and obstacles they face with regards to innovation. TFC 2019 placed special emphasis on TRIZ integration into recent research topics that present new opportunities for innovation breakthroughs for developing countries and emerging economies, such as but not limited to:

- Industrial R&D processes and innovation best practices
- Knowledge based engineering and computer-aided invention with TRIZ
- Creativity in Science, Entrepreneurship, Industry, and Education
- Opportunities and challenges of digitalization for innovation progress
- Integration of TRIZ Methodology into Innovation Design Process

This book constitues the proceedings of TFC 2019. It contains 41 papers divided into 7 themes. The first theme is dedicated to the 'Improvement of TRIZ theory, methods, and tools,' and includes seven articles proposing enhancements to TRIZ dealing with complexity, effectiveness, ideation, ontology, and patent integration. The second theme includes five papers dedicated to contributions that link TRIZ to other Innovation and R&D approaches such as frugal innovation, CK theory, FAST method, Lean, additive manufacturing, etc. A third theme is dedicated to TRIZ applications in technical design, an area addressed by authors within the nine papers. These first three themes confort the origin of TRIZ which was initially developed to address technical issues. The following theme leads us towards TRIZ applications in Eco Design, which addresses green issues and is becoming more effective. Therefore, this year's fourth theme includes eight papers and was the second most addressed area. Let us continue with the fifth theme. It is dedicated to associations between TRIZ and software engineering. This theme is composed of four papers that attempt to link TRIZ and the IA through Machine Learning or to use software techniques to help with problem solving in different areas. The sixth theme brings together five papers and addresses TRIZ applications in specific disciplinary fields such as healthcare, marketing, and farming. Finally, a seventh theme leads us to a series of three papers that address TRIZ in teaching, specifically through experimental studies with students.

Rachid Benmoussa
Roland De Guio
Sébastien Dubois
Sebastian Koziołek

Organization

Scientific Committee

Achille Souili	INSA Strasbourg, France
Alex Pinyayev	Technology Leader at Procter & Gamble, USA
Amadou Coulibaly	INSA Strasbourg, France
Amira Essaid	Institut Supérieur de Gestion de Tunis, Tunisia
Bakhturin Dmitri	Independent TRIZ-Specialist, Russia
Claude Gazot	ENSAM Paris, France
Claudia Hentschel	University of Applied Sciences HTW Berlin, Germany
David Oget	INSA Strasbourg, France
Davide Russo	University of Bergamo, Italy
Denis Cavallucci	INSA Strasbourg, France
Don Coates	Altshuller Institute for TRIZ Studies, USA
Fatima Zahra	BEN MOUSSA ENSA Marrakesh, Morocco
Federico Rotini	University of Florence, Italy
Gérard Griffay	ArcelorMittal R&D, France
Hicham Chibane	INSA Strasbourg, France
Horst Naehler	c4pi - Center for Product-Innovation, Germany
Ivana Rasovska	Université de Strasbourg, France
Jean Camille	LCPI, Arts et Métiers, France
Kai Hiltmann	Coburg University of Applied Science, Germany
Kalle Elfvengren	LUT University, Finland
KyeongWon Lee	Polytechnic University, South Korea
Leonid Chechurin	LUT University, Finland
Marc Trela	Product Management Director Bosch, France
Marco de Carvalho	Federal University of Technology - Paraná, Brazil
Nicolas Maranzana	Arts et Métiers ParisTech, France
Oleg Abramov	Algorithm Ltd., Russia
Oleg Feygenson	Samsung Electronics, South Korea
Oualid Kamach	ENSA Tanger, Morocco
Pavel Livotov	Offenburg University, Germany
Pei Zhang	University of Strasbourg, France
Rachid Benmoussa	ENSA Marrakesh, Morocco
Remy Houssin	INSA Strasbourg, France
Roland De Guio	INSA Strasbourg, France
Runhua Tan	Hebei University of Technology, China
Said Elfezazi	ENSA Safi, Morocco
Sébastien Dubois	INSA Strasbourg, France

Contents

TRIZ Applications in Technical Design

TRIZ Applications in Eco Design

TRIZ Improvement: Theory, Methods and Tools

If All You Have Is a Hammer: TRIZ and Complexity

Darrell Mann(✉)

Systematic Innovation Network, Devon, UK
darrell.mann@systematic-innovation.com

Abstract. TRIZ is essentially a distillation of the 'first principles' of problem solving. It was originally developed for complicated technical problem and opportunity situations and, through ARIZ, has been deeply optimized for such roles. Increasingly, however, the world has become dominated by complex, non-technical situations, and in these environments many of the tools, methods and processes of traditional TRIZ become highly inappropriate. Complex situations are characterised by an absence of 'root-causes', have cause-effect relationships that are frequently tenuous, and are vulnerable to highly non-linear 'butterfly effects'. The paper describes the creation and verification of coherent non-linear, iterative divergent/convergent processes that take advantage of the first principle nature of TRIZ, and complement them with essential pieces from other domains of science. In a final section, the paper provides change agents with a menu of heuristics for determining the most appropriate TRIZ and non-TRIZ tools and strategies for any given situation.

Keywords: Complexity · Cynefin · Complexity landscape model · Cybernetics · Law of requisite variety · ARIZ

1 Introduction

Genrich Altshuller starts The Innovation Algorithm [1] with the story of B. S. Egorov's journey to solve the problem of a winding machine to place coils of wire onto a small diameter toroidal transformer. In the story, Egorov is revealed to have already worked on what he thought was a similar problem, designing a machine to place coils onto an inductor for use in telephones. The problem was that the diameter of the toroidal transformer was significantly smaller than that of the telephone inductor coil, and unfortunately the system for 'threading' the wire with a needle, which was okay for the (7 mm+) diameter of the inductor coils was no longer viable at the new smaller (2 mm) diameter. A 'simple' problem had become a 'complicated' one. Had the new toroidal transformer been designed with a 6 mm diameter, he would have been able to simply scale the existing solution to the new diameter. No calculations would have been required, and there was little need for any actual thinking. But because the new diameter was smaller beyond a scaling threshold level, the needle solution would not work any longer. A contradiction had appeared, and as such it had become necessary to partake of some creative thinking. The contradiction needed to be solved. Or – as actually happened – Egorov had a flash of inspiration when he saw an analogous

Published by Springer Nature Switzerland AG 2019
R. Benmoussa et al. (Eds.): TFC 2019, IFIP AICT 572, pp. 3–15, 2019.
https://doi.org/10.1007/978-3-030-32497-1_1

solution in another domain, and was subsequently able to translate that solution into something that worked for the new 2 mm diameter transformer. The 'complicated' problem was successfully solved.

One might imagine that, over the course of time, the need for even smaller diameter coils would emerge. Egorov's new solution would perhaps continue to work down to 0.5 mm. Making a 1 mm coil would be 'simple'. But then another contradiction would emerge, and hence the problem would again become 'complicated'. This sequence of 'simple' scaling solutions followed by periodic arrival of 'complicated' contradiction problems would likely continue for some time. But, importantly, not forever. At some point, when the dimensions get small enough, the physics of the situation change. When – as we are beginning to see in the world of semi-conductor design – the physical dimensions have become so small that designers need to take into account quantum effects, the design challenge can be seen to have crossed another discontinuous problem-type boundary. A 'complicated' problem will, at small enough size scale, turn into a problem that is 'complex'. The point here being that when we cross the complicated-complex boundary, as when we cross the simple-complicated boundary, the method by which we need to tackle the problem makes a non-linear shift. These kinds of simple-to-complicated or complicated-to-complex phase boundary are important from the perspective of the tools and methods that problem solvers need to bring to bear if they are to make meaningful progress.

There are other ways that the toroidal transformer manufacture problem might cross the threshold from complicated into complexity. Traditional TRIZ was very much focused on technical problems. And moreover, the large majority of these technical problems turned out to be complicated. And so traditional TRIZ worked. In today's massively inter-connected world, however, it is increasingly rare that we find ourselves able to 'merely' focus on just the technical problem. The moment, for example, that we have to introduce our boss to the merits of our beautiful new contradiction-solving solution, we find ourselves having to acknowledge that bosses don't always do things for purely technical reasons. If the boss doesn't understand the new solution, there is the likelihood that they will become defensive. If the new solution causes the old solution to become redundant, and it was the boss who designed that old solution, their ego may easily become offended. If the boss is afraid of the next boss up the hierarchy, maybe they don't feel brave enough to argue the case for the new solution. Not to mention the customer, and what they might think about the risks associated with change. Do they trust us to deliver? The point, in any of these scenarios, is that our 'complicated' problem has become 'complex'. As soon as two or more human beings are present in the system, guaranteed it has become complex. People love change, but they hate being changed.

Increase the level of complexity sufficiently and we can easily find ourselves crossing another discontinuous, non-linear threshold. Complex systems, especially those involving humans and human behaviour have the occasional propensity to devolve into 'chaos'. Think of the devastation caused by Hurricane Katrina, or other extreme weather events, where quite clearly the 'recommended' rescue and recovery advice didn't work. When we find ourselves in chaos, it rapidly becomes clear that the usual 'rules' don't apply any more. The best thing we can do is either 'batten down the hatches' or get ourselves out of harm's way. Fortunately, chaos, because of its instability, tends not to last for very long. The hurricane passes. As far as Egorov's toroidal transformer situation is concerned, chaos could appear from a number of directions. The factory could burn down. Or the raw materials suffer a global shortage. Or we find ourselves subject to a public scandal and our main customer decides they don't wish to do business with us anymore.

Ultimately, the point of the discussion is this. A 'simple' problem is different to a 'complicated' one, is different to a 'complex' one, is different to a 'chaotic' one. Each demands a different strategy, methodology and potentially quite different tools if a viable set of solutions is to be delivered. Problem-solvers, in other words, if they are to stand the best chance of being successful, need to know what type of problem they are facing. It is to this identification issue that we now turn our attention.

2 A Complexity Landscape

The field of Complex Adaptive Systems (CAS) is still a relatively new one. Many authors and scientists are still caught in the struggle to find a coherent means of understanding and describing how problem-solvers and organisations might best operate under different complexity conditions. One of the most popular complex system frameworks is 'Cynefin' [2]. This framework divides the world into essentially the same four different types – simple (often labelled, 'obvious' in later iterations of the model), complicated, complex and chaotic – as used in the earlier description of the different variations of the Egorov toroidal transformer problem. As an orientation tool, Cynefin has found an audience mainly due to its elegant simplicity. If someone has never thought about what type of system they are operating within, it provides a ready supply of actionable insight. One of the main things it misses, however, is a means of describing the characteristics not just of a system under investigation, but also the characteristics and context of the surrounding environment within which that system is expected to operate. This shortfall has been addressed in the Complexity Landscape Model (CLM) reproduced in Fig. 1.

More details of this Model can be found in an ongoing series of papers [3, 4] and so only the basics will be reviewed here. Essentially the CLM comprises a 2-dimensional, 4×4 segment graph featuring the four different states of a system being analysed (y-axis) and the four different possible states of its surrounding ('super-system') environment. Importantly, to reflect the Cynefin insight that a 'simple' system can easily find itself tipping directly into a chaotic state, the 'system' axis is sequenced in such a way that these two states are positioned adjacent to one another. A significant aspect of this adjacency is that the world of 'Operational Excellence' has taught managers that the most efficient organisations are the ones in which as much as possible of the work needing to be performed has been standardized. Over-standardization (often referred to as the 'Dodo Effect'), however, means that what was eliminated from a system because it was thought to be 'waste' turns to have not been waste at all, but the resource needed to survive and thrive in turbulent times. When enterprises find themselves operating with a system that has become chaotic, they can be seen to have fallen past the Disintegration Line and into the Collapse Zone. Not surprisingly, this is an area of the Model organisations are well advised to avoid. The second noteworthy area of the

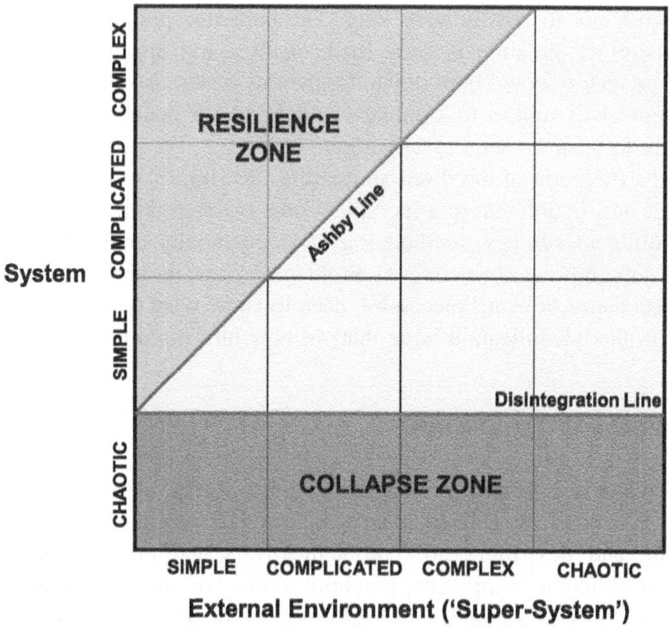

Fig. 1. Complexity Landscape Model (CLM)

Model is the Resilience Zone. The principle defining boundary for this Zone is the Ashby Line. The Ashby Line is named after the founding father of Cybernetics, Ashby [5] and specifically his Law Of Requisite Variety, which in simple terms states that if a system is to survive it must possess a level of achievable 'variety' greater than that of its surroundings: 'only variety can absorb variety'.

The Resilience Zone, then, defines the region of the CLM where Ashby's Law is satisfied. This is the Zone where every enterprise should aspire to operate.

Figure 2 takes the basic CLM and plots a number of the previously described Egorov problem scenarios. It is worth describing these in a little more detail in the context of the Model:

- The knowledge to reliably manufacture telephone inductor coils already existed. Assuming the enterprise is stably manufacturing such designs, the situation can be mapped into the Simple-Simple segment, above the Ashby Line.
- As soon as the market (external environment) demanded a 2 mm diameter transformer, this couldn't be achieved by simply scaling the original solution, but rather required a contradiction to be solved. Prior to Egorov's solution, the problem can be seen to have shifted to the Complicated-Simple domain. In this domain, no solution was possible, and it was only when Egorov's mind started thinking about contradictions and solutions from other domains that a solution became possible. When the solution did finally arrive it was because Egorov had (unknowingly) crossed the Ashby Line and entered the Complicated-Complicated domain: the solution generation strategy was now commensurate with the problem.

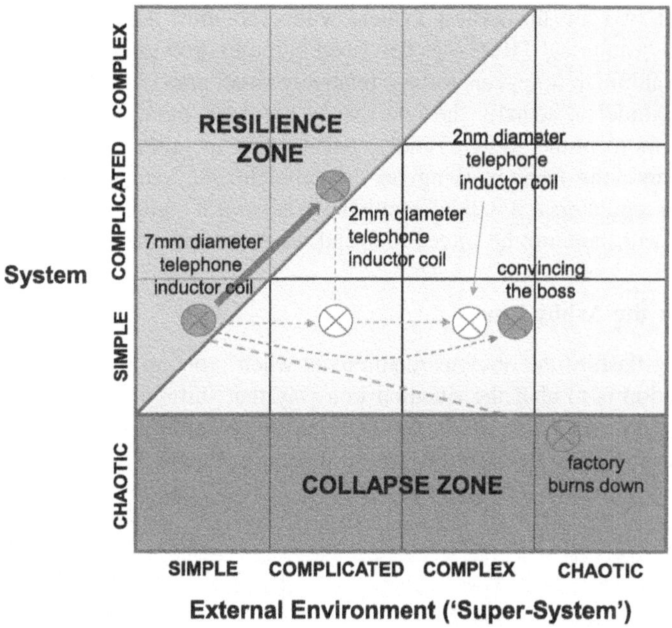

Fig. 2. Egorov problem scenarios mapped onto the Complexity Landscape Model

- If we can imagine further reducing the size of the coil to the level where quantum effects have started to become relevant, then the problem will become a complex one. As with the 'complicated' version of the problem, we will again only be able to solve the problem if we move our problem-solving system up above the Ashby Line and into the Complex-Complex segment of the Model.
- A similar shift takes place if the problem becomes 'convincing the boss' of the merits of our technical solution. And, again, we will only make meaningful progress on this version of the problem if we move into the region of the Complex-Complex segment above the Ashby Line.
- Finally, if the factory burns down, while the fire is burning, everything shifts into the Chaos-Chaos region. There is no hope for 'resilience' at this stage, but rather we must act to put the fire out and, as quickly as possible see what can be done to get back into the Complex super-system column of the Model.

Having now described how it is possible to map 'where' a problem sits on the Complexity Landscape, the next job is to establish the relevant solution approaches for each of the different scenarios. It turns out there are four that require step-change different shifts in approach:

(1) Below the Ashby Line
(2) Above the Ashby Line in the 'Simple' Super-System column
(3) Above the Ashby Line in the 'Complicated' Super-System column
(4) Above the Ashby Line in the 'Complex-Complex' triangle

The first two are the easiest to deal with. The third scenario is the one most amenable to 'traditional TRIZ' – as described in the Egorov toroidal transformer story. The fourth, although it appears to be a relatively small area of the overall Complexity Landscape Model is actually the one that is the most likely to be present. If only because the moment the 'system' under consideration includes humans – whether they be 'customers', the team working on the problem, the senior management of the enterprise or regulators – it will inherently have become a complex problem. This is the domain we will therefore be forced to spend the most time discussing.

2.1 Below the Ashby Line

The blinding-flash-of-the-obvious requirement when problem solvers find themselves in this situation is to alter the situation in a way that shifts it above the Ashby Line. Easy to say, not so easy to do. In no small part because the natural tendencies of the world serve to shift systems in the wrong direction. Figure 3 shows the two biggest 'natural' forces and the direction they act:

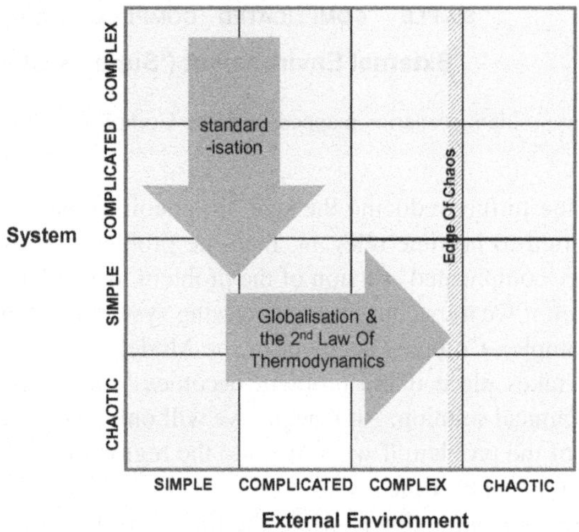

Fig. 3. 'Natural' forces act against resilience

(Whether 'standardisation' counts as a strictly 'natural' force is debatable. What is certain, however, is that ever since F. W. Taylor introduced 'Scientific Management' into the world of work in the early part of the 20th Century, standardisation has been the primary motivation of almost every manager and leader on the planet.)

As far as the Second Law Of Thermodynamics is concerned ('disorder (entropy) increases'), it is perhaps some consolation that it doesn't lead inevitably to 'Chaos'. As discussed earlier, chaos is a very unstable state, and as such, once a chaotic episode settles down, systems return to the Complex domain. More often than not, sitting in a sub-domain known as the 'edge of chaos' [6].

Figure 4 illustrates the human-instigated strategies that can be deployed to counter these natural forces in order to cross the Ashby Line:

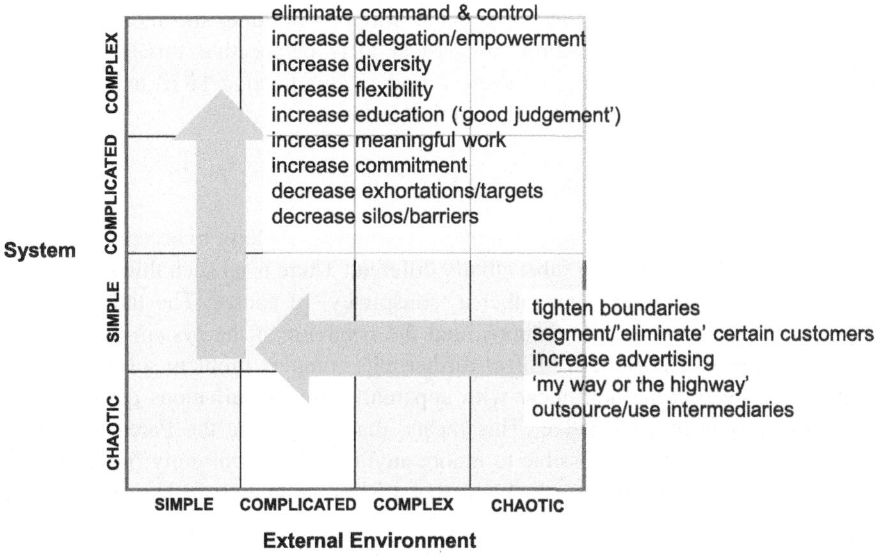

Fig. 4. Management strategies for shifting into the resilience zone

2.2 'Simple' and Above the Ashby Line

This is the place to be when it comes to minimum problem-solving effort. When a problem solver is literally able to replicate an existing known solution, or simply scale from that existing solution, there is no need for any kind of creativity. Or for tools and methods like TRIZ. This is definitely the 'cookie-cutter' segment of the CLM. No innovation required here. So long as the system sits above the Ashby Line, it doesn't particularly matter how far above. Although, having said that, the further above the line it is – if the system is, for example, designed to operate as a 'complicated' or, better yet, a 'complex' entity – then the level of resilience is increased. The idea of an 'Ashby Margin' [7] is something that organisations will shortly be able to objectively measure. The higher the margin, the more resilient the system will be, with, at the limit, the achievement of the ultimate level of resilience, 'antifragility' [8].

2.3 'Complicated' and Above the Ashby Line

Here is the domain of what might be thought of as 'traditional' TRIZ, whether at the level of individual tools, or overall start-to-finish processes like ARIZ. Complicated problems can be characterized in a number of different ways, but from a purely pragmatic perspective, there is a clear 'best' solution to the problem being addressed. Because this is the case, it is conceivable that the overall problem definition and solution generation process can be linear and sequential.

What this means in practical terms, too, is that it is appropriate for problem solvers to look for root causes, that there are clear connections between cause and effect, and that there are clear rules. Even if those rules are the TRIZ-based rules-for-breaking-rules. Constructing a Function Analysis diagram and/or Su-Field Analysis model makes for the most effective and systematic ways of building the required understanding of the current system. From a classical TRIZ perspective, this problem type domain hits a clear sweet-spot, and even a moderately effective TRIZ user will very likely be able to devise a meaningful, practical solution.

2.4 'Complex' and Above the Ashby Line

The moment we acknowledge that a situation is complex, we have to accept that we are operating in conditions that are substantially different. There is no such thing as a 'root-cause' in a complex system, but rather a 'conspiracy' of causes. The links between cause and effect or often quite tenuous, and the behavior of the system becomes an emergent property. The Butterfly Effect further tells complex problem solvers that the world can easily become non-linear with apparently tiny perturbations quickly magnifying to become transformative. This means that things like the Pareto Effect no longer have a role. It is not possible to ignore anything that is currently 'insignificant' since it could easily be the weak-signal that triggers a complete disruption of the current system.

Because of these fundamental shifts in behavior, problem solvers need to adopt a different approach. The famous H.L. Mencken aphorism, 'For every complex problem there is a solution that is clear, simple and wrong' offers problem solvers a clear, but we now know outdated piece of advice when working with complexity. What we now know is that for every complex problem there are thousands of clear, simple wrong answers. But we know too that there is also the possibility of a 'right' one. Provided we are able to understand the behavior of a system from a first-principles level. The fact that the original TRIZ research (unknowingly) sought to distil the world of technology down to such first principles, means that the tools continue to have a good deal of relevance. The Inventive Principles are in effect the 'first principle' level array of solution generation possibilities; forcing problem solvers to examine systems through the lens of function forces first principles thinking; the value equation is a first principles distillation of the fundamental direction of travel of successful systems.

But – and this is a big but – just because TRIZ has given problem solvers an array of 'first principle' tools does not mean that when we connect these tools together into a process we can deal with a complex problem in a linear fashion. In this respect, the currently fashionable 'Design Thinking' world has much to teach problem solvers. At least from a methodological level. When the dust finally settles on the 2000+ Design Thinking texts presently in circulation, what complex problem solvers will likely be left with at the first principle level is the need for an overall process that is iterative and which contains alternating periods of divergent ('exploration') and convergent ('consolidation') effort. That overall process will likely as not look something like the one reproduced in Fig. 5.

In true TRIZ, 'someone-somewhere-already-solved-your-problem' fashion, the benchmark for successful problem-solving in complex, edge-of-chaos situations can be

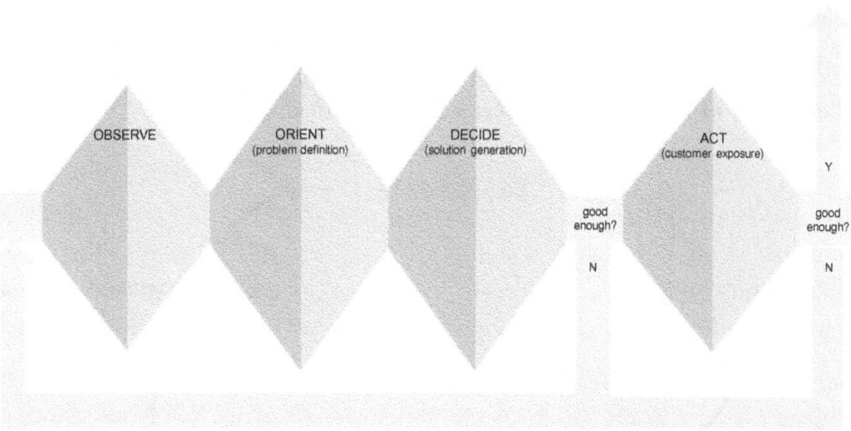

Fig. 5. Generic 'first principle'-level complex problem solving process

found with the pilots of military fighter jets. The best-of-the-best in this domain was very likely Colonel John Boyd of the USAF. The model he developed is now known as the OODA-Loop. Observe-Orient-Decide-Act. The victor in any aerial dogfight, Boyd determined, was the one with the shortest OODA Loop cycle time [9].

Translated into complex business and technical problem-solving terms, OODA translates to Observing the problem context and surroundings, Problem Definition, Solution Generation, and Prototyping. The fourth stage being the intention is to get a physical prototype into the hands of the intended customer as quickly as possible in order to learn what aspects of that solution do and don't work for said customer. If (when) we learn a solution is not yet good enough, the process requires innovators to cycle back to the beginning of the process and conduct another iteration.

Crucially, this cyclical process is built around the understanding that, first-principles or no, we can't actually 'know' what customers want until we deliver something to them and are able to obtain feedback from them when they're able to try something. In a complex environment, there is no such thing as the 'right' answer. Only 'right, right-now'. Or, perhaps more precisely, 'fittest for purpose at this moment in time'.

Also important to note is that the 'Systematic Innovation' methodology has been configured specifically with complex problems in mind. One of the basic tenets of SI is that, even though problem solvers can't know precisely what customers want, that doesn't mean that we can only make progress by trial and error. The TrenDNA toolkit [10], for example, seeks to distill a first-principle understanding of human behavior into a repeatable method that, when iterated, allows problems solvers to not only shorten their OODA Loop cycle time, but also require fewer iterations.

Sitting right at the heart of this 'first principles' story from the situation understanding perspective is the s-curve, and the dynamics associated with the discontinuous shift from one s-curve to the next that occur when innovation takes place. The basic shape of the s-curve remains the same whether the system under consideration is complex or not. When the system is complex, however, the dynamics of the curve are dictated by the presence of virtuous and vicious cycles. Virtuous cycles begin with weak signals that then take advantage of positive feedback effects. Figure 6 illustrates one such virtuous cycle. One that, over the course of the last ten years has seen the rise to dominance of the Magnificent Seven Big Data organisations [11].

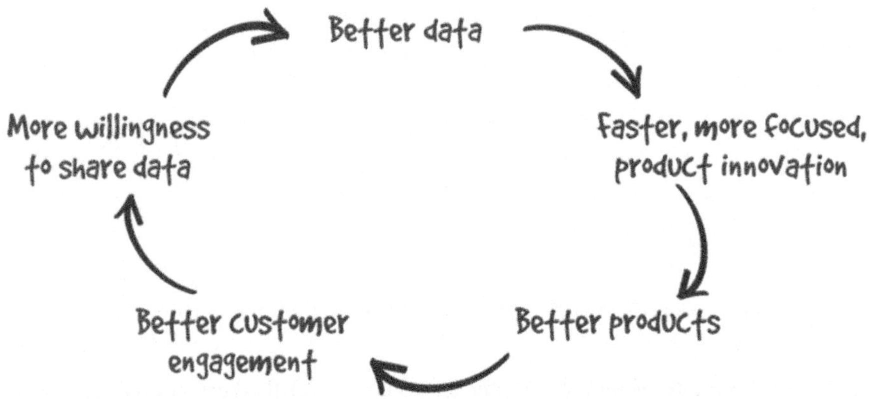

Fig. 6. Virtuous cycle responsible for the rise of the magnificent seven

At the other end of the s-curve come the vicious cycles. An illustration of the impact of vicious cycles on the failure of complex systems can be found in a recent analysis of the UK Brexit debacle [12]. The primary point of that paper was to register the need to break a vicious cycle as the only way to break out of the ever-more rapid tailspin into chaos. Breaking vicious cycles again becomes a task well suited to the TRIZ Contradiction tools. TRIZ is unable to reveal the vicious cycles (rather the Perception Mapping process [13] has become the go-to method for doing this job), but once they are revealed, only TRIZ provides the wherewithal to break them and point the way towards the possible step-change jumps to the next s-curve.

3 Conclusions: The Overall Role of TRIZ

98% of all innovation attempts end in failure. 98% of all TRIZ-originated innovation attempts end in failure. 98% of all Design-Thinking-originated innovation attempts end in failure. The same 98% figure applies to almost every problem-solving tool, method or strategy available to prospective innovators.

98% of innovation attempts fail because 100% of innovation problems are complex and 98% of the people tasked with conducting the work either didn't understand that or weren't using tools commensurate with the complexity.

So what did the 2% of successful attempts do? The clear answer is that they knowingly – or, occasionally, accidentally – found themselves in the right place at the right time with the right solution at the right price for the right customer. Getting all of these things right at the same time is a challenging task for which there is no 'formula', other than a recognition that the innovation project needs to be coordinated according to the demands of the Fig. 7 'Golden Triangle':

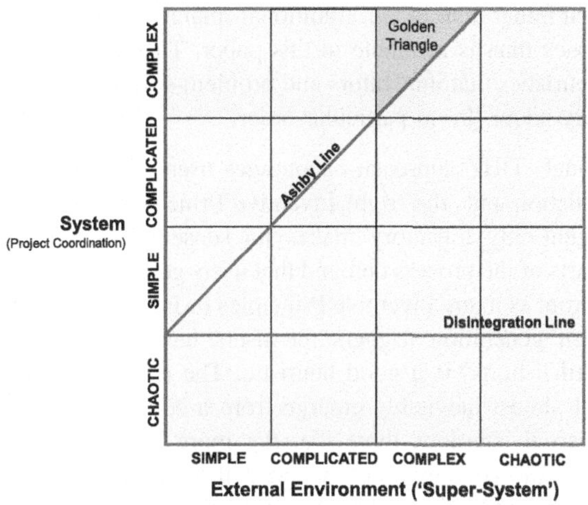

Fig. 7. 'The Golden Triangle' of successful innovation project coordination

Which in practice means the following:

Tangible skills:
Systems Thinking
Thriving in complexity - rapid-learning cycles, 'first principles', s-curves, patterns, 'critical mass at the critical point'
Understanding the customer/consumer say/do gap
Measuring what's important (rather than merely easy)
Having a clear compass heading
Knowing how to abstract problems to tap into solutions in other domains ('someone, somewhere already solved your problem')
Solving trade-offs & compromises

Intangible skills:

Innovation is largely about the individual & cultural intangibles ('Everyone has a plan until they get hit in the face' Mike Tyson)
Influencing others/working together in cross-disciplinary teams
Persistence/bloody-mindedness/willingness to stick-with-difficult-stuff
Learning to live with continual 'failure'
Acknowledging that 'ideas' have zero value
The Progress Principle [14]

Because TRIZ has effectively created a 'database' of first-principle level understanding of what success in technical problem solving looks like, it has a necessary but not sufficient role in enabling prospective innovators to have the best chance of ending up in the 2% of successful projects. Much of the original TRIZ research was performed on technical problems falling in to the 'complicated' category, and this is the domain where the tools are at their most effective. TRIZ continues to be relevant in the 'complex' domain too, provided that users deploy the various different tools in an appropriate fashion rather than in the 'traditional' manner. What this means in practice demands more space than is available in this paper. That said, there are a number of (first-principle) heuristics that innovators and problem-solvers working in the Complex domain can readily adopt. In no particular order:

(a) The 'traditional' TRIZ approach encourages users to progressively converge on 'the' contradiction and 'the' right Inventive Principle or Separation strategy, but this convergent-only trajectory makes no sense in the complex environment. Divergent parts of the process demand that users generate as many solution 'clues' as they can from as many Inventive Principles or Inventive Standards, or whatever other solution generation triggers the users have the time to work through. 'Diverge until it hurts' is a good heuristic. The eventual solution to a complex problem will almost inevitably emerge from a combination of partial solutions. The more partial solutions there are, the more likely it is that the necessary components of the winning combination will be present.
(b) The Trends and particularly the Evolution Potential version thereof are often referred to in the Classical TRIZ world as 'advanced'. When used in the Complex domain, however, the Trends are more frequently observed to be 'easy' since they are well-suited to the divergent idea-generation task. The TRIZ Trends effectively tell problem solvers what the answers are, without having to know what the problem being solved necessarily is. This 180degree switch is quite counter-intuitive in the 'Complicated' world, but rapidly becomes the most sensible way of moving forward in the 'Complex' world. Each Trend jump effectively points the way to the next s-curve on the road to the Ideal Final Result solution…
(c) …while apparently being one of the simplest tools in the TRIZ toolkit, the Ideal Final Result can rapidly come to cause problems in the 'Complicated' world. This is because it is almost inevitable that the IFR looks nothing like the solution that an organisation is currently selling to customers. And moreover, if it is ideal it will also be 'free', which then necessitates not just technical innovation but a host of business innovations to accompany it. And herein lies an enormous challenge for the large majority of all enterprises operating in the 21st Century: while the skills to innovate technically are well on their way to becoming a 'science', in the corresponding world of business and management, the innovation skills are still almost non-existent. The IFR tool is a tool for projects being coordinated in the Golden Triangle.
(d) Whether the word 'TRIZ' survives into the long-term future continues to be a matter of some considerable uncertainty. What will inevitably prevail, however, is the contribution made regarding the importance of revealing and resolving contradictions. Contradiction resolution is the primary mechanism for innovation. The Contradiction tools and methods were developed for complicated problems, but they apply to complex ones equally well. They are also the most effective means of shifting a project from a position below the Ashby Line to one within the Resilience Zone. Resilience, in almost all ways, comes from the ability of an enterprise to solve contradictions faster than their competitors.

References

1. Altshuller, G.: The Innovation Algorithm: TRIZ, Systematic Innovation and Technical Creativity, 1st edn. Technical Innovation Center, Worcester, MA (1999)
2. Snowden, D.J., Boone, M.E.: A Leader's Framework For Decision Making. Harvard Business Review, Boston (2007)
3. Mann, D.L.: A Complexity Landscape, 31 March 2019. www.darrellmann.com
4. Mann, D.L.: The Resilience Zone. Systematic Innovation E-Zine, Issue 205, April 2019
5. Ashby, W.R.: An Introduction to Cybernetics. Chapman & Hall, London (1957). http://pespmc1.vub.ac.be/books/IntroCyb.pdf
6. Pascale, R.T., Millemann, M., Gioja, L.: Surfing the Edge of Chaos: the Laws of Nature and the New Laws Of Business. Crown Business (2000)
7. Mann, D.L.: Calculating Ashby Margin. SI E-Zine, Issue 206, May 2019
8. Taleb, N.N.: AntiFragile: Things That Gain From Disorder. Random House, New York (2012)
9. Richards, C.: Certain to Win: the Strategy of John Boyd Applied to Business. Xlibris Corp, Philadelphia (2004)
10. Mann, D.L., Özözer, Y.: TrenDNA: Understanding Populations Better Than They Understand Themselves. IFR Press (2009)
11. Mann, D.L.: The Magnificent Seven Versus The Insurance Industry. Keynote address, Cardiff University Business School, 19 February 2019
12. Mann, D.L.: Unravelling The Brexit Debacle. EMBA Lecture Notes, September 2017
13. Mann, D.L.: Hands-On Systematic Innovation For Business & Management. IFR Press (2009)
14. Amabile, T., Kramer, S.: The Progress Principle: Using Small Wins to Ignite Joy, Engagement, and Creativity at Work. Harvard Business Review Press, Boston (2011)

Innovation Lab: New TRIZ Tools for Fast Idea Triggering

Davide Russo[1(✉)] and Paolo Carrara[2]

[1] University of Bergamo, 24044 Dalmine, Italy
davide.russo@unibg.it
[2] Warrant Innovation Lab S.r.l, 42015 Correggio, Italy

Abstract. During 2017, University of Bergamo and Warrant Innovation Lab have been starting a partnership to diffuse TRIZ in Italian SMEs. They aim to make SMEs perceive TRIZ as a time-saving methodology, the main needing expressed about innovation. The offering is a one-day problem-solving activity that aims at generating conceptual solutions, potentially patentable. First cases highlighted the reformulation was the trickiest phase: the extraction of the high-level technological alternatives cannot be supported by classical TRIZ tools (object-product transformation, ENV model, IFR, resources, evolutive laws, multiscreen, MTS) for both limited time and lacks in TRIZ skills of the customer. The staff overcomes such a double issue pre-processing the initial problem's information to extract insights from knowledge DBs. The results will be shown as visual-psychological triggers to stimulate the creativity of non-TRIZ-skilled users. The paper will disclose how visual triggers can work and how a triz expert facilitator can create them.

Keywords: Visual triggers · Serendipity · Innovation Lab · ENV model

1 Introduction

One of the most barrier to the innovation in SMEs is the lack in time and resources to spend on it [1]. The same is true also for TRIZ, which needs a long training period in order to become an efficient and effective resource. Because of it, the SMEs find it difficult to take advantage of TRIZ.

In SMEs, the incentive to innovate comes from the customers, who ask for improvement in performance or reduction in cost of the products, or from information given by the suppliers, who propose new technologies or products, or from the market competition, which forces toward cost reduction.

Irrespective of the reason for the request, SMEs rely on the insightful-ness, expertise and knowledge of their staff in order to innovate, who usually has traditional designing tools, but lacks in systematic methods specialized in innovation. They tend to outsource the R&D projects that are burdensome for the internal staff, both in time-consumption and in skills request.

Aiming to support SMEs in the most strategic phases of an innovation project, University of Bergamo (UniBG) and Warrant Innovation Lab (WIL) have been starting a partnership since 2017, relying on the Innovation Lab (IL): a consulting activity

Published by Springer Nature Switzerland AG 2019
R. Benmoussa et al. (Eds.): TFC 2019, IFIP AICT 572, pp. 16–25, 2019.
https://doi.org/10.1007/978-3-030-32497-1_2

expressly designed for SMEs and introduced in TFC 2018 [2]. It consists of a one-day team-working session of problem-solving.

To enhance the attitude of the team members, especially for the ones coming from the customer company who are not skilled in TRIZ, the IL exploits visual means to facilitate a serendipity process. They aim to carry the right information to the right person at the right time.

The IL staff can collect in a relatively simple way a large amount of information that are potential activator for serendipity. Furthermore, the people to which propose that information are the customer members of the team. The most difficult step for triggering the serendipity is the choice of the right time to transmit the information.

The visual means exploited by the IL lets the staff to separate in time the information offer from its receiving. Then, the visual means can be elaborated in back-office activity, before the one-day session, while the receiving time should happen during it.

As definition, serendipity means an unplanned, fortunate discovery [3]. It relies on the open-mindedness of the one who is looking for something other, the ability to catch the insight about a potential good idea while its thoughts are focusing on other topics.

In its definition, serendipity hides the overcoming of the psychological inertia.

To facilitate the occurrence of the right time, the staff takes advantage of a revised version of the ENV-model as psychological inertia inhibitor. It forces the company members of the team to leave the comfort-zone about ‘what I know to do’, calling into question their own problem perception, and going towards the attitude ‘what we should be able to do’.

The change of such a perspective let the customer to open their mindedness, overcome the psychological inertia and facilitate the occurrence of the *right time* for the serendipity.

This paper introduces the way IL exploits to push the serendipity mechanism. In Sect. 2, it illustrates which are the main goals of the customers involved in IL. Section 3 describes how WIL trains the customer participants to the innovation activity. Section 4 shows which are the tools exploited by the IL and which is the workflow of the activity. Then, in Sect. 5, details about Visual Triggers, how they work and how to prepare them, have been explained.

2 Customer Needs

Often, SMEs have not employees specifically dedicated to the R&D who are familiar with inventive problem solving, idea generation or patent literature. If R&D department exists in SME, in most cases it has not enough time to follow a wide-ranging innovation project.

WIL is a company devoted to facilitating and diffusing the systematic innovation in SMEs, through technology transfer and sharing of knowledge, ideas, technologies and methodologies, especially cooperating with universities and research centers. It offers services to fill in the lacks in innovation methodologies, establishing cooperation and partnership with suitable research teams.

Thanks to its long-lasting touch keeping with customers, WIL has been getting continuous up-to-date information about their innovation effort. This is the most important requirement to identify the actual goal of an innovation project. Indeed, customer rarely expresses clearly which they are, rather it asks for supporting in the development of an idea and translate it in an innovation project.

Thus, the first marketing activity about IL is understanding which the actual goals of the customer are. WIL offers the IL when it falls in one of main categories below:

1. Often, the customer wants to innovate a product/process for which it is not able to achieve a significant evolutive step. In such a case the customer takes the IL as the opportunity to test TRIZ, like it was a challenge, submitting a real and unsolved problem;
2. Before undertaking a R&D project, the customer wants to be sure it is going to undertake the less risky innovation path. By the means of the IL, it aims to widen the solution space in order to choose the most suitable conceptual solution for the development;
3. In some cases, especially with start-ups, the customer wants to achieve a new product/process about which it has not proficiency. This is interesting for IL when the customer requires the conceptual design of a new functional solution, that means it asks for inventive problem solving.

The IL was designed in order to save time for the first strategical phases of the innovation process. Nonetheless, it carries other added values.

First, the customer gets a new point of view about its system: tearing down the psychological inertia, IL supports the customer in uncovering new functional solutions, which are original for the reference market.

Widening the solution space, it allows the customer to consider several solving directions in order to plan an innovation and/or patenting strategy. This is particularly felt by start-ups which could get the high-level design of the solution to be developed.

3 Selection of Customer Participants

The IL requires the participants be willing to question their own point of view about the problem and its potential solutions. Further, it is appropriate to have different points of view about the product/process to innovate. Thus, not only technical profiles are required, rather, the presence of marketing employees and decision makers or CEO improves the IL performances.

Due to the long-lasting relationships between WIL and its customers, it enjoys credibility with them. This enables some important aspects for the success of the IL.

First, WIL gives to the customer some indications about the service and how it works. For example, giving them a smattering of TRIZ and/or describing how to difficult is for a specialist to overcome the psychological inertia. Using this opportunity, it can suggest to the customer which are the best employee profiles to involve in the IL. Eventually, it could assist the customer in the choice of people.

The second aspect is the preparation of the customer participants. Depicting the specific feature of the service is a way to prepare them for the work they will do with UniBG. They get upfront what to expect by the one-day innovation activity.

Lastly, together with what just said, the credibility of WIL with the customer is implicitly transferred to UniBG. This eases a lot the first phase of the IL, when the customer participants must be convinced about the goodness of the methodology behind the service.

4 Tools and Workflow

In the morning session of IL, the participants work on generalizing the problem and enlarging the space of its solutions. The TRIZ expert guides the participants along an innovation path [2] that include techniques of abstraction of the target product/process (functional modelling), suppression of the constraints (modified ENV model [4]), technological alternatives analysis (ENV model integrating the IFR [5] and IR tools specifically developed), management of requirements (market potential [6, 7]) and overcoming of psychological inertia (visual triggers).

In the afternoon session of IL, the participants choose the most interesting solving direction and develop it. The staff guides them exploiting the knowledge about physical contradictions, separation principles and other classic TRIZ tools, without explicitly describe them to the participants.

The ideas generated are tracked and organized according to the FBS ontology [8] on a map collecting high-level functional solutions (FBS map). Figure 1 shows the workflow of IL, the main tools exploited by the staff to lead the innovation path and how the FBS map works during the day.

More details about Visual Triggers and how to populate the FBS map are going to explain in next chapters.

5 Visual Triggers

Serendipity means an unplanned, fortunate discovery [3]. It is a common occurrence throughout the history of product invention and scientific discovery. The term is often applied to inventions made by chance rather than intent.

The goal of the IL staff is to create ‘a bump in the road’, so as to guide the accidental knowledge.

Many of the most well-known mechanisms for conducting a good problem solving path are those related to the sense of belonging to the problem: it is easier to passionately conduct a problem that is close to our heart, or a direction discovered by us rather than committing ourselves carry out the task assigned or discovered by someone else.

For this reason, the inventive idea must come from the customer experts and never from the staff! Even better when all the participants reach the idea at the same time, or if they are all aware that they could have grasped it by themselves.

It would be good whether nobody thought that an expert has dropped none of the ideas that come along. The ‘wow effect’ created by facilitators is one of the worst mistakes that can be made in this activity.

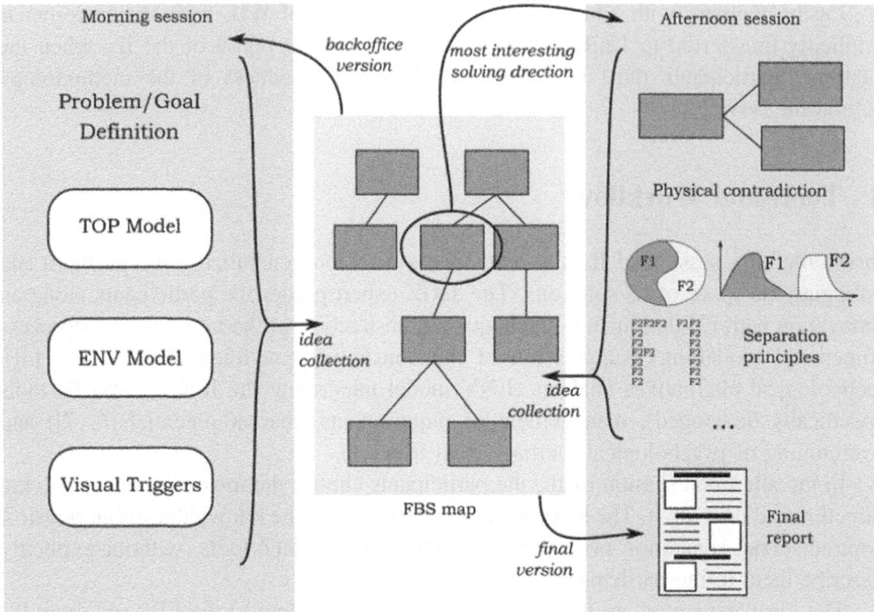

Fig. 1. Workflow and tools exploited by the IL. All interesting ideas are collected in the FBS map

On the contrary, all the participants must become actors, and to do this it is necessary to find an effective mechanism of *accidental knowledge*, capable of igniting the mysterious mechanism of serendipity.

Accidental knowledge means that knowledge that is acquired in a completely random way, through what is called the *knowledge accident*. This terminology belongs to that discipline called knowledge management, which studies how it is possible to ensure that "the right knowledge reaches the right person at the right time to be able to make the best possible decision".

Specifically, the *knowledge accident* represents a mechanism capable of conveying the right knowledge to the right person, not necessarily at the right time. This delay is an aspect that can completely frustrate the transfer of this knowledge.

Better to give the right information without the user having the perception of being guided in the choice, nor to arrive at the solution 'prepared' already by the staff.

In order to simulate *accidental knowledge*, a set of images, called visual triggers is prepared.

5.1 Triggers Functioning

The Images are designed to evoke functions or behaviors useful for identifying an alternative way for solving the initial problem.

According to FBS theory [8] a solution can be conceived as a set of elements (Structure) working together in order to realize a Behavior that allows the structure reaching a goal (Function).

Visual triggers are images of products, that being outside of our problem context, do not evoke structure analogies but only behavioral or functional alternatives.

They must be general enough to allow the user the freedom to decline it in the way he intends to use it for his own purposes.

For example, in a recent case, it was necessary to replace a cutting blade positioned with extreme precision inside a very heavy chassis. The changeover operation is frequent due to the high wear on the blade and every time an important machine stop is required with a very well-prepared intervention by the workers.

All the products sold by the company involved use the same maintenance process, which includes a "book" machine opening device to facilitate operator entry into the machine.

Visual triggers (shown in Fig. 2) help remove this type of condition, moving the problem to other areas.

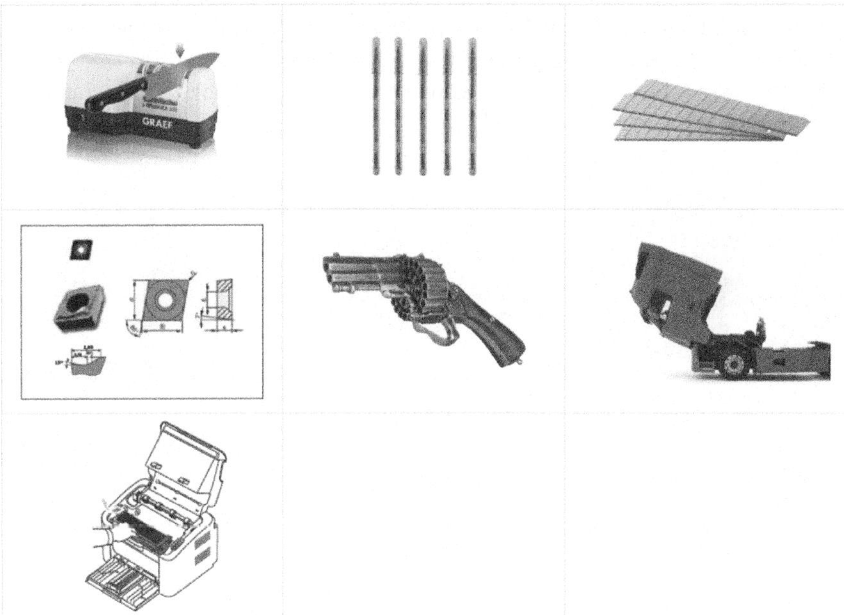

Fig. 2. Visual triggers at functional level, explain strategies for replace/restore the blade

For example, the first image is designed to suggest that you might not have to replace the blade in case someone is able to restore the thread. It may come out of refining methods or simply the idea of not having it sharpened anymore because it sharpens itself, or a blade that never loses the thread either because it has a much longer life, or because the system removes the condition so the blade loses the thread.

The second image indicates an alternative way of replacing things, restoring the blade with a ready one according to a precise and preset dynamic.

In a like manner, the cutter blades, the third visual trigger, produce a similar path but with completely different dynamics. Sometimes it is the union of several triggers that trigger the creative mechanism.

In the case of the cutting edges of image (Fig. 4) we have tried to explain how each blade has multiple profiles that can be used as cutting edges, instead of always putting a new one and having to recalibrate the system you could try to understand how to modify the housing for offer a new cutting edge. This image suggests using the same blade in a new position but does not say how.

Contrarywise, the subsequent images give us two different ways of preparing the new blade, respectively rotating or reversing.

The last case is the toner of the printer, which indicates a different way of inserting an object.

In the next figure we show an example of triggers focused on the goal of blocking. In them we suggest alternative ways at the level of Behavior.

As can be seen, the evocative level of these triggers is much more limited than in the previous case; the creative effort required of the user is undoubtedly much shorter. For each option the effort is only to imagine how to contextualize the solution to one's own field, assessing its technical feasibility and side effects.

What is shown in the Fig. 3 is a list of alternatives that could be generated automatically by a knowledge search tool.

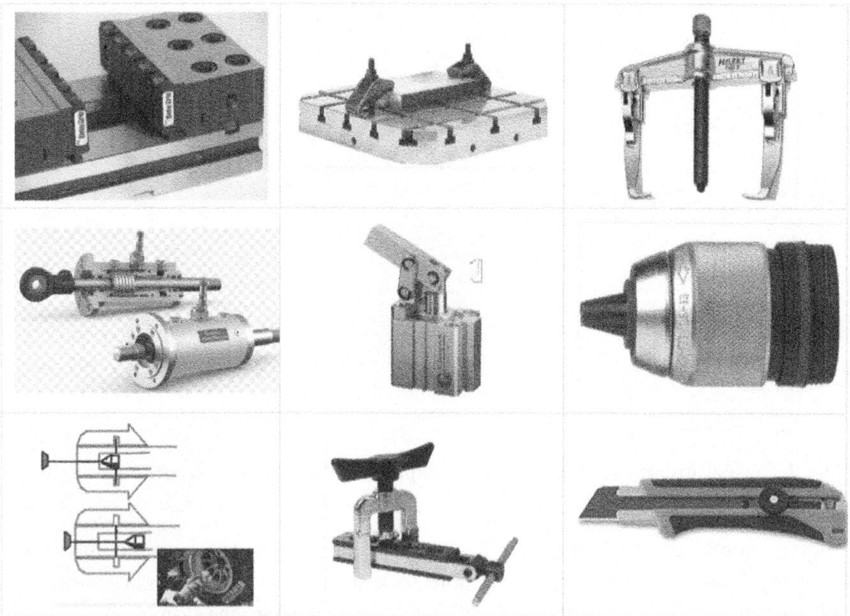

Fig. 3. Visual Triggers at behavioral level, explaining different ways of blocking something

The higher the degree of specialization of the triggers, the greater the possibility of automating the automatic content search process.

Similarly we look at the search for all the alternative ways in which a function can be exploited by exploring the various associated physical effects [9].

5.2 Triggers Preparation

For the construction of visual triggers, it is necessary to know very well all TRIZ tools. The most suitable tool for this purpose is the ENV model.

According to the OTSM TRIZ theory of Nikolai Khomenko [4], ENV model helps to describe one or more functions starting from its decomposition in features.

For each parameter/feature its value is described indicating to which element it is referenced. The function is defined as the variation of the feature value during the transformation induced by the function, before and after.

In this way it is possible to describe the main function of a system through a list of transformations, expressed as a variation of the value of the technical parameters.

To this, we can also add further information with respect to the value of the characteristic in the ideal situation.

The comparison between expected value (ideal) and obtained value (real) determines in the user an inventive trigger to improve the starting system.

The basic idea for the construction of the visual triggers is to work ahead of the day, applying this tool and defining an image for each suggested transformation, avoiding images taken from the context in which you are operating.

The choice of images is based on the number of constraints that can be removed during the day with the customer, as well as the number of unpublished prospects with which to address the problem.

The basic idea is to start from the main transformation of the system, imagining how the object of the main function is transformed into a desired product, and from here to hypothesize at a high level the alternative and integrative functions that could arise during the session, masking them with images that subliminally call the concept back without explicitly mentioning it.

The purpose of the triggers is to investigate possible alternatives at the function level. Once found, they must be hierarchically organized according to the following model (see Fig. 4). Once the map of alternatives is built, the facilitator can apply the other tools of the TRIZ methodology to formulate questions that push the experts of the sector to find further alternatives. IFR, multiscreen works very well both at the level of F and B.

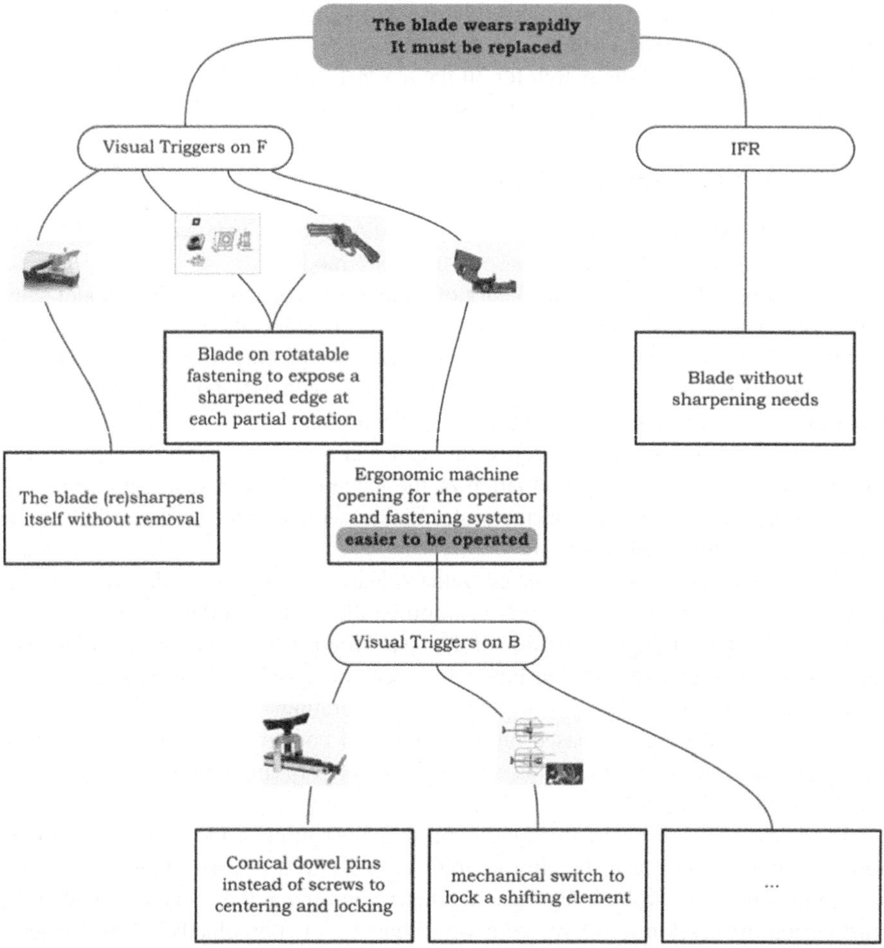

Fig. 4. Example of the hierarchical map of alternatives coming from F-level and B-level triggers and IFR

6 Conclusion

Warrant Innovation Lab and University of Bergamo have been starting a partnership that aims to support SMEs in the most strategic phases of their innovation projects limiting the time request to generate conceptual solutions. They offer the Innovation Lab, which is a TRIZ-based problem-solving activity that lasts one day and aims at generating conceptual solutions, potentially patentable.

The Innovation Lab adjusts the TRIZ-based innovation path to reach at least a conceptual solution within the limited time available. Especially, it exploits Visual Triggers, which are images representing functional examples able to convey insights in implicit manner. Thanks to this approach, the staff facilitates the *knowledge accident*, the idea generation mechanism behind serendipity.

The customers responded positively to the service, expressing satisfaction about the approach and results. Later to the Innovation Lab, all of them have been carring forward the innovation project. The knowledge uncover by the Innovation Lab allows them to save time also in the following development steps of the solution.

Irrespective to what initial attitude the customer had regarding the opportunity to patent the solution, all cases to date faced gave rise to a patent application. This proves even more the results are interesting and valuable for the customers.

Despite the advantages taken from the conceptual solutions the Innovation Lab allowed to grasp, the customers did not show interest in deepening their knowledge about TRIZ, for example through participating to learning or training courses. Rather, they consider the Innovation Lab the way to solve an inventive problem they are not able to overcome.

Of course, this is a positive result, but further developments on the Innovation Lab and on the approach to the customers must be considered to increase the interest about TRIZ.

References

1. Russo, D., Regazzoni, D., Rizzi, C.: A long-term strategy to spread TRIZ in SMEs. Analysis of Bergamo's experience. In: Koziołek, S., Chechurin, L., Collan, M. (eds.) Advances and Impacts of the Theory of Inventive Problem Solving, pp. 147–157. Springer, Cham (2018). https://doi.org/10.1007/978-3-319-96532-1_14
2. Russo, D., Carrara, P., Marusi, M.: Innovation lab: how to generate patents in one day. In: Cavallucci, D., de Guio, R., Koziolek, S. (eds.) TRIZ Future Conference 2018, Professional Proceedings (2018)
3. Serendipity | Definition of Serendipity in English by Oxford Dictionaries. https://en.oxforddictionaries.com/definition/serendipity. Accessed 11 May 2019
4. Cavallucci, D., Khomenko, N.: From TRIZ to OTSM-TRIZ: addressing complexity challenges in inventive design. Int. J. Prod. Dev. **4**, 4 (2007). https://doi.org/10.1504/IJPD.2007.011530
5. Altshuller, G.: The Innovation Algorithm – TRIZ, systematic innovation and technical creativity (Translated by Shulyak, L. & Rodman, S.) (2005)
6. Livotov, P.: Using patent information for identification of new product features with high market potential. Procedia Eng. **131**, 1157–1164 (2015). https://doi.org/10.1016/j.proeng.2015.12.438
7. Livotov, P.: Method for quantitative evaluation of innovation tasks for technical systems, products and processes. In: Proceedings of ETRIA World Conference "Synthesis in Innovation", pp 197–199 (2008)
8. Gero, J.S., Kannengiesser, U.: The situated function–behaviour–structure framework. Des. Stud. **25**, 373–391 (2004). https://doi.org/10.1016/j.destud.2003.10.010
9. Montecchi, T., Russo, D.: FBOS: function/behaviour-oriented search. Procedia Eng. **131**, 140–149 (2015). https://doi.org/10.1016/j.proeng.2015.12.363

Patent Based Method to Evaluate the Market Potential of a Product

Davide Russo(✉), Christian Spreafico, and Matteo Spreafico

University of Bergamo, Viale Marconi 4, 24044 Dalmine, BG, Italy
davide.russo@unibg.it

Abstract. Within TRIZ literature, only a small part is focused on the management of the requirements. In the majority of cases, they are treated at a mere technological level rather than marketing, by taking into account the requirements that have the greatest market potential.

According to the market potential technique, in the early stage phases of design, the product to be innovated is divided into a list of different properties that will be assessed individually in terms of importance and satisfaction. In order to support the evaluation made by product experts (R&D Team and Marketing Team), a search for knowledge must be carried out. This involves, for example, the research in each requirement for information contained in brochures, commercial catalogs, patents literature and scientific articles with the aim of extracting trends, statistics, emerging technologies and unresolved problems. This procedure requires time and a large economic investment, especially if integrated with market research, often costly and time consuming. To overcome these limitations, the novelty proposed in this article consists in a method to automate the estimation of the importance of each requirement, or at least those for which information is available in the various document sources.

An exemplary case dealing with an aerogel panel for civil application is proposed, stressing the geographical area in such a way as to define the investment and how it integrates into the potential market.

Keywords: Triz · Market potential · Problem solving · Patent

1 Introduction

This paper is addressing the main needs of the industrial sector regarding the definition of innovations tasks in the very early stage of the innovation process.

The present situation in planning and executing of innovation projects within industrial enterprises contains considerable drawbacks. These inconveniences can be summarized as the lack of tools for systematic task definition for short and long term innovation or low reliability of market success prediction for new product concepts in the early stages of innovation process [1].

Although the best endeavor to reduce risk of failures, the majority of all industrial innovation initiative offers only incremental improvements compared to the products on the market. The attempts to incorporate customers into new product development

Published by Springer Nature Switzerland AG 2019
R. Benmoussa et al. (Eds.): TFC 2019, IFIP AICT 572, pp. 26–35, 2019.
https://doi.org/10.1007/978-3-030-32497-1_3

require time-expensive interviews and surveys or extensive field research and rarely presents significant competitive advantages [1].

Using patent information makes the customer needs transfer feasible and manageable. The use of patents in order to estimate the market potential of a technique can be considered an efficient method to compare, monitor and analyze research activity in a specific sector of technology. Patent statistics are used as indicators of activity related to inventions. An analysis of patented technologies can provide information on technological trends. Like any methodology, the use of patents as indicators also has its limits: there is not always a correspondence between innovation and patented inventions, just as not all patented inventions have a technical value [2].

This procedure involves the following topics: analysis of market and technological trends. In order to predict costumer benefits, scholars employed the application of technological or market trends, TRIZ patterns of system evolution and trends of needs evolution.

Nevertheless, today the trend analysis delivers too general or to obvious results and can be considered as supplementary method only. The new TRIZ based approaches are too general or solution-oriented. For example, one method evaluates the relationships between market trends and TRIZ evolution patterns [3]. Based on the TRIZ laws of system evolution the universal trends of needs evolution can be formulated and applied for identification of hidden needs and for forecasting of new needs of customers [4].

Analysis of patent information: besides the mentioned approaches, this paper proposes the use of patent information for the identification of customer benefits. An important source of information to identify unsolved problems and to derive customer benefits is constituted by patent databases, which in fact is not available in any other source. According to the modern tools for patent text-mining and syntactic parsing tools, the information can be obtained more quickly and precisely. Moreover, with the patent analysis one can easily access and retrieve information for general inventive tasks and thus for benefits for the products from different industrial sectors with similar customer working processes.

Patent information enhanced through computer-aided classification and retrieval contributes significantly to the acceleration of innovation processes. The automatic retrieval of problems [5] or technical contradictions [6] helps experts to reduce the time needed for finding solutions. Analyzing and categorizing patents according to the TRIZ evolution patterns assists to identify the evolutionary potential and possible improvements of products. Patent analysis is hence applicable for forecasting emerging technologies, even if no historical data is available [7], and also for developing acquisition strategies [8].

Evaluation of market potential for customer benefits: according to [1], a new advanced computation algorithm includes a regression model which is suitable for calculation of the market potential as a function of importance and satisfaction for all values of the input variables.

According to the market potential technique, in the early stage phases of design, the product to be innovated is divide into a list of different properties that will be assessed individually in terms of importance and satisfaction. In order to support the evaluation made by product experts (R&D Team and Marketing Team), a search for knowledge must be carried out. This involves, for example, the research in each requirement for information contained in brochures, commercial catalogs, patents literature and scientific articles with the aim of extracting trends, statistics, emerging technologies and unresolved problems. The novelty proposed in this work consists in proposing a technique that integrates the technical approach just explained with an estimate of the investments in economic terms in order to establish how it integrates into the market potential.

Despite the many steps taken to improve the market potential, it remains today a tool that requires time and a large economic investment, especially if integrated with market research, often costly and time consuming. To overcome these limitations, at least partially, the article proposes a method to automate the estimation of the importance of each requirement, or at least those for which information is available in the various document sources.

The article presents an overview of market potential techniques in Sect. 2. In Sect. 3, it illustrates the methodological proposal to retrieve the state of the art and the way of proceeding conducted in this study. After, in Sect. 4, an example of the methodology through a case study is provided. In closing, Sect. 5, the conclusion.

2 Market Potential Techniques

Among the various approaches used to evaluate the market potential, a technique consists in the evaluation of a series of customer needs and requirements. These approaches are able to define customer needs or requirements, with a structured procedure to translate them into technical parameters and plans to produce products that essentially meet those needs. Benchmarking is one of the first form of structured product development. Products are compared with industry bests from other companies and improvements are planned to cover possible gaps or to overcome competitor's performances. In particular, satisfaction is a measure of how products and services supplied by a company meet or surpass customer expectation. In a scale from 0% to 100%, 0% is the absence of the feature or great dissatisfaction, 100% is maximum satisfaction. The aforementioned definitions are given to experts before the interviews for the evaluation (Fig. 1).

As shown in the example reported in the figure above, in which it is shown a market potential graph, the product that own the greater market potential is the product that presents the combination of greater importance levels and lower satisfaction levels among the various requirements treated.

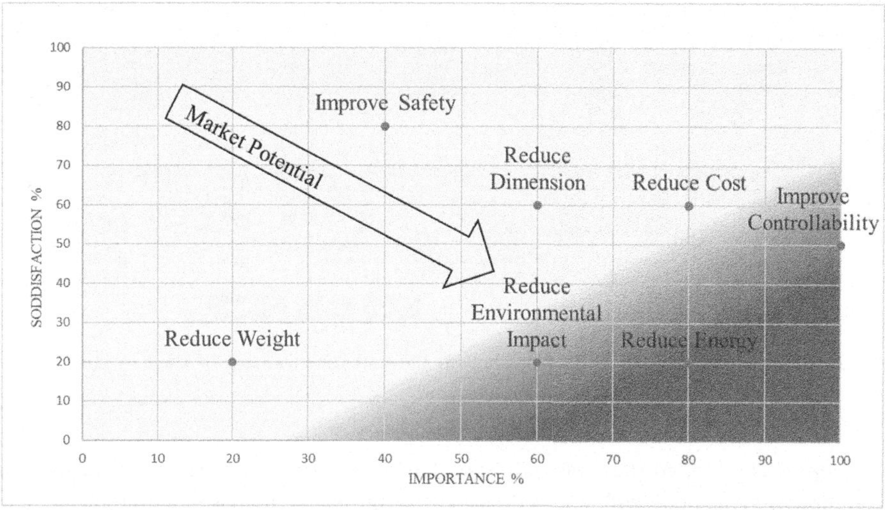

Fig. 1. Example of market potential graphical analysis

3 Proposal: Semantic Analysis and Documents Preparation

The punctual search for information through combinations of keywords represents an established fact [8], however in the last few years the business intelligence tools have made important steps forward, allowing us to hypothesize their use for delicate operations like these.

In the last years, in fact, thinking of basing a decision on a chart was quite risky. Business intelligence could help suggesting where to go for targeted research and punctual research.

The advent of semantics has transformed the potential of research, allowing us to obtain levels of precision in research that were unthinkable until now. The basic idea is to exploit this technology to produce graphics with high granularity and high precision, which can be used as quantitative comparison tools [9].

The process cannot be fully automated and still requires different expertise.

Step 1. First of all, an attempt is made to create the pool with maximum recall, extracting by content analysis tools the basic concepts in a fast and efficient way. This first screening helps to enter the subject, to find connections that are not obvious even for experts in the sector and helps not to lose potential requirements to be evaluated in the market potential that may not have come up in a preliminary planning (Fig. 2).

As it can be seen from the figure, by selecting a parameter it is possible to find all the correlations between the features, thus deducing dependency links and non-obvious relationships.

All information from this pool can be visualized in dashboard with automatic graphs.

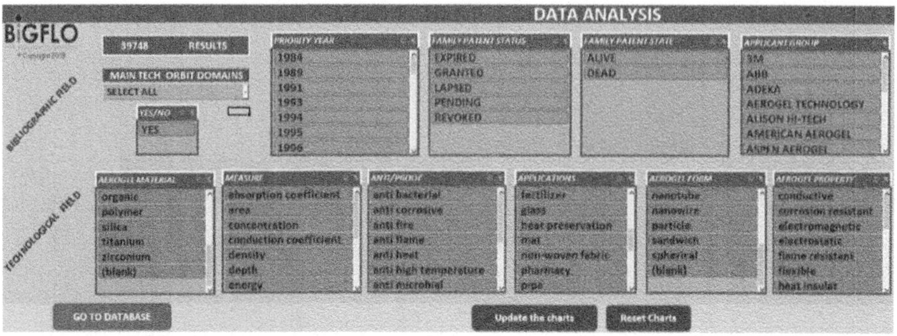

Fig. 2. Representation of the filters present on the software framework used to conduct the analysis

Step 2. The second step is to precisely define the pool that serves to evaluate each requirement. The pool will not necessarily be the same for each requirement. The semantic analysis is calibrated to identify only the features that are related to this pool.

The more complete the pattern network, the more reliable the final evaluation will be. Each requirement can be composed from a list of patterns that can be taken from, for instance: type of product, type of material, objective to be achieved, problem, parameter to be measured, parameter to be improved, product-proof, objects of a specific function, functions that the product receives, etc.

Table 1. Examples of pattern list used in the analysis

Patterns	
Goal to achieve	i.e. the **goal to achieve** of changing waste into valuables
Problem to be faced	i.e. insulation boards has **faced the problem** that the aerogel felt easily infiltrates steam and falls powder and not environmental protection
Product type	i.e. different **product types**: thermal insulation panel in nanoporous aerogel with support matrix in mineral fiber, resistant to compression, non-flammable
Kind of material	i.e. the three most common **kind of materials** are silica, carbon and metal oxides
Parameters to be measured	i.e. **measure parameters**, such as thermal performance or light perpendicularity
Parameters to be improved	i.e. insulating materials are provided to **improve** fire resistance and sound absorption rate
Proof	i.e. the invention relates to a wind-**proof**, rain-snow-**proof** and cold-**proof** thermal outdoor jacket
Technical functions	i.e. Aerogel materials presents, as **technical functions**: strength and durability expected of engineering materials
Agents involved	i.e. **Agents involved** in the sale of textiles, panels or boards

Compared to a search by keywords, the logic of constructing the result is reversed. In the first case we start with a very inaccurate result and manually clean up to obtain the desired precision, while with semantics we start from a precise search and add gradually many requests that could contain that information.

Special algorithms allow then to take almost similar concepts present in the different groups almost automatically.

In some cases, a manual refinement is still necessary, or a combination of the two techniques, but the fact of being able to work with semantics offers the undisputed advantage of almost always working with pertinent documents, allowing a much more effective degree of information acquisition and also much faster. Browsing for good documents also offers the possibility of creating a sector thesaurus with far fewer steps than searching for keywords.

Step 3. The third step consists in the creation of an infographic to be delivered to the evaluator during the audit carried out. This analysis can be totally qualitative or, if who performs the analysis is sufficiently skilled in the field, it is possible to set quantitative criteria to suggest to the evaluator a first numerical result.

Step 4. As for the final step, the audit is replicated for all the requirements involved in the analysis. Then the average of all is calculated and the market potential chart is realized.

4 Case Study on Aerogel Panel for Civil Application

As a means to test the method proposed in this work, the authors have considered the extraction in full text (i.e. title, abstract, description, claims and priority dates) regarding the whole patent set concerning the technology Aerogel. The technology itself is well enough developed as a result of work over the past decade by an international community of researchers. Several extensive substantial markets appear to exist for aerogels as thermal and sound insulators, if production costs can keep prices in line with competing established materials.

Step 1. The authors querying the worldwide patent database in order to interrogate scientific literature. The goal is to extract the largest set of documents with the aim to study the problem in a complete and exhaustive way. According to author's strategies, all sematic networks among words has been extracted along with the properties, functions, type, elements, market and technology applications in order to completely rebuild the technology being investigated.

The query is "AEROGEL OR AERO?GEL OR ((FROZEN OR SOLID OR BLUE) 1D SMOKE) OR (SOLID 1D CLOUD)/TI/AB/IW/TX" according to Orbit patent database syntax and producing a pool of 47593 results.

A more specific pool add "(PANEL? OR BOARD+) TI/AB/IW/TX" in full text according to Orbit Database syntax in order to limit the field of application to building panels (331 patents).

Requirements Selection Phase with Experts in the Field. In this case study, we consider Aerogel application related to panels for construction. Insulation with the highest performance and durability is chosen with aerogel insulating materials. Their use ensures maximum protection against winter cold, summer heat and humidity. The product range includes rigid and flexible mattresses, panels, coupled, suitable for the most diverse applications. Different coating characteristics, size and thickness make these innovative insulators the most advanced solution for the insulation of roofs, walls, facades, floors and thermal bridges. They are designed to meet the multiple requirements of building insulation applications for new buildings and restoration. The unique properties that characterize them make them indispensable in realizations that require maximum thermal performance with minimum thickness. The very low thermal conductivity, flexibility, compressive strength, hydrophobicity, breathability and ease of use make it the best thermal insulation currently available on the market, effectively representing the last frontier in thermal insulation (Fig. 3).

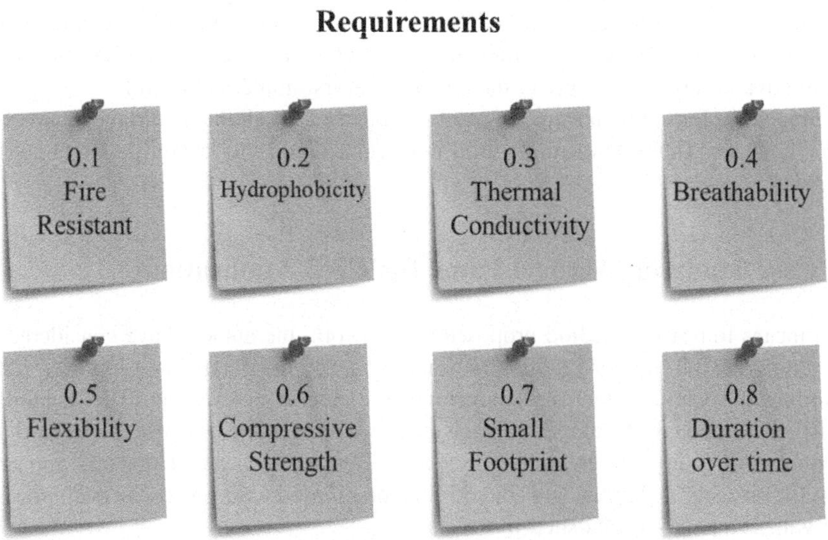

Fig. 3. List of the requirements of this study

Step 2. Any requirement is analyzed in detail by defining a specific pool of reference documents. In order to create the best pool of documents, a semantic based strategy is introduced. For instance, if we look for information related to the "*fire proof*" requisite, we can use many different patterns dealing with:

- parameters to be improved (i.e. *improve heat resistance*),
- the class of proof/resistant (i.e. *blaze, ignition, overheating, burning, flame, fire-proof/resistant*)

Another set of pertinent documents can be provided selecting all couples dealing with *fire* concept from a list of verb + object automatically extracted by the semantic parser (as reported in Table 1).

Table 2. List of Function + Object through semantic process

Function + Objects	
Reinforce panel, structure	**Reflect** light, mirror, radiation, sunlight, wave, ray
Reduce pollution, temperature, emission, consumption, noise	**Cover** surface, layer, glue
Improve resistance, strength, stability, conductivity	**Wrap** conductor, paper, tape
Insulate material, panel, board, structure, heat	**Increase** strength, temperature, capacity
Support structure, layer	**Convey** belt, pipeline, chain, pipe, fan
Adsorb contaminant, pollutant, substance, capacity	**Immobilize** microorganism
Form layer, structure, film, cavity, gel, groove, electrode	**Solve** pollution, waste, storage
Impregnate fabric, foam, blanket	**Protect** health, layer
Coat surface, substrate, layer, slurry, fabric, coating	**Resist** bacterium, corrosion, temperature, performance, heat
Block radiation, filter, transfer, ray, heat	**Restrain** growth
Deposit mask, metal, film, layer	

From that list for example we can analyze, for instance, patents containing the couple "*Reduce temperature, insulate heat, Impregnate fabric, Coat surface, Coat substrate, Coat layer, Coat slurry, Coat fabric, Coat coating, Block radiation, Block heat radiation, reflect light, reflect radiation, Protect layer, Resist temperature, Resist heat*" (Table 2).

The sum of all these combinations constitutes the pool of all the relevant patents of the dataset for any specific requirement.

Step 3. From the above mentioned patent dataset, we proceed now to understand and estimate the value of the importance (in terms of R&D investments).

The requirements that will be evaluated are:

- *Patent density/numerosity*: the number of patents applications during the years.
- *Relevance:* number of relevant patents
- *Investment trend*: This graph illustrates the evolution of applications over time, indicating the dynamics of inventiveness of the portfolio studied.
- *Number of patent families and global distribution*: size of the applicants' portfolios in the patent pool analyzed. This data is a good indicator of the level of inventiveness of the active players (Fig. 4).
- *Competitors analysis*: differentiation between dead and living patents
- *Legal status*: differentiation between dead and living patents

Step 4. In some cases it is easy to understand the value to be given, in others it is necessary to compare with the graphs found for other requirements. The final evaluation is always subjective, but the 360° vision in the form of concise graphs and

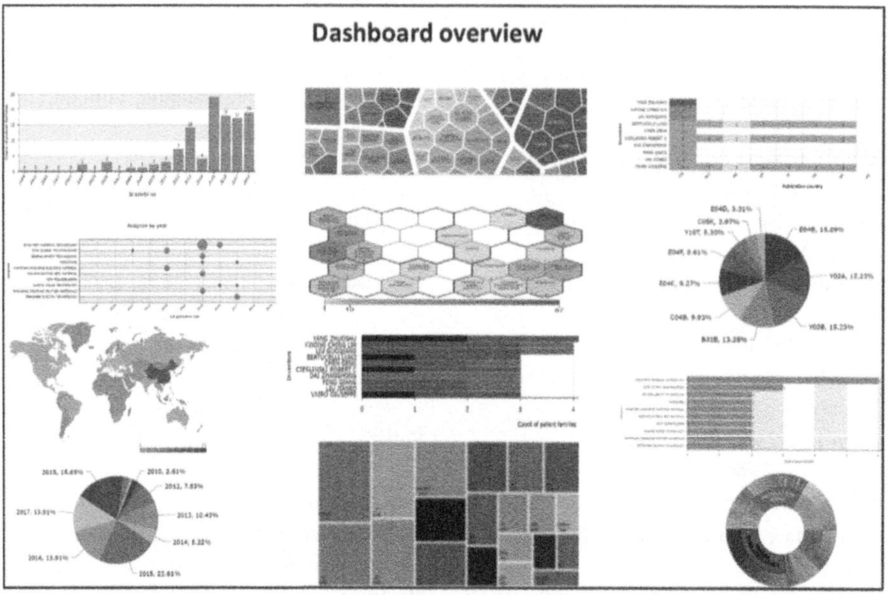

Fig. 4. Example of Infographic representation for the requirement monitoring

quantitative assessment helps to make more objective decisions. Once importance is fixed, marketing area and sales managers are interviewed for evaluating also satisfaction score.

The evaluation of importance and satisfaction is then replicated for all the requirements involved in the analysis. There are as many evaluations as there are participants. In the end, it gives an average and creates the final ranking and the market potential chart is realized.

5 Conclusion

This study proposes a method for the study of the market potential based on an automatic estimation of the importance of each requirement, or at least those for which information is available in the various document sources. The basic idea is to use this technology to produce graphics granularity and high precision thanks to the implementation of semantics, which can be used as quantitative comparison tools. Compared to a search by keywords, the logic of constructing the result is reversed, in the first case we start from a very inaccurate result and manually clean up to obtain the desired precision, while with semantics we start from a precise search and we add so many researches that could contain that information. Special algorithms allow then to take almost automatic analogous concepts present in the different groups. In some cases, it is still necessary a manual finishing, or a combination of the two techniques, but the fact that we can work with semantics offers the undisputed advantage of working almost always with pertinent documents, allowing a degree more effective and also much faster information acquisition. Browsing for good documents also offers the possibility of creating a sector thesaurus with far fewer steps than searching for keywords. In the end, the methodology provides infographics in order to have a clear picture in the most concise way.

References

1. Livotov, P.: Using patent information for identification of new product features with high market potential. Procedia Eng. **131**, 1157–1164 (2015)
2. Kostoff, R.N., Stump, J.A., Johnson, D., Murday, J.S., Lau, C.G., Tolles, W.M.: The structure and infrastructure of the global nanotechnology literature. J. Nanoparticle Res. **8**(3–4), 301–321 (2006)
3. Litvin, S.: Business to Technology – new stage of TRIZ development. In: Proceedings of the TRIZ Future Conference 2005, Graz, 16–18 November 2005, pp. 205–206. Leykam Buchverlag (2005). ISBN 3-7011-0057-8
4. Petrov, V.: Laws of development of needs. In: Proceedings of the TRIZ Future Conference 2005, Graz, 16–18 November 2005, pp. 195–204. Leykam Buchverlag (2005). ISBN 3-7011-0057-8
5. Souili, A., Cavallucci, D., Rousselot, F., Zanni, C.: Starting from patent to find inputs to the Problem Graph model of IDM-TRIZ. In: Proceedings of the 11th TRIZ Future Conference – Systematically Innovating for Sustainable Competitiveness, Dublin, 2–4 November 2011, pp. 177–190, 481p. (2011). ISBN 978-0-9551218-2-1
6. Cascini, G., Russo, D.: Computer-aided analysis of patents and search for TRIZ contradictions. Int. J. Prod. Dev. **4**(1/2), 52–67 (2007)
7. Daim, T.U., Rueda, G., Martin, H., Gerdsri, P.: Forecasting emerging technologies: use of bibliometrics and patent analysis. Technol. Forecast. Soc. Chang. **73**(8), 981–1012 (2006)
8. Moehrle, M., Geritz, A.: Developing acquisition strategies based on patent maps. In: Proceedings of the 13th International Conference on Management of Technology. R&D Management, Washington, pp. 1–9 (2004)
9. Russo, D., Duci, S.: Supporting decision making and requirements evaluation with knowledge search and problem solving. Procedia CIRP **39**, 132–137 (2016)

Evaluation of the Effectiveness of Modern TRIZ Based on Practical Results in New Product Development

Oleg Y. Abramov(✉), Alexander V. Medvedev, and Vladimir Y. Rychagov

Algorithm Ltd., 16 Ruzovskaya Street, St. Petersburg 190013, Russia
Oleg.Abramov@algo-spb.com

Abstract. Today's innovation processes used in industry are generally inefficient: various sources indicate that only one out of three-thousand, raw ideas yield a commercial product. Fortunately, most of the ideas are quickly rejected before much time and money are spent on their development. Still, approximately 300 of the raw ideas are normally selected for further investigation and development, which results in launching around 125 small pilot projects and in other time and money-consuming activities – all for the sake of a single commercially successful product. TRIZ-practitioners claim a much higher efficacy with the TRIZ-based innovation process because TRIZ provides a more systematic approach for innovation and dramatically speeds up the new product development (NPD) process. A number of case studies using TRIZ for NPD back up this statement; however, there is so far no solid quantitative data available to support this statement. In this paper, the authors have tried to evaluate the effectiveness of modern TRIZ in NPD by analyzing a pool of technical solutions for new products developed for different companies in actual TRIZ-consulting projects. For each solution, the authors have tried to identify whether the new product was ultimately launched. This analysis revealed the number of solutions/ideas that TRIZ consultants developed in order to launch one new product and the percentage of successful projects. The results show that using TRIZ improves the efficiency of the NPD process from about 5 to 12 times, which confirms that TRIZ brings high value to NPD.

Keywords: Innovation funnel · New product development · NPD · Quantum Economic Analysis · QEA · TRIZ

1 Introduction

Today's innovation process is known to be quite a wasteful practice for businesses. For example, Stevens and Burley [1] indicate that, on average, in order to obtain one commercially successful product about 3000 raw ideas are typically generated and almost all of these ideas are then rejected in the new product development (NPD) process. This innovation process, or innovation funnel, includes the following steps [1]:

Published by Springer Nature Switzerland AG 2019
R. Benmoussa et al. (Eds.): TFC 2019, IFIP AICT 572, pp. 36–44, 2019.
https://doi.org/10.1007/978-3-030-32497-1_4

- About 3000 raw ideas are generated and internally screened,
- Approximately 300 of these ideas are then submitted to decision makers,
- About 125 ideas are further developed in small projects/small efforts,
- On average, only 1.7 of those ideas result in product launch,
- Just one of the launched products is commercially successful.

Other authors indicate similar numbers characterizing the efficacy of the innovation funnel. For example, Staube in his post [2] indicates that out of 95 projects aimed at incremental innovations, just one results in launching a product, which is not necessarily commercially successful. These figures are nearly comparable to Stevens and Burley's data that 125 small-scale projects yield 1.7 launched products.

The common perception is that in order to increase the probability of obtaining a commercially successful product it is necessary to generate more ideas, the more the better. For example:

- In Design Thinking, as Dam and Siang [3] pointed out, "the goal is to generate a large number of ideas—ideas that potentially inspire newer, better ideas—that the team can then cut down into the best, most practical and innovative ones".
- The Systematic Inventive Thinking (SIT) approach by Boyd and Goldenberg [4] is also based on generating a multitude of creative ideas, but in this case the ideas are generated 'inside the box' just because "...the density of creative ideas is higher inside than outside".

In contrast, TRIZ offers a different way to improve the efficacy of the NPD process: generate fewer – but better and more targeted – ideas, as provided by the TRIZ-assisted Stage-Gate process [5]. The efficacy of TRIZ as a problem solving and problem finding methodology is confirmed in numerous papers, for example by Filmore and Thomond [6], Harlim and Belski [7].

Many case studies confirming the effectiveness of TRIZ have been published [8–11]. The case studies, however, represent only anecdotal data that illustrate how useful TRIZ is in solving technical problems, but do not disclose how many (if any) of the solutions obtained using TRIZ yielded commercially successful products. This leaves room for skepticism and questions about the effectiveness of TRIZ in terms of practical results for business.

For example, Ilevbare, Phaal, Probert et al. clearly expressed a common attitude toward TRIZ in their report [12]: "it appears to pay little attention to linking the inventive problems and their solutions to market needs and drivers. Therefore there exists the unpleasant possibility of TRIZ providing a solution to a problem which has little or no profitability or commercial benefit to an organization".

It should be said that such skepticism seems to be relevant for the older, "classical" TRIZ that utilizes only Altshuller's Contradiction Matrix, SU-Field Analysis and ARIZ, while modern TRIZ has tools such as Voice of the Product (VOP) [13] and Main Parameters of Value (MPV) Analysis [14, 15] to address business needs better.

In a recent conference paper [16], the authors presented solid quantitative data on the effectiveness of the modern TRIZ innovation funnel and contrasted it to that described by Stevens and Burley [1]. The data, derived by a statistical analysis of the outcomes of 161 actual TRIZ consulting projects in which the authors were involved, confirms that modern TRIZ is approximately ten times more efficient in NPD than the traditional approach researched by Stevens and Burley.

There are, however, researchers who believe that Stevens and Burley's data, obtained 22 years ago, is obsolete because the NPD process has become much more efficient due to advances in computer power and accessibility of information. Nevertheless, NPD has not become more efficient because, as practice shows, while these factors have indeed speeded up innovations, the level of wastefulness has changed little: in order to launch one commercially successful product, thousands of raw ideas must still be generated and hundreds of small projects performed.

In this paper, the authors aim to (1) refine the data on modern TRIZ efficacy by collecting more statistical information and (2) estimate the practical potential for further improvement of TRIZ effectiveness in the NPD process by using the Quantum Economic Analysis-based screening tool (further: QEA-screening) introduced and validated by Abramov et al. [17, 18].

2 Method

Just as in the previous paper [16], the authors statistically analyzed the outcomes of actual TRIZ-consulting projects in which they were involved.

The analysis includes the following steps:

1. Out of a pool of completed projects, only those aimed at NPD or at developing/improving a new technology for manufacturing an existing product were selected for further analysis. Projects that were a continuation of some previous project and aimed at developing the same product were not analyzed.
2. The outcomes of each selected project were identified: (1) the number of solutions/ideas submitted to the client after the problem solving stage of the project; (2) the number of solutions further developed (e.g. substantiation, prototyping or patenting efforts); (3) whether any of these solutions eventually yielded a launched product ("successful solutions"); (4) whether any of these solutions were rejected by the client ("unsuccessful solutions").
3. Percentages of successful solutions and projects (those that yielded launched products) were calculated.
4. The locations of all successful and unsuccessful solutions within the QEA business cube were determined – as was done previously by Abramov et al. [18].

The authors wish to make the following comments regarding this procedure:

- The number of raw ideas generated in each project could not be identified because (1) the TRIZ-based methodology used in these projects does not assume using brainstorming, SIT or other techniques for generating raw ideas and, therefore, (2) the raw ideas randomly generated in the projects were not documented.
- Since all of the projects analyzed are small (typically 8–12 weeks), they can be considered equivalent to the 'small projects' in Stevens and Burley's paper [1].

- It was not possible to identify just how many of the launched products were commercially successful because clients are not always willing to share this sensitive information.

3 Results

In this research the authors analyzed a pool of 178 TRIZ-consulting projects, which they carried out from 1994 through 2018. All of these projects were performed for different clients representing a variety of industries; all of them were aimed at NPD or at developing a new technology for manufacturing an existing product. In all projects the TRIZ-assisted Stage-Gate process [5] was employed.

Of the 178 projects in the pool, 40 were actually a continuation of one of the other 138 projects. That is, these 40 were aimed at further developing solutions generated in one of the 138 initial projects. For this reason, only these 138 initial ideation projects were extracted for further analysis.

The projects analyzed have, in total, yielded 1125 feasible technical solutions that were delivered to the clients after the problem solving stage.

Only 192 of these solutions were selected by the clients and further developed at the substantiation stage of the projects, which means that some ‘small efforts’ were put into them (e.g. proof-of-principle prototyping or patenting).

Of this number, the authors were only able to trace the fate of 70 solutions because clients seldom gave feedback on whether the solutions delivered to them were actually implemented. These 70 solutions include:

- 32 successful solutions (i.e. those actually implemented in launched products), and
- 38 unsuccessful solutions; that is, they were either abandoned by the clients or the clients tried to implement them, but did not succeed.

Table 1 summarizes the result of this research.

Table 1. Data obtained in this research is compared to Stevens and Burley data [1]

Item	Data derived in this research	Stevens and Burley data
NPD projects	138	No data
Submitted ideas	1125	300
Small efforts/patent submissions	192	125
Launched products (Successful solutions)	32	1.7
Rejected solutions	38	N/A

As can be seen from Table 1, TRIZ provides a much more efficient NPD process than the regular NPD used in industry. This can be characterized by the success rate at different NPD stages, i.e. by the percentage of submitted ideas and solutions invested with some ‘small effort’ that resulted in launched products, as shown in Fig. 1.

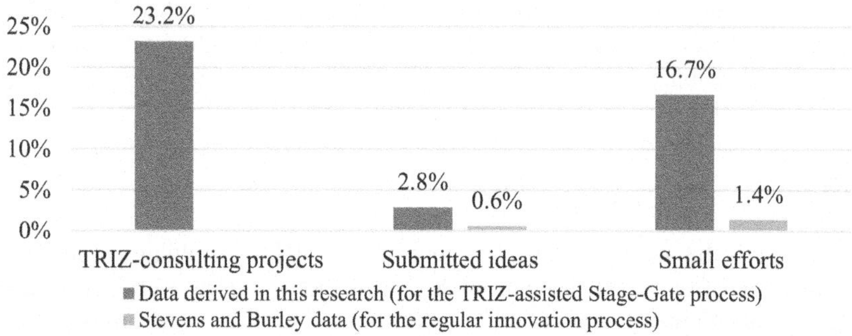

Fig. 1. Success rate at different NPD stages (calculated using the data from Table 1)

In addition to the calculated success rate of different NPD steps, Fig. 1 also shows the success rate of TRIZ-consulting projects in general.

Figure 2 represents the distribution of the 32 successful and 38 unsuccessful solutions within the QEA Business Cube, which was determined in the same manner as in our previous paper [18] that can be referred to for the details of this procedure.

Figure 2 shows that

- Out of 32 successful solutions, 28 fall into the QEA Allowed Set and only 4 do not;
- Out of 38 unsuccessful solutions, only 3 fall into the Allowed Set, while the rest 35 do not.

4 Discussion

As can be seen from Fig. 1, the modern TRIZ applied in the TRIZ-assisted Stage-Gate process for NPD is an order of magnitude more efficient than the regular NPD process with regard to the number of small efforts needed to launch one product. This confirms the results obtained in our previous paper [16].

The results of many projects analyzed in this research are, however, not known to the authors. Therefore, there is a possibility that some solutions resulting from these projects have actually been implemented by the clients, or their implementation is still in progress, which is quite likely for recent projects. This means that the number of successful solutions and successful projects may be higher than estimated in this paper. Therefore, the effectiveness of TRIZ evaluated by the method used in this paper should be considered a 'pessimistic estimation', while the actual effectiveness of modern TRIZ may be much higher.

In addition, it is important to note that all solutions, including those rejected by clients, were substantiated and proven technically feasible at the end of each project analyzed. The clients appreciated and accepted all of these solutions, but later rejected some of them for non-technical reasons.

As shown by the authors in a recent paper [18], while clients rejected a few solutions for personal or other subjective reasons, most solutions were rejected because

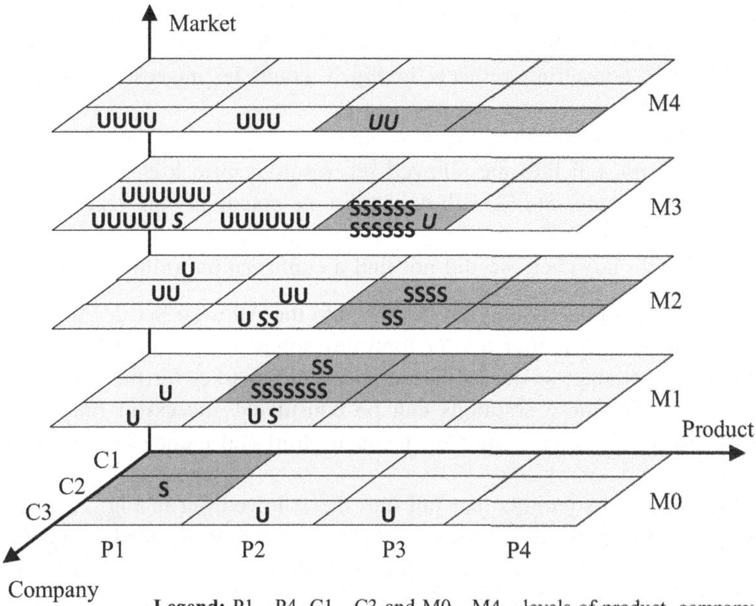

Legend: P1…P4, C1…C3 and M0…M4 - levels of product, company and market development, respectively.
Gray cells represent the combinations of these levels that are within the QEA Allowed Set.
Successful solutions that do not fall into the Allowed Set (*S*) and unsuccessful solutions that do fall into it (*U*) are indicated in red.

Fig. 2. Distribution of 32 successful (**S**) and 38 unsuccessful (**U**) solutions across the levels of the product, company and market development within the QEA Business Cube.

they were unpromising in terms of business impact. Such solutions could have been rejected early in the project by the TRIZ team if the new TRIZ tool called 'QEA-based screening' [17] had been employed.

For this reason, the authors believe that using this tool may further increase the effectiveness of modern TRIZ.

For example, based on Fig. 2, we can conclude that if QEA-screening had been used in the 138 projects considered in this paper, then out of 70 solutions analyzed only 28 successful solutions and 3 unsuccessful solutions would have been delivered to the clients, while the other 35 unsuccessful solutions and 4 successful solutions would have been discarded before delivery. This, then, would have saved the money and effort spent on developing 39 solutions, most of which were eventually rejected by the client.

It seems fair to assume that:

1. In real projects, the solutions rejected according to QEA will be replaced by others that pass QEA-screening, and
2. The success rate of promising solutions that pass QEA-screening will be about the same, as can be determined from Fig. 2, i.e. about 28 out of 31 solutions (approximately 90% of solutions) will be successful.

Under these assumptions, if the 39 solutions that did not pass QEA screening in this research were substituted by potentially successful solutions, then the overall success rate of 138 TRIZ consulting projects in Fig. 1 could be increased from 23.2% to about 46%.

Opponents might argue that QEA-screening (1) rejects some potentially successful solutions that do not fall into the allowed set, resulting in a loss of profit that these solutions would generate, and (2) still delivers some potentially unsuccessful solutions that fall into the Allowed Set.

In this research, however, we did not find a confirmation to this concern because:

- All 4 successful solutions that did not fall into the Allowed Set in Fig. 2 yielded a launched product only after a very long development process: when the product reached the next stage of its evolution and/or the market for the product became more mature. So, these solutions can be considered successful only with some reservations because they required far much effort and money before launching a product.
- All 3 unsuccessful solutions that fall into the Allowed Set in Fig. 2, were unsuccessful only for subjective reasons: in 2 cases clients decided to abandon the developed solutions and focus on some other products; in one case the client was technically unable to implement the proposed solution, although we delivered a working prototype of the product. In fact, all of these solutions could have been successful and should not have been rejected.

5 Conclusions

The results presented in this paper confirm the results reported in a previous paper [16]. The research shows that the effectiveness of modern TRIZ in the TRIZ-assisted Stage-Gate NPD process is at least ten times higher than the regular innovation process, and about 23% of TRIZ-consulting projects result in a launched product (pessimistic estimation).

The new TRIZ tool 'QEA-screening' may help to reduce the number of generated solutions that are unpromising businesswise, thus further increasing the effectiveness of modern TRIZ and the success rate of TRIZ-consulting projects (in terms of percentage of projects that yield a launched product) to about 46% or even higher.

Acknowledgements. The authors would like to thank Deborah Abramov for her helpful comments and for editing this paper.

References

1. Stevens, G., Burley, J.: 3,000 raw ideas equals 1 commercial success! J. Res. Technol. Manag. **40**(3), 16–27 (1997). https://doi.org/10.1080/08956308.1997.11671126
2. Steube, F.: The innovation funnel - infographic. A post on Twitter, 4 March 2018. https://twitter.com/steube/status/970318101425393664. Accessed 15 Apr 2019

3. Dam, R., Siang, T.: Stage 3 in the Design Thinking process: Ideate. Via Interaction Design Foundation. https://www.interaction-design.org/literature/article/stage-3-in-the-design-thinking-process-ideate. Accessed 15 Apr 2019
4. Boyd, D., Goldenberg, J.: Inside the Box: A Proven System of Creativity for Breakthrough Results. Simon & Schuster, New York (2013)
5. Abramov, O.: TRIZ-assisted Stage-Gate process for developing new products. J. Financ. Econ. **2**(5), 178–184 (2014). https://doi.org/10.12691/jfe-2-5-8
6. Filmore, P., Thomond, P.: Why reinvent the wheel? The efficacy of systematic problem solving method TRIZ and its value for innovation in engineering and its implications for engineering management. TRIZ J. (2006). https://triz-journal.com/reinvent-wheel-efficacy-systematic-problem-solving-method-triz-value-innovation-engineering-implications-engineering-management/. Accessed 15 Apr 2019
7. Harlim, J., Belski, I.: On the effectiveness of TRIZ tools for problem finding. Procedia Eng. **131**, 892–898 (2015). https://doi.org/10.1016/j.proeng.2015.12.400
8. Spreafico, C., Russo, D.: TRIZ industrial case studies: a critical survey. Procedia CIRP **39**, 51–56 (2016). https://doi.org/10.1016/j.procir.2016.01.165
9. Ramadurai, B.: TRIZ case studies. Blog on the Internet, 04 April 2017. http://balaramadurai.net/blog/2017/04/04/TRIZ-case-studies/. Accessed 15 Apr 2019
10. RMIT University website: "Case studies. TRIZ repository". https://www.edisons21.com/content/case-studies. Accessed 15 Apr 2019
11. Applied Innovation Alliance website: "AIA case studies briefings Part 1". https://www.appliedinnovationalliance.com/member-navigation/aia-case-studies-briefings-part1/. Accessed 15 Apr 2019
12. Ilevbare, I., Phaal, R., Probert, D., et al.: Integration of TRIZ and roadmapping for innovation, strategy, and problem solving: Phase 1 – TRIZ, roadmapping and proposed integrations. Report on a collaborative research initiative between the Centre for Technology Management, University of Cambridge, UK, and Dux Diligens, Mexico, July 2011. Via Institute for Manufacturing (IfM). https://www.ifm.eng.cam.ac.uk/uploads/Research/CTM/Roadmapping/triz_dux_trt_phase1_report.pdf. Accessed 15 Apr 2019
13. Abramov, O.: 'Voice of the Product' to supplement 'Voice of the Customer'. In: Proceedings of TRIZFest-2015 Conference, Seoul, South Korea. pp. 313–321. https://matriz.org/wp-content/uploads/2012/07/TRIZfest-2015-conference-Proceedings.pdf. Accessed 15 Apr 2019
14. Malinin, L.: The method for transforming a business goal into a set of engineering problems. Int. J. Bus. Innov. Res. **4**(4), 321–337 (2010). https://doi.org/10.1504/IJBIR.2010.033350
15. Litvin, S.: Main Parameters of Value: TRIZ-based tool connecting business challenges to technical problems in product/process innovation. Keynote presentation at 7th Japan TRIZ Symposium, Yokohama, Japan, 9 September 2011. http://www.triz-japan.org/PRESENTATION/sympo2011/Pres-Overseas/EI01eS-Litvin_(Keynote)-110817.pdf. Accessed 15 Apr 2019
16. Abramov, O., Markosov, S., Medvedev, A., Rychagov, V.: Innovation funnel of modern TRIZ: experimental study to show the efficacy of the TRIZ-assisted Stage-Gate process. In: Proceedings of the 14th MATRIZ TRIZfest-2018 International Conference, Lisbon, Portugal, pp. 105–110. https://matriz.org/wp-content/uploads/2019/01/TRIZfest-2018-Proceedings.pdf. Accessed 15 Apr 2019

17. Abramov, O.: Generating new product ideas with TRIZ-derived 'Voice of the Product' and Quantum-Economic Analysis (QEA). J. Eur. TRIZ Assoc. INNOVATOR **2**(04), 80–87 (2017). http://www.etria.eu/innovator/ETRIAjournal2017vol04.pdf. Accessed 15 Apr 2019
18. Abramov, O., Markosov, S., Medvedev, A.: Experimental validation of Quantum-Economic Analysis (QEA) as a screening tool for new product development. In: Koziołek, S., Chechurin, L., Collan, M. (eds.) Advances and Impacts of the Theory of Inventive Problem Solving, pp. 17–25. Springer, Cham (2018). https://doi.org/10.1007/978-3-319-96532-1_2

Applied Ideality: From Concepts to Inventive Problem Solving Algorithm

Evgeniy E. Smirnov(✉)

St. Petersburg International Public University of TRIZ, Saint Petersburg, Russia
triz-on@mail.ru

Abstract. The paper is devoted to the concept of an ideality and its derivatives: an ideal functional system and an ideal outcome. The differences between them and the scope of their practical application are studied.

The current state of art in modeling and problem solving algorithms in TRIZ are also highlighted.

A simple analysis-synthesis algorithm for inventive problem solving is proposed using the concept of an ideal outcome and a resource approach aimed to reducing the ideality of the result through a resource analysis of the situation. The proposed algorithm, in contrast to ARIZ, was created to solve problems with a single conflict, i.e., without related (conjugated) functions that form a contradiction of conditions. In addition to the concepts mentioned above, the algorithm relies on the "solution backwards" method and the use of element-functional modeling of conflicts (EFM.C).

The paper also provides an example of analysis-synthesis for a simple production problem in order to show the mechanics of individual steps of the algorithm, as well as the entire algorithm as a whole.

Keywords: Ideality · Ideal functional system · Ideal outcome · Ideal final result · Resource analysis · Analysis-synthesis algorithm · ARIZ

1 Introduction

The subjects of the study are concepts and toolkit of the science of creativity and its heuristic part – contemporary TRIZ, sharpened to solve non-standard (inventive) problems. There are many disagreements on various terms and concepts. In particular, this concerns one of the key concepts of TRIZ – ideality and its applications to the result and functional system.

At this point there are two main disadvantages in the interpretation of the stated subjects: (1) such concepts as value and ideality are placed on the same shelf; (2) the concepts of an ideal system and an ideal outcome are mixed.

There is also no simple tool for working with these concepts: for analyzing the conflict model and further synthesis of solution ideas.

All existing algorithms can be divided into two categories. The first one includes overly complex tools that contain almost all concepts – from conflicts and contradictions to resources and physical effects – for example, the algorithm of inventive problem solving (ARIZ). The second one includes tools that are weak in terms of

Published by Springer Nature Switzerland AG 2019
R. Benmoussa et al. (Eds.): TFC 2019, IFIP AICT 572, pp. 45–54, 2019.
https://doi.org/10.1007/978-3-030-32497-1_5

heuristics and dialectics, and they are not effective enough in solving complex extraordinary problems – for example, such sets of techniques as SIT, ASIT and so on.

For these reasons, it makes sense to deal with the aforementioned concepts and with the basic tool of contemporary TRIZ to increase the effectiveness of their application.

2 Background

In contemporary TRIZ, conceptual modeling is used. This implies precise definition of all the concepts used. To this end, the formula of concepts definition has been proposed [1].

The purpose of this study is to understand the ideality, its derivatives (an ideal functional system and an ideal outcome) and the development of practices for their application.

Historically, the ideal outcome in TRIZ is called the "ideal final result" (IFR). Such a name most likely implies a final solution that suits the inventor. But it has significant disadvantages. First, ideality itself is already a limiting abstraction. Secondly, the result finiteness creates a sort of psychological barrier which limits the search for possible alternative solutions to the problem.

It should be noted that IFR was not immediately introduced into the first versions of ARIZ, although it is analogous to an element of the well-known method of solution backwards, which was proposed by Pappus (III-IV centuries A.D.), a Greek mathematician and founder of Heuristics. In modern times this method was revived by George Polya (1945) [2].

However IFR is often used independently due to the fact that it has high heuristic power. And since "ideality" is the key concept here, it often happens that IFR is confused with another similar concept – the "ideal system".

For instance, the work [3, p. 76] states that the ideal final result can be achieved by the application of different tools through use of resources, and also that systems become simpler, not more complex, because: Ideality = ΣBenefits/(ΣCosts + ΣHarm). Although evolution is always a development which is the equivalent of the increasing complexity.

A similar definition of ideality is presented in many other works, for example, in the book [4]. At that, the authors write about the ideal result. Here is another vivid example when the ideal result is defined as an ideal system: "It's when something performs its function and does not exist" [5, p. 23].

On the other hand, one of the first definition of value is [6, p. 5]:

1. Value is always increased by decreasing costs (while, of course, maintaining performance).
2. Value is increased by increasing performance if the customer needs, wants, and is willing to pay for more performance.

Thus, it is necessary to precisely define all these concepts and figure out how to use them in practice to successfully solve inventive problems.

Today, the only tool within the classic TRIZ developed for this purpose is the ARIZ-85C (its latest version approved by Altshuller) [7]. In case of single conflicts, either inventive techniques or so-called Substance-Field (Su-Field) Analysis [7] are usually used. Both of these tools are seriously outdated and do not have acceptable, sufficiently effective analogues.

ARIZ-85C has a mechanism for using the concept of "IFR". But the algorithm is practically not used because it is complex, contains a large number of steps and it is necessary to formulate contradictions of different types.

In this connection, it is proposed to use a simplified version of the algorithm for solving problems without revealing contradictions. This new algorithm based on the key concepts of contemporary TRIZ: desired outcome, ideal outcome, and element-functional resources (EFR). For this, it is necessary to clarify these concepts, and outline ways of their practical application to eliminate conflicts in the framework of solving inventive (non-standard) problems.

3 Ideality and Outcome

If the value tends to infinity, it turns into the ideality. In other words, the ideality is the ultimate value. Taking value as the ratio of functionality to cost, it is possible to obtain a number of ways to idealize the target object (Fig. 1).

$$\begin{array}{l}\text{Ideality}\\ \uparrow\\ \infty\\ \uparrow\text{Value} \sim \dfrac{\sum F}{\sum C}\end{array}$$

Fig. 1. Representation of ideality.

The ideality can also be achieved in another way. Since the object model is an abstraction, the maximum abstraction assumes presence of only the most significant feature – the function. This also agrees with the value formula.

Next, it is necessary to make a clear choice about what outcome one needs to obtain under the problem conditions. This outcome will depend on the type of the function involved in the conflict model. All conflicts are associated with five types of actions (Fig. 2):

1. Infliction of harm.
2. Excessive or over activity.
3. Unstable (nonpersistent) action.
4. Weak or insufficient activity.
5. No activity or malfunction.

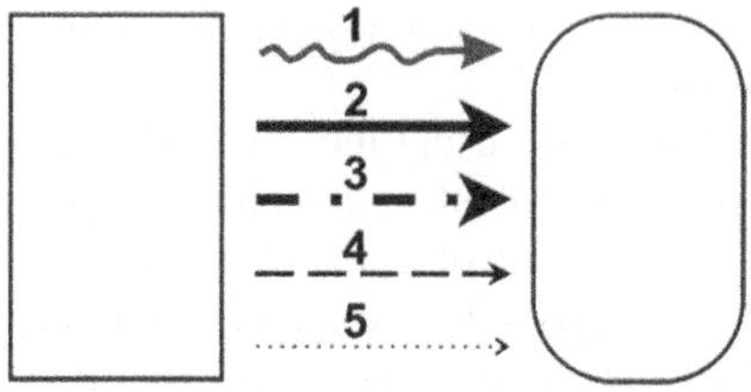

Fig. 2. Types of conflict activities.

Thus, the desired outcome will represent a new future state of the function: (1) harmful function – to eliminate or neutralize; (2) inadequate functions – to normalize; (3) missing function – to provide.

And only after the desired (or even required) outcome is determined, it is necessary to start its idealization.

4 Idealization – for System and Outcome

The science of creativity (or invention) and contemporary TRIZ deal with objects of reality while at the level of abstractions one develops models that allow of achieving goals and solving problems that stand in the way of these goals.

Real objects are modeled as functional systems (FS), which serve as one of the main subjects of study. The complete schematic of the functional system was presented in the author's work [1].

Modeling is the process of selecting the essential features of the object. Whereas idealization (or absolutization) assumes working with the most essential feature only, and is the highest form of abstraction. For functional systems, it is the function as a model for changing the object of function. And the outcome of the function implementation is the outcome of the change – the new state of the object of function (Fig. 3). This concept of the desired outcome is true for a useful, adequate (normal) function.

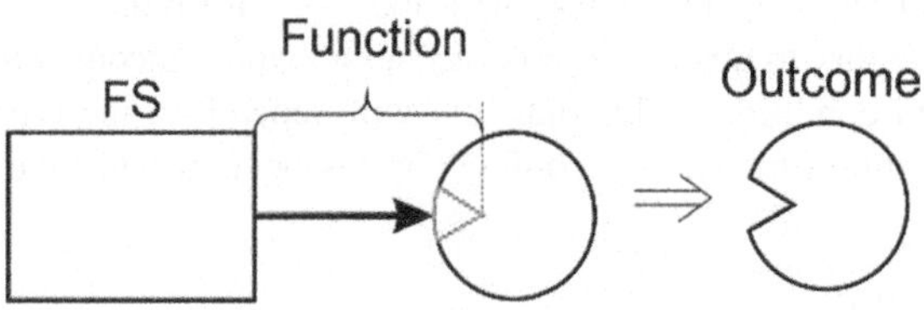

Fig. 3. Model of function and possible outcome.

It is for this reason that the ideal functional system (IFS) is reduced to a function. Cost is a relative or even subjective factor, and therefore is not taken into account in ideal models.

Thus, the IFS is formed by way of application of the idealization operator to the "functional system" concept, and has rather psychological meaning than the practical one.

The ideal outcome is designed to be used within the framework of algorithms, but it is often used independently, which, supposedly, is the reason for the loss of its original meaning.

The algorithmic approach uses the ideal outcome concept, when the desired state of a function (an object of function) is achieved **by itself**, with no costs for the process of obtaining it. The ideal desired outcome (IDO) as well as the ideal functional system are the benchmarks that make it possible to use resources for implementation of the required functions.

G. Altshuller proposed another version of the IDO – for detection and measuring problems – which was recorded only in the short video of 1974: "How to search for Cinderella? Formulate the ideal final result. How to make it perfect? There is no one except Cinderella <…>". For example, if it is required to find a needle in a haystack, then the IDO can be formulated in the same way – there is nothing but a needle. That is, generalizing this principle, everything that stands in the way (obstacle to the goal) should somehow disappear.

The direct interaction of the "ideal system" and "ideal outcome" concepts can occur when it is necessary to ensure the required action if there was a function missing in the original conflict. Here, ideally, the function should be implemented by the missing system that is the ideal system.

5 Basic Analysis-Synthesis Algorithm for Conflicts Resolving

To achieve the ideal desired outcome, a simplified algorithm based on mobilization of resources is proposed.

5.1 Analysis

At this stage the object under consideration is analyzed, and the environment is evaluated.

Step 1. Initial situation. Decomposition of form. It is necessary to make a list of all the elements available and their features. If the conflict is clearly localized, it is sufficient to specify only those elements which belong to the operational area.

Step 2. Revealed conflicts. Decomposition of structure and functions. It is necessary to highlight the main conflicts between the selected elements: obstacles, harm, inadequate or missing activity.

NB. It is possible to select all interactions between all the elements starting from the first step. But it will complicate the analysis process. If there are too many elements, then it is more convenient to switch to a purely analytical tool – for instance, value (triple) analysis. This particular algorithm is designed for the localized conflicts. Therefore, the number of such elements will be minimal.

Also, it is necessary to indicate here the type of each function: harmful, useful (excessive, insufficient and unstable), missing (see Fig. 2).

Step 3. Desired outcomes. It should describe the final outcomes that will suit you. That is, when there is no conflict, and everything works properly: there is no obstacle, no harm, the required interactions are ensured.

If several conflicts are considered, it is necessary to describe the outcome for each activity. The desired outcomes will depend on the function type and correspond to the number of harmful, inadequate and missing functions.

Step 4. Idealization of the desired outcomes. At this step, the ideal representation of all the desired outcomes (see Step 3) for each function (see Step 2) is carried out. In other words, the ideal processes for achieving the desired outcomes should be formulated. The results are achieved by themselves (automatically), with no cost.

"Self" is the key operator that tunes thinking process to a creative mode, and removes doubts about the feasibility of achieving the desired outcomes.

The ideal outcome is only the guiding star. It is necessary try to maximize the system value by changing the functionality and cost. This provides several ways to achieve perfection. For example, it is possible to add functions to the elements imagining that these functions are performed – themselves, without additional costs and support from other elements.

5.2 Synthesis – De-Idealization of Outcomes

At this stage, the fabulousness wrapper is discarded, and it is necessary to proceed to the new formulations of the process of achieving the specified ideal outcomes – it is achieved, but not by itself. Although the operator "itself" may be retained for greater effect.

It is necessary to start the search for resources and their application. But, in accordance with the proposed algorithm, most of the resources have already been collected in Steps 1 and 2. So, it remains to apply them. To do this, it is required to consistently insert the available resources (see Frame 1 and Frame 2 in the template – Fig. 4) in the following wording:

> <Resource or its feature> [itself] ensures the achievement of <the (ideal) desired outcome>.

Step 5. Use of conflict area resources to achieve ideal outcomes. The 1st step backward from the ideal outcomes: resource mobilization in the conflict areas – see Elements and Functions from Step 2. That is, now it is a retreat from the ideal, and anything will not happen by itself (not automatically), but with the use of assistants, some X-factors.

In this step, only those resources are used that are within the conflict operational space. That is, the interaction is normalized only at the expense of those elements which are involved in this interaction.

Each new formulation is an additional trigger for our thinking in search for new ideas. Much more paradox formulations appear. This is exactly the main objective of the algorithm.

Step 6. Use of remaining resources to achieve ideal outcomes. This is the 2nd step back from the ideal outcomes: mobilizing resources from the environment, system and supersystem. Here, resources should be taken from Step 1 – Elements and their Features; and from Step 2 – Functions, including space-time resources. If necessary, search for resources should be repeated.

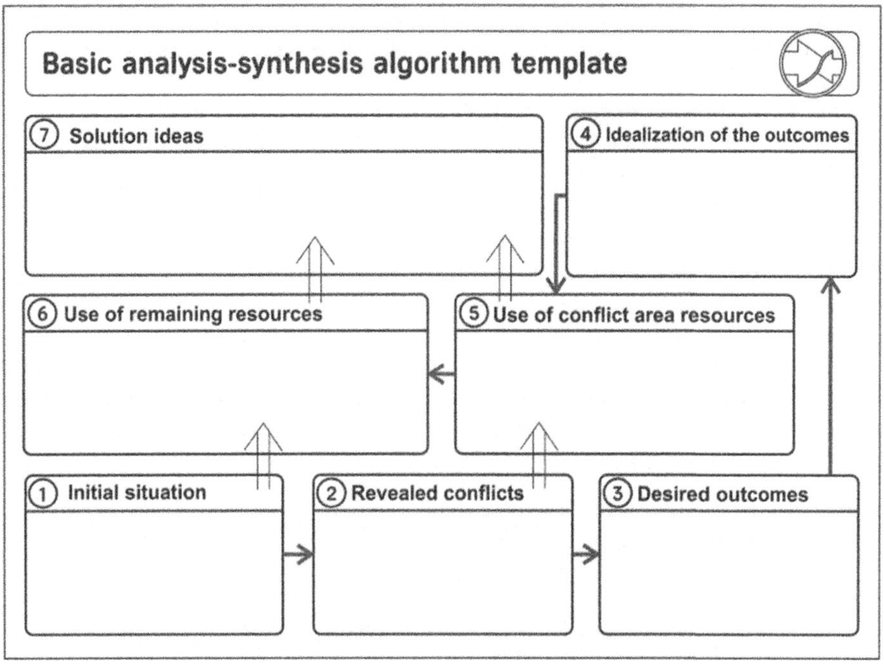

Fig. 4. Basic analysis-synthesis algorithm template.

The total number of formulations here will depend on the number of resources found. The bigger number of different resources are used, the grater departure from the ideal outcome will be.

Therefore, at this and previous steps, a number of quite specific challenges come up to be solved on one's own or delegated to appropriate specialists.

Step 7. Solution ideas. A frame for recording solution ideas (Fig. 4). If too many ideas spring up, it is better to use a special notebook for this purpose.

After the main resources are used – if an acceptable solution is not found or if more ideas are required – an additional step needs to be taken combining and modifying these resources (see ARIZ-85C, Part 4).

6 How to Use the Algorithm in Practice

In order to clarify the situation with the application of this algorithm, a simple example is offered. This will help to better understand the principles and concepts presented here.

The purpose of this example is only to demonstrate the mechanism of individual steps of the algorithm. There is no emphasis on solution ideas and their feasibility.

Part 1. Situation analysis.

Initial Situation. There is a furnace for heating workpieces. To unload workpieces after heat treatment and to load new workpieces, it is necessary to open the chamber by lifting the housing. This leads to negative consequences – hot air leaves the chamber and as a result there are excessive energy consumption and time wastes for new air heating.

Step 1. Identify all available components in the situation context.

It is better that this step is performed by an expert on the system in question.

The following components are available: chamber, housing, hot air, heater elements, electric drive, workpiece, etc.

Unrecorded resources can be added later.

Step 2. Determining the area (and time) of the conflict.

The main conflict occurs in the process of reloading the workpieces – when the housing is opened, the temperature inside the chamber goes down.

What element of the chamber is specifically designed to hold hot air? Camera housing. This means that it is necessary to formulate functional conflict between the housing and hot air during the restart of the process: housing is NOT holding hot air in the workpiece processing area (Fig. 5).

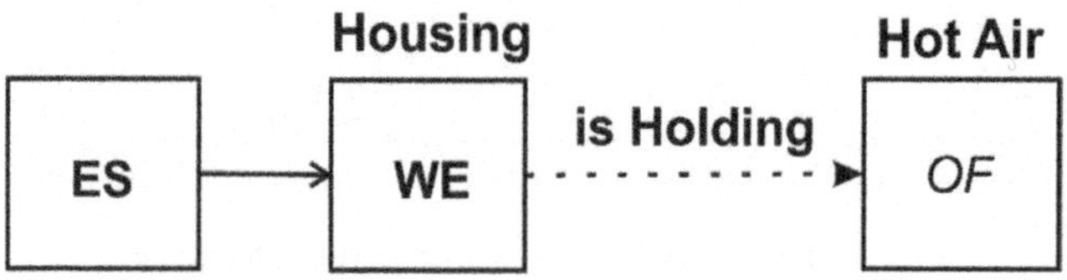

Fig. 5. Graphic representation of the element-functional model of conflict (EFM.C) [8]; where: ES – Energy Source; WE – Working Element; OF – Object of Function.

In this case, in the diagram the missing (or insufficient) action is shown as a dashed line. The word form does not contain a negative particle NOT.

Step 3. Desired outcome formulation.

The outcome is based on the type of conflict function from Step 2. It is necessary to ensure normal (adequate) performance of the function.

Desired outcome: housing is normally holding hot air in the workpieces processing area, that is, hot air remains within the chamber during its restart (reloading of workpieces).

Step 4. Idealization of the desired outcome.

It is necessary to formulate an ideal outcome based on how the desired outcome was set in Step 3.

Therefore, hot air **itself** has already remained in the chamber (during the restart).

It would be better to start this step with a mental representation. In order not to spoil the ideal image that the imagination painted, you should not write anything yet.

NB. This image is formulated in the perfect (completed) form. In the next steps with the use of resources, all formulations should be in the continued (process) form.

Part 2. De-idealization of outcome.

De-idealization of outcome is a synthesis of solution ideas using the resources collected during the analysis.

Step 5. Using conflicting elements as primary resources.

The formulation would be something like this: the hot air **itself** is holding hot air in the area during the restart process.

And here it is necessary to make another formulation – for the second element involved in the conflict (see the connection with Step 2 in Fig. 4): housing **itself** is holding hot air in the area inside, during the restart process.

Similar wording should also be added here for all characteristics of conflicting elements.

After that, they should be reformulated into tasks (specific challenges). It is these tasks that will need to be solved further. They are not quite inventive, but rather engineering.

For example, the task: how to make the thermal insulation layer is keeping the hot air in the process of restarting?

Such tasks should be distributed among the project participants.

Step 6. Using the remaining resources (from the system, supersystem and environment).

At this step, the resources that were taken into account at Step 1 are used.

New resources can also help other resources that are already working on achieving the ideal (desired) result from the previous step.

An example of new task: how to make cold air is keeping hot air from leaving the treatment area?

All relevant ideas should be recorded in the Frame 7: Solution ideas (see Fig. 4).

Thus, we are going from the initial situation through the inventive problem in the form of a functional conflict to engineering tasks. Some of these tasks can also be inventive problems and they must be rerun through this algorithm.

7 Conclusions

In the paper, the ideality idea is presented. The desired (required) and ideal outcome concepts are considered.

The differences between the ideal outcome and the ideal functional system are shown as well.

The algorithm for solving inventive problems, based on two fundamental mechanisms of thinking – analysis and synthesis – has been proposed: thinking goes through construction of the desired outcome, its idealization, and the reverse trace (de-idealization) using the rules for resource mobilization – that is, their search [analysis], choice [operational stage] and application [synthesis of solutions].

It is recommended to start learning and teaching the tools of contemporary TRIZ from this algorithm, because it is the assembly of the very first basic concepts that previously had to be studied individually: Element, Function, Functional System, Element-Functional Resources, Ideality, Ideal FS, Desired and Ideal Outcomes.

It can also be used for guided facilitation sessions for solving non-standard problems.

Also, the proposed algorithm works with single functions only. The algorithm can have at least two names, according to operating principle: Analysis-Synthesis Algorithm; and by function: Functional Conflicts Eliminating Algorithm (FCEA).

If contradictions arise, it is necessary to switch to more advanced algorithms, for example, ARIZ-85C. To work with the contradiction-removing algorithm, a preliminary study of additional concepts is needed, including: contradictions of conditions and contradictions of requirements [1].

References

1. Smirnov, E.E.: Formula of concepts definition and its application to basic concepts of contemporary TRIZ. In: TRIZ Future Conference 2018: Professional Proceedings, Strasbourg, France, 29–31 October 2018, pp. 213–223. https://tfc2018.fr/professional-papers
2. George Polya: How to Solve It. A New Aspect of Mathematical Method (1945)
3. Rantanen, K., Domb, E.: Simplified TRIZ: New Problem Solving Applications for Engineers and Manufacturing Professionals, 2nd edn., 272 p. Auerbach Publications (2007)
4. Gadd, K.: TRIZ For Engineers: Enabling Inventive Problem Solving. Oxford Creativity (2011)
5. Hipple, Jack: The Ideal Result. What It Is and How to Achieve It. Springer, New York (2012). https://doi.org/10.1007/978-1-4614-3707-9. ISBN 978-1-4614-3707-9
6. Miles, L.D.: Techniques of Value Analysis and Engineering. McGraw-Hill, New York (1961)
7. Altschuller, G.S., Zlotin, B.L., Zusman, A.V., Filatov V.I.: Search for New Ideas: from Insight to Technology (Theory and Practice of Inventive Problem Solving). Kartya Moldovenyaske, Kishinev, 381 p. (1989). (in Russian)
8. Smirnov, E.E.: Element-functional modeling of conflicts: EFM.C. In: Three Generations of TRIZ. Materials of the Annual Scientific and Practical Conference Dedicated to the 90th anniversary of G.S. Altshuller, pp. 4–13 (2016). http://ratriz.ru/konferentsii/tri-pokoleniya-triz-2016. (in Russian)

Deducing Altshuller's Laws of Evolution of Technical Systems

Justus Schollmeyer[1(✉)] and Viesturs Tamuzs[2]

[1] Second Negation, Berlin, Germany
justus@secondnegation.com
[2] Altshuller Institute, Worcester, MA, USA
viesturs.tamuzs@gmail.com

Abstract. According to Genrich Altshuller and most of his students, his eight laws of technical systems evolution were found by systematic patent analysis. In this paper, we show that not a single patent must be studied to derive the very same eight laws, but rather that they follow from an analysis of the concept of artificial instrumental systems in the context of a competitive world with scarce resources. Our investigation yields a clear definition of ideality which—insofar as certain constraints are respected—indicates multiple trends underlying the evolution of systems towards increased competitiveness when resources are scarce. By making the truth conditions for each law explicit, we attempt to explain why some high generality patents from the 20th century contradict some of Altshuller's laws. We conclude that although patents can be seen as a useful source for inspiration, validation and falsification of generalizations, they are not the most promising place to start to look for laws of system evolution, since mere induction from past examples cannot provide the justification needed to meaningfully inform engineers about how to develop systems in the future. Our approach suggest an alternative route for articulating and justifying such laws.

Keywords: Laws of system development · Technological forecast · Ideality

1 Goal and Structure of the Paper

In 1979, Genrich Altshuller published 8 laws of technical systems evolution [1], which according to him [2] can be found by systematic study of high generality patents. Both, critics [3] and advocates [4] of the usefulness of Altshuller's laws emphasize that thousands of patents were analyzed to discover these laws. Although there is an abundant literature proposing divergent formulations of these and other laws that are often called *trends* or *patterns* (see, for example, [5–10]), we will concentrate on Altshuller's initial formulation from 1979 [1].

Our paper aims to show that, in principle, not a single patent must be studied in order to arrive at Altshuller's eight laws of technical system evolution. Rather, they follow from the meaning of a *technical system* when understood as an *artificial instrumental system* in the context of a *competitive world with scarce resources*. This deductibility is the actual reason why they might be able to lay claim to some law-like

Published by Springer Nature Switzerland AG 2019
R. Benmoussa et al. (Eds.): TFC 2019, IFIP AICT 572, pp. 55–69, 2019.
https://doi.org/10.1007/978-3-030-32497-1_6

status[1]—at least as long as the respective conditions for their application are respected. This, however, does not imply that they should not be tested against the evidence from the patent stock (see Sect. 4).

The paper comprises three major parts. First, we will articulate in general terms what systems are by putting our focus on the notion of *instrumental systems*, which can either be *static* or *dynamic*, and *natural* or *artificial* (Sect. 2). Second, we will show that Altshuller's eight laws from 1979 can be inferred from the general statements explaining these distinctions—at least insofar as additional restrictions such as *scarcity of resources* and *competition* are assumed (Sect. 3). Third, we will reflect on the counterexamples from a patent analysis done by [19] and show how the derived truth conditions for Altshuller's laws help explain these contradictions (Sect. 4). Finally, we will summarize our findings and indicate how to proceed further (conclusions in Sect. 5).

2 General Reflection on Systems

2.1 Systems in General and Instrumental Systems in Particular

A system is a whole that consists of parts, which—insofar as the system is not an abstract one—can be anything that has some mass. Together these parts bring about effects. Systems are useful as long as they can be *controlled* such that their ability to realize effects makes it possible to employ them for particular purposes in particular contexts. When systems are employed for particular purposes, they are serving functions and will be called *instrumental.*

[1] Traditionally, the term law requires some form of deductibility. According to [11], the debate about the definition of *natural laws* falls into two camps: *systemic approaches* and *universal approaches*. In the case of systemic approaches, natural laws are viewed in the context of deductive systems. Deductive systems consist of axioms and their logical consequences: theorems. Some of them are stronger than others, which means they are able to explain more. Some others are simpler and thus less complex. Simplicity and strength are seen as competing virtues insofar as a system can be made simpler by reducing strength, which can be achieved easily by elimination of some of the axioms resulting in a simpler system (see [11]). As a proponent of the systems approach, [12] believes that an account of our natural laws can be found in the totality of our true deductive systems that have the best strength-simplicity ratio. In contrast, universal approaches think about natural laws in terms of particular things being seen as instantiations of their universals. For example, a law that states that *horses are mammals* would assume the existence of (i) the universals horse-ness and mammal-ness and (ii) a necessitating relation—i.e. a relation of causality that is not merely logical [13]—between horse-ness and mammal-ness, such that horse-ness necessitates mammal-ness. Making such necessitating relations explicit in the form of laws allows for deduction. In both types of approaches—systemic and universal ones—deductibility is crucial for calling something a law. The way in which Altshuller's laws are usually presented in the literature—i.e. as being found by comprehensive patent analysis—rather resembles the style of universal approaches. In contrast, we are going to show that they follow from a handful of axioms within a simple deductive system.

2.2 Living Systems with Needs and Desires

Living systems depend on instrumentalizing their environments. They must build cellular components from chemicals and energy (anabolism) and break down organic matter (catabolism) to either release energy or to serve anabolic reactions. These processes of metabolism require living systems to make use of what their environments provide. We will call a lack that would threaten a living system's healthy existence—if not satisfied—a *need*. In addition to needs, some living systems—in particular humans—have *desires*. They come as the feeling of wanting.

2.3 Satisfaction of Needs and Desires Requires Activity

In order to fulfill a desire or to satisfy some need, living systems must do something. Humans, for example, must breathe to enrich themselves with oxygen and plants must convert sunlight into chemical energy for growing. While—for most people—breathing is a subconscious activity most of the time, putting ourselves under water changes the situation entirely. Our standard technique of enriching our blood with oxygen will not work anymore.

2.4 Solving Problems with Techniques and Technical Devices

Living systems face problems, as soon as they are unable to fulfill some desire or to satisfy some need. Problems can be solved in a variety of ways. What can count as the most appropriate solution depends on context. Sometimes simple techniques such as breath retention can do the job. Sometimes, a basic technique is not enough, and some external enhancement is needed, for example a snorkel that allows us to breathe under water as long as the opening at the top of the snorkel remains above the waterline. In the latter case, we have employed something to help us satisfy our need to enrich our blood with oxygen by enabling us to breathe. We are not only using some technique but also some technical device.

2.5 Artificial and Natural Systems

While strolling around, we could be lucky and find some specially grown hollow wooden tree limb and use it is as a snorkel. Alternatively, we could make one on our own. In the first case, we would have to be able to recognize the *function* that the wooden limb could perform for us. In the second case, we will have to purposefully process something such that it can serve this function. In both cases, we must be able to recognize our need and understand that we are looking for something that makes it possible for us to breathe under water. It might already exist and we have to find it, or it might not exist yet and we must create it. We will call everything that was purposefully created or manufactured *artificial* to distinguish it from *natural* things that were not purposefully put together by someone.[2]

2.6 Functional Parts

In its simplest version, a snorkel is a hollow stick that is U-shaped at the bottom. The shorter leg fits into a human's mouth, while the longer leg is straight and reaches out of the water when used as a snorkel. Although the device consists of only one part, it can be called a system, because from a functional perspective, multiple parts can be distinguished: the "mouth part", the "channel part", and the "chimney part". Technically, functions are expressed in the form "part A + function (verb + measurable noun) + part B". Take, for example, the channel part (A), which constrains (verb) the movement (measurable noun) of the air flow (molecules [B]) within the snorkel.

2.7 Energy Transformation and Static Systems vs. Dynamic Systems

A function that can be executed while an equilibrium is reached such that the responsible parts do not have to expend any energy—as, for example, in "the screw positions the plate"—will be called *static*.[3] In contrast, functions will be called dynamic if their execution requires any of the responsible parts to expend energy, as in "the lever changes the position of the basket" (where something or someone needs to move the lever). Accordingly, we will speak of a *static system* when taking into account static functions alone—for example when reflecting on how the snorkel is constructed. Analogously, when taking into account dynamic functions as well, we will call the system *dynamic*. Since energy cannot be produced from nothing, dynamic systems have to be their own energy sources by somehow transforming energy from their environments. *Energy transformation* is thus a key feature of dynamic systems.

2.8 The Functions of Systems Show in the Respective Dynamic Super-Systems

Due to their dependence on dynamic systems, we would not be able to identify a static system's function if we were not able to imagine or observe it performing its roles within dynamic super-systems.[4] For example, a bicycle on its own is a static system. When being ridden, it is part of a dynamic super-system within which it serves a function. A bike has the disposition to become dynamic, but it is not dynamic in itself. The same holds for the snorkel. Only when used by someone for snorkeling does this

[2] The totality of roles that an artificial system can be employed for does not have to be equal to the set of roles it was designed for in the first place. A bridge, for example, can be designed for allowing cars to cross a river, but it might also provide shelter from rain.

[3] Note that this notion of a static function is an abstraction, since, upon closer consideration, functions can only be called *static* when abstracting from undesired dynamics—for example material wear in the screw that positions a plate.

[4] Note that some of the functions responsible for keeping the static system's form can be identified irrespective of the system's role in dynamic super-systems.

static system become part of a dynamic super-system and show its proper function. In one sentence: to understand functions of systems, we have to investigate them in the context of the dynamic super-systems where they satisfy some need or desire.

2.9 Hierarchical System Structure

Dynamic super-systems can themselves be systems in some wider dynamic super-system. A cyclist on a treadmill, for example, can be part of an energy generating fitness center. The treadmill (static system) and the cyclist (dynamic system) form a dynamic super-system, which is part of the larger dynamic super-super-system that consists of multiple ridden treadmills, a battery etc. Most of the time, systems exist in much more complex hierarchies than this one and it would be pointless to add the prefix "super" to each higher or "sub" to each lower level. From now on, we will therefore abandon this practice if no additional clarity can be gained by pointing out the different levels of hierarchy.

2.10 Energy Input as a Key Feature of Dynamic Systems

Although the ridden treadmill transforms mechanical energy into electrical energy, it is a static system because it requires a cyclist to receive energy in the first place. Therefore, the ability to transform energy is not enough for a system to be dynamic. Suppose the cyclist was replaced by a combustion engine providing the mechanical energy needed to turn the shaft of the pedals. As long as they are being fueled, engine (dynamic) and treadmill (static) would become a dynamic system. *Energy input* is thus a further key feature of dynamic systems. A dynamic system that is cut off from its energy source will sooner or later turn into a static system.

2.11 Dependence Versus Relative Independence

If a dynamic system does not have control over its own energy input, it is dependent on the dynamic system controlling it. This dependency comes in different forms. Electronic devices have power switches that are controlled by their users, solar thermal heating systems depend on whether or not the sun is shining and mammals have to find food or water to fuel their metabolism. Roughly speaking, the dynamic system controlling another's energy input determines whether or not the latter will remain dynamic or become static. Generally speaking, the more control a dynamic system gains over its fundamental operational functions such as energy input, the more independent it becomes.

2.12 Energy Conduction, Control, and Work as Key Features of Dynamic Systems

As far as we know, energy can neither be destroyed nor created, but only transformed from one form to another. That dynamic systems transform energy shows in their production of effects. Some of these effects might be useful for someone while others might not. This usefulness of the produced effects is the result of their work and it is also the reason why they are employed by others for their purposes. However, the work a dynamic system is employed for is different from the work carried out by the dynamic system's mechanism. When we want to turn a shaft by means of a combustion engine, the engine must burn fuel to transform chemical energy into mechanical energy. Besides guiding the input energy to its place of conversion and transforming it, the energy must be directed to where it can do the work it is supposed to do. Directing energy requires both control over the energy flow and the capacity to conduct energy from input, via transformation, to output. Figure 1 contains a summary of what we can say about dynamic systems in general terms.

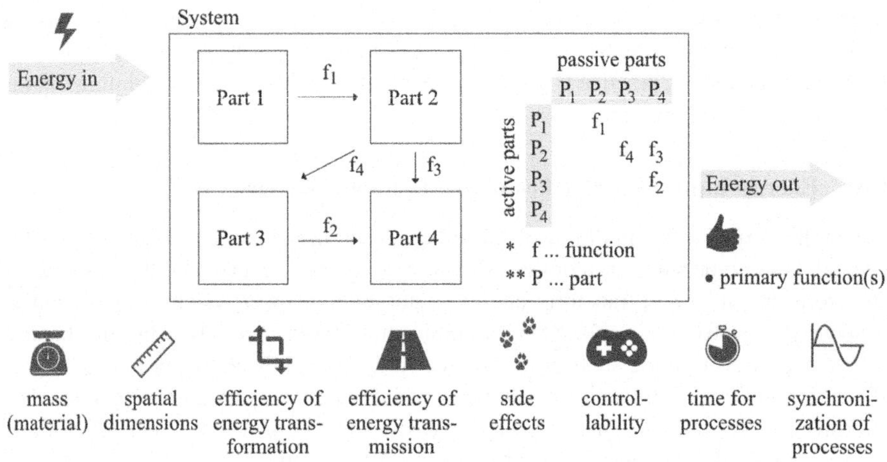

Fig. 1. The illustration captures necessary features of (instrumental) dynamic systems: They consist of parts which together bring about effects by transforming and directing energy such that it becomes useful for someone's purposes—primary function(s). The interactions of the parts can be described as processes that require a certain amount of time to be executed and that must be synchronized in order to work together under sufficiently controlled circumstances. The parts themselves have a mass and spatial dimensions. Insofar as we know the ratio between the amount of energy being consumed and being outputted in a useful manner, both energy transformation and transmission efficiency can be determined. Efficiencies lower than 100% result in side effects—i.e. in effects different from the system's primary function(s).

2.13 Scarcity of Resources and Efficiency

Those who employ a static or dynamic system for their own purposes are interested in the output produced by the dynamic super-system emerging during this process. The output shows in the work being done. This work comes at some cost. It is tempting to say that a dynamic super-system that consumes less energy to produce the same amount of work under similar conditions and with more or less the same undesired side effects is better than a system that consumes more. However this only holds if the energy resource we are talking about is scarce or at least hard to obtain. Assuming such scarcity, efficiency gains become desirable.

Departing from the above analysis of general features of dynamic systems (see Fig. 1), we can compare the efficiencies of systems serving the same primary functions by relating these functions to the invested energy (see Eq. (1)). This energy comprises (i) the energy being lost during operation, (ii) the energy contained in the useful work of the primary function(s), (iii) the energy required for manufacturing and (iv) the energy stored in the form of materials (mass). In order to increase a system's overall efficiency—which is desirable under the assumption that resources are scarce, we will have to choose one or multiple of the options expressed within the following equation:[5]

$$\begin{aligned} efficiency\uparrow &= \frac{primaryfunction\uparrow}{energy_{invested}\downarrow} \\ &= \frac{primaryfunction\uparrow}{energy_{lost}\downarrow + energy_{out}\downarrow + energy_{manuf}\downarrow + energy_{stored}\downarrow} \end{aligned} \tag{1}$$

2.14 From Efficiency to Ideality

While scarcity of resources makes efficiency gains desirable, it can be said that the pressure of competition forces systems to evolve towards being more efficient. Pushing the tendencies for increasing efficiency to their most extreme values (zero and max) or —as Altshuller would say—to their ideal forms, we will obtain Altshuller's famous definition of ideality (where no resources are needed to obtain the benefit of the system's function): *The ideal system is the fulfillment of the function without a system* [1]. Figure 2 summarizes these tendencies—and thereby the meaning of ideality—in one table. As a consequence, it can be said that a system that develops according to these tendencies is becoming increasingly ideal:

2.15 Integration in Wider Super-Systems

From the tendency to become increasingly ideal, a trend toward functional integration into larger super-systems can be inferred:[6] (i) A system that is serving multiple functions is more ideal than (ii) multiple systems that are serving all of these functions individually, assuming that (i) the multi-functional system consumes fewer resources (space, time, energy, materials) and (ii) that the quality of the execution of the functions does not suffer from the integration.

[5] An upward arrow stands for *increase* and a downward arrow for *decrease*. The upward arrow behind *primary function* indicates both quantitative and qualitative improvement, while quantitative improvement means larger amount of primary functions.

[6] See Fig. 2 "primary function(s)" (MAX).

Feature	Ideal value	Feature	Ideal value	Feature	Ideal value
energy in energy out	ZERO	efficiency of energy trans-formation	MAX	control-lability	MAX
primary function(s)	MAX	efficiency of energy trans-mission	MAX	time for processes	ZERO
mass (material)	ZERO	side effects	ZERO	synchroni-zation of processes	MAX
spatial dimensions	ZERO				

Fig. 2. The illustration shows the extreme values for each of the general features of dynamic systems, indicating the respective tendencies for an increase of the system's overall efficiency. Accordingly, both the energy put in and the energy (work) required to fulfill the primary function (s) should be zero as should be the parts' masses, spatial dimensions (when space is considered a scarce resource), side effects and execution time. In contrast, the amount and quality of the primary function(s) should be maximal, as should be the energy transformation and transmission efficiencies, overall controllability and synchronization of processes.

2.16 Integration Means Mediating Conflicts

Functional integration yields conflicts insofar as systems that are to be integrated compete over shared resources (space, time, material resources, energy). Systems that are able to integrate their sub-systems in a win-win fashion will be more efficient and therefore more competitive and more ideal than those that cap the potential of their individual sub-systems due to inner-systemic conflicts.

2.17 Increase of Efficiency Through Increase of Control Over More Fundamental Activities

When taking a look at the energy flow in dynamic systems above, we came across (i) energy input, (ii) energy transformation, (iii) energy conduction, (iv) energy control and (v) targeted energy output as necessary functions. The efficiency of each of these functions contributes to the system's overall efficiency. Loss of energy during any of these activities diminishes the system's overall efficiency and therefore provides opportunities for increasing ideality through problem solving.[7] Since energy cannot get lost, *loss of energy* refers to transformation of energy into a form that cannot be used for executing the system's functions and, in this sense, is wasted. The better a dynamic system controls the activities underlying these functions, the more it will get out from its initial energy input.[8]

The idea behind this principle is simple: intervening closer to where an activity originates allows for more controlled guidance of resulting effects as compared to intervention on the level of later emerging effects. For example, a central bank that aims at increasing investments into the economy by lowering interest rates cannot determine what banks will do with the cheap money. In contrast, direct control of the decision making of the banks would allow for more targeted intervention. The same holds for effects emerging from the activities of objects on an atomic and sub-atomic scale such as electromagnetism or material properties. The better we understand and control the origin of the effects of interest, the better we will control the effects themselves. Since increasing ideality is achieved by reducing losses while increasing functionality, systems that efficiently control the effects they exploit on the most fundamental level of their emergence, will turn out to be more ideal than systems operating at a later stage in the chain, where losses have already accumulated. If the origin of the effects exploited by some system resides at the sub-atomic scale, the system will have to obtain better control over the lower-scopic[9] levels to become increasingly ideal. As more refined physical cause-effect relationships become known for further exploitation, we will see an increase in systems using them for their purposes. This holds for both the creation of artificial instrumental systems and for our understanding of the causal mechanisms operating in natural dynamic systems.

[7] See Fig. 2 "efficiency of energy transmission" (MAX), "efficiency of energy transformation" (MAX), "energy in" (ZERO), "energy out"—corresponding to the work of the primary function (ZERO), "controllability" (MAX).

[8] How efficiently energy can be transformed by a given system depends on its ability to release the energy that is stored in what the system takes as input. Given that the maximal energy of a body is equivalent to its mass, a dynamic system can operate with increasing amounts of energy, the more control it gains over the matter it is dealing with. Burning a kilogram of dry straw provides approximately 16.8 MJ in energy. The loss of rest mass of about 1.9×10^{-7} g is so small that it is nearly impossible to measure. In contrast, when uranium decays, 0.1% of its mass is released as energy. After the reaction, the mass of the substance that initially was one kilogram of uranium is about one gram smaller, which is equivalent to a release of 9×10^{7} MJ. To use uranium as an energy source, we must be able to trigger the required chain reactions and control them adequately, which requires understanding and control of the processes on an atomic scale. In contrast, in order to burn and control one kilogram of straw, all we have to know is how to initiate and sustain a fire, which can be done on a macro-scale level. If we were able to transform the entire kilogram of anything's rest mass into energy, we would obtain roughly 9×10^{9} MJ. To do so we would have to be able to control the building blocks of matter on the lowest scale possible.

[9] We avoid the term "microscopic" since "micro" has the well-defined meaning of 10^{-6}. By coining the term lower-scopic, we want to convey the meaning of a spectrum for zooming out (macro-scale) and zooming in (towards sub-atomic scale).

3 Inferring Altshuller's Eight Laws of Technical Systems Development

This general understanding of systems is sufficient to derive Altshuller's eight laws as stated in 1979 [1]. Altshuller split them into three groups: (A) statics, (B) kinematics, and (C) dynamics. Note that Altshuller's usage of the terms "statics" and "dynamics" differs from our usage.

(A) The first class of laws deals with the beginning of a technical system's life, which is understood as the result of synthesizing parts into a whole
(1) *Law of system completeness:* The first law states that a technical system would not be able to perform its functions, unless at least the following four parts with their respective functions are present: engine (for energy conversion), transmission, working unit and control unit. At least one of these parts must be manageable to make the system manageable.

As we have seen, this statement only holds for dynamic systems. Static systems, such as tables, picture frames, plates, chairs, unridden bicycles, etc. do not have to transform energy in any meaningful manner in order to provide their functions.[10] The need for the five functions—(i) energy input, (ii) transformation, (iii) transmission, (iv) control and (v) targeted output (working unit in Altshuller's sense) follows from the fact that dynamic systems have to convert and control energy to bring about the effect that makes them instrumental for something (instrumental systems), themselves (self-sustaining living systems) or both (see Sects. 2.7, 2.10, and 2.12).

(2) *Law of energy conductivity:* Altshuller's second law states that a system's need for energy transformation requires the ability to conduct energy from the conversion unit to the working body. As we have seen, this can only be said about dynamic not static systems and is already contained in the meaning of *transmission/conduction* (see Sect. 2.12).
(3) *Law of synchronization:* The third law states that all parts of the system should work in coordinated rhythm.

Again, this only holds for dynamic systems and is due to the requirement that multiple parts have to contribute to the same process, which is the production of the system's effects through energy conversion and control. Insofar as the parts contribute to the same process their contribution has to be coordinated in time, which is just a different way of saying that coordination of rhythm is required.

(B) Altshuller put the second set of laws under the title "kinematics" stating that they refer to the development of technical systems irrespective of specific technical or physical factors contributing to the development.
(4) *Law of increasing degree of ideality:* Altshuller's fourth law is probably the most popular one and claims that all technical systems develop towards an increasing

[10] When zooming onto an atomic and sub-atomic level, we will find dynamic energy conversion, irrespective of whether we are analyzing a static or a dynamic system. However, this does not affect the meaning of the distinction between static and dynamic on a macro-level.

degree of ideality with the system's weight, volume and area tending towards zero, without diminishing its capacity to perform work, resulting in Altshuller's popular definition of an ideal technical system as function without a system [1]. In the TRIZ literature, it is common practice to understand ideality not only in terms of spatial and material resources, but also in terms of all resources (time, space, energy input, material resources) in the form of a qualitative cost-benefit equation with functionality above and costs and problems below the fraction line [14]. In [5], which is a translation of [15], ideality is defined as the ratio between useful and harmful effects.[11]

As seen above, the trend of increasing ideality (summarized in Fig. 2) is due to the need to increase efficiency (see Sects. 2.13 and 2.14). Increased efficiency, in return, provides a competitive advantage when resources are scarce. While the law of increasing ideality refers to both static and dynamic systems, it depends upon the assumption of competition and scarcity of resources. It would be an interesting thought experiment to investigate what would happen to the trend towards an increasing degree of ideality if the problem of scarcity of resources were solved.

(5) *Law of uneven development of a system's parts:* The fifth law states that the parts of a technical system develop unevenly. As a consequence, system conflicts arise, where one sub-system hinders the further development of another. Altshuller's example here is the insufficiency of brake systems in large ships [17].

This argument depends on two assumptions. The first is the system definition itself stating that systems bring about their effects by collaborative work of their parts. Due to the dependency of systemic effects on the interaction of all of the relevant parts of a given system, weaker parts will be bottlenecks for the stronger ones or the system will become unstable when weaker parts cannot balance out the stronger. The second assumption, which is not contained in the system definition itself, is that these parts do not develop simultaneously. This might be true if the system's designer was unilaterally focused. However, the law will collapse as soon as systems are developed from a holistic perspective by taking the functions of all sub-systems into account.

As we have seen above, there is another argument for the necessity of the outbreak of system conflicts that does not rely on assuming a limited perspective of the designer (see Sect. 2.16). Rather, it is based on resource dependency. Different sub-systems might exploit shared resources (energy, material, time and space), which will result in conflicts when these resources are scarce.

(6) *Law of transition to the super-system level:* Altshuller's sixth law states that when systems have exhausted their developmental potential, they become sub-systems within larger systems—that is their function is integrated into a super-system. As we have seen, this follows from the ideality statement under the condition that the function of the integrated systems is enhanced rather than worsened and that the

[11] According to [16], the translation contains slight modifications, but we currently have no access to [15] to judge whether or not they affect this definition of ideality.

non-integrated individual systems would require more resources for delivering their function (see Sect. 2.15).

(C) The third class of Altshuller's laws is titled "dynamics" and reflects the main trends in the development of technical systems in our—or rather Altshuller's—time; *Creativity as an Exact Science* was published in 1979 [1].

(7) *Law of transition from the macro- to the micro-level:* The seventh of Altshuller's laws claims that when a system's developmental potential is exhausted on the macro level, it will be fundamentally rebuilt with its working body acting on a lower-scopic level. As we have seen, this is due to the principle that the ability to control the more fundamental activities from where the effects emerge provides more control over the entire process. Therefore, less energy loss is accumulated, which results in higher efficiency and thus a higher degree of ideality. Moreover, the production of new effects is made available (see Sect. 2.17).

(8) *Law of increasing involvement of substance-field systems:* The eighth of Altshuller's laws finally states that the development of technical systems proceeds towards an increasing involvement of substance-field systems. In order to clarify the meaning of this statement, we first need to look at the role that substance-field (Su-Field) systems play in Altshuller's theory. Roughly, the Su-Field notation aims at representing problems in terms of cause-effect relationships by means of three major categories: *substances*, *fields* and *actions*. Fields are supposed to act upon and to be produced by substances. The actions of *being produced* and *acting upon something* are represented by means of arrows, which can highlight qualitative differences (harmful, useful, insufficient, and excessive). This notation is used to represent problems and can be converted into the notation of functional modeling where components (substances) act via functions (arrows) upon other components. The main difference between *function* and *field* seems to concern the level of abstraction. While fields are categories for physical effects, functions describe the activity by which one component acts upon another. In order to preserve the information represented in a Su-Field model which states that "A pushes B" by means of a mechanical field, we would have to say "A mechanically pushes B". Thus, in a Su-Field representation, the physical principles bringing about some effect are made explicit (something that is not necessarily shown in a functional diagram, but could easily be added).

Altshuller's eighth law states that no-field systems tend to develop into field systems (note that Altshuller's notion of a *no-field system* might be equivalent to what we are calling *static system*)[12], the number of connections between the elements of a system increases, the responsiveness of the system increases, and mechanical mechanisms are replaced by electromagnetic ones.

[12] Take for example a hammer, a nail and a wall. Without what Altshuller would call a mechanical field that is provided by, for example, someone's arm, the nail could not be hammered into the wall. According to our terminology, we need a dynamic system (the person who takes and controls the hammer) to turn the static systems—hammer, nail, wall—into a dynamic super-system: The person uses the hammer to hammer the nail into the wall.

All of these observations result from statements outlined before, namely that (i) the ability to efficiently control lower-scopic effects often makes it possible to influence matter more efficiently and extensively than handling them on a macroscopic mechanical scale (see Sect. 2.17) and that (ii) static systems are only useful insofar as they are integrated into dynamic super-systems (which refers to no-field systems turning into Su-Field systems) (see Sects. 2.7 and 2.8). Note that (i) is only true if we can control the lower-scopic behavior efficiently enough to gain an advantage over macroscopic mechanical control.

4 Patent Analysis for Validation/Falsification—not for Induction

We have shown that, without the study of a single patent, Altshuller's eight laws of technical system development from 1979 [1] can be derived from a reflection on the nature of systems, in general, and instrumental systems in particular. All in all, this shows that the law-like nature of these general statements about systems is due to their inferability from even more general statements. Instead of trying to derive laws of technical system evolution from patent analysis, it seems to be more promising to use the patent fund as resource for validation. In 2006, [19] tested Altshuller's laws in the following manner. From [20] they took the 68 highest generality US patents from 1963–1999, which are patents that are cited by subsequent patents belonging to a wide range of *International Patent Classification* (IPC) classes. For each of these patents, the authors studied the state of the art section in order to understand the transition from the state of the art situation to the solution in the respective patent. For each of the technical system evolution trends, they checked whether or not it could have been used for developing the solution and whether or not it contradicted the transition proposed in the patent. Altogether, the 68 patents provided examples for each of Altshuller's laws, while 3 patents provided counter-examples concerning *law (2)* energy conductivity, *law (5)* uneven development of a system's parts, and *law (8)* increasing use of su-fields. Despite our inability to get in touch with the authors of [19] to gain access to supplementary materials to view the counter-examples, our above analysis has shown that the contradicted laws are conditional, which might explain the contradictions: Law 2 does not hold for static systems, law 5 is not valid when the product was developed from a holistic standpoint, and law 8 depends on efficiency concerns, which allows for the possibility that a mechanical solution is more efficient than its non-mechanical predecessor.

5 Conclusion

As we have shown, Altshuller's eight laws of technical system evolution can be derived from a general reflection on *artificial instrumental systems* in the context of a *competitive world with scarce resources*. As a result, the conditions for applying the laws could be made explicit, which helped to hypothesize why 3 out of 68 high generality patents contradicted 3 out of 8 laws in the study of [19] (see Sect. 4). While patents are a useful source for inspiration, validation and falsification of generalizations, they are not the most promising place to start to look for laws of system evolution since mere induction from past examples cannot provide the justification needed to meaningfully inform engineers about how to develop systems in the future. Moreover, we drew the attention to *resource scarcity* as a fundamental condition for the validity of most of these laws, which allowed us to summarize the meaning of ideality in a deductive manner (see Fig. 2). Given that the number of general resource types is limited—time, space, material, energy—we believe that additional general statements about systems can be derived by further taking into account the general characteristics of each resource type in their respective contexts. Doing so might result in the formulation of trends similar to the patterns articulated in [18]. The same holds for (i) a more thorough investigation of the fundamental features of dynamic systems (see Figs. 1 and 2), (ii) a closer look at differences of employing living or non-living systems for certain jobs, and (iii) a definition by cases depending on whether the instrumental system is abstract (theories) or concrete (material).

References

1. Altshuller, G.: Creativity as an Exact Science: The Theory of the Solution of Inventive Problems. Studies in Cybernetics: A Series of Books and Monographs Covering All Aspects of Cybernetics, pp. 223–231. Gordon & Breach, New York (1984)
2. Altshuller, G.: Creativity as an Exact Science: The Theory of the Solution of Inventive Problems. Studies in Cybernetics: A Series of Books and Monographs Covering All Aspects of Cybernetics, pp. 30–36. Gordon & Breach, New York (1984)
3. Filkovsky, G.L.: Why laws of technical systems evolution can't successfully predict a system evolution. Anti TRIZ-J. **3**(1) (2004). http://www3.sympatico.ca/karasik/GF_why_LOTSE_cannot_predict_system_evolution.html
4. For example, Fey, V., Rivin, E.: Innovation on Demand by Victor Fey, p. 113. Cambridge Core, October 2005. https://doi.org/10.1017/CBO9780511584237
5. Altshuller, A., Zlotin, B., Zusman, A., Philatov, V.: Tools of Classical TRIZ. Ideation International Inc., Southfield (1999)
6. Savransky, S.D.: Engineering of Creativity: Introduction to TRIZ Methodology of Inventive Problem Solving. CRC Press, Boca Raton (2000)
7. Petrov, V.: The laws of system evolution. Triz J. (blog) (2002). https://triz-journal.com/laws-system-evolution/
8. Mann, D.: Hands on Systematic Innovation: For Business and Management. Edward Gaskell Publishers, Clevedon (2004)
9. Fey, V., Rivin, E.: Innovation on Demand by Victor Fey. Cambridge Core, October 2005. https://doi.org/10.1017/CBO9780511584237
10. Bukhman, I.: TRIZ Technology for Innovation. Cubic Creativity Company, Taipei (2012)
11. Carroll, J.W.: Laws of nature. In: Zalta, E.N. (ed.) The Stanford Encyclopedia of Philosophy (2016). https://plato.stanford.edu/archives/fall2016/entries/laws-of-nature/
12. Lewis, D.K.: Counterfactuals, p. 73. Blackwell, Oxford (1973)
13. Armstrong, D.M.: The identification problem and the inference problem. Philos. Phenomenol. Res. **53**(2), 421–422 (1993)

14. Fey, V., Rivin, E.: Innovation on Demand by Victor Fey. Cambridge Core, October 2005. https://doi.org/10.1017/CBO9780511584237, 17
15. Altshuller, G., Zlotin, B., Zusman, A., Philatov, V.: Search for New Ideas: from Insight to Technology (Theory and Practice of Inventive Problem Solving). Cartia moldovenyaske, Kishinyov (1989)
16. Domb, E.: Book review: tools of classical TRIZ. Triz J. (blog) (1999). https://triz-journal.com/book-review-tools-classical-triz/
17. Altshuller, G.: Creativity as an Exact Science: The Theory of the Solution of Inventive Problems. Studies in Cybernetics: A Series of Books and Monographs Covering All Aspects of Cybernetics, p. 229. Gordon & Breach, New York (1984)
18. Altshuller, A., Zlotin, B., Zusman, A., Philatov, V.: Tools of Classical TRIZ, pp. 11–23. Ideation International Inc., Southfield (1999)
19. De Carvalho, M.A., Da Rocha, L.L.V., Zanoni, A.P., Boell, H.F., Back, N., Ogliari, A.: Validity of technical system evolution trends – a patent study. In: Anais Do I Congresso Iberoamericano de Inovação Tecnológica. Asociación Mexicana de TRIZ (AMETRIZ), Puebla, México (2006)
20. Hall, B.H., Jaffe, A.B., Trajtenberg, M.: The NBER Patent Citations Data File: Lessons, Insights and Methodological Tools (2001). https://www.nber.org/papers/w8498.pdf

A New Way to Classify Physical Effects for Ontology Instantiation

Pei Zhang[1(✉)], Denis Cavallucci[1,3], and Cecilia Zanni-Merk[2]

[1] LGéCo (Design Engineering Laboratory), 67000 Strasbourg, France
pei.zhang@insa-strasbourg.fr
[2] INSA Rouen Normandie, LITIS, Normastic (FR CNRS 3638), Rouen, France
[3] INSA de Strasbourg, 24 boulevard de la Victoire, Strasbourg, France

Abstract. As one of the most important knowledge sources of TRIZ, the collection of Physical effects is currently searched in a very basic way. In order to enhance its use, different proposals have been brought to the community to classify effects into different categories. Among them, a rule-based approach classified the collection of physical effects into four categories and built a set of rules to facilitate its direct use. However, this approach is not robust enough due to the lack of instances of physical effects. In this paper, we propose a new approach to classify physical effects in order instantiate the existing ontology. In addition, preliminary results are presented to demonstrate the feasibility of the approach. The results brought us evidences that we facilitate the direct access to the collection of physical effects.

Keywords: TRIZ · Inventive design theory · Wikipedia · Physical effects

1 Introduction

According to Altshuller [1] the use of the scientific effects is one of the most important approaches that facilitates solution finding. For the reason that this collection of knowledge contains natural phenomena previously unused in the engineering domain. The use of this collection of effects often give rise to simple and reliable designs. In order to facilitate its use, the collection of physical effects provides the mapping between the technical functions and the available technical laws.

However, the technical functions and the available technical laws while the physical effects are a collection of physical phenomenon. They are at different levels of abstraction, thus making the access of the collection of physical effects from technical functions quite difficult. In order to address this problem, existing researches have proposed different ways to classify this collection of knowledge in order to ease its usage. These classifications are either based on the physical parameters that describe the effects or based on the categories defined by the constructed domain models such as ontologies. However, the existing classifications do not support the direct use of the collection of the physical effects, as a consequence, it requires knowledge both in engineering and physical domain.

Tackling at this drawback, existing research have proposed a physical effects ontology to facilitate its direct access by classifying the physical effects into two

Published by Springer Nature Switzerland AG 2019
R. Benmoussa et al. (Eds.): TFC 2019, IFIP AICT 572, pp. 70–78, 2019.
https://doi.org/10.1007/978-3-030-32497-1_7

categories (substance effects and field effects) [2]. However, the knowledge base is not complete thus limits its use. Therefore, in this paper, we focus on instantiating the existing physical effects ontology based on machine learning to support the construction and the population of the physical effect knowledge base, with the aim of support decision making by reusing existing ontology.

The remainder of this paper is organized as follows. In chapter two, we give a literature review about the existing classifications of physical effects and the need of ontology instantiation. In chapter three, we present the proposed method. In chapter four, we present the preliminary result to validate the proposed method. Finally, in chapter five, we conclude this paper by discussion and conclusion.

2 Literature Review

The classical way to classify the physical effects is by their functions, which is knownas the pointers to scientific-engineering effects (as it is depicted in Fig. 1). The pointers classified the effects by different technical functions they perform. For example, the technical function *Change shape* can be achieved by the use of the effects like *Curie point, Evaporation, Ferromagnetism, crystallization etc.*

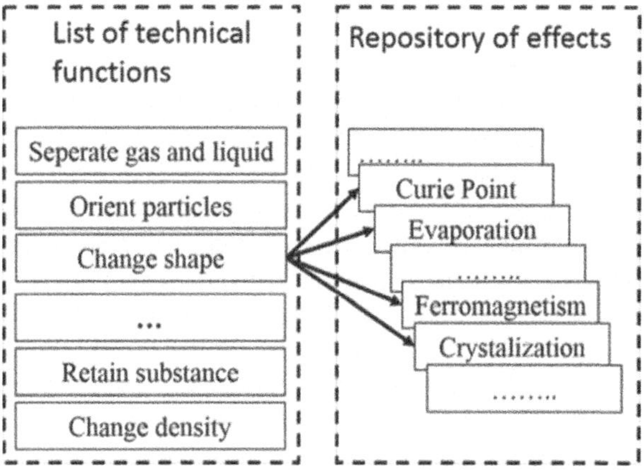

Fig. 1. Pointers to scientific-engineering effects

In this way, the effects can be accessed by searching for the technical functions. However, the use of the scientific-engineering depends on the user's experience in the engineering domain to map between conceptual (technical functions) and actual (scientific-engineering effects) solutions. Therefore, this type of classification is useful for experienced users but making its use for novice users very difficult.

Apart from the pointers to scientific-engineering effects, the classification of effects based on the construction of a domain ontology is getting more and more attention. This is because the construction of an ontology not only facilitates the description of the modeling domain, but also enables the knowledge induction by the establishment of rules. Combined together, the construction of ontology enables the automatic inference of needed knowledge without the intervention of human.

An ontology is a formal and explicit specification of a shared conceptualization. It is composed of classes, instances and their binary relations that are used to express knowledge about the domain of interest. In an ontology, classes are abstract collection of objects. The instances are concrete objects of its class. Relations are links between pairs of classes, pairs of instances or between classes and instances. Rules are another form of expressing knowledge in the domain of interest [2]. They are used to reflect the notion of consequence and are in the form of IF-THEN-constructs. In this way, rules are able to express complex statements of different types. Based on the construction of rules, techniques of automated reasoning allow a computer system to draw conclusions from the existing ontology.

The work of [3] organized the effects by a chain of design elements at different abstraction level. It creates the causal relationship between the functions and structures by physical variables. It is based on the fact that most of the physical laws include variables and constants. And the application of these physical laws depends on such descriptors. The work in [4] constructed an ontology that classifies the physical effects based on the language descriptors. In this ontology, the classes are input, output and object. The relations for representing the interactions between the classes are: Cause Action, EffectAction and ActionObject. In this way, different effects can be classified and represented by different text descriptors that are extracted from natural language texts. Other direction of this research has conducted by authors in [5] as well, who proposed a dynamic approach that does not rely on the classification in advance.

The work in [6] developed the physical effects ontology that classified the physical effects into two categories: Sub_PE and Field_PE (Fig. 2) in order to facilitate its use with the Inventive Standards. The physical effects ontology classified the physical effects based on the substances and fields it concerns. Along with it, this work also constructed the rules based on the Inventive Standards. These notions are particularly interesting because they enable the user to access directly to the needed effects by reasoning on rules once they have obtained the substance-field model of the his/her problem. Therefore, the novice user can access to the needed effects through the substance-field model without understanding what function that is performed by which effects. However, even though the physical effects ontology has been built, it should be instantiated largely in order to provide enough knowledge for the users. Therefore, we should consider a method to instantiate the physical effects ontology to facilitate its reuse.

Ontology instantiation is the process of building the knowledge base. It consists of adding new instances of concepts and relations into an existing ontology. This process usually starts after the conceptual model of ontology is built [7].

The construction of the knowledge base makes it possible to perform reasoning tasks with the aim of assisting decision making. However, to construct a knowledge base is not an easy task because it is based on the capture of categorized knowledge. Therefore, it is often done manually by domain experts.

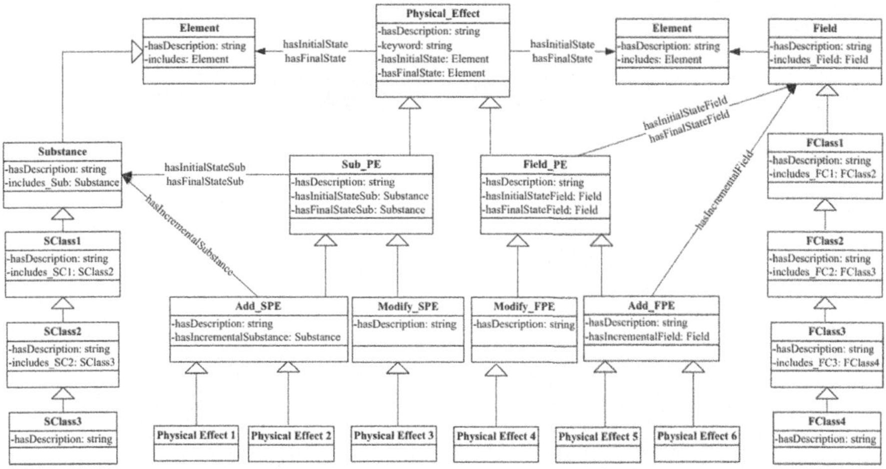

Fig. 2. The physical effects ontology (from [5])

In order to solve this problem, we adopt machine learning to automatically classify the physical effects in order to instantiate the physical effect ontology and in this way, constructing the physical effects knowledge base.

3 Methodology

In this chapter, we propose a new approach based on machine learning which enables the instantiation of physical effects knowledge base. The proposed approach is implemented to classify the collection of physical effects as two classes (Sub_PE and Field_PE). The proposed methodology is composed of three steps as it is illustrated in Fig. 3:

- Step1: data collection
- Step2: feature extraction
- Step3: classification and ontology instantiation

The first step is to collect the data needed. In here, the data should be in the machine interpretable form in order to apply the classification techniques later. However, there are two main difficulties. One is that the physical effects are in the form of natural language and we need to find a way to represent them in a computer process able way. The other is to find an appropriate text similarity measure in order to perform the classification task.

We address these problems by using Wikipedia[1] as a knowledge base to create a graph for each effect based on the Wikipedia category network. In this way, each

[1] https://en.wikipedia.org/wiki/Main_Page.

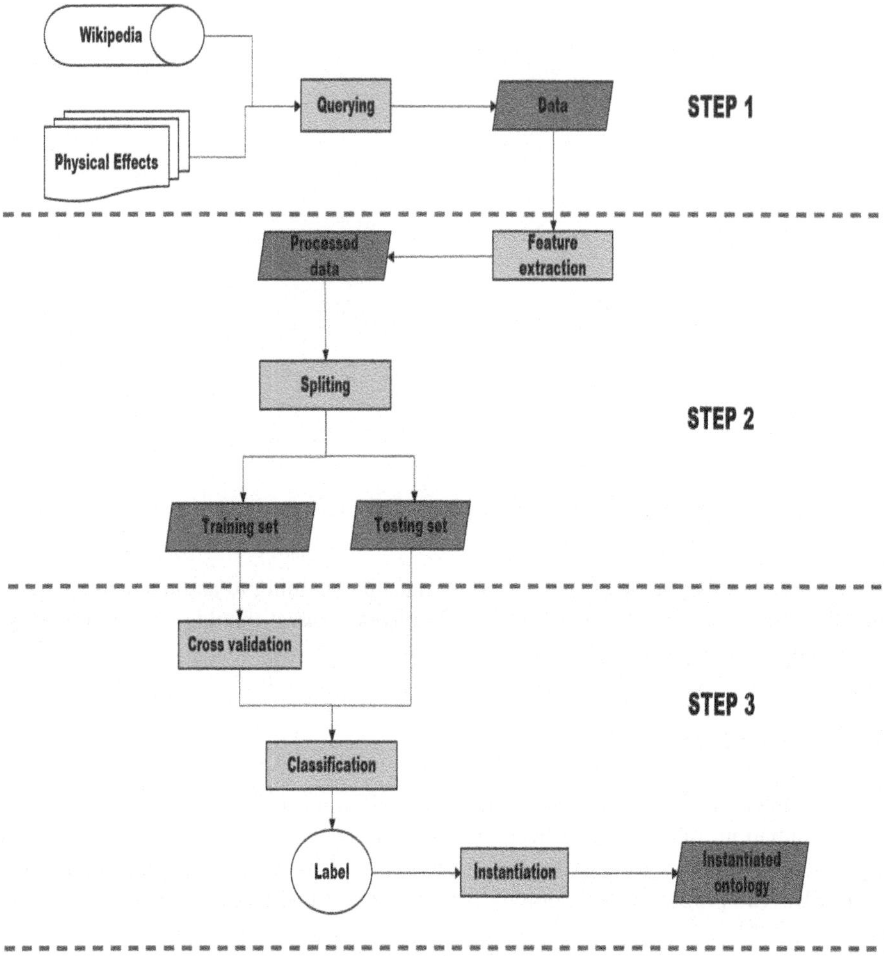

Fig. 3. The proposed methodology

physical effects will be represented as a hierarchical graph composed of a set of its related categories.

The second step is feature extraction. Based on the characteristics of the obtained graphs, which are not suitable for applying classification algorithm, we have to find a way to extract features from them. Feature extraction consists in transforming arbitrary data, such as text or images, into numerical features usable for machine learning tasks (e.g. classification task). In order to extract features from the obtained graphs, we are inspired by the vector-space model [8] and represent each effect by all the categories associated with it. We assign the value of each feature by the distance between the effect and each category on the shortest path from the effect to the category. In this way, we obtained a multi-dimensional vector for each effect, where each category related to this effect on the retrieved graph corresponds to an axis. Such that the values along the axes for the effect correspond to the distance between this category and the effect on the shortest path linking them.

In this way, we can construct a large feature matrix where each row corresponds to an effect and each column corresponds to a category that is retrieved from the Wikipedia network. However, the resulting feature matrix is too large which will increase the training time. Therefore, we have to reduce the dimensions of the matrix by preserving the most significant features to shorten the training time for the predictive model. To do so, the Principal Component Analysis (PCA) is applied to achieve this goal.

Once the feature extraction is done, we can apply the classification algorithm to classify the data. To do so, we have to train a classifier. A classifier is a function that maps an unclassified piece of data to a class by applying an induction algorithm, which builds a classifier from a given dataset [9]. In order to train the classifier, we have to apply a proper classification algorithm [10] on the training set obtained from the previous step. One of such method is the k-Nearest Neighbor algorithm (kNN) [10]. The advantages of applying the kNN classification algorithm is obvious: There is no existing model to classify the physical effects but a collection of correctly classified effect instances that is labelled by the domain experts. kNN method assumes that the observations which are close together will have the same classification, making it possible to classify the given effects based on the effects with a label. Once the classifier is obtained, we can instantiate the physical effect ontology based on the obtained label.

4 Preliminary Result

In our experiment, we try to validate the proposed approach to classify the physical effect Boiling. We take 11 physical effects to conduct our experiment. Among them, we use 10 as the training set and 1 as the testing set. The aim is to classify the effect boiling into one of the two categories.

Firstly, we have to obtain the graph of each effect. It is obtained by retrieving the Wikipedia category network. Therefore, for each effect, we obtain a category graph by querying Wikipedia. In Fig. 4, an excerpt of the obtained graph of boiling is presented. Once the graph of each effect is obtained, we eliminate the irrelevant categories. For example, at the first level of the category graph of boiling, there are two irrelevant categories. They are All_Articles_needing_additional_references and All_Articles_needing_additional_refences_from_June_2017. In Fig. 4, these irrelevant categories presented by the red nodes. In our approach, these categories are deleted in step 1.

The next step is to apply the feature extraction method to transform the obtained graph into a multi-dimensional vector. To achieve this goal, we assign the shortest distance between a category and the effect on the shortest path between them. For example, the value of feature Phase_transitions is 1 because the distance between the category Phase_transitions and the effect Boiling on the shortest path is one. In addition, a special case is that there is no path between the effect and a category, for example, the category Electromagnetic_radiation, Electrodynamics and Radiation. In this case, we assume that the distance is 11. This is because in our graphs, the distance from an effect to the Contents category (root node) ranges from 3–10, therefore, 11 means that the value is infinity.

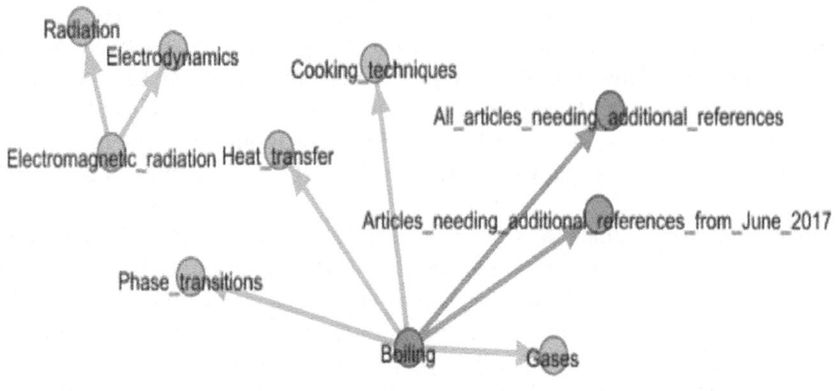

Fig. 4. An excerpt of the effect Boiling

Once the vector of each effect is obtained, we construct a feature matrix with 11 rows and 89 columns where each row corresponds to an effect and each column corresponds to a category that is retrieved from the Wikipedia network (as it is presented in Fig. 5). With the obtained matrix, PCA method is employed for feature selection. We fit the PCA preserving 95% of components and obtained a new matrix with 11 rows and 5 columns, where each row corresponds to an effect and each column corresponds to the assigned k principle components after the feature selection.

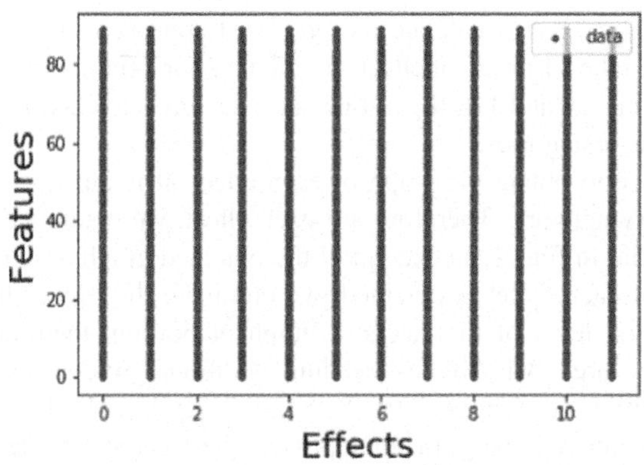

Fig. 5. Visualization of the feature matrix

Then, the obtained training set is used as the input for classification task by applying the kNN method. And finally the 10-fold cross validation is applied to determine the value of k. To do so, we divide the training set into 10 subsets of equal size and repeat the 10-fold cross validation 10 times, where each time one subset is assigned as the Testing_set_cv and the rest are assigned as the Training_set_cv. Therefore, each time the cross validation is performed, we can evaluate its performance by calculating its accuracy rate. The accuracy rate is obtained by dividing the sum of

TP and TN by the sum of P and N, where TP is the number of true positive samples, TN is the true negative samples, P is the number of positive samples and N is the number of positive samples. In this way, the mean accuracy rate is obtained by calculating the sum of the 10 accuracy rates and divide it by 10 as it is depicted by Eq. (1).

$$\text{ACC\_mean} = \frac{\sum_{x=1}^{10} (TP + TN)/(P + N)}{10} \tag{1}$$

The 10-fold cross validation is used to determine the value of k, which is the number of the nearest neighbors. We varied the value of k from 1 to 5 and the ACC_mean of k = 1, k = 2, k = 3 and k = 5 are respectively presented in Table 1. From this result, we can observe that k = 5 is a better choice than the others since it yields a better accuracy rate than the other values of k.

Table 1. Experiment result

Category	K = 1	K = 2	K = 3	K = 5
Substance_effect	0.5	0.5	0.873	0.955
Field_effect	0.5	0.7	0.7	0.873

5 Discussion and Conclusion

In this paper, we proposed a new approach to classify the physical effects based on machine learning. More specifically, it is based on the use of Wikipedia and kNN method. The proposed method can be applied to instantiate the physical effects database automatically which contributes the reusability of domain ontologies and the independence from domain experts.

The preliminary result showed that we have successfully applied the proposed method to classify the physical effects, and achieved the mean accuracy of 0.995 when k = 5. This encouraging result enables further directions of research:

- To largely populate the physical effects into two classes by a bigger data set;
- To populate the relations of the physical effects ontology with more refined classifications.

However, the proposed method relies on labelled data which is sometimes difficult to obtain, therefore, there is a need to find some ready to use dataset in order to instantiate the physical effects ontology with more individuals. Moreover, it is also interesting to test other machine learning techniques on a larger dataset in order in increase the precision of the classification result, such as naive bayes classifiers [11], support vector machines [12], radial basis function (RBF) networks [13] etc.

References

1. Altshuller, G., Shulyak, L.: And Suddenly the Inventor Appeared: TRIZ, the Theory of Inventive Problem Solving. Technical Innovation Center, Inc. (1996)
2. Grimm, S., Hitzler, P., Abecker, A.: Knowledge Representation and Ontologies Logic, Ontologies and Semantic Web Languages (2007)
3. Rihtaršič, J., Žavbi, R., Duhovnik, J.: Application of wirk elements for the synthesis of alternative conceptual solutions. Res. Eng. Des. **23**(3), 219–234 (2012)
4. Korobkin, D., Fomenkov, S., Kamaev, V., Fomenkova, M.: Multi-agent model of ontology-based extraction of physical effects descriptions from natural language text. In: Information Technologies in Science, Management, Social Sphere and Medicine (2016)
5. Russo, D., Montecchi, T., Caputi, A.: Tech-finder: a dynamic pointer to effects. In: 16th International TRIZ Future Conference, vol. 1, no. 3, pp. 79–87 (2018)
6. Yan, W., Zanni-Merk, C., Rousselot, F., Cavallucci, D., Collet, P.: A heuristic method of using the pointers to physical effects in su-field analysis. Procedia Eng. **131**, 539–550 (2015)
7. Makki, J., Alquier, A.-M., Prince, V.: Semi automatic ontology instantiation in the domain of risk management. In: Shi, Z., Mercier-Laurent, E., Leake, D. (eds.) IIP 2008. ITIFIP, vol. 288, pp. 254–265. Springer, Boston, MA (2008). https://doi.org/10.1007/978-0-387-87685-6_30
8. Salton, G., Wong, A., Yang, C.S.: A vector space model for automatic indexing. Commun. ACM **18**(11), 613–620 (1975)
9. Kohavi, R.: A study of cross-validation and bootstrap for accuracy estimation and model selection. IJCAI **14**, 1137–1145 (1995)
10. Cover, T.M., Hart, P.E.: Nearest neighbor pattern classification. IEEE Trans. Inf. Theory **13**(1), 21–27 (1967)
11. Rish, I.: An empirical study of the naive Bayes classifier. In: IJCAI 2001 Workshop on Empirical Methods in Artificial Intelligence, vol. 3. no. 22 (2001)
12. Joachims, T.: Text categorization with support vector machines: learning with many relevant features. In: Nédellec, C., Rouveirol, C. (eds.) ECML 1998. LNCS, vol. 1398, pp. 137–142. Springer, Heidelberg (1998). https://doi.org/10.1007/BFb0026683
13. Howlett, R.J., Jain, L.C.: Radial basis function networks 2: new advances in design, vol. 67. Physica (2013)

TRIZ and Other Innovation Approaches

TRIZ-Assisted Frugal Innovation

Oliver Mayer[1] and Tiziana Bertoncelli[2](✉)

[1] Bayern Innovativ, Nuremberg, Germany
o.mayer@ibom.de
[2] Danfoss Silicon Power GmbH, Ismaning, Germany
tiziana.bertoncelli@ieee.org

Abstract. Frugal Innovation is an unorthodox approach to product design recognized in many developing countries, where creativity is essential to generate solutions that increase economic and social value while fewer resources, usually taken for granted are available, if at all, keeping the focus on delivering the main function with state-of-art technology. Big companies are also applying a similar philosophy, called "disruptive innovation" or "reverse innovation", to meet the needs of potential customers with limited buying power and enter new markets, introducing novel business models. The peculiar attentiveness to the sparse usage of raw materials and resources offered by frugal innovation is also relevant for rethinking the design process in view of sustainable development.

The present paper will review some examples and show how the TRIZ thinking frame can effectively assist frugal innovation projects, formulating the Ideal Final Result and formalizing a dedicated process, based on Resource Analysis, Functional Analysis and Trimming.

Keywords: Frugal innovation · Resources · Ideal Final Result

1 Frugal Innovation: Definitions, Features and Methods

Frugal Innovation emerged as an unorthodox approach adopted in the Global South to address basic needs and offer state-of-the-art solutions [1] characterized by high level of creativity. It was sparked in India, favoured by several socio-economic and cultural factors [2], i.e. the need for "affordable excellence", availability of technological expertise and a positive attitude towards frugality. It praises solutions that allowed to get more value a better social impact from limited resources and at lower cost. Frugal Innovation states a different Value Proposition, reversing the notion of product innovation based on added functionalities (previously in the "nice to have" space foreseen by the Kano model) and increased complexity, leading to a more attractive and expensive high-end product.

Moreover, the ability to generate a positive impact on sustainability and progress for a larger group of people otherwise out of the picture is thought to be a source of soft power and influence [3], aligned with the Sustainable Development Goals [4]. It has been recognized and investigated with growing interest in the scientific community, in association with keywords like Bottom of the Pyramid, Emerging Markets, Jugaad, Reverse Innovation, Disruptive Innovation, Low-Cost Innovation [5]. It is expected to be in demand also globally, in view of the growing need for social innovation and

Published by Springer Nature Switzerland AG 2019
R. Benmoussa et al. (Eds.): TFC 2019, IFIP AICT 572, pp. 81–92, 2019.
https://doi.org/10.1007/978-3-030-32497-1_8

sustainability [6]; in fact it quickly found a big resonance in the western countries [7] as the a way to address new urgent global needs world-wide, i.e. connecting a larger base of customers with limited purchasing power. In Europe efforts are made to define the relevant space with several studies requested by the European Commission [8, 9], where it emerged that challenges posed by environmental awareness, climate change, excessive complexity and financial austerity would increase frugal solution success in Europe, along with the opportunity to reformulate design approaches for cheaper and smarter solutions.

Multinational companies like GE, Siemens, Philips, Bosch already recognized in the early 2000s that affordability brings about big opportunities to open market segments in emerging countries and allows to retain market position; in order to diffuse products and solutions it is possible to sacrifice some "nice to have features" while focusing on the delivering of the minimal function with state of art technology, bridging the gap between pricey products and the basic needs of customers without money. For a product success, defeaturing was recognized not to be enough, but a need to rethink the entire design process was stated, paying attention to the local peculiarities, thus paving the way for the so-called "Disruptive Innovation" or "Reverse Innovation" [10], later also called "Corporate Frugal Innovation" [11].

A big effort has thus been undertaken to define Frugal Innovation as a concept and frame it as a process. At first, many definitions based on descriptive criteria to qualify a solution as frugal have been proposed, highlighting cost reduction, concentration on core functionalities, and optimized performance level [12]. In [13] a longer list of features is compiled: Affordability, Simplicity, Robustness, User friendliness, Economies of scale, Quality, Locality, Sustainability, this last one underlining the opportunity to support greener solutions.

Most of literature contributions offer definitions and identify processes, gathering countless case studies and formulating statements to changing the operating mode, mostly adopting empathic methodologies, but pragmatic proposals of a structured workflow to organize a frugal innovation project are still rare. A seminal example is presented in [14], where a combined approach of VAVE (Value Analysis/Value Engineering) and TRIZ tools allows to removing all unnecessary features from a product and reducing the cost. The workflow is organized according to the SAVE Template [15], where TRIZ is used after a value Analysis, during the creativity phase, focusing on Trimming and Function Oriented Search applied on the generated function modeling and identification. In this paper it will be discussed how TRIZ could offer a stand-alone workflow dedicated to frugal innovation, offering the tools to overcome technical issues. The list of Frugal innovation features can be used as idea-downselection criterion.

2 TRIZ Tools Relevant to Frugal Innovation

The tools that so far have been identified in literature relevant to Frugal Innovation are Trimming and Function Oriented Search: this is consistent with Frugal Innovation most evident attributes:

- Focus on functionality: a previous step of Function Analysis (be according to VAVE or Modern TRIZ schema) to identify the most expensive functions and establish a function ranking, along with a systematic the pathway for simplification;
- Defeaturing: trimming and radical trimming to maintain the focus on main functions and redistribute or eliminate the remainder, so as to "do more with less";
- Function oriented search to "do better and cheaper", leveraging from existing alternative technologies and adapting to frugal environments.

In this paper the focus is on a workflow entirely based on TRIZ, and the discussion on the relevance of approach offered by other TRIZ tools, like:

- Ideal Final Result (IFR): to give an essential formulation of the need to cover;
- Resource Analysis: to systematically analyze what is available to solve the problem;
- Function Level Analysis/Trend of increasing Coordination: to enhance the focus on functionality and take the appropriate steps in the decision-chain;

These observations led to the identification of a dedicated TRIZ-based workflow, as explained in Sect. 3.

As far as the S-Curve analysis is concerned, the classic TRIZ theory foresees a First and a Transitional Stage with focus on delivering the Main Function and a Second Stage, when the product reaches market success, when functionality increases quickly to gain new customers; a frugal approach would need to review this formulation.

3 TRIZ-Assisted Systematic Process for Frugal Innovation

The proposed workflow foresees the following steps:

1. Ideal Final Result Formulation
2. Resources Analysis
3. Level of Functionality – Trend of Decreasing Human Involvement
4. Idea generation
5. Selection vs. Frugal Innovation Criteria
6. Business model formulation
7. Implementation

A case study to showcase this workflow in presented in Sect. 4.

4 Example: GIZ Water Supply Project in Uganda

Water is essential for any civilization. Still today about two billion people don't have access to clean and potable water. Water scarcity already represents one of the most important global challenges [16], expected to be exacerbated by the climate change, representing a crucial problem to be solved for sustainable development. The following example reports a frugal innovation experience from The GIZ project in Kabale, Uganda, addressing a water supply scarcity issue.

Typically, western countries want to address this problem with the western State-of-the-Art: use high technological solutions to pump and clean water. The current solutions are photovoltaic pumping systems. They consist of the following basic components (Fig. 1):

Fig. 1. Usual non-frugal approach components: top left, clockwise: Photovoltaic Modules, Inverter, Water Tank & Piping, Motor/Pump combination

- PV Modules that have to be imported and that are expensive;
- Inverter to convert the PV power into power to drive a submersible pump: this part is as well expensive and produces in developed countries;
- Submersible motor/pump combination: also to be imported;
- Water tank, pipes, hydraulic fitting (usually available in the country), which make ~10% of whole value chain.

Such a high technology system is furthermore usually designed for usage by proper trained persons and for good environmental conditions. The operation is done by a switch (on/off) and the operation is indicated by a LED: green – system operates, red – system failure. A repair on site by local people is not possible. The following pictures show the elements of such a PV Pumping System.

It is evident that in such a case an ordinary well-known solution would represent not only a non-affordable product, but also deliver an unsatisfactory performance regarding the life-cycle behavior. It is not adopted to the needs, skill set and requirements onsite.

We will now demonstrate how a TRIZ-assisted frugal innovation approach would address this issue by using the proposed workflow.

4.1 Ideal Final Result (IFR)

The IFR can be formulated as a **System, that always and safely delivers water** by itself.

4.2 Resource Analysis

A Resource Analysis was performed, leading to the list of the all available water reservoirs:

- Water itself
- Water holes (water is scooped)
- Deep wells
- Surface wells
- Rivers
- Handpumps
- Sakieh (Fig. 2)
- Atmospheric Humidity

Fig. 2. Sakieh

This list will also serve as a checklist for Trimming (described in Sect. 4.5), while brainstorming how to redistribute the functions to the external environment.

4.3 Level of Functionality – Trend of Decreasing Human Involvement

In this chapter we detect the level of functionality for the different resources, so as to assess the adaptability to the selected frugal environment. The Trends of Decreasing Human Involvement is used as a tool since it is very helpful as a rating criterion as a system evolves. The levels are defined according to Fig. 3:

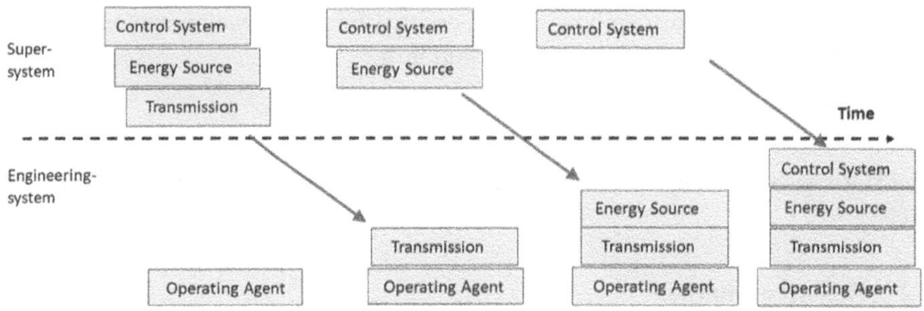

Fig. 3. Template for level of functionality analysis for the different resources

The engineering system ALWAYS consists at least of the operating agent. That is the functionality it was designed for. Control system, energy source and transmission are part of the super system. Over time transmission, energy source and control may move from the super system to the engineering system. This includes a reduction of human involvement. E.g. 1st automobile was the chassis and the motor. The driver had to do everything – start motor by hand, move wiper, move flasher, etc. Now we have lots of assistant systems in a car that help support the driver and we are nearby "autonomous driving" where even the control system moved to the engineering system.

For the resources listed in Sect. 4.2, human involvement is very high for all systems, but the handpump and the Sakieh.

One could improve the reduction of human involvement by using motorized systems like diesel fueled systems or photovoltaic systems. For the motor pumps, human involvement would be needed to start/stop of the system, refueling and maintenance. The operation affords technical expertise, but since combustion vehicles are well known, the skills are available. A system where controls are moved as well is a photovoltaic system. It operates fully autonomous (Fig. 4).

Fig. 4. Motorized systems used for water supply

4.4 Idea Generation: From Resources

As already presented, there are already existing solutions available to pump water with different levels of human involvement. The more autonomous the engineering system is, the more complex it is (and thus usually more expensive). So, the higher these solutions rank according to the Trend of Decreasing Human Involvement, the less frugal they are. **The frugal approach aims to concentrate on what is the maximum**

reduced functionality in order to meet the fundamental basic need. And based on this thought to develop ideas.

In this example the following ideas have been generated by asking: "How can <*resource*> help to pump water in the easiest way?".

A possible list of concepts in this case are reported below:

Fog nets collect the water out of the atmosphere. There is no pumping needed, no mechanics. It is simple, can be built by anybody on his own. But the capacity is limited and depends on the air humidity (Fig. 5).

Fig. 5. Fog nets

Water Wheel Pumps (Fig. 6) are simple constructed pumps for low heads (~6 m). They consist of a tube that is wind up in a spiral towards the middle. This spiral is mounted max. half sunk in the river. The flow of the river rotates the spiral und by this the water is pumped. This again is a very simple construction that can be made on-site as well.

Fig. 6. Water wheel pumps

Handpump with motor (Fig. 7) is a simple solution to move the transmission and energy to the system. Instead of the person pumping the water, a motor does the job. If it is not working, you can still pump manually. As motor an electric motor power by PV can be used which then needs again to be imported. An alternative could be a wind powered pump, constructed out of available waste materials.

Fig. 7. Handpump with motor

4.5 Idea Generation: Trimming

Another way to find ideas for solution is to use the trimming tool of TRIZ. For an existing system a function analysis is performed. Then trimming is used to simplify the system down to its basic functionality, fitting very well the frugal philosophy.

In the shown example we have a photovoltaic system. The solar irradiation energizes the PV module with photons. They are converted into electric current and power the inverter. The electronic inverter converts the electric power into AC current with variable frequency. This is powering the motor that feeds back the EMK as a control signal to the inverter. The motor rotates the pump and pressurizes the water in the well into the pipe. The Function Model is shown in Fig. 8.

In a first round of trimming (Fig. 9) the inverter unit was put at disposal. The task to solve was: how can the PV module power the motor directly? And the solution should be as simple as possible. The following figure shows one solution idea. Replace the inverter by a negative temperature coefficient (NTC-) resistor and a DC motor. This would work under less efficiency, but as reduced cost of about 1.000€ and much simpler.

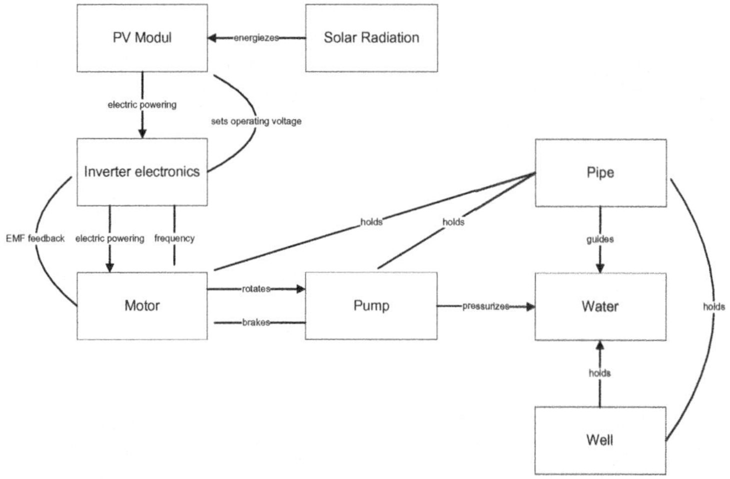

Fig. 8. Function Model of a photovoltaic system to power a water pump

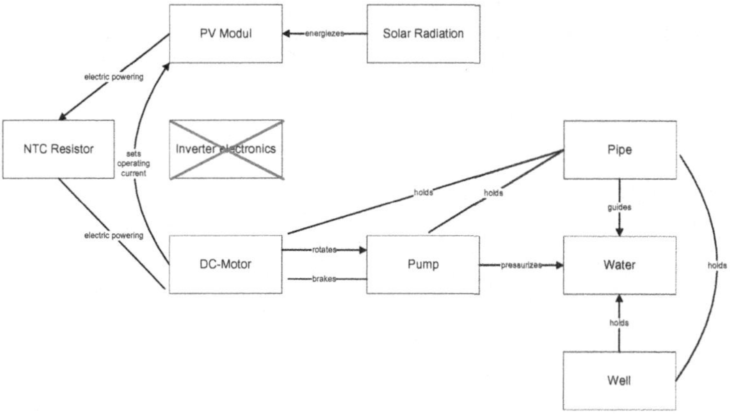

Fig. 9. Function Model after trimming the inverter unit

In a further step additional trimming is done (Fig. 10): Trimming of PV module, NTC-resistor and DC-motor. As a new component a low-temperature Stirling engine (LTSE) could move the pump. An LTSE is a low-tech product that can be manufactured in the local country.

Further trimming of solar irradiation usage and LTSE (Fig. 11) leads to the question if the water can pump itself, getting closer to the formulated IFR? A solution was show above with the water wheel pump, that can be built easily as well on site.

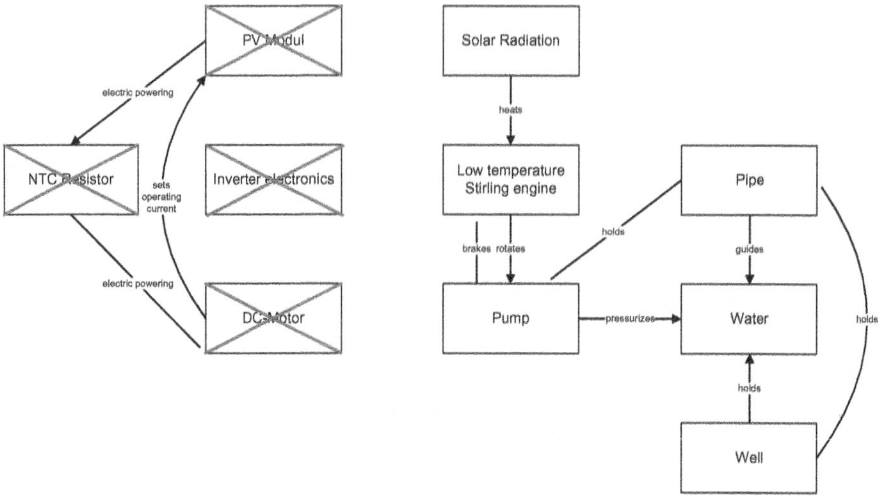

Fig. 10. Function Model after trimming the PV module

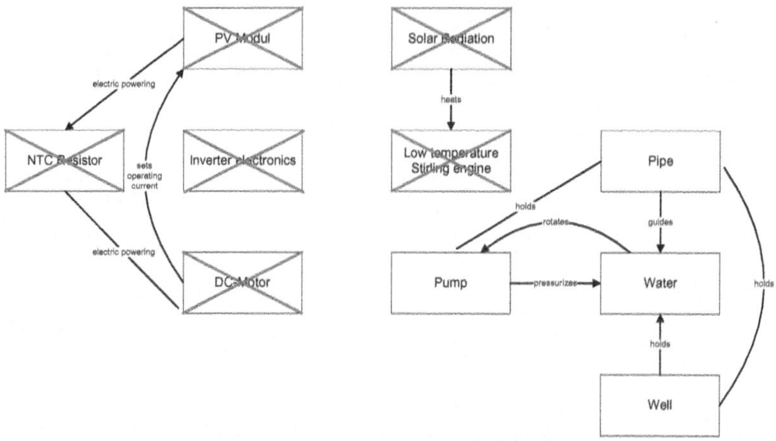

Fig. 11. Function Model after trimming solar irradiation

4.6 Selection vs. Frugal Innovation Criteria

For the selection of the best technology under frugal conditions, we have defined FOR THIS PROJECT the following criteria, normalized between 1 and 10 for comparability (Table 1):

- Performance (1 worse-10 good): How good and continuously the system is performing, quantified by water flow
- Cost (10 worse-1 good): Cost of the system in the site of application
- Usability (1 worse-10 good): States to extent to which the solution can be implement locally, i.e. percentage of locally manufactured components

Table 1. Idea down-selection according to frugal-criteria

	Performance	Cost	Usability	Transfer function
Weight	3	8	10	
Fog Nets	2	8	8	150
Water Wheel Pump	4	8	5	126
Handpump with electric motor	8	4	4	96
Handpump with wind power	4	7	7	138
PV pump	9	1	6	95
PV pump with NTC-resistor	7	4	8	133
LTSE pump	5	5	7	125
Dieselpump	10	2	8	126

In this list Performance maps Quality, Cost maps to Affordability and Usability maps to Simplicity, Robustness, User friendliness, and Locality, mentioned before.

The transfer function is calculated as:

$$F = \text{Performance} \times \text{weight} + \text{Cost} \times \text{weight} + \text{Usability} \times \text{weight}.$$

This shows that under the given assumptions fog nets and handpumps powered by wind make great sense.

4.7 Business Model Formulation

When the technology was selected the last step is to define a business model that will work for the manufacturer and for the customer. This will be based very much on the local conditions. Ideally the technology should be available/manufacturable locally.

5 Conclusions

The idea of frugal innovation addresses the needs of the bottom of the pyramid and allows to opens new business opportunities in new markets. A TRIZ-assisted workflow to generate frugal solutions, based on the understanding of the basic functionality needed in the target country for the product, has been presented, where the frugal thinking permeates the process at all stages. The TRIZ tools "IFR", "Resource analysis" and "Trimming" are valuable tools to generate ideas for a frugal product. The presented structured approach showed that TRIZ is a very valuable tool to assist frugal innovation; the next step will be to wholly deploy a TRIZ workflow for full optimization.

References

1. Radjou N.: Creative problem-solving in the face of extreme limits. TED Talk, 12 January 2015. https://www.youtube.com/watch?v=cHRZ6OrSvvI

2. Tiwari, R.: India's potential as a lead market for frugal innovation and the role of socio-cultural context factors. Working Paper 94, Hamburg University of Technology (TUHH) Institute, August 2016
3. Tiwari, R., Prabhu J.: Soft power of frugal innovation and its potential role in india's emergence as a global lead market for affordable excellence. Working Paper 104, Hamburg University of Technology (TUHH) Institute, August 2018
4. https://www.un.org/sustainabledevelopment/sustainable-development-goals/
5. Tiwari, R., Kalogerakis, K.: A bibliometric analysis of academic papers on frugal innovation. Working Paper 93, Hamburg University of Technology (TUHH) Institute, August 2016
6. Tiwari, R., Kalogerakis, K.: Frugal innovation in germany: a qualitative analysis of potential socio-economic impacts. Working Paper 94, Hamburg University of Technology (TUHH) Institute, March 2017
7. https://www.economist.com/special-report/2010/04/15/first-break-all-the-rules
8. Cheaper, Better, more Relevant: is Frugal Innovation an Opportunity for Europe? Fraunhofer ISI, Nesta. https://www.isi.fraunhofer.de/en/competence-center/politik-wirtschaft-innovation/projekte/frugal_innovations.html
9. https://www.rdm.iao.fraunhofer.de/en/research/organisation-fue/frugal-innovation.html
10. Immelt, J.R., Govindarajan, V., Trimble, C.: How GE Is Disrupting Itself. Harvard Business Review, October 2009. https://strategicdesignthinking.files.wordpress.com/2012/11/hbr-ge.pdf
11. "Low-Cost Innovation" Fraunhofer, IAO. https://wiki.iao.fraunhofer.de/images/studien/low-cost-innovationen.pdf. (in German)
12. Weyrauch, T., Herstatt C.: What is frugal innovation? three defining criteria. J. Frugal Innov. **2**, Article no. 1 (2016). https://jfrugal.springeropen.com/articles/10.1186/s40669-016-0005-y
13. Koch, C., Täube, F.A., Bernheim, E.: A teething smile: frugal innovation and global chain upgrading in India. Conference Paper, January 2018
14. Nanrudaiyan, N., Potdar, Y.: Value Engineering Tool for Frugal Innovation. www.valueanalysis.ca/publications.php?file_id=448
15. https://www.value-eng.org/default.aspx
16. World Economic Forum: Water scarcity is one of the greatest challenges of our time. https://www.weforum.org/agenda/2019/03/water-scarcity-one-of-the-greatest-challenges-of-our-time/

How Can TRIZ Tools Tremendously Stimulate the Lean Canvas Analysis to Foster Start-Up Business Model and Value Proposition?

Pascal Sire[1(✉)], Eric Prevost[2], Yves Guillou[3], Alain Riwan[4], and Pierre Saulais[5]

[1] innoppie & VP TRIZ France, Strasbourg, France
pascal.sire@innoppie.com
[2] Oracle Corp & President TRIZ France, Paris, France
president@trizfrance.org
[3] Guilbert EXPRESS & Secretaire TRIZ France, Paris, France
secretaire@trizfrance.org
[4] CEA, LIST, Interactive Robotics Laboratory, Paris, France
alain.riwan@cea.fr
[5] Mines Telecom Institute, Paris, France
pierre.saulais@telecom-em.eu

Abstract. TRIZ is a well-known innovative problem solving method, massively implemented within big industrial groups to boost their efficiency in innovation process. TRIZ is also a creativity technique providing a wide set of methodological formalized concepts applied through numerous tools. Case studies showed how start-ups can benefit from business innovation methodological good practices by enforcing the link between invention, innovation and intellectual property. This paper aims at demonstrating the ability of the formal TRIZ approach to contribute to the feasibility of the next step: helping entrepreneurs and start-ups' stakeholders in accelerating their «serial innovation» capability while keeping the control of the Lean process. To achieve this ambitious and crucial objective, the team will share its best practices of TRIZ expertise aiming at fostering the Lean canvas in-depth analysis thanks to the powerful TRIZ appropriate tools in order to dramatically reinforce and secure the pioneer spirit.

Keywords: Creativity · Entrepreneurship · Lean canvas · Start-up · TRIZ

1 Introduction: Which Business Model for Start-Up Creativity?

TRIZ is a well-known innovative problem solving method, massively implemented within big industrial groups to boost their efficiency in innovation process, and also a creativity technique providing a wide set of methodological formalized concepts applied through numerous tools (Altshuller 1988).

Published by Springer Nature Switzerland AG 2019
R. Benmoussa et al. (Eds.): TFC 2019, IFIP AICT 572, pp. 93–105, 2019.
https://doi.org/10.1007/978-3-030-32497-1_9

Case studies, in an industrial group and a start-up environment, have illustrated the power of the formalism of problem solving by applying the "start-up spirit" for efficient creativity (Sire et al. 2018).

We now want to ever more focus on the innovative start-up context, from both inventive activity and project management points of view.

The first purpose of this paper is therefore, regarding inventive activity point of view, to analyze how the young or recent entrepreneurs can take advantage of the formalism and analogy of the TRIZ state of mind, which is rigorous and oriented toward the search for progress, to foster their innovative activity (Sect. 2).

The second purpose of this paper is, regarding project management point of view, to explore the well-known business models in industry like the Business Model canvas and some derived approaches like Lean Start-up dedicated to a flexible early stage of development, in order to include the Lean canvas in stakeholder strategies (incubators and start-ups, innovative firms) (Sect. 3).

The third purpose of this paper is to illustrate in a start-up context how to easily fill the Lean canvas thanks to TRIZ methods and tools (Sect. 4).

The conclusion summarizes the lessons learned, limitations and perspectives of the paper.

2 How Can TRIZ Take Benefit of the Links Between Invention and the Inventive Intellectual Corpus to Foster Innovation?

2.1 Links Between Intellectual Property Rights and Invention

Our aim here is to show the contribution of information protected by intellectual property rights to the capacity for invention, whether directly (informational support) or indirectly (methodological support).

Direct Support of Invention Patents. Published patents help researchers to explore new fields (knowledge of what exists and of what is protected, understanding of past stages and humility in the face of the future, descriptions of prior art and traceability of technical design choices); patents and publications complement each other.

Publications focus on explaining phenomena while patents are positioned further on in the process, on results, applications and the means used for these applications (Breesé and de Kermadec 2004). Invention patents have acted as the innovation memory for two centuries (Breesé and de Kermadec 2004).

The patent also has as a counterpart to meet its obligation to disseminate the scientific and technical content of the invention, allowing "skilled individuals" to be able to reproduce it. The fact that the patent does not protect the idea (or the knowledge), but its materialization allows to insure compatibility between private incentive to invention (by increasing the personal yield from the invention) and technical progress (by disseminating knowledge).

A patent describes the prior art and explains how the proposed solution differs from the existing one, thereby allowing an excellent level of traceability in the choice of technical designs (Breesé and de Kermadec 2004).

Indirect Methodological Support for Invention Patents. Formalizing an innovation "like a patent" (de Kermadec 2001), that is, by describing certain aspects with documents that follow the editorial rules of patents, can contribute to strengthening this common vision of the work being created (What field is the invention in? What is the problem to be solved? How is the problem currently solved?) in such a way that, by appropriating the specific style of invention patents, the team behind the innovative project:

- Clearly defines its objectives;
- Find out the state of the art;
- Can imagine a wide variety of solutions;
- Compare its solutions to others in a synthetic way;
- Strictly formalizes what it wants to do;
- Communicates more effectively;
- Is more aware that it is teamwork that allows "the best solution" (de Kermadec 2001) to be created.

Formalizing and creating are therefore indivisible (de Kermadec 2001); "patent style" formalization is particularly suited to the inventive approach. Pierre Breesé and Yann de Kermadec confirm that reinvention is highly expensive and a record of the company's creations should be kept.

Using an innovation-base (that is, a knowledge base dedicated to innovation products and processes) allows ideas to be saved so that they can be used at the right time, as well as avoiding reinvention, and identifying problems, solutions and the people to contact. It contains innovation files, innovation memos, patents, files of inventions that have not been retained, and so on (Breesé and de Kermadec 2004).

In this way, the link between industrial property and innovation is shown in the fact that databases of invention patents are unrivaled and often exclusive sources of technological and scientific information, presented according to powerful formalism, methodologically speaking.

2.2 Reciprocal Links Between Inventive Activity and the Inventive Intellectual Corpus

Our ICAROS® method uses analysis of the inventive intellectual corpus to stimulate inventive activity (Saulais and Ermine 2016a); the inventive intellectual corpus of an organization contains basic elements that allows for the representation of a certain number of inventive trajectories undertaken by the organization's knowledge actors by linking the inventive intellectual traces that have been left (patents, theses, reports of advanced studies). A reasoned analysis of the traces thus restores the intellectual path drawn by the trajectories of these traces, giving a strategic evolution of the inventive intellectual corpus that has been inventoried over several years.

The assessment obtained by this process of collecting and explaining inventive knowledge that has led to a new design, is then put into perspective with the potential knowledge in each field (representing an absolute reference) to form a cognitive stimulus applied to experts representing each area of knowledge, who individually have potential elements for the identification and the explanation of which they have to be guided in order to help them develop a forward-looking vision of their field (Saulais and Ermine 2016a).

The reciprocity is expressed through the analysis, extraction and implementation of the inventive knowledge, with this new inventive knowledge going on to enrich the inventive intellectual corpus (Saulais 2016b), (Saulais 2016c), as illustrated by Fig. 1, which focuses on the dossier on inventive activity called Invention & Innovation File.

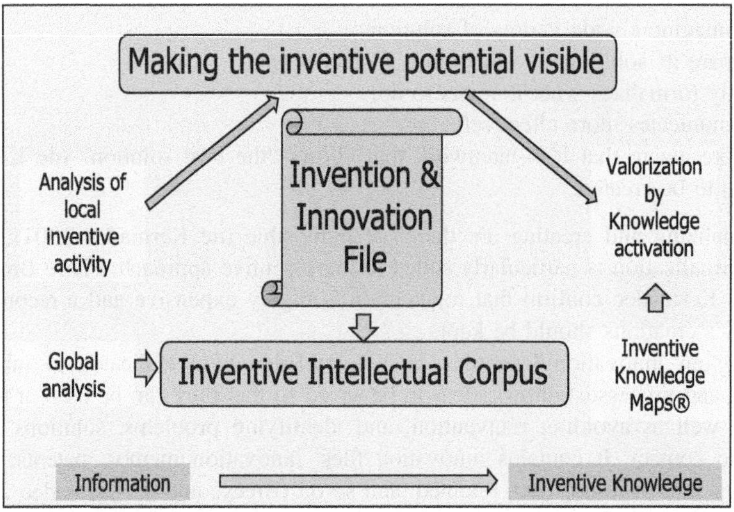

Fig. 1. Analysis of inventive activity – Source: author

Figure 2 illustrates the applications of analysis of overall inventive activity (contained within the inventive intellectual corpus) to support decision-making in different fields.

2.3 Synthesis

We defined invention, innovation and intellectual property rights as objects of knowledge.

We thus presented each of the three objects of knowledge, primarily the act of innovating and its outcome, followed by the ability to invent, and lastly the inventive intellectual corpus and intangible capital. By considering each object of knowledge to represent its own field of knowledge, we have examined the links between the three fields both in a static sense and in a dynamic sense of one thriving on the other, in a pure start-up spirit.

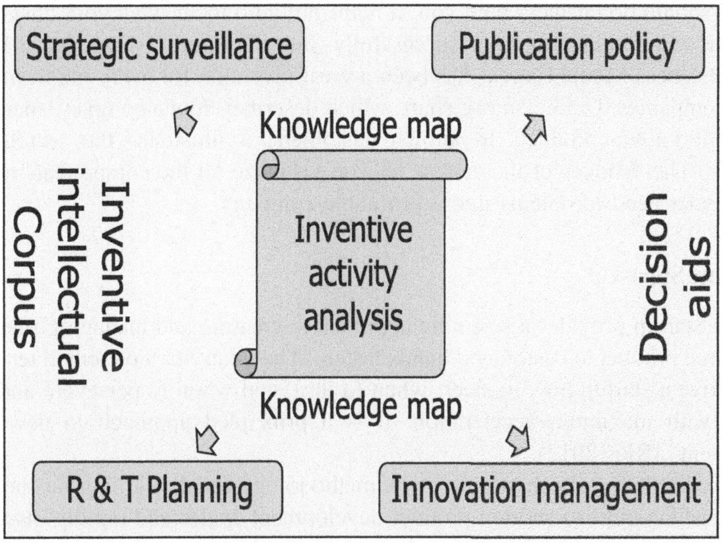

Fig. 2. Applications for showing analysis of inventive activity in knowledge maps – Source: author

Having highlighted the benefits of applying a structured and reasoned method to technical fields of innovation, we now want to explore its application to other fields of innovation, mainly in the management domain. This is the ambition of Sects. 3 and 4.

3 From Business Model to Lean Canvas

How can an organization innovate? "To achieve organizational innovation, every facet of a business needs to move together in the same direction. That can be difficult without a clear visual of what your business model is and how your activities should be aligned. You need to identify what your company wants -and is prepared- to do before innovation can turn from a buzzword into an action" (Hemmer 2016).

3.1 Business Model Canvas

The Business Model Canvas is a methodology on the rise that helps companies visualize and position their business models for growth and innovation. Strategyzer defines it as "a strategic management and entrepreneurial tool. It allows you to describe, design, challenge, invent, and pivot your business model." (Strategyzer 2019).

It breaks your business model down into easily-understood segments: Key Partners, Key Activities, Key Resources, Value Propositions, Customer Relationships, Channels, Customer Segments, Cost Structure, and Revenue Streams.

"It also reveals clear paths on which to build your organizational innovation strategy. It helps you communicate your goals to your team. It helps communicate to clients why they should do business with you. It helps pull into focus what your business does and how it will continue to do it -successfully- into the future." (Hemmer 2016).

The Business Model Canvas has been a great invention for everyone from startups to large companies. Unlike an org chart, which describes how a company manages the delivery of known products to known customers, it illustrates the search for the unknowns. The 9 boxes of the canvas let you visualize all the components needed to turn customer needs/problems into a profitable company.

3.2 Lean Start-Up

The Lean Startup provides a scientific approach to creating and managing startups and get a desired product to customers' hands faster. "The Lean Startup method teaches you how to drive a startup-how to steer, when to turn, and when to persevere-and grow a business with maximum acceleration. It is a principled approach to new product development" (Ries 2012).

Wikipedia defines Lean startup as "a methodology for developing businesses and products, which aims to shorten product development cycles and rapidly discover if a proposed business model is viable; this is achieved by adopting a combination of business-hypothesis-driven experimentation, iterative product releases, and validated learning".

Central to the lean startup methodology is the assumption that when startup companies invest their time into iteratively building products or services to meet the needs of early customers, the company can reduce market risks and sidestep the need for large amounts of initial project funding and expensive product launches and failures (Wikipedia 2019).

The Lean Startup is the way most innovators build startups and innovate inside of existing companies. As a formal method, the Lean Startup consists of three parts:

- The Business Model Canvas – to frame hypotheses
- Customer Development – to test those hypotheses in front of customers
- Agile Engineering – to build Minimum Viable Products to maximize learning.

3.3 Lean Canvas

The Business Model Canvas was proposed by Alexander Osterwalder based on his earlier book: Business Model Ontology. It outlines several prescriptions which form the building blocks for the activities. It enables both new and existing businesses to focus on operational as well as strategic management and marketing plans.

The Lean Canvas, on the other hand, has been proposed by Ash Maurya as a development of the Business Model Generation. It outlines a more problem-focused approach and it majorly targets entrepreneurs and startup businesses (Canvanizer 2019).

Ash Maurya's main objective with Lean Canvas was making it as actionable as possible while staying entrepreneur-focused. The metaphor he had in mind was that of a grounds-up tactical plan or blueprint that guided the entrepreneur as they navigated their way from ideation to building a successful startup.

He had already been working with Lean Startup principles which had a big influence on the design. His approach to making the canvas actionable was capturing what was most uncertain, or more accurately, what was most risky (Maurya 2015).

Unlike Business Model Canvas, the Lean Canvas focuses on: Problem understanding (avoiding working on the wrong problem), Solution (purposefully within a small box to avoid spending time and resources), Key metrics (just a very few that matter), and Unfair Advantage (another name for competitive advantage or barriers to entry) (Fig. 3).

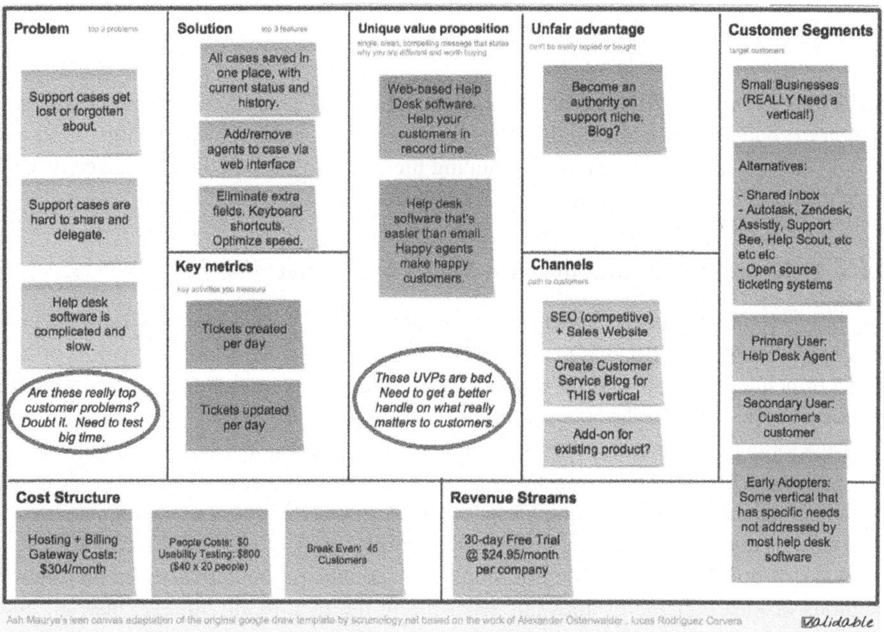

Fig. 3. Lean Canvas (Keylime example) – source Steve Mullen

"Going through the nine steps on Lean Canvas helped me to understand what information really matters in creating a start-up. I feel that identifying the problem and the solution are the most important steps in the Lean Canvas process. They are the sole purpose of your product and you must ensure that a problem does exist in order for your product to be successful." (Nancyaviles 2012).

The Lean Canvas is a one-page strategic tool, in the Lean Startup spirit, that defines a startup or product and helps document and validate an inventive business plan (Table 1).

How to help entrepreneurs and start-ups'stakeholders in accelerating their «serial innovation» capability while keeping the control of the Lean process?

If identifying the problem and the solution are the most important steps, what about the ability of the formal TRIZ approach to contribute to the feasibility of this ambitious and crucial objective?

Table 1. Lean Canvas details and suggested order – source: Ash Maurya

Product			Market	
2-Problem Top 3 problems	**4**-Solution Top 3 features	**3-Unique Value Prop**	**9**-Unfair Advantage	**1-Customer Segments**
2b-Existing Alternatives	**8**-Key Metrics Key activities	*3b-High level Concept*	**5**-Channels to Customers	*1b-Early Adopters*
7-Cost structure (fixed, variable)			**6**-Revenue streams (sources)	

4 TRIZ Helps Filling the Lean Canvas

According to authors (Maia et al. 2012), "Lean and TRIZ share a main idea: design and delivery products to the clients that they really want. In order to achieve this, both use principles and tools having in mind reducing the waste or minimizing the usage of new resources and both uses a procedure of continuous improvement".

4.1 TRIZ and Systematic Business Model Innovation

As early as 2010, Valeri Souchkov presented at the TRIZ Future Conference in Bergamo an approach to Business Model Innovation based on a combination of key TRIZ principles and tools and a new approach to business modeling which introduces building blocks to describe and represent business models.

Developing a competitive business model is essential for any business organization since the model defines the company strategy and future on the market. However in the modern times of accelerated innovation business models might not remain static: ever changing business environment requires continuous innovation of both technology and the ways of doing business. The traditional way of innovation which relies on random methods of idea generation does not seem fitting the picture any longer. Instead, new systematic and structured methods supporting continuous process of new business ideas generation are emerging.

Application of key TRIZ tools and concepts such as Ideality, Contradictions, Resources and Trends of Business Systems Evolution within the context of business models was discussed. Such a combination helps to:

- represent business models in terms of building blocks and describe business models clearly and in a structured way without overloading it with numerous details;
- systematically assess and analyse business models with TRIZ analytical tools; locate and define problems, contradictions and areas with high evolution potential;
- apply the TRIZ tools for business and management problem solving and ideas generation to innovatively modify existing business models or to design new, innovative business models for a specific market or industry (Souchkov 2010).

As an example was shown a contradiction mapping revealed with RCA+ to relevant building blocks of a business model.

4.2 TRIZ Method Aligns with Organizational Practices for Innovation

At TFC 2012, Helena Navas studied the TRIZ-Lean Environment: "The Lean approach is to find the best compromise between contradictions, whereas the TRIZ approach is to eliminate contradictions avoiding the compromise or trade off. TRIZ can be seen as a Lean tool. There are many Lean techniques and concepts where TRIZ might be applied." (Navas 2015).

As an example, in "8 Discipline" (8D), one of the Lean problem solving tools, TRIZ may help in the 8D problem solving process: in D2 step (Describing the Problem) to identify contradictions and to define and to valuate problems, in D5 step (Choosing Corrective Actions) with many and varied generic solutions available with several TRIZ tools, etc. The TRIZ tools would help to 8D become more systematic, effective and successful method of problem solving. Also, TRIZ might help with waste reduction, the TRIZ concept of ideal system presents similarities with the Lean search for systems without cost or harm (without waste), etc.

According to Paul Hobcraft, the use of the Lean management as above have shown "a consistent change over the years to move towards a more inventive engineering and discovery mindset within our innovation approaches." (Hobcraft 2017). It started in manufacturing, continued in logistics and supply chain and evolved in labs and thinking to keep advancing processes, thinking and growth inside our organizations. Far more outside is now looked to connect into the customer's specific needs.

"The Lean Startup movement has been a significant part of the fusing of internal learning becoming more agile and understanding of what customers really want. It takes agility as central to this evolving through learning and constant discovery.", he says (Hobcraft 2017). Minimum viable propositions are now built into problem-solving thinking, extending prototyping into discovery process, and learning to pivot on the go.

Designing the Business Model through the Canvas has appealed to those that believe they are visionaries, game changers, and challengers striving to defy outmoded business models and design tomorrow's enterprises. This has spawned a variety of visual tools, different canvases as strategic and operational ideas and tools, and makes them easy to implement in any organization.

"TRIZ is a problem solving method based on logic and data, not intuition, which accelerates the project team's ability to solve these problems creatively. TRIZ also provides repeatability, predictability, and reliability due to its structure and algorithmic approach. New TRIZ tools are being developed, with active groups working on this. These are more advanced tools applied to help in: functional oriented search (FOS), main parameters of value (MPV) analysis, Voice of the Product (VOP), etc." (Hobcraft 2017).

4.3 Lean Canvas with TRIZ Tools

At TFC 2014, Teemu Toivonen proposed forming a hybrid "continuous innovation" model by combining Toyota Kata with TRIZ techniques. He said: "It is only one possible solution and there is a lot of room for different approached due to the large amount and flexibility of TRIZ techniques available".

A guiding principle for the author has been to try to evaluate not only how well an individual technique works, but how well it fits together with the other techniques. The idea has not been to map all possible TRIZ techniques to Toyota Kata, but rather to give examples of how that mapping can be done (Toivonen 2014).

With such a spirit, the authors would like to share an easy to use, quick and efficient way to fill the Lean Canvas boxes using some of the well-known Classical TRIZ tools. This was done several times, within incubators for a few start-ups at early stage, and within a worldwide-class SMB wanting to take advantage of the "start-up spirit" (Table 2).

Table 2. Lean Canvas boxes and an example of TRIZ toolkit – source: authors

Lean Canvas boxes	Example of TRIZ toolkit
1. Problem	– Thinking in Time and Space
2. Customer Segments	– Trends of Technical Evolution
3. Unique Value Proposition	– Contradictions
4. Solution	– Resources
5. Channels	– Ideality
6. Revenue Streams	– Functional Analysis
7. Cost Structure	– 40 Inventive Principles
8. Key Metrics	– 76 Standard Solutions
9. Unfair Advantage	– Size-Time-Cost, etc.

Among the many possibilities of cross-linkage, the Fig. 4 proposes one case, without content in the Lean Canvas boxes due to IP reasons (Prevost et al. 2014).

For example, to be discussed during the TFC presentation, some suggestions:

- first step in to get a textual explanation of the customer issues using the TRIZ contradiction schema to summarize the owner's vision of the problem to solve;
- filling the box 2 "Customer segments" using the TRIZ Time & Operational zones;
- filling the box 3 "Unique Value Proposition" thanks to the TRIZ ideality;
- filling the box 4 "Solution" is quite easy with TRIZ as problem-solver;
- etc.

Last but not least, Fig. 5 show resonance from startups (Prevost et al. 2014). For example: the start-ups' owners discovered the power of the Evolution Laws to imagine the next innovation after their first one, they were confortable with the Time zone and Operational zone to focus on when and where do the customer pains occur, the multi-screen was appreciated to understand the different layers of systems and times around their innovative product or service, also ideality and S-Curve, etc.

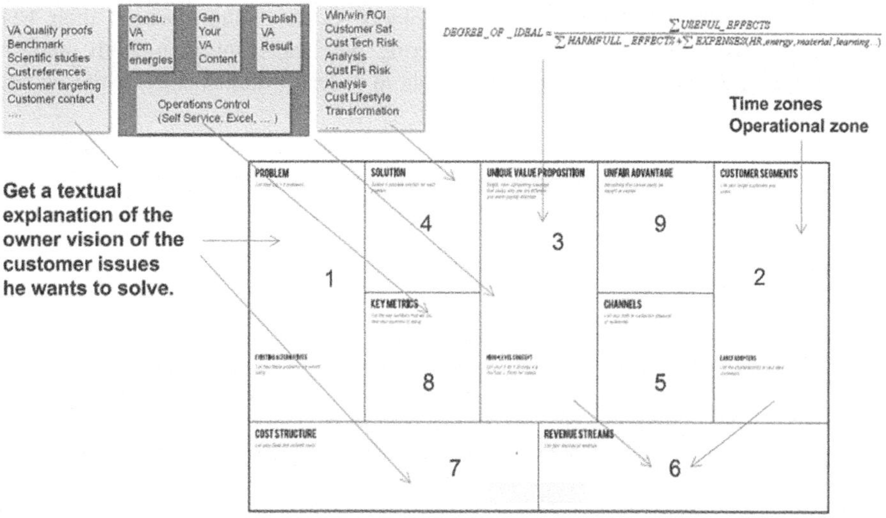

Fig. 4. Lean Canvas boxes filling with TRIZ tools – source: authors

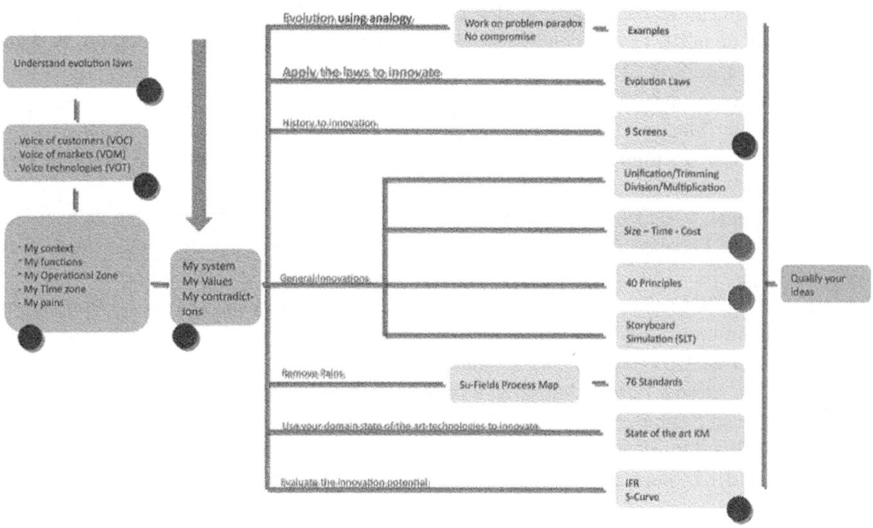

Fig. 5. LeanCanvas and TRIZ feedback from startups – source: authors

5 Conclusion

In this paper aims, we demonstrated the ability of the formal TRIZ approach to contribute to the feasibility of the next step: helping entrepreneurs and start-ups'stakeholders in accelerating their «serial innovation» capability while keeping the control of the Lean process.

To achieve this ambitious and crucial objective, the authors shared their best practices of TRIZ expertise aiming at fostering the Lean canvas in-depth analysis thanks to the powerful TRIZ appropriate tools in order to dramatically reinforce and secure the pioneer spirit.

Next step would be to carry over other real-life case studies. Does the TRIZ community have such examples or experiences to share and learn from?

References

Altshuller, G.: Creativity as An Exact Science: The Theory of the Solution of Inventive Problems. Gordon & Breach, New York (1988)

Sire, P., Prevost, E., Guillou, Y., Riwan, A., Saulais P.: TRIZ and intellectual property to strengthen the start-up spirit. In: TRIZ Future Conference, Strasbourg, France (2018)

Breese, P., de Kermadec, Y.: La Propriété intellectuelle au service de l'innovation. Nathan, Paris (2004)

de Kermadec, Y.: Innover grâce au brevet. Dunod, Paris (2001)

Laperche, B.: Brevets et normes techniques: de l'incitation à l'invention au contrôle de l'innovation. Dans Propriété industrielle et Innovation, de Blandine LAPERCHE, pp. 81–98. L'Harmattan, Paris (2001)

Saulais, P.: Application de la gestion des connaissances à la créativité des experts et à la planification de la R&T en milieu industriel de haute technologie. Thèse de doctorat, Télécom Ecole de Management (2013)

Saulais, P.: Mise en visibilité du potentiel inventif et représentation du patrimoine intellectuel inventif. Veille Mag, no. 155 Spécial Gestion des Connaissances (2016b)

Saulais, P.: Analyse, cartographie et mise en action de la connaissance inventive. GeCSO, Paris (2016c)

Saulais, P., Ermine, J.-L.: Emergence d'innovation technologique incrémentale par aplication, à des experts, de l'analyse du patrimoine intelectuel inventif. Édité par De Boeck. Innovations 49, no. 1, pp. 103–140 (2016a)

Hemmer, M. (2016) https://blog.onefire.com/why-a-business-model-canvas-is-important-to-organizational-innovation

Strategyzer: Canvas (2019). https://www.strategyzer.com/canvas

Wikipedia: Lean Startup (2019). https://en.wikipedia.org/wiki/Lean_startup

Ries, E.: The Lean Startup, Pearson (2012). http://theleanstartup.com/principles

Canvanizer (2019). https://canvanizer.com/how-to-use/business-model-canvas-vs-lean-canvas

Maurya, A. (2015). https://www.linkedin.com/pulse/why-lean-canvas-vs-business-model-ash-maurya

Nancyaviles (2012). https://nancyaviles.wordpress.com/2012/10/27/lean-canvas-lessons-learned

Maia, L.C., Alves, A.C., Leao, C.P.: How could the TRIZ tool help continuous improvement efforts of the companies? TFC (2012)

Navas, H.V.G., Machado, V.A.C.: The Lifeline of Technical systems in a TRIZ-LEAN environment. Procedia Eng. **131**, 232–236 (2015). TFC 2012

Souchkov, V.: TRIZ and systematic business model innovation. In: Proceedings of the "TRIZ Future Conference 2010", Bergamo, Italy, 3–5 November 2010, pp. 189–197. Bergamo University Press. https://triz-journal.com/triz-and-systematic-business-model-innovation. ISBN: 978-88-9633359-4

Toivonen, T.: Continuous innovation – combining Toyota Kata and TRIZ for sustained innovation. Procedia Eng. **131**, 963–974 (2015). TFC 2014

Prevost, E., Bruno, G., Guillou, Y., Sire, P., Conrardy, C.: What roles can TRIZ play in Start-up incubators? In: Global TRIZ Conference 2014, Seoul, Korea (2014)

A Proposal for a Methodology of Technical Creativity Mixing TRIZ and Additive Manufacturing

Armand Lang[1(✉)], Claude Gazo[1], Frédéric Segonds[1], Fabrice Mantelet[1], Camille Jean[1], Jerôme Guegan[2], and Stéphanie Buisine[3]

[1] Arts et Métiers, LCPI, 151 boulevard de l'Hôpital, 75013 Paris, France
armand.lang@ensam.eu

[2] Université Paris-Descartes, LATI, 71 avenue Edouard-Vaillant, 92100 Boulogne-Billancourt, France

[3] CESI, LINEACT, 93 boulevard de la Seine, 92000 Nanterre, France

Abstract. The industry has quickly realized the importance of bringing creativity into product design. The industrial context requires robust and efficient methods and tools to access untapped sources of ideas.

Furthermore, Additive Manufacturing (AM) offers a large potential of creativity for product design. This potential is particularly significant at the level of Intermediate Objects. Previous works have demonstrated the interest of AM Intermediate Objects (Rias, 2017) in creativity phases. This new manufacturing process is revolutionizing the value chain associated with product design, from the ideation to the industrialization.

The purpose of this paper is to describe the bases for proposing a methodology of technical creativity based on TRIZ and Additive Manufacturing.

Keywords: TRIZ · Creativity · Design for Additive Manufacturing (DFAM) · Intermediate objects

1 Introduction

In recent years, Additive Manufacturing (AM) has become a major technology in modern manufacturing. It includes all manufacturing processes from an object designed in digital format (CAD) to a physical object; this manufacturing is done layer by layer by adding material. The gradual shift from prototyping to manufacturing of functional parts manufacturing is revolutionizing product design in all areas of industry, particularly in the automotive, aeronautics, aerospace and medical industries.

This technology is totally different from traditional manufacturing processes. Today, however, design teams rely on traditional processes to idealize, design and manufacture a product. A designer has cognitive barriers that will prevent him from innovating with AM processes. The challenge is therefore: how to structure a methodology that will make it possible to overcome these cognitive barriers? The issue is also: which design tools has to be integrated in the methodology?

R. Benmoussa et al. (Eds.): TFC 2019, IFIP AICT 572, pp. 106–116, 2019.
https://doi.org/10.1007/978-3-030-32497-1_10

Thus, in this article, we will present the structure of a methodology of innovation and creativity by additive manufacturing, using the tool and the way of thinking of TRIZ.

The first part will focus on the literature on additive manufacturing, on Design for Additive Manufacturing (DfAM) and on TRIZ. In the second part, the methodological approach will be presented according to the findings of the work presented in the first part. Then in a last part, we will develop a tool based on the 40 principles of TRIZ and on the capabilities of additive manufacturing.

2 State of the Art

2.1 Design and Manufacturing

This part will help to define additive manufacturing and understand the difference and links between additive manufacturing and other manufacturing processes.

Design

Manufacturing is a technique of transforming or modifying raw materials or basic products into a finished product. This technique is therefore the tool that makes it possible to satisfy product design; that is, to complete and validate the design process. Indeed, design is the process from the identification of the problem to the manufacturing of the product, going through generation of concepts, analysis and evaluation (technical, economic, ergonomic, aesthetic, etc.) [1, 2].

In the literature, there are several design characterizations. Some studies distinguish four types of design from creative design to routine design, with innovative design and redesign in between [1, 3, 4]. The differentiation between creative and innovative design is characterized by the distinction between designs coming from innovative concepts and designs coming from concepts based on knowledge without existing conceptual development. Some authors group these two types into innovative design, but distinguish within this notion, breakthrough innovation and continuity innovation [5]. The definition of redesign is rather vague because it is only a question of making an improvement to the product; therefore, it is not possible to say with this definition if the improvement is an innovative function or not.

In our study, we will work with two types of designs and not with a scale of four designs. These two types of design are [6]:

- Innovative design. It is the set of designs that provides a solution to a problem that has never been solved. It can be a redesign with a new function, as well as a fundamentally new product.
- Routine design. It is the set of designs that is based on solutions already known. Often a routine design is an improvement in response to a competitor's innovative design.

This bipolar distinction will allow us not to differentiate between innovative design and creative design. We will talk about innovative design based on the result of the finished product, and we will talk about a creative approach for the process from problem to solution.

Manufacturing

In the context of a physical product design, manufacturing is a tool for developing the product. There are several types of manufacturing processes (Fig. 1).

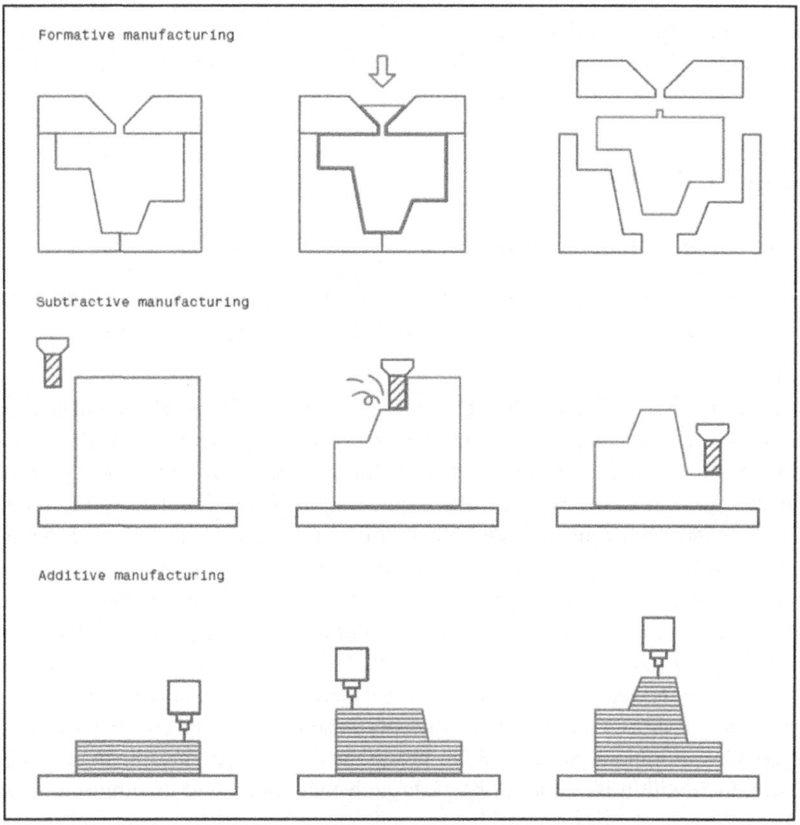

Fig. 1. The three types of manufacturing [6]

Additive manufacturing is a layer-by-layer manufacturing process by adding material; it is a generative manufacturing process. This technology is often referred to with other terms, considered reductive such as 3D printing or layered manufacturing.

Additive manufacturing disrupts traditional manufacturing techniques such as:

- Formative manufacturing: the material is brought into a liquid or viscous state, then the shaping is carried out by flowing this material into a mold (ex: foundry).
- Subtractive manufacturing: The product is made from a raw part on which the material will be removed in order to obtain the desired final shape(ex: machining).

2.2 Design for Additive Manufacturing (DfAM)

In order to operate and leverage additive manufacturing for product innovation, it has become imperative to structure and develop design tools and methods through additive manufacturing for design teams. In order to stimulate creativity through additive manufacturing, the designer needs a tool-based methodology to take into account the specificities of these new manufacturing processes in order to overcome the cognitive barriers printed in the customs and practices of design teams. To this end, several studies are focusing on Design for Additive Manufacturing so as to develop methodological supports that meet the needs of promoting the potential of additive manufacturing.

DfAM is "the set of methodology and tools that help the designer to take into account the specificities of additive manufacturing (technological, geometrical, pre/post processing …) during the design stage" [7]. Despite this definition, which highlights the design phases, many studies are working more particularly on product redesign, i.e. on designing with additive manufacturing an existing product usually build in traditional manufacturing.

Depending on the different approaches of Design for Additive Manufacturing, some authors will propose tools for analysing design problems, while others will rather propose tools for generating ideas.

Works on tools for analysing design problems are based on parametric optimization [8] or axiomatic design [9]. Studies oriented towards tools for generating ideas will instead use databases of additive manufacturing functionalities [10] or associations with intermediate objects during creativity sessions [11].

But current Design for Additive Manufacturing methods have certain limits because they do not take advantage of the potential of additive manufacturing, on creativity and innovation as early as possible in the design and innovation process of a product, at the ideation level. In order to really overcome cognitive barriers, the need to bring a methodology is found at the earliest stage in the design phase, during the phase of creativity and of intermediate object design [11].

2.3 Design with Additive Manufacturing (DWAM)

Laverne et al. propose a methodology adapted from Design with X (DWX): Design With Additive Manufacturing [12]. DWX objective is "to inspire designers and supports them in creating product because DWX focuses on innovations so the product design solutions have always an innovative character" [13]. The purpose of this methodology is therefore to provide designers with knowledge during the design phases and particularly in the upstream phases.

Unlike DfAM, which focuses on additive manufacturing technology, DWAM will expand the solution space by providing designers with new knowledge on additive manufacturing elements and characteristics. The DWAM allows the characteristics of intermediate representations to be linked with characteristics of products designed in additive manufacturing.

The advantage of DWAM is that it can be used in the upstream phases. However, this methodology is not intended to guide designers entirely towards one or more design solutions.

The approach of an innovative design consists in starting: from a problem, analysing this problem to arrive at solutions, then deepening the solutions to arrive at a feasible technical solution. To ensure that a methodology is in the early design phase, it is necessary to define how to introduce tools to benefit from the potential of additive manufacturing during the study of the problem, and not only during the study of the solution. This work on technical problems sends us to the theory of inventive problem solving (TRIZ).

2.4 Inter-methodological Gateway Between TRIZ and DfAM

The TRIZ invention approach consists in modelling the problem to achieve a solution through a solution model [14]. The tools used in TRIZ make it possible to go beyond cognitive limits by directing designers towards research areas to be developed. It is unlike other creative tools, which rather encourage them to deepen their own research areas. The 40 innovation principles guide designers towards innovation axes according to design problems.

Several studies have proposed inter-methodological bridges between TRIZ and other design methods. The work of Durand et al. presents several applications of methodologies that mix TRIZ with other design methods, such as Functional Analysis, FMECA or Quality Function Deployment [15].

In this perspective, it is interesting to look at the literature mixing TRIZ and DfAM. Gross et al. will propose a new TRIZ matrix, specific to additive manufacturing by defining the characteristics of additive manufacturing as the criteria for innovation [16]. This study uses the way of working defined by the TRIZ matrix but does not include any historical notion of the TRIZ theory.

Kretzschmar et al. sought an example for the 40 TRIZ principles in additive manufacturing, focusing both on the characteristics of a product made of additive manufacturing, and those of additive manufacturing processes (material extrusion, vat polymerization, powder bed fusion, material jetting, binder jetting) [17]. The articles from Kamps et al. focus on the intersection of TRIZ, biomimicry and DfAM. In these articles, the authors explain that the designers start with the function of the product and a product with a basic design, then the product is improved through a biomimicry database. The integration of a biomimetic design into the design is carried out through a TRIZ invention process [18].

The work mixing TRIZ and DfAM does not meet the need defined above: to have a methodology at the earliest in the design and innovation phase of a product, at the ideation level. This need will therefore be the challenge of our model.

3 Methodological Approach

3.1 Schematization

A TRIZ application associated with additive manufacturing capabilities can be used as a tool for generating ideas that can then generate innovative solutions to initial design problems. This methodology will force designers to expand their creativity with the technical potential of additive manufacturing. The purpose of using the TRIZ method is to expand this creative potential that designers can exploit.

Figure 2 below shows the schematization of our methodology. We can find all the elements presented in the above parts. The design includes all manufacturing processes, there is a distinction between traditional manufacturing (formative and subtractive) and additive manufacturing.

Within the "design" set, we observe a "creativity" set that corresponds to the innovative design, the rest being the routine design.

In the overall "creativity", one part represents the creative potential of traditional manufacturing and the other part represents the creative potential of additive manufacturing. Today, due to cognitive barriers, only a small part of this potential is exploited by designers. That is, a large part of it is not exploited.

The purpose of the TRIZ tool is therefore to guide designers towards solutions available in this untapped part.

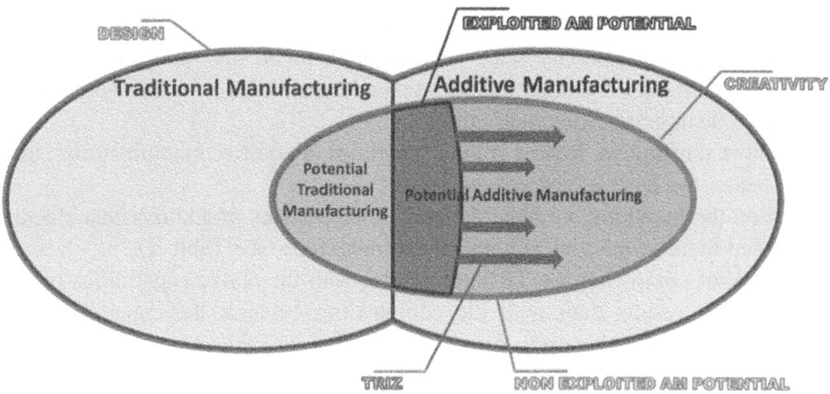

Fig. 2. Schematization of the methodology

3.2 Structuring the Link Between TRIZ and DfAM

In order to guide designers towards additive manufacturing, a link must be created between TRIZ and DfAM.

To create this link, we first focused on the capabilities of additive manufacturing. This technology has unique characteristics (inclusion, cavity, lattice structure…). In 2010, Gibson et al. presented these unique characteristics through four complexities [19]:

- Shape complexity: With additive manufacturing, it is possible to manufacture any shape within the constraints of the printing machine.
- Hierarchical complexity: Additive manufacturing makes it possible to design a product by varying the microscopic structure according to the technical needs of each part of the product.
- Functional complexity: It is possible to manufacture functional devices in a single construction, not just simple parts.
- Material complexity: Additive manufacturing makes it possible to build multi-material parts.

Gibson's four complexities are used as the basis for all DfAM approaches. We have therefore chosen to start from these complexities and compare them with one of TRIZ's tools, the 40 principles of innovation. For each of the principles, a team of eight people defined whether an additive manufacturing application did correspond. This team was composed of complementary profiles: a designer, two ergonomists and five engineers (a TRIZ specialist, two creativity specialists and two AM specialists). The result showed us that the complexity scale was too high to do this study. For functional complexity in particular, the latter includes several capabilities, which it would be more interesting to distinguish from each other.

To achieve a result, we looked at the capabilities of additive manufacturing; that is, the level below the level of complexity.

Based on the literature, we have defined 13 capabilities of additive manufacturing and classified them in relation to Gibson's complexities (see Table 1).

The work of comparing the TRIZ principles with the above capabilities provided more interesting results than with the complexities because the capabilities corresponded to fewer principles each. This work resulted in Table 2.

Two levels of links have been created, the "full" level (represented in red and with "X") and the "partial" level (represented in orange and with "x").

The "full" level was chosen when the capability fully corresponds to the TRIZ principle; i.e. all designs with this characteristic comply with the principle of innovation. When only a part of the designs with a given capability meets a principle, the level is defined as "partial". If no design with a given capabilities corresponds to the principle of innovation, then the box is not checked.

Finally, we note that 10 principles do not correspond to any of the capabilities. Conversely, some principles correspond to several capabilities. For example, the principle of local quality corresponds perfectly to 7 capabilities and partially 4 others.

Table 1. Complexity and capabilities of additive manufacturing

Additive manufacturing complexities	Additive manufacturing capabilities	Definitions
Shape complexity	Free form shapes	Possibility to build almost any shape
	Objects from 3D scans	Possibility to manufacture parts corresponding to scanned objects
Hierarchical complexity	Microstructure variation	The density of the parts can vary according to the porosity choices
	Texture	Possibility to create variant surfaces
Functional complexity	Monoblock	AM reduces the number of parts of a product
	Topology optimization	With finite element analysis, it is possible to integrate it into the AM
	Non-assembled mechanisms	Possibility of making kinematic joints
	Segmentation	Possibility to manufacture the parts separately to create a kit
	Embedded components	Possibility to trap an element in the part during manufacturing
	Internal channels	Possibility to design an internal network during manufacturing
	Infilling	The shapes of the inside of the structure can be adjusted according to the need
	Auxetics structure	Possibility to vary the Poison module of a room thanks to the structure
Material complexity	Material choices	Wide choice of AM materials
	Multi-materials	Possibility to design multi-material parts

3.3 Methodology Integration

We have seen the structure of the methodology through its schematization and the link between TRIZ and DfAM through the correspondence table between the 40 principles of innovation and the 13 capabilities of additive manufacturing.

The challenge now is to integrate this work into creative sessions to observe the results and see if designers will exploit the potential of additive manufacturing and if this method will overcome cognitive barriers.

The use of the TRIZ matrix, during modelling a problem, allows us to guide the designer towards one or more innovation principles. Once the principle(s) have been defined, the TRIZ/DfAM correspondence table will guide the designer towards characteristics specific to additive manufacturing.

Table 2. Table of correspondences between the 40 principles of TRIZ and the capabilities of additive manufacturing

	Shape Complexity		Hierarchical Complexity		Functional Complexity								Material Complexity	
The 40 TRIZ Principles	Freeform shapes	Objects from 3D scans	Microstructure variation	Texture	Monoblock	Topology optimization	Non-assembled mechanisms	Segmentation	Embedded components	Internal channels	Infilling	Auxetic structure	Material choices	Multi-materials
Segmentation			x	x			x	X	x			x		x
Extraction					x	x		x						
Local quality	x	x	X	X		x	X		X	x	X	X		X
Asymmetry	x	x				x					x			
Combination					X		x	x	x					x
Universality							X		x	X	x			x
Nesting			x						X	x				x
Counterweight			x							x	x			x
Prior counteraction														
Prior action		x					x	x	x					
Cushion in advance								x						
Equipotentiality														
Inversion							x							
Spheroidality	x					x					x			
Dynamicity							X		x			X		
Partial, overdone or excessive action				X							x		x	x
Moving to a new dimension	x													
Mechanical vibration														
Periodic action														
Continuity of useful action														
Rushing through														
Convert harm into benefit				x										
Feedback														
Mediator							x	x	x					x
Self-service									x					
Copying	X	X									x		x	
Inexpensive short life		x	x	x		x					x		X	
Replacement of a mechanical system														
Use pneumatic or hydraulic systems									x	x				
Flexible film or thin membranes	x					X		x			x	x		x
Use of porous materials			X						x					
Changing the colour			x										x	x
Homogeneity													x	x
Rejecting and regenerating parts			x	x				x			x			x
Transforming physical or chemical states			X	X					x		x			X
Phase transition													x	x
Thermal expansion									x				x	X
Use strong oxidisers														
Inert environment														
Composite materials									x		x			X

Keys: X (dark) The AM capability fully corresponds to the TRIZ principle; x (light) Only a part of the designs with a given AM capability meets a TRIZ principle

4 Future Work

The aim of this article was to propose a structure of creativity methodology combining TRIZ and additive manufacturing. Through the literature, we have observed that there is a real need for a methodology, and that it should stimulate the creativity of designers as early as possible in the design process. The use of a methodology at the beginning of the design process best allows designers to overcome cognitive barriers and thus allow them to innovate with the under-exploited additive manufacturing potential.

The creation of a correspondence between TRIZ's innovation principles and the capabilities of additive manufacturing makes it possible to guide the designer towards solution models specific to additive manufacturing.

To go even further upstream in the design process, it would be interesting to start from the notion of physical contradiction. The physical contradiction makes it possible to move more quickly from the problem to the principles of innovation and therefore to the additive manufacturing capabilities.

In addition, the use of terms for additive manufacturing capabilities may limit the creativity of designers. It would therefore be interesting to design intermediate objects beyond the terms that correspond to these capabilities [11]. This would increase the level of creativity.

Acknowledgements. This research was carried out as part of project CREAM (CREativity in Additive Manufacturing), funded by the National Research Agency (project ANR-18-CE10-0010) in France.

References

1. Sriram, D., Stephanopoulos, G., Logcher, R., et al.: Knowledge-based system applications in engineering design: research at MIT. AI Mag. **10**(3), 79 (1989). Author, F., Author, S.: Title of a proceedings paper. In: Editor, F., Editor, S. (eds.) CONFERENCE 2016, LNCS, vol. 9999, pp. 1–13. Springer, Heidelberg (2016)
2. Audoux, K., Segonds, F., Kerbrat, O., et al.: Toward a customized multicriterion tool for product evaluation in the early design phases: the CMDET methodology. Int. J. Interact. Des. Manuf. (IJIDeM), **3**(3), 981–993 (2019)
3. Bonjour, E., Deniaud, I., Micaëlli, J.-P.: Conception routinière ou innovante: quels apports de l'ingénierie système?. Revue Française du Génie Logiciel **100**, 9–15 (2012)
4. Howard, T.J., Culley, S.J., Dekoninck, E.: Describing the creative design process by the integration of engineering design and cognitive psychology literature. Des. Stud. **29**(2), 160–180 (2008)
5. Hatchuel, A., Weil, B.: A new approach of innovative design: an introduction to CK theory. In: DS 31: Proceedings of ICED 03, the 14th International Conference on Engineering Design, Stockholm (2003)
6. Redwood, B., Schffer, F., Garret, B.: The 3D Printing Handbook: Technologies, Design and Applications. 3D Hubs (2017)
7. Laverne, F., Segonds, F., Anwer, N., et al.: DFAM in the design process: a proposal of classification to foster early design stages. In: CONFERE, Sibenik, Croatia (2014)

8. Vayre, B., Vignat, F., Villeneuve, F.: Designing for additive manufacturing. Procedia CIrP **3**, 632–637 (2012)
9. Salonitis, K.: Design for additive manufacturing based on the axiomatic design method. Int. J. Adv. Manuf. Technol. **87**(1-4), 989–996 (2016)
10. Bin Maidin, S., Campbell, I., Pei, E.: Development of a design feature database to support design for additive manufacturing. Assem. Autom. **32**(3), 235–244 (2012)
11. Rias, A.-L., Segonds, F., Bouchard, C., et al.: Towards additive manufacturing of intermediate objects (AMIO) for concepts generation. Int. J. Interact. Des. Manuf. (IJIDeM), **11**(2), 301–315 (2017)
12. Laverne, F., Frédéric, S., et al. Enriching design with X through tailored additive manufacturing knowledge: a methodological proposal. Int. J. Interact. Des. Manuf. (IJIDeM) **11**(2), 279–288 (2017)
13. Langeveld, L.H., et al.: Design with X is new in product design education. In: DS 36: Proceedings DESIGN 2006, the 9th International Design Conference, Dubrovnik, Croatia, pp. 1179–1186 (2006)
14. Altshuller, G.: The Innovation Algorithm: TRIZ, Systematic Innovation and Technical Creativity. Technical Innovation Center, Inc. (1999)
15. Durand, J., Weite, P.-A., Gazo, C., et al.: Determination and evaluation of the possible links and sequences between TRIZ and other design methods. In: ICED 2007, p. CD ROM-11 pages (2007)
16. Gross, J., Park, K., Kremer, G.E.O.: Design for additive manufacturing inspired by TRIZ. In: ASME 2018 International Design Engineering Technical Conferences and Computers and Information in Engineering Conference. American Society of Mechanical Engineers, pp. V004T05A004–V004T05A004 (2018)
17. Kretzschmar, N., Chekurov, S.: The applicability of the 40 Triz principles in design for additive manufacturing. In: Annals of DAAAM & Proceedings, vol. 29 (2018)
18. Kamps, T., Gralow, M., Schlick, G., et al.: Systematic biomimetic part design for additive manufacturing. Procedia CIRP **65**, 259–266 (2017)
19. Gibson, I., Rosen, D.W., Stucker, B., et al.: Additive manufacturing technologies. Springer, New York (2014). https://doi.org/10.1007/978-1-4939-2113-3

FAST for TRIZ

Kai Hiltmann(✉)

Coburg University of Applied Sciences and Arts,
Friedrich-Streib-Str. 2, 96450 Coburg, Germany
kai.hiltmann@hs-coburg.de

Abstract. The functional framework of FAST, which C. Bytheway originally published in 1971, has been widely employed in several variants in Value Engineering, but is not common in TRIZ. However, the original, logically consistent and unabbreviated form Bytheway originally proposed can be an instructive way to model a landscape of functions that can be used in TRIZ for a variety of purposes. Among these are landscaping the functions of the system and its super systems, including neighbouring systems and subsystems, thus depicting a system in new coordinates. In contrast to Function Analysis, possible ways of functional integration and evolution of a system can be modelled and explained; moreover, the technique constitutes a creativity tool and a strategic tool indicating disruptive innovations.

Keywords: Functions · FAST · Map of functions

1 Introduction

The notion of function was coined by L. Miles in 1947 [1, p. xxi], so G. Altshuller does not seem to have known it before about 1980 [2]. Altshuller instead used the term of field to express the influence of one object onto another, even though the concepts of field and function are not equivalent [2]. Moreover, he used the term of ideality to describe the main function of an engineering system (**ES**) and to relate a function to the cost and effort required for its realization. Highest ideality thus means pure fulfilment of the main function at no cost [3, ch. 2, p. 83].

In TRIZ, Gerasimov et al. first employed the term of function in 1990[1] in the context of Functional Value Analysis [2, 5] with the definition "*function is the man ifestation of the properties of a material object, consisting in its action (influence or interaction) on the change in the state of other material objects*". In 1992, Gerasimov and others introduced function analysis, which models the interactions between the components of an engineering system and its environment – the super system – [6]. The functional model thus enlarges the substance-field model from the conflicting pair to the complete system and connects the notions of field and function. In 1996, Terninko and Zusman used the term in a generalized meaning of events or states of a system in their tool "Problem Formulation" [7, 8].

[1] Souchkov [4] mentions the year 1988 but we could not identify the source.

Published by Springer Nature Switzerland AG 2019
R. Benmoussa et al. (Eds.): TFC 2019, IFIP AICT 572, pp. 117–134, 2019.
https://doi.org/10.1007/978-3-030-32497-1_11

As will be shown, there are different concepts of functions and of their relations with different models addressing different objectives. This often causes difficulties in adequately formulating functions.

At the task of product planning and development, it is necessary to analyse the functionality of products in order to define new products, to seek new applications, and to match market needs with the uses that products offer. A further objective in TRIZ itself is to understand the mechanisms of the so-called laws or trends of system evolution. The functional models in use do not support this objective.

C. Bytheway developed his *"Function Analysis System Technique, FAST"* in 1963 [9, sec. A2.3.2], which he originally intended as a support for the value analyst in correctly composing the hierarchy of functions in a functional tree [10]. To achieve this, he introduced a logical scheme of "*how? vs. why?*" into the functional tree, corresponding to the direction of hierarchical level. In doing so, he additionally attributed a new meaning to the tree structure. In addition, the two questions can trigger creativity to find alternative ways of performing a function or finding new uses to it. The questions of how and why do not have to end at the system boundaries, though. If the logic is extended consistently, a functional structure is achieved that functionally connects a product with its environment and indicates chances for further evolution. This produces a functional map of needs and their fulfilment – extending from basic human activities and natural resources until basic human needs – in which the borders of the product are outlined.

A part of this work was presented earlier on TRIZfest conference 2018 [11] and has been complemented since.

2 Function Modelling

Gerasimov's definition has largely purported the definition in standard VDI 4521-1 [12] as "*influence from a system or a system component upon one or more others which changes, eliminates, or maintains a parameter of the other component or system*". The TRIZ Function Model is a directed graph that models the components as nodes and their functions – i.e. relations between the components – as edges [13]. Standard EN 1325 for value engineering (**VE**) also defines a function as an "*action of a product or of a component of its*" [14], even though value analysts in practice attach more importance to formulations that inspire phantasy than describe measurable effects [15].

Other function models are [16]:

- the flow-oriented model, i.e. a block diagram with flows of energy, substance, and information as system quantities
- the relation-oriented model, which describes interrelations between functions as the problem formulation does,
- and the functional tree as a hierarchical system of functions.

Reports on function models have been compiled by Ponn [17], Stetter [18], and others.

The different models picture different relations, with only the two TRIZ models considering the interrelation of a system with its super system.

3 The FAST Model

Bytheway's method proved its value to determine the basic (main) function of the ES. It was quickly modified by others: Ruggles introduced "*the notions of superordinate functions, essential functions, secondary functions, permanent functions, simultaneous functions, design objectives, and problem domains*" [1, pp 11]. Snodgrass determined a fixed format, "*refers to superordinate functions as "tasks" and below them places essential functions and four supplementary functions. He designates these four supplementary functions as assuring convenience, reliability, satisfaction, and appeal, and writes that their purpose is to secure customer "acceptance" of the product.*

The Ruggles and Snodgrass versions of FAST, with their patterned, formulaic diagrams, represent interpretations not seen in Bytheway's FAST. We can fairly say that FAST has changed course as its significance and emphasis have shifted from the application process to the diagrammed result". We are reporting these modifications in order to justify a use of FAST differing from its standard application in VE. The current formats used in VE are reproduced in Fig. 1 for standard EN 12973 (preliminary version) and in Fig. 2 for German standard VDI 2803.

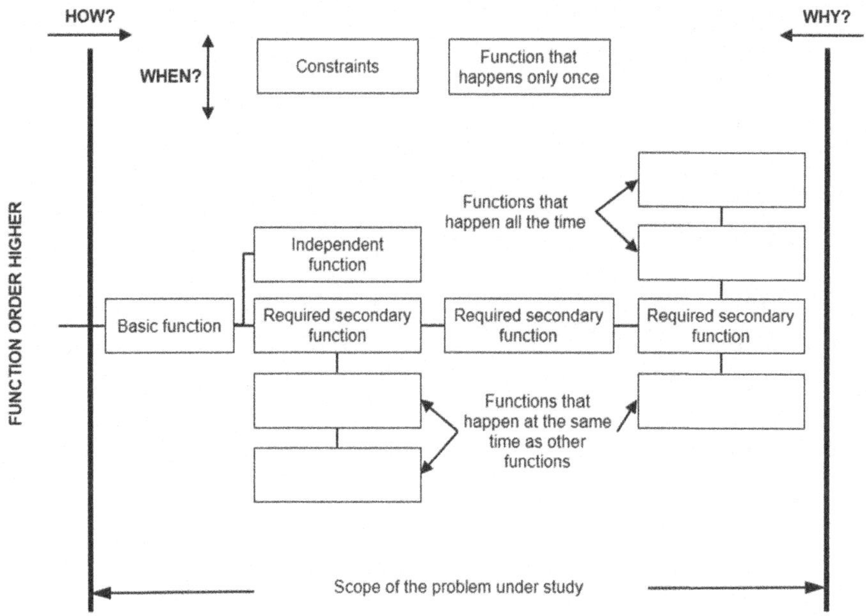

Fig. 1. FAST Diagram acc. to prEN 12973:2017. Note constraints and rarely occurring functions inserted on top and without connections. "Functions that happen at the same time as other functions" are also called "simultaneous functions".

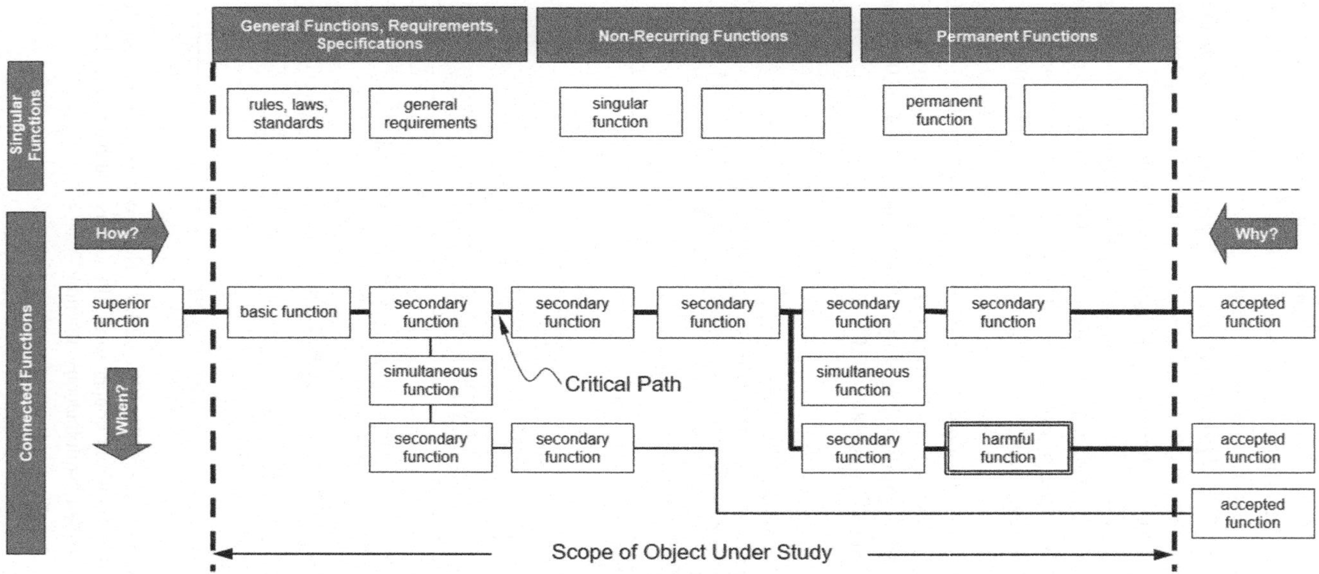

Fig. 2. FAST Diagram acc. to German standard VDI 2803: 2017. Note the "accepted functions" delivered by the super system on the right. Translation by the author; "harmful function" is called "problem domain" by Ruggles

4 Modifying FAST for TRIZ

4.1 Basic Concept

The modification we suggest for use in TRIZ is just based on Bytheway's original logics of "why" and "how". To make it compatible with TRIZ conventions, we formulate functions according to the definition given above. The basic model is shown in Fig. 3: The ES performs the functions enclosed in the system boundary (replacing the Scope Lines in VE). With the "how" direction extending to the right (the coordinate system may actually be oriented arbitrarily), the first function right to the left boundary is the system's main function (or basic function in VE). Ikovenko gives a training example of a projectile hitting a soldier's helmet and asks for the function of the helmet [19]. This may be to "deflect bullet". Asking "how is 'deflect bullet' performed?" one may find several subfunctions ("secondary functions" in VE) to be required. It may be, however, that a helpful answer is "accelerate bullet [sideways][2]". In this case, subfunction 1 would be a mere reformulation of the function ("deflect bullet" = "accelerate bullet"). In the second step, asking "how is 'accelerate bullet [sideways]' performed?", a few subfunctions may be identified, one of them being "transfer IMPULSE[3] [to bullet]". Transferring impulse means simultaneously transferring a counter-impulse, in this case to the head, which constitutes a *harmful simultaneous function*.

Often, functions require secondary functions that are performed not by the system itself but by super system components; these are marked as "*accepted functions*". Typical accepted functions are "control system", "provide electric energy[4]" or "position helmet" as in the example.

On the other hand, one will ask "*why is 'deflect bullet' performed?*". The answer is the purpose of the ES: the main function is performed in order to fulfil its super function, which should be formulated in a user-related way [14], i.e. "protect head". One may continue to ask "why should 'protect head' be performed?". This will lead to a secondary super function "keep body alive". At this point, a basic boundary is reached: A human being is not an engineering system and thus has no purpose to meet, so no reason is required for staying alive and the functional tree has reached its root point.

Please note in the diagram of Fig. 3 that in contrast to VE, a situation mentioning solely one single subfunction corresponds to a mere reformulation. Sometimes, however, more subfunctions may exist but are not considered relevant and therefore are neglected. In the example, "protect head" and "keep body alive" require more functions than just deflecting projectiles. We mark this situation with an additional line ending in a bullet (as an abbreviation for "…"). In the diagram, this situation is also indicated after subfunction 3.

---

[2] Since correct function formulations are difficult for beginners, we use to write the attributes of the function in [brackets].

[3] We use to write FIELDS in a different font.

[4] We regard "provide energy" a correct formulation because (a) electric energy has parameters voltage and amps, can influence components and be influenced, and (b) "providing" changes these parameters.

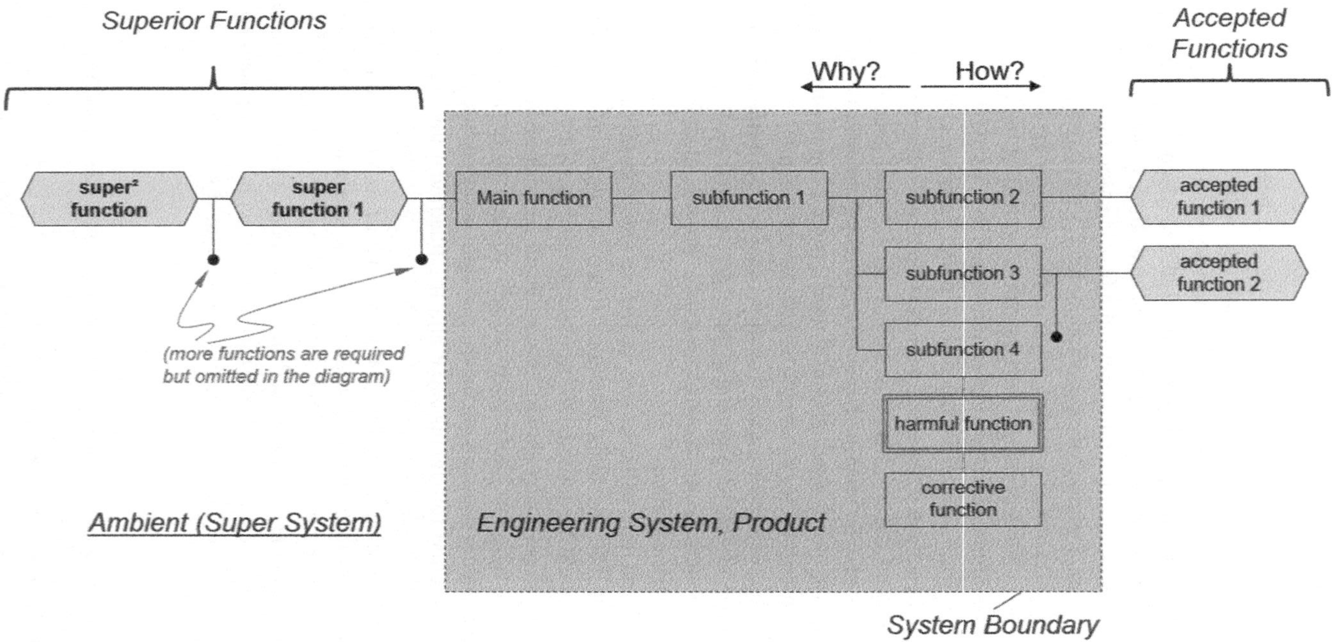

Fig. 3. Basic concept of FAST for TRIZ. We use to draw supersystem functions in hexagons.

As a rule, every function in the ES is supposed to possess a super function, i.e. a neighbour to its "why" side. Otherwise, the respective function would be evidently useless. Therefore, we do not suggest to insert any general, singular, recurring etc. functions in this diagram as isolated boxes. The only exception to this rule are simultaneous functions, first of all harmful ones, which of course do not serve a useful purpose (they may possess harmful functions as their super functions, though, see Fig. 8). We have also marked a corrective function associated to the harmful one in Fig. 3. At least, the fact that corrective functions lack super functions is both plausible and agrees with trimming rules for processes [19].

Please also note that the configuration of the system modelled may not be constant over time – depending on the phase in its life cycle or its momentary use, super functions, accepted functions, and even the internal functional structure may change. The diagram must therefore be redrawn for differing situations or this variability should be indicated by suitable means.

4.2 Assistance in Formulating Functions

Identification of functions is required for various reasons. These include TRIZ Function Analysis [20], which, in turn is used for system improvement, problem solution, or cost reduction, for description and understanding the objectives of the customer as well as of an ES's structure and operation, and for analysis of a projected design task for subsequent search for partial solutions [16, 21].

When working with functions, users often encounter difficulties finding the correct formulation. Despite the definition of a function seems simple and logical, even experts get into predicaments in practice. Indeed, there are different concepts of functions as Pulm points out [16, 22]. The official VDI 4521 definition regards functions as relations between system components. Correspondingly, in his lessons Ikovenko asks for the function of an open door [19]. The answer is "none" since the open door does not interact with persons travelling through. If however doors had no function, there would be no reason to build them[5]. The concept of functions is thus closely related to the specific functional model chosen [22]. It therefore seems appropriate to translate formulations from one concept to another, which can be done easily in the FAST model. In the helmet example, "protect head" would then be a reasonable *user-related formulation* which is translated via secondary function into the *system-related* formulation "deflect bullet".

Another difficulty lies in interface functions: If the functionality of a hammer is only described as "drive nails", its usability for the worker will be neglected – a mistake that has been made by engineers for long times. Practitioners therefore use to formulate "hammer permits/enables/supports use", which is not correct from the standpoint of system theory since "use" is not a component and "permit" is not an influence. The FAST model though can easily consider interface functions: Due to the separation in system and super system functions, there is no more need to formulate

[5] A formal argumentation in TRIZ might be to formulate a harmful function of a wall "block persons" and to counterweigh it with the corrective one of the door "remove wall".

"hammer supports use" but "move/accelerate/guide/…/hammer" in FAST is a function of the super system.

By asking "how is <function> performed?", the structure of the system is detailed further until a satisfying level of detail is reached. Subfunctions of this level are called "elementary functions" [23 pp. 30, 24 p. 423]. It depends on the system and its user to decide which degree of refinement is elementary, as is the rule in TRIZ function analysis [20]. A machine designer will consider a motor and its function "transform electrical energy [to mechanical]" as an elementary component whereas a motor producer has to consider the components of the motor and their respective functions.

In the process that standard VDI 2221 recommends for mechanical design, function analysis among others serves to identify subordinate problems. After these have been found, their corresponding requirements ought to be conveyed to the specification sheet. We do so by first inserting comments into the diagram, Fig. 4, and then collecting the comments in the specification sheet.

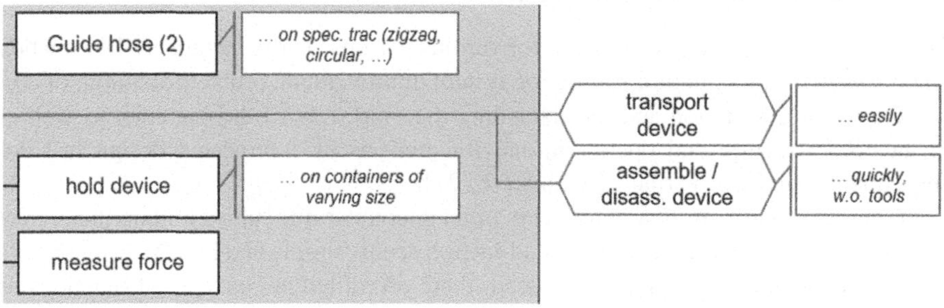

Fig. 4. Part of a FAST diagram for a fire-fighting device with comments

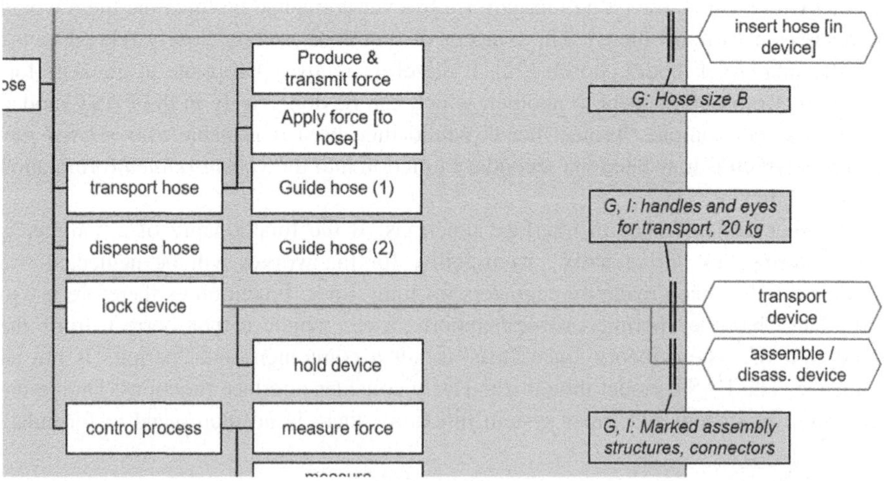

Fig. 5. Interface parameters (**G** geometric, **I** information, **E** energetic) entered in the model

It may further be helpful to indicate interface parameters, especially if functions are to be performed by differing function carriers as in highly modular systems. These parameters can be entered into the model as shown in Fig. 5:

4.3 Landscape of Functions/Functional Map

Typically, a system fulfils not just a single basic function, i.e. an effect on its super system, but several, including harmful ones and aesthetical functions. For instance, an electric drilling machine serves for drilling workpieces. Besides this, it can also be used to produce chamfers, for threading etc., but also to stir paint and for countless other applications. We call these functions "*Additional*" ones, Fig. 6. Which of these basic functions is the main function is arbitrary and again depends on the user and the considered phase of the product life cycle. The argument, the main function was the one the ES was built or bought for does not hold since depending on the situation and the life cycle phase, the main function may change [25, 24 p. 423].

A question that comes up when searching for additional functions is "which exactly are all the functions, also unknown ones, a system can perform?" One tool to identify possible additional functions is Anticipatory Failure Determination [26, 27], another Reverse Function-Oriented Search [28] but more work is needed on this subject.

An ES always serves a superior function[6]; since this is a user-related function, usually a use aspect and an aesthetic aspect must be distinguished [14]. Each ES therefore uses to serve *at least two superior functions* but the ES is not sufficient in fulfilling these. If it was, the ES's basic function would be just a reformulation of the superior function. For instance, a hammer serves to impact on an object and the user needs this action to drive a nail into a wall. Obviously, two more ES's are required: The nail and the wall (and the worker). All these three (four) systems together with their respective functions can fulfil the user's desired function which requires mutual matching.

Functions that are fulfilled externally from the ES and support the ES in serving a common superior function we call "*Neighbouring Functions*". Neighbouring functions may be performed by one or more systems in the neighbourhood of the system, i.e. in its super system. The concept of neighbouring functions is important for matching their parameters, in order to increase the functionality of the ES (neighbouring functions are prone for integration into the ES), and to organize ES's into systems of ES's. This latter point is required when a product portfolio shall be defined or when an ES is to be organized into modules.

One tool of "classical" (Altshuller's) TRIZ is the system operator. The system operator compares a system at different times and may be used to estimate the future evolution of the system. In addition, several levels in system hierarchy are considered: The system itself, its subsystems, and its super system(s). We suppose that the diagram drawn for different situations may help clarify the interrelation of ES and super systems. However, more experience is needed on this subject.

[6] … which follows from its definition "man-made assembly […] which meets a purpose" [11].

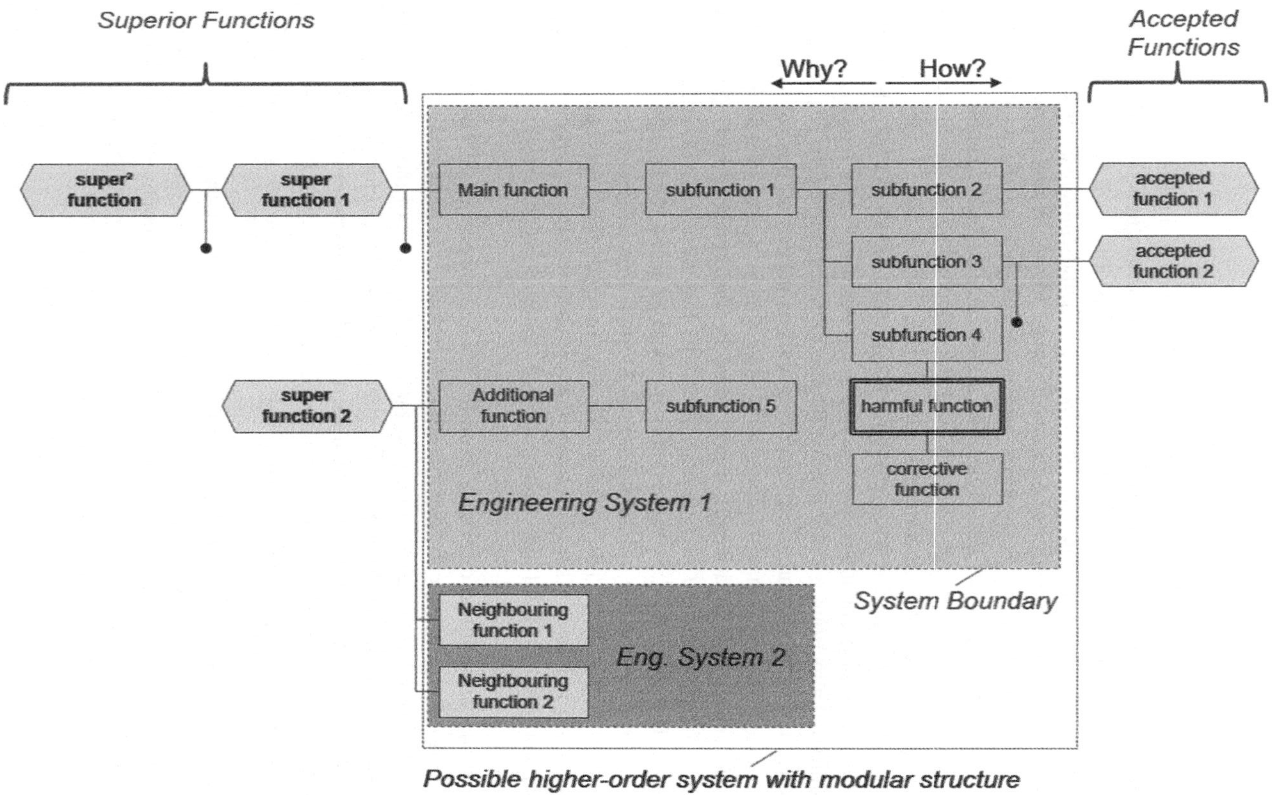

Fig. 6. A system performs several functions on its super system. On the other hand, it contributes only partially to super functions

4.4 Illustrating and Explaining the Laws of Evolution of Engineering Systems

G. Altshuller formulated laws that governed the way engineering systems evolve over time. According to Schollmeyer [29] and Karasik [30], these laws resulted from Altshuller's understanding of Soviet books on the history of technology (first of all aviation technology) of his time and reflect the principle of dialectics in the system of Marx and Engels. To our knowledge, Altshuller does not explain why, in what limits, and how exactly he expected these laws to apply.

The first of these laws is the "*law of the completeness of parts of the system*" stating that "*each technical system must include four basic parts: an engine, a transmission, a working organ and an organ of steering*" [3].[7] In the scheme of GenTRIZ, an engineering system acquires these functional elements in the order of *Operating Element – Transmission – Energy Source – Control* [19].

Obviously, the first stage in the evolution of an engineering system (tool) is characterized by a situation without this tool, i.e. naked man who provides solely of his body to perform the functions he desires, Fig. 7. Improving the system will include first absorbing the operating/working function, and consecutively the remaining ones.

As an example, Fig. 8 reproduces Hodler's painting of a lumberjack who constitutes in combination with his axe a complete (although, as a human, not necessarily an engineering) system. Please note that the axe itself – though incomplete – is a functioning system as well, provided that it can borrow the missing functions from its super system. We consider this observation important since it draws a link to well-adjusted systems of ES's and touches the aspect of how much functionality an optimally fitted system should contain.

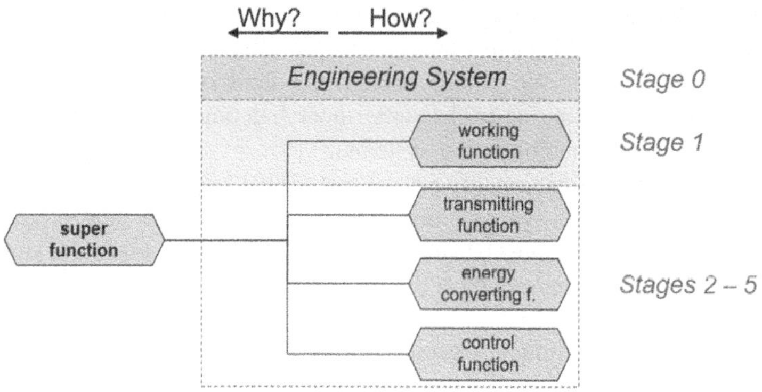

Fig. 7. An engineering system evolves from a situation before its creation (man performs all required functions with his body) until a complete system, gradually absorbing all the functions required.

[7] Hubka mentions in "Theory of Technical Systems" [31] that Borgnis in 1818 [32] distinguished six classes of machine elements (engines, transmissions, transformers, supports, control, and working organs). Marx, whom Altshuller might have referred to, mentions only three elements (motor, transmission, and working organ) [33 p. 261].

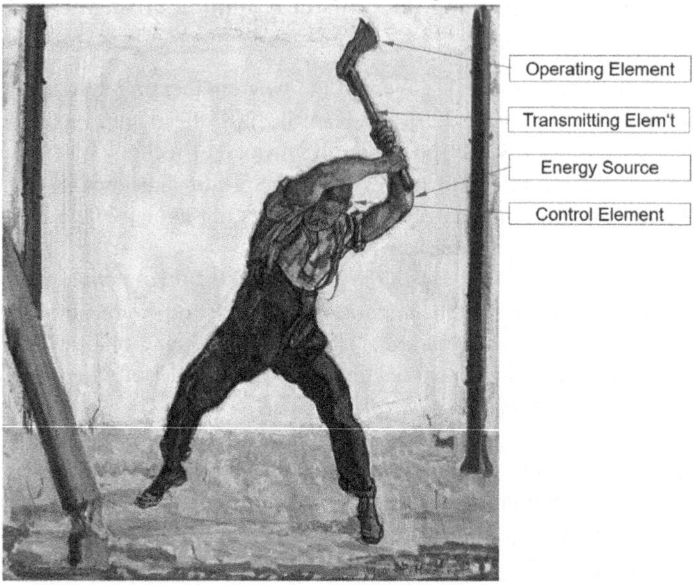

Fig. 8. Complete system consisting of axe + lumberjack. The axe itself will be a working system if it borrows the functions of energy conversion and control from its super system [using 34].

4.5 Increasing Product Functionality, Updating the Product Portfolio

One way to increase the value of an ES is to increase its functionality as is recommended especially in the first phases of the S curve [35 p. 168; 19; 36]. Prushinskiy recommends to merge (hybridize) the ES with an alternative one that performs the same main function [37]. We would enlarge the field of search for hybridization partners to systems contributing to the same super function, i.e. systems that perform neighbouring functions (neighbouring systems).

With value V = total functionality F/total cost C [19], cost must be kept low in spite of rise in functionality, so synergy must be used [38] and the new products to be integrated into the portfolio must be similar to the existing ones. From the viewpoint of an engineer, similarity means technical or technological similarity. From the marketer's viewpoint however, similarity means similarity of market. The highest similarity of market is achieved with products serving the same super function, i.e. the same need.

Likewise, new functions to be integrated into a product must use technical synergies and/or serve a known market – if possible, the same marked as covered before.

The network of functions displayed by the FAST diagram supports both identification of neighbouring functions serving the same need/super function and technical synergies. We have therefore varied the functions and extended the notion of neighbouring ones, Fig. 9. This diagram uses concepts of systems with varied parameters and competing systems that Ikovenko presented with the GenTRIZ system of evolutionary laws, first of all the *law of transition to the super system* [19]: According to the

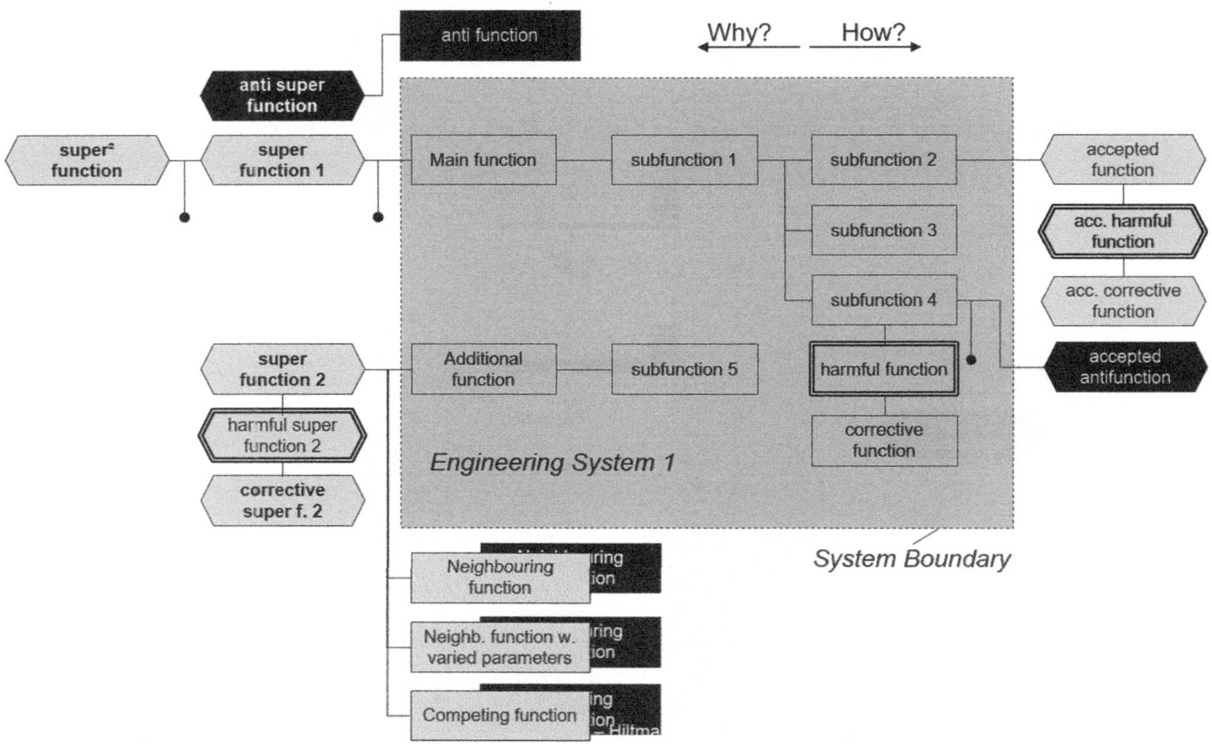

Fig. 9. FAST diagram with varied functions, see text

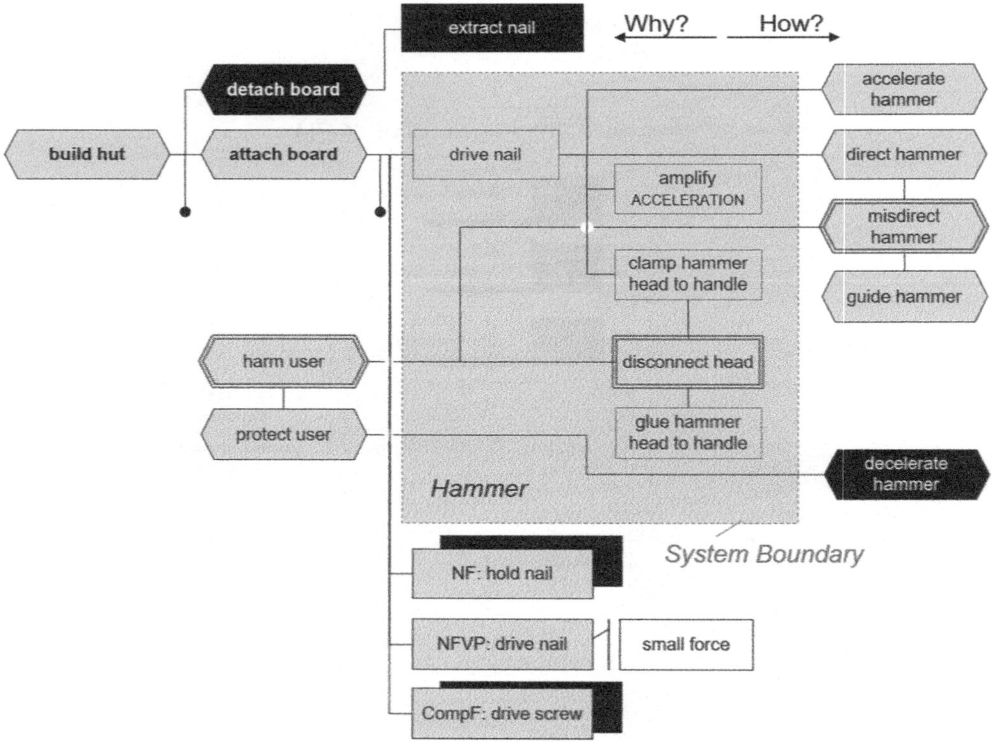

Fig. 10. Varied functions on hammer example. Example is shown for main function, but can be applied to any subfunction.

first subtrend, the parameters of the integrating system become increasingly different from those of the Engineering System.

Let us explain the scheme given above using again the example of a hammer, Fig. 10. With "attach board" being the super function, "detach board" is the anti super function. Both are required to fulfil the secondary super function. However, the simple hammer does not serve "extract nail" which a gripper is needed for. Other functions required for attaching boards are neighbouring function "hold nail", driving a small nail with lesser force (varied parameter, lesser hammer), and "drive screw" (competing function) together with their respective anti functions of "let nail go" and "extract screw".

On the input side, the user will accelerate and direct the hammer at which activity he mail fail, requiring a correcting function, or which he may perform in an opposite way.

In accordance with the law of evolution, the diagram now suggests extending the functionality of the hammer "horizontally" by including the functions of extracting nail, holding the nail, driving with reduced force, or driving screws. "Vertical" integration would mean to have some of the accepted functions included, e.g. accelerating and directing the tool. Vertical integration may as well extend to the "why" direction, realizing a complete system with "attaching boards" as its main function.

Search for technically similar products is done by regarding the functionality of the ES and searching for alternative uses, e.g. using Reverse Function-Oriented Search.

4.6 Finding Threats of Substitution

An ES is a means to fulfil a need (its super function) and it is created in order to achieve the need using the available resources efficiently [39 p. 23]. The FAST model illustrates this situation by arranging the ES between the needs on the "why" side and the resources (via accepted functions) on the "how" side. One may imagine a flow of resources streaming from "how" to "why" into the fulfilment of needs. Since there use to be competing systems, the main functions of which deliver an alternatively viable means to fulfil the need, the ES may lose the race in favour of its competitor, and vanish. Examples for this are the steam engine or the mechanical typewriter.

It must be kept in mind that the FAST model represents first of all a model of functions into which we draw the allocation with systems. Basically, the model is self-similar: What has been said above may be applied to any super or subsystem, as big or small as it may be. Therefore, in general, every subfunction has its neighbouring, competing etc. functions, which may replace it, thereby eliminating all its direct subfunctions. Likewise, a super function may vanish as it is replaced by a competing one[8]. The model thus permits consideration of alternative ways to fulfil a need and to monitor threats of substitution. What is still missing however, is the assessment of the risk, see discussion.

[8] It is an open question if the "final" super function can vanish or not. Since it constitutes a basic human need, it is expected to last as long as mankind.

5 Conclusion and Discussion

We have proposed for application in TRIZ a variant of the FAST model and diagram that omits changes which had been introduced for specific needs of Value Engineering compared to Bytheway's original approach. On the other hand, we added concepts of function which result from considerations within TRIZ. The resulting scheme depicts a landscape of functions which is associated with the boundaries of engineering systems. The scheme is self-similar and applies to all hierarchical levels of functions.

The advantages of the model are seen primarily in product development: Similar to the flow-oriented model it permits to enter specifications of functions and interface parameters as well as demarcation of system levels – at least as long as they correspond with the functional hierarchy. In addition, it can present a map of needs and their fulfilment (a market-related view) and correlates this with the functionality of a product. The optimal set of functionality can be checked using a list of potential functions:

- standard functions (acc. to Altshuller [3], Borgnis [32], Linde [40, p. 264], Bettencourt [41])
- anti functions
- competing functions
- parameter-varied functions
- harmful together with failure functions and their corrective ones
- neighbouring functions
- higher superiour functions

The developer should decide if incorporating these functions or trimming and borrowing them from super system would increase the value of the ES.

The aspects of trimming the model and optimal design of functionality, linking to and optimizing the super system as well as possible mechanisms of laws/trends of system evolution have not yet been treated in this paper and remain for later research.

What we mentioned are changing conditions in the life cycle of a system. Souchkov pointed out that due to changes in the super system – super functions vanishing or resources running dry – systems may face becoming obsolete [42]. Evidently, a time-dependent format of the model would be desirable.

The FAST model as described here displays functions, however for strategic system planning, ideality or value is a needed information to assess future development. A task to be solved in the future therefore is how to integrate the aspect of cost. A vague idea may be to compare the flow of resources through the system with an electrical circuit or "potential problem" with cost being represented by the respective electrical "function resistances".

References

1. Akiyama, K.: Function Analysis. Productivity Press, Cambridge (1991)
2. Zlotin, B., Zusman, A.: Introduction of the concept of function in TRIZ; private email. Sent: 2018 June 06

3. Altshuller, G.S.: Creativity as an exact science. Gordon and Breach, New York (1987)
4. Souchkov, V.: A brief history of TRIZ. TRIZ J (2015). https://triz-journal.com/a-brief-history-of-triz/. Accessed 01 June 2018
5. Gerasimov, V.M., et al.: ТРИЗ-ФСА - Методические рекомендации 1990 [TRIZ-FVA – Methodologic Recommendations 1990]. MATRIZ, St. Petersburg. http://triz-summit.ru/triz/metod/204080/204081/, updated 01 May 2006. Accessed 01 June 2018. (in Russian)
6. Gerasimov, V., Litvin, S.: Main principles and postulates of the methodology for the performance of the TRIZ based value engineering analysis. TRIZ J. **3**(2), 7–45 (1992)
7. Zusman, A., Terninko, J.: TRIZ/ideation methodology for customer driven innovation. [cited after [8]]. In: 8th Symposium on Quality Function Deployment, The QFD Institute, Novi, MI, June 1996
8. Terninko, J., Zusman, A.V., Zlotin, B.L.: Systematic Innovation. St. Lucie Press, Boca Raton (1998). http://www.gbv.de/dms/hbz/toc/ht008711909.pdf. Accessed 01 June 2018
9. Standard prEN 12973:2017: Value Management. Beuth, Berlin (2017)
10. Bytheway, C.W.: The creative aspects of FAST diagramming. In: Society of American Value Engineers (ed.) Proceedings of the SAVE Conference 1971, Miami, Florida, 24–26 May 1971, Smyrna, Ga 1971. (SAVE proceedings, 6), pp. 301–312 (1971)
11. Hiltmann, K.: The fast diagram for TRIZ. In: Mayer, O. (ed.) TRIZfest - 2018. The 14th International Conference, Lisbon, Portugal, 2018, pp. 136–147 (2018). ISBN 978-0-942442-95-3
12. Standard VDI 4521-1: 2016-04: Inventive problem solving with TRIZ - Fundamentals, terms and definitions. www.vdi.eu/4521. Accessed 01 June 2018
13. Bruns, M.: Systemtechnik [Systems Engineering]. Springer, Berlin (1991). https://doi.org/10.1007/978-3-642-95646-1
14. Standard EN 1325: 2014-07: Value Management - Vocabulary - Terms and definitions. Beuth, Berlin (2017)
15. Bolton, J.D., et al.: Function Analysis Guide: A Supplement to the SAVE Body of Knowledge. Interspiral Press, Saline (2016)
16. Standard VDI 2221-1: 2018-03: Entwicklung technischer Produkte und Systeme – Modell der Produktentwicklung [Development of engineering products and services – model of product development]. http://vdi.eu/2221. Accessed 01 June 2018
17. Ponn, J., Lindemann, U.: Konzeptentwicklung und Gestaltung technischer Produkte [Concept development and design of engineering products], 2nd edn. Springer, Berlin (2011). https://doi.org/10.1007/978-3-642-20580-4
18. Stetter, R., Assmann, G., Viertlboeck, M.: Functional product modelling – new methods for the generation of product functions. In: Culley, S. (ed.) Design Research, Theories, Methodologies, and Product Modelling. 13th International Conference on Engineering Design: ICED 01: Glasgow, UK, 21–23 August 2001. Institution of Mechanical Engineers (WDK publications, 28), Bury St Edmunds, pp. 493–500 (2001)
19. Ikovenko, S.: MA TRIZ Level 3 Training 2013/14. Jantschgi C&R, AT – Wolfsberg (2014)
20. Standard VDI 4521-2: 2016-12: Inventive problem solving with TRIZ - Description of objective, problem definition, and prioritisation of solutions. www.vdi.eu/4521. Accessed 01 June 2018
21. Standard VDI 2222-1: 1997-06.: Konstruktionsmethodik - Methodisches Entwickeln von Lösungsprinzipien [Methodics of design – methodic development of basic solutions]. Beuth, Berlin (1997)

22. Pulm, U., Lindemann, U.: Enhanced systematics for functional product structuring. In: Culley, S. (ed.) Design Research, Theories, Methodologies, and Product Modelling. 13th International Conference on Engineering Design: ICED 01: Glasgow, UK, August 21–23 2001. Institution of Mechanical Engineers (WDK publications, 28), Bury St Edmunds, pp. 477–484 (2001)
23. Koller, R.: Konstruktionslehre für den Maschinenbau [Design theory for mechanical engineering], 3rd edn. Springer, Heidelberg (2011)
24. Ehrlenspiel, K., Meerkamm, H.: Integrierte Produktentwicklung [Integrated Product Development], 5th edn. Hanser, München (2013)
25. Hentschel, C.: Unorthodox use: TRIZ for non-intended product use. TRIZ J. http://www.triz-journal.com/archives/2008/02/03/, updated 04 February 2008. Accessed 01 June 2018
26. Visnepolschi, S.: How to Deal With Failures (The Smart Way): Anticipatory Failure Determination". Ideation International, Farmington Hills (2008). http://whereinnovationbegins.net/build/publication.asp. Accessed 01 June 2018
27. Standard VDI 4521-3: 2018-x: Inventive problem solving with TRIZ - Problem Solution. www.vdi.eu/4521. [to appear by December 2018]
28. Feygenson, O.: Tutorial. Part #2: elements of advanced function approach. In: Pre-Conference Training Session at TRIZfest 2017. MATRIZ. Krakow. 13 September 2017
29. Schollmeyer, J.: Wie kam TRIZ zur Dialektik? [How did TRIZ get dialectic?]. [Lecture] University of Applied Science, Hamburg, 01 February 2019
30. Karasik, YB.: Why was TRIZ born in Baku? [Editorial]. Anti TRIZ-J. **9**(2) (2010). http://www3.sympatico.ca/karasik/why_was_triz_born_in_baku.html
31. Hubka, V., Eder, W.E.: Theory of Technical Systems, 4. print. Springer, Heidelberg (1988) https://doi.org/10.1007/978-3-642-52121-8. ISBN 978-3-642-52123-2
32. Borgnis, J-A.: Traité complet de mécanique appliquée aux arts, vol 1. Composition des machines. Bachelier, Paris (1818)
33. Marx, K.: Capital. Moscow, USSR: Progress Publishers. Volume 1 Book One. https://www.marxists.org/archive/marx/works/download/pdf/Capital-Volume-I.pdf. Accessed 28 July 2019
34. Hodler, F.: Lumberjack. 1910, São Paulo Museum of Art. https://commons.wikimedia.org/w/index.php?curid=7018049. Accessed 10 May 2016
35. Fey, V., Rivin, E.I.: Innovation on demand. Cambridge University Press, Cambridge (2005)
36. Abramov, O.Y.: Product-oriented MPV analysis to identify voice of the product. In: The 12th MATRIZ TRIZfest-2016 International, Beijing, China, 28–30 July 2016, pp. 1–12 (2016)
37. Prushinskiy, V.: Tutorial: Part 1 - Basics of Hybridization. Pre-conference Training Session at TRIZfest 2017. MATRIZ, Krakow, 13 September 2017
38. Welge, M.K., Al-Laham, A., Eulerich, M.: Strategisches Management [Strategic Management], 7th edn. Springer-Gabler, Wiesbaden (2017)
39. Hubka, V., Eder, W.E.: Theory of Technical Systems, 4th edn. Springer, Berlin (1988). https://doi.org/10.1007/978-3-642-52121-8
40. Linde, H., Herr, G.: World opening innovation strategy and the contributions of Altshuller. In: Rizzi, C. (ed.) Proceedings of the 10th ETRIA World TRIZ Future Conference, pp. 257–264. University of Bergamo, Bergamo (2010)
41. Bettencourt, L.A., Ulwick, A.W.: The Customer-Centered Innovation Map. Harv. Bus. Rev. **86**(5), 109–114 (2008)
42. Souchkov, V.: The trend of functionality evolution. In: Aoussat, A., et al. (ed.) Proceedings of the 13th ETRIA World TRIZ Future Conference 2013. Paris, 29th–31st October 2013. ETRIA. Langres (FR): La Manufacture (No. Imprimeur 13814), p. 779–788. http://www.xtriz.com/publications/Souchkov_TrendFunctionalityEvolution.pdf. Accessed 01 June 2018

Differences and Complementarities Between C-K and TRIZ

Sébastien Dubois(✉), Roland De Guio, and Hicham Chibane

CSIP, ICube Laboratory, Strasbourg, France
sebastien.dubois@insa-strasbourg.fr

Abstract. TRIZ and C-K are both presented as theories aiming to facilitate innovations. In recent years several authors have published articles enlightening differences between TRIZ and C-K. C-K was initially a descriptive theory of innovation, which has gradually been developed into methods with an operational focus.

To clarify if both TRIZ and C-K could be recognized as theories, a first question will be considered, what is a theory? Are then TRIZ and C-K design theories, and if so, is it possible to consider two different theories of a single subject? This article is a first step in a more global perspective aiming at clarifying what a design theory should be and how these two proposals give part of answers, and they could be complementary.

Keywords: Design theory · TRIZ · C-K

1 Introduction

Design methods have been widely proposed in literature, widely spread, and widely used in industries. One can cite, among the most famous ones, Axiomatic Design, Value Analysis, Quality Function Deployment, and so on… But a question remains about what is really designing, and can a theory of design be proposed? Speaking about theory is quite common in sciences such as mathematics, physics, … but as soon as we consider human-centered subjects, lot of divergences could appear. Is designing a human activity? If so, has it to be considered as a cognitive description of activities? Lot of approaches, even based on TRIZ, aim at automatizing the design process, thus making this question a question of algorithms, and computerization. In this article, the authors propose to consider the design as a human activity.

On the basis of this hypothesis, we consider on the one hand C-K as a design theory, and on the other hand, TRIZ as a theory of inventive problem solving which is often presented as a design theory… Are they really design theories, and if so, do they differ? Do they contradict each other? Or are they complementary? To answer these questions, this article proposes to first give a presentation of these two theories, and then to give a pattern to analyze the requirements a theory should satisfy. Then C-K and TRIZ will be described through this list of requirements. Finally, a comparison and conclusion for discussion will be proposed.

Published by Springer Nature Switzerland AG 2019
R. Benmoussa et al. (Eds.): TFC 2019, IFIP AICT 572, pp. 135–143, 2019.
https://doi.org/10.1007/978-3-030-32497-1_12

2 Materials and Method

2.1 C-K Theory

"The name "C-K theory" reflects the assumption that Design can be modelled as the interplay between two interdependent spaces with different structures and logics: the space of concepts (C) and the space of knowledge (K)." [1] This theory has been introduced in 2003 by Hatchuel and its main assumption is that designing, and in particular innovative design, is based on cognitive processes between true facts, true assumptions, that composed the space of Knowledge; and undecidable propositions, that composed the space of Concepts.

Moreover, these two spaces are defined as being expandable, the space K containing all established, true, propositions, whereas the space C contains "concepts" which are undecidable propositions in K (neither true nor false in K). These two spaces can also be partitioned, and two kind of partitions have been proposed [2]:

- Restrictive partitions add to a concept a usual property of the object being designed.
- Expansive partitions add to a concept novel and unprecedented properties

The expansion of the two spaces are enabled due to 4 operators [3]:

- K → C operator, which adds or subtracts properties from K to concepts in C, a way to create alternatives;
- C → K operator, which seeks for properties in K that could be added or subtracted to reach propositions with a logical status;
- C → C operator, which is at least the classical rules in set theory that control partition or inclusion;
- K → K operator, which is at least the classical rules of logic and propositional calculus that allow a knowledge space to have a self-expansion.

Thus, the design process could be represented as conjunctions and disjunctions between the two spaces as illustrated on Fig. 1.

2.2 TRIZ Theory

Another theory well known in design, and more specially in creative design is TRIZ. TRIZ has been developed by G. Alsthuller to help designers to be more creative and it has first been a set of tools, which were later organized in a method, before being defined as a theory [4]. The last step of method development, under Altshuller's supervision is ARIZ-85C. G. Altshuller concluded that ARIZ- 85C was a complete tool for solving inventive problems, and did not need to be improved further very much since its application had been tested on thousands of real problems and proven to be effective [5]. This version contains considerable generalizations of all the underlying elements of TRIZ and has been recognized as a Meta-Algorithm [6].

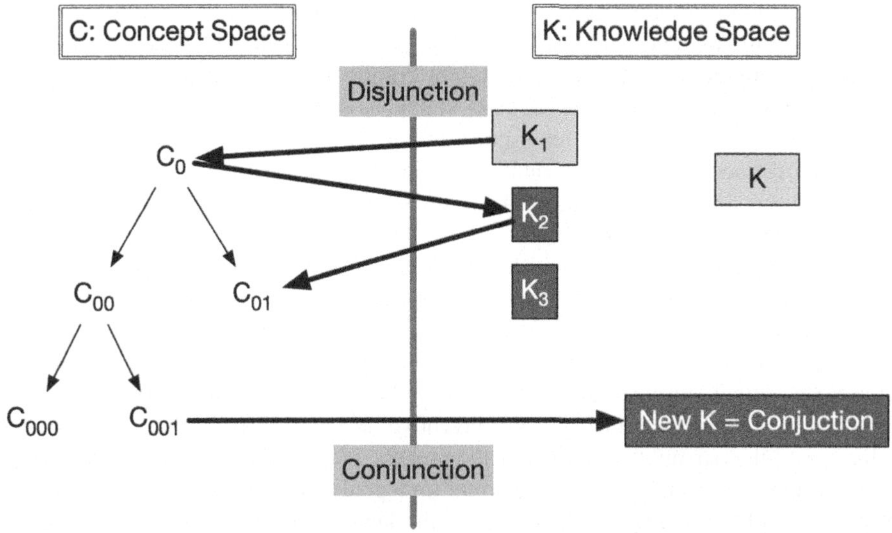

Fig. 1. C-K design process and its operators

Following the elements constituting the TRIZ theory, which are recognized as being the 3 main axioms on which any TRIZ based method has to be built:

- The laws of technical systems evolution: the evolution of a technical system is guided by a set if tendencies that are common to any system;
- Any problem has a hidden contradiction: to evolve a technical system has to overcome the contradictions related to its level of maturity and in accordance with its environment;
- Specific conditions: the way a technical system will solve the contradiction depends of the available resources, as formulated by the Ideal Final Result.

The elements have historically defined throughout the evolution of ARIZ and could be found in [7, 8]. Some authors recognize TRIZ as "the only constructive theory of invention and, based on its essence, of engineering creativity." [6] Moreover TRIZ is described as a theory providing models, rules, for thinking.

2.3 Method of Analysis

To analyze and compare TRIZ and C-K, the authors propose to first give a definition of what should be a theory, and then analyze C-K and TRIZ methods in regard of the definition. A theory should have a predictive and explicative role about the world, being thus a representation and inference tool [9]. Based on this working definition of what is a theory it is necessary to clarify the object of the world a theory should explain. Our general topic is inventive design, thus how can we define exactly what is inventive design?

In engineering domain, a creative product is often called an invention [10]. Both creative and inventive design problems are considered as requiring creative and inventive thinking in order to propose new, original, different and efficient solutions. Inventive design involves the creative thinking, and are considered as non-routine and ill-defined activities by Reitmann [11]. For Simon [12] to design is to solve ill-structured problems. Boden [13] suggests that achieving creativity is only possible by going beyond the bounds of a representation, and by finding a design that could not have been defined by that representation. If referring to a more engineering point of view, and according to Gero [14], creativity in design is concerned with the introduction of something new leading to a result that is unexpected.

In general, the cognitive scientists rely the creativity to three main concepts [15]: the creative person (defining a creative person as one who can tolerate ambiguity), creative product (defining a creative product as a new product qualitatively different from other products of the same type) and creative process (defining a creative process as a process involving integration of new knowledge in a problem model).

Then, if considering a theory about inventive design, this theory has to clarify the subject; is it the person, the product or the process? For Altshuller, TRIZ "is a system of many approaches and methods providing for a goal-oriented direction of the process of problem-solving based on knowledge of the laws of development of the objective reality" [7]. If considering one of the pioneer in design theorizing, Simon considered designing as a problem solving activity [16, 17]. One of the similarities for the two approaches of C-K and TRIZ is to be human-centered and not to aim at proposing an automatization of the process. It seems then interesting to consider designing, and so, problem solving, under a cognitive point of view. In [18], 4 general strategies: means-end analysis, subgoals, analogy, and diagrams are described that can be solicited during problem solving. Designing, as an open-ended and ill-structured problem [19], can then easily be regarded throughout the solicitations of these 4 strategies. Another key aspect is the co-construction of the problem and search space [18, 20], the problem defining the number of possible choices and paths that could be followed in searching for a solution (the search space), whereas the problem solver determines which of these he will explore (the problem space).

Considering these last points, problem solving and problem formulating could not be considered separately. Nevertheless, Novick pointed out that it is "important to distinguish, to the extent possible, how solvers represent the information in a problem from how they use that information to solve the problem" [21]. Novick also proposed that a good representation is one for which all of the important components of the problem are interconnected.

In conclusion of the elicited characteristics of design, and if aiming at proposing a design theory, we will confront both proposals, C-K and TRIZ throughout the following points:

- Object: what exactly do the proposed theory study?
- Problem/search space: do the proposals consider the construction of these two spaces, and do they make the link between them?
- Explicative: do the theory enable to explain how the design occurs?
- Predictive: do the theory propose means to foresee how solutions will appear and propose a formal model to make these predictions?
- 4 strategies, do the theories consider the 4 main strategies of problem solving?

3 Analysis of the Theories

3.1 Critical Analysis of C-K

Object of C-K

The C-K theory aims at describing how information are treated throughout the problem resolution process, characterizing information in regard of its and how to build partitions and make the information evolve by the use of the 4 operators. Thus the question of what does the C-K theory model and analyze and what it enables to study would rather find an answer in regard of the cognitive process. One can say that the C-K does not really consider the design process itself but rather the way the designer is thinking during the process. Indeed, the 4 operators do not describe the way information has to be processed to transform a problem into a solution, but they rather clarify how the information status (is it a concept? Is it a knowledge?) evolve during the resolution process.

Problem/Search Spaces and C-K

If considering that a problem is an objective which the designer does not know how to satisfy, one can easily recognize that a problem is such an information that cannot be considered neither true nor false, thus the Concept space could be referred as the problem space.

Is then the Knowledge space the search space? It is obvious that these two spaces are connected, as any satisfying and feasible (or not) solution found is both an element of the search space and of the K space (as the value of the element will be true if it is feasible, or false otherwise). But the search space is not necessarily composed of valued information, and the K space could be full of information not directly linked to problem. To conclude solutions concepts for which feasibility is known are common elements of both K space and search space, but these two spaces are not similar.

Is C-K Explicative?

Does the theory enable to understand how a design problem is solved? It, at least, enables to illustrate and follow the way ideas are generated and valuate the information in regard of their feasibility. Based on this, the C-K does not detail the mechanisms of change; but it could rather be defined as a macro model of cognitive processes to explain how the flow of information is processed during the design process.

Is C-K Predictive?

This question arises another one, what does it mean being predictive? In regard of what a theory should be, it should give the rules and a model to predict how a phenomenon will occur. As explained previously the object of C-K is more the cognitive process of the designer rather than the object of design, so, one can consider that C-K is predictive, as it specifies the mental operations the designer will have to follow to progress from a problem, a concept in C space, to a feasible solution, an information in K space.

Strategies of Problem Solving and C-K

Considering the strategies again in regard of C-K, the 4 operators do not consider how to progress from a given problem to a solution, but rather explains how the use of any of these strategies will impact the value of the information. It can be seen as a meta model modelling the way new information is built, this point is seen by C-K authors as helping in the exploration of new alternatives [3].

If considering the 4 main strategies, one can consider that both sub-goals and diagrams could be recognized as partitions in the Concept Space. But either means-ends analysis, or analogies could imply any of the 4 operators of the C-K theory. The operators will enable a description of the nature of the information generated by the strategies.

As described in [22], C-K theory proposes a model to evaluate creative design, it introduces metrics, it "offers a controllable model on the evaluation of creative design." This idea is reinforced in [23] by the terms of C-K theory offering an interpretative tool supporting critical discussion on design and creativity.

Critical Analysis of TRIZ

Object of TRIZ

The first aim of G. Altshuller was to start to develop tools to help engineers to be more creative [24]. Step by step, he understood that not only the tools were required, but also the good way to use them, and then the need of methods arose. The last method developed by Altshuller personally is ARIZ-85C [25]. This is the result of many versions throughout the years, which have been built and tested by hundreds of engineers on many problem resolutions [8]. TRIZ gives the axioms on which any method has to be built, if aiming at proposing robust concepts to solve technical systems problems.

Problem/Search Spaces and TRIZ

In TRIZ methods, in the different versions of ARIZ, two main processes are recognized, problem formulating, and problem solving. The formulation of problem is the identification of a goal, a specs, that have to be fulfilled, and also a set of constraints that have to be considered. The set of specs, of constraints, could be recognized as a list of Evaluation Parameters, on which Systems of Contradictions will be built, and this list of Evaluation Parameters (and their required value) and of Systems of Contradictions is the problem space.

Then the solution space could be recognized as the way one particular System of Contradictions will be chosen and how it will be treated throughout its resolution.

Is TRIZ Explicative?

Does TRIZ enable to understand how a design problem is solved? ARIZ-85C, for example, proposes a set of steps that have to be performed to step-by-step transform the mental representation of a problem till the formulation of a feasible concept of solution. It, thus, explains, the path followed from a given problem to a solution concept, based on a well-formulated System of Contradictions. For this, one can say that TRIZ plays an explicative role in design problem solving.

Is TRIZ Predictive?

Does TRIZ methods give the rules and a model to predict how a phenomenon will occur? The assumption of G. Altshuller is that any problem, to be solved, has to first be formulated in the shape of a contradiction. This is the predictive model of TRIZ. Solving a problem thus require to identify, formulate and solve the inherent contradiction. Does TRIZ give a set of rules? For sure, ARIZ-85C proposes the ways to well formulate and solve the problem, each step giving a pattern for respecting these rules.

Strategies of Problem Solving and TRIZ

Talking about TRIZ and about the 4 main strategies highlights immediately the question of analogies. It is obvious that the way the inventive principles, the methods of separation of physical contradictions, and also the 76 standards have been defined and are used is an illustration of analogies.

Does TRIZ use the 3 others strategies? One can recognize some aspects of means-ends analysis or sub-goal strategies in the methods used for the Analysis of Initial Situation, but these strategies here are more used to well choose a priori problem to be considered, rather than to search for solution. It seems thus that TRIZ consider mainly only one of the 4 strategies.

3.2 Comparison

The Table 1 summarizes all the previously described elements of C-K and TRIZ in regard of the required elements for a theory.

An analysis of one TRIZ-based method, ASIT [15], throughout the C-K paradigms has been proposed in [22]. It reveals how C-K theory enables to well capture "the activities of a creativity method" and also that the theory "says nothing about 'how' expansive partitions should be generated from K". This could be recognized as a limitation, but in fact it is quite consistent, as the object of the C-K is not the design process itself, but rather the cognitive processes and their impact on the information, during this design process.

Table 1. Table captions should be placed above the tables.

<table>
<tr><th colspan="2"></th><th>C-K</th><th>TRIZ</th></tr>
<tr><td colspan="2">Object</td><td>Design cognitive process</td><td>Design process</td></tr>
<tr><td colspan="2">Problem space</td><td>The Concept Space could be recognized as the problem space</td><td>The problem space is built on the list of Evaluation Parameters and of Systems of Contradictions</td></tr>
<tr><td colspan="2">Search space</td><td>The search space is a combination of both the Knowledge and the Concept Spaces</td><td>The search space is defined by one chosen System of Contradictions and how it is resolved</td></tr>
<tr><td colspan="2">Explicative</td><td>It defines a macro model of the cognitive processes</td><td>As a meta-algorithm it gives the clue to explain the design process</td></tr>
<tr><td colspan="2">Predictive</td><td>The 4 operators specify the kind of operation have to be performed during design process</td><td>The methods of TRIZ (ARIZ-85C) give a predictive description of the process</td></tr>
<tr><td rowspan="4">Strategies</td><td>Means-end</td><td rowspan="4">The 4 operators describe the results in regard of the quality of information but do not define the way to act on information</td><td rowspan="2">Partially performed by the Analysis of Initial Situation</td></tr>
<tr><td>Subgoals</td></tr>
<tr><td>Analogy</td><td>Resolution tools</td></tr>
<tr><td>Diagrams</td><td>Not used</td></tr>
</table>

With TRIZ, the object is the design process itself, it has the explicative and predictive aspects, but one interesting question is, could TRIZ methods take benefits of using the 4 generic operators for problem resolution?

4 Conclusion and Discussion

One of the main conclusions of this analysis and comparison of C-K and TRIZ is that both are non-conflicting theories as they do not focus on the same object. An interesting question is thus about their complementarity. Could each theory benefit of the other? Is it possible to propose cross-fertilization between both? It seems that the answer is yes, as TRIZ proposes, with the resolution tools, precise processes to act on information, and as, on the other side, C-K, gives a way to analyze the completeness of a design process in regard of the 4 proposed operators.

A future study will be performed to analyze, during a case study performed with TRIZ-based methods, how C-K elements give elements to describe more precisely and to give clues to be more complete, in regard of the way information are treated.

References

1. Hatchuel, A., Weil, B.: C-K design theory: an advanced formulation. Res. Eng. Des. **19**(4), 181–192 (2009)
2. Kazakçi, O.A.: A formalization of CK design theory based on Intuitionist Logic. In: Chakrabarti, A. (ed.) ICORD 2009, 2nd International Conference on Research into Design, Bangalore, India (2009)
3. Hatchuel, A., Le Masson, P., Weil, B.: C-K theory in practice: lessons from industrial applications. In: Marjanovic, D. (ed.) DESIGN 2004, the 8th International Design Conference, Dubrovnik, Croatia, pp. 245–258 (2004)
4. Souchkov, V.V.: A brief history of TRIZ. TRIZ J. (2015)
5. Madara, D.S.: Theory of inventive problem solving (TRIZ): his-story. IJISET-Int. J. Innov. Sci. Eng. Technol. **2**(7), 86–95 (2015)
6. Orloff, M.A.: Inventive Thinking Through TRIZ: A Practical Guide, 2nd edn. Springer, Heidelberg (2006)
7. Altshuller, G.S.: Creativity as an Exact Science. Gordon and Breach, New York (1988)
8. Altshuller, G.S.: The Innovation Algorithm: TRIZ, systematic innovation and technical creativity. Technical Innovation Center, Inc., Worcester (1999)
9. Vorms, M.: Qu'est-ce qu'une théorie scientifique? Philosophie des Sciences. Vuibert (2011)
10. Maimo, O.Z., Horowitz, R.: Sufficient Conditions for Inventive Solutions. IEEE Trans. Syst. Man Cybern. Part C Appl. Rev. **29**(3), 349–361 (1999)
11. Reitman, W.R.: Heuristic decision procedures, open constraints and the structure of Ill-defined problems. In: Shelly, M.W., Bryan, G.L. (eds.) Human Judgments and Optimality. Wiley, New York (1964)
12. Simon, H.A.: The structure of ill-structured problems. Artif. Intell. **4**, 181–201 (1973)
13. Boden, M.A.: What is creativity? In: Dimensions of Creativity, pp. 75–117. Massachussets Institute of Technology (1994)
14. Gero, J.S., Computers and creative design. In: T.F.A.o.A. SAFA (ed.) ArchComp 1995, Helsinki, Finland, pp. 1–13 (1995)

15. Horowitz, R.: Creative problem solving in engineering Design. Tel-Aviv University, Tel-Aviv (1999)
16. Newell, A., Simon, H.A.: Human Problem Solving. Prentice-Hall, Englewood Cliffs (1972)
17. Simon, H.A.: Problem forming, problem finding, and problem solving. In: 1st International Congress on Planning and Design Theory, Boston, USA (1987)
18. Reed, S.K.: Cognition. Theory and applications, 7th edn. Thompson/Wadsworth, Belmont (2007)
19. Bonnardel, N.: Towards understanding and supporting creativity in design: analogies in a constrained cognitive environment. Knowl. Based Syst. **13**, 505–513 (2000)
20. Rasovska, I., Dubois, S., De Guio, R.: Mechanisms of model change in optimization and inventive problem solving methods. In: International Conference on Engineering Design, ICED 2009, Stanford, CA, USA (2009)
21. Novick, L.R.: Representational transfer in problem solving. Psychol. Sci. **1**(2), 128–132 (1990)
22. Reich, Y., et al.: A theoretical analysis of creativity methods in engineering design: casting and improving ASIT within C-K theory. J. Eng. Des. **23**(1–3), 137–158 (2012)
23. Hatchuel, A., Le Masson, P., Weil, B.: Studying creative design: the contribution of C-K theory. In: Studying design creativity: Design Science, Computer Science, Cognitive Science and Neuroscience Approaches, Aix-en-Provence, France (2008)
24. Starovoytova, D.: Theory of inventive problem solving (TRIZ): his-story. IJISET Int. J. Innov. Sci. Eng. Technol. **2**(7), 86–95 (2015)
25. Altshuller, G.S.: Algorithm of Inventive Problem Solving (ARIZ-85C). OTSM-TRIZ Technologies Center, Minsk, Belarus, p. 32 (1985)

TRIZ Applications in Technical Design

An Approach Merging the IDM-Related Knowledge

Xin Ni[1(✉)], Ahmed Samet[2(✉)], and Denis Cavallucci[1(✉)]

[1] ICUBE/CSIP, INSA of Strasbourg, 24 Boulevard de la Victoire, 67084 Strasbourg, France
{xin.ni,denis.cavallucci}@insa-strasbourg.fr
[2] ICUBE/SDC, INSA of Strasbourg, 300 Bd Sébastien Brant, 67412 Illkirch, France
ahmed.samet@insa-strasbourg.fr

Abstract. Patents are one of the main innovation knowledge sources for engineers and companies. Inventive Design Method (IDM) – results from a research that extends from TRIZ and contains formal knowledge description components using ontologies, such as problems, partial solutions, and parameters. In this paper, we introduce IDM-Similar model that extends existing research work in IDM-related knowledge. A neural network named Word2vec and cosine similarity approach are used to build this model to compute the similarity among problems in wide range domains' patents covering from the chemistry to mechanics and the computer to physics. Our model assumes that a partial solution of a patent could be used to solve the problem of another patent from a different domain if these two problems are similar enough. Experiments show that our model is a promising alternative to classical TRIZ for engineers to associate their problems in a field to solutions from patents of another field. Consequently, the step dedicated to solution concepts ideation is improved using our work.

Keywords: TRIZ · Inventive Design Method · Word2vec · Similarity computation

1 Introduction

TRIZ is the theory of inventive problem solving [3] and its derived approach Inventive Design Method (IDM) was created to assist engineers in their invention process [2]. Moreover, IDM-related knowledge mainly is hidden in patent documents. And also, more than 80% of man's technical knowledge is described in patent literature [2] and the World Intellectual Property Organization revealed that 90% to 95% of all the world's inventions are found in patent documents [1]. Therefore, the patents now are the most useful reference materials for engineers to find out innovative solutions.

However, most companies, nowadays, still rely on engineers' experience or brainstorming among different domain's experts or manual work on searching knowledge from patent documents to promote the advancement of products. These types of methods now cannot fit the current rise of infinite and permanent renewal of

R. Benmoussa et al. (Eds.): TFC 2019, IFIP AICT 572, pp. 147–158, 2019.
https://doi.org/10.1007/978-3-030-32497-1_13

information and data's throughout all domains. At the same time, engineers are traditionally using the patent to check if their idea has already been exploited by somebody else or to browse large quantity of images to check the state of the art around their project in order to be aware of what exists. Further, some innovative solutions or methods might be from other domains, which normally could not be found by engineers via conventional search methods because their lack of expertise. The limitation of the knowledge that engineers have and the inefficiency of searching patent documents have become a big obstacle to promote the development of innovation.

Thus, finding an innovative solution for some special industrial problem from a wide range of patent documents is of paramount importance. Moreover, engineers usually are unable to find out breakthrough inventive solutions, key to competitiveness, using classical methods. To address this issue, we propose to use Google's neural network named word2vec [6] to obtain the sentence vector for every problem in patents. Then, we compute the cosine similarity between the pairs of sentences in order to retrieve similar problems from other patent documents. Consequently, we can successfully merge three of the similar IDM-related knowledge from patent documents that are problems, partial solutions, and parameters [4]. This approach should be helpful to engineers to easily and effectively find out similar problems from other patent documents. The latter could suggest more inventive solutions mined from a wider range of industrial domains so that they could be better assisted in Research & Design development activities [3, 5].

The final experimental results on real-world dataset show that the approach we used achieve promising results on finding similar problems from a large amount of patent documents as well as corresponding solutions. This greatly speeds up the whole efficiency for seeking innovative solutions and emerging IDM-related knowledge. Particularly, we show that our work successfully finds out two typical similar problems that are just matched with the vibration and data retention problems as well as corresponding solutions from different domain's patents. The contribution of this paper is that we mix the use of neural networks and IDM-knowledge to facilitate the merging of IDM-knowledge of different domains' patent documents in order to promote R&D activities. Besides, no other work, to the best of our knowledge, has been introduced so far.

The paper consists of the following sections. Section 2 introduces a brief state of art about similarity computation on patent documents. Section 3 and Sect. 4 separately details the IDM ontology as well as the methodology of the Word2vec, Sentence2vec, and similarity computation. We expose the experiments validating our model and the case study detailly in Sect. 5. We finally conclude our work and show perspectives for future works.

2 Related Work

Similarity computation is one of the most important tasks in natural language process. At the same time, there are many research achievements that use content of patent documents. These research achievements usually are valuable for product innovation. Significant efforts have recently been recorded in the similarity computation on patent documents, especially in word similarity computation [7, 8, 10] and document similarity computation [11–18].

In the study of word similarity computation, Dagan et al. [7], at 1993 year, proposed that the feature according to contextual information in documents can be used to better compute the similarity among words when we have a large-scale corpus. Most of the following research is then based on this achievement to further improve the final performance. Further, Pilehvar et al. [8] used an iterative method for calculating topic-sensitive PageRank [9] to construct each semantic signature in order to compute the similarity between two words. In addition, Terra et al. [10] investigated frequency estimates for co-occurrence that are based both on documents and on a variety of different window sizes, and examine the impact of the corpus size on the frequency estimates. They found that the size of a context for the target word will notably affect the result of the similarity computation on words.

The study of the document similarity computation is mainly as follows. In the beginning, Kessler et al. [11] and Small et al. [12] separately proposed Bibliographic Coupling and Co-citation Analysis methods at 1963 and 1973 year to analyze the similarity among different patents. Besides, a patent classification system using co-citation analysis has been also proposed by Lai et al. [13] to compute the patent similarity. Further, McGill et al. [14] and Mowery et al. [15] computed the similarity of firm patents via cross-citation rate when analyzing patent citation data. Moehrle et al [16] and Bergmann et al [17] also used natural language process methods to extract a subject–action–object–format (SAO) structures in patents first and then built similarity matrices for patents to evaluate their similarity. In addition, some indexes as centrality index, technology cycle index, and technology keyword clusters in patents are also used for in-depth quantitative analysis in order to compute the patent similarity [18].

The above similarity computation approaches on patent documents now mainly are applied on wide fields like evaluating the risk of patent infringement [17], discovering competitive intelligence [19], identifying technology opportunities [20], measuring the novelty of patents [21], making the technological roadmap [22], detecting the similarity between patent documents, and scientific publications [23], etc. Our work achieves also some inspiration from the above similarity computation methods that are used on real applications. However, we found that few of existing similarity computation methods or models which have been used on IDM-related knowledge, especially computing the similarity among different problems in patents. In this paper, we try to fill the gap of similarity computation on the field of IDM-related knowledge implementation by using the word vector model in order to improve the efficiency of finding similar problems and corresponding solutions from patent documents as well as expand the border of finding solutions.

3 IDM Ontology

Inventive Design Method (IDM) is based on the Theory of Inventive Problem Solving - the translation of the acronym TRIZ. It represents an extension of TRIZ and is usually perceived as more guided, therefore easier to teach to others since it is more formally described. It aims at assisting companies and engineers to solve complex and multi-disciplinary problems in creative ways.

Different from other ontologies, IDM ontology is generic and applicable in all fields [25]. In addition, Cavallucci et al. [26] proposed the main concepts of IDM that are problems, partial solutions, and contradictions including element parameters and values. In patents, problems normally describe unsatisfactory features of existing methods or situations. Partial solutions provide improvements or changes to the defined problems. Each problem may cause one or more contradictions the patent solves. Besides, partial solutions must be the simplest possible. Elements are components of the system and parameters qualify the element with certain specifics. Parameters are also qualified by values. The knowledge contained in these key concepts of patents usually has great value for engineers. Thus, we try to maximize this knowledge, hidden in patents unstructured text, to find out relevant inventive and potential solutions to a given problem in order to assist creative R&D departments.

4 Methodology

In this section, we introduce a new model named IDM-Similar for IDM-related knowledge similarity computation. Our work aims to find out similar problems to a given problem from the large-scale patent corpus in order to merge IDM-related knowledge. We first extract problems as well as corresponding partial solutions and parameters from several patent corpus using IDM-related knowledge extraction tool [24]. Then, we compute the similarity between these problems.

Formally, the extracted IDM-related knowledge set $K_i = \{P_i, PS_i, PA_i\}$ is from i-th patent document where P_i, PS_i, and PA_i are problems, partial solutions, and parameters respectively in the i-th patent document. Given the j-th problem $P_i^j = \left(w_i^{j_1}, w_i^{j_2}, \ldots, w_i^{j_{|w_i|}}\right)$ in the i-th patent document where $w_i^{j_{|w_i|}}$ is the $|w_i|$-th word in the j-th problem sentence, and we compute its similarity between to the other considered problems P.

4.1 Word Vector

We aim at using Word2vec to compute every word's vector in training corpus. Indeed, we integrate open source Wikipedia corpus to train Word2vec model. Word2vec is a type of word embedding model that proposed by Google first. This two-layer neural network can be trained by a large-scale corpus to achieve a vector in the space for each unique word in the corpus. Word vector is positioned in the vector space such that words that share common contexts in the corpus are located in close proximity to one another in the space [6]. The trained Word2vec model can simplify the processing of the considered text into n-dimensional space vector operation. Thereby, the similarity in vector space can represent the semantic similarity of text. In addition, the process of training on Word2vec is unsupervised and this two-layer neural network turns text into a numerical form that deep networks can understand so that it can be run on the computer efficiently.

The continuous bag-of-words (CBOW) and skip-gram [6] are two types of model architectures that are used on Word2vec to produce a distributed representation of words. These two architectures are similar at an algorithmic-wise but the main difference between them is that CBOW predicts the target word according to the context words around the original word. On the contrary, skip-gram predicts each context word via the target word. For instance, as shown in Fig. 1, CBOW predicts that the blank (target word) is "*mat*" when it encounters "*The dog sits on the _. It looks like a cat.*". For skip-gram, it will predict that the context of the center word "*mat*" is "*The dog sits on the*" and "*It looks like a cat*" when it reaches "_ _ _ _ _ *mat.*-_ _ _ _ _". Further, the CBOW smoothly processes the distributed information, such as treating a whole piece of context as a single observation set. In many cases, it is normally helpful for processing the small-sized dataset. In contrast, the skip-gram combines every context and target word as a new observation set and it normally works well on the large-sized dataset. Moreover, skip-gram does a better job for infrequent words. In this paper, we use Word2vec that is with skip-gram because there are many infrequent words in Wikipedia corpus comparatively to any other corpus.

4.2 Sentence Vector

As illustrated in Fig. 2, we choose to work with unsupervised text matching method to obtain each sentence's vector. Matched sentence problems in patent documents are extracted by the IDM-related knowledge extraction tool. We achieve the sentence vector $\vec{\boldsymbol{p}}$ by calculating the average vector of all words in each sentence. The calculation is defined as:

$$\vec{\boldsymbol{P}} = \frac{\sum_{i=0}^{j} \overrightarrow{\boldsymbol{w_i}}}{j} \tag{1}$$

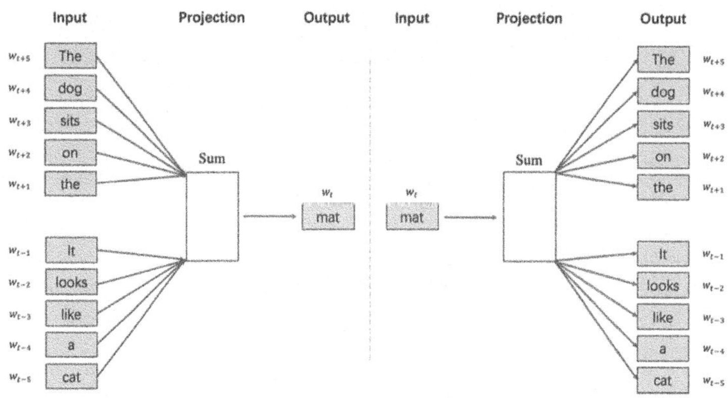

Fig. 1. CBOW (left) and skip-gram (right)

4.3 Cosine Similarity

We first compute the cosine distance between the given problem's sentence vector $\overrightarrow{P_i}$ and another sentence vector $\overrightarrow{P_j}$:

$$CosineDistance = \frac{\overrightarrow{P_i} \cdot \overrightarrow{P_j}}{|\overrightarrow{P_i}||\overrightarrow{P_j}|} = \frac{\sum_{i,j=1}^{n} P_i \times P_j}{\sqrt{\sum_{i=1}^{n} (P_i)^2} \times \sqrt{\sum_{j=1}^{n} (P_j)^2}} \tag{2}$$

Next, the cosine similarity is defined as:

$$Cosine\ Similarity = 1 - Cosine\ Distance = 1 - \frac{\overrightarrow{P_i} \cdot \overrightarrow{P_j}}{|\overrightarrow{P_i}||\overrightarrow{P_j}|} \tag{3}$$

Overall, if the value of cosine similarity is closer to 1, the similarity between pairs of sentences increases.

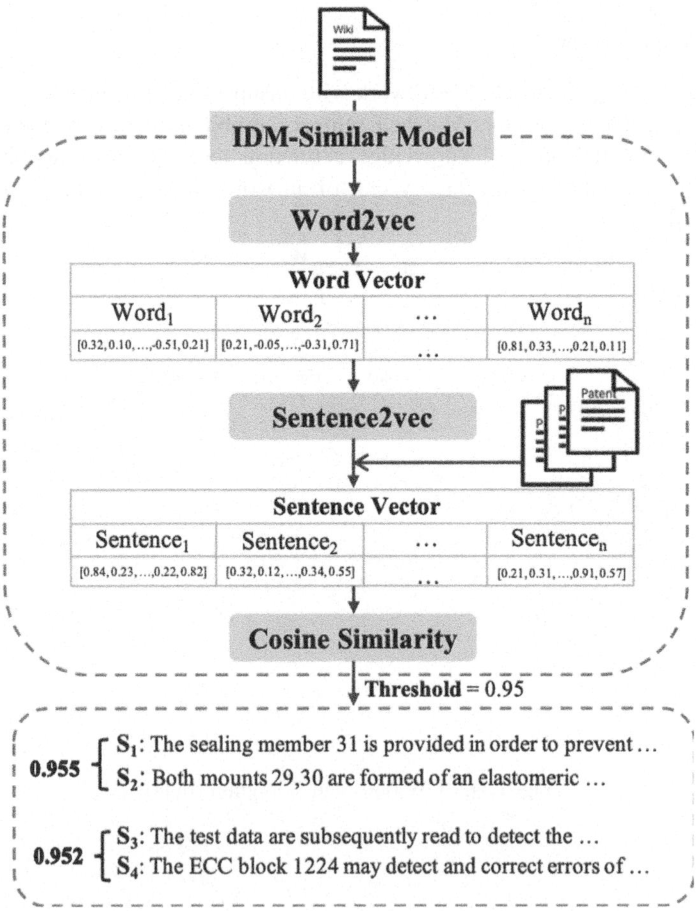

Fig. 2. An overview of our model

As illustrated in Fig. 2, we first employ the open source Wikipedia corpus to train Google's neural network Word2vec [6] in order to achieve every word's vector. After that, we adopt the trained word vector model to obtain the sentence vector for every inputting problem sentence. Finally, we apply the similarity computation approach to calculate the cosine similarity among each pairs of problem sentences and then find out those similar problems whose value are greater than the threshold as well as their corresponding solutions and parameters.

5 Experiments

5.1 Datasets and Evaluation Metrics

In this paper, we use the clean version of the English Wikipedia dataset [27] to train our Word2vec model. It only contains regular article text but removes tables and links to foreign language versions. Also, in this dataset, citations, footnotes, and markup were removed as well as hypertext links were converted to ordinary text. Furthermore, we also evaluate the similarity computation method on the Utility Patent datasets of US Patent Grant dataset [28].

US patents are mainly classified to three types: utility patent, design patent, and plant patent. According to the USPTO, utility patents are granted to anyone who invents or discovers any new and useful process, machine, article of manufacture, or composition of matter, or any new and useful improvement. Design patents are granted to anyone who invents a new, original, and ornamental design for an article of manufacture. Plant patents are granted to anyone who invents or discovers and asexually reproduces any distinct and new variety of plant. But 90% of US patents are utility patents, which protect the utility or functional aspects of an invention and they normally contain some kind of similarity on invention domains with each other compared to other types of patents. Therefore, in this paper, we use utility patent dataset as the test dataset to check the performance of the similarity computation approach. Utility patent dataset contains a total of 6,161 documents.

Finding the "gold-standard" ground truth of verifying the similarity among different sentences always is an open problem, especially for the sentences that are from different domains, and no work solved this problem. In this paper, we referred to 3 experts who are respectively from mechanics, chemistry, and architecture to verify the experimental results manually. A cross-checking among them is made to ensure the authenticity of the final results.

5.2 Experimental Settings

In order to achieve an optimal word vector model, in this paper, we tune our Word2vec model on the training dataset by using different parameters. At the same time, we also optimize the efficiency and accuracy for training the model. The final parameters of our Word2vec we set are shown in Table 1.

The number of dimensions in the created vectors is defined by *#size*. Hence size here means each document receives a 100-dimensional vector from training.

More dimensions usually mean slower training and we may risk having overfitting when the model works on small-sized datasets. The *#window* indicates how many words before and after a given word would be included as context words of the given word. Those words in training corpus that the minimum frequency of words is below the threshold of frequency will be discarded by *#min_count*. It is helpful to filter out those extremely rare or wrong words in the corpus. Word2vec model will use the hierarchical softmax as the loss function when we set *#negative* > 0 and *#hs* = 1 as well as we set 3 noise words in the model when the value of *#negative* is 3. The *#sample* represents the threshold of sampling. Those words with higher frequency in the training dataset will be randomly down-sampled.

Furthermore, in the cosine similarity computation, as mentioned in Sect. 4, if the similarity value between the two sentences is closer to 1, they are considered as similar. We finally fix the threshold of the similarity to 0.95 for performance reasons upon carrying out several tests and optimizing the size of the output.

Table 1. Parameters of the Word2vec model

Parameter	#size	#window	#min_count	#negative	#sample	#hs
Value	100	5	5	3	0.001	1

5.3 Overall Results

In this part, we carry out the performance analysis of our model on the US patent dataset and offer some further analysis. At first, as illustrated in Table 2, Patent Extractor [24] we used has extracted three types of IDM-related knowledge from 6,161 US patent documents. We used 4,574 problems among them as input dataset to Sentence2vec model. We compute the similarity between any two different problems via IDM-Similar model. The performance of our model on US patent dataset is shown in Table 3. From the results, we can observe that IDM-Similar model finally gives us 1,121 pairs of similar problems when the similarity threshold is set as 0.95. Through three experts' cross-checking, the number of true positive (TP) and false positive (FP) of final results are 1,000 and 121 respectively so that the precision of similarity is 89.21%. It demonstrates that our model can efficiently find out similar IDM-related knowledge from a large amount of patent documents belonging to different domains.

Table 2. Performance of Patent Extractor on US patent dataset

Model	Patent Extractor		
IDM-related knowledge	Problem	Partial solution	Parameter
Number	**4,574**	17,971	29,264

Table 3. Experimental results on US patent dataset

Model	IDM-Similar			
Metric	TP	FP	Total	Precision
Number	1,000	121	1,121	**89.21%**

5.4 Case Study

The objective of this part is to demonstrate the practical value of our model on merging IDM-related knowledge from different domains' patents. Two case studies on chemistry/mechanics and computer/physics domains respectively assess the performance of our model.

1. **Chemistry/Mechanics:** "Collector for bipolar lithium ion secondary batteries (US9537152B2)" and "Vacuum cleaner with motor between separation stages (US9532691B2)" are two US patents that are from chemistry and mechanics respectively. As shown in Fig. 3, our model finds out a pair of similar problems: "*The sealing member 31 is provided in order to* ***prevent contact*** *between the current collectors 11 adjacent to each other inside the battery and prevent a short circuit caused by slight unevenness at edge portions of the single cell layers 19 in the power generation element 21.*" and "*Both mounts 29, 30 are formed of an elastomeric material and act to* ***isolate*** *the second dirt-separation stage 7 and thus the remainder of the dirt separator 3 from the vibration generated by the vacuum motor 6.*" After analyzing the whole two patents, experts think that both problems are linked and belong to different domains. It is possible to solve the short circuit problem in US9537152B2 patent with the provided solution of the elastomeric material in US9532691B2 patent and vice versa.

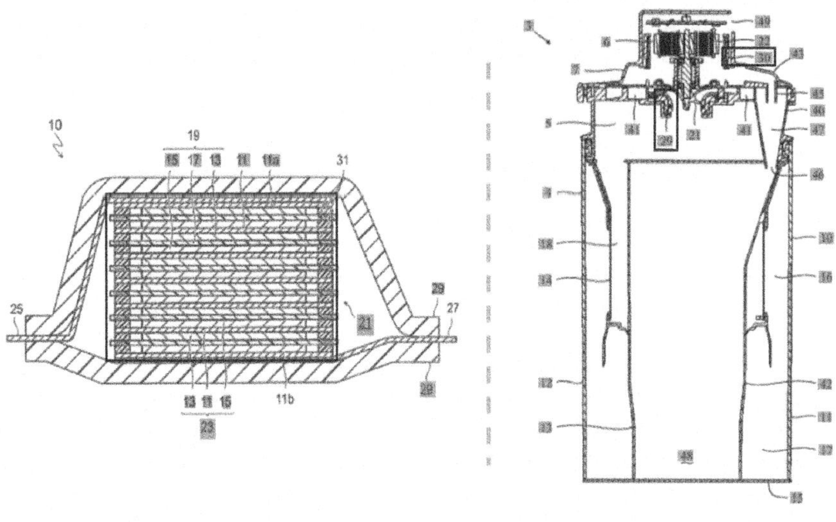

Fig. 3. Diagrams of the sealing member (left) and the elastomeric material (right)

2. **Computer/Physics:** "Hybrid-HDD with improved data retention (US9536619B2)" and "Semiconductor device and method of fabricating the same (US9536897B2)" are two US patents that are from computer and physics respectively. Two similar problems our model found are illustrated in Fig. 4: "*The test data are subsequently read to detect the possibility of data retention* ***errors*** *that may occur when reading the associated* ***user data***." and "*The ECC block 1224 may* ***detect and correct errors of data*** *which are read out from the memory device 1210.*" We think there is a kind of possibility to add ECC block using US9536897B2 patent into the left device to solve the data retention errors that mentioned in US9536619B2 patent. This case is from two similar domains and also was extracted by our model successfully.

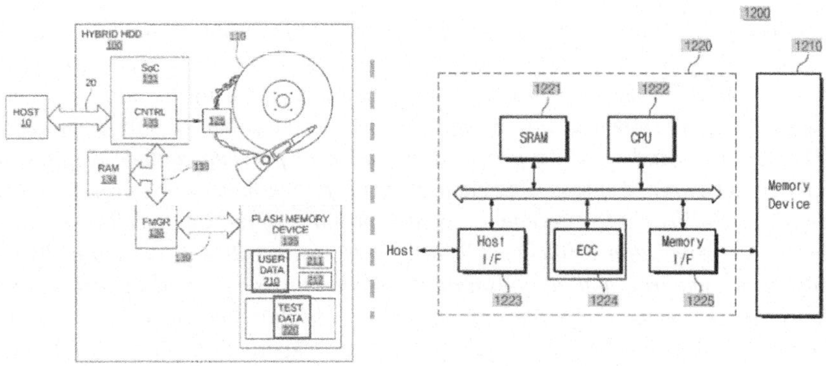

Fig. 4. Diagrams of the hybrid HDD (left) and the memory systems (right)

In conclusion of these cases, we note that the final similar problems our IDM-Similar model found from different domains' patents have a significant practical value for inventive solutions. In fact, these experimental results on the real-world dataset are a great encouragement for us.

6 Conclusion and Future Work

In this paper, we propose an IDM-Similar model to compute the similarity of the different pairs of sentences in order to merge the IDM-related knowledge that are from different domains' patent documents. Our model can make full use of the IDM-related knowledge in patents and find out similar problems from different domains. In the experimental results, we show that our model has good precision and significant practical value. In particular, we demonstrate two real cases that the problems can be solved by inventive solutions from another domain using our model. It will significantly improve the efficiency for engineers to find out innovative solutions and promote R&D activities for companies.

In the future, we will explore the following directions:

1. An accurate IDM-related knowledge extractor can further improve the performance of our model. We will explore how to effectively and accurately extract IDM-related knowledge from unstructured patent documents to further enhance the performance.
2. The different size and types of training datasets can affect the performance of the Word2vec model. We will try to utilize some larger patent corpus to train Word2vec model to improve its performance.

Acknowledgments. This work is supported by China Scholarship Council (CSC).

References

1. Yeap, T., Loo, G.H., Pang, S.: Computational patent mapping: Intelligent agents for nanotechnology. In: International Conference on Mems, Nano and Smart Systems. IEEE (2003)
2. Souili, A., Cavallucci, D., Rousselot, F.: A lexico-syntactic pattern matching method to extract IDM-TRIZ knowledge from on-line patent databases. Procedia Eng. **131**(Complete), 418–425 (2015)
3. Altshuller, G.S.: 40 Principles: TRIZ keys to technical innovation (Lev Shulyak et Steven Rodman, Trans.), 1st edn, 141p. Technical Innovation Center, Inc., Worcester (1998). ISBN-10: 0964074036
4. Zanni-Merk, C., Cavallucci, D., Rousselot, F.: Using patents to populate an inventive design ontology, Proceedings of the TRIZ Future Conference 2010, Bergamo, 3–5 November 2010, pp. 52-62. Elsevier Ltd. (2010)
5. Cavallucci, D., Khomenko, N.: From TRIZ to OTSM-TRIZ, Addressing complexity challenges in Inventive design. Int. J. Prod. Dev. **4**, 4–21 (2007)
6. Mikolov, T., et al.: Efficient estimation of word representations in vector space. arXiv preprint arXiv:1301.3781 (2013)
7. Dagan, I., Marcus, S., Markovitch, S.: Contextual word similarity and estimation from sparse data. In: Proceedings of the 31st annual meeting on Association for Computational Linguistics. Association for Computational Linguistics (1993)
8. Pilehvar, M.T., Jurgens, D., Navigli, R.: Align, disambiguate and walk: a unified approach for measuring semantic similarity. In: Proceedings of the 51st Annual Meeting of the Association for Computational Linguistics (Volume 1: Long Papers), vol. 1 (2013)
9. Haveliwala, T.H.: Topic-sensitive PageRank. In: Proceedings of the 11th international conference on World Wide Web. ACM (2002)
10. Terra, E., Clarke, C.L.A.: Frequency estimates for statistical word similarity measures. In: Proceedings of the 2003 Conference of the North American Chapter of the Association for Computational Linguistics on Human Language Technology-Volume 1. Association for Computational Linguistics (2003)
11. Kessler, M.M.: An experimental study of bibliographic coupling between technical papers. No. 62 673TN1. Massachusetts Inst of Tech Lexington Lincoln Lab (1962)
12. Small, H.: Co-citation in the scientific literature: a new measure of the relationship between two documents. J. Am. Soc. Inf. Sci. **24**(4), 265–269 (1973)
13. Lai, K.-K., Shiao-Jun, W.: Using the patent co-citation approach to establish a new patent classification system. Inf. Process. Manag. **41**(2), 313–330 (2005)

14. McGill, J.P.: Technological knowledge and governance in alliances among competitors. Int. J. Technol. Manag. **38**(1), 69 (2007)
15. Mowery, D.C., Oxley, J.E., Silverman, B.S.: Technological overlap and interfirm cooperation: implications for the resource-based view of the firm. Res. Policy **27**(5), 507–523 (1998)
16. Moehrle, M.G., et al.: Patent-based inventor profiles as a basis for human resource decisions in research and development. R&D Manag. **35**(5), 513–524 (2005)
17. Bergmann, I., et al.: Evaluating the risk of patent infringement by means of semantic patent analysis: the case of DNA chips. R&D Manag. **38**(5), 550–562 (2008)
18. Yoon, B., Park, Y.: A text-mining-based patent network: analytical tool for high-technology trend. J. High Technol. Manag. Res. **15**(1), 37–50 (2004)
19. Shih, M.-J., Liu, D.-R., Hsu, M.-L.: Discovering competitive intelligence by mining changes in patent trends. Expert Syst. Appl. **37**(4), 2882–2890 (2010)
20. Yoon, B., Park, Y.: A systematic approach for identifying technology opportunities: keyword-based morphology analysis. Technol. Forecast. Soc. Change **72**(2), 145–160 (2005)
21. Gerken, J.M., Moehrle, M.G.: A new instrument for technology monitoring: novelty in patents measured by semantic patent analysis. Scientometrics **91**(3), 645–670 (2012)
22. Lee, S., et al.: Business planning based on technological capabilities: patent analysis for technology-driven roadmapping. Technol. Forecast. Soc. Chang. **76**(6), 769–786 (2009)
23. Magerman, T., Van Looy, B., Song, X.: Exploring the feasibility and accuracy of Latent Semantic Analysis based text mining techniques to detect similarity between patent documents and scientific publications. Scientometrics **82**(2), 289–306 (2009)
24. Souili, A., Cavallucci, D.: Automated extraction of knowledge useful to populate inventive design ontology from patents. TRIZ – The Theory of Inventive Problem Solving, pp. 43–62. Springer, Cham (2017). https://doi.org/10.1007/978-3-319-56593-4_2
25. Bultey, A., De Bertrand De Beuvron, F., Rousselot, F.: A substance-field ontology to support the TRIZ thinking approach. Int. J. Comput. Appl. Technol. **30**(1), 113–124 (2007)
26. Cavallucci, D., Rousselot, F., Zanni, C.: Initial situation analysis through problem graph. CIRP J. Manuf. Sci. Technol. **2**(4), 310–317 (2010)
27. Wikipedia Dataset. http://mattmahoney.net/dc/textdata.html. Accessed 13 Apr 2019
28. US Patent Dataset. https://bulkdata.uspto.gov/data/patent/grant/redbook/fulltext/2017/. Accessed 13 Apr 2019

How to Find Disruptive Technologies Systematically?

Jianguang Sun(✉), Zhitao Song, Kang Wang, Haoyu Li, and Runhua Tan

Hebei University of Technology, Tianjin 300401, China
sjg@hebut.edu.cn

Abstract. This article describes an empirical study focusing on the systematic innovation process for finding disruptive technology opportunities. In the first part, the concept of the disruptive technology based on the bifurcation point of routes of system evolution of technology system is defined. The authors address three research questions. First, how does disruptive technology define? Second, what disruptive technologies of new product are most attractive in terms of interest from the customers from fuzzy front end of NPD? Third, in order to accurately find disruptive opportunities during the process of product detail design, how to establish models of function and find solutions from components of supersystem? The most notable achievement is a systematic flow constructed for achieving disruptive technologies systematically. Thus, the article provides a practical support for the methods to achieve disruptive technologies and the process is verified by case studies about copier and children's phone.

Keywords: Disruptive innovation · Disruptive technology · Model of function · Supersystem component

1 Introduction

Disruptive innovation refers to the development of products whose performance is not as good as that of mainstream products but which have other characteristics of attracting insignificant users and new users [1, 2]. From the beginning these products enter the low-end market or new markets, then gradually replace the finalized products of the mainstream market, and finally the enterprises that own these products will replace the incumbents [3]. This process is called disruptive innovation, and the technology used in new products is disruptive technology. Disruptive innovation products initially fail to meet the needs of mainstream customers because they may lack some features or functions of mainstream goods. However, they are typically simpler, more convenient, and less expensive. It is these characteristics that attract new users and existing low-end users, allowing emerging companies to enter the mainstream market to compete with incumbents. Disruptive innovation usually destroys the original market competition structure and constructs a new market pattern [4].

Published by Springer Nature Switzerland AG 2019
R. Benmoussa et al. (Eds.): TFC 2019, IFIP AICT 572, pp. 159–173, 2019.
https://doi.org/10.1007/978-3-030-32497-1_14

Danneels holds the view that disruptive technologies change the bases of competition because they introduce a dimension of performance along which products did not compete previously [5]. Adner states that as disruptive technologies mature they will alter industry boundaries by displacing established technologies from mainstream segments [6]. Christensen believes the industry's leading firms almost always triumphed in battles of sustaining innovation and that entrant firms typically beat the incumbent leaders when disruptive innovations emerged [7]. Hardman et al. mentioned the threat of the new technology is not often recognized by existing market leaders. Disruptive technologies are initially more expensive than the incumbent technologies. The quality of the disruptive technology initially is often worse than the quality of the technologies they seek to replace. The technologies have some form of 'added value' to the consumer [8]. Govindarajan and Kopalle hold the view that the disruptive-technology framework does indeed help us make ex ante predictions about the type of firms likely to develop disruptive innovations [9]. Bower and Christensen pointed out that the key is to manage strategically important disruptive technologies in an organizational context where small orders create energy, where fast low-cost forays into ill-defined markets are possible, and where overhead is low to permit profit even in emerging markets [10]. Bergek doubts the creative destruction of existing industries as a consequence of discontinuous technological change. He argues that creative accumulation requires firms to handle a triple challenge of simultaneously (a) fine-tuning and evolving existing technologies at a rapid pace, (b) acquiring and developing new technologies and resources and (c) integrating novel and existing knowledge into superior products and solutions [11].

Disruptive innovation is a special branch of technological evolution route. Unlike sustaining innovation, disruptive innovation technology does not pay much attention to promoting mainstream functions constantly. Technology forecasting based on technology evolution route can achieve the forecasting process of disruptive technology [12]. The implementation of disruptive innovation technology has two modes: requirement-driven and technology-driven. Requirement-driven originates from market, and disruptive innovation strategies are formulated in the light of the demand of new market. Technology-driven comes from the prediction of the technical status of the target product.

Although scholars have done a lot of research on disruptive innovation, its application still remains in the business model innovation in the field of management. Such innovation often solves the problem of fuzzy front end, and its implementation and verification are not clear enough [13]. In order to apply the process of disruptive innovation to the field of technological innovation, this paper proposes a systematic method of realizing disruptive innovation, which integrates disruptive technology as a solution into the solution set of innovative problem solving, effectively achieving the integration and application of multiple methods.

2 Concept Definition

2.1 Disruptive Innovation Concept by Christensen

The concept of disruptive innovation was first formally put forward by Clayton Christensen in his book The Innovator's Dilemma: When New Technologies Cause Great Firms to Fail and it has become a theory of technological innovation after the continuous improvement of later research [14–16]. Disruptive innovation refers to the introduction of products with lower performance than mainstream market products, but with some characteristics that attract unimportant users or new users. And with the development of these products, they can not only gradually gain a firm foothold in the low-end market and new market, but also replace the finalized products in the mainstream market. Companies that own these products, namely emerging enterprises, will replace incumbents, which means that disruptive innovation is completed. In terms of product technology evolution, the definition of disruptive innovation is summarized as follows: Disruptive innovation is a branch taking place on the route of product technology evolution, which occurs in the mature period of product life cycle, and the formation of this evolutionary branch make products have the ability to attract low-end users and new market users so that disruptive innovative products quickly form market scale and make a profit. It should be noted that although the performance of disruptive innovative products is poor in the introduction stage, it is generally cheaper, simpler, smaller, and more convenient to use. It is some of these features that enable them to compete with finalized products in the mainstream market. The disruptive innovation model and sustaining innovation model proposed by Christensen are shown in Fig. 1:

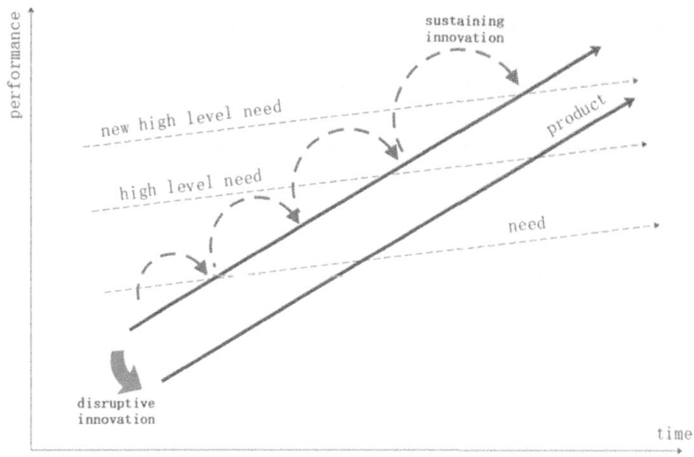

Fig. 1. Disruptive innovation model by Christensen

2.2 Concept of DI Based on Technological Evolution

In order to adapt to the living environment, biological systems are constantly mutating and evolving, and the driving force of their evolution is the surrounding environment, that is, the so-called survival of the fittest. Similar to the process of biological evolution, products are constantly evolving [17] to adapt to market changes, and the market is driven by demand. In other words, product evolution is the result of adapting to current and future needs, and demand is the driving force of product evolution. Future demand promotes the evolution of current products, transforming their functions from the current state to the future state. To meet the constantly changing needs of the market and consumers, companies have designed ever-changing products. These products, similar to biological individuals, have genetic information that determines their structure, identity, and function, and have evolved from generation to generation. However, in order to capture the market in the future, it is not enough for enterprises to compete passively with their competitors, but to continuously develop the new market space with huge demand and realize the strategic action of "value innovation" [18, 19]. This process is consistent with the concept of disruptive innovation proposed by Christensen. Therefore, we have redefined disruptive innovation in the field of technological evolution, aiming to improve the effectiveness of innovation, break away from the passive inherent evolutionary route, and make technological prediction of disruptive technology.

It is generally considered that innovation is divided into three categories: Incremental Innovation (II), Radical Innovation (RI), and Disruptive Innovation (DI). The evolution process of product technology is usually represented by a series of head-tail S-curves. It includes many evolutionary branches, and different branches of technological evolution determine the classification of innovation [20]. As shown in Fig. 2, the innovation process occurring on the same S curve segment usually involves solving local conflicts and improving performance, and has a fixed path of evolution [21]. This process is called Incremental Innovation, such as the technological innovation that happens from B to C in Fig. 2. During the exit state of the S-curve, the re-sources for improving the prior art have been exhausted, the technical performance has reached the limit, however, the market requirements cannot be met. At this time, new alternative technologies must be developed to achieve a breakthrough in technical performance and principles. This innovative process is called Radical Innovation [22], which is characterized by the end of one S-curve connected to the head of next adjacent S-curve, as shown in Fig. 2 (from C to D). Disruptive Innovation takes place in the mature period of the S-curve, and there are two types. One is the short-term retrogression of technological evolution, such as the technological innovation in the evolution process from B to A in Fig. 2. The other technological innovation is shown as a jump between different S curves during the mature state (from B to E in Fig. 2). The former is called Low-end Disruptive Innovation, while the latter is called New market Disruptive Innovation.

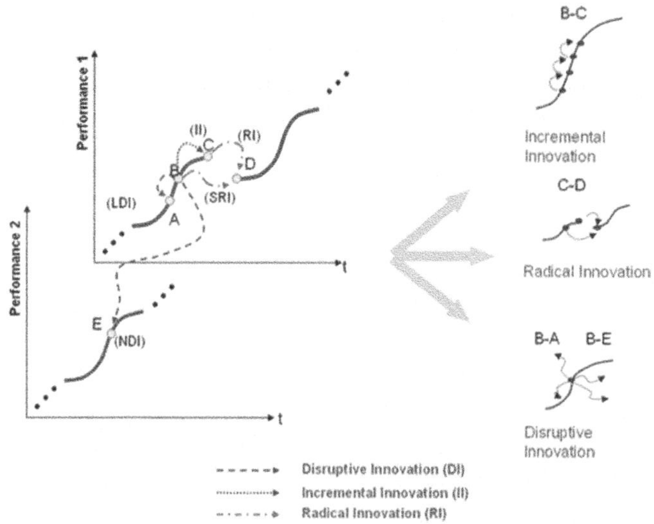

Fig. 2. Innovations in the process of technological evolution

3 Systematic Methodology

3.1 Problem Definition

The systematic product innovation process includes five stages: Fuzzy Front End (FFE), New Product Development (NPD), Conceptual Design, Detailed Design, Production Process and Commercialization, as shown in Fig. 3. During the fuzzy front end stage, various ideas should be generated based on market opportunities, and according to enterprise capabilities, several ideas should be determined through evaluation, and new product development projects should be launched on the basis of these ideas. After the subsequent conceptual design, detailed design, production process design and manufacturing, the ideas input in the previous stage are transformed into products and exported to the commercialization stage. After the operation of the market, the products are transformed into enterprise benefits in the commercialization stage, thus completing the whole process of effective product innovation.

Innovation is a complex process that needs to constantly solve the problems that arise at each stage. During the fuzzy front end stage, it is mainly about how to generate innovative ideas and how to make a choice from these ideas. In the product development phase, it mainly involves how to turn selected innovation ideas into real products and the problems at different stages of development are different. In the commercialization stage, it is mainly a question of how to carry out the commercialization operation so that the product can produce benefits. In the process of product innovation, technological innovation is mainly reflected in the stage of fuzzy front end and new product development, which realizes product innovation by constantly discovering and creatively solving the technical problems. With regard to the obstacles encountered in the stage of commercialization, on the one hand, it can be solved by management innovation methods, and at the same time, the technological environment of the society can be utilized to create more market-oriented approaches.

The disruptive innovation problem solved by Christensen is mainly concentrated in the fifth stage mentioned above, namely the commercialization stage. For the systematic innovation problem, it exists in the whole life cycle of the product, so the problems that arise in the remaining four stages also have the disruptive innovation solutions.

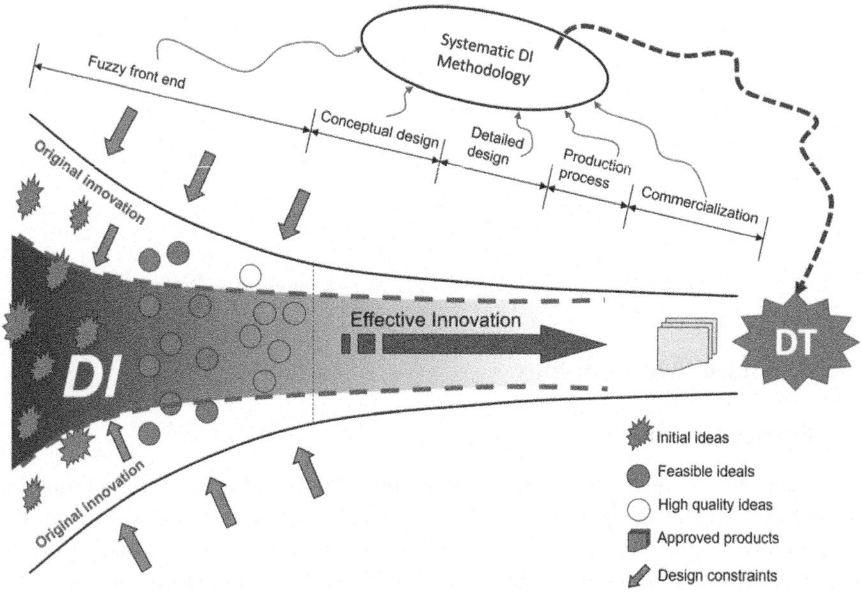

Fig. 3. The innovation process of products development

3.2 DI Process for Fuzzy Front End

In a market environment full of risks and fierce competition, it is difficult for emerging enterprises to enter a mature market because incumbents already occupy a large amount of resources [23], such as technology, patents, markets, people and so on. For them, traditional incremental innovation cannot compete with incumbent enterprises, while radical innovation must solve the technical bottleneck problem of upgrading mature products in the industry, and emerging enterprises generally do not have this ability. For emerging enterprises, disruptive innovation is an effective method. Only through disruptive innovation can they enter the market in the initial stage and change their passive position in the competition, which often occurs in the fuzzy front end stage of product development.

As shown in Fig. 4, it is a disruptive technology implementation process for the fuzzy front-end stage based on the analysis of technological system evolution.

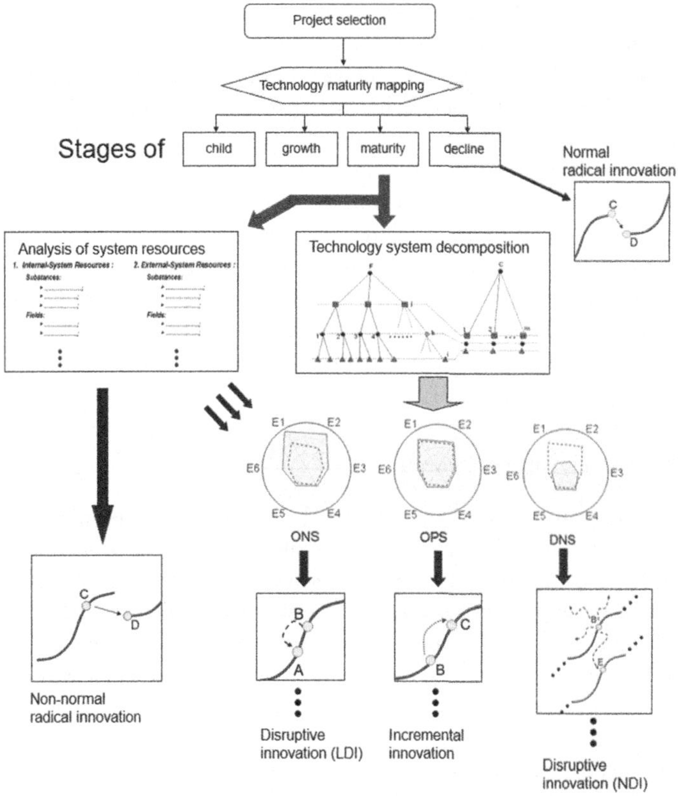

Fig. 4. Innovation process for the fuzzy front-end stage

First, according to the product structure of the enterprise, the innovation object is selected, and the technical maturity analysis of the innovation object is carried out. In the mature stage, products are facing fierce market competition. The performance improvement brought by incremental innovation is not obvious, and the cost performance is not high, but the implementation effect of disruptive innovation is pretty good. Therefore, products that are in mature period are preferred for disruptive innovation.

Second, the target product is decomposed into a number of technical systems. Similar to the functional structure of the product, the technical system that constitutes the product consists of subsystems at all levels. Each subsystem has a complete system structure, which can be analyzed as a complete technical system, resulting in multiple technical subsystems.

Third, demand evolution analysis is carried out. Aiming at a specific new market, the law of demand evolution is selected and used to determine the evolutionary direction of related technical subsystem functions. According to the principle of demand evolution and the designer's experience, the potential demand is predicted, and then the possible additional auxiliary functions are determined. Through market survey, the market demand of adding auxiliary function is investigated to prepare for the subsequent evolution analysis of the technical subsystem.

Fourth, carry out the evolutionary analysis of technical subsystem. By comparing the existing functional state of each technical subsystem with the result state of demand evolution analysis, the evolutionary state diagram of the technical subsystem is drawn. According to user demand, if the technology subsystem is in the over-satisfied need state (ONS), Low-end Disruptive innovation can be achieved by reducing excessive performance. If current or future new market user needs are in the dis-satisfied need state (DNS), the New market Disruptive Innovation strategy can be implemented.

Fifth, evaluate the design results. Evaluate the results of innovative design, mainly to assess whether it brings new technical conflicts, whether it causes the increase of costs, and whether it meets the market demand. After the evaluation, the product can enter the detailed design stage.

3.3 DI Process for Design Process

Target of innovation is effective innovation. There exists many problems to be solved in the process of product design, so what is the target for solving these problems? Perhaps you will answer: The target is to improve the performance of the product, but for the enterprise, making profits is seen as the most important goal. If a product with excellent performance cannot bring benefits to the enterprise (because of high cost, complicated operation, high energy consumption, etc.), this product will be declared a failure. From the angle of innovation, this innovation is ineffective. In conclusion, in the process of product design, the target of solving the problem is to achieve effective innovation, that is to say, to bring expected benefits to enterprises.

Search technology opportunities based on effective innovation. The goal of the sustaining innovation process is to improve the performance of the product. The process of solving the problem is illustrated in Fig. 5. Define the problem first, then establish the function model [24, 25] and carry out the root cause analysis. Determine the available resources of the system through resource analysis, and finally solve the problem by using the tool of TRIZ. But in the mature period of product evolution, the market competition is fierce, the available resources are scarce, and the improvement of performance often faces a large number of conflict problems that are difficult to resolve. In this case, effective innovation can be achieved by adopting a compromise method to eliminate conflicts and modifying the supersystem to meet user needs.

Function analysis for disruptive innovation: Complex user requirements are often achieved by a number of interrelated functions. In order to facilitate the search for a principle scheme that satisfies the total function of the product, or to make the solution of the problem simple and convenient, the total function is usually decomposed into sub-functions with relatively low complexity, and sub-functions are decomposed into next level sub-functions until they are decomposed into function units. The decomposition process is called functional decomposition. The total function of the product refers to the total relationship between input and output of the product or system to be designed. The entity that inputs and outputs is called a flow. After a high level of abstraction, the flow is divided into matter flow, energy flow, and information flow. The sub-function is a part of the total function, and its relationship with the total function is controlled by the constraint or the relationship between input and output. Function unit is the abstraction of existing components and processes. The substance-field model expresses the functions of two components through field interaction. The technical system is composed of different components interconnecting and interacting with each other. Every two interacting components can construct a substance-field model and all elements of the system form a complex material-field model system through field connections. And then the function model of the system can be established by expressing the "field" with "action".

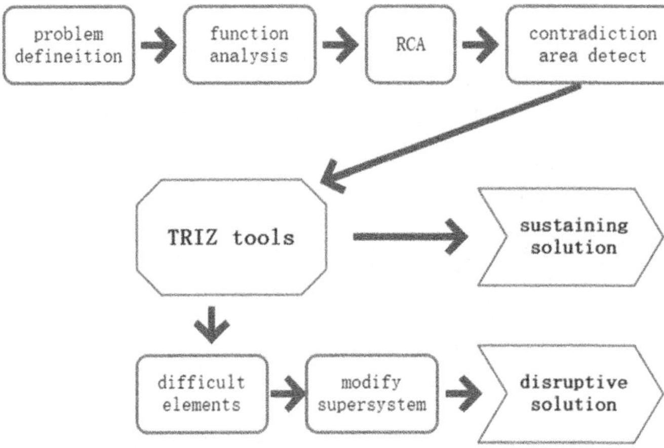

Fig. 5. Systemic innovation process of product

Any product can be represented by a function model. There are many problems encountered in the process of product design and improved design, and the process of solving these problems is the process of innovation. In the expression of a function model, there are products, components, supersystems, and the relationship between them. For example, as illustrated in Fig. 6, there is a problematic product that requires technological innovation to correct the insufficient effect a6 and harmful effect a11 (see Unit1). Under the guidance of the principle of TRIZ, such as conflict theory, standard solutions of substance-field, trimming, technological evolution and so on, components 2, 3, 5 have been changed, eliminating the insufficient effect a6 and harmful effect a11 (see Unit2). However, the above process of solving problems is a typical sustaining innovation process, the purpose of which is to improve the performance of the system, and changes to products and supersystems are not allowed. By changing products and supersystems, it is often possible to reduce the difficulty of solving problems and achieve disruptive innovation. As show in Fig. 6, low end disruptive innovation can be achieved by changing the product, and new market disruptive innovation can be realized by changing the supersystem (see Unit3).

The process method is as follows:

First, describe the problem to be solved and clarify that the ultimate target of solving this problem is to achieve an effective innovation of the product.

Second, establish the system function model, which is composed of components, supersystems, products, and the interactions between them. Current system problems can be expressed as harmful or insufficient effects between components, between components and supersystems, and between components and products.

Third, after the root cause analysis (RCA), TRIZ tool is used to solve the problem of function model. If the solution process is not so complicated, multiple solutions can be obtained according to the steps of sustaining innovation.

Fourth, try to change the supersystem and adjust the corresponding components until the harmful and insufficient effects between the components are eliminated for obtaining a new solution and the corresponding disruptive innovation is formed.

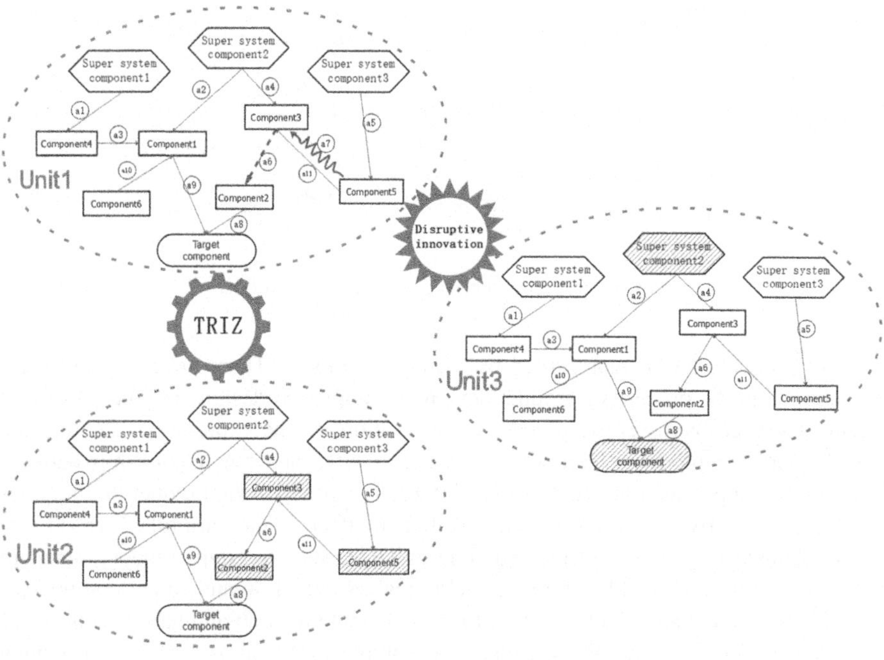

Fig. 6. Innovation process based on function model analysis

4 Case Study

4.1 Canon Copier

In 1976, Canon avoided the fierce competition in the Red Ocean market of large duplicators and entered the small duplicator market which everyone ignored and looked down upon. As a result, it created an amazing business myth in this Blue Ocean market, with almost no obstacles. From 1976 to 1981, Xerox's market share in the photocopier market plummeted from 82% to 35%. Although it took Xerox more than a decade to deal with the threat of Canon's entry into home offices and small businesses, it was too late to shake Canon's leading position in the market. In this process, Canon adopted disruptive technology.

The function of a copier is to copy the original into multiple copies. The principle is as follows: Light shining on the item to be copied is reflected by the lens onto a photosensitive (selenium-coated) drum to form an image. The selenium drum's surface charge varies with the light and dark areas of the image. The toner drum delivers tiny black particles (toner) to the dark, charged areas of the image. The toner-based image is then transferred to the paper rolled onto the drum, the negatively charged toner particles being attracted by a positive charge under the sheet, and the paper is heated to fix the toner. The copy paper itself originally provided the treated surface, but the innovation of the selenium-coated drum made it possible to use the ordinary paper. Light projection permits the printed image to be enlarged or reduced by any desired percentage.

The function model of the Ricoh copier is shown in Fig. 7. The problem with current system is that it is necessary to further expand the market and improve the competitiveness of products. The main parameters of the copier are: copy speed, copy format and copy definition. In order to achieve this goal, it is necessary to modify each function unit to solve a large number of conflict problems. There are many difficult function units, which make the solution of the problem quite complex in this process. A compromise approach can be adopted to modify the supersystem and products so that problems can be solved and a disruptive innovation opportunity arises. The following steps are adopted:

(1) Problem Description: New enterprises are supposed to develop a high-performance photocopier to form effective innovation if they are willing to enter the existing photocopier market.
(2) The copier's function model is established, as shown in Fig. 7. In order to improve the performance of the copier, it is important to increase the copying speed, increase the copy size, and improve the clarity of the copy. Since the product is monopolized by the existing leading enterprises and the available resources are scarce, it is extremely difficult to solve the corresponding function model, which means that there is no way to form an effective solution of sustaining innovation.
(3) Change the user which belongs to the supersystem. The former user is a professional operator for large and medium-sized enterprises, while the current user is transformed into a domestic user and a small company user. The problem of insufficient copy size can be solved, and the requirements of simple operation is put forward. Change the product to reduce the size of the paper to be copied. The above measures solve the problem of current performance improvement.
(4) The resulting disruptive technology products are: a small, lightweight, inexpensive, and easy-to-operate copier for domestic users and small company users. Compared with mainstream engineering copiers in the market, it has low speed, small format, and low definition requirements.

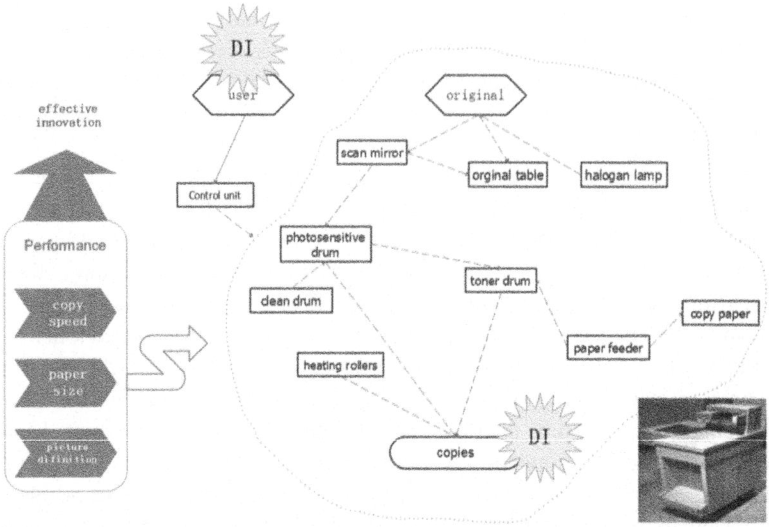

Fig. 7. Innovation process of copier

4.2 Child's Phone

The functional model of smartphones is shown in Fig. 8. The existing problem of the current system is that the emerging enterprises want to enter the mobile phone market, but they are weak in technology and lack of funds. Therefore, there are a lot of difficult function units in the function model of the system. In the process of solving these difficult function units using traditional TRIZ theory, due to the lack of resources, the solving process can not be completed and effective innovation can not be achieved. Disruptive innovation methods can be used to change the supersystem and products of the system, so that problems can be solved and opportunities for disruptive innovation emerge. The following steps are adopted:

(1) Problem Description: New enterprises need to develop a new mobile phone to enter the existing mobile phone market.
(2) Establish the function model of mobile phone, as shown in Fig. 8. If we design according to the idea of improving the performance of mainstream products, we need to improve the performance of most of the key components. Because of the lack of resources in emerging enterprises, it will lead to the increase of costs and can not achieve effective sustaining innovation.
(3) Change the user which belongs to the supersystem. The original user is aimed at the adult user market. By turning users into children, the problems of insufficient performance and high cost can be solved. Meanwhile, the requirements of simple operation, protecting eyesight and preventing addiction to games are put forward. Change the product. Replace the mainstream high-resolution touch screen with low-resolution small screen with a few function keys, and remove the photo function.

(4) The ultimate disruptive technology is: a special mobile phone with simple function, easy operation, low cost and no entertainment function for children users. On the basis of guaranteeing basic communication functions, compared with mobile phones in the mainstream market, children's mobile phone has low cost, simple structure and low performance requirements. It avoids fierce competition with the mainstream market of mobile phone and opens up the Blue Ocean market.

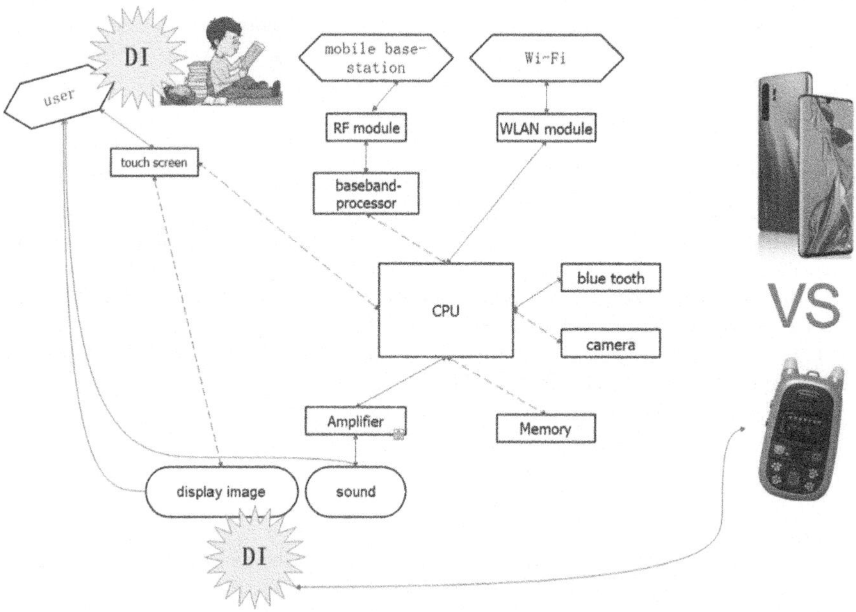

Fig. 8. Innovation process of Child's phone

5 Conclusion

In this study, disruptive technology is introduced into the process of product technology innovation, which enlarges the application scope of this technology. It is not only applied to the business model innovation in the field of management, but also used in the field of technology innovation, which is a complement to the traditional innovation methods. It is reflected in the following points:

(1) In the process of solving problems with TRIZ, if the resources are insufficient, it will make it extremely difficult to solve the problem, and sometimes the problem cannot be solved. The application of this method can effectively solve the problem of insufficient innovation resources, and introduces a large amount of available resources through changes to the supersystem.

(2) The problem of solving difficult function units is solved by disruptive innovation technology. Difficult function unit is a great obstacle to solve problems by using TRIZ. The application of this method changes the attributes of difficult function units by changing supersystems and products, so that they are no longer obstacles to innovation.

(3) The usual process of sustaining technological innovation is dedicated to solving the problems in technical systems by eliminating the insufficient and harmful effects of the system with TRIZ tools. Changes to supersystems and products are not allowed in this process. The method proposed in this study allows modification of supersystems and products based on the target of effective innovation.

Acknowledgements. This research is supported by the National Innovation Method Fund of China (2017IM040100), Erasmus+ Programme of European Union (586081-EPP-1-2017-1-FI-EPPKA2-CBHE-JP), the Natural Science Foundation of Hebei province of China (Grand No. E2017202260).

References

1. Adner, R.: When are technologies disruptive? A demand-based view of the emergence of competition. Strat. Manag. J. **23**(8), 667–688 (2002)
2. Christensen, C.M.: The Innovator's dilemma: When New Technologies Cause Great Firms to Fail. Harvard Business School Press, Boston (1997)
3. Christensen, C.M., Baumann, H., Ruggles, R.: Disruptive innovation for social change. Harv. Bus. Rev. **84**(12), 94–101, 163 (2007)
4. Christensen, C.M., Rosenbloom, R.S.: Explaining the attacker's advantage: technological paradigms, organizational dynamics, and the value network. Res. Policy **24**(2), 233–257 (1995)
5. Danneels, E.: Disruptive technology reconsidered: a critique and research agenda. J. Prod. Innov. Manag. **21**(4), 246–258 (2010)
6. Adner, R., Zemsky, P.: Disruptive technologies and the emergence of competition. RAND J. Econ. **36**, 229–254 (2005). https://doi.org/10.2139/ssrn.293686
7. Christensen, C.M.: The ongoing process of building a theory of disruption. J. Prod. Innov. Manag. **31**(1), 39–55 (2005)
8. Hardman, S., Steinberger-Wilckens, R., Dan, V.: Disruptive innovations: the case for hydrogen fuel cells and battery electric vehicles. Int. J. Hydrog. Energy **38**(35), 15438–15451 (2013)
9. Govindarajan, V., Kopalle, P.K.: The usefulness of measuring disruptiveness of innovations ex post in making ex ante predictions. J. Prod. Innov. Manag. **23**(1), 12–18 (2005)
10. Bower, J.L., Christensen, C.M.: Disruptive technologies: catching the wave. Harv. Bus. Rev. **73**(1), 43–53 (1995)
11. Bergek, A., Berggren, C., Magnusson, T.: Technological discontinuities and the challenge for incumbent firms: destruction, disruption or creative accumulation? Res. Policy **42**(6–7), 1210–1224 (2013)
12. Sun, J., Tan, R.: Method for forecasting DI based on TRIZ technology system evolution theory. Int. J. Innov. Technol. Manag. **9**(02), 1250010 (2012)
13. Reinhardt, R., Gurtner, S.: The overlooked role of embeddedness in disruptive innovation theory. Technol. Forecast. Soc. Change **132**, 268–283 (2018)
14. Christensen, C., Raynor, M.: The innovator's Solution: Creating and Sustaining Successful Growth. Harvard Business School Press, Boston (2003)
15. Christensen, C.M., Bower, J.L.: Customer power, strategic investment, and the failure of leading firms. Strat. Manag. J. **17**(3), 197–218 (1996)

16. Christensen, C.M., Overdorf, M.: Meeting the challenge of disruptive change. Harv. Bus. Rev. **78**(1), 67–76 (2000)
17. Nelson, R.R., Winter, S.: An Evolutionary Theory of Economic Change, vol. 32, no. 2. Social Science Electronic Publishing (1982)
18. Kim, W.C., Mauborgne, R.: Blue Ocean Strategy: How to Create Uncontested Market Space and Make The Competition Irrelevant. Harvard Business School Press, Boston (2005)
19. Kim, W.C.: Blue Ocean strategy: from theory to practice. Calif. Manag. Rev. **47**(3), 105–121 (2005)
20. Sun, J., Tan, R.: Methods for roadmapping mutational innovation based on technological evolution bifurcations. Comput. Integr. Manuf. Syst. **19**(2), 253–262 (2012)
21. Sun, J., Tan, R., Guo, J.: Research on IFR of technological evolution bifurcations. In: TRIZ Future Conference, Paris, France, pp. 377–390 (2013)
22. Sood, A., Tellis, G.J.: Technological evolution and radical innovation. J. Mark. **69**(3), 152–168 (2005)
23. Zlotin, B., Zusman, A.: The Concept of Resources in TRIZ: Past, Present and Future. Ideation International, Farmington Hills (2005)
24. Altshuller, G.: The Innovation Algorithm: TRIZ, Systematic Innovation and Technical Creativity. Technical Innovation Center, Worcester (1999)
25. Altshuller, G.: Creativity as an Exact Science: The Theory of the Solution of Inventive Problems. Gordon and Breach Science Publishers, New York (1984)

Research of the Possibilities for Using and Linking TRIZ Methods with Systems Engineering

Ovidiu Bielefeld[1(✉)], Vladimir Sizikov[2], and Nadine Schlüter[1]

[1] University of Wuppertal, Gaußstraße 20, 42119 Wuppertal, Germany
bielefeld@uni-wuppertal.de

[2] Robert Thomas Metall- und Elektrowerke GmbH & Co. KG, Hellerstraße 6, 57290 Neunkirchen, Germany

Abstract. Increasing complexity and global competition are forcing product development to develop faster products that are marketable and innovative. Thereby, key issues are increasing product functionality and user-friendliness. The significant engineering contradiction is: How can user-friendliness of the products be optimized for the customer without adversely affecting the functionality of the product? This requires a systematic consideration of the interactions between the customer and the product as well as the effects and interactions of the functions within a product. TRIZ provides a variety of methods to analyze and solve problems, incl. resolving of engineering contradictions. In addition, an interdisciplinary and transparent model can be created with Model-Based Systems Engineering (MBSE) to improve product understanding.

The scope of this research is to combine the potential of MBSE with TRIZ in order to generate an optimal approach regarding implementation and networking from TRIZ function models in to a MBSE overall model. Based on the MBSE overall model both usability and system functionality (especially harmful function) should be considered.

Keywords: TRIZ · Model-Based Systems Engineering (MBSE) · System model · Vacuum cleaner · Engineering contradiction · Function analysis · Function model

1 Introduction

In product development it is important not only to focus on its functionality or primary useful function(s) (PNF) according to TRIZ, but also to deal with the context of application and handling to improve the ergonomy and usability of products. Due to the technological development the complexity of products is increasing significantly. Usability is a topic of many scientific researches and practical efforts. Especially TRIZ has powerful tools for analysis and understanding of development problems. Also very complex problems can be handled with both classic and advanced TRIZ tools. A further alternative solution in product development is provided by the MBSE. Because only when the product is understood as a model, the complexity can be made tangible

Published by Springer Nature Switzerland AG 2019
R. Benmoussa et al. (Eds.): TFC 2019, IFIP AICT 572, pp. 174–186, 2019.
https://doi.org/10.1007/978-3-030-32497-1_15

and manageable [1]. Based on the principles of the MBSE, interactions and dependencies between different functions and components within a system can be displayed transparently. Furthermore, it is theoretically possible to model several (sub) models (e.g. function models) from TRIZ in an overall model or a super system that can serve as the basis for a common understanding within a multidisciplinary team. Consequently, MBSE is very suitable as a supplement for TRIZ. The goal of this research is to combine the potential of MBSE with TRIZ in order to generate an optimal approach regarding implementation and networking from TRIZ function models into a MBSE overall model. Based on the MBSE overall model both usability and system functionality (especially harmful functions) should be taking into account. In order to explain how the approach was developed, in Sect. 2 selected methods and tools of TRIZ will be presented. Section 3 gives a short introduction to MBSE. This is to better understand the approaches presented in Sect. 4 for the combinations of TRIZ and MBSE. The new approach is presented using the vacuum cleaner as an example. Finally, the results in the last section are discussed and an outlook on the further research work is given.

2 TRIZ Methods

2.1 Problem Analysis with Classical TRIZ

Classic TRIZ includes the methods for clarifying the task, determining the functions and abstraction of the problem as well as finding a solution with various tools [2].

Function modeling is used to analyze the functioning of a technical system. It defines a target component (from the Super System) that is served with the primary useful function of a technical system [3]. The problem analysis focuses only on this target component. In the problem analysis for consumer goods, the authors have discovered a special feature. A an engineering system addresses two target components from the Super System:

1. An item treated by the given system (main function of the system).
2. The human, who uses the given system (customer experience).

As a case study, the vacuum cleaner was taken. Formulation of the primary useful functions, which occur at the same time, is shown in Fig. 1.

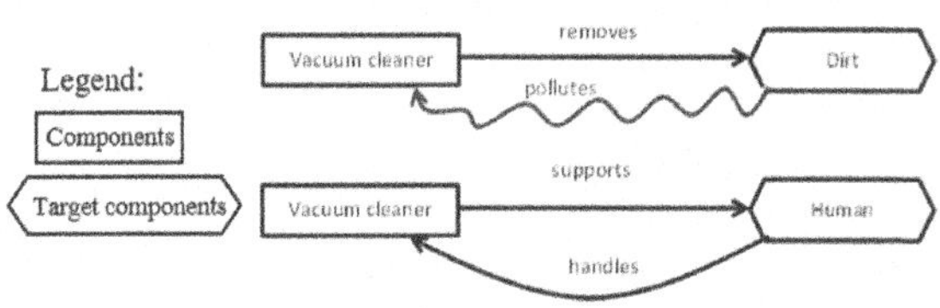

Fig. 1. Target components for vacuum cleaners as a technical system

In this illustration, the vacuum cleaner is mapped as a component with all subsystems. Details on the case study, including subsystem components as well as useful and harmful functions follow in Sect. 4.

In the interaction between vacuum cleaner and dirt, dirt exerts a harmful function on the vacuum cleaner. But the function "removes" is not affected. Harmful effects of the function "pollutes" appear in the other function model by the interaction between human and vacuum cleaner (preparation, vacuuming, and emptying/cleaning). Therefore, the dirt increases the operating effort. Though the vacuum cleaner supports the human in various ways. For example ergonomically (the person does not have to bend down), health-wise (no inhalation of dirt) and saves time (little effort). In the example shown, two function models are to be constructed, whereby some functions from one model influence the functions of the other model. Due to the fact that the use of the vacuum cleaner by humans displays a process with three phases, as described above, the TRIZ Function-Analysis for processes [4] is relevant for the case study.

The process steps are also called use case processes. Use case is defined as the description of an intended (or existing) use process that describes the user's handling of the system [5].

Also, in the process analysis for the case of the vacuum cleaner two target components are relevant: dirt and human. This results in two different processes:

1. The use case processes of dirt handling (remove from the ground, suck in, catch in the filter system, etc.)
2. The use case processes of handling the device by a human (add filter medium, assemble, operate and clean the device).

The following difficulties have come with the problem analysis by means of the described tools of the classical TRIZ:

1. Simultaneous addressing of two target components. These two target components appear in two different functional models. The problems of individual models are interlinked with other models.
2. A special challenge for the functional analysis is to identify the customer experience (soft and emotional factors).

The tools of the classic TRIZ were used in the project (case example vacuum cleaner). The core problems (engineering contradictions), however, could not be identified due to the problem complexity. Therefore, further research was done in order to analyse further development of the TRIZ methodology. The results of this analysis will be described in the next section.

2.2 Further Research for TRIZ-Based Problem Analysis

As described in Sect. 2.1, applications of the tools of the classical TRIZ in analyzing the problems with the focus in the field of customer experience encounter several difficulties. In science and practice through further development of the TRIZ methodology (so-called Advanced TRIZ), various tools have emerged for the analysis of complex questions. This section discusses their relevance. After the research and pre-selection, the authors considered the following tools from Advanced TRIZ:

1. OTSM-TRIZ (Russian acronym for General Theory of Powerful Thinking)
2. IDM (Inventive Design Method)
3. FA+ (Function Analysis Plus)
4. Cause Effect Chain Analysis (CECA)

As summarized by [6], OTSM consists of the following elements: problem technology, partial solution technology, contradiction technology, and problem flow technology. Based on these four elements, a network of problems is developed, which is used to describe the actual state. The graphical representation of problems and partial solutions help to identify the main engineering contradictions. The strength of OTSM is the simultaneous consideration of problems and solutions as well as building the causalities between individual elements in the network of problems.

IDM Methodology [7] has further deepened and automated the treatment of problem networks. The problem analysis with IDM creates a problem graph. Through structured syntax and algorithmic evaluation of existing relationships, it is possible to automatically extract the contradictions from the problem graph. The methodology also takes up a search for solutions. Thus, the tracing of the contradictions eliminated by a solution is possible. Also, change from a problem graph is representative (transition of a model of problem into the model of solution).

FA+ is another method in consideration of existing research. In the work of Lee [8], the TRIZ function modeling is combined with the Inventive Standards and Cause-Effect Chain Analysis. The objective here was the synthesis of a practical and systematic method for simplifying the search for solutions. FA+ uses classic functional modeling with the help of innovative standards to detect causalities and temporal relation between individual components and functions. The advantage of this method is a combination of problem models (functional analysis) and solution models (innovative standards) in one presentation.

Cause Effect Chain Analysis (CECA) is another TRIZ-tool for problem analysis. It would be also possible to visualize the dirt handling and the process of device handling with the help of CECA. But CECA treats only disadvantages or negative effects of the system as nodes [3]. So modelling with CECA would bring the same disadvantages as a function model. Furthermore CECA deals with negative effects of useful functions only. That's why the authors didn't use CECA in the project.

The four described approaches from Advanced TRIZ have the following features compared to classic tools:

1. A higher degree of abstraction in problem formulation.
2. Consideration of possible solutions already in the problem description.
3. Systematic detection of contradictions (or standard solutions).
4. A visualization that allows detection of one or more critical problems. At the same time, the problems are also prioritized.

This state of research has given important directions for problem analysis in customer experience. These are, among other things, consideration of all problems of the technical system in one model, search for algorithms and automated problem analysis, and quick integration of the solution search in a model. Nevertheless, based on the findings from classical and advanced TRIZ in relation to the scope of this paper following issues still remain unanswered:

1. How interact two or more target components from two or more function models (problem model) with each other? In the case of customer experience, this is at least one target component of the technical function (e.g., dirt, see Sect. 2.1) and the human being, as a user of a technical system.
2. How use case processes can be taken into consideration in a same model? This means that the relationships between components and functions happen in various use case processes (e.g. one of the use case process of the vacuum cleaner is "dirt suction").
3. How contradictions between compontens, useful function and harmful function in a same model with technical parameters (e.g., filter effect) can be taken into consideration in a same model?

Those issues could be solved by a new approach based on TRIZ and MBSE. Using MBSE a overall model can be created in order to map two or more target components from two or more function models. Moreover, use case processes could also be considered in the same model. And also contradictions between compontens, useful functions and harmful functions could be shown. To meet these goals, MBSE has been examined to detect its potential (Sect. 3). Finally, a new approach based on TRIZ and MBSE has been developed and tested using a case study (Sect. 4).

3 Systems Engineering, Model-Based Systems Engineering and Demand Compliant Design

To master the complexity of products it is helpful to understand the product as a system. This can be done on the basis of a holistic and transdisciplinary model according to the basic principles of MBSE [1]. In addition a system model forms the basis for a common understanding of system behavior within a multidisciplinary team [1, 9]. The model enables a systematic identification of the dependencies between different system elements (e.g., system component, target component, functions, etc.).

This systemic thinking from MBSE arose from Systems Engineering (SE), which already has been used in the aerospace industry in the 1950s [10]. SE is defined as "an interdisciplinary approach and should make the development of systems methodically possible. SE focuses on a holistic and collaborative understanding of stakeholder requirements, discovery of solution options and documentation of requirements as well as synthesizing, verifying, validating, and developing of solutions. The whole problem is considered from concept development to system development and the SE provides suitable methods, processes and best practices for this" [11]. As an interdisciplinary discipline, SE acts as a "link" between the different disciplines [12].

The model-based implementation of the SE is the MBSE. Through the MBSE, a system model can be created. There are different modeling languages and approaches in MBSE (e.g., SysML, Modelica or CONSENS), but for this work and due to the positive experiences several years of project work from the Demand Compliant Design (DeCoDe) approach is selected. DeCoDe is an approach for a standardized description to model technical systems under the principles of systematic thinking and acting [1]. Modeling with DeCoDe is matrix based i.e. data and information about the system is recorded in a structured way and systematically reproduced. To analyze the system it can be examined based on "classic views" of product development: Requirements, Components, Functions and Processes. These views are linking goal-oriented by using the DeCoDe Main matrix within the DeCoDe-Tool (see Fig. 2).

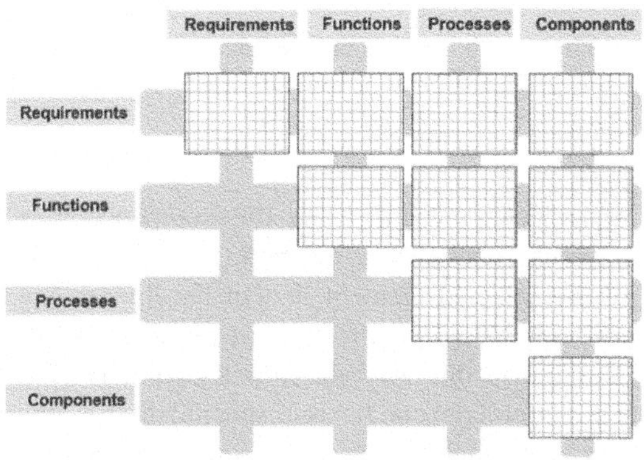

Fig. 2. The Main matrix of DeCoDe with its 4 views [in compliance with 14]

The complete linking of views makes a multidimensional view of the entire system possible. This is realized by the so-called Multi-Domain Matrix (MDM). Basically, in matrix-based modeling, there are three types of matrices:

- Domain Structure Matrix (DSM): describes the interlinking within a view (e.g., within the components-components matrix the components structure can be described).
- Domain Mapping Matrix (DMM): describes the interlinking between two views (e.g., the components-processes matrix describes the relationship between the components and processes).
- Multi-Domain Matrix (MDM): describes a multi-dimensional view of the entire system by mapping all views with their system elements and relations [13].

For the implementation of the DeCoDe approach, the complexity management software Loomeo® is used. The software not only enables the presentation of the DeCoDe data, but also the graphical visualization of the DeCoDe element types and their relations (see Fig. 3). By focusing on an element and its relations, individual cause-and-effect relationships can be discussed as part of workshops in the interdisciplinary development team through various other elements related to the focused element, as Fig. 3 shows.

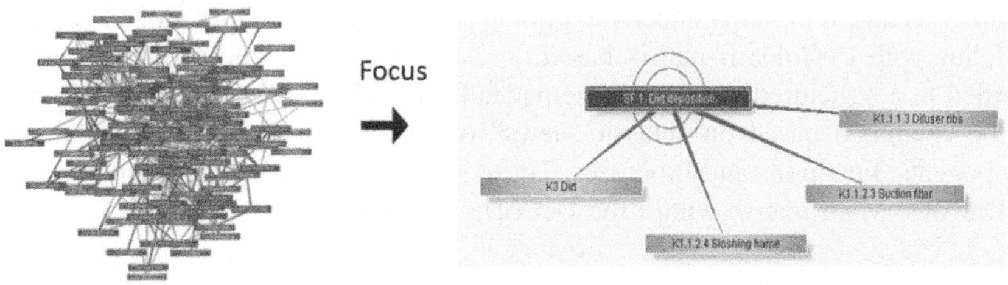

Fig. 3. Exemplary visualization of the identification of cause-and-effect relationships for individual elements through focusing by using Loomeo® function "Environment's Fokus" [Principle diagram].

By selecting a system element and using the Loomeo® "Environment's Focus" feature can bee seen which elements are interacting with each other. For example, in case of the failure of the selected element, it will be obvious via the corresponding relations which components would be affected directly or indirectly. The relationships and dependencies identified in this way are stored separately with a unique ID. This information from the system model can be used specifically for different TRIZ methods from the phases of problem analysis processes and problem-solving processes. The knowledge transfer between MBSE and TRIZ methods is shown in the next section.

4 Investigation of Possibilities for Combinability Between TRIZ Methods and Systems Engineering

The goal of this study is to combine the potential of MBSE with TRIZ in order to generate an approach regarding implementation and networking from TRIZ function models into overall model based on MBSE.

The chapter is divided into three subchapters, which together represent the new approach for combination of TRIZ methods and MBSE (see Fig. 4). The first phase contains the classic functional model according to TRIZ. In this phase, according to TRIZ and to the methods presented in Sect. 2, the functional model is created. Building on the first phase, the functional model according to TRIZ is extended by using the tools and the procedure from MBSE, which were presented in Sect. 3. The third phase contains an analysis and a targeted search for problems and causalities in the context of the entire system model. By means of the focus function from Sect. 3 relationships and dependencies of functions and components will be identified. Finally, the findings from the analysis will be presented. The focus here is to show what concrete benefits the MBSE approach has for TRIZ. The approach will be explained in more detail with by showing the vacuum cleaner as application example.

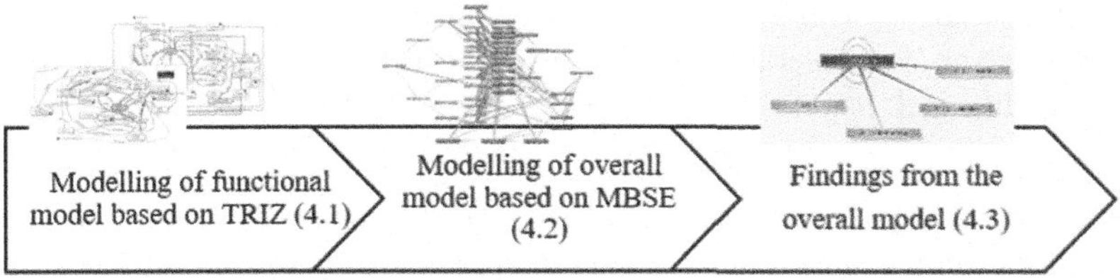

Fig. 4. Approach for the combinability between TRIZ methods and SE

4.1 Modelling of Functional Model Based on TRIZ

THOMAS vacuum cleaners have special filtration technologies. Aqua-Fresh-Air-Box uses water as a filtration medium. The advantages for target groups are the following:

(1) Humidification of dust and capture even fine particles inside the filtering unit. This function is very important for allergic sufferers.
(2) Water can also bind smell, odors and formaldehyde. It is an advantage for households with cats and dogs.

The technical function (filtering) does not have any problems. Far over 90% of all dirt particles are catched within the Aqua-FreshAir-Box. Due to the fact that the contaminated water cannot be kept for a long time, there is a need to wash out the dirt after using of the vacuum cleaner. By collecting the information from different sources (promoters, market research, online reviews) the project team identified the demand for improving of customer experience with the filtration unit. It refers to the handling of vacuum cleaner: preparation, vacuuming (collecting the dirt) and cleaning of the filtration unit (Fig. 5).

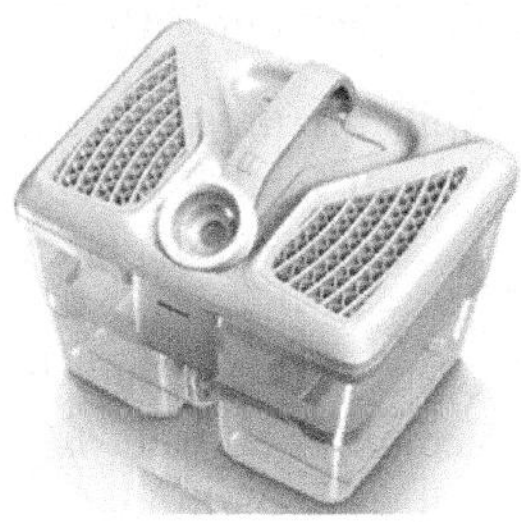

Fig. 5. Aqua-FreshAir-Box as a component form the vacuum cleaner system

As described in the Sect. 2.1, there are two targets components for the given engineering system: dirt (technical function – filtering) and human (usability, handling, etc.). Follow-ing steps were done with TRIZ, addressing the problem of customer experience:

(1) innovation checklist,
(2) function analysis with dirt as a target component,

(3) function analysis with human as a target component,
(4) flow analysis for materials: air, dirt (which can be differed from fine dust and coarse dirt, incl. hairs).

Both function models (see Fig. 6), which are created according to classic TRIZ, describing respectively filtering and handling, were complicated. There are 13 components of the engineering system, having multiple useful and harmful functions.

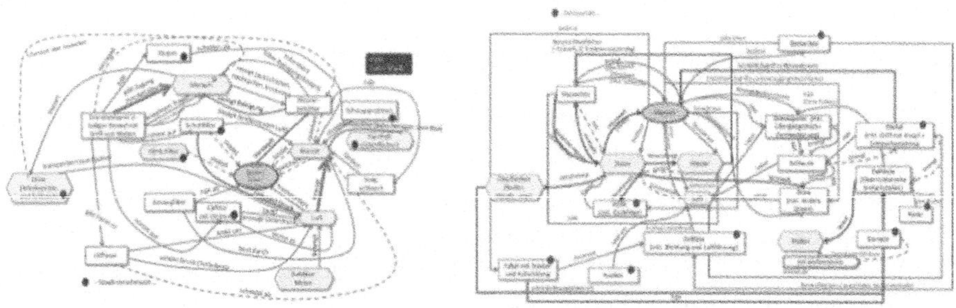

Fig. 6. Exemplary visualization of both functional models (left – dirt as a target component, right – human as a target component) [Principle diagram].

As mentioned in the Sect. 2.1, several useful and harmful functions from one model have influence at the another model. These models were shown as examples, an entire presentation would be too unclear. In addition, the data is confidential and cannot be published. Furthermore, these functions models serve as a basis for one overall model which is created with MBSE.

4.2 Modelling of Overall Model Based on MBSE

The extended modelling begins with the transfer of the function model (see Fig. 6) from Sect. 4.1 into the MBSE overall model. In addition to the functions and the components, the usage processes are also integrated into the system model. The meshing is template-based according to the principles and using the DeCoDe main matrix, which were presented in Sect. 3. The graph below outlines a schematic representation of the components hierarchy (as well as target components Human and Dirt), the useful functions (as well as a harmful function) and the three processes involving the components (see Fig. 7). Based on this graphical representation, the overall system or the Super System to be analyzed can be viewed in a structured manner. Furthermore, several functional models based on TRIZ can be transferred into this one overall model, so that just a single model is available for multiple problem analysis. The functions, whish are interlinked with the components, could be the same but also similar.

Based on the extended model, the next phase will analyze the problem according to the TRIZ principles.

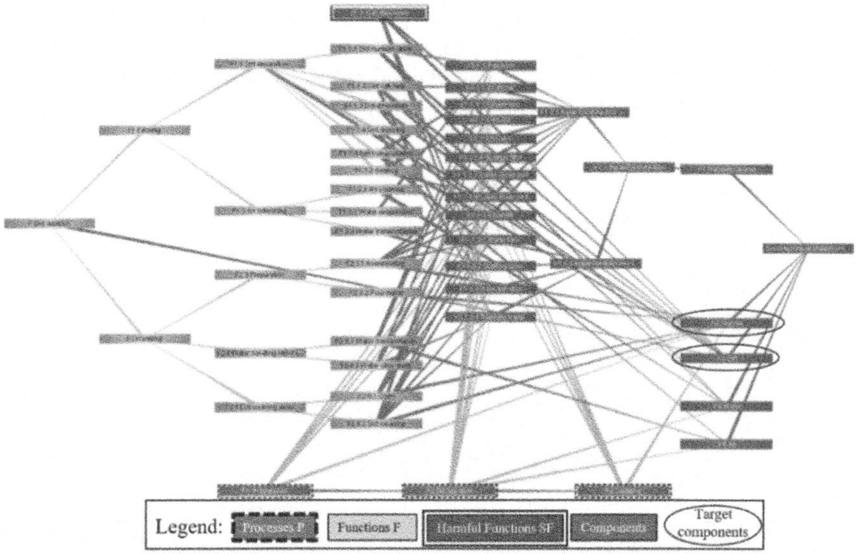

Fig. 7. Schematic representation of the extended model according to Systems Engineering with useful functions, harmful functions, components, target components and use case processes [Principle diagram].

4.3 Findings from the Overall Model

The analysis begins based on the TRIZ methodology, i.e. with the problem search or problem definition [3]. For this purpose, the overall model from Sect. 4.2 is used as well as the focus function for a specific search for possible problems and causalities within the Super System. First the focus function was used for the target component Human, then the focus will be put on the harmful function "Dirt deposition".

Using the focus function and spatial separation provide a quick way to identify the components that perform the harmful "Dirt deposition" function (see Fig. 8).

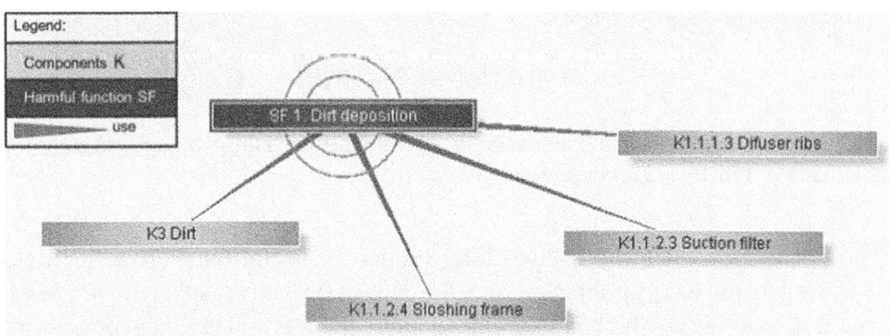

Fig. 8. Correlation between the harmful function of "Dust deposition" and the components that implement this function (e.g. Suction filter, Sloshing frame and Diffuser ribs)

Thus, it was thus possible to identify that the components Suction filter, Sloshing frame and Diffuser ribs and the target component "Dirt" are involved in this harmful function. At the same time, it was found that the components "Diffuser ribs" and "Sloshing frame" also realize the useful function of "Water slow down" (see Fig. 9).

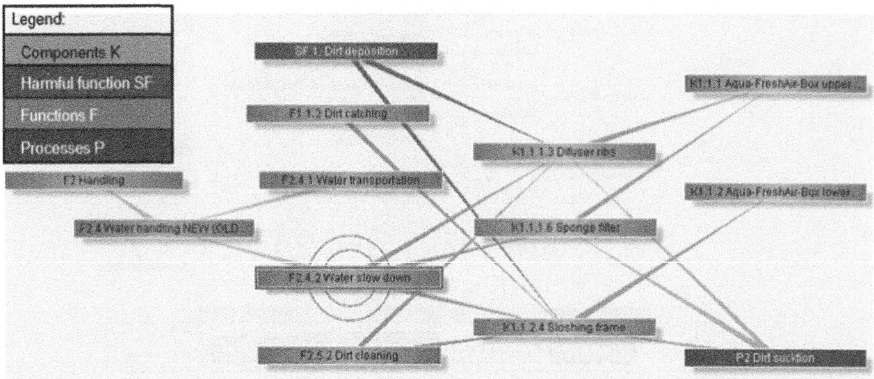

Fig. 9. The components Sloshing frame and the Diffuser ribs realize the useful function "Water slow down"

In this way, the engineering contradiction could be identified. Furthermore, it has been focused on the component "Suction filter" to find out which useful functions this component implements in the model (see Fig. 10).

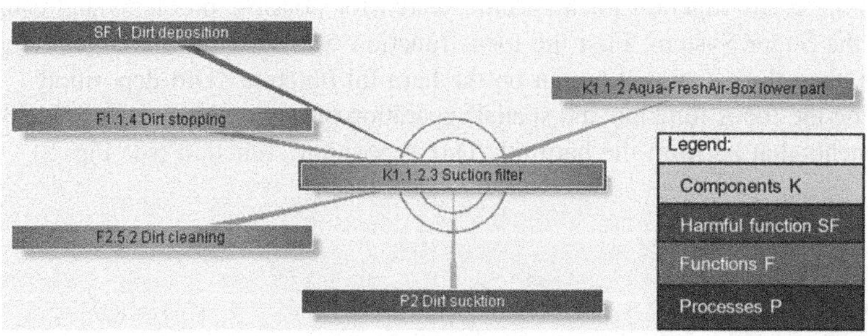

Fig. 10. The component Suction filter realize the useful function "Dirt stopping" and at the same time the harmful function "Dirt deposition"

The figure shows that the Suction filter fulfills the useful function of "Dirt stopping" as well as the harmful function of "Dirt deposition" simultaneously. In addition, the "Suction filter" is involved in the "Dirt suction" process and is a sub-component of the Aqua-Fresh-Air-Box (see Fig. 10). The involvement of the component "Suction filter" in one useful function and one harmful function forms this engineering contradiction in the model (parameter of suction filter is the size of the grid cell):

IF the suction filter has a big grid cell, THEN it does not deposit the dirt, BUT it does not stop the dirt. The inverse engineering contradiction is: IF the suction filter has a small grid cell, THEN it stops the dirt, BUT it deposits the dirt.

A physical contradiction here is: Grid cell must be big and small. Identification of engineering and physical contradiction with classical function modelling (Sect. 4.1) was not possible. The useful function "Dirt stopping" belongs to the model with dirt as a target component (filtering). While the harmful function "Dirt deposition" appears at the model with human as a target (usability). The identification of the two engineering contradictions provides a good basis for a well-founded problem definition and the continuation of the problem-solving process according to TRIZ. In the same way the model described in the Sect. 4.2 enabled identification of further engineering contradictions.

5 Conclusion and Outlook

The goal of this research paper was to combine the potential of MBSE with TRIZ in order to generate an optimal approach regarding implementation and linking from TRIZ function models in to a MBSE overall model. Furthermore, the overall model to detect the impact between usability (use case processes) and the system functionality (especially harmful function).

It can be shown that tools from MBSE are useful for the TRIZ analysis methods in order to transparently depict relationships, dependencies, and causalities (see Sect. 4.3). Using MBSE a overall model was created. The model allows an efficient and quick search for problems (TRIZ problem-solving process) and formulation of both engineering and physical contradictions. In addition, several target components and functions are mapped in a transparent model. Also the hierarchic structure of functions according to MBSE allows fast identification of components, having same or similar functions.

However, this research is at the beginning and many more investigations remain open. Further research is planned, such as the implementation of a quantitative evaluation by means of the software in the analysis, so the components and functions as well as their relations can be weighted. Furthermore, it is necessary to investigate whether a change in the procedure of the analysis, e.g. focus on the use case process (useability) and not on the harmful functions, leads to different results. These aspects could form an integral part of further research into the combinability between TRIZ and SE.

References

1. Winzer, P.: Generic Systems Engineering - Ein methodischer Ansatz zur Komplexitätsbewältigung. Springer, Heidelberg (2016). https://doi.org/10.1007/978-3-642-30365-4
2. VDI-Standard: VDI 4521 Blatt 1, VDI, Dusseldorf (2016)
3. VDI-Standard: VDI 4521 Blatt 2, VDI, Dusseldorf (2018)
4. MATRIZ Homepage. https://matriz.org/. Accessed 28 Mar 2019

5. Jacobson, I.: Object-oriented development in an industrial environment. In: Meyrowitz, N. (Hg.) OOPSLA 1987 Conference Proceedings. Object-Oriented Programming Systems, Languages and Applications, S. 183–191. ACM, New York (1987). SIGPLAN Notices Spec. Iss, 22, 12
6. Nagel, T.: Application of OTSM-TRIZ for definition of engineering process model and related deployment strategy. Papers Presented at the 14th International TRIZ Future Conference – Global Innovation Convention, Lausanne/CERN, 29–31 October 2014, pp. 57–60. ETRIA e. V., (2014)
7. Cavallucci, D., Fuhlhaber, S., Riwan, A.: Assisting decisions in Inventive Design of complex engineering systems. Procedia Eng. **131**, 975–983 (2015)
8. Lee, M.-G.: How to generate simple model solutions systematically from function analysis diagram. Selected Papers Presented at the 16th International TRIZ Future Conference, 24–27 October 2016, Wroclaw, Poland, pp. 42–47, ETRIA e. V., (2017)
9. Haberfellner, R., Fricke, E., de Weck, O., Vössner, S.: Systems Engineering - Grundlagen und Anwendungen Orell Füssli Verlag Zürich (2012)
10. Gausemeier, J., Dumitrescu, R., Steffen, D., Czaja, A., Wiederkehr, O., Tschirner, C.: Systems Engineering in der industriellen Praxis (Studie). wentker druck GmbH, Paderborn (2013)
11. INCOSE Systems Engineering Handbook – A Guide for Systems Life Cycle Processes and Activities. Wiley, Hoboken (2015)
12. Weilkiens, T.: Systems Engineering with SysML; Modeling, Analysis, Design. Morgan Kaufmann OMG Press/Elsevier, Amsterdam (2007)
13. Lindemann, M.M., Braun, T.: Structural Complexity Management. Springer, Heidelberg (2009). https://doi.org/10.1007/978-3-540-87889-6
14. Winzer, P., Sitte, J.: Demand compliant design. IEEE Trans. Syst. Man Cybern. Part A **41**, 434–448 (2011)

An Approach for Customer Requirements Acquisition Based on Time Iteration

Wen-Dan Yang[1,2(✉)], Guo-Zhong Cao[1,2], Jun-Lei Zhang[1,2], and Chuan He[1,2]

[1] Hebei University of Technology, Tianjin 300401, China
ellen0745@163.com
[2] National Engineering Research Center for Technological Innovation Method and Tool, Tianjin 300401, China

Abstract. Acquiring customer requirements (CRs) is important for enterprises to compete in marketplace since inexhaustible innovation chances could be discovered from CRs. However, it is insufficient to generate ideas for innovation solely depending on the market-pull CRs acquisition method or technology-driven CRs acquisition method. From the time dimension, these two traditional methods put different emphasis on CRs: the market-pull method focusing on digging CRs for design improvement from existing products while the technology-driven method pays more attention on CRs that future products need to satisfy sustainability in the market. This paper proposes a systematic approach for CRs acquisition on the basis that CRs at different time period have different impacts on innovation. The two traditional acquisition methods can be integrated based on time iteration. Firstly, CRs are divided into past customer requirements (PCRs), current customer requirements (CCRs) and future customer requirements (FCRs) in time dimension. Secondly, we believe that PCRs and their potential evolution information can be acquired by analysis of patents, CCRs can be identified by making use of tools in the market-pull CRs acquisition method, and FCRs can be predicted through evolutionary knowledge in TRIZ. Finally, a case study is provided to validate the feasibility of the approach.

Keywords: Customer requirements (CRs) acquisition · Time iteration · Market-pull CRs acquisition method · Technology-driven CRs acquisition method · Patent analysis · Evolutionary knowledge

1 Introduction

Defining and predicting customer requirements (CRs) is crucial in order to satisfy customer needs and ensure supplier success for the present and future [1]. But neither engineers in sales department nor engineers in R&D department have no systematic approach to comprehensively and accurately discover, identify and predict CRs throughout the whole time range, since sales department engineers always focus on

Published by Springer Nature Switzerland AG 2019
R. Benmoussa et al. (Eds.): TFC 2019, IFIP AICT 572, pp. 187–203, 2019.
https://doi.org/10.1007/978-3-030-32497-1_16

capturing the voice of their current and future customers [2] and R&D department engineers pay more attention on CRs that lied in existing products and future technologies [3].

The method of using customers as the research source for CRs acquisition is usually considered as the market-pull CRs acquisition method [3], and its research data include the customer satisfaction, user experience, and users' behavior in online data systems. Customer satisfaction analysis [4] can describe CRs qualitatively to sort CRs for importance as well as explain the ambiguity of them, but it cannot discover CRs since CRs are inputs of this type of analytical method. The user experience analysis [5] investigates the reliability, validity and sensitivity of standardized questionnaires, sample sizes and usability problems to improve the accuracy of market-pull CRs acquisition tools both from pre-acquisition and post-analysis. The analysis of users' behavior in online data system focuses on collecting CRs efficiently under extreme data condition [6]. Further, the importance of quick response to dynamic CRs has been considered, Chong et al. [7] suggested using neural network techniques to capture new CRs in the temporal space between the product conceptualization and market introduction. Although the market-pull method takes a glimpse of the dynamics and inducible property of CRs, it can only manage CRs that currently active. What's more, past states of CRs are missed leading to a lack of objectivity and continuity of needs, and unexpected needs which would made the product a top shot in the market have not been considered as well.

The method of using products as the research source for CRs acquisition is usually considered as the technology-driven CRs acquisition method [3], and its research data concentrate on products and patents. Cao et al. [8] demonstrated that CRs can be obtained through the patent technical information analysis. He also presented the innovation direction of a product in different development cycles based on laws of needs evolution after sorting CRs of several mature products [9]. Zhang et al. [10] proposed a CRs acquisition process model which integrates laws of needs evolution with laws of the technology evolution in TRIZ to predict future CRs qualitatively from both macro and micro levels. However, the technology-driven method does not have continuous communication with customers in the CRs analysis model, resulting in a decrease in the accuracy of the results. Ding [3] discussed that the integration of market-pull and technology-driven model would be a main way to determine CRs. More precisely, he proposed using market-pull methods to interact with customers before the detail design whereas the proposed approach highlights roughness and did not reveal the intrinsic mechanism of the combination of those two traditional methods.

In this article, a systematic CRs acquisition method is proposed based on time iterations to acquire past customer requirements (PCRs), identify current customer requirements (CCRs) and predict future customer requirements (FCRs). Comparison of tools in the market-pull CRs acquisition method and technology-driven CRs acquisition method in time dimension is discussed in Sect. 2 along with the intrinsic mechanism of combining those two methods is stated. The approach for the CRs acquisition based on time iteration is illustrated in Sect. 3 followed by introducing seven steps of this approach. Hand installation pincers for operating the spring band hose clamps is selected as an example to implement CRs reacquisition in Sect. 4, followed by the conclusions in Sect. 5.

2 Two Traditional Acquisition Methods in Time Dimension

Kano divided CRs into basic requirements, regulate requirements, attractive requirements, indifferent requirements and reverse requirements [11]. But it cannot help to inspire as one partake in a creative action, although this classification method can differentiate CRs as it is more of an analytical tool. For different characteristics of CRs in different time dimension, we firstly make the following classification: CRs that have been realized in the past of the product, CRs that customers currently request for design, and CRs that future products need to satisfy in the market. They are briefly referred as past customer requirements (PCRs), current customer requirements (CCRs), and future customer requirements (FCRs). Therefore, tools of the market-pull method and technology-driven method are analyzed according to the performance of obtaining these three types of CRs.

Market-pull methods take customers as research subjects. Customers' current problems and feedback from the products on hand are the main research data [12]. Therefore, this type of methods can capture CCRs well. Moreover, as the potential (unexpressed) needs of customers are continuously tapped, the ambiguity of CCRs will continue to weaken, and research results will become more comprehensive and accurate. However, CRs that have been well achieved and performed in past and existing products are often easily be overlooked by customers during communication, which means the depth and width of PCRs are inferior to those of the CCRs. Although, the scope of research data sources of PCRs can expand to some extent with the help of users' online behavior analysis, PCRs obtained from the market-pull method remains limited. For FCRs which can help facilitate innovation, the market-pull method is short of inducible research data, and can only rely on the expert system to provide guidance, so it is difficult to carry out more in-depth investigation.

Technology-driven methods take products as research subjects. Function is the nature of survival of a product, thus CRs can be acquired through the function analysis of existing products [3]. More precisely, the hierarchical function model and TRIZ substance-field model, two of the most common used tools for the function analysis, can help sort out relationships between PCRs and identify FCRs caused by non-standard functions. Petrov [9] suggested that CRs can be implemented through known and new functions, presented five laws of needs evolution to predict FCRs. Patent library collects all solutions of every development cycle of a product, therefore analysis of patents ratio analysis of products can obtain a wider range of PCRs [8]. In particular, the development of the patent map technology can not only effectively deal with the information displayed by documents of one patent, but also take groups of patents as a system to explore its potential information. LESE (Laws of Engineering System Evolution) developed by analysis of patents is one of the contributions that engineers have proved useful to generate a requirements list [13]. However, technology-driven method suffer a poor performance in acquiring CCRs compared to market-pull method. First, the documents of a patent is publicized until 18 months from its filing date. Therefore, new patents, also can be identified as new CRs, generated during this temporal space cannot be included in their analysis model. Secondly, the continuous communications with customers are missing in technology-driven method, its understanding of CCRs lacks credibility.

In summary, the suggested tools in market-pull methods and technology-driven methods are scored according to the performance in acquiring PCRs, identifying CCRs and predicting FCRs (they are called functions in this paragraph). We used a five-tiered scale to define a measurement logic. The value does not have a specific meaning, what is important is the gap between the values. Firstly, identify the tools that perform best for each function, giving a maximum of 5 points. For example, the 'analysis of patent technical information and patent mapping technology' scored 5 points for acquiring PCRs, the 'laws of engineering system evolution' scored 5 points for identifying CCRs and the 'mining potential needs of customers' scored 5 points for predicting FCRs. Secondly, compared the other 7 tools with the best performing tool for each function, a five-level division of performance for the same function is obtained. At last, compared the degree to which the three functions are implemented by the same tool to revise the scores. For visualization, the scores are plotted in a radar chart. Axes on the right correspond to four tools in market-pull methods, and axes on the left correspond to four tools in market-pull methods. The radius indicates a performance score in Fig. 1. The smaller the radius, the lower the score.

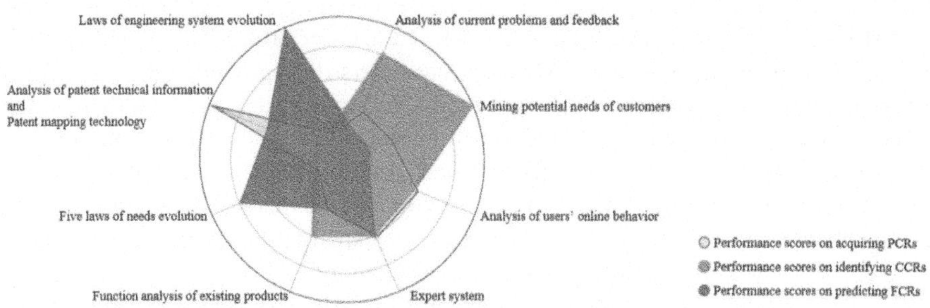

Fig. 1. The performance scores on the radar chart.

There are trade-offs for acquiring CRs both in the market-pull method and technology-driven method. More precisely, analysis of patent technical information and patent mapping technology performs the best in all tools in acquiring PCRs. Mining potential needs of customers does the best in identifying CCRs. Laws of engineering system evolution dose the best in predicting FCRs. Therefore, if a combined approach is formed to exploit the positive characteristics of all the tools, the comprehensiveness and accuracy of research results will be increased to lead successful designs.

3 Customer Requirements Acquisition Based on Time Iteration

All CRs as follow-up product design's inputs can be divided into past customer requirements (PCRs), current customer requirements (CCRs) and future customer requirements (FCRs) through a time frame. Depending on different roles they play, we split PCRs into no longer exiting (or unneeded) ones and everlasting (until now) ones. We define that CCRs are made up of everlasting ones and new generated ones, and FCRs are the ones predicted by evolution knowledge for future products. Hence, CRs are divided into four parts as shown in Fig. 2: ① PCRs that have ceased to exist; ② CCRs that evolved from PCRs until now; ③ CCRs that newly generated; ④ and FCRs predicted by evolutionary knowledge. The collection of CCRs and FCRs, shown on the Fig. 2 as ②③④, constitutes CRs as follow-up product design's inputs. The detail approach for identifying each type of CRs are discussed as follow.

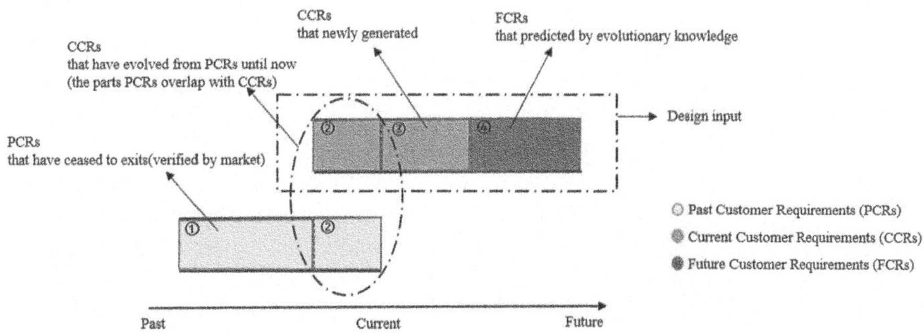

Fig. 2. A Classification of customer requirements in the time dimension.

3.1 Acquisition of Past Customer Requirements

As one of the best tools to obtain PCRs, analysis of patent technical information and patent mapping technology can not only acquire PCRs but also extending evolutionary patterns of PCRs.

Leagans defined needs as the gap between the present situation or status quo and a new or changed set of conditions assumed to be more desirable, so the gap between effect of a patent and its technical background at that time can be seen as PCRs. After rough reading patent's 'abstract' and 'summary', sentences describe the effect of it can be extracted, and by comparing 'background of the invention' with the way it achieves its effect, the gap between the status quo and the desirable status can be determined.

Especially, PCRs are described with standard technical expressions, such as '[Direction of improvement], [Object of control], [Parameter]', or '[Direction of improvement], [Parameter]'. On one hand, patent maps, such as an effect matrix, should be constructed under constraints of elements of specific expressions to analyze potential evolution patterns of PCRs. On the other hand, specific expressions will be exploited as inputs of interview's questionnaires or field investigation's preparation files to prevent customers from expressing CRs in casual.

Mastering PCRs can help engineers fully conversant with products and understand origins of CCRs more accurately. PCRs may become more and more important for product design over time, or may no longer exist due to the development of technology and policies. However, the current states of CRs must be determined through communicating with customers. Therefore, the next step will be focusing on customer data.

3.2 Identification of Current Customer Requirements

To identify CCRs means to find no longer existed PCRs, and PCRs that have evolved into CCRs, and whether there are new CRs generated or not. In this paper, customer interviews and field investigations are promoted simultaneously. Before carrying out interviews, it is necessary to define the purpose of the research first.

First, needs of different customers for a same product may vary distinctly. Therefore, differentiating different customers or groups of customers can help better hold opportunities to make decisions made by stakeholders scientifically and commercially [12]. Secondly, customer's behavior in purchasing products is actually 'hire' products to do specific 'jobs' [14]. Therefore, by abstracting higher levels of 'jobs', we can formulate assumptions about CCRs more open to bring more opportunities. Third, CCRs are generated due to constantly appealing for the product design improvement, which is determined by product problems built by customers. All in all, [Type of Customer], [Job], and [Question] constitute CCRs.

The identification of CCRs can be developed as follows. Firstly, product's workflows or functions are extracted from previously acquired PCRs, then they are abstracted as assumptions of [Job] of CCRs. Secondly, an expert team is built for listing all the [Type of customer] (here, pay more attention to the unique attributes of the customers, such as job scenarios, behavioral habits, etc.). [Question] customers may encounter through doing a specific [Job]. Thirdly, [Type of customer], [Job], and [Question] are arranged to build several hypotheses: '[Type of Customer] encountered [Question] when executing [Job]'. Finally, customer interviews and field investigations are conducted to validate and eliminate these hypotheses, as well as to reconstruct other new hypotheses until no new elements are discovered and no hypothesis is denied. By verifying the CCRs expressed in a hypothetical form, the objective can be achieved during identifying CCRs [12].

To make products a top shot in the market, stakeholders often want their products satisfy FCRs. However, FCRs cannot be expressed by customers. On the contrary, it depends on the designer's keen sense of market trends or through the technology-driven power.

3.3 Prediction of Future Customer Requirements

Predicting FCRs in the market-pull method is usually based on experts' subjective experience. In 1986, Hippel suggested lead users' present requirements will become general in a marketplace in the future and gave detailed implementation for utilizing lead users in marketing research [15]. However, this method is only clear to those with technical expertise [16]. Since there is no stable basis for neither trend identification nor lead user identification. In fact, to improve the accuracy of predictions, predicting FCRs depends on objective criteria. In addition, the TRIZ-based prediction results based on the objective LESE can provide a high accuracy.

The prediction of FCRs based on LESE can be developed as follows. Firstly, patents are selected and read for solutions to problems of a product, and determine the technological evolution level of the product through analyzing the patterns of the time-varying solutions in the patents. Secondly, the technological evolution law is determined for its application. Thirdly, one or several technological evolution routes are selected using this law to predict future states of the product. Finally, the development cycle of the product is identified followed by acquiring the effective future evolutionary states of it, which are FCRs, using several innovative strategies suitable for this stage of the product, such as applicable laws of development of needs.

The pre-verification of the problem identified before improving the accuracy of the predictive process's inputs, and the post-confirmation of innovative strategy can improve the convergence of the predictive process's outputs.

3.4 Workflow of Customer Requirements Acquisition Based on Time Iteration

A complete workflow of the proposed approach is shown in Fig. 3, which consists of 7 steps as follows.

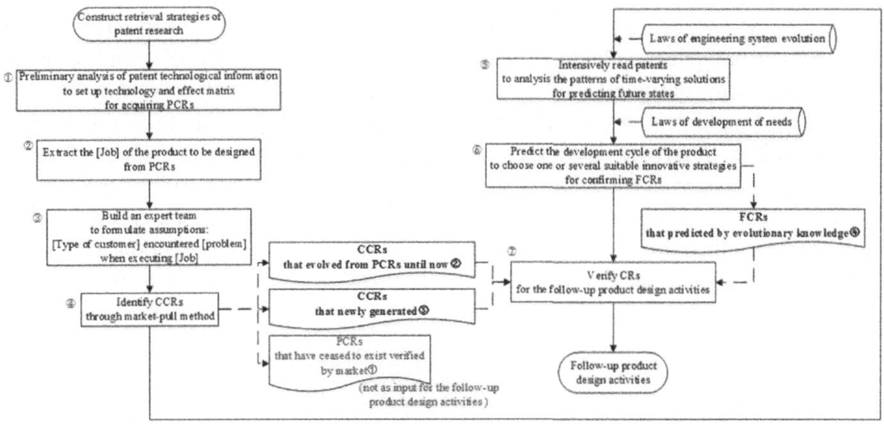

Fig. 3. Workflow of CRs acquisition based on time iteration.

Step 1: Construct retrieval strategies of the patent research by information of products such as business background and working principle followed by a preliminary analysis of the patent technological information to set up the technology and effect matrix for acquiring PCRs.

Step 2: Extract the [Job] of the product to be designed from PCRs.

Step 3: Build an expert team to formulate assumptions: [Type of customer] encountered [problem] when executing [Job].

Step 4: Identify CCRs through customer interviews, field investigations and other tools in market-pull methods. After customer requirements are obtained, so they divided as CCRs that evolved from PCRs until now, CCRs that newly generated, and PCRs that are no longer existed.

Step 5: Intensively read patents to analysis patterns of time-varying solutions for predicting future states of the product.

Step 6: Predict the development cycle of the product to choose one or several suitable innovative strategies for confirming FCRs to be implemented.

Step 7: Verify customer requirement inputs to carry out subsequent design activities.

4 Case Study

The spring band hose clamp, stamped from 65Mn spring steel, is a preferred connection standard part for connecting rubber hoses in cooling system vehicle power system, i.e. engine, power battery, etc.). The pincers are used to press the clamp's ears of the outer ring to make the inner ring larger enough to wrap a hose. At present, the most commonly used tools for operating the spring band hose clamps are hand installation pincers, as shown in Fig. 4. To liberate the workforce, the handle transmission part of such a hand tool is designed with a force-increasing mechanism, like a spring shown in Fig. 4(b), or a locking mechanism, like a lock hook shown in Fig. 4 (c), as well as lengthen the force arms and shorten the resistance arms (Fig. 4(c)). Moreover, to prevent the clamp from ejecting and accidentally injuring the operator, the jaw is usually designed with a card slot (Fig. 4(b)). Nevertheless, they are still laborious and inefficient in mass production, and it is still impossible to avoid personal injury caused by improper operations or negligence of the operator.

Improved designs of such a product are based on CRs of 'labor-saving' and 'safety' acquired under the guidance of two traditional CRs acquisition methods, it is difficult to trigger radical innovations of such a dedicated tool. The following section reanalyzed the CRs of such a product using the approach proposed in this paper to facilitate the acquisition process.

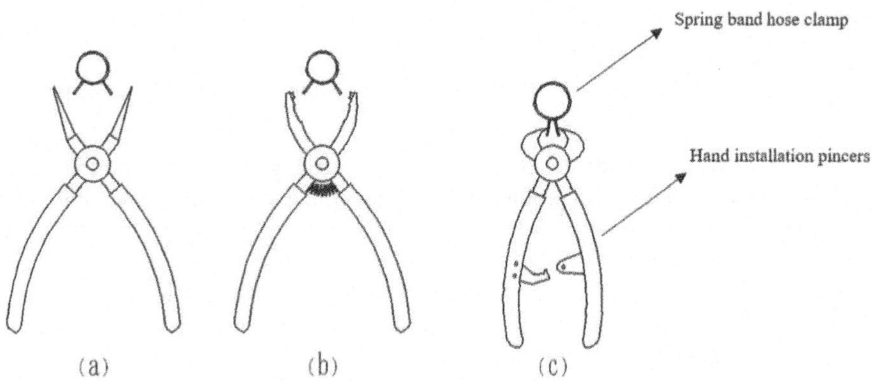

Fig. 4. Three typical designs of hand installation pincers.

Step 1: Through a Patent Search and Analysis Platform (https://www.zhihuiya.com/), we download all the patents related to design for operating spring band hose clamps. Then we analyze those patents' technical information first and a patent efficacy analysis table is established, as shown in Table 1. 'Effect' extracted from a patent is the PCRs it discloses. All PCRs acquired from patents are listed in Table 2. In this case, we describe [Object of control] as super-system, working unit, energy converter, energy source, control unit, and action objects. When devoted to other products, the perspective and decomposition degree of these parts should be determined according to the specific situation.

From the information in Table 1, we establish a metric about distribution of patents at different times and different effects (Fig. 5) and another metric about distribution of patents at different times and different system compositions (Fig. 6) for analyzing the trends of PCRs. The larger the diameter of the pie, the greater the number of patents filing for that year. As we can see from Fig. 5, 'Labor-saving' and 'Safety' were the principal PCRs of pincers since 2011. 'Suit for small working space' was fascinated until 2014 and it was gradually ignored and replaced by 'Work-efficiency' and 'Multi-functionality' in 2015. New PCRs like 'Anti-error' and 'Automation' were emerged in 2015. According to Fig. 6, the working unit, the energy converter and energy source are governing systems for designer to improve of pincers catering to the PCRs. In 2017, the application of source of the action objects reached a new height, it is nevertheless that the design and improvement ratio of the control unit, the action objects and the super-system is smaller compared with other three items.

Table 1. List of patents and efficacy analysis results.

No.	Pub. no.	Filing date	Effect	Direction of improvement	Object to control	Parameter
1	CN202045610U	2011-01-26	Labor-saving	Enlarge	Energy source	Working force
			Safety	Eliminate	Clamp	Movement
			Work efficiency	Reduce	Working unit	Working time
2	CN205184158U	2015-09-30	Labor-saving	Enlarge	Energy source	Working force
			Safety	Enlarge	Working unit	Pre-force
			Multi-functionality	Improve	Working unit	Dimensional flexibility
			Anti-damage	Increase	Number of functions of control unit	
			Mistake-proof	Increase	Number of functions of working unit	
3	CN206578769U	2017-02-09	Safety	Increase	Working unit	Force area
			Labor-saving	Increase	Number of energy source	
4	CN108312556A	2017-12-25	Work efficiency	Change	Principal function of the product	
			Automation	Increase	Number of auxiliary function	
5	…	…	…	…	…	…

Table 2. PCRs extracting from effects of patents.

No.	Past customer requirements (PCRs)
1	Labor-saving
2	Safety
3	Work efficiency
4	Multi-functionality
5	Anti-damage
6	Suit for small working place
7	Anti-error
8	Automation

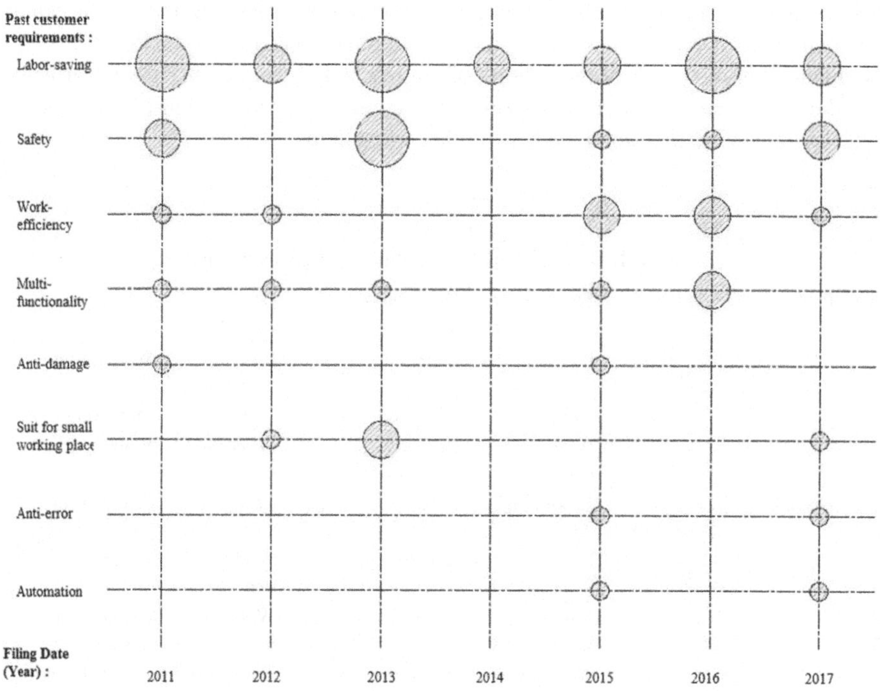

Fig. 5. Distribution of patents at different times and different effects.

Step 2: The 'jobs' of designs for operating spring band hose clamps can be extracted from PCRs: "put pressure on ears of clamp in prior", "positioning joint", "positioning hose", "positioning clamp", "operate clamps in high-volume", "clamp multiple types of clamps" and so on.

Step 3: Engineers, craftsmen, sales personnel, etc. are grouped to formulate the assumptions of [Type of customer] and [Problem], respectively. Consequently, assumptions of [Type of customer] include [Workers in pre-assembly line], [Workers in assembly line], [maintenance personnel], etc.; Assumptions of [Problem] include

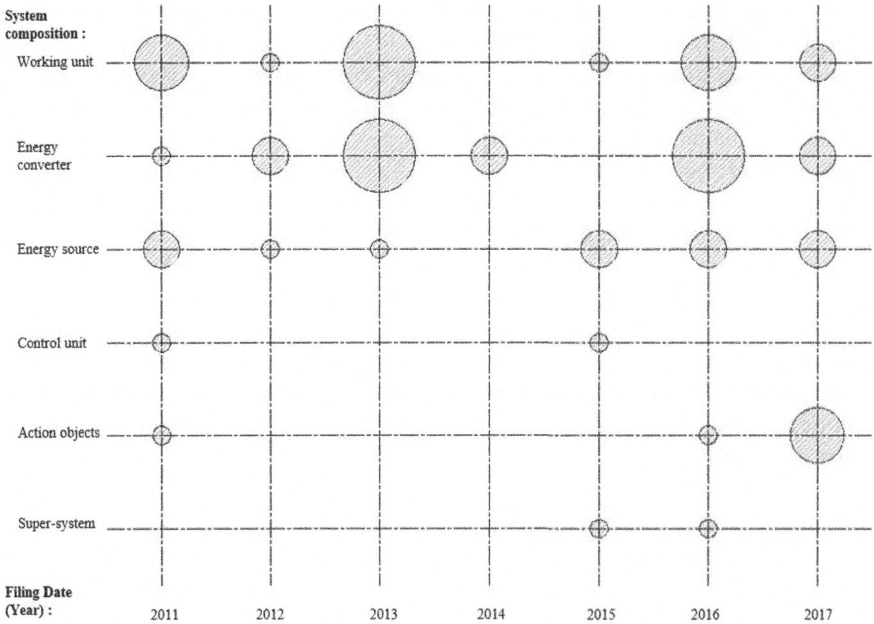

Fig. 6. Distribution of patents at different times and different system compositions.

[Clamp repeatedly lead to intensity of labor], [Too much courses lead to low efficiency], etc.

Step 4: Proposal of a questionnaire for customer interviews and field investigations. Eventually, we determine [Type of customer] as 'Workers in pre-assembly line' and verify their problems as 'Clamp repeatedly lead to labor intensity', 'Too much process lead to low efficiency' and 'Poor consistency of clamping position', which are classified into two groups as CCRs that evolved from PCRs until now and CCRs that newly generated. The results are shown in Table 3.

Table 3. CCRs of designs for operating spring band hose clamps.

Type of customer	Job	Problem	Source
Workers in pre-assembly line	Put pressure on ears of clamp in prior	Clamp repeatedly lead to labor intensity	CCRs that evolved from PCRs until now
	Positioning joint	Too much process lead to low efficiency	
	Positioning hose		
	Positioning clamp		
	Operate clamps in high-volume	Poor consistency of clamping position	CCRs that newly generated

Step 5: Read intensively the patents that focus on solving the problem of 'Clamp repeatedly lead to labor intensity'. Figure 7 illustrates the change in objects that improved versus time: The cumulative number of patents for implementing working unit improvements before 2013 has been higher than for other unit of the product; In 2015, the cumulative number of patents for energy converter system improvements has surpassed other units; While at the same time, although the cumulative number of patents for implementing energy source and control unit has increased continuously, they are not significant enough to catch up with. It can be inferred that dealing with this customer requirement, the technical evolutionary route roughly conforms to the 'the law of system completeness'. Specifically, we obtain two future evolutionary states of the product from 'the law of increasing information saturation of a system': 'Introduce a more efficient energy source' and 'Increase energy supply control for energy source'.

Similarly, read intensively the patents that focusing on solving the problem of "Too much process lead to low efficiency", more future states can be obtained. The results are listed in Table 4.

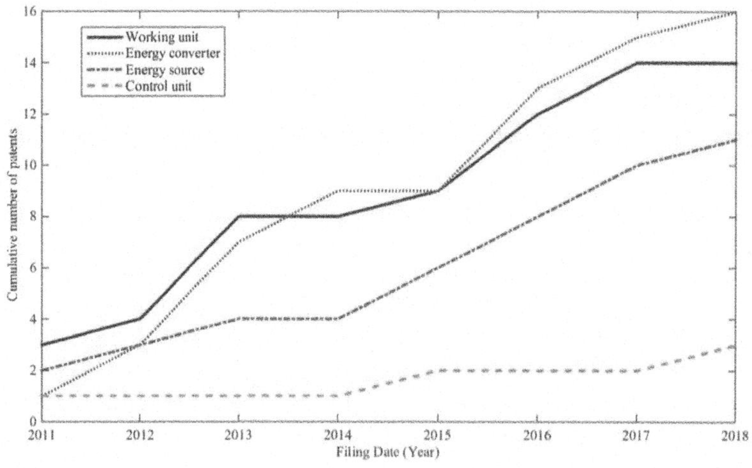

Fig. 7. Change in objects that improved to solve 'Clamp repeatedly lead to labor intensity' versus time.

Sep 6: Calculate the technical growth rate (the ratio of invention patent applications or authorizations in a certain technical field to the total number of invention patent applications or authorizations in the technical field in the past 5 years [17]) to predict the development cycle of designs for operating spring band hose clamps. As we can see from Table 5, the technical growth rate was increasing from 11.1% in 2015 to 27.8% in 2016 to 28.6% in 2017, as well as the interpolation curve of cumulative number of patents granted by years (Fig. 8), which devotes to predict the maturity of a product, we predict that the development cycle of products for operating spring band hose clamps has gradually moved from Infancy to Growth.

Table 4. Future states predicting from evolutionary knowledge.

Problem	Law of technical system	Technological evolutionary route	Future state
Clamp repeatedly lead to labor intensity	The law of system completeness	Increasing information saturation of a system	Introduce a more efficient energy source
			Increase energy supply control for energy source
Too much courses lead to low efficiency	The law of increase of the degree of ideality	Increase of a number of delivered functions	Incorporate the previous or subsequent courses into the principal function
			Adding more craft processes' requirements to the principal functions, such as cleaning the pipeline, sealing the pipe, etc.
		Elimination of undesired effects	Connect hoses without clamp
		Reduction of cost	Use expensive materials in necessary zones only
	Irregular evolution of system parts	Irregular evolution of system parts	Improve degree of idealization of the previous or subsequent courses

In the Growth stage, a large number of new functions, enhancement of performance and brand effects should be the main innovative directions [8], reflected in the laws of development of needs is the following three: First, integration. The pre-operation and post-process are summed up and intensified. Second, specialization, i.e., specific products should be targeted to specific people. Third, coordination. Coordination could be dynamic, in particular, it can be also understood as intensification of the maximum difference between CRs.

The above-mentioned future evolutionary states were matched with the laws of development of needs, and according to the results in Table 6, 'Connect hoses without clamp' and 'Use expensive materials in necessary zones only' should be deleted.

Step 7: Organize CCRs that are evolved from PCRs until now, CCRs that are newly generated and FCRs that are predicted by evolutionary knowledge as effective CRs for follow-up product design activities, as shown in Table 7.

Table 5. CCRs of designs for operating spring band hose clamps.

Filing date (Year)	2011	2012	2013	2014	2015	2016	2017
Filing number of patents	5	3	6	2	2	5	6
Technical growth rate	\	\	\	\	11.1%	27.8%	28.6%
Cumulative number of patents	5	8	14	16	18	23	29

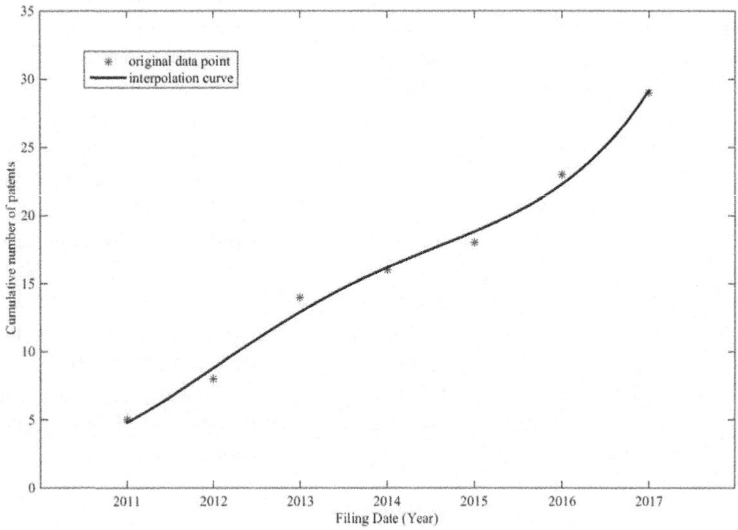

Fig. 8. Cumulative number of patents for operating spring band hose clamps granted through years.

Table 6. CCRs of designs for operating spring band hose clamps.

Future state	Corresponding laws of development of needs
Introduce a more efficient energy source.	Coordination
Increase energy supply control for energy source.	Dynamization
Incorporate the previous or subsequent courses into the principal function.	Idealization, Integration
Adding more craft processes' requirements to the principal functions, such as cleaning the pipeline, sealing the pipe, etc.	Idealization, Specialization
~~Connect hoses without clamp.~~	~~Idealization~~
~~Use expensive materials in necessary zones only.~~	~~Idealization~~
Improve degree of idealization of the previous or subsequent courses.	Integration, Specialization, Corodination

Table 7. Customer requirements (CRs) of schemes for operating spring band hose clamps.

No.	Customer requirements (CRs)	Source
1	Solve the problem of "Clamp repeatedly lead to labor intensity"	CCRs that evolved from PCRs until now
2	Solve the problem of "Too much process lead to low efficiency"	
3	Solve the problem of "Poor consistency of clamping position"	CCRs that newly generated
4	Introduce a more efficient energy source	FCRs that predicted by evolutionary knowledge
5	Increase energy supply control for energy source	
6	Incorporate the previous or subsequent courses into the principal function	
7	Add more craft processes' requirements to the principal functions, such as cleaning the pipeline, sealing the pipe, etc.	
8	Improve degree of idealization of the previous or subsequent courses	

5 Conclusions

The approach proposed in this paper integrated the market-pull CRs acquisition method with technology-driven CRs acquisition method based on time iteration for providing useful indications to support follow-up product design activities. More precisely, we listed a total amount of eight tools that split into the market-pull and technology-driven methods representing different performance of acquiring PCRs, identifying CCRs and predicting FCRs.

As a result, we observed that the market-pull method performs better than the technology-driven method in identifying CCRs, while the latter exceeds the former both in acquiring PCRs and in predicting FCRs. We highlighted that the gap between patents' effect and technical background is PCRs; Patent maps are built based on the PCRs display for the potential evolutionary information of PCRs; Expression elements took the PCRs heritage exploited as inputs of interview's questionnaires, or field investigation's preparation files would prevent customers from expressing CRs in casual to improve the consistency between statements of CRs and representations of engineering designs. Objective laws of the engineering system evolution have good maneuverability for FCRs prediction. Moreover, the statement of the integration of two traditional CRs acquisition methods is a more comprehensive. The accurate way to capturing CRs is observed and confirmed.

With the rapid development of economic environment, companies are no longer satisfied with incremental innovations. They need to generate radical innovations. This proposed approach is especially suitable for conducting radical innovations. Since incremental innovation features improvements in existing requirements, while radical innovation emphasizes new markets, new users, new technology and long-term development platforms. Due to the uncertainty of radical innovation and a passive role of users, companies will face severe challenges when they participate in the radical innovation process based on customers. Because users might not be able to or not want to contribute to indiscernible ideas. Thus, we might prefer to use technology-based innovation processes and design-based innovation processes.

It should be noted that the prediction of FCRs in this paper only took into account the chain-type evolutionary routes. In fact, CRs may be developed in a tree-shaped evolutionary patterns. It is necessary to provide a more comprehensive description to apply the proposed approach in the future.

Acknowledgement. This paper was sponsored by the National Science and Technology Basic Project of China (Grant No. 2017IM040100), Support Scheme for 100 Outstanding Innovative talents in Colleges and Universities in Hebei Province (SLRC2017030).

References

1. Agulyansky, A., Talalaevkski, A., Roggel, A.: TRIZ Usage for Customer Needs Identification Part1. https://triz-journal.com/innovation-methods/innovation-triz-theory-inventive-problem-solving/triz-usage-customer-needs-identification-part-1/. Accessed 16 Apr 2019
2. Mann, D.L.: Capturing the voice of the customer before the customer knows what they want: TRIZ, spiral dynamics, and the fourth turning. Procedia Eng. **9**, 573–581 (2011). https://doi.org/10.1016/j.proeng.2011.03.143
3. Ding, J.W., Yang, D.T., Bao, Z.Q.: Research on capturing of customer requirements based on innovation theory. In: 2012 Conference on Applied Physics and Industrial Engineering, pp. 1868–1880. Elsevier (2012). https://doi.org/10.1016/j.phpro.2012.02.275
4. Violante, M.G., Vezzetti, E.: Kano qualitative vs quantitative approaches: an assessment framework for products attributes analysis. Comput. Ind. **86**, 15–25 (2017). https://doi.org/10.1016/j.compind.2016.12.007
5. Sauro, J., Lowis, J.R.: Quantifying the User Experience: Practical Statistics for User Research, 2nd edn. Elsevier, Waltham (2012)
6. Qia, J.Y.: Mining customer requirements from online reviews: a product improvement perspective. Inf. Manag. **53**(8), 951–963 (2016). https://doi.org/10.1016/j.im.2016.06.002
7. Chong, Y.T., Chen, C.H.: Management and forecast of dynamic customer needs: an artificial immune and neural system approach. Adv. Eng. Informatics **24**, 96–106 (2010). https://doi.org/10.1016/j.aei.2009.06.003
8. Cao, G.Z., Tan, R.H.: The Principle and Application of Function Design, 1st edn. Higher Education Press, Beijing (2016). (in Chinese)
9. Petrov, V.: Laws of development of needs. https://triz-journal.com/laws-development-needs/
10. Zhang, J.H., Li, Y., Zhang, P., Zhang, W.M.: Customer needs acquisition by integrating needs evolution with technology evolution. J. Mach. Des. **34**(7), 15–22 (2017). https://doi.org/10.13841/j.cnki.jxsj.2017.07.003. (in Chinese)
11. Walden, D.: A special issue on: Kano's methods for understanding customer-defined quality. Cent. Qual. Manag. J. **2**(4), 1–37 (1993)
12. Lowdermilk, T., Rich, J.: The Customer-Driven Playbook: Converting Customer Feedback into Successful Products, 1st edn. O'Reilly Media, Sebastopol (2017)
13. Fiorineschi, L., Frillici, F.S., Rotini, F.: Enhancing functional decomposition and morphology with TRIZ: literature review. Comput. Ind. **35**, 1–15 (2018). https://doi.org/10.1016/j.compind.2017.09.004

14. Christensen, C.M., Raynor, M.E.: Innovator's Solution: Creating and Sustaining Successful Growth, 1st edn. Harvard Business School Press, Boston (2003)
15. Hippel, E.V.: Leader users: a source of novel product concepts. Manag. Sci. **32**(7), 791–805 (1986). https://doi.org/10.1287/mnsc.32.7.791
16. Ross, R., Rouen K., Austin-Breneman J.: Extending lead user theory to participatory co-design: a case study in a base of the pyramid context. In: Proceedings of the ASME 2018 International Design Engineering Technical Conferences and Computers and Information in Engineering Conference, ASME, vol. 7. American Society of Mechanical Engineers, New York (2018). https://doi.org/10.1115/detc2018-86009
17. Chen, Y., Huang, Y.Y., Fang, J.G.: Patent Information Collection and Analysis, 2nd edn. Tsinghua University Press, Beijing (2006). (in Chinese)

Method of Identification of Useful Functions in the Scope of Technical System Development

Marek Mysior[1(✉)], Witold Hnat[2], and Sebastian Koziołek[1]

[1] Department of Machine Design and Research, Wroclaw University of Science and Technology, Łukasiewicza 7/9, 50-371 Wroclaw, Poland
marek.mysior@pwr.edu.pl

[2] Mine Master Sp. z o.o., Wilków ul. Dworcowa 27, 59-500 Złotoryja, Poland

Abstract. Proper understanding of customers' needs is of great importance in developing strategy for a technical system development. Current description of those needs is based on customers' opinions and experience. This description rarely resembles parameters of the system-to-be-developed that are changing in time. The aim of this study was to develop a method for useful function identification that will take into account evolution of not only a technical system, but also customers' needs. This approach consists of problem identification in the context of an expected outcome in order to identify customers' needs in the form of evaluation parameters. Those parameters are further analyzed to define required functions of the system-to-be-developed by means of functional analysis. During the study, such TRIZ tools like Function Analysis and System Operator were implemented to model useful functions and context of development of technical system. Innovation Assessment methodology was applied to assess obtained results of the study. Application of proposed method of identification of useful functions during technical system development makes it possible to create product development strategies that take into account evolving needs of customers at early design stages. This allows reduction of R&D costs and resources usage in the design process.

Keywords: TRIZ · Function analysis · Inventive engineering · Useful function

1 Introduction

Nowadays, design of inventions is not an easy task. According to TRIZ [1–4], ideality of technical system is never declining throughout its evolution, what translates into necessity of new functions being implemented to the system with simultaneous reduction in harms and costs. On top of that, needs of customers evolve in time, creating new perspectives for technical system development. People get used to solutions that are available on the market, which makes products outdated. As shown in [5], to maintain stable level of innovativeness of the products and/or processes, it is necessary to maintain a specific share between attributes of attractiveness, linear quality and must be within the system. This is especially difficult if one take into account evolving needs of customers, which makes this share change. This creates an urgent need to take into account migration of attributes, so that the system designed will

Published by Springer Nature Switzerland AG 2019
R. Benmoussa et al. (Eds.): TFC 2019, IFIP AICT 572, pp. 204–215, 2019.
https://doi.org/10.1007/978-3-030-32497-1_17

maintain its high, stable level of innovativeness in response to those changes. To do this, it is necessary to have knowledge on which functions of a technical system will be attractive to customers in the future, which will be linearly related to customers' satisfaction and which will represent basic requirements. One solution to that may be the use of technology forecasting and roadmapping methods [6–12] to determine priorities in research and to specify what the system to be forecasted will look like in the future, but even if applied, technology roadmapping often do not result in positive innovation performance outcomes [8, 13, 14]. This knowledge, even if obtained and used with success, gives only an overview of both expected technical system traits and customers' needs, but there is very limited concern in assessment of innovativeness of systems-to-be-designed with respect to those evolving needs. There are several methods on how to measure innovativeness of products that were summarized in [5], but there is lack of method that would take into account evolution of needs and changes in useful functions. This paper proposes novel approach in design systems to-be in the future taking into account evolving needs of customers. As a base for this work, Innovation Assessment Method shown in [15, 16] was chosen and extended for the scope of defined task.

2 Materials and Methods

The proposed method of identification of useful functions in the scope of technical system development is based on forecasting future needs and taking them into consideration at the stage of parameters selection for innovation assessment. In this work, step-by-step approach was described how to determine useful functions of a technical system, how to identify their evolution and how to take them into account during innovation assessment method. In the later part of this work, proposed approach was shown on real life example of underground mining bolting machine used in Copper Mines in Poland. Proposed method consists of 3 steps as described on Fig. 1. For each step, set of tools was proposed, based on [15, 17]. At first it is necessary to define and formulate a problem that is being dealt with. This problem formulation includes, but is not limited to functional modelling of the system that helps to fully understand the core of the problem from the point of view of useful and harmful functions. Having functions defined, the next step is to determine system parameters[1] describing those functions in a measurable way on a level of system, super-system and sub-system. Those parameters are required to determine key parameters[2] of the technical system, which are parameters that describe useful functions of the analyzed system and represent add-ed value to the customer. In TRIZ, those parameters are often referred to as MPV (Main Parameters of Value), which are parameters that create customer satisfaction and play important role in customer purchase decision [18]. There are other works in which authors identified MPVs of products to plan their development, which involved application of fuzzy logic [19] and S-curve analysis [20]. The approach

[1] System parameters- parameters describing functions of a technical system.

[2] Key parameters- system parameters that represent value for customers.

proposed by Malinin [19] makes it possible to identify development strategies based on MPVs in a systematic way. There is however very limited description on how to identify those parameters in a systematic way. Identification of MVPs proposed by Lok [18, 20] concentrates on qualitative market research methods to identify MPV, which do not form a scientific evidence and confidentiality in proper selection of those parameters.

In this paper, authors present a novel approach to identify useful functions and their key parameters in a systematic way through functional decomposition of a system. In the following chapters, each step of the proposed approach is described and application of this method is presented.

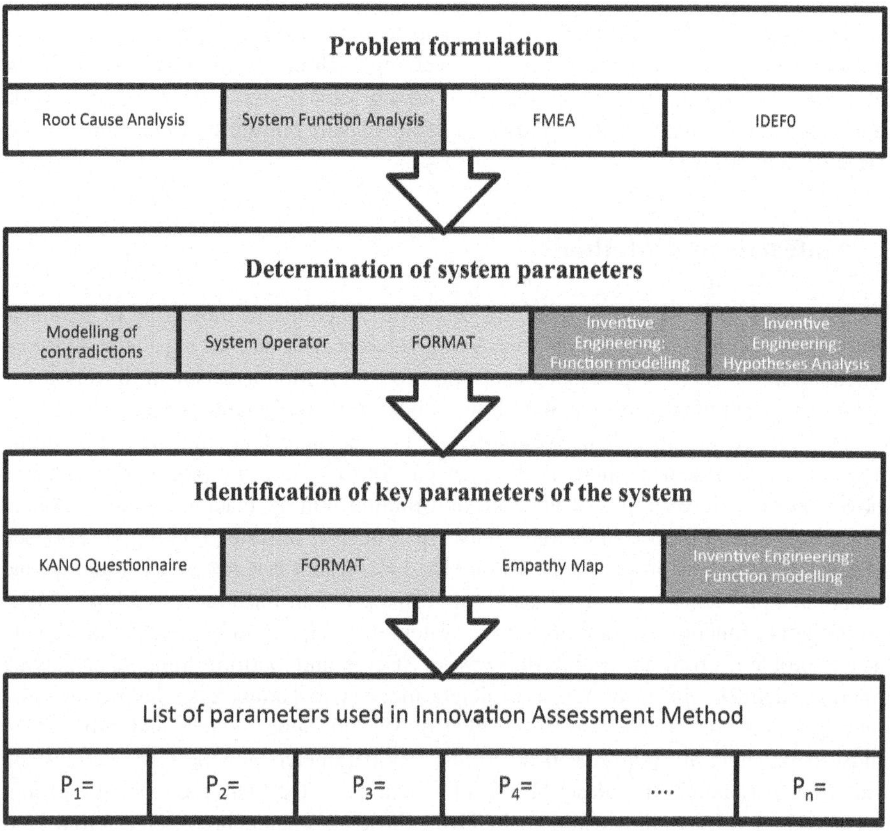

Fig. 1. Overview of the proposed method of identification of useful functions

The first step in a proposed approach is to formulate the problem that limits development of a specific product. According to TRIZ, technical systems evolve by elimination of contradictions and thus increase of their ideality [4]. This problem can be referred to as a main function being realized by a technical system. For example, technical system being dedicated to transport and storage of compressed biogas has a main outcome of <delivered biogas>, which is a result of a function <to transport> [21]. Determination of a main outcome of a given system and its main function can be determined using various tools like IDEF0, System Function Analysis or Root Cause Analysis.

Having main function defined, it is important to identify parameters describing effectiveness (performance) of the analyzed system. Those parameters describe its behavior in respect to all the actions that are being realized by the system as a result of interaction of system components with each other and with supersystem. For example, biogas transportation system can be described by such parameters as storage pressure [Pa] and volume [nm^3], methane content [%] etc. Those parameters can be obtained using several TRIZ tools, for example System Operator (9 boxes) or modelling of contradictions or tools described in Inventive Engineering, such as function modelling and hypotheses analysis [15].

Having those parameters described, it is necessary to identify those that contribute to customers' value. For this purpose, technology forecasting methods may be used in order to identify Main Parameters of Value (MPV) and choose them for further analysis in innovation assessment method. It is also possible to question customers on what is important for them (Kano Questionnaire) or use an Empathy Map to identify customers' needs. Those parameters are being referred to as key parameters and are subjected to innovation assessment in order to identify development strategy for a given technical system [5].

3 Results: Case Study

Results of application of proposed approach are shown on an example of underground roof bolting machines used in copper mines. Roof bolting process is a very dangerous process in which free walls and ceiling of the mine face is being bolted with adjacent layers of rock in order to minimize a risk of roof fall, which is one of the biggest threads in underground mining both in Poland [22] and worldwide [23]. This process consists of several steps which require both manual and automatic work of the machine, operated by operator. The aim of this case study was to design a roof bolting machine that will be innovative and will address customers' needs in the most appropriate way both in the short-term and long-term future. For this to be possible, it was necessary to define key parameters of roof bolting machines that are today and those that will be significant in the future.

3.1 Problem Formulation in Design of Bolting Machine

At first problem formulation step was performed in which the process of bolting was described using IDEF0 function modelling [24] to name useful functions of the system. This is shown on Figs. 2 and 3. This tool is very efficient in knowledge acquisition for every analyzed system or process. The main outcome of the bolting machine is bolted ceiling that protects operators and miners in harsh environment near the mine-face. This area is one of the most dangerous areas in the mine, that is why ceiling in those places has to be secured as soon as possible. This means, that efficiency of bolting is directly related to efficiency of the entire copper extraction process.

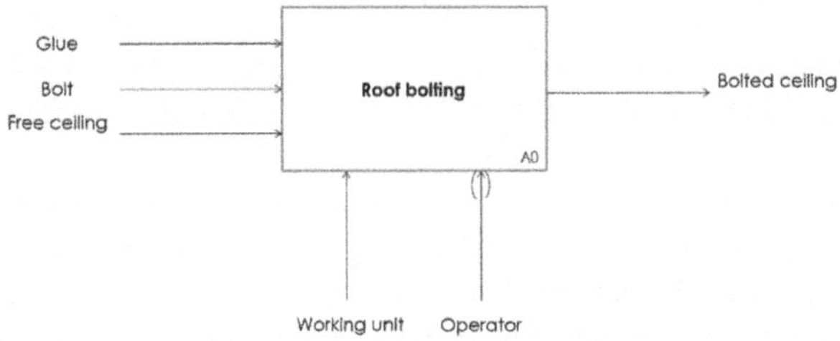

Fig. 2. IDEF0 of the roof bolting process, node A-0.

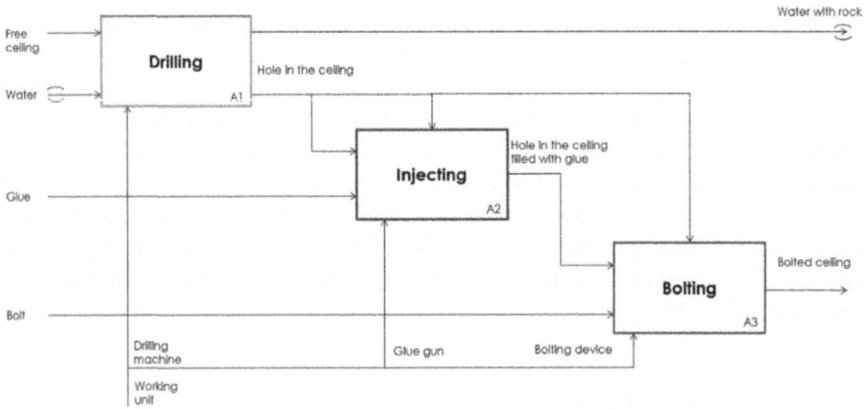

Fig. 3. IDEF0 of the roof bolting process, node A0.

Based on functions defined in IDEF0, it was possible to define useful functions of the system that were further used to evaluate measurable parameters of a roof bolting machine.

3.2 Determination of System Parameters

Having functions of the system identified it is important to define parameters describing those functions in quantitative way. This may be performed using many different tools, but in this case study, tabular method based on definition of functions, their requirements and methods on how to satisfy those requirements was used. This method was described on an example of thermal insulation materials in [16]. Results of this analysis are presented on Fig. 4.

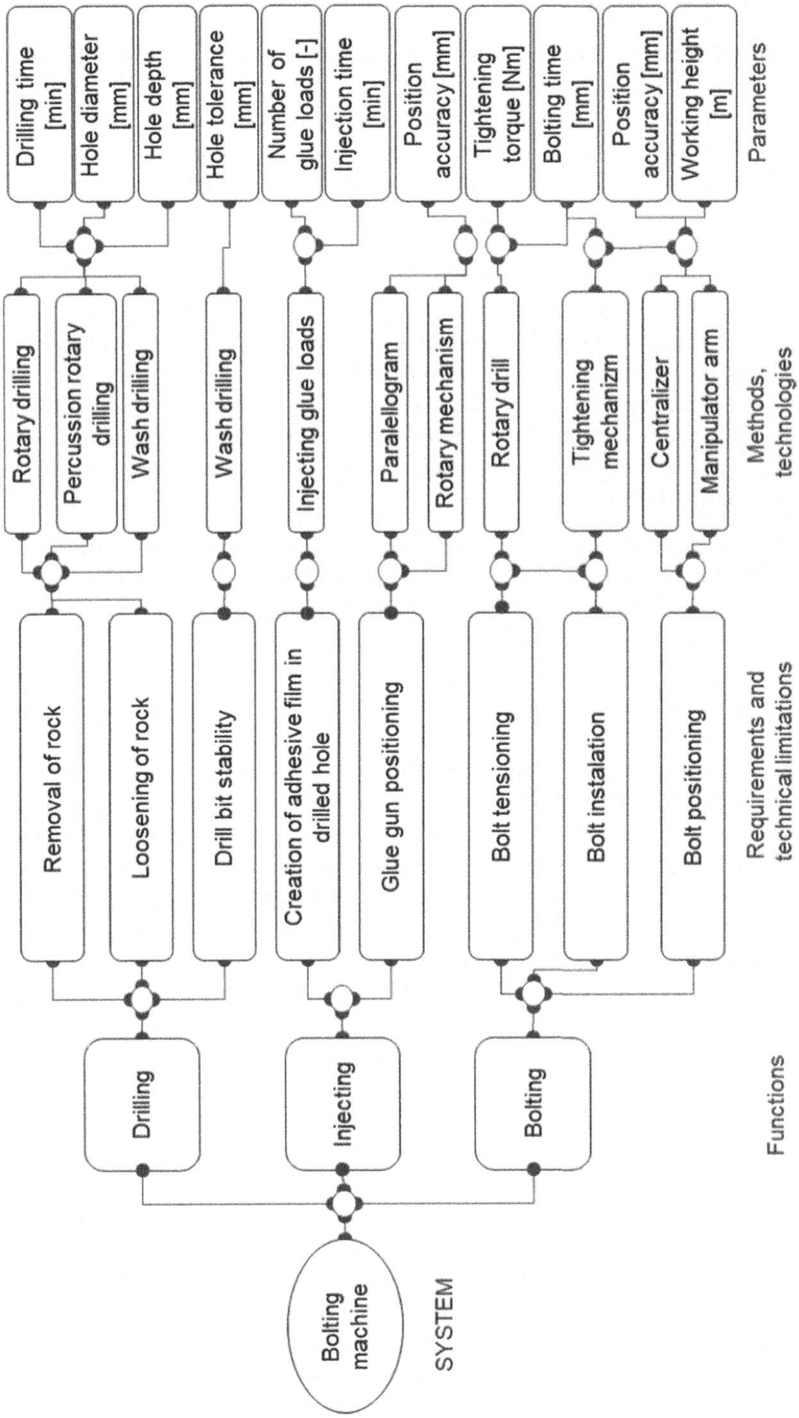

Fig. 4. Model of extraction of parameters from useful functions

As it was shown on Fig. 2, there are 3 main functions that can be identified within the process of roof bolting:

- drilling, in which hole in roof/wall is being prepared that is dedicated for mounting of bolts. Usually, drilling is realized by drill rod with cutting rods using various types of equipment, such as rotary drills, percussion drills and so forth. Some methods involve also drilling with water (wash drilling) to eliminate loosened rock from the hole as drilling progresses. Alternative method to this include Airmist and Air spraying;
- injecting. In this operation, glue is being delivered to the drilled hole that will serve as adhesive holding rocks together after bolting. There are several ways of injecting glue into the hole, but the main result is the same. There are also important considerations regarding positioning of glue gun in the axis of previously drilled hole, which is very important for the process to be effective;
- bolting. This is the process in which actual bolt is being screwed into the drilled hole, mixing injected glue and attaching to layers of rock in the roof or walls. There are several types of bolts used, but for the purpose of this work only expandable bolts were analyzed.

Each function above was described in terms of requirements, **which** are conditions that have to be satisfied in order to deliver desired outcome, methods on **how** to satisfy those conditions and parameters describing **how effective** those conditions are satisfied, which translates directly to effectiveness of the realized function.

Similar outcome may be achieved using other tools, such as Hypotheses Analysis that is part of Inventive Engineering [25], TRIZ Contradiction Modelling [17, 26] and many others.

Parameters described on Fig. 4 are related to the system being analyzed. For the analysis to be complete and to make it possible to identify key parameters of the roof bolting machines, it is necessary to determine even more parameters that are related to the customers needs. Because roof drilling machine being the scope of this work works in underground copper mine, as a **super-system, underground copper mine** was defined. **Sub-system** of the roof drilling machine **is defined as bolts, drills and other equipment used to make roof bolting operations**.

System Operator of roof bolting system in underground copper mine is presented on Fig. 5. Results presented on the Fig. 5 were obtained using technology forecasting method FORMAT and are presented in the form of a single picture showing evolution of a mine, bolting machines and bolting equipment.

From the point of view of a copper mine, the most important parameter that resembles customers' needs is extraction depth. Polish copper mines, in order to satisfy slightly decreasing extraction rate need to explore ores that are deeper underground [27]. This creates set of problems that have to be addressed in the nearest future. As it was shown in [28], exploration of deeper ores means reduction in ore height, what has a great impact on a roof drilling machines. The smaller the ore height, the lower machine should be to be effectively operated in future mine. The significance of the problem is additionally shown on Fig. 6 which shows share of ore extraction in biggest copper mines in Poland, for every which ore height is shown [28]. It can be observed, that there is a trend in increase rate of extraction of copper and silver ore from mines having

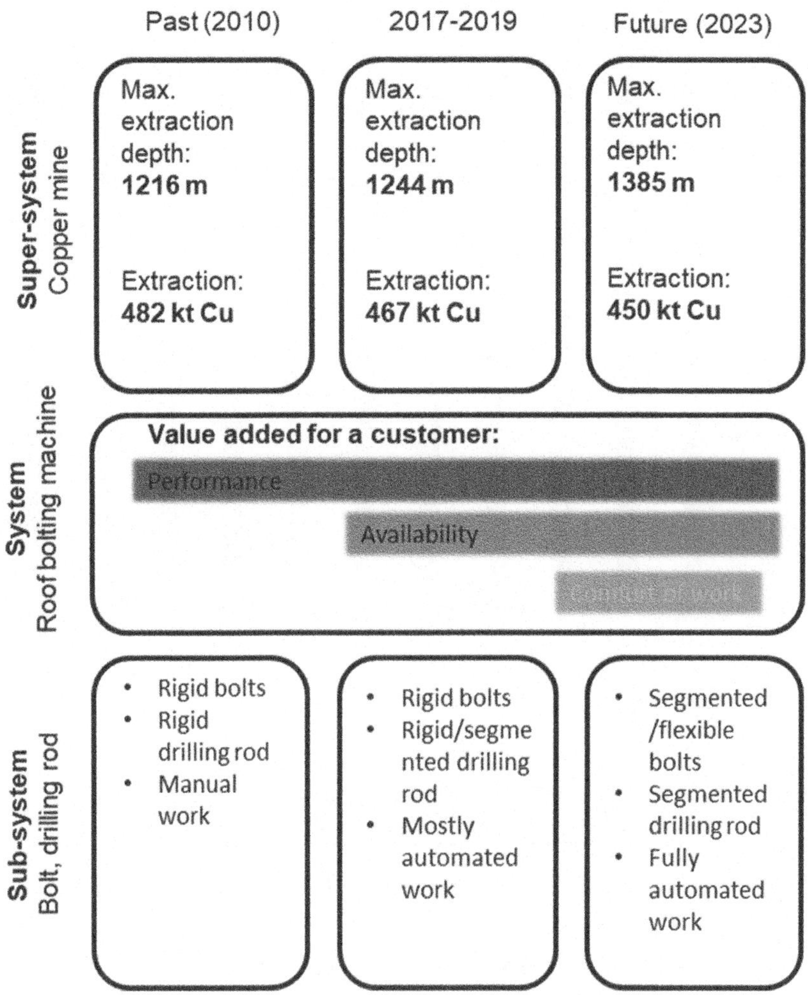

Fig. 5. System Operator of roof bolting system

low ore which means, that it is getting more and more important to design machines capable of working in smaller working height. What is also important, the higher the depth, the higher the temperature in the mine, making very harsh environment for the operator to work in. This makes it necessary to limit amount of time the operator spends outside of the machine.

Results of technology forecasting, combined with parameters describing technical system, it is possible to define key parameters of the roof bolting machine.

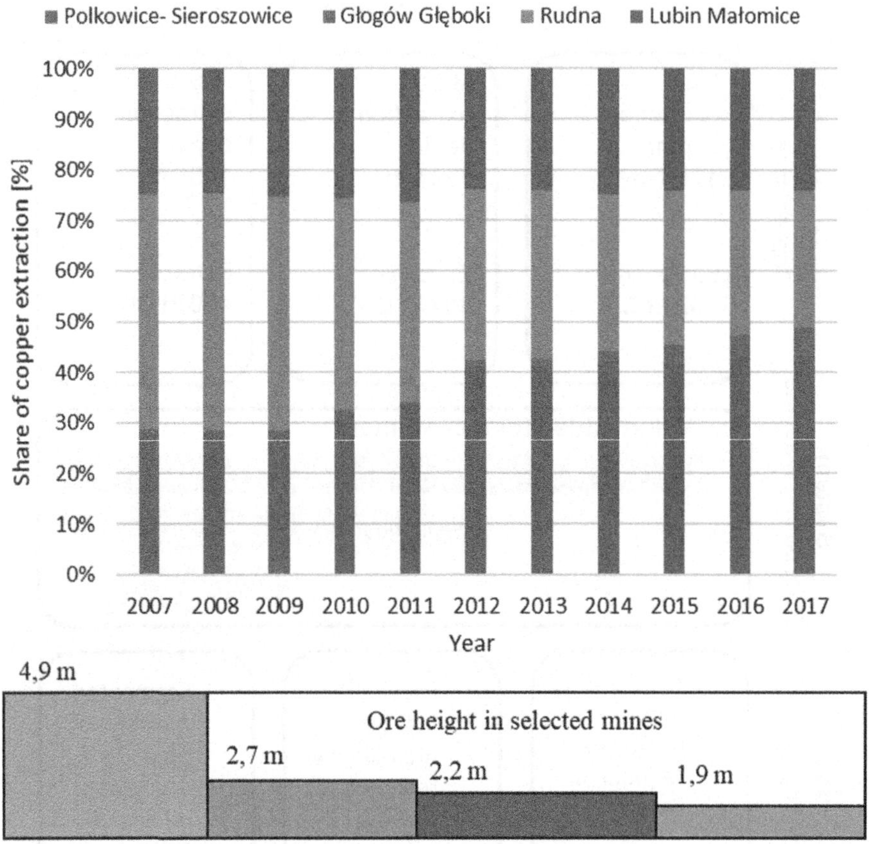

Fig. 6. Share of copper extraction in polish mines and average height of ore in those mines.

3.3 Identification of Key Parameters of the System

Key parameters of the system are being extracted based on results of technology forecasting method in the form of parameters describing super-system of a designed system. It was shown, that the most important parameters describing future mine are:

- SS1: depth of copper and silver ore extrusion [m],
- SS2: height of the copper and silver ore, determining height of the front of the mine [m],
- SS3: temperature in the mine [°C],
- SS4: Ore extraction [kt/year].

Those parameters are then verified, if they influence any of the parameters describing the technical system. Results are shown in Table 1 which shows matrix of influence of super-system parameters on system parameters. Those parameters of the system that are being influenced by super-system parameters are called key parameters and represent value added to customers and users of those machines.

Table 1. Influence of parameters of super-system on system parameters

	Drilling time [min]	Hole diameter [mm]	Hole depth [mm]	Hole tolerance [mm]	No. of glue loads [-]	**Injection time [m]**	Position acc. [mm]	Torque [Nm]	**Bolting time [min]**	Position acc. [mm]	**Working height [m]**
SS1											
SS2											X
SS3	X[a]					X			X[a]		
SS4	X					X			X		X
	Key parameter P_1					Key parameter P_2			Key parameter P_3		Key parameter P_4

[a]Temperature in mine influences drilling time only if work is being done manually by the operator. If an operator is separated from harsh environment, this is not important.

The table above summarizes, which parameters describing useful function of roof bolting machine are related to customers' satisfaction, thus being key parameters of the designed system.

4 Discussion

As a result of conducted case study and developed method, it was possible to determine key parameters that are responsible for customers' satisfaction in the future based on results of technology forecasting. Those parameters are summarized once again in Table 1. It was shown in the case study, that for development of roof bolting machines it is important to concentrate on aspects connected with working height of the machine, because future working environment will be getting lower. This is a direct result of necessity of extraction of copper ore from deeper levels in order to maintain nearly stable extraction rate. This in turn means, that environmental conditions will be getting more and more difficult for operators, which will require either minimizing of time spent outside of the machine by operator or introduction automated machines in which operator sits in air conditioned cabin, separated from harsh environment.

Key parameters at the super-system level	Key parameters at the system-level
SS1: Depth of ore extrusion [m], **SS2:** Height of the copper and silver ore, determining height of the front of the mine [m], **SS3:** Temperature in the mine [°C], **SS4:** Ore extraction [kt/year].	$\mathbf{P_1}$: Drilling time [min] $\mathbf{P_2}$: (Glue) injection time [min] $\mathbf{P_3}$: Bolting time [min] $\mathbf{P_4}$: Working height [min]

Key parameters describing a technical system being developed should be then assigned attributes of attractiveness, linear quality or must be and further evaluated to present innovativeness of specific technical solution, as shown in [5].

5 Conclusions

In the article, method of identification of useful function in the scope of product development was developed. In this method, key parameters of system to be designed are determined based on results of technology forecasting and functional analysis of the system. After this, dependence of parameters of super-system, sub-system and system is defined, which makes it possible to identify key parameters representing customers' needs. Proposed approach is not limited to technology forecasting and roadmapping, but also makes it possible to assess innovativeness of the developed products based on forecasted needs, reducing R&D costs and increasing probability for successful implementation of a solution to the market. It is yet to be determined, how to verify if the list of key parameters that was defined is complete. That will require further work in case studies based on proposed approach and verification of its effectiveness on other examples outside mining industry.

Acknowledgements. Research conducted by Marek Mysior was funded by the Ministry of Science and Higher Education in Poland, grant number 0402/0072/18, dedicated to young researchers.

References

1. Zlotin, B., Zusman, A.: Directed Evolution: Philosophy, Theory and Practice. Ideation International Inc., Farmington Hills (2001)
2. Orloff, M.: Inventive thinking through TRIZ: a practical guide (2006). https://doi.org/10.1007/978-3-540-33223-7
3. Altshuller, G.S.: The innovation algorithm: TRIZ, systematic innovation and technical creativity (2007)
4. Altshuller, G.: And Suddenly the Inventor Appeared. Technical Innovation Center (2004). https://doi.org/10.3324/haematol.2009.020586
5. Pryda, B., Mysior, M., Koziołek, S.: Method of innovation assessment of products and processes in the initial design phase. In: Cavallucci, D., De Guio, R., Koziołek, S. (eds.) TFC 2018. IFIPAICT, vol. 541, pp. 75–83. Springer, Cham (2018). https://doi.org/10.1007/978-3-030-02456-7_7
6. Abe, H., Ashiki, T., Suzuki, A., Jinno, F., Sakuma, H.: Integrating business modeling and roadmapping methods - the Innovation Support Technology (IST) approach. Technol. Forecast. Soc. Change (2009). https://doi.org/10.1016/j.techfore.2008.03.027
7. Daim, T.U., Oliver, T.: Implementing technology roadmap process in the energy services sector: a case study of a government agency. Technol. Forecast. Soc. Change (2008). https://doi.org/10.1016/j.techfore.2007.04.006
8. Carvalho, M.M., Fleury, A., Lopes, A.P.: An overview of the literature on technology roadmapping (TRM): Contributions and trends. Technol. Forecast. Soc. Change **80**, 1418–1437 (2013). https://doi.org/10.1016/j.techfore.2012.11.008
9. Saritas, O., Aylen, J.: Using scenarios for roadmapping: the case of clean production. Technol. Forecast. Soc. Change (2010). https://doi.org/10.1016/j.techfore.2010.03.003
10. Lee, S., Lee, S., Seol, H., Park, Y.: Using patent information for designing new product and technology: keyword based technology roadmapping. R D Manag. (2008). https://doi.org/10.1111/j.1467-9310.2008.00509.x

11. Groenveld, P.: Roadmapping integrates business and technology. Res. Technol. Manag. (2007). https://doi.org/10.1080/08956308.2007.11657472
12. Cascini, G., et al.: Knowing the future is possible. The handbook (2015)
13. Vatananan, R.S., Gerdsri, N.: The current state of technology roadmapping (TRM) research and practice. Int. J. Innov. Technol. Manag. **09**, 1250032 (2012). https://doi.org/10.1142/S0219877012500320
14. Cooper, R.G.: Product innovation and technology strategy. Res. Technol. Manag. (2000). https://doi.org/10.1080/08956308.2000.11671329
15. Koziołek, S.: Inżynieria Wynalazczości. Metodologia projektowania innowacyjnych systemów technicznych. Oficyna Wydawnicza Politechniki Wrocławskiej, Wrocław (2019)
16. Koziołek, S.: Design by analogy: synectics and knowledge acquisition network. In: Rusiński, E., Pietrusiak, D. (eds.) RESRB 2016. LNME, pp. 259–273. Springer, Cham (2017). https://doi.org/10.1007/978-3-319-50938-9_27
17. Bukhman, I.: TRIZ Technology for Innovation. Cubic Creativity Company (2012)
18. Lok, A.: Combination of Hidden Customer Needs tools and MPV to generate product concept. Presented at the MATRIZ TRIZfest 2016 International Conference (2016)
19. Malinin, L.: Technology selection based on main parameters of value and fuzzy logic. Int. J. Bus. Innov. Res. **11**, 431 (2016). https://doi.org/10.1504/IJBIR.2016.10000079
20. Lok, A.: MPV-based engineering system evolution. In: Proceedings of the MATRIZ TRIZfest 2017 International Conference, Kraków (2017)
21. Koziołek, S., Białowiec, A., Mysior, M., Ptak, M., Słupiński, M., Derlukiewicz, D.: Rozproszone systemy dystrybucji biogazu: badania, projektowanie i rozwój. Oficyna Wydawnicza Politechniki Wrocławskiej, Wrocław (2017)
22. Karliński, J., Ptak, M., Działak, P., Rusiński, E.: The approach to mining safety improvement: accident analysis of an underground machine operator. Arch. Civ. Mech. Eng. **16**, 503–512 (2016). https://doi.org/10.1016/J.ACME.2016.02.010
23. Helander, M.G., Krohn, G.S., Curtin, R.: Safety of roof-bolting operations in underground coal mines. J. Occup. Accid. **5**, 161–175 (1983). https://doi.org/10.1016/0376-6349(83)90002-0
24. Inc, K.S.: IDEF0
25. Mysior, M., Koziołek, S., Rusiński, E.: Problem formulation of screw feeding system of fibrous materials using TRIZ. In: Koziołek, S., Chechurin, L., Collan, M. (eds.) Advances and Impacts of the Theory of Inventive Problem Solving, pp. 57–64. Springer, Cham (2018). https://doi.org/10.1007/978-3-319-96532-1_5
26. Gadd, K.: TRIZ for Engineers: Enabling Inventive Problem Solving. Wiley, Hoboken (2011)
27. KGHM Polska Miedź SA: Strategy for 2023 (2017)
28. Konopko, W., Piernikarczyk, A.: Koncepcja technologii eksploatacji cienkiego złoża rud miedzi. CUPRUM – Czas. Nauk. Górnictwa Rud. **4**, 17–33 (2014)

Improving Inventive Design Methodology's Agility

Masih Hanifi[1(✉)], Hicham Chibane[1], Rémy Houssin[2], and Denis Cavallucci[1]

[1] ICUBE Laboratory-CSIP Team, INSA of Strasbourg, 24 Boulevard de la Victoire, 67084 Strasbourg, France
masihhanifi.mh@gmail.com

[2] ICUBE Laboratory-CSIP Team, University of Strasbourg, 3-5 rue de l'Université, 67084 Strasbourg, France

Abstract. Inventive Design (ID) methodology has been developed in four main phases, from initial situation analysis to solution concept, in order to overcome TRIZ limitations. However, this methodology needs to optimize its performance, because it takes a lot of time to obtain the best solution concepts. In addition, the ability of ID to give the best result depends on individual knowledge and experience of designer, and correctness of initial situation analysis. The proposed methodology in this article uses a collection of tools and combines a long-term vision for continuous improvement. This improvement method focuses on removing the non-value added activities during the process and maximizing the quality of the results. Integration of this proposed methodology with ID framework will eliminate the wastes, which occur in different phases of ID method and increase its overall efficiency and agility.

Keywords: Inventive design · TRIZ methodology · Efficiency · Agility

1 Introduction

Ability of organization in innovating and introducing new high quality products at a quicker rate than competitors lead to success of any business. There is a clear evidence that increasing of efficiency, effectiveness and agility of innovation process, which is believed a bottleneck to new product introduction, is key to survival of the enterprises in the competitive global environment. This incites the companies to track continuously the methods and techniques more cost-effective and time-efficient to boost the performance. Among these methods, we choose to investigate Lean product development theory.

Lean Manufacturing theory was originated by Toyota Company in the early 1950 s based on its product development process and make it to become one of world's leading car producer [1]. Nowadays, Many organizations have adapted lean in an attempt to reduce cost, decrease time, and maximize value in product development [2]. Where Lean Product Devolvement (LPD) is developed to be applied in design process. Lean philosophy takes a look at continuous eliminating nonvalue adding activities in

Published by Springer Nature Switzerland AG 2019
R. Benmoussa et al. (Eds.): TFC 2019, IFIP AICT 572, pp. 216–227, 2019.
https://doi.org/10.1007/978-3-030-32497-1_18

order to achieving the excellence, as well as inserting set of practices that help to reduce the cost and time while improving the performance of process [3].

TRIZ [4] or Theory of Inventive Problem Solving consider that technical systems will be developed in similar ways. In fact, it says that any problem can connected to a general situation independent of original domain of the technical system. As a result, designer is able to extend the solution space into various domains of knowledge and apply problem-solving techniques from different fields of knowledge [5–7]. However, this theory supplies many ideas and has the following defects: it could not guarantee a solution and its feasibility, TRIZ provides only concepts and it could not directly propose implementable solutions [8].

INSA of Strasbourg has developed Inventive Design Methodology (IDM), which is an extension of TRIZ, in four main phases, from initial analysis to choice of solution [7, 9]. ID Methodology has not only inherited drawbacks of TRIZ but also has its own problems. For this reason, this methodology needs improving its performance because it takes time to give the best concepts. In addition, the ability of IDM to give the best result depends on the individual knowledge and experience of designer, and correctness of initial analysis. We propose to integrate IDM and LPD to solve these problems. In fact, this integrated framework can continuously help in removing wastes within the process; it can decrease lead-time of the phases. In summary, this combination has to improve performance of IDM's process and to increase its efficiency and agility.

This paper deals with Inventive Design Methodology and aims to propose the first integration of LPD in this methodology, with the goal of increasing its efficiency and agility. This paper is organized in four sections. In Sect. 2, we present the state of art of Inventive Design Methodology, Lean, and its implementation in the sectors beyond manufacturing. The Sect. 3 present our proposition of integration of LPD in IDM. The paper finishes by the conclusion in Sect. 4.

2 Literature Review

2.1 Inventive Design Methodology

Nowadays, companies to survive in global market need to invest in systematic innovation, which is crucial for raising design effectiveness, increasing competiveness and profitability [10]. Inventive Design Methodology (IDM) is a systematic approach, which has been developed within several years of research at INSA of Strasbourg to solve classical TRIZ limits, and to complete its body of knowledge with other theories such as graph theory or Pugh's theory [7, 9].

IDM is a framework, which consists four main phases, Fig. 1, from initial situation analysis to the choice of solution concepts [7, 9, 11]. We briefly describe here these four phases, the employed tools or techniques in each step:

1. Initial Situation Analysis: This phase is to collect all the knowledge related to a problem and translate it to into graphical model in order to facilitate decision-making. In fact, this knowledge comes from (a) patent, relevant literature, and company's internal documents (b) existing data's regarding the targeted subject and (c) tacit know-how of experts concerned by the treated subject [9, 11, 12].

The applied tool in this step is problem graph. A problem graph is a set of problems, which are defined as a barrier that prevents the achievement of what has to be done, and a set of solutions, which represent an outcome that is known in the domain and verified by experience [13]. Nevertheless, in order to use TRIZ techniques to solve the problems and to gain solution concepts, it is necessary to translate the problems and the partial solutions to parameters. In this way, each problem can be derived in one or several evaluation parameters, and partial solutions into one or several action parameters. Then, these parameters will be applied to formulate the contradictions [13].

2. Contradictions Formulation: After completing the first phase, the initial situation analysis becomes visible as a reduced set of problems and partial solutions. It is used as departure point for formulating a range of poly-contradiction, from which the contradictions will be adapted [12, 13]. These contradictions are physical and technical issues, which represent bottlenecks in the development of system [9, 12]. The following sub-steps such as formulation of poly-contradictions, Extraction of contradictions, and classification of the significance of contradictions according to the specific of scenario are done within this phase [12]. The extracted contradictions become an input point for applying the different tools of TRIZ.
3. Solution Concept Synthesis: Once problems structured as contradictions, different TRIZ methods are applied to boost creation process, and to solve the precedence contradictions. These methods are the technical contradiction resolution matrix that relates to inventive principles, the substance-Field modeling related to the Inventive Standards system and the ARIZ-85C algorithm [12]. Contradiction Matrix is the most famous TRIZ tools. It is a matrix, which includes 39 improving parameters and 39 worsening parameters that are ordered on vertical and horizontal axis to interact with one another. This matrix is used to point out to the inventive principles that can be applied to eliminate the contradiction [14, 15]. Substance field analysis represents graphically the interaction, which there are between two components in a technical system, by a triangle model. Each triangle consists of one substance S1 that acts on substance S2 by a field, which is a kind of energy, acting on the instrument to adjust its interaction with the substance. A field can be thermal, chemical, magnetic, acoustic, electric, or electromagnetic. After developing the substance field models, Identification of system's problems is possible through further analysis. In order to solve revealed problems, TRIZ proposes 76 inventive standards, which helps us consider ideas from the world's knowledge bases [16, 17]. ARIZ or the algorithm for inventive problem solving is defined as a structured process that includes a series of steps integrating numerous TRIZ tools to formulate initial problems as well as resolve these problems [18]. It is known as the most appropriate for complex problems [15]. Since 1956, the different versions of ARIZ have been introduced. However, ARIZ-85-C, which is well improved compared to the other versions, and includes S-Field, operators, resources, etc., is the last version of ARIZ. This version of ARIZ contains nine steps including three steps to analyze and reformulate the original problem, the next three steps to eliminate the contradictions, and the final three steps to analyze the solution [19].
4. Solution Concept Selection: In this phase, measurement of the impact of each solution concept on the problem graph explained in the first phase will be done [9].

For this purpose, external experts should weigh the impact of each Solution Concept on Evaluation Parameter by filling out Pugh's like evaluation grid. In fact, if SC can make the EP develop in the desired direction, the assigned weight is positive, and if it could not make the evolvement in the favorable sense, the weight is negative [1].

Despite all the advantages that this four-phased framework to the designers presented, today, it does not have sufficient efficiency and agility to suggest the best solution. In fact, the identified areas of inefficiencies of each step of IDM are as the following: 1. Initial analysis: the essential time to collect and analyze the data, 2. Contradictions formulation: required time for this step, formulation of unnecessary contradictions, and inaccuracy in expressing the term, 3. Concept synthesis: time needed to understand the knowledge base, and errors in estimating the interest of new element of knowledge.

For improving the performance of ID methodology, we propose to integrate this framework with other methodologies or theory like Lean Product Development (LPD), which by continuously removing the wastes within ID process, can help to increase the efficiency and agility.

2.2 Lean Philosophy

Lean philosophy was originated in the practices of Toyota Motor Corporation in the 1950 s [1]. However, its introduction to the business world has been done through the books such as "Lean thinking" written by Womack and Jones in 1996, and "The Machine that Changed the World", which documents results of a study performed at the Massachusetts Institute of Technology (MIT), composed by Womack in 1990 [3]. Although, the concentration of these books was on the manufacturing aspect of business rather than engineering and design, the authors emphasized that the same principles can be implemented to remove all types of waste in various industrial sectors [3, 20].

Lean philosophy is based on the fundamental goals of the Toyota Production System (TPS) and can be understood as a set of practices, principles and techniques, which looks for removing continuously all types of waste in order to attain cost decrement, quality, efficiency and agility improvement with less endeavor [20–22]. According to lean, waste is defined as everything that does not directly add value to product or service [23]. In addition, this philosophy has recognized wastes in seven forms, Fig. 5, that have been classified as follows [24]:

a. Overproduction: generating too soon and more than requirements, which causes a weak stream of information or products, and unneeded inventory.
b. Defects: products or information that do not meet expectation because of problem quality, common mistakes in paperwork, and week delivery performance.
c. Excessive inventory: unnecessary raw material stores, work in process (WIP), finished stock storage, and retardation of information or products, resulting in extreme cost and poor service.

d. Unsuitable processing: unnecessary process steps, or processes that uses the wrong set of tools, procedures or systems, often when easier approach could have more effectiveness.
e. Unnecessary transportation: any movement of products, information or people that is not an added value process step, and causes wasted time, effort and cost.
f. Waiting: Idle time for information, people or products, which results long lead-time and weak flow.
g. Excessive motion: poor structure of the work place, which causes extreme stretching and repeatedly missing items.

After introduction of Lean, there were the authors, which they have gone beyond the boundaries of manufacturing and adapted these wastes to other departments of business. Among these authors, it is possible to point out to (Ohno 1998; Liker 2004; Morgan 2005; Reinertsen 2009), which they have defined them in Product Development Process [25]. However, in order to remove waste and deliver improvement in specific area, it is fundamental understanding Lean Thinking principles.

"The Machine that changed the world" and "Lean Thinking" have articulated a universal Lean philosophy base on five key principles, which are essential to eliminate the seven wastes. Furthermore, these books have showed that how this concept by using these principles could be extended beyond manufacturing to any sector or department. The five principles and their brief description are as follows [24, 26]

a. Specify value: define value precisely from perspective of customer in terms of specific product. Everything that absorbs resources but could not create value, it is kind of waste and should be eliminated.
b. Identify value-stream: recognize all the activities required across the whole value stream to ensure that each of them provides value, and highlight non-value adding waste.
c. Make value flow: make value-stream flow without discontinuity, waiting, deviation or scrap.
d. Pull: provide or design what they are required on customer demand.
e. Strive for perfection: continuous elimination of consecutive layers of waste when they are detected.

However, fulfillment of these principle needs application of some practices, which are activities applied to improve the organizations. These practices are implemented by set of tools and techniques [20].

Techniques and tools are essential to implementing Lean. In fact, application of these tools and techniques could be considered as a facility of defining, evaluating, and attacking sources of inefficiency in a specific manner [27] Some of the widely acknowledged Lean tools and techniques are as follows: (a) Value Stream Mapping or VSM: to detect non-value-added activity, (b) Cause-and-effect: to prioritize the root causes, (c) DSM (Design Structure Matrix): to understand the nature and root cause of waste, (d) Single-piece flow: to employ the concept of single piece flow to remove waste time, (e) A3 reports: to describe in one sheet the problem, solution alternatives, and the best commendation to solve the problem, (f) Kaizen: to detect and eliminate waste according to Plan-Do-Check-Act, (g) Kanban: a visual signal to support flow,

(h) Quality Function Deployment (QFD) to identify critical customer attributes and to create a link between the attributes and design parameters) and Multi Criteria Decision Making: to weigh all the criteria against each other before making the final decision [25, 28–31]. Integration of these tools and techniques are helpful for various of issues [27].

The principles of Lean philosophy have made it applicable to other sectors of industry, including innovation process, which plays today an important role in success of the business.

2.3 Implementation of Lean in the Sectors Beyond Manufacturing

Todays, most of the authors have written about application of Lean philosophy in manufacturing process. However, there have been the writers, which pays attention to integration of this philosophy in information management, innovation and product development process, because of its ability to increase efficiency and agility.

Within the information management, Hicks [32] propose application of Lean thinking to support the improvement of the performance of the overall information management, which is defined as the process of adding value to information by organizing, visualizing and representing, and enabling information to flow to the information customer.

In product introduction, which involves flows of information within the product development process rather than physical circulation of materials through the cases of manufacturing [2], Haque and James-Moore [26] describe the application of the five Lean Thinking principles to New Product Introduction (NPI) process. In fact, in their paper each principle is characterized within the context on NPI. In addition, they introduced the key methods and tools that enable Lean in NPI, and they discussed about the essential modifications to the manufacturing definitions of value and waste in order to incorporate to demands of effective and efficient NPI. In this field, Nepal [25] has proposed an integrated framework for increasing capability of identifying and eliminating of waste in Product Development Process by integrating LPD tools with DSM and Cause and Effect Matrix, which allows analysis of underlying complexity of PD, and facilitates specification of root causes of useless rework. In the same way, Anand and Kodali [3] have had a proposed conceptual framework for Lean New Product Development. The authors additionally integrated different tools and techniques to make NPD leaner.

By looking at the presented examples of Lean applications to the sectors beyond manufacturing, and by considering this point that Inventive Design Methodology involves the flow of information, it can be concluded that the principles of Lean and also its tools and techniques, which needs some modifications, are applicable to ID methodology.

3 Application of Lean Philosophy to Inventive Design Methodology

In this section, in order to apply Lean philosophy within Inventive Design Methodology process we propose five steps methodology, Fig. 1. The purpose of this applying, it is to continuously remove the wastes in ID process and increase its efficiency and agility by applying different tools and techniques of Lean. In this methodology, the five steps, described below, explain how it is possible to constantly improve the process.

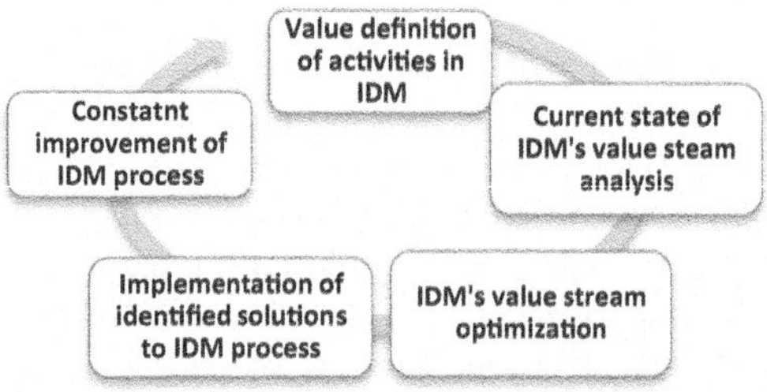

Fig. 1. The five steps methodology introduced to improve Inventive Design Methodology

1. Value definition of activities in IDM process: In this stage, the value of each activity should be defined according to the objective, which is convincing the designer.
2. Current state of IDM's value stream (process) analysis: This stage includes creation of value stream mapping of actual ID process, as well as wastes definition and analysis.
   a. Value stream creation of the current process of IDM: in order to analyze the IDP, the activities within this process should be categorized as Non Value Added (NVA) activity, and Value Added activity (VA). For this purpose, it is possible to employ Value Stream Mapping (VSM), Fig. 2, which is a proven analytical tool for demonstrating flow of information in IDM process, and identifying different types of wastes.
   b. Wastes and problems identification of the actual process of IDM: After mapping the needed steps of IDM by VSM, it is necessary to identify different types of wastes according to the adaptation that has been done in the second step, as well as the methods that should be changed.
      (1) In the Initial Analysis step, the user needs time to collect and analysis all the data as problems and partial solutions without paying attention to use of them in solution step. Figure 3 demonstrates a graph problem of a performed project, which has been done for this article to demonstrate IDM's drawbacks. As shown in this figure, the user has collected 22 problems and 5 partial solutions.

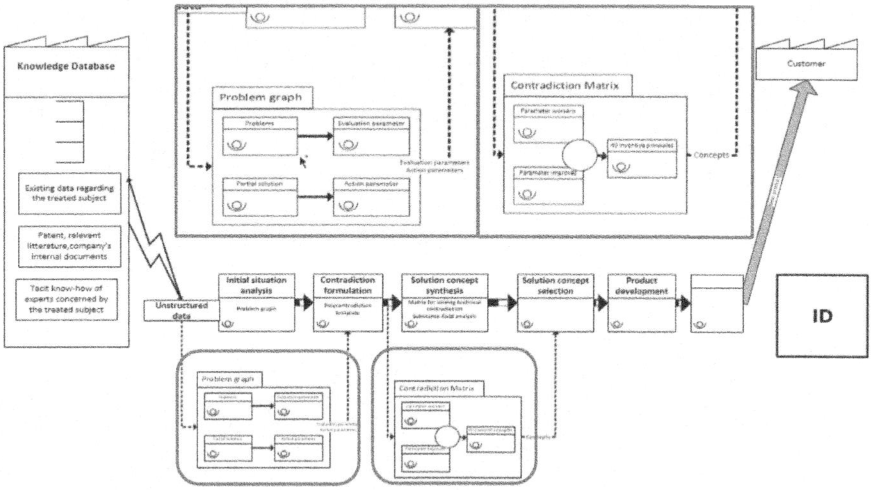

Fig. 2. Value Stream Mapping (VSM) of Inventive Design Methodology

(2) Contradictions formulation step: the users requires time to formulate all the contradictions that sometimes are useless. Figure 4 shows the formulated contradictions related to the graph problem of Fig. 3.

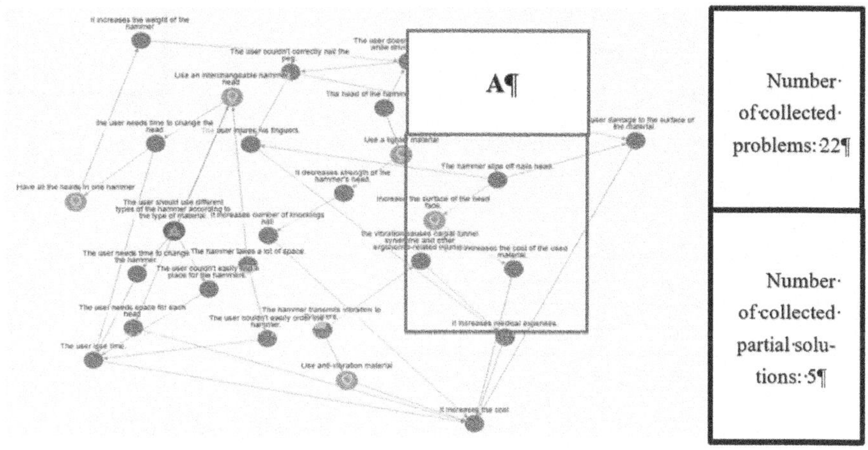

Fig. 3. Graph problem of a realized project (brown circles shows problems; green circles shows partial solution) (Color figure online)

(3) Solution Concept Synthesis step: the designer requires allocating a lot of time to understand the knowledge base. Furthermore, he could make errors in estimating the more interest of new knowledge element.

(4) Solution Concept Selection step: of ID process, it is remarkable that after creating a network of a lot of problems and partial solutions in the first stage, and formulating all the possible contractions in the second stage, the designer applies just some of them to create the solution. For example, as shown in Fig. 5, in the presented project of step one, the designer has used just one of the contractions to formulate the solution. After verifying and comparing this project with other projects been realized by other designer, we received to the same results. Figure 6 demonstrates results of this review.

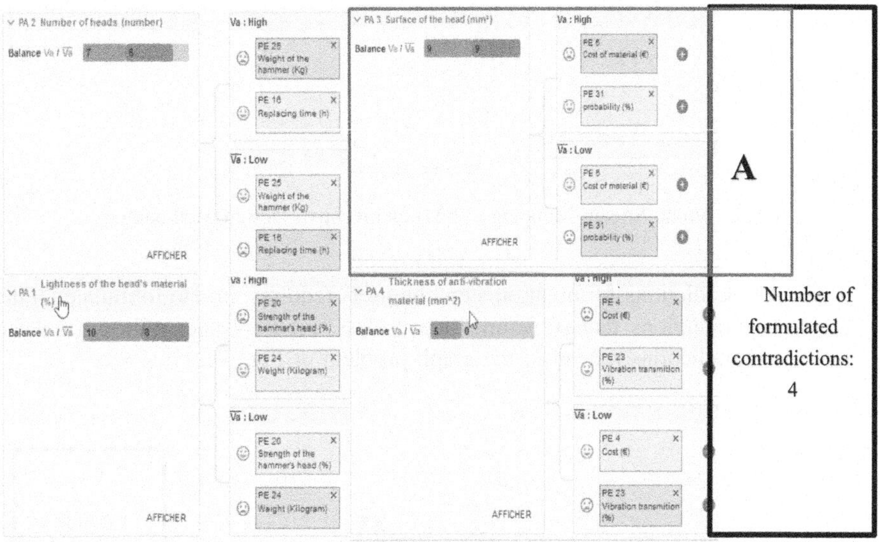

Fig. 4. Formulation of contradictions related to problem graph of Fig. 3

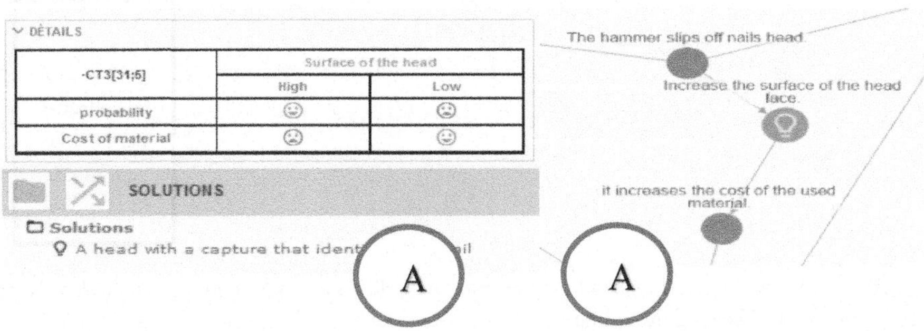

Fig. 5. The applied problem and contradiction to receive an innovative solution

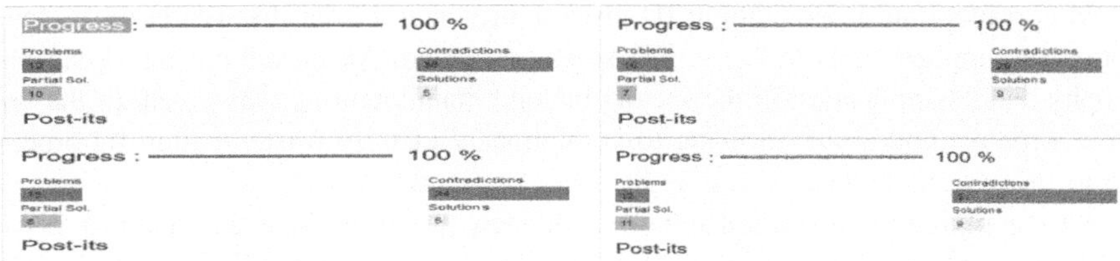

Fig. 6. The results of review of other projects

c. Wastes analysis: This stage has been defined to find root causes of identified NVA activities in the previous steps and to prioritize them with respect to their impact on IDM process.
   (1) To understand the root causes of wastes: in Inventive Design Methodology process, it is possible to use the tools such as cause and effect chain or Why-Why analysis.

3. IDM's value stream (process) optimization: After understanding the root causes of wastes, it is the stage of identifying the possible solutions to remove wastes and propose the solutions to improve the process.
   a. Identify the possible solutions to make the stream of information flow: suitable techniques or tools should be used to create flow of information. For example, it is possible to reduce the size of batch, apply the concept of single-piece from the initial phase of IDM to eliminate waiting time.
   b. Identify the possible solutions to create a pull stream of information between downstream activity and upstream activity: the goal is to able the process to develop the information based on request of its immediate customer. In other words, each phase of IDM will produce information when is needed without break.
   c. Estimate the future state of value stream of IDM according the identified solutions: After identifying all types of waste within IDM's process, the future VSM could be developed by predicting how Inventive Design process will be when the identified wastes are eliminated.
4. Implementation of the identified solutions to IDM process: the potential solutions could be implemented on Inventive Design Methodology in order to increase its efficiency and agility.
5. Constant improvement of IDM process: Continuous improvement is integral part of Lean philosophy. In fact, the goal here is to continuously improve IDM process by focusing on eliminating as many waste activities as possible while increasing the activities that generate value.

4 Conclusion

This paper dealt with innovation process and aimed to apply Lean, as philosophy to continuous eliminating wastes within the processes in order to achieve the excellence, in Inventive Design Methodology.

After a literature review about ID process in which a brief discussion on its main phases and applied tools in these phases was provided. An introduction to Lean philosophy and its application in the sectors beyond manufacturing was given. In the last, a five steps methodology, allowing to continuously identify wastes within ID process and to increase its efficiency and agility, was presented.

After applying the identified solutions, the new proposed algorithm and process, of the step 3 of the methodology into IDM process, we will have a flow of information from initial phase without waiting time. In addition, the information will be developed within the process base on the needs of the designer. The proposed methodology has to have also possibility to identify continuously wastes in ID process, and to propose the solutions to eliminate them. The final and the most important result of this five steps methodology, it is to constantly increase the efficiency and agility of Inventive Design Methodology.

In the future research work, we will present a new algorithm and a new process in order to increase the agility of Inventive Design methodology. Furthermore, the step 4 of methodology, which is implementation of the identified solutions to ID process, will be done.

References

1. Chen, H., Taylor, R.: Exploring the impact of lean management on innovation capability. In: PICMET 2009 - 2009 Portland International Conference on Management of Engineering and Technology, Portland, OR, USA, pp. 826–834 (2009)
2. Letens, G., Farris, J.A., Van Aken, E.M.: A multilevel framework for lean product development system design. Eng. Manag. J. **23**(1), 69–85 (2011)
3. Anand, G., Kodali, R.: Development of a conceptual framework for lean new product development process. Int. J. Prod. Dev. **6**(2), 190 (2008)
4. Altshuller, G.: And Suddenly The Inventor Appeared TRIZ. Technical Innovation Ctr; Édition: 2, 1 mai 1996
5. Houssin, R., Renaud, J., Coulibaly, A., Cavallucci, D., Rousselot, F.: TRIZ theory and case based reasoning: synergies and oppositions. Int. J. Interact. Des. Manuf. (IJIDeM) **9**(3), 177–183 (2015)
6. Houssin, R., Coulibaly, A.: An approach to solve contradiction problems for the safety integration in innovative design process. Comput. Ind. **62**(4), 398–406 (2011)
7. Chinkatham, T., Cavallucci, D.: On solution concept evaluation/selection in inventive design. Procedia Eng. **131**, 1073–1083 (2015)
8. Casner, D., Souili, A., Houssin, R., Renaud, J.: Agile'TRIZ framework: towards the integration of TRIZ within the agile innovation methodology. In: Cavallucci, D., De Guio, R., Koziołek, S. (eds.) TFC 2018. IFIPAICT, vol. 541, pp. 84–93. Springer, Cham (2018). https://doi.org/10.1007/978-3-030-02456-7_8
9. Cavallucci, D., Strasbourg, I.: From TRIZ to Inventive Design Method (IDM): towards a formalization of Inventive Practices in R&D Departments, p. 2 (2012)
10. Navas, H.V.G.: TRIZ: design problem solving with systematic innovation. In: Coelho, D. (ed.) Advances in Industrial Design Engineering. InTech (2013)
11. Zanni-Merk, C., Cavallucci, D., Rousselot, F.: Use of formal ontologies as a foundation for inventive design studies. Comput. Ind. **62**(3), 323–336 (2011)

12. Cavallucci, D.: Designing the inventive way in the innovation era. In: Chakrabarti, A., Blessing, L.T.M. (eds.) An Anthology of Theories and Models of Design, pp. 237–262. Springer, London (2014). https://doi.org/10.1007/978-1-4471-6338-1_12
13. Cavallucci, D., Rousselot, F., Zanni, C.: Initial situation analysis through problem graph. CIRP J. Manuf. Sci. Technol. **2**(4), 310–317 (2010)
14. Childs, P.R.N.: Mechanical Design Engineering Handbook. Butterworth-Heinemann, Amsterdam (2014)
15. Ilevbare, I.M., Probert, D., Phaal, R.: A review of TRIZ, and its benefits and challenges in practice. Technovation **33**(2–3), 30–37 (2013)
16. Zhang, X., Mao, X., AbouRizk, S.M.: Developing a knowledge management system for improved value engineering practices in the construction industry. Autom. Constr. **18**(6), 777–789 (2009)
17. Gadd, K.: TRIZ for Engineers: Enabling Inventive Problem Solving, pp. i–xviii. Wiley, Chichester (2011)
18. Chou, J.-R.: An ARIZ-based life cycle engineering model for eco-design. J. Clean. Prod. **66**, 210–223 (2014)
19. Mishra, U.: An introduction to ARIZ. SSRN Electronic Journal (2013)
20. Ugochukwu, P., Engstrom, J., Langstrand, J.: Lean in the supply chain: a literature review. Manag. Prod. Eng. Rev. **3**(4), 10 (2012)
21. Hallam, C., Contreras, C.: Integrating lean and green management. Manag. Decis. **54**(9), 2157–2187 (2016)
22. Vinodh, S., Joy, D.: Structural Equation Modelling of lean manufacturing practices. Int. J. Prod. Res. **50**(6), 1598–1607 (2012)
23. Bakri, A.Hj., Rahim, A.R.A., Yusof, N.Mohd., Ahmad, R.: Boosting Lean Production via TPM. Procedia Soc. Behav. Sci. **65**, 485–491 (2012)
24. Hines, P., Taylor, D.: Going Lean: A Guide to Implementation. Lean Enterprise Research Centre, Cardiff (2000)
25. Nepal, B.P., Yadav, O.P., Solanki, R.: Improving the NPD process by applying lean principles: a case study. Eng. Manag. J. **23**(3), 65–81 (2011)
26. Haque, B., James-moore, M.: Applying lean thinking to new product introduction. J. Eng. Des. **15**(1), 1–31 (2004)
27. Moehrle, M.G.: What is TRIZ? From conceptual basics to a framework for research. Creat. Innov. Manag. **14**(1), 3–13 (2005)
28. León, H.C.M., Farris, J.A.: Lean product development research: current state and future directions. Eng. Manag. J. **23**(1), 29–51 (2011)
29. Melton, T.: The benefits of lean manufacturing. Chem. Eng. Res. Des. **83**(6), 662–673 (2005)
30. Dombrowski, U., Zahn, T.: Design of a lean development framework. In: 2011 IEEE International Conference on Industrial Engineering and Engineering Management, Singapore, Singapore, pp. 1917–1921 (2011)
31. Verma, A.K., Das, L.K., Erande, A.S.: Creative Lean Design Process, p. 8
32. Hicks, B.J.: Lean information management: understanding and eliminating waste. Int. J. Inf. Manag. **27**(4), 233–249 (2007)

A Multi-perspective and Multi-level Based Approach to Organize and Represent Inventive Knowledge

Longfan Liu[1,2(✉)], Denis Cavallucci[2(✉)], and Yan Li[1]

[1] School of Manufacturing Science and Engineering, Sichuan University, NanYihuan Road No. 24, Chengdu 610065, Sichuan, China
liulongfan@sina.com

[2] ICube (UMR-CNRS 7357), 24 Boulevard de la Victoire, 67000 Strasbourg, France
denis.cavallucci@insa-strasbourg.fr

Abstract. Through analyzing the solving mechanism of product inventive design problem based on TRIZ theory, we propose in this paper a multi-perspective and multi-level knowledge organization model, so as to fill the "GAP" between the general solution and the particular solution in the process of solving inventive problems. We labeled here design knowledge by five attributes, i.e., TRIZ, function, behavior-flow, effect, and domain, each of which includes respectively three levels that are conceptual level, semantic level and factual resource level. Thereby, a multi-perspective and multi-level local knowledge base is established. Besides, we put forward also a card-type knowledge representation template, which divides the traditional cases, patents and other knowledge into several independent parts, and each of them can be displayed and pushed to designers in form of cards. Thus, it's conductive to stimulate designers' analogy and association. One multi-perspective and multi-level knowledge organization based inventive problem solving model is conclusively established, which supports analysis and problem-solving in different perspectives and at different levels. A conceptual design of an ultrasonic washing machine is illustrated at the end as an implemented example for this proposed model.

Keywords: Knowledge representation · Inventive problem solving · TRIZ

1 Introduction

Product design is a continuous and purposive kind of creative thinking activity, which is carried out to meet certain needs of knowledge [1]. From the cognitive perspective, the process of solving the design problem can be regarded as that of "the correlation mining between the problem and the existing knowledge, as well as the knowledge transfer and combination" [2]. The knowledge requirement runs through the entire life cycle of product design.

Bringing knowledge forward and making it explicit is one of the key roles of knowledge representation [3]. Recent studies about the organization and representation

Published by Springer Nature Switzerland AG 2019
R. Benmoussa et al. (Eds.): TFC 2019, IFIP AICT 572, pp. 228–239, 2019.
https://doi.org/10.1007/978-3-030-32497-1_19

are based on artificial intelligence, which focuses on the computer processing of knowledge. All the presentations and organizations of knowledge are structural, which the computer can handle and be regarded as a set of structural data and a set of correlative operation. Cong et al. [4] and Paul et al. [5] put forward a method of patent knowledge classification based on inventive principles, as well as assisted by ontological reasoning technique. And it can also automatically provide the relevant patent knowledge to designer during the solving process of TRIZ problem. Yu et al. [6] and Park et al. [7] proposed to analyze and retrieve the patent items with the help of the trend of evolution so as to solve the current problem. Zhang et al. [8] proposed a semantic ontology based knowledge representation model for invention principles. Qin et al. [9] proposed a Requirement-Function-Behavior-Structure-Evolution (RFBSE) model to obtain useful knowledge and experience in the design process. There are also some innovative design knowledge management platforms including Aulive [10], Pro/Innovator [11], PIXSEB (Driving innovation through the semantic extraction of patent content) [12], Creap (Creativity Design Service Platform) [13] CREAX [14] etc. However, the former research in knowledge representation model emphasized chiefly the description of connection between design objects and design processes, and nevertheless lacked an efficient systematic approach that can integrate the design object, problem-solving process, as well as recognition strategies.

Inventive design is people-centered, and people should be finally engaged in design. Knowledge must be oriented to comprehension and motivation of humans. Knowledge representation should pay attention to human's reading, understanding, association. However, the kind of knowledge presented to people is rather important. The main role of computers is to organize, and to represent knowledge. In fact, it is a state in which human-machine forms a joint cognition, that is to say, the combination of artificial intelligence and human cognition forms a cognitive channel that is conducive to innovation. Therefore, the organization and representation of knowledge must satisfy [15]: (I) It should be benefit of the designer's perception. (II) It should be in favor of the designer's association analogy and knowledge transfer. (III) It should make for computer retrieval and push forward. (IV) It should avail the expansion of knowledge and the use of resources.

Besides, the design problem is typical ill-structural problem [16]. The design problem solving process is a process of clarifying and refining the initial problem, along with repeated iterations in different abstraction level, i.e. designers may need the knowledge of different abstraction levels at different time to solve the problems. Knowledge organization and representation for product innovative design requires different abstraction levels of design knowledge to assist designers to obtain knowledge information of different levels, which facilitates thereby the analysis and problem-solving from different conceptual levels and different perspectives.

2 The Mechanism of Creative Problem Solving Based on Multi-perspective and Multi-level

TRIZ (theory of inventive problem solving) is presented by G.S. Altshuler from the Soviet Union and his studying team, as a complete methodological and theoretical system for inventive problem solving, which can accelerate the process of invention and obtain the productions of good quality [17]. The flow of TRIZ application can concluded to solve the inventive problem as Fig. 1: Firstly, We can use TRIZ, FBS and other ways to represent engineering problem and transform it into a general problem. And then, the general solution is retrieved by using the inventive tools. Finally, the designer transforms the general solution into a particular solution with the help of analogy, as well as his own domain knowledge and design experience.

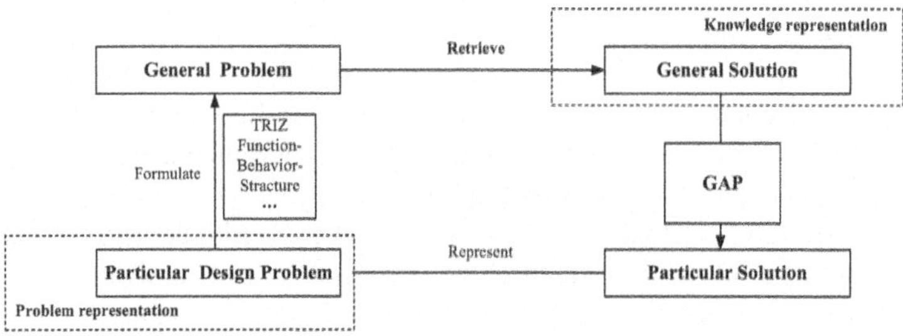

Fig. 1. The Flow of TRIZ Application

The general solution is not the final solution to the problem, it provides the designer with a new possible approach to solve the problem. The general solution is a highly abstract one. A gap exists between general solution and particular solution. The transformation process to a particular solution still requires the immense amount of knowledge from different practical domains, but the designer himself cannot grasp all the supporting knowledge needed for solving the problem, which results in the lack of knowledge and increases the difficulty to the inventive design.

As shown in Fig. 2, in order to help designers to get over the "gap" between the general solution and particular solution, we propose a multi-perspective and multi-level based inventive problem solving model. In this model, the design task is represented from 4 perspectives basing on human comprehension of processing problems of product inventive design, including "*what do you want to design?*" (Considering inventive problem in a visual perspective, specific design objects included, with certain limitations, easy to cause mindsets, not easy to acquire creative solutions.), "*What is it used for*" (Considering the ultimate goal of design, representing the problem on the overall goal. By completely eliminating the existing production system limitations, to describe the inventive problem from the functional level.), "*How to achieve it?*" (Thinking about the implementation of this design problem, transforming the design principles into concrete operations.) and "*Which problem do you have?*" (considering the current problems is the driving force for the transformation between problem levels, including technical principles and design thinking, and five abstract attributes corresponding to domain information, functions, behavior-flow, scientific effects, and invention principles.) Designers could reconstruct a new problem representation by this way.

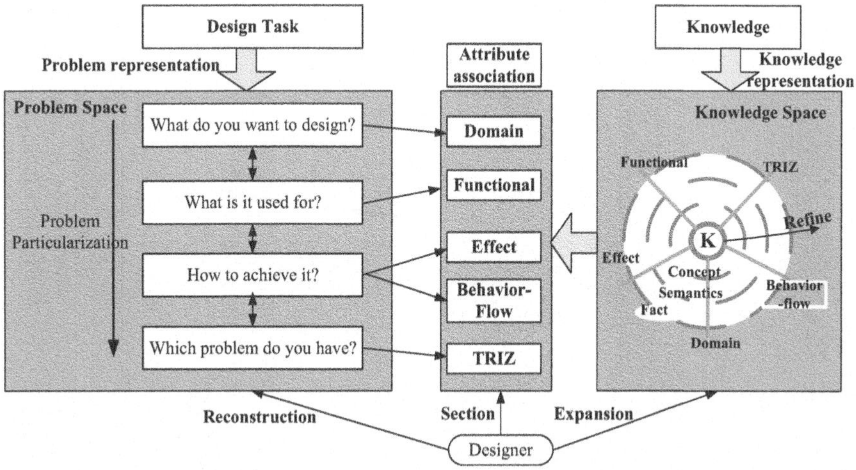

Fig. 2. A multi-perspective and multi-level based inventive problem solving model

Besides, we extract five attributes of design knowledge—TRIZ, function, behavior-flow, effect, and domain attribute. An attribute is regarded as a description perspective and a retrieval perspective of knowledge. Each attribute is described from three levels from abstract to specific: concept, semantics and fact resources, which forms a multi-perspective and multi-level local knowledge base. Designers could choose any perspective and any level to understand the knowledge.

Finally, according to the relationship between attributes, the semantic ontology of attributes is established. Relevant knowledge is searched and mined from patent database and network resources. Through semantic similarity calculation, knowledge within domain, in closing domain and in further domain are provided for inventive design. Supporting designers to analyze and utilize knowledge from different perspectives as well as at different levels is beneficial to motivating designers to make analogy and complete knowledge transfer, thus facilitating the transferring process of general solutions to particular solutions.

3 The Organization and Representation of Design Knowledge

3.1 The Computer-Oriented Knowledge Organization

Upon the type of knowledge in the product inventive design process, we here divide the attributes of product design knowledge into TRIZ attribute, function attribute, behavior-flow attribute, effect attribute, and domain attribute, in order to make up for the "gap" between the general solution and the particular solution. Meanwhile, each attribute is described by different levels knowledge. Each level corresponds to different abstract levels, including conceptual layer, semantic layer and factual resource layer, we can thereby establish a multi-perspective design knowledge organization and representation model. As the figure shown in Fig. 3:

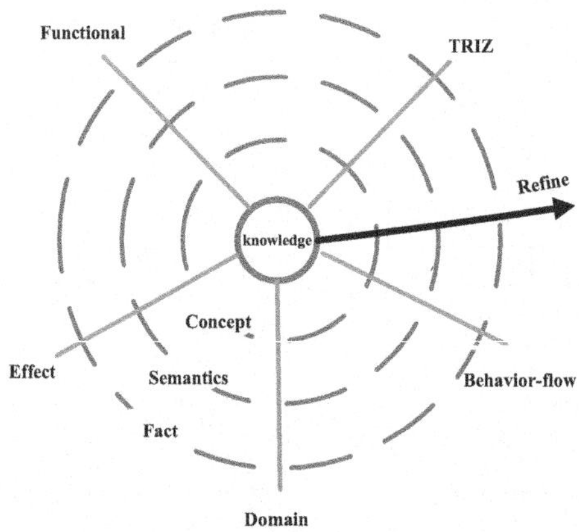

Fig. 3. A multi-perspective and multi-level based knowledge representation model

Conceptual Layer Knowledge Organization: The conceptual layer is a highly abstract representation of attributes and also the basic unit of the attribute description. A concept may contain many sub-concepts and may be sub-concept of another concept. A set of concept can form a grain, and a multi-granular and multi-level attribute concept description is formed by organization of the concept layer. The granularity conceptual structure of each attribute is expressed as follows.

TRIZ attribute: It describes and expresses the principle, general solution and technological evolution rule of TRIZ, as shown in the Fig. 4:

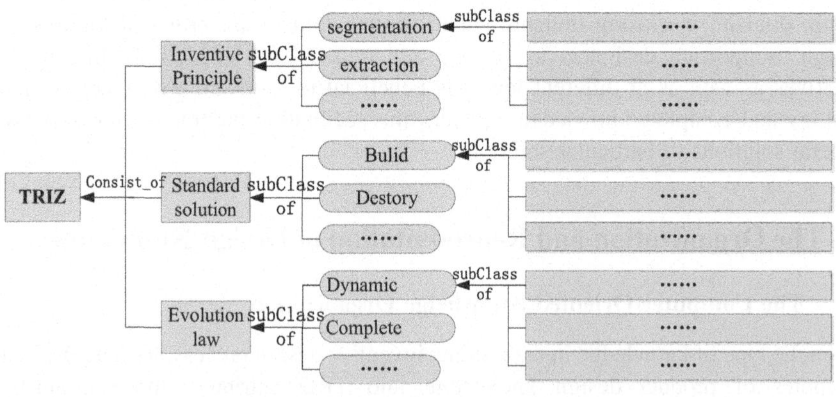

Fig. 4. The conceptual layer of TRIZ attribute

Semantic Layer Knowledge Organization: The semantic layer is a description of attribute content and the relationship between semantics, including attribute description and attribute association. Attribute is a description of the characteristics, which is meanwhile a concrete manifestation of attribute characteristics in knowledge, which is convenient for designers to understand quickly knowledge and establish the relationship between attributes through the relationship between attribute semantics.

Factual Layer Knowledge Organization: Facts refer to detailed descriptions of practical case. Resources refer to resource content obtained through attribute semantic description and Internet information expansion, including patent knowledge and extended knowledge of network resources within domain, in closing domain, and in further domain.

Through the attribute concept and ontology association, the external network resources are retrieved by knowledge, and then the semantic similarity between the search result document and the attribute description is calculated to sort and classify the searched results according to the knowledge of the domain, the adjacent domain and the further domain. The vectorization of the text can be expressed as:

$$d_j = (w_{1j}, w_{2j}, \ldots, w_{nj})$$

Where dj represents the document j, w_{ij} represents the weight value of the word t_i, and the weight of a word is calculated using TF-IDF (word reverse document frequency). The idea of TF-IDF is that the more a word appears in a document, the greater the weight value it has. The less common a word is in the document, the greater its weight value is, that is to say the word has a good distinguishing ability. The formula for calculating TF-IDF is as follows:

$$w_{ij} = \frac{f_{ij}}{\max\{f_{1j}, f_{2j}, \ldots, f_{nj}\}} * \log \frac{N}{df_i}$$

Here f_{ij} is the number of times the word t_i appears in the document dj, N is the total number of documents, and d_{fi} is the number of words t_i in the document. The similarity between the document q and the document d_j is calculated as follows:

$$sim(d_j, q) = \frac{\sum_{i-1}^{n} w_{ij} \times w_{iq}}{\sqrt{\sum_{i=1}^{n} w_{ij}^2} \times \sqrt{\sum_{i=1}^{n} w_{iq}^2}}$$

(Note: the similarity value is within (0,1))

While $sim \in [0.7, 1)$,, the document d_j belongs to within domain of the document q.

While $sim \in [0.4, 0.7)$, the document dj belongs to closing domain of the document q.

While, $sim \in [0, 0.4)$, the document dj belongs to further domain of the document q.

The problem solving is a process of cooperation between relevant knowledge, and it cause easily mind-set relying on one single domain of knowledge, which is adverse to generation of new ideas. In this Internet era, the connection between local knowledge basis and internet resource should be well established during the organization and representation of knowledge, which helps the knowledge extension, as well as expands the knowledge space of designer.

3.2 The User-Oriented Knowledge Representation

The design knowledge representation avails not only computer retrieve and storage, but makes also for users' reading comprehension so as to stimulate efficiently associative thinking. Based on the analysis above, we propose here one card-type multi-perspective and multi-level design knowledge representation template. The traditional cases, patents and other knowledge are divided into relatively independent parts according to different attributes, and each part is displayed in the form of card. Each card describes the knowledge from the conceptual, semantic and factual layers of each attribute. Designers can start reading knowledge from any card and form a multi-perspective and multi-level knowledge structure, which is convenient to understand and knowledge transfer. In addition, the knowledge is marked by multiple attributes to form a structured text, which is beneficial for computer processing. An example of a design knowledge representation template shown in Fig. 5.

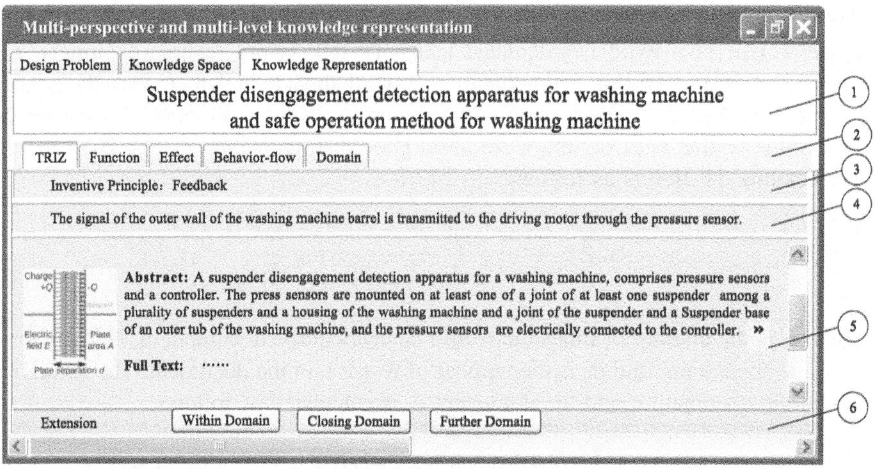

Fig. 5. Knowledge representation template

Where, 1 is the title bar, displaying the name of the knowledge item; 2 is the attribute tab bar, including TRIZ, functions, effects, behavior flow and domain. Designers are free to choose any attribute tag for browsing and reading; 3, 4, 5 are respectively the conceptual layer, the semantic layer and the factual layer of attributes; 6 are the extension layer of knowledge item, referring to semantic similarity algorithm, with which knowledge can be retrieved within domain, in closing and in further domain.

The user retrieves knowledge through the attribute tag, selects the content of interest in the knowledge space, and browses the knowledge item. Through the knowledge representation of card-type, the user does not need to read the full text, and can understand the content from different perspectives, thereby reducing the cognitive load of users, as well as improving the efficiency of knowledge application.

4 Case Study

As a mature household appliance, this paper takes the innovative design of the washing machine as an example to show the application process of the above model.

4.1 Problem Representation

As shown in Fig. 6, the design task can be described as "Please use your imagination to provide an innovative design for the washing machine". There is relatively fewer restricted conditions, which is easy for designer to consider the problem from any angles.

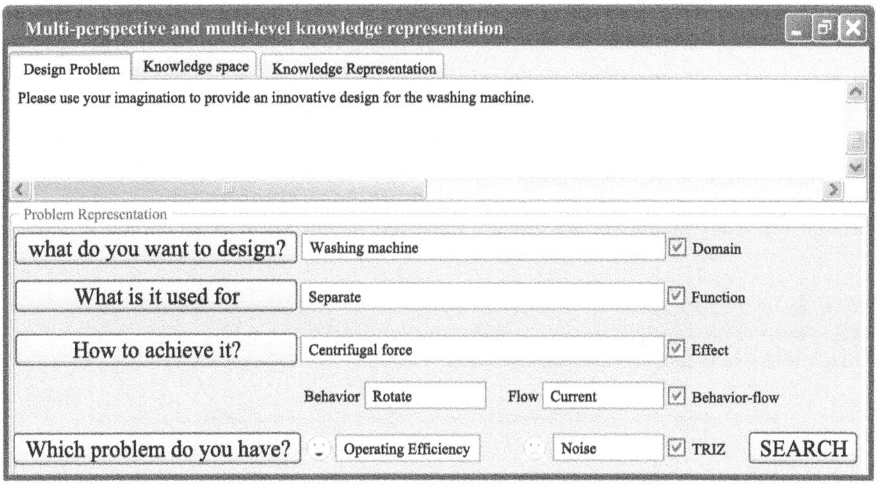

Fig. 6. The interface of problem representation

i. Problem representation from "domain" perspective: Designers can type "Washing Machines" in "What are you design?" Input box to retrieve relevant knowledge so as to understand the current development and main problems of "Washing Machines".
ii. Problem representation form "functional" perspective: The main function of the washing machine is to clean the stains on the clothes whose functional basis can be expressed as "separate/remove solid". Therefore, type "separate" in input box "what is used for?", to get all the patent knowledge that implements the "separation" function.

iii. Problem representation from "effect" perspective: Currently, the washing machine mainly includes a pulsator washing machine and a drum washing machine. Both of them are applied to reach the function of the product realized by "centrifugal force".
iv. Problem representation from "behavior-flow" perspective: Nowadays, the washing machine drives the engine to rotate by electric current, and generates centrifugal force to separate the stain from the clothes. In input box "how to achieve it?", we can enter "rotation-current" to get a case of using "centrifugal force" to achieve product function.
v. Problem representation from "TRIZ" perspective: The existing washing machine consists of a box body, an engine, a base and the other elements. Thus it is very cumbersome and occupies a large area. So it is only suitable for household use. But when the people are traveling, they also need an equipment to help them clean their clothes. The adaptability and the volume of washing machine form a set of technical contradictions. In input box "which problem do you have?", we can input "adaptability" into the harmful factors and put "the volume of stationary object" into the favorable factors to retrieve the knowledge to solve this contradiction.

Through these five perspectives to characterize the design problem, it can assist the designer to fully understand the design problem and find a breakthrough. The designer can select any one or more of the attributes to combine multiple knowledge for retrieval. In this paper, all five perspectives are settled as examples.

4.2 Knowledge Representation

Through the analysis above, we got the retrieved patent knowledge shown in Fig. 7.

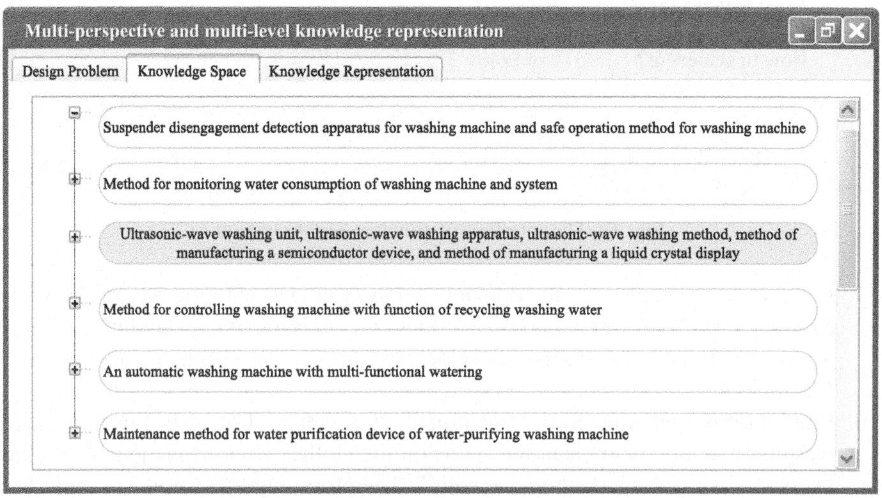

Fig. 7. The interface of knowledge space

We choose one of the knowledge items to browse. As shown in Fig. 8(a, b, c, d, e), we can read this knowledge from five perspectives. This is an ultrasonic cleaning unit that uses a sound wave with a frequency exceeding 20 kHz beyond the human hearing range. The dirt layer is dispersed, emulsified, and stripped to arrive at cleaning purposes by direct and indirect effects on liquids and dirt from cavitation, and acceleration. At present, ultrasonic cleaning machines can be used in the machinery industry, the pharmaceutical industry, and the textile industry, etc.

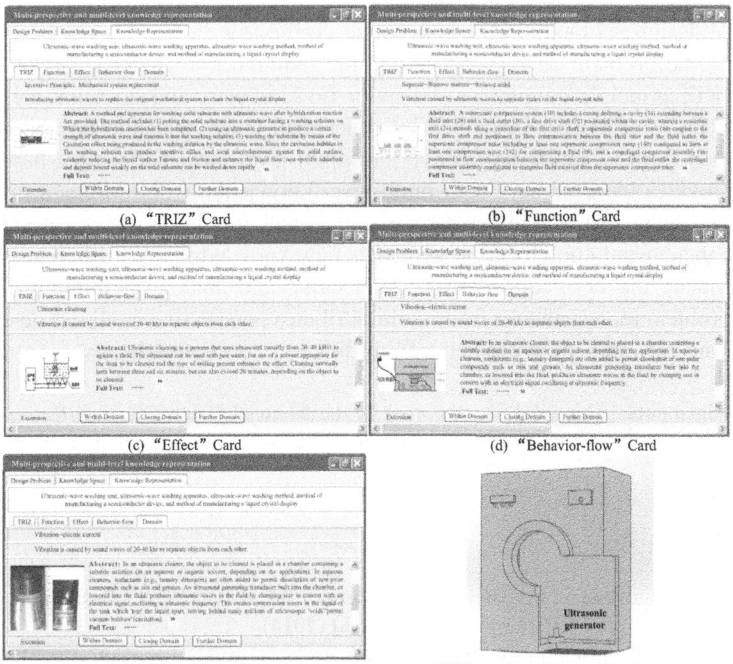

(a) "TRIZ" Card
(b) "Function" Card
(c) "Effect" Card
(d) "Behavior-flow" Card
(e) "Domain" Card
(f) Ultrasonic washing machine conceptual plan

Fig. 8. The interface of knowledge representation for conceptual design case

Based on this, we created a conceptual solution to design an ultrasonic washing machine. The conceptual diagram is shown as in the Fig. 8(f). An ultrasonic generator is used replacing the rotary pulse generator. In addition, the ultrasonic device is compact, and a 20 kHz ultrasonic generator device has a size of 160 mm * 100 mm * 120 mm, which is easy to carry. Users can carry it in their backpacks. When you want to wash your clothes, you only need to fill the pool with water and your clothes, then put the ultrasonic generator into it. solving thereby the contradiction between "operational efficiency" and "noise".

5 Conclusion

According to the problem of transforming from the general solution to the particular solution during inventive problem solving, this paper proposes a multi-perspective and multi-level knowledge representation method from the perspective of human cognition and knowledge transfer, and provides knowledge of different abstraction degrees to the designer in the product design process, such to compensate for the lack of knowledge between the general solution and the particular solution. And finally, it assists the designer to make association and analogy, so as to quickly and effectively propose innovative design solutions in the conceptual design stage.

Due to the problem characteristics and the required knowledge types at different stages, TRIZ principles, functions, behavior flow, effects, and domains are used as attributes. Each attribute is described by conceptual layer, semantic layer and factual layer, which forms a multi-perspective and multi-level local knowledge base. Moreover, it provides the designers with multi-level knowledge within domain, in closing domain and in further domain, which is convenient for the designer to understand. Focus on the current knowledge, it generates new knowledge from different levels, so as to stimulate the designers to make associative and analogical thinking. Besides, through problem representation from multi-attributes perspective, it allows designers to observe, analyze, and solve problems from different conceptual levels.

Acknowledgements. This work is supported by the National Natural Science Research Foundation of China (NSFC) (No. 51435011) and the China Scholarship Council (CSC).

References

1. Lutters, E., van Houten, F.J., Bernard, A., Mermoz, E., Schutte, C.S.: Tools and techniques for product design. CIRP Ann. **63**(2), 607–630 (2014)
2. Horvath, I.: A treatise on order in engineering design research. Res. Eng. Des. **15**(3), 155–181 (2004)
3. Chandrasegaran, S.K., et al.: The evolution, challenges, and future of knowledge representation in product design systems. Comput. Aided Des. **45**(2), 204–228 (2013)
4. Cong, H., Tong, L.H.: Grouping of TRIZ inventive principles to facilitate automatic patent classification. Expert Syst. Appl. **34**(1), 788–795 (2008)
5. Prickett, P., Aparicio, I.: The development of a modified TRIZ technical system ontology. Comput. Ind. **63**(3), 252–264 (2012)
6. Yu, H., Fan, D.: Man-made boards technology trends based on TRIZ evolution theory. Phys. Procedia **33**(6), 221–227 (2012)
7. Park, H., Ree, J.J., Kim, K.: Identification of promising patents for technology transfers using TRIZ evolution trends. Expert Syst. Appl. **40**(2), 736–743 (2013)
8. Zhang, Y., Luo, X., Li, J., Buis, J.J.: A semantic representation model for design rationale of products. Adv. Eng. Inform. **27**(1), 13–26 (2013)
9. Qin, H., Wang, H., Johnson, A.L.: A RFBSE model for capturing engineers' useful knowledge and experience during the design process. Robot. Comput. Integr. Manuf. **44**, 30–43 (2017)
10. Aulive Homepage. http://www.aulive.com/. Accessed 10 July 2019

11. Pro/innovator Homepage. http://www.iwint.com/en/products/pro_innovator-20081208-211930.html. Accessed 02 May 2019
12. PIXSEB Homepage. http://pixseb.com/. Accessed 02 May 2019
13. CREAP Homepage. http://www.creap.cn/. Accessed 02 May 2019
14. CREAX Homepage. https://www.creax.com/en/create/product-innovation. Accessed 10 July 2019
15. Liu, L., Li, Y., Ma, J., Du, X., Liu, H.: Application of TRIZ in creative design based on knowledge granularity. J. Mech. Eng. **52**(5), 22–32 (2016)
16. Cross, N.: Designerly Ways of Knowing. Springer, London (2006). https://doi.org/10.1007/1-84628-301-9
17. Yan, W., Liu, H., Zanni-Merk, C., Cavallucci, D.: IngeniousTRIZ: an automatic ontology-based system for solving inventive problems. Knowl. Based Syst. **75**, 52–65 (2015)

Conceptual Design of the Technical System Using Complementary Use of TRIZ Function Analysis and Patent Information

Sehoon Cho[1(✉)], Kyeongwon Lee[2], and Yongwon Song[2]

[1] Hanwha Precision Machinery, Seongnam-Si, Gyeong-Do, South Korea
sehoon.cho@hanwha.com, sh68.cho@gmail.com
[2] Korea Polytechnic University, Siheung, Gyeonggi-Do, South Korea

Abstract. In general, patents are the outcome of research and development. TRIZ is making a real contribution to solving many problems in new research and development. Such contributions create new patents. Patent and TRIZ have an interdependent relationship from the beginning. In most cases, TRIZ will have a chance to contribute when there is a real engineering problem or when the problem is expected. This study attempts to verify that the above-mentioned relationships are made more active by increasing the interaction, and that the technology systems we want and planned are optimized more quickly. Especially, it is useful in the initial concept design phase of the product, and it is more useful in the new product design situation where the background knowledge of the product or the design experience is low or not. In brief, we propose a tear-down analysis of products that are most similar to the target technology system, or search for prior patents based on 'technology tree' and function. The patent research will acquire the keywords necessary for the patent search by analyzing the function or performance keyword and the similar product by the new VOC, VOB. Through this process, the core technology necessary for the initial conceptual design of the target system and the patent information to be utilized are obtained. From the obtained patent information, we get a hint about the technical components and the interaction relationship for the new system. This facilitates conceptual design for the new technology system.

Keywords: Conceptual design · Tear down analysis · Patent search and analysis · Optimal design · Function analysis · Trimming · Design around · FOS

1 Introduction

1.1 Patent and TRIZ

In general, patents are the outcome of research and development, and TRIZ is known as a problem solving methodology obtained through studying the characteristics and

S. Cho—Ph.D. student at Korea Polytechnic University.

Published by Springer Nature Switzerland AG 2019
R. Benmoussa et al. (Eds.): TFC 2019, IFIP AICT 572, pp. 240–256, 2019.
https://doi.org/10.1007/978-3-030-32497-1_20

patterns of a large number of patents. TRIZ is making a real contribution to solving many problems in new research and development. Such contributions create new patents. Patent and TRIZ have an interdependent relationship from the beginning. In most cases, TRIZ will have a chance to contribute when there is a real engineering problem or when the problem is expected. This relationship is often regarded as a passive relationship. This study attempts to verify that the above-mentioned relationships are made more active by increasing the interaction, and that the technology systems we want and planned are optimized more quickly.

1.2 Patent Information

Patents and their legislation have different standards and operating systems in different countries. This paper briefly examines the meaning of patent information in the US patent system as an example and introduces the basis of what this paper uses. Normally, when a patent application is filed with the US Patent and Trademark Office (PTO), it is firstly confirmed whether the PTO's employee conforms to the format required for the application, and an examiner will be appointed to examine the relevant technical field. The examiner will first look at the specification and the claim, and find that the invention is '35 U.S.C. §101' of the patent. The examiner shall review the details of the description and review the prior art after reviewing the conformity to the requirements for registration (35 U.S.C. §112). The examiner will review the research result to see if there is a "novelty" (35 USC § 102) and "unobviousness" (35 USC § 103) and then decide whether to issue a patent or reject it.

"The specification shall contain a written description of the invention, and of the manner and process of making and using it, in such full, clear, concise, and exact terms as to enable any person skilled in the art to which it pertains, or with which it is most nearly connected, to make and use the same, and shall set forth the best mode contemplated by the inventor of carrying out his invention." This is summarized in (a) a "written description" requirement, (b) a "enablement" requirement, and (c) a "best mode" requirement. Here, the enablement requirement can be divided into the "how to make" requirements and the "how to use" requirements, which will enable a person skilled in the art to make and use an invention It should be taught in the specification. The case is explained as follows.

"To be enabling, the specification of a patent must teach those skilled in the art how to make and use the full scope of the claimed invention without 'undue experimentation.'" In re Wright, 999 F.2d 1557, 1561 (Fed. Cir. 1993).

In the end, it can be seen that the patent information contains essential components for its specific function, performance implementation and technical effect, its interactions and concrete examples. Analyzing one patent means analyzing one technology system. The elements constituting the claim are components of the technical system, and the contents described in order to obtain the function and performance describe the interaction of the components.

1.3 Use of Patent Information and Problem Solving

Patent information having the legal requirements described above has been utilized in various ways by industry.

1.3.1 Prior Patent Research (PSR)

Before proceeding with research and development, basically, developers list up the products to be used for business planning or R & D and the technologies used in the products and perform 'Prior Art Research'. Researchers look for the presence of prior art or patents that are the same or similar to the technology of interest. If there are patents that are substantially the same as or similar to the technology of interest in the results, a review of the patent matter should be done first.

The person in charge of the assignment judges whether or not to do 'Design around' to solve the patent problem. Another example of use is that prior to filing the invention with the Patent Office, the inventor or the patent expert of the company conducts 'Prior Art/Patent Research' and judges whether the application is filed at the Patent Office according to the result of the review.

1.3.2 Patent Map (PM)

Company researchers or planning departments use patent information to prepare new projects or to investigate industry trends. It draws a kind of map with time and technology center with patent information. The company searches and analyzes the patent information on the subject such as country, competitor, product, technology, specific researcher, period, region according to purpose. The results of this research provide information that suggests the flow of development of a specific technology, a technology strategy of a company, a patent strategy, a portfolio of a business, or a future product. It also allows you to predict which researchers are organized and when new features will be added to which products.

1.3.3 Function Oriented Search (FOS)

FOS is one of the useful problem solving methods to find out from various information (resources) when there is a task to be solved or a function required in one technical system is determined.

FOS is similar to 'Prior Patent Search', but it defines the function to be searched and performs function-oriented research. Function-Oriented Search (FOS) is a problem solving tool based upon identifying existing technologies worldwide, using function criteria [1]. If the problem (task) to be solved is defined, investigate whether there is an identical or similar case attempted for the problem solving (function). The flow consists of four steps and there are detailed steps. As an example, proceed as follows. Each step can have sub-steps.

Table 1 shows that the FOS is modified to correspond to the patent database. The following table shows a brief table of methods and procedures that I use mostly.

Table 1. Function-Oriented Search (FOS)

Main Steps	Sub Steps	Guidance
Definition of main function	Definition of key issues to be solved	
	Define the function to be performed	Combination of words to be searched and search expression
Generalization of function	Change function to be performed to generalized function	What (subject) + predicate, maintenance or change of parameter
	Key word extraction from the point of substance-function-problem	
Find case and idea	International patent (technology) survey	Using patent classification table
	Selection of Leading Area	Selection of industry group that is widely used by quantitative analysis
Create solution	Select the most suitable technology/solution to perform necessary functions	
	Identification of possible problems in applying selected technology and application of solution	

The Function-Oriented Search is to find the problem and the functions, hits, or principles needed to solve it. However, if there is only a principle or function itself to solve the contradiction, new sub-problems may arise in the process of using them. So far, the purpose and effects of some cases of using patent information can be basically summarized as a process in which a rough technical system is defined, finding a comparative object, or finding similarities of some of the functions.

There are various examples and studies that TRIZ is very useful as a tool and method for dealing with patent problems [4–7]. It has also been verified through various attempts and exploits that patent information is useful for solving problems [15]. In this paper, we are going to use patent information to solve the problems of the existing technology system, that is, the initial conceptual design to achieve it when a new function or performance is required.

1.4 New Threat of Patent Information

The obtained patent information is beneficial but at the same time has new risk factors. Because patents are information that is proprietary to the technology for a certain period of time, users should be very careful according to their usage patterns.

There are a number of studies that use TRIZ to solve problems in patent disputes [18–20]. There are cases where research results are used in practice. However, the fact that the problem is resolved in the solution of the patent law and commercial problem solving are often different. It is desirable to judge whether all problems or tasks are solved based on the actual profit or value obtained from the whole point of view. It should not be judged simply by technically solving the problem. Simply implementing the desired functionality and performance does not solve the problem. The solution should not create serious subsequent problems. In particular, if the contradictory solution or concrete solution created or presented by the TRIZ expert infringes the patent of the third party, it becomes a new big problem. If a new problem can not be resolved in a timely manner, or if the resources and costs needed to solve it exceed the problem owner's expectations, then the attempted solution is not a solution. Therefore, when dealing with patent information, it should be cautious of the claim.

Patent information is the best information resource that must be utilized in the process of solving technical problems. The reason was verified by case and theoretically. In particular, there is the usefulness of patent information at the point of conceptual design without concrete problem situations. It is one of the implications of this paper that the existing application area extends to a wider area. The solution derived through this process will have both applicability and patentability at the same time.

2 The Reality of the Planning of a Typical New Product or System

Research and development of most technical systems starts with people's needs. Whether it is convenience, comfort, or pleasure, it comes from seeking something better developed from the current state. A technology system that people are currently using or have experienced in the past is the starting point. It may not be a problem of the present technology system itself. It is a new requirement and expectation for technical systems by a human.

2.1 Design Motivation for New Systems

Voice of Customer (VOC) and Voice of Business (VOB) have similar and different appearance, but individual keywords are the same. That is, the new functions, improved performance, convenience, low price, and new value are the keywords. In this case, low price has a difference in terms of suppliers and recipients in 'manufacturing cost' and 'purchase price', but the essence is the same. Specific efforts or attempts to reach new demands or expectations are made in the laboratory. The problem is that there are various constraints and new problems in the process of such efforts or attempts. Development period, quality verification, product price, manufacturing cost, technology barrier, patent problem, and the like.

Especially when the new expectations are beyond the developers' experience, skills and knowledge. Sometimes the content and desired level of a technical problem goes beyond common sense. These situations can be called contradictory situations.

2.2 New Needs and New Challenges

Most of the work in the laboratory of the company is the extension of the existing company's products. Much of the additional functionality and performance enhancements are made. However, when existing products do not meet the ongoing needs and expectations of customers in the marketplace, or when the appearance of alternative systems is anticipated, new challenges arise. Also, when a competitor has already made a new product and put it on the market, it will reach similar difficulties. Sometimes it can be a challenge to develop without causing conflicts with competitors' patents.

Difficulty here can mean that developers need to work with new approaches and other unfamiliar ways. It may be a situation that requires different approaches and new methods and efforts compared to the technology, experience and knowledge contained in the current product. In many cases, the company may be in a situation where it needs to establish new business strategies or plan new products. It is foolish to expect new products using the same methods and materials [Albert Einstein].

2.3 Beginning and Limitations of Conceptual Design

In order to develop most new products, concept design will be done first. It is practically very difficult to manufacture a product with a complex technology system in a single attempt. In particular, the needs and expectations of customers are often unclear in the marketplace, and sometimes requests or expectations from managers are frustrating for developers. Researchers strive to establish clearer technical goals from VOCs in the market and from VOBs of managers. The beginning of conceptual design is designed by a few people who are rich in experience, knowledge and skills relative to the business or product or technology involved in the organization. They define the approximate composition, function, and performance of a product that reflects more or less specific requirements from VOCs and VOBs. Most companies prepare their business and products with a long-term plan. Predict market and technology trends and develop key technologies in advance, bringing new products to market in a timely manner. There are prepared developers and engineers in this process.

At times, however, there is no planner suitable for the company. Even if there are designers who have similar experience and knowledge, it is difficult to predict the actual technical problems that will be encountered in developing the conceptual designs made by them and developing them to make actual products. Many issues remain, such as the required period of time for the final product to be made, money, developer, major component supply, and so on. In actual product development, it is very difficult to obtain results that satisfy both VOC and VOB. Developers study functionality and performance as final goals, and product planners plan products for sales and profit. Products with potential problems are under development. Most of the time when the market demands and the timing and methods of supplying are inconsistent. Therefore, despite the fact that many products are planned in technology management, the proportion of products that are successful in the market is very low, so that there are cases in which it is not certain whether a product that succeeds in actual market is thoroughly planned. Figure 1 is an example of statistics showing this situation.

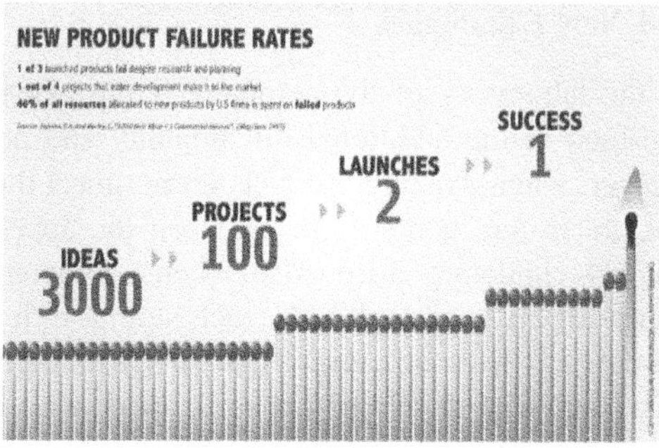

Fig. 1. New product failure rate [2]

These results, together with the need for the development of a new methodology, continue to analyze the successful cases of the relatively good group and make them more aware of the need for active use. Many researchers have attempted to combine the potential difficulties of conceptual design with a variety of methodologies to solve problems and errors in the process. Samsung incorporated several research methodologies, including 'Technology Road Map' and 'Technology Tree' around 2000.

In addition, research has been conducted on how various methodologies can be applied in the process of delivering products and services from mid- and long-term business planning to customers. Figure 2 shows the appropriate time for the various methodologies to be used step by step throughout the entire R & D process [22]. Here, 'Technology Tree' has a feature that combines 'Logic Tree' and 'Technical classification'. It means that the technology and the components of a technology system are structured logically and systematically.

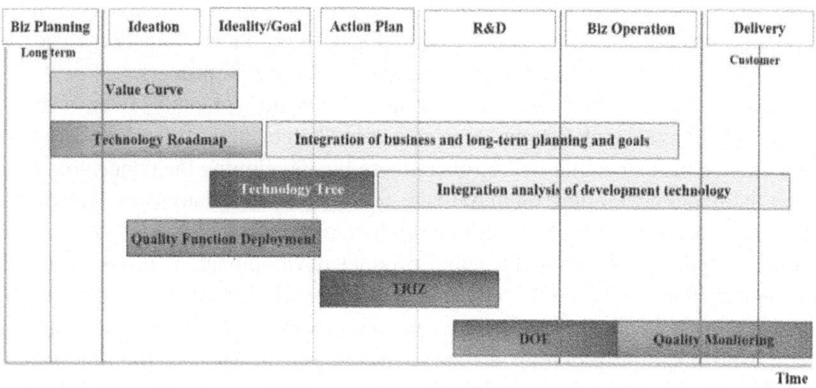

Fig. 2. R & D process and methodology of research methodology [22]

'Technology Tree' can be a good tool to systematically view the current technology system, to improve the technical system by grasping the level of research field, element technology, adding or removing new functions, and reducing manufacturing cost. Figure 3 is a conceptual diagram that predicts which element technology needs further research and which product is likely to be applied [22]. Interaction or combination of these methodologies can be a good approach for predicting future products or selecting targets for strategic technology development. In addition, by combining 'Quality Function Deployment' and 'Technology Tree', VOC can be easily converted into an engineering language and contribute to understanding the related element technology. However, it does not provide the necessary methods, hints or layouts for designing new products for new VOCs or VOBs.

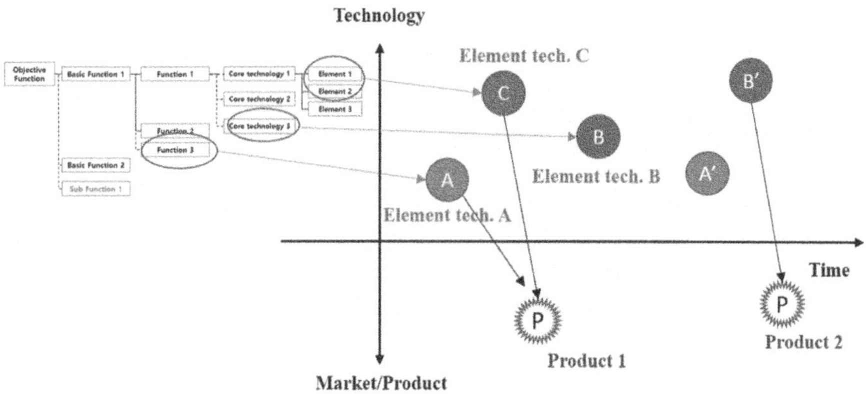

Fig. 3. Technology Tree application in Technology Roadmap [22]

In the field of TRIZ, various methods and applications of tools and new attempts are continuing. It is not a real solution if existing methods create new problems or have potential problems. In Part 7 (7.2) of ARIZ [3], Altshuller asks whether each solution meets the requirements of IFR-1. Recently, Pahl and Beitz proposed the hybrid method of TRIZ method and SDA (Systematic Design Approach) [12]. Fundamental understanding of conceptual design, safety and problem solving resulted to a systematic yet simple optimization process simultaneously changing the perspective of creative problem solving as a whole [12].

Segmenting the system and structure of a prototype into F3(Form-Fit-Function) can help designers plan and organize resources, such as technology concept, incorporation of new materials and time taken to develop the system pertaining to the constraints [13]. The combined methodology of TRIZ with the constraint-based approach sanguinely increases the capability to design with constraint management [13]. Also, an integrated model of the Conceptual Design Process was presented, which is based on QFD, Functional Analysis and TRIZ [9, 10]. Here, the information obtained during the Functional Analysis was used to identify the product structure which reveals the technical parameters needed for the QFD process [9]. This is very useful in deriving the functions required in a technical system in conjunction with a contradiction matrix.

Another attempt has been proposed by the Analytical Hierarchy Process (ARI) to enhance the three main stages of the TRIZ methodology: problem definition, root cause identification and solution generation [21]. There are also studies to explore the symbiotic relationship between axiomatic design and TRIZ, to utilize the strengths of each method, and to complement vulnerabilities [11]. However, there is a fundamental need for professional experience such as various situations, constraints, and resource analysis to be considered in conceptual design [14].

Until now, various methodologies including TRIZ have been integrated or partially complemented. And the results obtained good results corresponding to the purpose of each attempt. Normally, the company checks the business risk through 'Freedom To Operate Analysis (FTO)' before the product is released to the market [15]. Likewise, the final stage of problem solving requires patent analysis. In other words, we must review whether the beneficial solution infringes the patents of third parties.

3 Additional Attempts at Conceptual Design

It is very useful to use some TRIZ tools, including essential patent information at the stage of planning a product or technology system in terms of the final Goal and total cost, before specific engineering problem exists. This procedure minimizes new risks or problems in the use of the final solution.

3.1 Basic Flow for the Conceptual Design

An in-depth analysis of the product planning stage in conceptual design has (a) Identification of needs and opportunities, (b) Resource assessment, (c) Definition of a first product requirement list to be updated during the design process [14]. The TRIZ-SDA Conceptual Design Framework (CDF) consists of eight steps [16]: (a) Identifying and Understanding, (b) Formulating Ideas and Finding Solution, and (c) Evaluating and Confirming. Table 2 shows the flow of the method presented in this paper as 4 main steps and 8 sub steps. This can be called patent information-based problem solving (PIPS).

Table 2. Patent information-based problem solving

Main steps	Sub Steps	Guidance
Definition of functional requirements in system	VOC & VOB review	QFD, HOQ, ENV
	Similar/basic system review	Tear Down Review (TDR) analysis Gap information
	Technology tree draft for target system	Keywords list up based on function
Generalization/search of the functions	Prior art (patent) search	World patent database, FOS
	Patent information classification & analysis	IPC. CPC, grouping
Developing solution	Function analysis	Trimming
	Implementation the solution	Resource analysis
Solution enhancement	Patent apply & portfolio	Claim structuring

3.2 Detail Flow for the Conceptual Design

The flow of problem solving using patent information presented in this paper and presented experimentally is explained in more detail as follows.

3.2.1 VOC and VOB Review

As at the roof of the HOQ are identified the contradictory relationships among the design parameters, it seems straightforward to use these identified contradictory parameters to find a link to Altshuller's Technical Contradiction Matrix [9]. These can be used to derive functional and performance words from the VOCs and VOBs that the customer ultimately expects or requires. Of course, you can create a list using the ENV (Element, Name of Feature, Value) Model. It is desirable to draw as many functional words as possible.

3.2.2 Similar/Basic System Review

It is difficult to design a new technology system from the start with general knowledge and skills. Therefore, it is recommended to find a system that is similar to the function and performance currently required. If the actual product is obtained, test the function and performance before disassembly, and obtain the gap information of required function and performance. Then, the decomposition process is performed while sequentially estimating the components and functions. This Tear Down Review (TDR) analysis can be a very important process in determining functionality, performance, structure, components, materials and pricing information from a similar system to a new target system. Electronic components provide individual manufacturers and pricing information, and PCBs can infer module-level functionality. It is appropriate that TDR should be conducted by three or four people with different technical fields.

3.2.3 Technology Tree (TT) Draft for Target System

The purpose of this step is to extract the keywords for the function based search. The structural approach to the construction of the technical system can be developed using 'Technology Tree (TT)'. The 'Technology tree' is a method to define functions for the purpose of the system and to organize the detailed functions for implementing the functions and the components for creating each function. When the objective function of a new technology system to be created by a new requirement or need is roughly defined, subdivide it into main functions and additional functions and list the configurations for making each function. Although TT itself does not provide a clue for new ideas or solutions, it is useful for understanding the components for exploring new technology systems as functions. Figure 4 shows the development of the basic TT. TT can be diagrammed with function and performance list, gap information obtained from TDR analysis, unit module information of similar system, component parts, function and performance information.

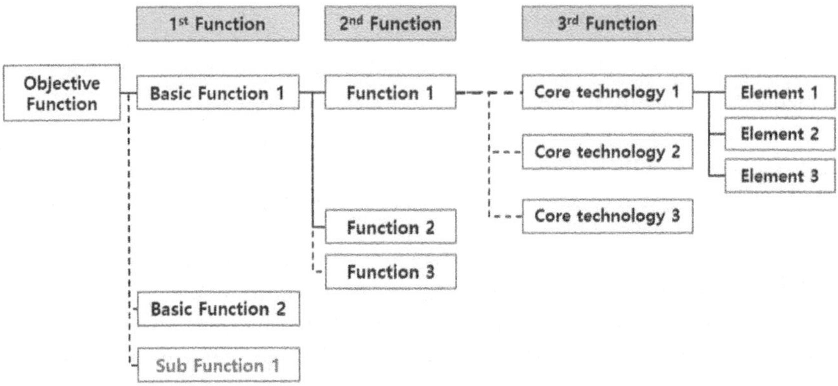

Fig. 4. Technology Tree [22]

3.2.4 Prior Art (Patent) Search Based on Function

The TT, which is primarily made, is partially completed with functions and capabilities to meet customer needs and expectations. In other words, there are situations where functions or performances that can be obtained or completed by existing similar systems, as well as features and capabilities that are missing or lack items. Here, function-based keywords for searching prior art and patents can be extracted. Create a function-based keyword for each function, and separate the function to be created and the function to be created, respectively. The patent searches are conducted through function-oriented keywords according to the number of kinds of functions to be found. Patent information is provided by the patent office of most countries. Apply FOS well known in TRIZ field.

3.2.5 Patent Information Classification and Analysis

The prior art and the patents found are classified according to the presence or absence of the function. Regardless of the classification, additional procedures should be followed if living patents are consistent with the functionality and performance within the TT Draft. The discovery of the problem patent and the procedure for solving it can be done using the procedures and tools of the previous studies using TRIZ [18–20].

The degree of completion of the TT Draft can be increased from the patent information found. First, it is necessary to partially complement the functions and performance learned through the TDR of the similar system to improve the completeness. Functionality and performance inferred from the characteristics or shape of a component may occasionally include errors. It is necessary to analyze the interactions between the components and the components necessary for implementing the existing functions and performance before implementing the new functions and performance. This is essential for resource analysis of the configuration that a subsequent existing system requires and for analyzing interactions between new components for added functionality and performance implementation.

Then analyze patents for missing or incomplete functions in the current TT Draft. Similar configurations will be found in different patents from those described in detail for the same or similar functions from multiple patents. From this patent information, we raise the level of completion of TT.

3.2.6 Function Analysis

Based on the completed TT, it is possible to analyze the interaction relation with the components, that is, the function analysis of TRIZ. It is possible to derive the technical contradiction and the physical contradiction through the interaction relation between the added component based on the existing component and the existing function and the newly added function. Trimming through system analysis, system optimization can be performed subsequently.

3.2.7 Implementation the Solution

The patent information used in the process of this step includes a detailed description of each functional implementation. Thus, such information is the source of information that implements the functionality and performance of the intended technology system without further experimentation or special difficulties. In addition, the functional analysis is deepened, and the system is optimized by performing resource analysis on the components. Subsequent steps will improve the system's completeness through partial detail design if necessary.

3.2.8 Patent Apply and Portfolio

In addition, the function of patent application and its components are easily extracted in the process of classifying and analyzing patent information. New patents are created, including interrelated configurations. New variations of patents can be made in various combinations of candidate components in functional implementation.

4 Case Study

The case of this paper is a case based on VOC or VOB at the business planning stage of the company or university and individual business. Most of the cases are undergoing the development stage for actual commercialization after the planning stage and also the patents have been made. In addition to the following examples, drone, cosmetics, and mechanical systems were also useful for solving real problems and developing patents.

4.1 Case (1) Video Image Problem of Surveillance Camera for Outdoor

The needs of external customers, VOCs, are addressing the problem of losing specific surveillance areas caused by reflected spotlight problems. Most surveillance camera manufacturers have responded to these customer requests to understand them as physical phenomena. It is also installed in a lower area than the installation position in the surveillance camera installation and surveillance area. Despite various attempts to solve the problem, the solution was not obtained. There was a solution that showed some effect, but it was not applicable because it caused a lot of manufacturing cost and it affected profit and loss. The problem was that both VOC and VOB were not resolved.

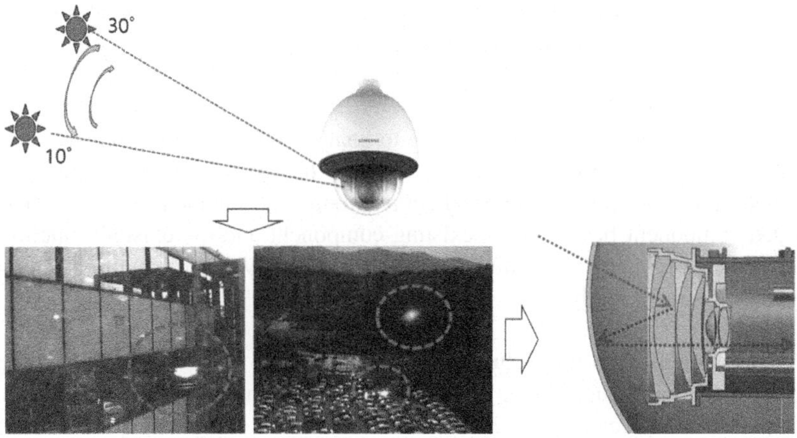

Fig. 5. Reflected spot light problem situation

Figure 5 shows the ‘Reflected spot light’ problem situation. External installation The surveillance camera sometimes monitors higher than the camera installation position to monitor a large area. The figure illustrates the problem that occurs.

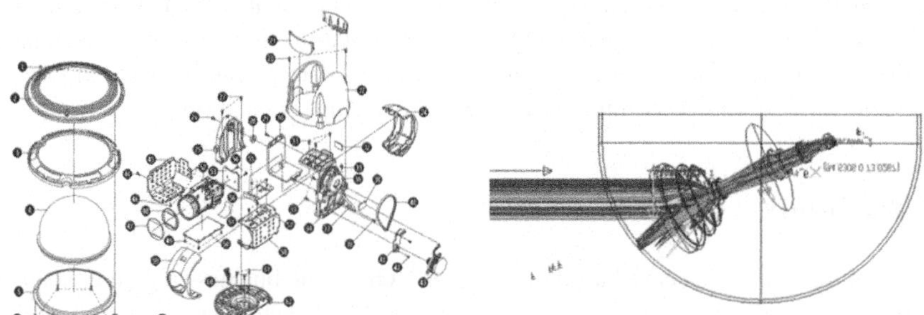

Fig. 6. TDR and problem analysis, solution principles and results

In accordance with the procedure presented in this paper, we performed camera disassembly and function development of our company and competitors, and followed FOS according to the keywords. The patent search did not provide information on the required function implementation. I found information on physical phenomena at Goldfire. However, there is no implementation example, so we tried to analyze the resource for implementing new function. Figure 6 illustrates an example of application to real products based on similar phenomena. And Fig. 7 shows the actual images comparing the post-war situation according to the application of the solution.

Before

After

Fig. 7. Comparison of effectiveness of solution application

Case 1's solution has been patented and registered in several countries including the United States [23]. Although a new alternative has been introduced to the market as a replacement for the structure with a transparent cover removed, the technical problem that has not been solved for a long time has been resolved. This has shown that the difficult problem that the company has long given up solving can be solved through TRIZ.

4.2 Case (2) Large-Area Graphene Transfer System Problem

In 2010, Andre Gamem and Konstantin Novoselov won the Nobel Prize for physics for separating graphene from graphite and became known worldwide. At that time, we were jointly developing large area graphene synthesis technology for commercialization. As shown in Fig. 8, the graphene is synthesized and subjected to a transfer process for actual use. The third party had patents on these processes. There were situations with high royalties and some physical problems. This task was a problem of patent problem solving and improvement of manufacturing method based on VOB.

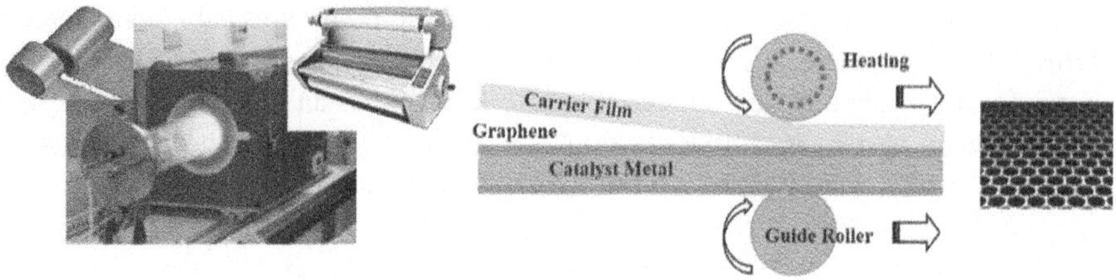

Fig. 8. Concept of transfer method after synthesis of graphene

The serious problem is that the current process is a graphene with a thickness of 0.2 nm, (1) Degradation of surface properties of graphene after transfer, (2) Surface damage of graphene due to mechanical pressure of roller, (3) the graphene to control the gap and the contrast roller. Since the patent has been started, TT was created through TDR and claim chart of experimental manufacturing equipment. The patent search provided a technique for manufacturing thin plates using rollers, but it was not suitable for handling the thickness of graphene. Finally, in the conceptual diagram obtained from TDR as shown in Fig. 9, a method of attaching different thin plates in a physical and non-contact manner was devised from a device for cleaning the surface of the thin plate with the air included in the thin plate manufacturing process.

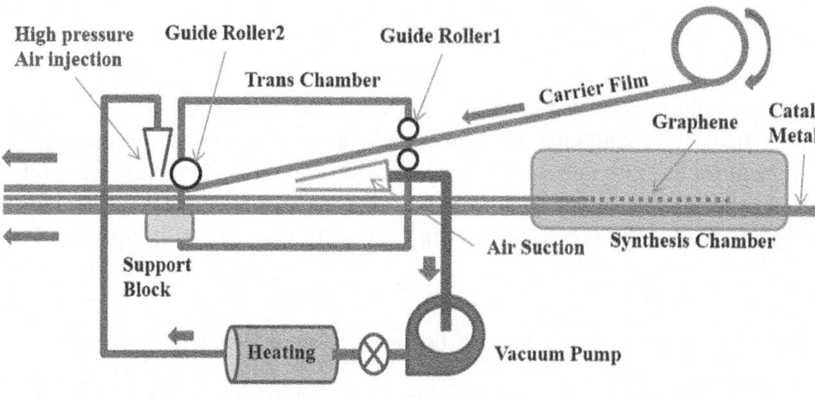

Fig. 9. Conceptual diagram of sheet metal attachment using air pressure

Case 2's solution was filed and registered as a patent in several countries, including the United States [24]. Based on this conceptual design, several processes have been further improved and additional patents have been filed. The solution to this task is to be set up as a subsequent process necessary to produce large area graphene.

In addition to the above examples, many cases have been based on the present study and a good solution has been obtained.

5 Conclusions

It is a bit hesitant to define a good problem solver or an appropriate methodology to solve a problem well in a skill area that is familiar to them. It is a true TRIZ expert's role if you find clues in solving unfamiliar technical areas and finding and providing directions and technical principles and resources to solve problems.

VOC, VOB, new business planning, concept design of new products, product configuration in the basic design phase, problems of technical design and technical implementation, there have been various studies and efforts to solve this problem. Rather than new research, it is necessary to use them well and settle and spread with more general methodology. This paper shows how the features of patent information are used in such a process to obtain useful results in the industry and the possibility.

The result of the patent information survey can be expanded to add new resources or analyze in-depth system resources (derivative resources, modified resources), modification of purpose, etc., depending on the presence or absence of necessary information.

When the required end customer's demand and expected function or performance is set, the technical patents are searched in the patent as the preparation for the technical system design to implement it. In the analysis process, the technology system to be implemented by functional analysis of TDR, Technology Tree and TRIZ We have shown that it is advantageous to classify the necessary functions and to use patent information for empirical information to implement each function.

An additional research task is the attempt to conceptualize a future technology system using patent information, such as new material and its characteristics, new unit module, etc., which have the potential role of resources to create a new technology system of the future.

References

1. Litvin, S.S.: New TRIZ-Based Tool — Function-Oriented Search (FOS), 13 August 2005
2. New product failure rate. https://visual.ly/community/infographic/business/new-product-failure-rates
3. Altshuller, G., The Innovation Algorithm: TRIZ, Systematic Innovation and Technical Creativity, Worchester, MA (1999)
4. Ikovenko, S.: Strategies for patent busting using function analysis and TRIZ. In: TRIZCON 2004 (2004)
5. Ikovenko, S., Kogan, S.: TRIZ application for patent strategies development. In: Proceedings of TFC, Graz, Austria, 16–18 November 2005, pp. 427–434 (2005)
6. Ikovenko, S.; Kogan, S: Patent practices of addressing doctrine of equivalents and its substitutes with G3:ID/TRIZ. In: TRIZfuture 2006 (2006)
7. Ikovenko, S. TRIZ Application for IP Strategies Development, Referat to obtain the TRIZ master title, Boston (2006)
8. Park, Y.T., Kuk, K.H.: Structure development of systematic conceptual design process for designing engineering systems. J. Korean Soc. Precis. Eng. **24**(9=198), 86–94 (2007)
9. Leon-Rovira, N., Aguayo, H.; A new model of the conceptual design process using QFD/FA/TRIZ. In: Quality Function Deployment 1998, pp. 437–444 (1998)

10. Hua, Z., Wang, W.: Method of product conceptual design by integrating QFD and TRIZ technical tools. Comput. Integr. Manuf. Syst. **10**(12), 1588–1593 (2004). ISSN 1006-5911
11. Ogot, M.: Conceptual design using axiomatic design in a TRIZ framework. Procedia Eng. **9**, 736–744 (2011). TFC 2006
12. Kamarudin, K.M., Ridgway, K., Hassan, M.R.: Modelling the conceptual design process with hybridization of TRIZ methodology and systematic design approach. Procedia Eng. **131**, 1064–1072 (2015)
13. Kamarudin, K.M., Ridgway, K., Hassan, M.R.: Modelling constraints in the conceptual design process with TRIZ and F3. Procedia CIRP **39**, 3–8 (2016)
14. Frillici, F.S., Fiorineschi, L., Cascini, G.: Linking TRIZ to conceptual design engineering approaches. In: TFC 2014 (2014)
15. Cho, S., Lee, K.: Strategic patent development using TRIZ and patent information in industry. In: TFC 2018 (2018)
16. Kamarudin, K.M., Ridgway, K., Hassan, M.R.: Modelling the conceptual design process with hybridization of TRIZ methodology and systematic design approach. In: TRIZ Future Conference 2014. Procedia CIRP (2014)
17. Kamarudin, K.M., Ridgway, K., Ismail, N.: Abstraction and generalization in conceptual design process: involving safety principles in TRIZ-SDA environment. Procedia CIRP **39**, 16–21 (2016). ISSN 2212-8271. TFC 2015
18. Hung, Y.-C., Hsu, Y.-L.: An integrated process for designing around existing patents through the theory of inventive problem-solving, 1 January 2007
19. Yao, B., Jiang, P., Zhang, T., Ma, Q.: A study of designing around patents based on Function Trimming. In: 2010 IEEE International Conference on Management of Innovation and Technology (ICMIT), pp. 214–219 (2010). https://doi.org/10.1109/icmit.2010
20. Jiang, P., Zhai, J., Chen, Z., Tan, R.: The patent design around method based on TRIZ. In: IEEE International Conference on Industrial Engineering and Engineering Management, IEEM 2009, pp. 1067–1071 (2009)
21. Rosli, M.U., Ariffin, M.K.A., Sapuan, S.M., Sulaiman, S.: Integrated TRIZ-AHP support system for conceptual design. Appl. Mech. Mater. **548**(549), 1998–2002 (2014)
22. Gil, Y., et al.: Study on the research methodologies for strategy-integrated R&D. Science & Technology Policy Institute (2002)
23. Cho, S.: US 10,084,977 Camera system and photographing method, 25 September 2018
24. Cho, S., Won, D.: US 8,419,880 Method of transferring Graphene, 16 April 2013

TRIZ Barcamp Exercise: Ideas for Wearable Defibrillators

Tiziana Bertoncelli[1(✉)], Barbara Gronauer[2], and Horst Nähler[2]

[1] TRIZ Consulting Group, Sulzbach-Rosenberg, Germany
bertoncelli@triz-consulting.de
[2] TRIZ Akademie, Hünfeld, Germany
{barbara.gronauer,horst.naehler}@triz-akademie.de

Abstract. A wearable external defibrillator is usually an option for all patients at risk for sudden cardiac arrest (SCA) for whom the very invasive surgery intervention to implant an internal defibrillator is not viable. The metallic paddles that convey the electrical discharge have to stay attached to the skin for effectiveness of the device, but such a solution presents several problems, i.e. lack of comfort, difficulties in usage for overweight people, skin rash and burns, itching, sleep disturbances. Moreover, the vest be removed to shower or bathe. As a result, many patients stop using it, putting themselves at a very high risk. Such a system presents a lot of issues and contradictions and an effective use of TRIZ methodology could be very helpful to identify the needed improvement actions. The present paper will show a case study model developed for the first TRIZ Barcamp, with strong focus on the modelling peculiarities required by a very short session, the ideas generated by the participants and the learnt lessons.

Keywords: Wearable defibrillator · Barcamp · Contradictions · Functional analysis

1 A TRIZ Session for a Wearable Defibrillator

1.1 The TRIZ Barcamp Experience

The present paper will show a case study model developed for the first TRIZ Barcamp, focusing on the modelling peculiarities required by a very short session; also the ideas generated by the participants and the learnt lessons will be discussed. The first TRIZ Barcamp took place in Fulda, Germany, in Februar 2018, organized and led by the TRIZ Akademie, following the international format spread by the Barcamp International Network [1]. Originated in the Information Technology field, especially for web application, this unconference concept spread very fast to many other fields.

The content of such an open workshop is chosen at the beginning of the session by the participants themselves.

During the TRIZ Barcamp, attended by ~25 people, different topics were presented introduced at the very beginning, presented as problems to be tackled by means of TRIZ; every short oral presentation was actiually actually a call for participants, where the number of people, the level of needed TRIZ expertise and the approximated required

Published by Springer Nature Switzerland AG 2019
R. Benmoussa et al. (Eds.): TFC 2019, IFIP AICT 572, pp. 257–265, 2019.
https://doi.org/10.1007/978-3-030-32497-1_21

time were stated. After the brief topic introductions, the participants declared their interest and willingness to attend the dedicated session (about 20 min 45 min each), and both the content and the agenda of the workshop were organized accordingly.

1.2 The Wearable Defibrillator Session

The wearable defibrillator topic was proposed and selected by the Barcamp participants for a 20-min 45 min session, for which all level of TRIZ expertise were welcome. It was introduced explaining which kind of patient need such a device and the issues it poses, as explained in detail in Sect. 2. Since a very short time was allocated for the Barcamp exercise, the TRIZ modelling phase had already been sketched during a pre-work session and presented to the participants. The proposed TRIZ tools to be dynamically selected for the problem-solving tools were Physical Contradictions and Substance-Field modeling. A Function Model was also prepared, to serve as an example and guideline. Goal of the workshop was to identify solutions as effective as the implanted defibrillator, but with a lesser degree of invasiveness; the workshop was kicked off posing no boundary to the kind of ideas and with the statement that ideas were to the be released and published afterwards.

2 Wearable Defibrillator: Importance and System Description

The wearable external defibrillator is regarded as a valuable option for all patients at risk for sudden cardiac arrest (SCA). Many cardiovascular conditions require continuous monitoring and the possible intervention with a defibrillator, i.e. recent myocardial infarctions, inherited arrhythmias, and congenital heart diseases [2–6]. The usual way to prevent a sudden arrhythmia in a patient is to implant an internal defibrillator, with a very invasive surgery intervention. When surgery is not possible or before it, the wearable defibrillator offers an alternative. This solution nevertheless poses issues that impair its long-term usage and effectiveness. A substantial improvement of such a system would be of major impact also for patients with limited access to healthcare for geographic and economic reasons, i.e. the ones living in rural areas, and the ones for whom surgery is an economical challenge.

The system typically [2–6] comprises a lightweight vest, a monitoring system and the necessary electrodes to perform the monitoring function and to convey the electrical discharge when an anomaly is detected, as shown in Fig. 1.

The usual reported problems are:

- The person wears the defibrillator all day, but it must be removed to shower or bathe, exposing the patient at risk
- The electrodes need to press against the chest firmly enough to detect heart rhythm changes, but not so tightly that they trigger false alarms
- The defibrillator vest is not comfortable
- It is difficult to use if person is overweight
- Up to one in five people stop using it because of: skin rash, itching, sleep disturbances, skin burns

These issues represented the starting point of the TRIZ modelling effort, explained in Sect. 3.

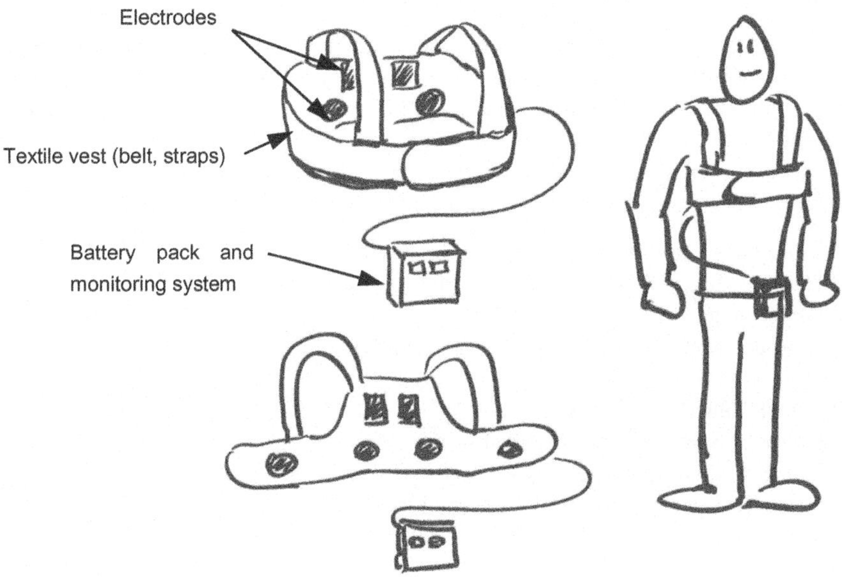

Fig. 1. Sketch of a typical wearable defibrillator.

3 Wearable Defibrillator: Main Aspects and TRIZ Modelling

In addition to the well-known disadvantages listed in Sect. 2, the main aspect that can be expressed as an Engineering Problem is the following: the metallic paddles needed to convey the electrical discharge have to stay attached to the skin for effectiveness of the devices; nevertheless such a solution is not practical since the metallic material damages the skin in the long run. This disadvantage has a very localized operating zone and depicts a harmful interaction; it can be thus very effectively modeled by means of Physical contradictions and a Su-Field Models, as shown in details in Sects. 3.1 and 3.2. Those models were prepared as a pre-work prior to the Barcamp day; the 20 min 45 min session would have not allowed both a modelling and a problem solving stage, so it was preferred to involve the participants in the latter only; the two chosen modeling approaches, being the Su-Field model visual and the physical contradictions focused on the core physics of the problem have been also proven to be the most effective for very short sessions, especially when the participants have little or no previous TRIZ experience [7].

3.1 Physical Contradictions

The physical contradiction presented to the session participants was formulated as follows:

Electrodes SHOULD BE attached to the skin
to monitor heart and convey electrical discharge
Electrodes SHOULD NOT BE attached to the skin
not to irritate, damage or burn it

The workshop participants immediately observed that the approach Separation in Space was not an option, being the electrode placement fixed; nevertheless they recognized quickly that the requirements to fulfill could be expressed as two functions: Monitoring and Convey Electrical Discharge, to be delivered at two different times; a more precise modelling would have demanded to address the two operating modes separately. For this reason, the physical contradiction was refined and split accordingly:

Monitoring Function
Electrodes SHOULD BE attached to the skin
to monitor heart
Electrodes SHOULD NOT BE attached to the skin
not to irritate or damage it
Restart Heartbeat Function
Electrodes SHOULD BE attached to the skin
to convey electrical discharge
Electrodes SHOULD NOT BE attached to the skin
not to irritate, damage or burn it

3.2 Substance-Field Model

The most acute harmful interaction occurs between the defibrillator paddles (electrodes) and the skin; during monitoring because of the mechanical friction and during the electrical discharge because of the electric current and the associated thermal field, as summarized in Fig. 2:

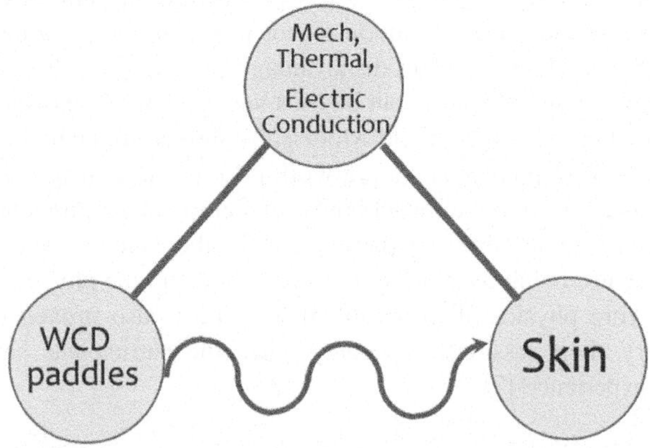

Fig. 2. Substance-field model for a wearable cardioverter defibrillator (WCD): the electrode paddles generate mechanical friction, electric conduction and heat, damaging the skin (harmful interaction).

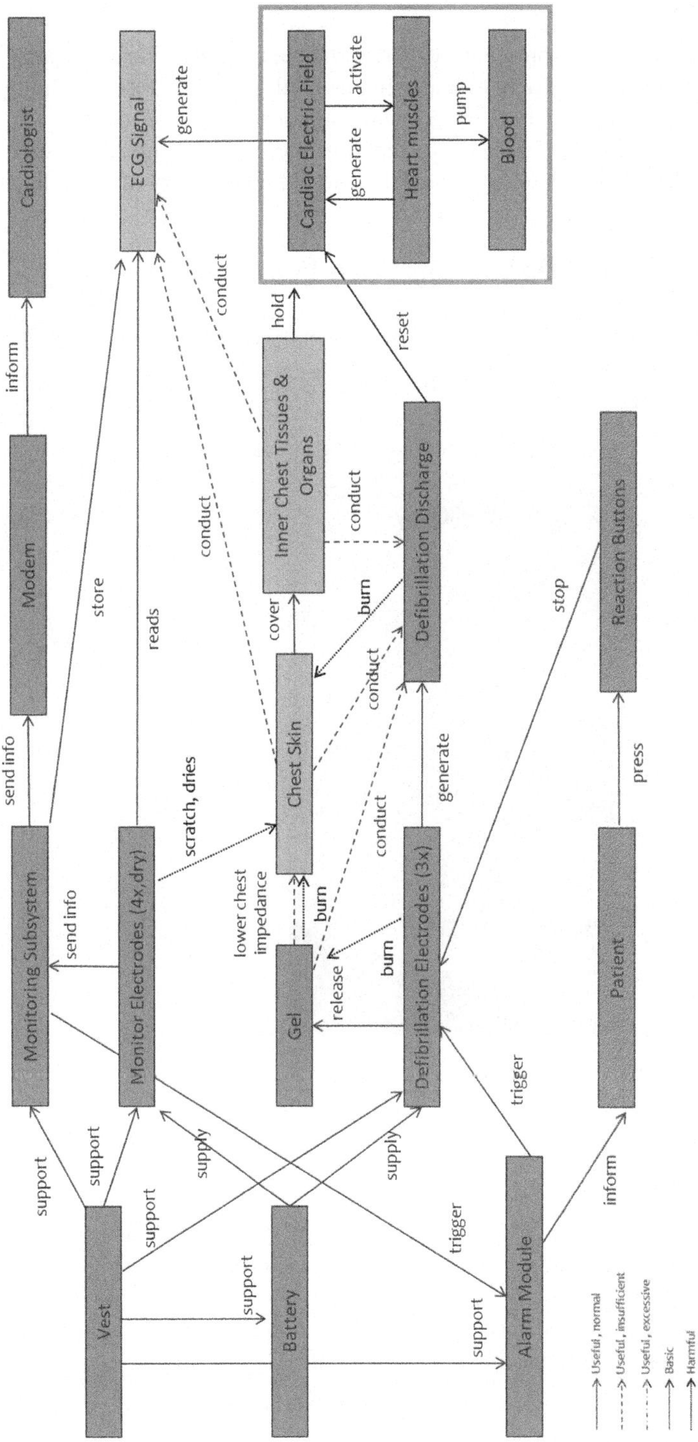

Fig. 3. Function model for a wearable defibrillator (Color figure online)

3.3 Functional Analysis

This function model was briefly presented to the participants, mostly for illustrating purposes, to showcase this approach to the newbies and as a back-up for future inspiration. It reported in Fig. 3, where the System component are depicted in green, the Supersystem ones in blue; the Target of the main function is highlighted in cyan; it is composed of heart muscles, heart electric field and blood for simplicity of modelling.

4 Idea List Description, Discussion, Open Points

Many ideas (~20) were generated (Fig. 4) and subsequently grouped according to the kind of proposed intervention.

Fig. 4. Generated ideas

Modify Vest

1. Use an actuator that compresses shock electrodes on the skin only when arrhythmia detected, using same mechanism (pump) that pushes conductive gel to attach electrodes
2. Use segmented pads: single pad surface so small that skin not damaged, with many small contact surfaces, like lotus-effect or gecko-foot

Modify Monitoring

1. Monitor also through blood pressure
2. Monitor by means of a smartwatch-like device (recognized in a commercial product in November 2018)

Minimize battery size for low weight Vest

1. Use smaller battery + condensator
2. Make it chargeable with net current, auto with a sensor signaling when recharge is needed
3. Use piezo-actuators with body movements

Use other fields (not electrical)

1. T-Shirt with monitoring + mechanical cardiac massage
2. Use piezo-strips for the abovementioned cardiac massage
3. Restart heartbeat not with an electrical shock, but with acoustic field
4. Restart heartbeat not with an electrical shock, but mechanically
5. Activate heart muscles with other impulses (e.g. microwaves?)
6. Use a mixed approach, implementing a smaller shock + mechanical cardiac massage

Act on ECG

1. Produce an artificial ECG
2. Study energy optimization of the needed electric pulse: amplitude & duration

Use another substance S3* between pads and skin to improve conductivity – Modified T-shirt

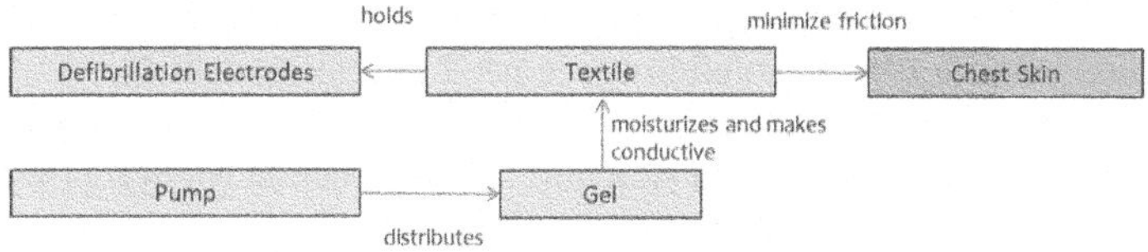

Fig. 5. Function model of a solution

1. Just under the electrodes use a patch of special textile that gets conductive when wet conductive gel is pumped on it
2. Use a mixed textile: e.g. combination of cotton + metal (Fig. 5)

Use another substance S3* between pads and skin to improve conductivity – use available body fluids

1. Blood
2. Sweat
3. Skin Moisture

5 Conclusions: Lessons Learnt

The conclusions can be grouped in two categories: First the immediate observations and the feedback of the participating group, second the observations from the external viewpoint of the TRIZ-facilitator.

Conclusions from immediate observation and feedback:

- The number of ideas and the engagement of the participants confirmed the effectiveness of visual methods like Su-Field models and Physical contradictions
- TRIZ-initiated participants appreciated the pre-prepared modelling effort and enjoyed the creative process
- Non-TRIZ experts were intimidated by the TRIZ-jargon and expressed their wish for more background information about the topic, that resonated quickly but the impact of which needed to be better clarified
- During the idea generation process the time was too short to address more technical questions, i.e.: how much energy is needed for a defibrillator discharge, which is the maximum time window for defibrillator intervention and how many people are affected.

Conclusions from external observations from the viewpoint of TRIZ-facilitator/moderator:

- For short TRIZ sessions it is crucial to have a thoroughly prepared problem analysis to point out the crucial key problems to be addressed during the session. The Innovation Situation Questionnaire [8] could be used for preparation. The goal of the session and the desired solution space need also to be defined.
- The use of graphical representations is extremely helpful for explaining context and correlations regarding the system structure (TRIZ Function Model) or the problem situation (Substance Field Model, Contradictions). These tools, when used with common language, are also understandable for the "TRIZ-newcomer".
- The language and syntax used in the TRIZ Function Model helps to quickly understand the system structure and interactions, enabling participants from all different kinds of knowledge background to collectively focus on the task at hand.
- The TRIZ solution models (e.g. Standard Solutions, Inventive Principles, Separation Principles) need explanation or even re-wording by the moderator, ideally also prepared in advance. Examples for the problem models help understand the underlying meaning of the solution model and help overcoming the psychological inertia and look in different directions offered by TRIZ. Unmodified use of e.g. the

standard solutions is likely to alienate the TRIZ newbie, making it harder to focus on idea generation because it takes time to figure out what the solution model is about.

- The role of a moderator is mandatory, especially for short, focused TRIZ sessions. It is compulsory that the process of the TRIZ session is monitored as well as the discussions between the participants. Especially short TRIZ sessions need a "game plan" and a structure beforehand, balancing time for analysis, discussion, free association and guided idea generation with TRIZ tools. Discussions between the participants need to be monitored and limited if necessary, to stay on track. If TRIZ newbies are participating, it is even more needed to have a "translator" for the TRIZ-specific syntax and wording.

The generated ideas were encouraging and it is planned to look for practical implementation of the most promising concepts.

Acknowledgments. The authors would like to thank Ms. Paola Mainardi for passionately raising the topic during a TRIZ discussion and Dr. Raffaella Boise for her engaging lecture about cardiovascular diseases.

References

1. https://en.wikipedia.org/wiki/BarCamp
2. http://lifevest.zoll.com/de/medical-professionals/
3. https://en.wikipedia.org/wiki/Wearable_cardioverter_defibrillator
4. Francis, J., Reek, S.: Wearable cardioverter defibrillator: a life vest till the life boat (ICD) arrives. Indian Heart J. **66**(1), 68–72 (2014). https://doi.org/10.1016/j.ihj.2013.12.050. https://www.ncbi.nlm.nih.gov/pubmed/24581099. Accessed 18 Sep 2019
5. Wäßnig, N.: Experience with the wearable cardioverter-defibrillator in patients at high risk for sudden cardiac death. Circulation **134**(9), 635–643 (2016). https://doi.org/10.1161/circulationaha.115.01912. https://www.ncbi.nlm.nih.gov/pmc/articles/PMC4998124/. Accessed 18 Sep 2019
6. https://www.hrsonline.org/content/download/18186/804164/file/Wearable-Cardioverter-Defibrillator.pdf. http://electrophysiology.onlinejacc.org/content/3/3/251. Accessed 18 Sep 2019
7. Bertoncelli, T., Mayer, O., Lynass, M.: Creativity, learning techniques and TRIZ. In: ETRIA TRIZ Future Conference 2015, Berlin, 26–29 October 2015
8. Terninko, J., Zusman, A., Zlotin, B.: Systematic Innovation: An Introduction to TRIZ (Theory of Inventive Problem Solving). CRC Press, Boca Raton (1998)

TRIZ Applications in Eco Design

Sustainable Innovation in Process Engineering Using Quality Function Deployment Approach and Importance-Satisfaction Analysis of Requirements

Mas'udah(✉), Pavel Livotov, and Arun Prasad Chandra Sekaran

Offenburg University of Applied Sciences, Badstr. 24, 77652 Offenburg, Germany
masudah@hs-offenburg.de

Abstract. Growing demands for cleaner production and higher eco-efficiency in process engineering require a comprehensive analysis of technical and environmental outcomes of customers and society. Moreover, unexpected additional technical or ecological drawbacks may appear as negative side effects of new environmentally friendly technologies. The paper conceptualizes a comprehensive approach for analysis and ranking of engineering and ecological requirements in process engineering in order to anticipate secondary problems in eco-design and to avoid compromising the environmental or technological goals. For this purpose, the paper presents a method based on integration of the Quality Function Deployment approach with the Importance-Satisfaction Analysis for the requirements ranking. The proposed method identifies and classifies comprehensively the potential engineering and eco-engineering contradictions through analysis of correlations within requirements groups such as stakeholder requirements (SRs) and technical requirements (TRs), and additionally through cross-relationship between SRs and TRs.

Keywords: Sustainable innovation · Eco-design · Process engineering · Quality Function Deployment · Importance-Satisfaction Analysis

1 Introduction

Development of green and efficient intensified process technologies in process engineering (PE) plays a fundamental role in society and global economy. Moreover, with the increasing interest towards sustainable innovation design, anticipating possible negative side effects either of technical or environmental origin becomes more important in the early phase of innovation design and process development [1]. Numerous approaches, methods and tools have been developed in the last decades to support the sustainable and environmentally friendly product and process development, as presented in the reviews [1, 2]. To the well-established one belongs the concept of Eco-Design, which is defined by the International Standard Organization (ISO 14006:2011) as "integration of environmental aspects into product design and development, with the aim of reducing adverse environmental impacts throughout a

Published by Springer Nature Switzerland AG 2019
R. Benmoussa et al. (Eds.): TFC 2019, IFIP AICT 572, pp. 269–281, 2019.
https://doi.org/10.1007/978-3-030-32497-1_22

product's life cycle". In the field of process engineering are well known the Green Process Engineering [3], Process Intensification [4], and Process Design for Sustainability [5]. Nevertheless, the process innovation activities in industrial companies are still usually driven primarily by costs and quality concerns. As a result, both ecological and technical problems subsequently lead to increase of capital expenditures (CAPEX) and operating expenditures (OPEX) [6]. Therefore, the comprehensive sustainable innovation in process engineering should lay much greater emphasis on higher productivity and quality, as well as on lowering environmental footprint and increasing resource and energy efficiency, as illustrated in Fig. 1.

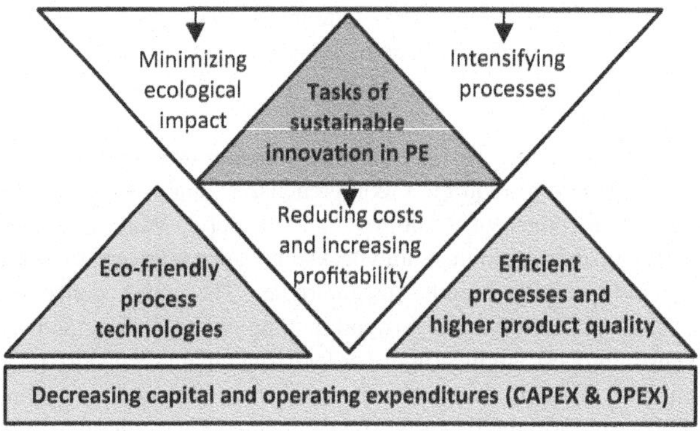

Fig. 1. Tasks and outcomes of sustainable innovation in process engineering

The success of any innovation process depends on how its outcomes meet the needs and expectations of all beneficiaries – in first place the customer groups, and other internal and external stakeholders of industrial companies. The Process Mapping method for systematic and comprehensive identification of engineering and stakeholder requirements in process engineering is a part of the Advanced Innovation Design Approach for PE [7]. One of the widely used methods for collection and evaluation of the customers' priority criteria in innovation design is the Quality Function Deployment (QFD) with the concept of the Houses of Quality (HoQ) as its core part [8]. QFD helps to translate customers' requirements into the corresponding technical requirements in each stage of product development and manufacturing. Various models and applications of the QFD are known in the literature [9–11]. In the field of eco-design, one should mention in the first place the Quality Function Deployment for Environment (QFDE) [12]. However, the practical QFD application for process intensification and environmental innovation in process engineering remains relatively seldom in comparison with the product innovation. Therefore, the presented paper conceptualizes a new method based on integration of the Quality Function Deployment approach with the Process Mapping [7] and the Importance-Satisfaction Analysis of requirements [7, 13].

Process Mapping is an easy-to-use technique to identify problems and innovation tasks, formulated as solution-neutral process intensification requirements. This method involves breaking down of a complete industrial production process into process steps to capture in each step the information on process equipment, processing methods, input/output quality parameters, product, available resources, and environment, as illustrated in Fig. 2. Process Mapping results in comprehensively capturing and ranking of all existing problems, needs, requirements and possible improvements or optimization opportunities of the technologies and equipment in each process step and in production process in whole. It delivers reliable results for existing technologies or well-known processes [7]. The systematically identified requirements and innovation tasks can be separated in three major groups: (a) enhancement of positive functions or properties; (b) elimination of harm or undesired properties, including environmental impact; (c) raising degree of controllability, accuracy, and automation of the process. The pair-by-pair comparisons of requirements allow to systematically identify all possible engineering and eco-engineering contradictions [1].

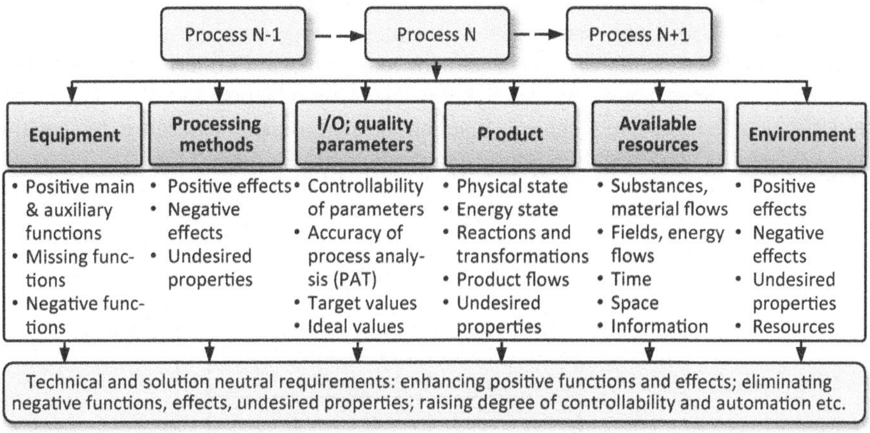

Fig. 2. Fragment of Process Mapping adapted from [7]

The Importance-Satisfaction Analysis (ISA) is applied for requirement ranking and for the fast and objective identification of the high priority process intensification problems. The average values of Importance and Satisfaction are based on the independent judgements of the experts. The concept of the QFD House of Quality is used for a systematic identification and fast visualization of the positive and negative interactions between technical requirements and functions (TRs) and requirements of different stakeholders (SRs). In other words, the proposed method identifies and classifies comprehensively the potential engineering and eco-engineering contradictions through analysis of correlations within different requirements groups in complex problem situations in process engineering. The paper introduces new metrics, such as Synergy Index and Contradiction Index in correlations between SRs and TRs, which can be used in optimization algorithms for selection of the process intensification and innovation strategies.

2 Integrating Quality Function Deployment and Importance-Satisfaction Analysis

The proposed method includes modifications of five phases of building the first House of Quality, known in the classical QFD. These modifications, presented in Fig. 3, are essential for the application in process engineering in general and for the requirement ranking and Importance-Satisfaction Analysis in particular. In accordance to the modification of the phase 1, the roof of the HoQ contains the TRs correlation matrix of technical functions and requirements of process equipment and steps. In the phase 2, the voice of the customer is rearranged into stakeholder requirements (SRs) with at least two groups of requirements - the solution-neutral engineering requirements and environmental issues. The interaction between different stakeholder requirements is documented in the SRs correlation matrix. Both the TRs and SRs correlations matrices indicate with the correlation coefficients c_{TR} and c_{SR} equal "−1" a possible negative correlation (contradiction), with "+1" a possible synergy impact, and with "0" - a neutral or unknown relationship between two requirements. Furthermore, the correlations matrices are extended by the Synergy and Contradiction Indexes. These new metrics characterize each technical function or requirement regarding its positive impact (synergies) and negative impact (contradictions) on other TRs.

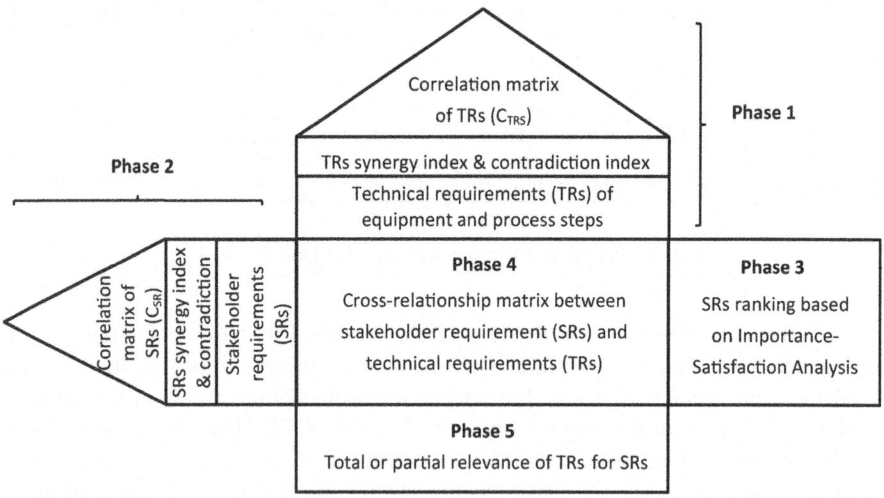

Fig. 3. Modification of the House of Quality for requirements ranking in process engineering

In the phase 3 the importance of each stakeholder requirement and its current performance (defined as satisfaction with its fulfillment in existing process) is evaluated by the experts from a stakeholders' point of view using a scale from 0% to 100% (100% - very high level of importance or performance, 80% - high, 60% - middle, 40% - low, 20% - very low importance or performance). In accordance to the Importance-Satisfaction Analysis [7, 13], the requirements with higher importance and lower performance have a higher ranking in a process innovation strategy.

The phase 4 comprises the cross-relationship analysis of the stakeholder requirements SRs and technical requirements TRs. The results of this analysis are documented in corresponding cells in the body of the House of Quality. The cells contain the impact factor F of each technical requirement TR on the stakeholder requirement SR. The impact factor has a positive value from 0 to 1, if a TR increases the satisfaction with a stakeholder requirement. On the other hand, the impact factor has a negative value from -1 to 0, if a TR decreases the satisfaction with a stakeholder requirement. The simplest and fastest way to classify a relationship for each pair of SRs and TRs is to apply the binary method. In accordance to the binary classification, the YES-option (impact factor $F = 1$ or $F = -1$) is applied if a SR is affected positively or negatively by the corresponding TR. Whilst the NO-option (impact factor $F = 0$) is indicated if a TR shows neither improving nor worsening effect on a SR.

Finally, the phase 5, includes the calculation of the total, positive or negative relevance of each TR for all stakeholder requirements SRs. Additionally, the partial relevance of each TR for a specific SRs group, for example the partial relevance of each TR to the eco-requirements group, can be estimated in this step. The relevance values of TRs identify technical functions with higher priority for process intensification in order to fulfill the stakeholder requirements with higher ranking, as it has been defined in the phase 3.

3 Illustrating Case Study

The proposed concept for integration of the Quality Function Deployment and Importance-Satisfaction Analysis is illustrated below using an industrial case study dealing with the ceramic powder granulation [14] as presented in Table 1.

Table 1. Function analysis of ceramic powder granulation (fragment of Process Mapping).

Process step	Equipment	Positive functions	Negative functions and harm
1. Raw material preparation	Piles and silos	Maintain humidity of raw materials prior to milling	– Humidity changes in raw materials – Blocking over bottom part of silos – Dust generation & material losses
	Excavator and crusher	Reduce size of raw materials	– Dust generation – High energy consumption
	Scales	Weigh raw materials	– Inaccuracy of measurement – Dust generation

(continued)

Table 1. (*continued*)

Process step	Equipment	Positive functions	Negative functions and harm
2. Wet milling	Dosage tank	Binds ceramic powders	– Clogging/discharge problem & Material losses
	Ball mill	Mixes & homogenizes powders	– High energy & water consumption – Fouling & blocking of equipment
…	…	…	…
6. Drying	Spray dryer unit	Dries slurry	– High energy consumption – Fouling & blocking of equipment – Exhaust gas & material losses
7. Utilities processing	Cleaning and treatment units	Clean facility and remove dust; recycle waste water	– High cleaning efforts – High water consumption – Low quality of recycled water

Based on the information collected by the Process Mapping, the creation of the House of Quality and requirements ranking can be carried out in the following phases.

1. Generating a correlation matrix of technical requirements (TRs):
   (a) Listing all TRs in each unit operation (process step and corresponding equipment) identified by Process Mapping and Function Analysis.
   (b) Classifying each TR to technical function (T), and to environmental function (E) for further correlation analysis.
   (c) Evaluating the correlations between TRs using (−1) as negative correlation, (+1) as positive correlation and (0) as neutral correlation.
   (d) Calculating the Synergy (i_s) and Contradiction (i_c) Indexes for each TR respectively as a number of positive (+1) and a number of negative correlations (−1)

$$\textit{TR Synergy Index,} \qquad i_{s,TRx} = \sum\nolimits_{j=1}^{j=n} C_{TRxj}(C_{TR} = +1) \qquad (1)$$

$$\textit{TR Contradiction Index,} \qquad i_{c,TRx} = \sum\nolimits_{j=1}^{j=n} C_{TRxj}(C_{TR} = -1) \qquad (2)$$

where:

$i_{s},_{TRx}$ – Synergy Index of a technical requirement x;
$i_{c},_{TRx}$ – Contradiction Index of a technical requirement x;
C_{TRxj} – correlation factor between technical requirement x and other TRs;
n – total number of technical requirements.

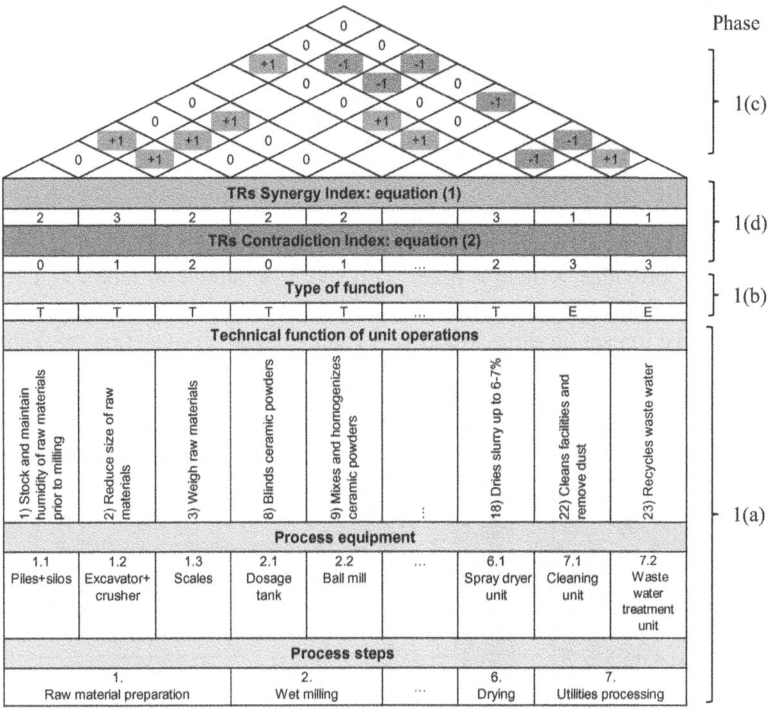

Fig. 4. Structure of correlation matrix of technical requirements TRs

As depicted in Fig. 4, the correlation matrix of TRs (C_{TR}) presents Synergy Index (i_s) and Contradiction Index (i_c) of each technical function. For example, technical function *Drying slurry* (process step 6) has a positive correlation with three TRs (i_s = 3) and a negative correlation with other two TRs (i_c = 2).

2. Generating a correlation matrix of stakeholder requirements (SRs):
   (a) Listing all stakeholder requirements (SRs) based on Process Mapping results.
   (b) Categorizing SRs to technical or engineering requirements (T), and to the environmental requirements (E).
   (c) Evaluating the correlations between SRs using (−1) as negative correlation, (+1) as positive correlation and (0) as neutral correlation.
   (d) Calculating the Synergy (i_s) and Contradiction (i_c) Indexes for SRs respectively as a number of positive (+1) and a number of negative correlations (−1)

$$SR\ Synergy\ Index: \qquad i_{s,SRx} = \sum_{j=1}^{j=m} C_{SRxj}(C_{SR} = +1) \tag{3}$$

$$SR\ Contradiction\ Index: \qquad i_{c,SRx} = \sum_{j=1}^{j=m} C_{SRxj}(C_{SR} = -1) \tag{4}$$

where:

$i_{s,SRx}$ – Synergy Index of stakeholder requirement x;
$i_{c,SRx}$ – Contradiction Index of stakeholder requirement x;
C_{SRxj} – Correlation factor between stakeholder requirement x and other SRs;
m – total number of stakeholder requirements.

In the same way as presented in Fig. 4, the correlation matrix of SRs (C_{SR}) shown in Fig. 5 also provides Synergy Index (i_s) and Contradiction Index (i_c) of each stakeholder requirement. For instance, the requirement on *Reducing air pollution* has a positive impact on three SRs ($i_s = 3$) and a negative impact on two other SRs ($i_c = 2$).

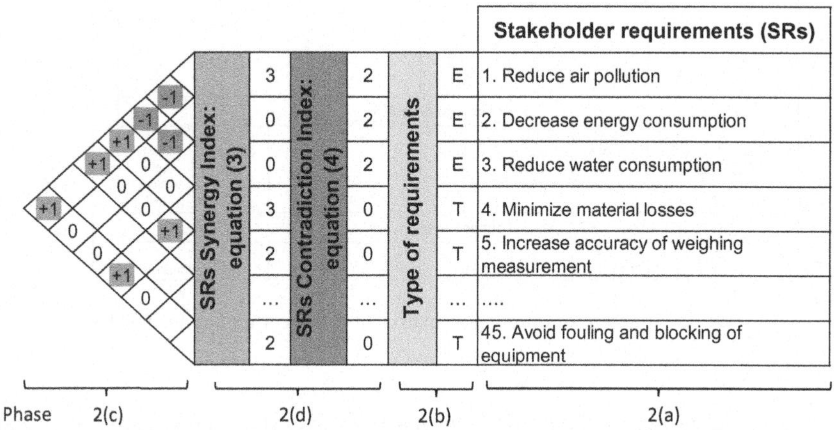

Fig. 5. Structure of correlation matrix of stakeholder requirements

3. Determination of SRs ranking using Importance-Satisfaction Analysis (ISA):
   (a) Rating the current SRs importance (I_{SR}) and satisfaction (S_{SR}) with the following scale from 0% (lowest value) to 100% (highest value) with interval of 25%.
   (b) Obtained importance and satisfaction mean values allow one to calculate the ranking of each stakeholder requirement using the following equation [15]:

$$Rank_{SRx} = \frac{\{I_{SRx} + aI_{SRx}(I_{SRx} - S_{SRx})(1 - S_{SRx})\}}{\sum_{x=1}^{x=m}\{I_{SRx} + aI_{SRx}(I_{SRx} - S_{SRx})\}} \quad (5)$$

where:

$Rank_{SRx}$ – ranking of stakeholder requirement x (SR_x), %;
I_{SRx} – importance level of SR_x, 0 …100%;
S_{SRx} – satisfaction level of SR_x, 0 …100%;
m – total number of stakeholder requirements;
a – adjustment coefficient; $a = 1$ recommended for PE [7].

If we define the “ideal process” as a process with all stakeholder requirements satisfied to 100%, the ranking value $Rank_{SRx}$ in the formula (5) corresponds to a maximum contribution of one requirement to the growth of total process ideality towards 100%. An example of problem ranking by one expert is illustrated in the Table 2 below. Decreasing energy consumption has been identified here as the highest priority requirement among other SRs.

Table 2. Example of stakeholder requirements ranking using Importance-Satisfaction Analysis.

Stakeholder requirements SRs	Importance	Satisfaction	Ranking Eq. (5)
1. Reduce air pollution	75	50	1,4%
2. Decrease energy consumption	100	25	4,0%
3. Reduce water consumption	100	50	2,3%
4. Minimize material losses	50	75	0,3%
5. Increase weighing accuracy	100	75	1,0%
…	…	…	…
45. Avoid fouling of equipment	75	75	0,6%

4. Defining the cross relationship between TRs to SRs in the House of Quality: evaluating the effect of each single technical requirement TR on stakeholder requirements SRs, using simplified binary approach, as illustrated in the Fig. 6:

   YES - if TR has an effect on SR, either improving ($F = 1$) or worsening ($F = -1$);
   NO - if TR has no influence on SR (impact factor $F = 0$).

Technical requirements (TRs)	Technical function of unit operations								
	1) Stock and maintain humidity of raw materials prior to milling	2) Reduce size of raw materials	3) Weigh raw materials	8) Blinds ceramic powders	9) Mixes and homogenizes ceramic powders	…	18) Dries slurry up to 6-7%	22) Cleans facilities and remove dust	23) Recycles waste water
	Process equipment								
	1.1 Piles+silos	1.2 Excavator + crusher	1.3 Scales	2.1 Dosage tank	2.2 Ball mill	…	6.1 Spray dryer unit	7.1 Cleaning unit	7.2 Waste water treatment unit
Stakeholder requirements (SRs)	Process steps								
	1. Raw material preparation			2. Wet milling		…	6. Drying	7. Utilities processing	
1. Reduce air pollution	YES	YES	YES	NO	NO	…	YES	YES	NO
2. Decrease energy consumption	NO	YES	NO	NO	YES	…	YES	NO	NO
3. Reduce water consumption	NO	NO	NO	NO	YES	…	NO	YES	YES
4. Minimize material losses	YES	YES	YES	YES	YES	…	YES	NO	NO
5. Increase accuracy of weighing measurement	NO	YES	YES	NO	NO	…	NO	YES	NO
….	…	…	…	…	…	…	…	…	…
45. Avoid fouling and blocking of equipment	YES	NO	NO	YES	YES	…	YES	YES	NO

Fig. 6. Example of cross-relationship between TRs and SRs (simplified binary approach)

5. Calculating the total relevance of a technical requirement x (TR_x) for all stakeholder requirements SRs using the Eq. (6):

$$Rel_{TRx \rightarrow SRs} = \sum_{j=1}^{j=m} \left(Rank_{SRj} \times |F_{xj}| \right) \quad (6)$$

where:

$Rel_{TRx \rightarrow SRs}$	– total relevance of technical requirement x (TR_x) for all SRs;
$Rank_{SRj}$	– ranking of a stakeholder requirement j (SR_j), %;
F_{xj}	– impact factor of a TR_x to a stakeholder requirement j (SR_j): $F_{xj} = 1$ if TR is improving SR, or $F_{xj} = -1$ if TR is worsening SR (YES-option); $F_{xj} = 0$ if TRs have not influence on SRs (NO-option) – see phase 4;
m	– total number of stakeholder requirements.

Following example illustrates calculating the total relevance of technical function (*Drying slurry*) from drying process step 6 to all stakeholder requirements (see the complete modified House of Quality in Appendix A): $Rel_{TRx} \rightarrow {}_{SRs} = (1.4\% \times 1) + (4.0\% \times 1) + (2.3\% \times 0) + (0.3\% \times 1) + (1.0\% \times 0) + \ldots + (0.6\% \times 1) = 6.3\%$.

In the same manner, one can calculate the total positive relevance considering the improving impact factor ($F_{xj} = 1$) or total negative relevance considering the worsening impact factor ($F_{xj} = -1$) only. It is also possible to calculate a partial relevance considering the impact of technical requirements TRs on, for example, environmental stakeholder requirements SRs only.

4 Conclusion

The proposed approach of integrating Quality Function Deployment (QFD) and Importance-Satisfaction Analysis (ISA) aims to identify and classify comprehensively the potential engineering and eco-engineering contradictions in process engineering. As shown in Fig. 7, the method investigates correlations within different requirements groups in complex problem situations using Function Analysis and Process Mapping and combining importance-satisfaction evaluation with visualization of the metrics and correlations between technical and stakeholder requirements in a modified House of Quality.

In general, the proposed approach can contribute to the practical needs of innovation tasks ranking for process intensification using current importance and satisfaction with process key performance parameters by considering not only process efficiency and product quality but also environmental concerns. The estimation of proposed metrics, such as Synergy and Contradiction Indexes of requirements, Ranking of stakeholder requirements and Relevance of technical requirements, helps to define the appropriate process innovation strategy and to select or develop the optimal process intensification technology without secondary problems. Based on obtained

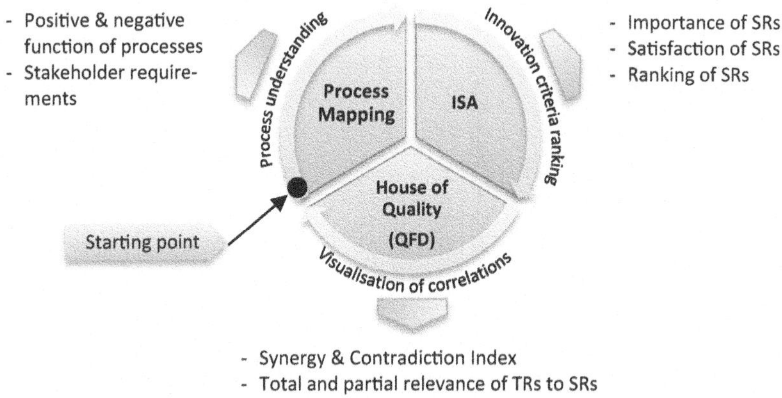

Fig. 7. Concept and main outcomes of integrating Quality Function Deployment and Importance-Satisfaction Analysis for process engineering

information, the computer-aided multi-parameter optimization of processes can be applied to reduce environmental impact and to improve performance of new technologies with the inventive tools of the Theory of Inventive Problem Solving (TRIZ) and Process Intensification methods. However, the application of the proposed method requires specific expert knowledge and practical experience to define and evaluate the correlations of stakeholder and technical requirements. Also, the introduction of the qualitative and quantitative cause-effect relationship between partial problems and requirements will be a part of the future work.

A Appendix

Example of the modified House of Quality and requirements ranking for ceramic powders granulation process (fragment).

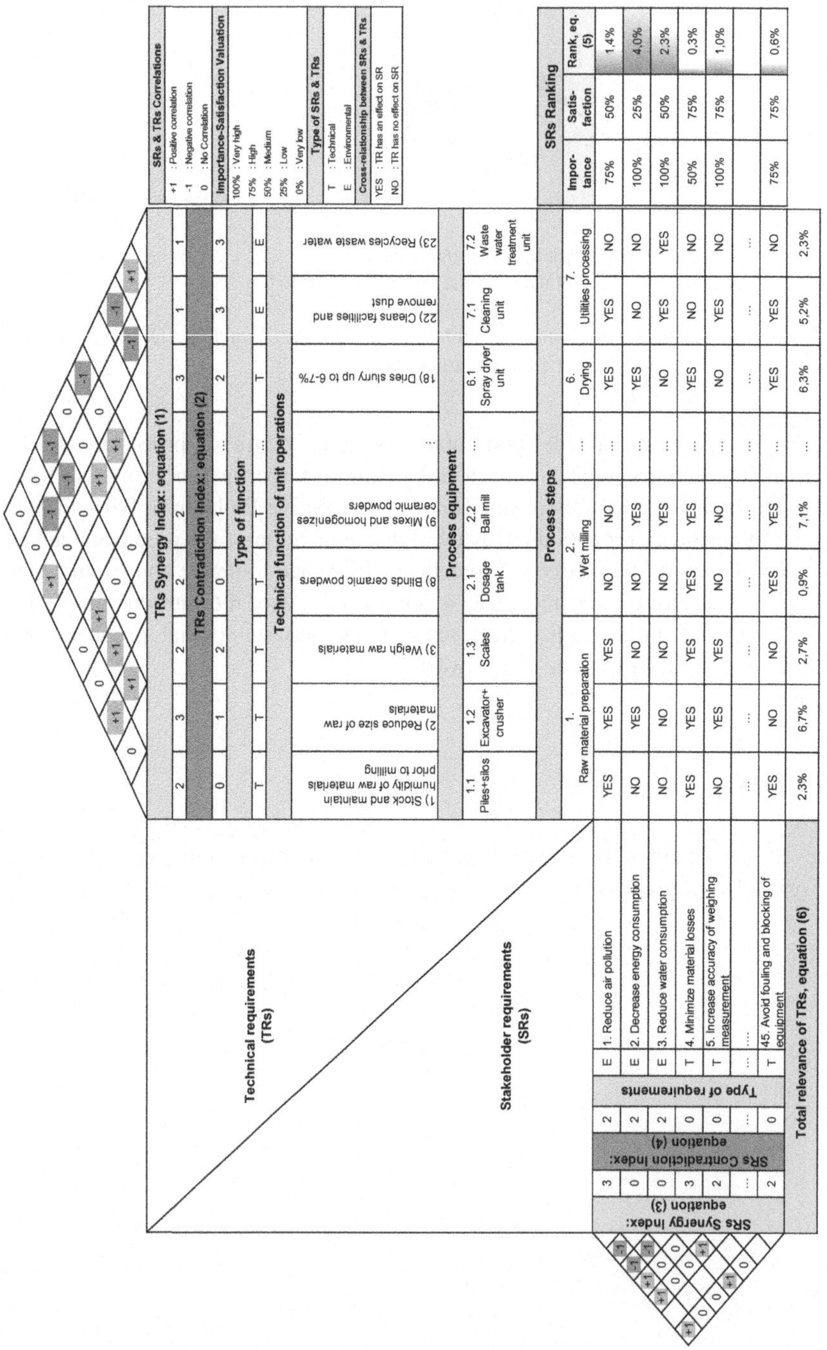
SRs & TRs Correlations
+1 : Positive correlation
-1 : Negative correlation
0 : No Correlation
Importance-Satisfaction Valuation
100% : Very high
75% : High
50% : Medium
25% : Low
0% : Very low
Type of SRs & TRs
T : Technical
E : Environmental
Cross-relationship between SRs & TRs
YES : TR has an effect on SR
NO : TR has no effect on SR
TRs Synergy Index: equation (1)
TRs Contradiction Index: equation (2)
Type of function
Technical function of unit operations
1) Stock and maintain humidity of raw materials prior to milling
2) Reduce size of raw materials
3) Weigh raw materials
8) Blinds ceramic powders
9) Mixes and homogenizes ceramic powders
18) Dries slurry up to 6-7%
22) Cleans facilities and remove dust
23) Recycles waste water
Process equipment
1.1 Piles+silos
1.2 Excavator+ crusher
1.3 Scales
2.1 Dosage tank
2.2 Ball mill
6.1 Spray dryer unit
7.1 Cleaning unit
7.2 Waste water treatment unit
Process steps
1. Raw material preparation
2. Wet milling
6. Drying
7. Utilities processing
Technical requirements (TRs)
Stakeholder requirements (SRs)
SRs Synergy Index: equation (3)
SRs Contradiction Index: equation (4)
Type of requirements
1. Reduce air pollution
2. Decrease energy consumption
3. Reduce water consumption
4. Minimize material losses
5. Increase accuracy of weighing measurement
45. Avoid fouling and blocking of equipment
Total relevance of TRs, equation (6)
2,3% 6,7% 2,7% 0,9% 7,1% 6,3% 5,2% 2,3%
SRs Ranking
Impor-tance
Satis-faction
Rank, eq. (5)
1,4%
4,0%
2,3%
0,3%
1,0%
0,6%

References

1. Livotov, P., et al.: Eco-innovation in process engineering: contradictions, inventive principles and methods. Therm. Sci. Eng. Prog. **9**, 52–65 (2019). https://doi.org/10.1016/j.tsep.2018.10.012
2. Tyl, B., Legardeur, J., Millet, D., Vallet, F.: A comparative study of ideation mechanisms used in eco-innovation tools. J. Eng. Des. **25**(10–12) (2014). https://doi.org/10.1080/09544828.2014.992772
3. Poux, M., Cognet, P., Gourdon, C.: Green Process Engineering: From Concepts to Industrial Applications. CRC Press, Boca Raton (2015). ISBN 9781482208177
4. Boodhoo, K., Harvey, A.: Process intensification: an overview of principles and practice. In: Boodhoo, K., Harvey, A. (eds.) Process Intensification for Green Chemistry, pp. 1–31. Wiley (2013). https://doi.org/10.1002/9781118498521.ch1
5. Azzaro-Pantel, C.: Green process engineering design methodology: a multicriteria approach. In: Poux, M., Cognet, P., Gourdon, C. (eds.) Green Process Engineering: From Concepts to Industrial Applications, pp. 3–26. CRC Press, Boca Raton (2015). ISBN 9781482208177
6. Livotov, P., Mas'udah, Chandra Sekaran, A.P., Law, R., Reay, D.: ecological advanced innovation design approach for efficient integrated upstream and downstream processes. In: Proceedings of the International Conference on Engineering Design, ICED 2019, Delft, 5–8 August 2019, vol. 1, Issue 1, pp. 3291–3300. Cambridge University Press (2019). https://doi.org/10.1017/dsi.2019.336
7. Casner, D., Livotov, P.: Advanced innovation design approach for process engineering. In: Proceedings of the 21st International Conference on Engineering Design (ICED 2017), vol. 4: Design Methods and Tools, Vancouver, pp. 653–662 (2017)
8. Akao, Y.: Quality Function Deployment. Productivity Press, Cambridge (1986)
9. Chan, L.K., Wu, M.L.: Quality function deployment: a literature review. Eur. J. Oper. Res. **143**, 463–497 (2002)
10. Akao, Y., Mazur, G.H.: The leading edge in QFD: past, present and future. Int. J. Qual. Reliab. Manag. **20**(1), 20–35 (2003)
11. Sisasamy, K., Arumugan, C., Devadasan, S.R.: Advanced models of quality function deployment: a literature review. Qual. Quant. **50**, 1399–1414 (2016). https://doi.org/10.1007/s11135-015-0212-2
12. Masui, K.: Quality function deployment for environment: QFDE - a methodology in early stage of DfE. In: Proceedings of Second International Symposium on Environmentally Conscious Design and Inverse Manufacturing, Japan, pp. 852–857. IEEE (2001)
13. Bettencourt, L., Ulwick, A.: The customer-centered innovation map. Harv. Bus. Rev. **86**(5), 109–114 (2008)
14. Livotov, P., Mas'udah, Chandra Sekaran, A.P.: On the efficiency of TRIZ application for process intensification in process engineering. In: Cavallucci, D., de Guio, R., Koziołek, S. (eds.) TFC 2018. IFIPAICT, vol. 541, pp. 126–140. Springer, Cham (2018). https://doi.org/10.1007/978-3-030-02456-7_11
15. Livotov, P.: Method for quantitative evaluation of innovation tasks for technical systems, products and processes. In: Proceedings of ETRIA World Conference 2008 "Synthesis in Innovation", Enschede, 5–7 November 2008, pp. 197–199. University of Twente, Enschede (2008). ISBN 978-90-365-2749-1

Investigating the Value Perception of Specific TRIZ Solutions Aimed to Reduce Product's Environmental Impact

Lorenzo Maccioni(✉) and Yuri Borgianni

Faculty of Science and Technology, Free University of Bozen-Bolzano, 39100 Bolzano, Italy
lorenzo.maccioni@natec.unibz.it

Abstract. Understanding the impact of inventive solutions on consumers' value perception is essential to develop successful products. This applies particularly to sustainable solutions, which need to penetrate the market to pursue environmental objectives. This paper explores the value perception of three categories of TRIZ-oriented sustainable solutions, namely designs that have undergone dynamization, change of the physical state or the field exploited. Through an experimental study with 43 participants, supported by a specific questionnaire and biometric measures (eye tracking, skin conductance), self-assessments and unconscious behavioral aspects were gathered while a series of 18 product pictures was shown. Out of them, 9 products implement one of the above TRIZ-oriented principles and 9 constitute same-category products with a higher environmental impact. The results show that the different categories of TRIZ solutions give rise to diverse nuances of value perception. This outcome triggers further considerations concerning the ease of interpreting design modifications steered by TRIZ concepts and heuristics.

Keywords: Human perception · Eco-design · Eco-innovation · TRIZ-oriented sustainable solutions · Biometric measures

1 Introduction

Although TRIZ methodology supports the individuation of technical problems (i.e. what are the problems?) and provides frameworks to solve them (i.e. how to solve the problems?), many scholars argue that the contextualization of the problems (i.e. why should these problems be solved?) has to be entrusted to complementary methods [1, 2]. Therefore, especially when the problem solving process is set in a Business-to-Consumer product development context, TRIZ suffers from a limited understanding of human values, product meanings, and unspoken needs [3]. To this respect, many attempts to integrate human factors into TRIZ can be found in the literature.

Wang [4] developed a Kansei-TRIZ framework, where the design philosophy proposed by Nagamachi [5], aimed to consider the cognitive and emotional dimensions of designs, has been integrated with the 39 engineering parameters and the 40 inventive principles.

Published by Springer Nature Switzerland AG 2019
R. Benmoussa et al. (Eds.): TFC 2019, IFIP AICT 572, pp. 282–294, 2019.
https://doi.org/10.1007/978-3-030-32497-1_23

Borgianni et al. [6] developed a method able to take into account both the customers perceived benefits and the engineering resources exploited trough the combination of the Kano model [7] and specific TRIZ knowledge. The combination of Kano model and TRIZ can be found also in [8], where an integrated framework was proposed, and in [9], where a combination of Kano model and Su-Field Analysis was suggested.

In their review, Batemanazan et al. [2] highlight the pro and cons to combine usability criteria (to understand the user perspective and context) and TRIZ (to help the problem abstraction). In addition, the scholars stressed the importance to envision a holistic perception of products and criticized the products' characterizations solely based on a sum of the implemented functions. Filippi and Barattin [1] developed a framework to relate constructs of interactive design (i.e. principles, guidelines and heuristics aimed to improve the product's acceptance and reliability) with inventive principles. Lin and Luh [10] emphasized how TRIZ thinking should be enriched in a holistic view to support radical innovation through the human-centered value creation. In the same direction, Ávila et al. [11], exploring the combination of TRIZ and the User Centered Design approach, concluded that an inventive product cannot be successful if it does not create enough value for the consumers compared to alternative solutions.

Therefore, understanding how to create value for the consumer through inventive solutions (which include tangible and intangible elements) is the main way to innovate, and to achieve radical innovation [12]. This leads to the need to develop inventive solutions (exhibiting an evident technical improvement) that have a positive impact on human life through their use, acceptance and diffusion.

It is worth noting how the same challenges are shared by research in sustainable development [13, 14]. Indeed, in order to outline sustainable development, designers are urged to develop eco-innovative products and services, i.e. solutions able to drastically reduce the environmental impact (compared to existing ones) and to increase people's quality of life [15, 16]. Although the focus of many scholars was on developing and testing TRIZ-based tools and methods for achieving solutions with lower environmental impact, the literature offers a limited contribution for understanding how these TRIZ-Oriented Sustainable Solutions (TRIZ-OSSs) can be perceived, adopted and used. An experiment was conducted by the authors with the aim to study, among the others, the Consumer Value Perception (CVP) of TRIZ-OSSs [17]. The results of the experiment are used to provide a better understanding on the perception of TRIZ-OSSs.

The present paper is structured as follows. In Sect. 2, an overview of the relationship between TRIZ and eco-innovation is shown in order to clarify how TRIZ-OSSs can be obtained. In Sect. 3, the concept of CVP and the way adopted to measure it is explained. The method is illustrated in Sect. 4. Results are presented in Sect. 5 and discussed in Sect. 6. Conclusions are drawn in Sect. 7.

2 TRIZ and Eco-Innovation

The application of many TRIZ tools and principles directly provide benefits for the environment [18]. Russo [19], exploring different eco-design methods, claimed that integrating TRIZ into eco-design leads to effective methods in both eco-improvement and eco-assessment perspectives. Bocken et al. [20] emphasized how the eco-TRIZ literature supports radical eco-improvements and provides many conceptual eco-assessment indicators.

Tyl et al. [15] stressed the remarkable contribution of TRIZ-based tools in eco-innovation process, especially in the ideation phase. In addition, the close relationship between TRIZ and eco-innovation was highlighted in a recent contribution [21], where more than 60 pertinent scientific works published in 2000–2018 were collected and analyzed.

The overlapping between TRIZ and eco-design had already been noticed by Jones and Harrison at the very beginning of this century [22]. In their work, they compared the eco-compass headlines [23], i.e. mass intensity, energy intensity, extending service and function, health and environmental risk, resource conservation, and revalorization, with the 39 engineering parameters. Chang and Chen [24] developed a CAD software by integrating the same 39 parameters into the 7 major eco-efficiency elements identified during the World Business Council for Sustainable Development [25], i.e. material reduction, energy reduction, toxicity reduction, material retrieval, sustainable resources, product durability and product service. The same research team provided, for each of the 40 inventive principles, at least one successful eco-innovative product that implements it [26]. With the same aims of the previous authors, Cherifi et al. [27] developed a framework that supports the identification of the most suitable inventive principles to solve contradictions on specific eco-design parameters e.g. material consumption, energy consumption, releases, use of parameters, ownership of eco-design.

Inventive principles and engineering parameters were not the only TRIZ tools able to support eco-innovation. For example, the eternal struggle between technological and biological interest was dealt with in Bio-inspired TRIZ tools [28] and many other TRIZ concepts [29] e.g. biomimetic, ideality, function analysis and laws of evolution. Laws of evolution and evolution trends in an eco-innovation context have been explored in various papers [19, 30, 31].

The usefulness and the applicability of the evolution trends in eco-design was discussed in [31]. Russo [19], pivoting on the concept of ideality, resources and laws of evolution, developed 8 guidelines aimed at driving eco-design towards innovation. Based on the results of this work, Russo et al. [30] developed an evaluation method to assess a solution and to support the design towards the ideal solution (also exploiting the concept of Energy, Material, Signal [32] and standard solutions). This method was fine-tuned in SMEs [33] and subsequently, an advanced CAD system was created [34].

However, the integration and the application of TRIZ in the eco-innovation processes still presents some limitations. For instance, most of TRIZ approaches require a good level of expertise, and therefore, an effective application of TRIZ entails time and training to be successfully applied by novices in the TRIZ field [35]. In order to overcome these limitations, Russo et al. [36] proposed guidelines for non-expert users, collected in a framework called iTree; in addition, an advanced version thereof was developed in an online CAD tool [37]. Moreover, as emphasized in the introduction, specific TRIZ methods are limited to work only under well-defined boundaries [35].

Although this section stress the goal to link TRIZ with eco-innovation and the introduction highlights some attempts that link TRIZ with human-related issues, in the literature, only few contributions can be found that try to link these tree areas (TRIZ, eco-innovation and human-related issues). The main attempt to expand the ECO-TRIZ knowledge towards human-related issues are reported in the followings.

D'Anna and Cascini [38] developed a method integrating the humankind into TRIZ for identifying needs through the combination of System Operator and Maslow's Hierarchy of needs [39]. With the aim of achieving sustainable objective, the voice of the consumer was taken into consideration by the combination of TRIZ, Eco-Quality-Function-Deployment and Analytical Hierarchy Process in [40]. Recently, a Kansei ECO-TRIZ technique was developed [41], where Kansei Engineering has been juxtaposed with the 39 engineering parameters and the 7 Eco-efficiency elements proposed in a previous study [24].

Therefore, this paper aims to expand the ECO-TRIZ knowledge towards studying the CVP of specific TRIZ-OSSs.

3 Consumer Value Perception

The CVP drives the consumer behavior in a decision-making context, affects their preferences and purchase intention, and, consequently, the adoption and the success of the solution [42]. Woodal [43] conceptualized CVP as a comparison between benefits, in terms of advantages that the ownership (or the use) of the solution provides to the consumer, and sacrifices, in terms of resources that the consumer has to spend for the ownership (or the use) of the solution. Although this definition is similar to the TRIZ concept of Ideal Final Result, it not only includes the utilitarian/functional dimension but also a hedonic/emotional one. In addition, Holbrook [44] emphasized how the CVP is not a property of the solution itself but it is an experiential characteristic of the interaction between the consumer and the product. Then, the proper way to study the CVP is to capture consumers' perception about functionalities, feelings, experiences, emotions and behaviors during an interaction with the solution (or its representation).

The perception of utilitarian/functional dimensions is usually investigated trough surveys. However, it is claimed that the exclusive use of self-assessment methods might fail to capture human factors in a reliable way, especially when sustainability-related themes are involved [45]. To overcome these limitations, the exploitation of biometric instruments are increasingly diffused in experimental design research [46], especially Eye-Tracking (ET) technologies and Galvanic Skin Response (GSR) meters. The ET allows recording the ocular behavior by understanding what a participant is looking at, for how long, with which observation strategy, how often s/he blinks and how the pupils' size changes. These data can be interpreted as attention, interest, involvement, curiosity, cognitive load other psychological and behavioral terms. GSR meters measure skin conductance and markedly the micro-sweat changes that are ascribable to emotional arousal. The combination of surveys, for studying the utilitarian/functional dimensions, with biometric instruments, for exploring the unconscious behavioral and emotional reactions, is the last frontier of the study of the CVP [17].

4 Materials and Method

The goal of this paper is to understand how the implementation of TRIZ-OSSs affects the CVP. In order to pursue this goal, the following steps were performed.

1. Three common TRIZ-OSSs, easily identifiable in everyday products, were selected. Pictures of these products in a baseline version (presenting specific environmental issues) and in the TRIZ-OSSs version (presenting an eco-improvement) were collected (Sect. 4.1).
2. The pictures of each product were shown singularly to 43 participants (individually) in a PC screen. The participants were asked to evaluate each picture by filling in a 5-point Likert questionnaire, according to their perception of the products. Meanwhile, their visual approach and behavior were monitored through an ET and their level of emotional arousal was captured by a GSR (Sect. 4.2). This is part of a larger study described in [17].
3. The data collected were statistically elaborated in order to highlight differences in CVP characteristics and to understand if these are statistically influenced by the type of TRIZ-OSS (Sect. 4.3)

4.1 Characterization of the Stimuli

Nowadays, the excessive use of resources, the amount of wasted packaging and the toxicity of energy systems are environmental problems designers are asked to solve. TRIZ offers many strategies to deal with these problems and, since the proposed experimental procedure (Sect. 4.2) is time-consuming, this paper explores a subset of these strategies. Therefore, among the most common implemented TRIZ strategies, the authors focused on the following ones, which were empirically identified as very diffused in innovative product design.

- Dynamization, which saves material (allowing the replacement of worn components only), space and energy resources (improving the adaptability of the product during various phases of its life)
- Change the product's Substance (solid, liquid, gas), often allows reducing the environmental impact of its packaging or of its transportation
- Change a Field that performs a function (mechanical, chemical, electromagnetic), which often allows reducing the related toxic emissions.

For these reasons, for each of the three above-mentioned TRIZ-OSSs, three pairs of everyday products were collected (3 TRIZ-OSSs and the 3 corresponding baseline products).

- Dynamization: disposable razors vs. razors with interchangeable blades, common toothbrushes vs. toothbrushes with interchangeable bristles, common water bottles vs. space-saving water bottles.
- Substance: liquid laundry detergent in a plastic packaging vs. washing powder in a cardboard packaging, a liquid shampoo in a plastic container vs. a solid shampoo in a paper container, couches vs inflatable couches.
- Field: battery torches vs. hand-powered torches, gasoline cars vs. electric cars, gas cookers vs. induction cookers.

A summary is shown in Fig. 1.

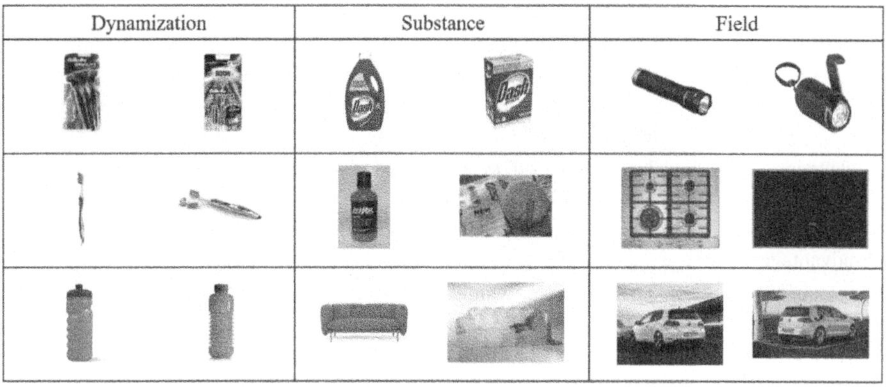

Fig. 1. The products are presented in pairs - the baseline version on the left, the TRIZ-OSS on the right. Product pairs implementing the same TRIZ-OSS are grouped in the same column

4.2 Procedure

Forty-three volunteer participants were involved in this experiment and all product pictures were shown randomly in two sessions at least two days apart. All the participants were students, lecturers and administrators of research institutions in South Tyrol, Italy. Their sensitivity to sustainable themes was monitored through a preliminary questionnaire, which was a primary research goal explored in [17].

In addition to the 18 products illustrated in the previous subsection, other 22 product's images were selected with similar criteria, and shown in the same way for other purposes [17].

The baseline products and the TRIZ-OSS alternatives were equally distributed between the two sessions and the products of the same pair have never been shown in the same session. The participants were informed that the aim of the experiment was to evaluate products and that biometric instruments would have been used. They were unaware of the type of products to be evaluated, the actual goal of the experiment, as well sustainability-related terms have never emerged during the experiment.

While the image of a product was shown on a PC screen, the participants were invited to observe it, to fill in a questionnaire (in which their level of agreement with statements associated with the variables summarized in Table 1 was gathered) and to estimate the product's price. In the meantime, they were wearing a GSR sensor, in the non-writing hand, and a remote ET, arranged at the bottom of the screen, was recording their ocular behavior. In this way, the functional dimensions of CVP were investigated trough a self-assessment questionnaire, while the unconscious emotional and behavioral dimensions were studied trough the afore-mentioned biometric instruments. The whole sample of collected data is available in [17].

Table 1. Variables explored through a 5-point Likert scale questionnaire.

Variables	Meaning Level of agreement of the participant in affirming that:
Knowledge	The participant knows the specific product, they use it, they have bought it in the past and they know similar products
Interest	The aim of the product is relevant to their daily life, they are interested in this kind of products and they can benefit from it
Quality	The participant believes that it the product is of high quality and is able to meet their expectations
Advantages	The product offers advantages if compared to similar products and it has valuable characteristics
(Absence of) Disadvantages	The product has (not) disadvantages if compared to similar products
Preference	The participant would likely choose this product instead of a similar one
Novelty creativity	The product has novel or original characteristics and it proposes innovative or brilliant solutions
Willingness to pay	The participant considers appropriate that the depicted product is more expensive than the average in its category

4.3 Data Elaboration

The raw data collected through biometric instruments were elaborated by a specific MATLAB routine in order to obtain indicators related to the interaction between each participant with each products. The biometric indicators were combined with the indicators extracted through the questionnaire. A series of bivariate Spearman correlations, involving the whole samples of indicators was performed. When two indicators showed correlations greater than 0.8, one of the two was discarded to facilitate following statistical processes. In this way, the independent indicators who passed the Spearman test were 35 out of the initial 93 ones. In order to reduce the complexity of the phenomenon to be studied, a Principal Component Analysis was then performed on these 35 variables. The "principal" function in the statistical software R was used for the PCA. Keeping factors with eigenvalues higher than 1 resulted in obtaining 10 principal components (PCs) explaining 68% of the variability of the observed phenomenon. An interpretation of these 10 PCs was given in [17] and it is summarized in Table 2.

Data related to products implementing a TRIZ-OSS (including the relative baseline products) were extrapolated from the whole dataset. Subsequently, this data was subdivided between Dynamization, Substance, Field and the amount of valid observations (in the PCs coordinates) were 204, 202 and 196 respectively.

The implementation of a given category of TRIZ-OSS has been considered as a dummy variable in the products pair (1 if the product implements the TRIZ-OSS, 0 if the product is the alternative baseline). Therefore, two different kind of regressions were carried out through R software.

1. In order to study the overall phenomenon, linear regressions between every category of TRIZ-OSSs (as independent variables) and every PCs (as dependent variables) were carried out.
2. In order to provide results that can be simply interpreted on CVP perspective, ordinal logistic regressions between every category of TRIZ-OSSs (as independent variables) and the answers to the 5-scale questionnaire (as dependent variables).

Table 2. Interpretation of the PCs emerged by the experiment.

Principal components	Interpretation
Consciously Approaching the Task (CAT)	It is related to those processes occurring while consciously approaching the task (looking at the screen many times, fast answers etc.)
Level of Arousal (LA)	It defines the emotional involvement
Implicit Task Effort (ITE)	It describes implicit task effort, being related to the activation of the autonomous nervous system combined with long time to complete the evaluation task
Information Foraging (IF)	It describes the tendency to search many information
Innovative Value (IV)	Beyond quality-related aspects, this component is characterized by the perceived presence of novel or creative aspects
Price Overestimation (PO)	It describes the tendency to overestimate the product's price
Voluntary Wide Exploration (VWE)	The variables explain the typical behavior occurring when eyes were pointing to different targets
Pupil Dilation (PD)	It is deemed as a descriptor of phenomena involving large pupil dilation
Curiosity and Exploration (CE)	Curiosity- and exploration-related factors appear as determinants (long eyes movements and large dimension of pupils)
Ordinary Value (OV)	Knowledge and interest dimensions are fundamental dimensions for this component

5 Results

The influence of the TRIZ-OSSs on PCs is shown in the upper part of Table 3, while the influence of the TRIZ-OSSs on the variables investigated through the questionnaire is shown in the bottom part of Table 3. For every relationship, the regression coefficient and the p-value are reported in the Table. Relationships with p-value higher than 0.1 are written in light gray as considered not statistically significant, while the relationships characterized by 0.1 > p-value > 0.05 are indicated with (.) after the coefficient. The regression coefficient can be read as metric of the specific TRIZ-OSS's power to positively (negatively) affect the dependent variable if it is positive (negative).

Table 3. Results of the linear regressions between TRIZ-OSSs and PCs, and ordinal logistic regressions between TRIZ-OSSs and questionnaire variables

Independent Variables →	**Dynamization**		**Substance**		**Field**	
Depenent Variables ↓	**Coeff.**	**p-value**	**Coeff.**	**p-value**	**Coeff.**	**p-value**
CAT	0.255	0.047	0.101	0.464	-0.053	0.703
LA	-0.037	0.765	-0.065	0.661	-0.062	0.659
ITE	0.086	0.608	0.557	0.000	0.007	0.962
IF	-0.054	0.674	-0.040	0.753	0.144	0.391
IV	0.256	0.050	0.327	0.012	0.335	0.023
PO	-0.105	0.425	0.077	0.550	-0.072	0.656
VWE	-0.391	0.001	0.109	0.265	-0.035	0.799
PD	0.782	0.000	-0.200.	0.093	0.460	0.000
CE	0.545	0.000	0.320	0.018	-0.115	0.296
OV	-0.437	0.000	-0.923	0.000	-0.647	0.000
Knowledge	-0.544	0.001	-0.749	0.000	-0.647	0.000
Interest	-0.011	0.943	-0.472	0.003	0.173	0.274
Quality	0.565	0.001	-0.736	0.000	-0.125	0.447
Advantages	0.826	0.000	-0.148	0.349	0.737	0.000
Absence of Disadvantages	-0.216	0.167	-0.682	0.000	-0.445	0.005
Preference	0.498	0.002	-0.402	0.011	0.164	0.293
Novelty Creativity	1.568	0.000	0.661	0.000	1.334	0.000
Willingness_to_Pay	0.676	0.000	-0.291.	0.065	0.337	0.032

6 Discussions

All the TRIZ-OSSs showed a significantly increased IV and diminished OV. The participants revealed a low knowledge of these TRIZ-OSSs and changing Substance displays the lowest acceptance level. Indeed, although TRIZ-OSSs implementing change of Substance are considered more new and creative than baseline solutions, these lead to a negative perception of quality, a low level of interest and a negative preference. In addition, this is followed by a negative Willingness to Pay (WTP), by a perception of disadvantages and a not clear perception of advantages. Moreover, the low level of affordances was highlighted by the significant positive effect on ITE and negative on PD. This result suggests that solutions implementing this TRIZ-OSS may not be competitive with the baseline one. However, these solutions could be successful in specific market sectors targeted to peculiar consumers.

TRIZ-OSSs implementing change of Field are perceived undoubtedly new and creative but the advantages, clearly perceived by participants, are counterbalanced by disadvantages noticed in the solutions. In addition, a positive WTP has emerged while a significant preference, interest and perception of quality have not. These results could mean that solutions changing Field are perceived innovative but not sufficiently mature. Therefore, further efforts should be made to reduce their real or perceived disadvantages.

TRIZ-OSSs implementing Dynamization showed a clear perception of quality, advantages and preference enhanced by novelty and creativity that lead to a positive WTP. The PCs related with biometrics measures indicate how the evaluation process takes place through a careful, curious and meticulous observation of the solutions. These solutions seems to be the most valued by the participants, and a possible explanation can be found in the ability of the products to meet participants' expectations. Indeed, the TRIZ-OSSs offer comparable (or better) performances compared with the baseline ones and provide additional benefits that can be directly exploited during the products' use. In particular, they provide useful functions for both the user and the environment without perceivably increasing costs and/or harmful effects.

Furthermore, by comparing the TRIZ-OSSs investigated, it is possible to note differences in the way solutions provide benefits to consumers. Indeed, while all the solutions provide direct benefits for the environment, only the Dynamization provides direct benefits for the user e.g. the possibility of replacing only the worn blades or bristles instead of buying a completely new product. In the used case studies, this is accompanied by a change in business model. The effects brought on by more dynamic solutions are worth investigating further; in particular, it should be studied whether these remarks emerge because of the specific products leveraged in the experiment or have general validity.

7 Conclusions

The paper provides an overview of the literature involving humankind and/or ecological issues in the TRIZ methodologies. It highlights how the contextual analysis of both perspectives is limited. Accordingly, the authors performed an experimental study aimed with a dual purpose: to provide a methodological framework to investigate the CVP from functional, hedonic and behavioral perspectives and to capture differences in CVP between baseline products and the alternative TRIZ-OSSs, i.e. potentially inspired by Dynamization, Substance and Field. Different TRIZ strategies resulted in marked differences in terms of CVP.

Indeed, the results showed how the change of Substance leads to decrease the solutions' acceptance while improving the environmental performances, which limits the competitive advantages compared with baselines solutions. Innovative advantages are perceived in the solutions performing functions through a different Field, but the perception of disadvantages could be the main barrier to their preference and adoption. Solutions implementing Dynamization give rise to better feedback from participants in many dimensions that are fundamental for successful innovation.

Two considerations emerge from these results. Firstly, the preferred TRIZ-OSSs combine environmental and humans' benefits with no performance drop, delivering new valuable attributes. Secondly, the TRIZ-OSSs with lower acceptance levels are more suitable for radical product changes while the most appreciated ones are more suitable for incremental innovations.

These results enrich the ECO-TRIZ knowledge by providing a general perspective on the perception of products implementing specific strategies. This information increases the designer's awareness of possible risks related to the radical change of a solution and the need to involve potential consumers in order to be able to develop acceptable solutions with, consequently, enhanced success chances. This newly generated knowledge is, however, constrained by the limited number of TRIZ-OSSs; this represents a trigger for future research.

References

1. Filippi, S., Barattin, D.: Exploiting TRIZ tools in interaction design. Procedia Eng. **131**, 71–85 (2015)
2. Batemanazan, V., Jaafar, A., Kadir, R.A., Nayan, N.M.: Improving usability with TRIZ: a review. In: Badioze, Z.H., et al. (eds.) Advances in Visual Informatics IVIC 2017. Lecture Notes in Computer Science, vol. 10645. Springer, Cham (2017). https://doi.org/10.1007/978-3-319-70010-6_58
3. Van Pelt, A., Hey, J.: Using TRIZ and human-centered design for consumer product development. Procedia Eng. **9**, 688–693 (2011)
4. Wang, C.H.: Combining rough set theory with fuzzy cognitive pairwise rating to construct a novel framework for developing multi-functional tablets. J. Eng. Des. **29**(8–9), 430–448 (2018)
5. Nagamachi, M.: Kansei engineering: a new ergonomic consumer-oriented technology for product development. Int. J. Ind. Ergon. **15**(1), 3–11 (1995)
6. Borgianni, Y., Cascini, G., Rotini, F.: Process value analysis for business process re-engineering. Proc. Inst. Mech. Eng., Part B: J. Eng. Manufact. **224**(2), 305–327 (2010)
7. Kano, N.: Attractive quality and must-be quality. Hinshitsu Quality. J. Jpn. Soc. Qual. Control **14**, 39–48 (1984)
8. Chen, L.S., Hsu, C.C., Chang, P. C.: Developing a TRIZ-Kano model for creating attractive quality. In: 2008 4th International Conference on Wireless Communications, Networking and Mobile Computing, pp. 1–6. IEEE (2008)
9. Wu, C.T., Shao, M.H., Huang, C.L., Chen, C.H., Pan, T.S.: A kano-based evaluation model for extensive innovation procedure. In: 2013 Second International Conference on Robot, Vision and Signal Processing, pp. 178–181. IEEE (2013)
10. Lin, C.C., Luh, D.B.: A vision-oriented approach for innovative product design. Adv. Eng. Inform. **23**(2), 191–200 (2009)
11. Ávila, J., González, S., Borja, V., Espinosa, A.: Using TRIZ tools at early stages of a user centered design process. In: ASME 2013 International Mechanical Engineering Congress and Exposition, pp. V012T13A038-V012T13A038. American Society of Mechanical Engineers (2013)

12. Toivonen, T., Siitonen, J.: Value stream analysis for complex processes and systems. Procedia CIRP **39**, 9–15 (2016)
13. Vezzoli, C., Manzini, E.: Design for Environmental Sustainability. Springer, London (2008). https://doi.org/10.1007/978-1-84800-163-3
14. Navas, H.V.: Radical and systematic eco-innovation with TRIZ methodology. In: Azevedo, S., Brandenburg, M., Carvalho, H., Cruz-Machado, V. (eds.) Eco-Innovation and the Development of Business Models, pp. 81–95. Springer, Cham (2014). https://doi.org/10.1007/978-3-319-05077-5_5
15. Tyl, B., Legardeur, J., Millet, D., Vallet, F.: A comparative study of ideation mechanisms used in eco-innovation tools. J. Eng. Des. **25**(10–12), 325–345 (2014)
16. D'Anna, W., Cascini, G.: Adding quality of life to design for Eco-Efficiency. J. Clean. Prod. **112**, 3211–3221 (2016)
17. Maccioni, L., Borgianni, Y., Basso, D.: Value perception of green products: an exploratory study combining conscious answers and unconscious behavioral aspects. Sustainability **11**, 1226 (2019)
18. Russo, D., Serafini, M., Rizzi, C.: Is TRIZ an ecodesign method? In: Setchi, R., Howlett, R. J., Liu, Y., Theobald, P. (eds.) Sustainable Design and Manufacturing 2016. SIST, vol. 52, pp. 525–535. Springer, Cham (2016). https://doi.org/10.1007/978-3-319-32098-4_45
19. Russo, D.: TRIZ-driven eco-design and Innovation. In: ICORD 09: Proceedings of the 2nd International Conference on Research into Design, Bangalore, India, pp. 105–112. Design Society, Glasgow (2009)
20. Bocken, N.M.P., Allwood, J.M., Willey, A.R., King, J.M.H.: Development of an eco-ideation tool to identify stepwise greenhouse gas emissions reduction options for consumer goods. J. Clean. Prod. **19**(12), 1279–1287 (2011)
21. Livotov, P., Sekaran, A.P.C., Law, R., Reay, D., Sarsenova, A., Sayyareh, S.: Eco-innovation in process engineering: contradictions, inventive principles and methods. Thermal Sci. Eng. Prog. **9**, 52–65 (2019)
22. Jones, E., Harrison, D.: Investigating the use of TRIZ in Eco-innovation. In: TRIZCON2000 Conference Proceedings, Altshuller Institute, USA (2000)
23. Fussler, C., James, P.: Eco-Innovation: A Breakthrough Discipline for Innovation and Sustainability. Pitman, London (1996)
24. Chang, H.T., Chen, J.L.: The conflict-problem-solving CAD software integrating TRIZ into eco-innovation. Adv. Eng. Softw. **35**(8–9), 553–566 (2004)
25. DeSimone, L.D., Popoff, F.: Eco-Efficiency: The Business Link to Sustainable Development. MIT press, Cambridge (2000)
26. Chang, H.T., Chen, J.L., Tainan, T.: Eco-innovative examples for 40 TRIZ inventive principles. TRIZ J. 1–16 (2003)
27. Cherifi, A., Dubois, M., Gardoni, M., Tairi, A.: Methodology for innovative eco-design based on TRIZ. Int. J. Interact. Des. Manufact. (IJIDeM) **9**(3), 167–175 (2015)
28. Bogatyrev, N., Bogatyreva, O.: BioTRIZ: a win-win methodology for eco-innovation. In: Azevedo, S.G., Brandenburg, M., Carvalho, H., Cruz-Machado, V. (eds.) Eco-Innovation and the Development of Business Models. GINS, vol. 2, pp. 297–314. Springer, Cham (2014). https://doi.org/10.1007/978-3-319-05077-5_15
29. Chen, J.L., Yang, Y.C.: Eco-innovation by integrating biomimetic with TRIZ ideality and evolution rules. In: Hesselbach, J., Herrmann, C. (eds.) Glocalized Solutions for Sustainability in Manufacturing, pp. 101–106. Springer, Berlin, Heidelberg (2011). https://doi.org/10.1007/978-3-642-19692-8_18
30. Russo, D., Regazzoni, D., Montecchi, T.: Eco-design with TRIZ laws of evolution. Procedia Eng. **9**, 311–322 (2011)

31. Chulvi, V., Vidal, R.: Usefulness of evolution lines in eco-design. Procedia Eng. **9**, 135–144 (2011)
32. Pahl, G., Beitz, W., Feldhusen, J., Grote, K.H.: Engineering Design: A Systematic Approach. Springer, London (2007). https://doi.org/10.1007/978-1-84628-319-2
33. Russo, D., Schöfer, M., Bersano, G.: Supporting ECO-innovation in SMEs by TRIZ eco-guidelines. Procedia Eng. **131**, 831–839 (2015)
34. Russo, D., Serafini, M., Rizzi, C.: TRIZ based computer aided LCA for ecodesign. Comput. Aided Des. Appl. **13**(6), 816–826 (2016)
35. Tyl, B., Legardeur, J., Millet, D., Falchi, A., Ranvier, B.: A new approach for the development of a creative method to stimulate responsible innovation. In: Bernard, A. (ed.) Global Product Development, pp. 93–104. Springer, Heidelberg (2011). https://doi.org/10.1007/978-3-642-15973-2_10
36. Russo, D., Rizzi, C., Montelisciani, G.: Inventive guidelines for a TRIZ-based eco-design matrix. J. Clean. Prod. **76**, 95–105 (2014)
37. Russo, D., Rizzi, C., Spreafico, C.: How to build guidelines for eco-improvement. In: Campana, G., Howlett, R.J., Setchi, R., Cimatti, B. (eds.) SDM 2017. SIST, vol. 68, pp. 879–887. Springer, Cham (2017). https://doi.org/10.1007/978-3-319-57078-5_82
38. D'Anna, W., Cascini, G.: Supporting sustainable innovation through TRIZ system thinking. Procedia Engineering **9**, 145–156 (2011)
39. Maslow, A.H.: A theory of human motivation. Psychol. Rev. **50**(4), 370 (1943)
40. Vinodh, S., Kamala, V., Jayakrishna, K.: Integration of ECQFD, TRIZ, and AHP for innovative and sustainable product development. Appl. Math. Model. **38**(11–12), 2758–2770 (2014)
41. Chen, H.-C.: Green innovation design model of kansei engineering. In: Lokman, A., Yamanaka, T., Lévy, P., Chen, K., Koyama, S. (eds.) Proceedings of the 7th International Conference on Kansei Engineering and Emotion Research 2018. AISC, vol. 739, pp. 267–276. Springer, Singapore (2018). https://doi.org/10.1007/978-981-10-8612-0_29
42. Swait, J., Sweeney, J.C.: Perceived value and its impact on choice behavior in a retail setting. J. Retail. Consum. Serv. **7**(2), 77–88 (2000)
43. Woodall, T.: Conceptualising 'value for the customer': An attributional, structural and dispositional analysis. Acad. Mark. Sci. Rev. **12**, 1–42 (2003)
44. Holbrook, M.B.: Consumer Value: A Framework for Analysis and Research. Psychology Press, London (1999)
45. Tseng, S.C., Hung, S.W.: A framework identifying the gaps between customers' expectations and their perceptions in green products. J. Clean. Prod. **59**, 174–184 (2013)
46. Lohmeyer, Q., Meboldt, M.: The integration of quantitative biometric measures and experimental design research. In: Cash, P., Stanković, T., Štorga, M. (eds.) Experimental Design Research, pp. 97–112. Springer, Cham (2016). https://doi.org/10.1007/978-3-319-33781-4_6

TRIZ Applied to Waste Pyrolysis Project in Morocco

Davide Russo[1(✉)], Paolo Peri[2], and Christian Spreafico[1]

[1] University of Bergamo, Viale Marconi 4, 24044 Dalmine, BG, Italy
davide.russo@unibg.it
[2] Synecom srl, 24040 Stezzano, Bergamo, Italy

Abstract. The methods and technologies of waste disposal are characterized by a slow evolution. A system that can bring great benefits, in economic and environmental terms is pyrolysis. A technology that instead of burning waste, gets products for industrial use.

The technology offers many advantages, among which they allow drastically reduce the ashes deriving from the reaction compared to those deriving from normal combustion, it also produces reaction gases and oils that have a high calorific value and are suitable for conversion into other energy such as electricity, district heating or cold, compressed air.

In order to make this technology usable today we need an important scale up in response to the many pilot projects around the world.

In this article we can show some examples of how an Italian-French industrial group, active in pyrolysis has implemented TRIZ to develop a large-scale technology for urban waste recycling. In particular, the ongoing project in Agadir area in Morocco will be presented.

The project will be shown in the article and how the sponsoring company is using TRIZ to develop its technology worldwide.

Keywords: Triz · Pyrolysis · Problem solving · Evolutive tree

1 Introduction

In recent times, the quantity of the produced wastes has considerably increased: everyday over three million tons of waste are produced. As a result, the problem of their disposal has become a crucial point. Traditional methods, such as storage and incineration, are no longer effective and environmentally sustainable due to the high impact of the pollutants produced.

A less impactful alternative is represented by the pyrolysis, or the thermal decomposition of materials at high temperatures inside a not oxidant atmosphere.

Moreover, such process is able to generate products (i.e. gas, liquid and solid) with interesting qualities in terms of composition and heating value, with a relative distribution dependent on several parameters (e.g. time, temperature, waste composition).

Despite pyrolysis is a technology known for centuries, its application in the field of waste disposal is considerably newer and for this reason it is still under development and with huge industrial potential.

Published by Springer Nature Switzerland AG 2019
R. Benmoussa et al. (Eds.): TFC 2019, IFIP AICT 572, pp. 295–304, 2019.
https://doi.org/10.1007/978-3-030-32497-1_24

Since the most important feature of pyrolysis is the calorific value and the energy content of the exhaust gases, the comparison with a traditional incineration system is very significant. The comparison can involve the processed products, the required energy, the versatility and the dimensions of the plants. In general, while the products obtained from an incineration plant are only pollutants to be destroyed with a little advantage deriving from their combustion, those from pyrolysis are interesting resources for different markets (e.g. fuels). The process also requires less energy due to the to the low operating temperature, which is around 500–800 °C, unlike the 1000 °C needed for the traditional combustions. Other advantages include the possibility of building the reactor with less valuable materials to save costs.

Today there are many pyrolysis technologies: Fluidized bed combustion, Cyclonic, Rotative screws, electric induction, microwave, laser-assisted and plasma assisted). Any technology can work with different operative parameters in a multitude of design variants.

Some of them are almost fully operative while others are still at experimental and, in general, the most important requirements driving their development are:

(1) Ensuring the full disposal of a greater flow of raw materials, deriving by the increasing in the total production of waste.
(2) Reducing the time required for processing the waste within the reactor or its residence time.

The two requirements are clearly in contradiction: the complete waste disposal in a pyrolysis reactor generally requires a long time for carrying out all the chemical reactions involved occurring inside the reactor, which typically imply large volumes of the reactor chamber for storing the entire mass of waste.

However, this problem cannot be solved by directly applying TRIZ separation principles, because of the lack of knowledge about the operative parameters and their combinations governing its functioning.

The contradictions work well when the conflicting parameters can be considered reasonably independent of each other, otherwise the formulation of the contradiction tends towards tautology, resulting therefore impossible to separate. During the heating with the thermal vector and immediately after in the cooling phases, the chemical reactions between the reactants and the continuous recombination of the products are very difficult to predict and describe, because they depend on hundreds of factors: it can almost be said that every chemical process has its peculiar dynamic! If we cannot start with a bottom-up approach, we can instead create contradictions starting instead from the results of field experiments. Hence the idea of collecting and organizing all the information on the subject with an evolutionary approach and in particular the evolutionary tree of Shpakovsky [1].

The starting point concerns the recovery of information through the collection and analysis of experimental results from the scientific literature. Through the Shpakovsky evolution tree, the recovered technologies were then classified. Therefore, the same tree is used to select the technologies and to visualize the operational parameters that come into conflict with each other in order to identify the physical contradictions. The structure of the paper is as follows: Sect. 2 presents the state of the art on the operational parameters of pyrolysis, Sect. 3 proposes the use of the evolutionary tree to organize information on pyrolysis technologies, Sect. 4 draws conclusions.

2 State of the Art

The process of the pyrolysis is too complex because of the multitude of involved parameters (e.g. temperature, time of reaction, typology and granulometry of the processed material) and the nature of their mutual correlations affecting the quality (e.g. heating value) and the quantity of the obtained products (i.e. gas, liquid and solid).

In addition, today, a lack of knowledge still persists, as testified by the interest of the scientific community in proposing always new experiments, and by the many contradictory obtained results.

On a practical level, this lack is detectable on the insufficient flexibility of the numerous commercial and semi-commercial plants of pyrolysis, which are forced to work in too narrow ranges of function for not compromising the performances.

For this reason, we carried out an analysis of the existing technologies, both from patent and papers and an analysis of the operative parameters based on the experimental results of the test from scientific literature.

The research of the technologies of pyrolysis has been carried out on patents and papers on the international databases (i.e. Espacenet, SCOPUS and Google Scholar) by using generic keywords (i.e. "pyrolysis" and "gasification").

The result shows that the number of documents is very high, both as regards the number of scientific articles and the number of patent documents. The goal was to extract correlations between physical-chemical parameters of the pyrolysis process in order to be able to set contradictions.

2.1 Analysis of the Operative Parameters

The first parameter searched in the document pool is the temperature at which the pyrolysis process takes place. According to [2], each chemical reaction of each element of the pyrolyzed waste has a precise threshold value. In general, we noticed how the increase of temperature leads to an increase in the gases produced, while the fraction of liquids and solids is reduced even if with different quantities [3].

Another main parameter is the reaction time which substantially discriminates the two main pyrolysis mechanisms: the fast, which occurs in a few seconds (less than 5) and the so-called "traditional", which times are always longer than 10 min. A lot of authors (e.g. [4]) studied the combination between temperature and time of reaction by deepening the effects deriving from the heating rate and the permanence at the peak temperature.

Also, the raw material within the reactor, the shape of the reactor and the agitation mechanism of the raw material can strongly influence the reaction (e.g. [5]).

This framework is then complicated by the comparison of the influence of these parameters on different feeding materials (e.g. rubber, wood, paper), by their shape of aggregation (e.g. dust or pellet) and by the percentage of the contained humidity (e.g. [6]).

The analysis of the product also considers other evaluations in addition to the quality and the quantity of the products, such as the reactivity of the ashes, or its ability to keep suspended in the produced gas (e.g. [4]).

Figure 1 summarizes different correlations between the operative parameters and the obtained products found in literature. As can be seen, there is no correlation factor between the increase in temperature and the modification of the percentages of pyrolysis products. The different processed materials, even very similar to each other, behave in unpredictably: some improve with the increase in temperature while others get worse. These dynamics have been identified for most of the analyzed literature and for all types of parameters.

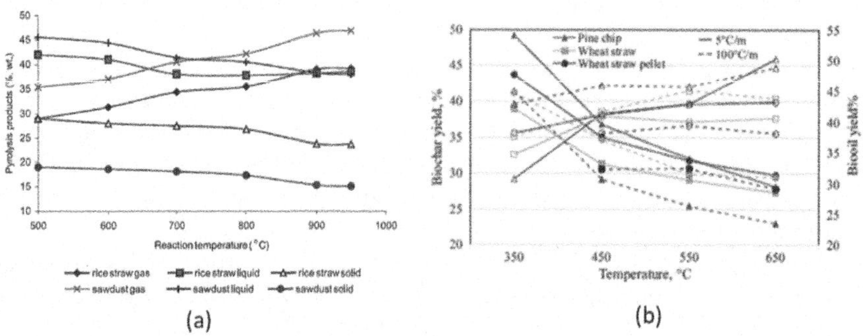

Fig. 1. Different influences of the operative parameters on the pyrolysis products from literature (a – [7] Chen et al. b – [6] Roy and Dias 2017).

3 Proposal

The collected technologies have then been related to those regarding the operative parameters and then they have been organized through the logics of the evolutive theory and the tree of Shpakovski (i.e. [1]).

The starting point of this logic are the Laws of Technical System of Evolution [8] and the related patters, which are the most general trends for describing the evolution of technical systems and they are reported to be one of the most used TRIZ tools within the case studies from literature [9]. During the years, the Laws have been applied in several fields, and, in particular, along with the evolutive trees, they have been exploited for classifying technical systems according to their level of evolution [10].

The first pattern (Evolution Toward Increased Ideality) is based on the assumption that every system has both useful and harmful effects and it is used for classifying the systems in order to maximize their ratio of useful to harmful effects and approach ideality. The second pattern (Stages of Technology Evolution) is a sort of an S-curve for mapping the technological maturity of the systems. The third pattern (Non-Uniform Development of System Elements) explains that different systems could evolve by their different schedules, since they are affected by different constraints during different period. The fourth pattern (Evolution Toward Increased Dynamism and Controllability) states that the evolution of the systems passes through the increasing of their dynamism and controllability. The fifth pattern (Increased Complexity, Then Simplification) explains that there is an initial tendency to add functionalities to the systems, by increasing their complexity, and then to divide them into simpler systems that provide the same, or more, functionality. The sixth pattern (Evolution with Matching and Mismatching Elements) states that evolving system elements are matched or mismatched to improve performance or compensate for undesired effects. Seventh pattern (Evolution Toward the Micro-level and Increased Use of Fields) explains that technological systems tend to transition from macro- to micro-systems, and that different types of energy fields are used to achieve better performance and control during this transition. The last pattern (Evolution Toward Decreased Human Involvement) explains that evolution of the system passes through the decreasing of the human involvement.

Their improvements and combinations have been proposed by several authors.

[11] found hidden patterns in technological evolution by exploring the relationships between the evolution of products from the point of view of TRIZ's patterns of evolution and new emerging information technologies (semantic web, data mining, text mining, theory of chaos and evolutionary algorithms).

[12] proposed an algorithm to perform functional analysis for building a network of evolutionary trend for a given technical system and they integrated it with well known models for function representation (e.g. Energy Material Signal -EMS- model).

[13] proposed an automated method for identifying TRIZ evolution trends from patents which consists of extracting binary relations of verb, nouns and adjectives from patents using natural language processing, defining a 'reasons for jumps' rule base that arranges trend-specific binary relations for trend identification, and determining specific trends and trend phases by measuring semantic sentence similarity between the binary relations from patents and the binary relations in the rule base.

[14] presents a forecasting novel model to acquire innovative ideas more easily to design eco products, followed by evaluation of whether the new design is more effective than currently available ones in the concept design stage based on TRIZ evolution patterns, in which the index system of case-based reasoning connects the innovative idea to cases located in a database to accelerate the process.

[15] identified promising patents for technology transfer by adopting TRIZ evolution trends as criteria to evaluate technologies in patents, and Subject–Action–Object (SAO)-based text-mining technique to deal with big patent data and analyze them automatically [16] explained how they can be used to construct a technology road-map that profiles the life curves of considered technical system. In particular, the author used the patterns of evolution to define the fuzzy edge of what we will be tomorrow compared with what we are today.

Among all these approaches, one of the most simple and immediate way to organize information, especially for novice designer, is the work about the evolutive trees carried out by Shpakovski (2006). The peculiarity of this approach consists in using the so-called "Evolution Tree" – an organized set of technical system evolution patterns - to structure technical and patent information. The result is a certain hierarchy of actions, as shown in Fig. 2, performed during the system transformation, as well as the hierarchy of evolution patterns formed as a result of each of these actions:

(1) Introduction of new or segmentation of existing objects, processes, fields and forces.
(2) Coordination the shape, size, and properties of the surfaces with the internal structure of the system's elements, process parameters, fields, and forces,
(3) Dynamization of sets of objects, processes, fields, and forces.
(4) Providing controllability of the system's elements,
(5) Coordination the action of the system's elements.

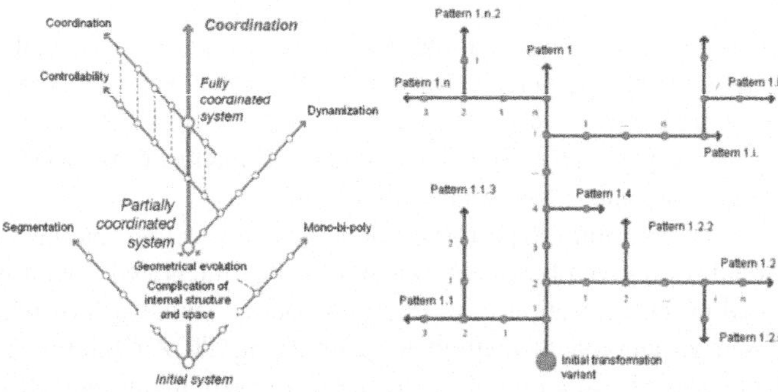

Fig. 2. (a) Hierarchy of actions aimed at the transformation of the system's elements and (b) the structure of the Evolution tree (Shpakovski 2006).

3.1 Application of the Evolutive Theory to Pyrolysis

Within the obtained evolutive tree in Fig. 3, the pyrolysis technologies have been divided into different groups based on the trends involved and ordered based on them. Trends act on two hierarchic levels of detail.

The main vertical branch considers the different modes of interaction between the heat vector and the raw material to be subjected to pyrolysis, considering in particular the activation energies of the pyrolytic combustion. The direction of the path follows the "Transition from macro to micro level" evolutionary law. At the bottom of the evolution the heat transfer is limited to one single surface of the raw material, then with 2 or many surfaces till to move to a new level of granularity with an interaction with small parts of raw material and finally to a total decomposition in small particles. In the same way, the same tendency can also be observed on the thermal vector that begins with a hot surface, breaks down into different surfaces and then into an increasing number of parts (small spheres) until it takes the form of micro plasma molecules. The secondary horizontally branches collect main variants from the different pyrolysis technologies. A short selection of inventive principles was used to organize and hierarchize these variants according to an evolutionary type criterion (#1 Segmentation, #3 Local quality, #5 Merging, #7 Nesting, #14 Spheroidality, #17 Another dimension).

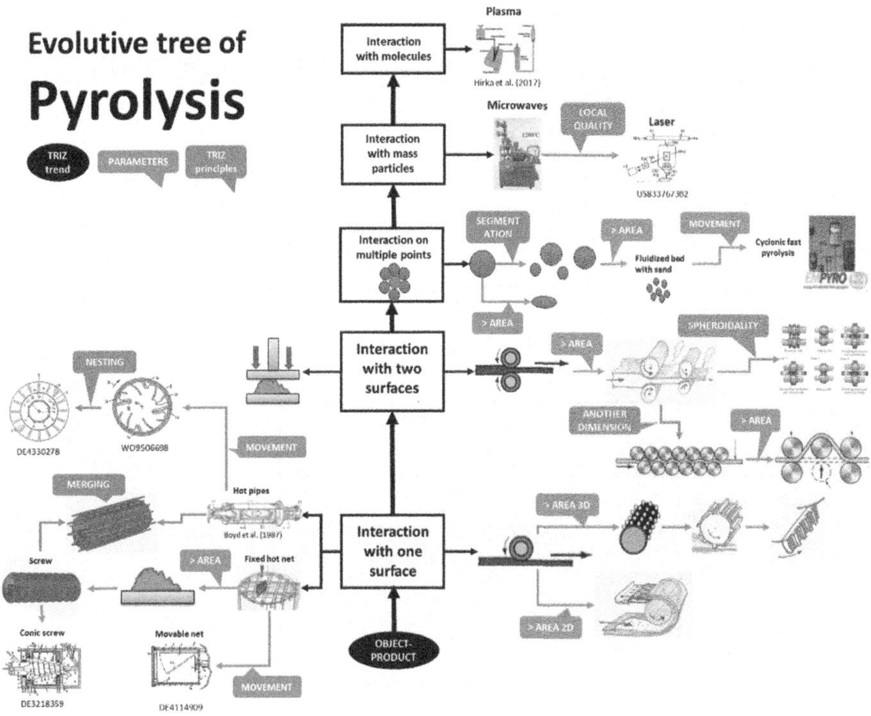

Fig. 3. The proposed evolutive tree for organizing the technologies for the pyrolysis.

3.2 Idea Generation

The starting point of the problem-solving activity was the hot screw reactor produced by the company. Among the many contradictions faced in the process of improving the screw technology, we take for example the one aimed at improving productivity in terms of the quantity of raw material processed. One of the possible ways to improve it is to increase the temperature of the heating mantle. However, this modification seriously undermines the seals of the system, which must have well-controlled thermal expansions to prevent the entry of oxygen into the inert environment. Otherwise serious safety problems may occur; more generally, there are complications in terms of overall structural resistance and a deterioration in the useful life of the plant. A physical contradiction has been set identifying two situations, the "current cold" one which does not guarantee a high productivity and a "warmer" one that gives problems of resistance and tightness, which is showed in Fig. 4.

For solving this contradiction, we have then applied the principle of the separation in space identifying the operative zones of Control Parameters inside the screw structure. As shown in Fig. 5, the parts in contact with raw materials have to reach a high temperature, in order to ensure a more efficient pyrolysis, while seals have to be maintained at a lower temperature for guarantee safety.

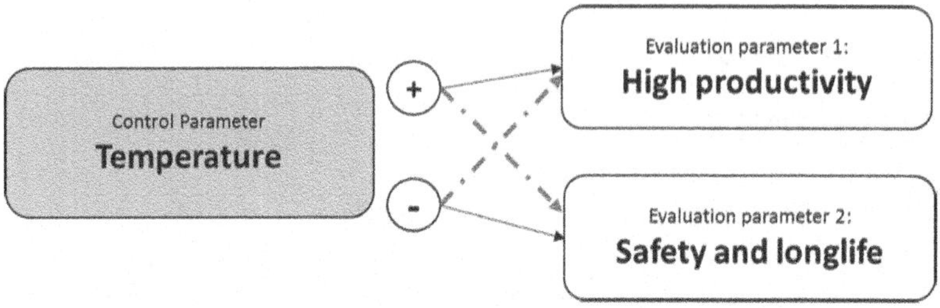

Fig. 4. One physical contradiction affecting the hot screw reactor.

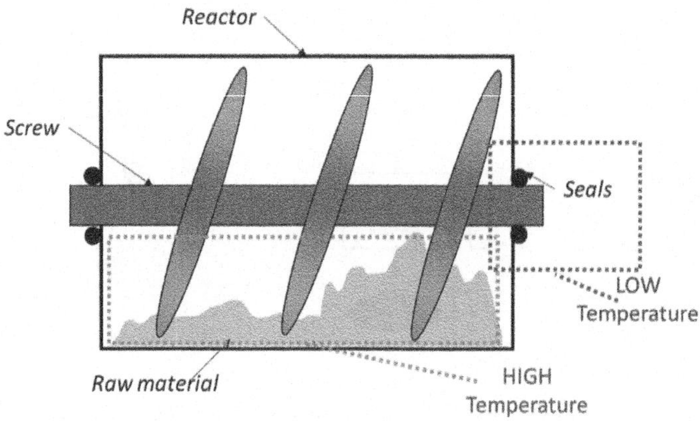

Fig. 5. An application of the spatial Separation principle.

We have then applied principle n°14 – Spheroidal, and in particular its suggestion about the introduction of spheres within the technical system.

The derived solution, please refer to Fig. 5, is made by the same reactor where the screw is heated at same "low" temperature (i.e. 400 °C), and the introduction of hot spheres with a high temperature (i.e. 1000 °C), which are moved by the contact with screw rotation within the reactor.

4 Conclusions

The subject of pyrolysis is of great interest at present. Despite the great experimental interest, the laws that govern it have not yet been well circumscribed. The study of the available literature on pyrolysis has identified the lack of information as the biggest obstacle to conduct a more classic TRIZ approach: the initial representation of the process through totally reliable models of physics and chemistry prevents the formulation of equally reliable contradictions. Hence the risk of investing in solutions that may not be sufficiently effective. However, the vast literature is an important resource that has been exploited by the authors to extract those correlations that, considered individually, are certainly true as they are tested. The shape of a rector and its operating parameters, we know that they have produced a certain result even if we are not able to understand exactly which process dynamics took place within it.

Hence the choice to work at a high level of detail. The evolutionary graph has proved to be a very versatile tool, able to give order to the enormous amount of material available, to guide research according to a reasonable criterion; it has also proved to be a valid communication tool to discuss the client and overcome it as to resolve some contradictions that were evolutionarily more advantageous than others that on paper without other criteria could have seemed so interesting.

The tree also offered a valuable contribution to systematizing the technological hybridization process, resulting simple and orderly. It has been also used for formulating physical contradiction like the one shown in the paper showing the transition from a warm mantle technology with a screw to technology integrated with hot spheres.

A hybridization project of some pyrolysis technologies is ongoing. It concerns a plant in Morocco that will be built in the next 3 years at Agadir. It will have to process more than 1000 tons of solid urban waste per day with an innovative technology in a plant that will also be a showcase of green technological solutions involving solutions for exhaust heat storage, energy production and treatments foe ashes and pollutants.

References

1. Shpakovsky, N.: Evolution Trees. Analysis of technical information and generation of new ideas. TRIZ Profi, Moscow (2006)
2. Demirbaş, A.: Kinetics for non-isothermal flash pyrolysis of hazelnut shell. Biores. Technol. **66**(3), 247–252 (1998)
3. Lopez, A., De Marco, I., Caballero, B.M., Laresgoiti, M.F., Adrados, A.: Influence of time and temperature on pyrolysis of plastic wastes in a semi-batch reactor. Chem. Eng. J. **173**(1), 62–71 (2011)
4. Solar, J., et al.: Influence of temperature and residence time in the pyrolysis of woody biomass waste in a continuous screw reactor. Biomass Bioenerg. **95**, 416–423 (2016)
5. Promdee, K., Vitidsant, T.: Synthesis of char, bio-oil and gases using a screw feeder pyrolysis reactor. Coke Chem. **56**(12), 466–469 (2013)
6. Roy, P., Dias, G.: Prospects for pyrolysis technologies in the bioenergy sector: a review. Renew. Sustain. Energy Rev. **77**, 59–69 (2017)
7. Chen, G., Andries, J., Spliethoff, H.: Catalytic pyrolysis of biomass for hydrogen rich fuel gas production. Energy Convers. Manag. **44**(14), 2289–2296 (2003)
8. Altshuller, G.S.: Creativity as an Exact Science: The Theory of the Solution of Inventive Problems. Gordon and Breach, New York (1984)
9. Spreafico, C., Russo, D.: TRIZ industrial case studies: a critical survey. Procedia CIRP **39**, 51–56 (2016)
10. Russo, D.: Dalla multidisciplinarietà degli ingegneri del rinascimento alla gestione della complessità nei processi di innovazione e Forecasting tecnologico. Ph.D. thesys. University of Florence (2007)
11. Leon, N. (2006). Trends and patterns of evolution for product innovation. Journal of TRIZ
12. Cascini, G., Rotini, F., Russo, D.: Functional modeling for TRIZ-based evolutionary analyses. In: DS 58-5: Proceedings of ICED 09, the 17th International Conference on Engineering Design. Design Methods and Tools (pt. 1), Palo Alto, CA, USA, 24–27 August 2009, vol. 5 (2009)

13. Yoon, J., Kim, K.: An automated method for identifying TRIZ evolution trends from patents. Expert Syst. Appl. **38**(12), 15540–15548 (2011)
14. Yang, C.J., Chen, J.L.: Forecasting the design of eco-products by integrating TRIZ evolution patterns with CBR and Simple LCA methods. Expert Syst. Appl. **39**(3), 2884–2892 (2012)
15. Park, H., Ree, J.J., Kim, K.: Identification of promising patents for technology transfers using TRIZ evolution trends. Expert Syst. Appl. **40**(2), 736–743 (2013)
16. Slocum, M.: Use the eight patterns of evolution to innovate. TRIZ J. (2014)

TRIZ Directed Evolution for Automobile Fuel

Mohd Roshdi Hassan[1(✉)] and Yaser Yahya Al-Kodami[2]

[1] Department of Mechanical and Manufacturing Engineering, Faculty of Engineering, Universiti Putra Malaysia (UPM), 43400 Serdang, Selangor, Darul Ehsan, Malaysia
roshdi_hassan@upm.edu.my

[2] Yemen LNG Company Ltd., Adhban Building, P.O. Box 15347 Sana'a, Republic of Yemen

Abstract. Recently, Global Warming effect and Green House Gases (GHG) emissions have become one of the main concern for environment that principally come from the exhaust of fossil fuel combustion process (i.e. coal, crude oil, and natural gas). Electric Vehicles (EVs) industry has started taking the lead and showing significant competition in the market via Plug-in Hybrid Electric Vehicle (PHEV) and fully Battery Electric Vehicle (BEV) over the conventional fossil fuel powered vehicles which are going to ban (prohibit) within coming two decades as officially announced by many of global countries. Battery is the backbone of this evolution and it encourages many researchers and scientists to expedite their studies, experimental tests to discover the best reliable, sustainable, and safe resource of energy to meet the customers' (vehicles users) values, satisfactions and expectations. This study aims to scientifically predict and analyze the future battery generation that last longer up to (500 km) with improved charging time (less than 30 min). A systematic evolution method called TRIZ (Theory of Inventive Problem Solving) was used in this paper to link the historical data with present timeline in order to improve the main characteristics of the battery (e.g. energy density, durability, charging time and safety). TRIZ has variety of inventive tools (9 – Windows, S – Curve and Function Analysis), these tools are efficiently assist to predict and achieve the next generation of the future battery. By using the tools of Directed Evolution (DE) and utilizing Level of Innovation Domains, battery development is going to be deeply illustrated. Finally, logical recommendations were proposed to those personnel in charge to move forward to approach the future battery system with targeted features and characteristics.

Keywords: Battery Management System (BMS) · Directed Evolution · Greenhouse Gases (GHG) · Theory of Inventive Problem Solving (TRIZ)

1 Introduction

Practically, fossil fuels as coal, crude oil and natural gas were formed anciently and nowadays they perform an essential influence in humankind's global evolution. Unfortunately, the burning fossil fuel releases toxic gases which in turns make a contribution to acid rain and global warming effect. However, the main source of automobiles energy is "Fossil Fuel" and the total oil production reached a peak during

Published by Springer Nature Switzerland AG 2019
R. Benmoussa et al. (Eds.): TFC 2019, IFIP AICT 572, pp. 305–313, 2019.
https://doi.org/10.1007/978-3-030-32497-1_25

this century. Recently, the recent assessments, environmental associations' policies, and restrictions show that petroleum-based fuels is going to be prohibited by the year 2042. The engine's fuel evolution has grown up rapidly and has obviously followed the behaviour of matter status as Solid (coal), Liquid (petrol/diesel), Gas (NG) and Field (electrical). Batteries industry and its high technologies have been significantly improving. Since early 1990's, Lithium battery's technology has taken the lead of the era of electronic devices evolution (e.g. cell phones, laptops, and smart watches) as well as the automobile industry [1, 2].

2 Evolution of Technologies

2.1 Fuel Evolution of Vehicles' Engine

Engine is the key part of vehicle and simply considered as the heart of automobile and even functioning likewise. In general conventional sense, engine converts the chemical energy in fuel (petrol, diesel and NG) into mechanical energy of moving a vehicle forward. The engine's fuel evolution has grew up rapidly and has obviously followed the behaviour of matter status as Solid (coal), Liquid (petrol/diesel), Gas (NG) and Field (electrical) [3–6].

2.2 Batteries at Electric Vehicles

A battery is a generator of electrons via electro-chemical reactions, it has positive (+) and negative (−) terminals. The early battery was launched in 1859 by lead-acid battery, and then the advanced batteries have been introduced to market with better performance, more efficiency, environmentally safe and even cheaper. At the beginning of this century, batteries was utilized for EV's industry with Lead-acid battery. After that, other technologies joint the market such as Nickel-Metal Hydride (Ni-MH), Fuel Cell, Super-capacitor and Lithium-ion batteries [7–10] as shown in Fig. 1.

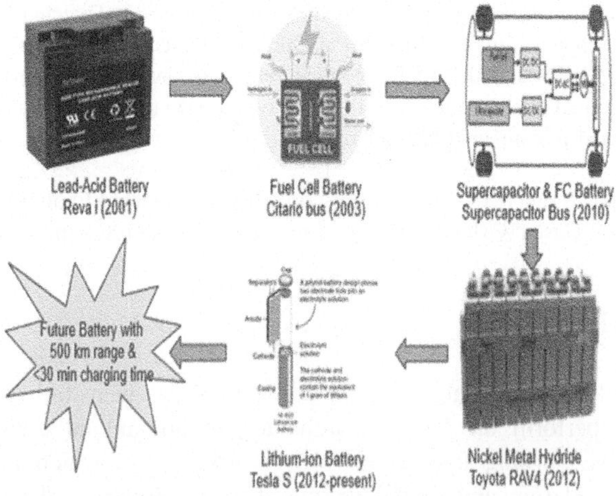

Fig. 1. Batteries at electric vehicles evolution

2.3 Electric Vehicles Classifications

The EV's present a good successor of existing petroleum automobile for many reasons, the key words that show societies prefer EVs comparing to conventional vehicles are the No-gas emission and less noise pollution. Due to air pollution and gas emission laws, the automobile producers were requested to produce vehicles with matching emission specifications which in turns lead to significant improvement of the electric vehicle industries. EV's have three categories based on the engine vs. battery installation as well as its charging technology [11]; these three categories are

Hybrid Electric Vehicle (HEV), Plug-in Hybrid Electric Vehicle (PHEV) and Battery Electric Vehicles (BEV).

3 Directed Evolution Method

3.1 TRIZ Method

TRIZ is a Russian phrase "Teorija Rezhenija Izobretatelskih Zadach", that means "Theory of Inventive Problem Solving". It is demonstrated systematic method to solve problems. It was developed when the scientist and engineer Genrikh Altshuller reviewed thousands of patents in 1946. He revealed that a technical system evolution of is not a randomly occurs but overseen by guaranteed objective rules [12, 13]. TRIZ has valuable and significant tools that have different features to support the scientific prediction of the future generation, which include 40 inventive principle, Contradiction Matrix, 9-Windows, S-Curve and Function Analysis.

3.2 Directed Evolution Method

The Directed Evolution (DE) is a proactive technique that utilized by an organization assigned for the development of new system, products, processes, services and technology. It is the preparation of an inclusive scenarios that helps for future planning and current development to achieve the proper successor [14, 15]. Five stages of DE are shown in Fig. 2.

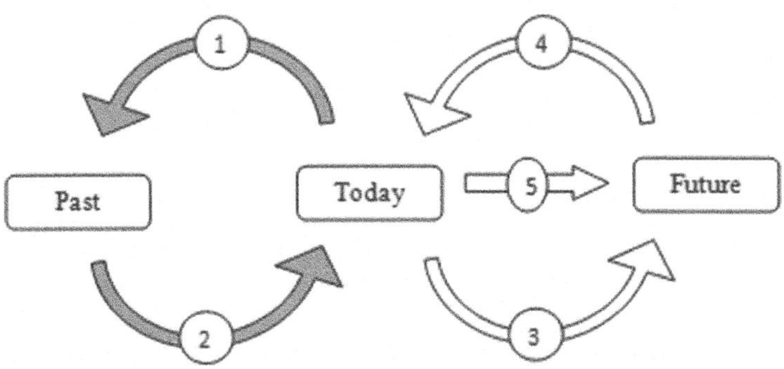

Fig. 2. Stages of directed evolution

1. Collection of historical data.
2. Directed evolution diagnostics.
3. Synthesis of ideas.
4. Decision making.
5. Supporting the process evolution.

4 Result and Discussion

4.1 Collection of Historical Data

Lithium-ion batteries (LIB), is one of the most familiar rechargeable sources of energy, it has led in portable electronic items in markets for last 25 years. Nevertheless, the existing technology of LIBs which just about reach the theoretical capacity and leave little competition space for further assessment which is not able to hold the current applications requirements (e.g. Electric Vehicles) that need more capacity and better lifecycle. With huge demand and massive market prospective, re-chargeable source of energy with greater density and lower cost remain crucially under investigation [16–19].

Table 1 shows the relationship of battery technology among Past-Present-Future stages and taking in consideration the influence of internal and external factors.

Table 1. TRIZ 9-Windows for battery technology

	Past	Present	Future
Super-system	- RoHs Standards – Battery Supplier	- RoHs Standards – Battery Supplier - Charging Station – Local Authority	- RoHs Standards – Battery Supplier – Charging Station – Local Authority – Replacement System – BMS
System	Rechargeable Battery (Lead Acid) (LIQUID)	Lithium-ion (Li-ion) Battery (FIELD – Single material)	Battery of 500 km capacity range and less than 30 min charging time (FIELD-Hybrid)
Sub-system	- Anode (Lead) - Cathode (lead-dioxide) - Electrolyte (Sulphuric acid) - Wiring Connection	- Anode (Graphite, LTO) - Cathode (Li,Al,Ni, Co) - Electrolyte (Solid) - Quick Connection - Separator (polyethylene) - Battery Modules	- Anode (Sn-Li, Sn-Na Hybrid) - Cathode (Li,NCA,S) - Electrolyte (Solid) - Separator (Tin, polymer) - Rack Mounting - Flat Shape - Monitoring Sensors

In the past, a Lead Acid rechargeable battery with basic internal (sub-system) component (e.g. anode, cathode, liquid electrolyte and wiring connection), while external components (super-system) were limited to safety and raw material concerns.

In present, Lithium-ion technology is improved and its "Battery Pack" version has taken the lead in automobiles industry via its additional (sub-system) components (e.g. different substances of and cathode, solid electrolyte, separator and battery modules).

Its related (super-system) components encourage the process development (e.g. charging stations policies and local authority).

In the future, the new vision of battery technology is going to be enhanced components. The researches for sub-system components help to predict the next generation technology with hybrid anode and cathode using more effective substances (e.g. Sn-Li, Sn-Na), solid electrolyte, CAN communcation system, new flat shape and rack mounting design, installing smart monitoring sensors).

4.2 Directed Evolution Diagnostics

As the main step of this strategy, the diagnostic stage needs more concentration, brainstorming and connection of all collected data that were got about the history of battery, competitors, advantages & disadvantages, etc. By applying a dedicated knowledge of 9-windows and data collection, S-curve analysis can help to identify how the correct directions for future development to achieve the targeted specifications as shown in Fig. 3.

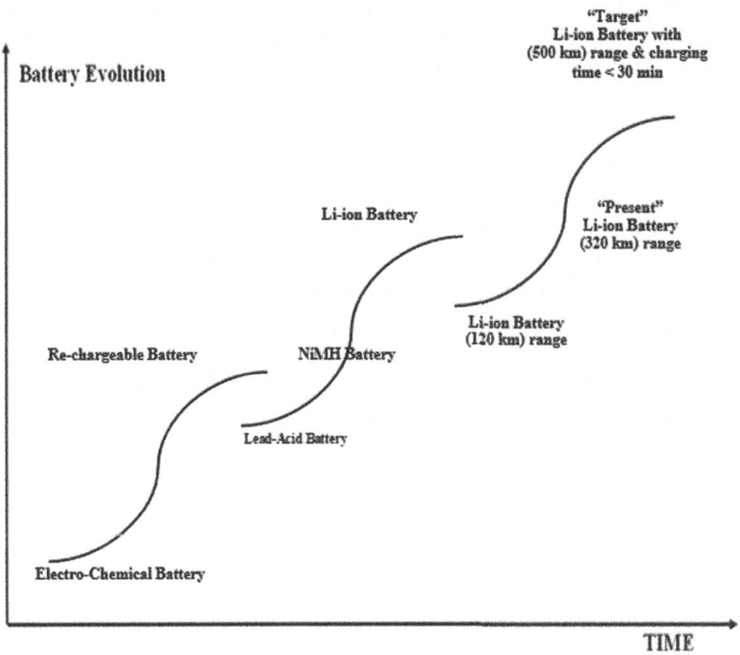

Fig. 3. Lithium battery prediction S-curve

4.3 Synthesis of Ideas

This stage aims to create ideas which will transfer the recommended battery to the next step of evolution. Tools and techniques to be utilized are Ideation brainstorming and Evolutionary Analysis.

Based on 40 inventive principles, some principles have been useful in generating the idea of future battery.

For Principle 3 (Local Quality), changing the structure of the battery is one of the improvement modifications and the flat shape of the future battery is going to have many advantages for utilizing efficiently the maximum available size and even to save more space on the vehicle.

For Principle 8 (Anti-weight), the new rack mounting design will decrease significantly the weight of the battery system which in turn will save more money of the vehicles price.

For Principle 10 (Preliminary action), easy and immediate battery switching feature by providing the vehicle with a redundant battery system (one in duty & one stand-by). This technique will increase the available energy density (distance range) and dragging the charging time to zero.

For Principle 12 (Remove Tension), changing the operating conditions by changing to new substances and hybrid electrodes (e.g. Tin-Sn and sodium-Na) more effective substances with better performance characteristics, current limitations and even cheaper of commercial materials.

For Principles 13 (The other way round), this principle gives a hint to the manufacturers to utilize the reverse concept of charging/discharging. Battery is moving the vehicle during discharging phase, so why not to be recharged using the rotational movement of the vehicle itself.

For Principle 28 (Mechanics substitution), installing the future battery with smart sensors and replacing the conventional wiring connection of the battery by CAN (Controller Area Network) communication system which provides monitoring, controlling and protection features for the battery system.

For Principle 31 (Porous materials), it is one of the important principles and adding a catalytic element such as Graphene is going to improve the charging time due to its superior physical, chemical and mechanical properties.

For Principle 35 (Parameter change), changing the structure of the future battery to be more flexible will have positive impact on physical (less weight), technical (less effected by external environmental conditions) and even safety characteristics (no leak or vibration).

4.4 Decision Making

Since this stage needs personnel in sale, marketing, procurement and finance to be involved, so we are not going deeply and will just utilize the questionnaire analysis tool to recommend the needful to those in charge personnel.

As part of marketing and providing redundant battery, many customers have no objection to pay a reasonable amount of deposit while having a quick battery replacement and negligible recharging time.

4.5 Supporting the Process Evolution

It is not enough to have good plans, there will always be unexpected deviations and out of control issues. Therefore, the earliest four stages can generally be done in a fairly short time. Certainly, they are a preparation for this critical stage of supporting the process, which comprises the process continuous monitoring and making proper corrections if needed. The next concerns need be monitored during the system's development:

- Looking for potential abnormalities in the charging stations environment.
- Predicting deviations analyzing planned versus actual results
- Correction of scenario.

Tools and techniques to be utilized:

- System training to assigned team.
- Continuous data collection of customers' feedback and suggestions.
- Installing battery management system (BMS) including:

Data acquisition, Safety protection, Battery charging/discharging Controlling, Cell balancing, Showing battery status and certification at the user interface, extending the battery life (charging and discharging cycles).

5 Conclusions

The battery industry is one of the most rapidly improved recently and many researches have being conducted even at the moment of writing these words. The understanding of the battery structure and its made substances will lead effectively to the right improvement directions and create a new generation of battery that has significant features and characteristics such as energy density (Capacity), durability, charging time and safety.

Based on TRIZ inventive tools and Directed Evolution (DE) process, the dedicated physical, chemical and mechanical states of the battery can be improved using the 40 Inventive Principles to predict the next generation of battery system which is expected to have some (or even all) of the following characteristics:

Structure: It has two effected parts,

- Adding catalytic element such as Graphene.
- Using new substances and Hybrid electrodes (e.g. Tin-Sn and sodium Na)

Design: It has three effected parts,

- New flat and flexible shape.
- Changing the state of electrolyte to solid.
- New rack mounting installation.

Charging System: It has two effected parts,

- Including redundant battery system.
- Utilizing the vehicle's rotary motion to for recharging.

Control Technology: It has two effected parts,

- Changing to CAN communication connection.
- Installing smart sensors for monitoring and protection.

References

1. Palihawadana, A.: A Literature Review of the Electric Vehicle Battery Management System. Thesis for: Mechatronic Engineering (MEng), University of Wolverhampton (2016). https://www.researchgate.net/publication/309281477_A_Literature_Review_of_the_Electric_Vehicle_Battery_Management_System. Accessed 24 May 2018
2. Changfu, Z., Lei, Z., Xiaosong, H., Zhenpo, W., Torsten, W., Michael, P.: A review of fractional-order techniques applied to lithium-ion batteries, lead-acid batteries, and supercapacitors. J. Power Sources **390**, 286–296 (2018)
3. Whitmore, M.: Development of coal-fired steam technology in britain. J. Encycl. Anthropocene **1**, 285–305 (2018)
4. Moore, J.: The History of Fossil Fuels. https://www.justenergysolar.com/blog/the-history-of-fossil-fuels/. Accessed 27 May 2018 (2016)
5. MacLean, H.L., Lave, L.B., Lankey, R., Joshi, S.: A life-cycle comparison of alternative automobile fuels. J. Air Waste Manag. Assoc. **50**(10), 1769–1779 (2000)
6. Werpy, M., Santini, D., Burnham, A., Mint, M.: Natural Gas Vehicles: Status, Barriers, and Opportunities. Argonne National Laboratory: Center for Transportation Research, Energy Systems Division (2010)
7. Deyab, M.A.: Ionic liquid as an electrolyte additive for high performance lead-acid batteries. J. Power Sources **390**, 176–180 (2018)
8. Deok, H., Ho, H., Dae-Ung, K., Sungtack, H., Young-Hoon, Y., Byeong, O.: Development of an optimal charging algorithm of a Ni-MH battery for stationary fuel cell/battery hybrid system application. Int. J. Hydrogen Energy **38**, 9008–9015 (2013)
9. Lin, C., Leon, L.: Recent advances in lithium-sulfur batteries. J. Power Sources **267**, 770–783 (2014)
10. Hannan, M.A., Azidin, F.A., Mohamed, A.: Hybrid electric vehicles and their challenges: a review. J. Renew. Sustain. Energy Rev. **29**, 135–150 (2014)
11. Ralston, M., Nigro, N.: Plug-In Electric Vehicles: Literature Review. Centre for Climate and Energy Solutions, Arlington (2011)
12. The Altshuller Institute for TRIZ Studies (2013). What is TRIZ? https://www.aitriz.org/triz. Accessed 29 May 2018
13. Georges, A.: Can we equitably manage the end of the fossil fuel era? J. Energy Res. Soc. Sci. **35**, 217–223 (2018)
14. Prushinskiy, V.: Triz and Hybridization Algorithms for Innovative Economy. Develop Great Innovation Triz, Malaysia (2016)
15. Zlotin, B., Zusman, A.: Directed Evolution: Philosophy, Theory and Practice. The Triz Journal. Ideation International Inc., Michigan (2001)
16. Ghassan, Z., Rodolfo, D., Monica, C., Guzay, P.: The lithium-ion battery: State of the art and future perspectives. J. Renew. Sustain. Energ. Rev. **89**, 292–308 (2018)
17. Guorui, Z., Siji, L., Zhanguo, W., Weige, Z., Zeyu, M.: State of energy estimation of lithium titanate battery for rail transit application. J. Energ. Procedia **105**, 3146–3151 (2017)

18. Liqiang, W., Zichao, W., Qun, J., Wei, W., Zhanguo, W.: Characteristic analysis of lithium titanate battery. J. Energ. Procedia **105**, 4444–4449 (2017)
19. Tan, P., et al.: Advances and challenges in lithium-air batteries. J. Appl. Energy **204**, 780–806 (2017)

Classification of TRIZ Inventive Principles and Sub-principles for Process Engineering Problems

Arun Prasad Chandra Sekaran(✉), Pavel Livotov, and Mas'udah

Offenburg University of Applied Sciences,
Badstr. 24, 77652 Offenburg, Germany
arun.chandra@hs-offenburg.de

Abstract. The paper proposes a classification approach of 40 Inventive Principles with an extended set of 160 sub-principles for process engineering, based on a thorough analysis of 155 process intensification technologies, 200 patent documents, 6 industrial case studies applying TRIZ, and other sources. The authors define problem-specific sub-principles groups as a more precise and productive ideation technique, adaptable for a large diversity of problem situations, and finally, examine the anticipated variety of ideation using 160 sub-principles with the help of MATCEM-IBD fields.

Keywords: TRIZ · 40 Inventive Principles · Process engineering · Process innovation

1 Introduction

The scope of process innovation and intensification in process engineering (PE) is interdisciplinary, diverse and complex. It focuses on design, operation, control, and optimization of chemical, physical and biological processes and has applications in a wide range of industrial sectors. However, the typical scenarios for developing vital innovations in PE are not easy as it may be initially perceived. Process engineering problems are specific and complex situations involving multiple physical-chemical parameters, processing methods, and process equipment [1]. Furthermore, process intensification (PI) and implementation of new technologies and eco-innovative solutions in process engineering often lead to numerous additional negative side effects and secondary problems, resulting in three types of engineering contradictions [2], as illustrated in Fig. 1.

The Theory of Inventive Problem Solving (TRIZ) is one of the most comprehensive, systematically organized invention and creative thinking methodologies for enhancing the intensification of processes in PE [3, 4]. One of the main advantages of TRIZ is that it helps to find new inventive solutions for a given problem in a systematic way by using the entire potential of science, engineering and outside of the originally formulated problem field [5, 6].

TRIZ has already found successful applications in PE, such as new development of chemical or biochemical products and technologies [7–9], problem-solving with

Published by Springer Nature Switzerland AG 2019
R. Benmoussa et al. (Eds.): TFC 2019, IFIP AICT 572, pp. 314–327, 2019.
https://doi.org/10.1007/978-3-030-32497-1_26

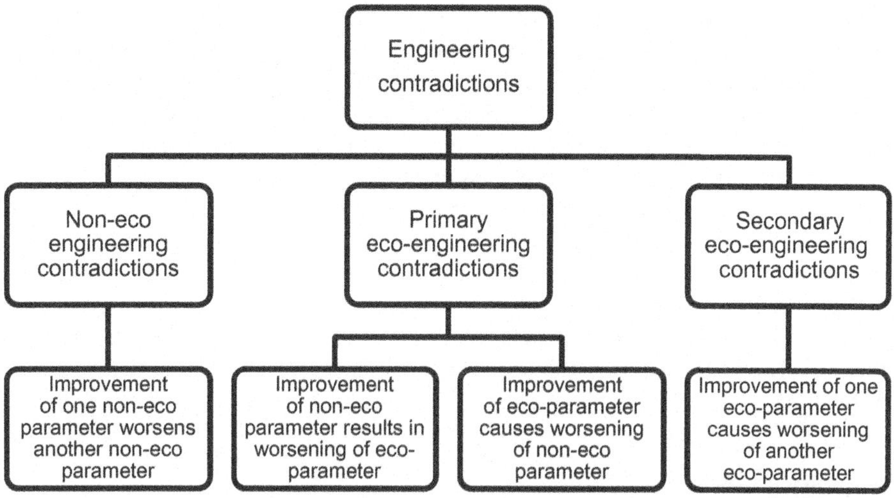

Fig. 1. Types of engineering contradictions in process intensification [2]

inventive principles and standard solutions [10, 11], TRIZ evolutionary forecast of equipment [12] and technologies [13]. Authors outline in their recent paper [3] that the fundamentals and objectives of Process Intensification [14–17] are highly consistent with the evolution laws of technical systems in the TRIZ methodology. Among numerous components of TRIZ, the 40 Inventive Principles belong to the tools most frequently mentioned in research papers [18] and used in practice [19].

Over the past decades, the 40 TRIZ Inventive Principles have been widely used to solve technical contradictions in various engineering domains and enhanced through adjustments, illustrations and examples for specific fields of application. The 40 Inventive Principles are good for newcomers to TRIZ, simple to use or modify for specific technical domains and can be easily integrated into brainstorming or daily engineers work [3]. Moreover, several studies on Inventive Principles have been conducted to improve the quantity and quality of ideation process for the various engineering domains. The study [20] has grouped Inventive Principles in redesign service approaches (RSA) to solve service problems. Russo and Spreafico [21] classified Inventive Principles through functional behaviour structure (FBS) ontology. Livotov and Petrov [6] established specific groups of Inventive Principles for industrial and business practices. Mann [22] proposed a classification of the Inventive Principles based on three areas of intervention: space, time and interface. Further, the Inventive Principles also have been enhanced by providing engineering interpretations and examples for chemical engineering [23, 24]. Recently, Petrov (2018) presented the "universal" 40 Inventive Principles with engineering illustrations with changed or extended names or formulations of certain principles and sub-principles [25].

Even though many studies have expanded and enhanced Inventive Principles and sub-principles to a broader range of applications, the major challenge for the engineers remains a precise selection of the strongest principles or sub-principles for specific problems and fast solving of primary and secondary contradictions. Therefore, this study classifies and proposes sets of recommended 40 Inventive Principles with 160 sub-principles for different domains in process engineering such as, for example, reduction of environmental impact, intensification of processes involving solids handling, reduction of energy and material losses. The classification method summarizes and evaluates the recent research studies of the authors [2–4, 26] on further development of TRIZ principles for PE, based on thorough analysis of 200 patent documents, 155 process intensification technologies, and 6 comprehensive industrial case studies. Authors of the paper also recommend the specific sub-principles groups as a promising more precise and productive ideation technique, adaptable for a large variety of problem situations. Furthermore, the anticipated variety of ideation using 160 sub-principles is verified with the help of nine MATCEM-IBD fields (Mechanical, Acoustic, Thermal, Chemical, Electric, Magnetic, Intermolecular, Biological and Data Processing).

2 Methodology

In the authors' previous studies [2–4, 26] the top 10–20 most effective and frequently used Inventive Principles in process engineering (PE) have been identified in PE patents, process intensification (PI) technologies, and industrial case studies, and compared with the inventive principles recommended by process intensification strategies [27] and the classical Altshuller matrix [5]. It is important to note that the performed analysis was carried out using the extended version of 40 Inventive Principles with 160 sub-principles proposed in [3] and presented in Appendix, which addresses the needs of process engineering regarding multiple physical-chemical parameters, processing methods, and process equipment. Furthermore, compared with the original number of sub-principles varying between 85 and 95 [5], the new version of the Inventive Principles contains at least 65 additional sub-principles relevant for process engineering. Additionally, the sub-principles have been assigned to MATCEM-IBD fields of interactions in order to evaluate the anticipated variety and completeness of ideation with sub-principles for PE problems.

2.1 Identification and Analysis of Inventive Principles in Patent Documents

The patent literature is the most important and complete source for actual technical information [28, 29]. Identification of inventive principles from the PE patents has been associated with invention goals, processing methods or equipment, and with the specific PE sub-domains. Thus, 150 patent documents in the field of solids handling and 50 patent documents in the field of eco-friendly process intensification technologies, published between 2000 and 2017, were selected and analyzed for this purpose [3, 26]. For example, in the eco-technology patent document US20140299028A1 the goal of invention is the reduction of environmental pollution and fouling, when burning coal by adding sorbents to raw material (powder components containing calcium, alumina, silica, iron, magnesium, and a halogen sorbent). The corresponding associated inventive sub-principles are (9a) Counter harm in advance and (11b) Preventive measures.

2.2 Identification and Analysis of Inventive Principles in PI Technologies

In addition to the patent documents, the identification of inventive principles typical for process engineering has been performed by analysis of the existing process intensification (PI) technologies. The PI technological databases are continuously evolving and currently cover a wide range of more than 155 processing methods and equipment, such as equipment involving and not involving chemical reactions, multi-functional reactors, hybrid separation methods, alternative energy sources and others [14, 15]. Many of these PI technologies are not only fully described and documented but also validated or implemented in the industry. The obtained information about underlying inventive principles in PI technologies is as a rule more precise and reliable in comparison to the inventive principles derived from the patents only. For example, our research paper [3] shows the identification of TRIZ inventive principles and sub-principles in a Spiral Flash Dryer [30], a new compact equipment combining the advantages of a flash dryer and of a fluidized bed. Corresponding inventive sub-principles for spiral flash drier are (29a) Gas as a working element; (29d) Fluidization of powders or granulates; (14b) Use sphere, cylinders, cones; (14d) Swirling motion; (17e) Increase contact area between objects or substances; (21b) Boost the process that may result in new useful properties.

Among 155 analyzed PI technologies about 58 technologies can be assigned to the thermal operations and methods. These thermal technologies can be recommended for solving of eco-problems such as high energy consumption and energy losses. The example of the microwave heating technology in Table 1 illustrates the identified characteristic pair of inventive sub-principles, such as (28a) Use electromagnetics and (35d) Change temperature.

Table 1. TRIZ Inventive Principles assigned to the microwave heating technology

N	Key characteristics of the PI technology	TRIZ Inventive Principles	Corresponding sub-principles (inventive operators)
1	Heating of dipole molecules such as water	35 Transform physical and chemical properties	(35d) Change temperature
2	Microwaves enhance the motions of free ions/ionic species resulting in even heating	28 Replace mechanical working principle	(28a) Use electromagnetics

Additionally, analysis of 15 strongest process intensification strategies [27] helps to point out the corresponding TRIZ Inventive Principles and sub-principles, as illustrated in Table 2 [26].

2.3 Analysis of Inventive Principles Applied in Industrial Case Studies

In 6 case studies the Advanced Innovation Design Approach (AIDA) and TRIZ Inventive Principles have been applied by the authors for process intensification in the

Table 2. Classification of TRIZ Inventive Principles in 15 process intensification strategies in PE (fragment)

15 Process Intensification strategies [27]	40 TRIZ Inventive Principles
1. Modification of operating conditions: temperature, pressure, concentration 2. New solvents to reduce environmental impact of processes 3. Modification of fluid phase properties by change of pressure or temperature	35. Transformation of the physical and chemical properties: Change an object's aggregate state (35a), change the object's concentration or consistency (35b), change the object's temperature (35d), change process chemistry (35e)
3. Modification of fluid phase properties by addition of gas bubbles or solid particles	40. Composite materials: composition of materials in different aggregate states (40e)
4. Inert species addition in multiphase flow: emulsifying additives, viscosifying agents …	39. Inert environment: Inert coatings or additives (39d) 24. Mediator: intermediate object (24a)
…	…
10. Parallelism in the process, multi-scale design 15. Coupling with separation	5. Combining: parallel operations (5a), combine process steps to perform parallel or contiguous operations (5b)

field of chemical, pharmaceutical, ceramic, and mineral industries: (1) Separation of ceramic-metal powders, (2) Dry granulation of ceramic powders, (3) Metal ore beneficiation, (4) Granulation of pharmaceutical powders, (5) Drying of pharmaceutical powders, and (6) Mixing of chemical reagents [4]. After the performed problem definition and ranking, the process engineers and researchers applied the enhanced version of 40 Inventive Principles with in total 160 sub-principles. The application of the principles has been performed for each partial problem separately in the recommended order proposed in Table 3 [6], whereby each idea generation phase has been started with statistically strongest principles (group 1), optionally followed by the group 2 in case of design problems or by the group 3 for process optimization problems. The application of TRIZ inventive principles resulted in 234 new solution ideas and 28 patentable concepts, whereby each idea was assigned to one or more inventive sub-principles. To the outcomes of the study [4] belongs the identification of the most effective inventive principles and corresponding sub-principles, which have led to the strongest ideas integrated in 28 innovation concepts.

2.4 Identification of Inventive Principles for Solving Eco-Contradictions with the Altshuller Matrix

In their prior research work [26], the authors have applied the classical 39 × 39 TRIZ Contradiction Matrix, also known as Altshuller matrix [5], for identification of the inventive principles for eco-engineering contradictions in PE with 5 ecologically relevant parameters, such as *Energy consumption of the moving object* (n19) and of the *non-moving object* (n20), *Energy losses* (n22), *Material losses* (n23), *Amount of substance* (n26). The mentioning frequency of the inventive principles has been evaluated from the following eco-contradictions regarding efficiency of energy or material utilization:

Table 3. Recommended order for application of 40 Inventive Principles in the case studies [6]

Group 1: Statistically strongest principles	(35) Transform physical and chemical properties, (10) Prior useful action, (1) Segmentation, (28) Replace mechanical working principle, (2) Leaving out/ Trimming, (15) Dynamism and adaptability, (19) Periodic action, (3) Local quality, (17) Shift to another dimension, (13) Inversion, (18) Mechanical vibration, (26) Copying
Group 2: Principles for solving design problems	(6) Universality, (5) Combining, (29) Pneumatic or hydraulic constructions, (30) Flexible shells or thin films, (7) Nesting/ Integration, (8) Anti-weight, (4) Asymmetry, (40) Composite materials, (24) Mediator, (14) Sphericity and Rotation, (23) Feedback and automation, (31) Porous materials, (25) Self-service
Group 3: Principles for specific problems in Process Engineering	(16) Partial or excessive action, (27) Disposability, (20) Continuity of useful action, (32) Change colour, (21) Skipping/ Rushing through, (11) Preventive measure, (33) Homogeneity, (22) Converting harm into benefit, (39) Inert environment, (37) Thermal expansion, (36) Phase transitions, (38) Strong oxidants, (34) Rejecting and regenerating parts, (12) Equipotentiality, (9) Prior counteraction of harm

(a) 65 primary eco-contradictions resulting from improvement of parameters *Energy consumption of the moving object* (n.19), *Energy consumption of the non-moving object* (n.20), and *Energy losses* (n.22) on the one hand and worsening of the other 34 non-ecological parameters of the Altshuller matrix on the other hand.

(b) 64 primary eco-contradictions resulting from improvement of parameters *Material losses* (n.23), *Amount of substance* (n.26) on the one hand and worsening of the other 34 non-ecological parameters of the matrix on the other hand.

In general, a comparison of most frequently recommended top 10 inventive principles from the Altshuller Matrix with the top 10 inventive principles extracted from 50 eco-patents or 58 thermal operations [26] reveals about 50% overlapping of principles in different top 10 lists.

3 Results

3.1 Identification of Strongest Inventive Principles and Sub-principles in PE

Table 4 summarizes the recommended or statistically most frequently applied TRIZ Inventive Principles and sub-principles, which were extracted from 8 different sources of information and analysis, such as PE patents, PI technologies, industrial cases studies, scientific literature, classical Altshuller matrix and recommendations presented in the Table 3. Additionally, the ranking method [26] using mean occurrence frequency of principles and sub-principles in different sources allows one to select and to recommend top 10 or top 20 lists of principles and sub-principles for different applications and tasks in process engineering, as shown in the Table 5.

Table 4. Identified most frequently used or recommended TRIZ Inventive Principles and sub-principles for PE problems

Sources	Problem category	Inventive Principles	Sub-principles
(1) 150 solids handling patents [3]	Intensification of processes involving solids in ceramic and pharmaceutical industries	40, 35, 14, 29, 5, 24, 6, 33, 1, 18, 9, 15, 20, 25, 28, 31, 13, 17, 22, 34	40a, 35b, 40c, 6a, 33a, 29a, 20a, 24a, 31a, 9a, 34a, 35d, 1e, 3a, 14a, 14b, 14c, 15c, 18a, 22a
(2) 100 eco-patents [26]	Environmental problems and eco-engineering contradictions in PE	25, 2, 22, 15, 9, 1, 29, 34, 35, 40, 5, 21, 33, 10, 11, 14, 28, 37, 3, 8	2a, 25b, 22a, 25a, 15a, 21a, 29a, 33a, 34a, 1a, 5b, 9a, 9b, 10a, 11b, 35b, 37a, 40a, 3a, 14a
(3) 155 PI-technologies [3]	Intensification of processing technologies, equipment and methods	14, 29, 35, 2, 5, 36, 6, 28, 24, 18, 30, 1, 10, 7, 13, 8, 15, 17, 19, 20	36a, 2e, 14c, 29e, 6b, 28a, 14b, 35a, 35d, 5a, 30e, 18a, 24b, 29a, 35b, 2a, 5b, 10a, 20a, 19d
(4) 58 thermal PI technologies [26]	Reduction of energy consumption and losses	35, 5, 2, 29, 28, 36, 10, 20, 24, 30, 7, 13, 6, 17, 1, 15, 31, 34, 3, 9	29e, 2e, 35d, 35a, 36a, 5a, 28a, 5b, 10a, 20a, 30e, 35b, 2a, 6a, 13d, 24b, 5c, 7a, 7b, 24a
(6) 15 PI strategies [27]	Supporting of process intensification strategies	35, 40, 39, 24, 17, 8, 5, 1, 3, 19, 15, 25	35a, 35b, 35c, 35d, 35e, 40e, 39a, 24a, 17e, 17b, 8d, 5a, 5b, 1a, 3a, 19a, 15a, 25b, 25c
(7) 6 industrial case studies [4]	Processes involving solids handling	35, 14, 13, 3, 28, 1, 5, 22, 2, 16, 17, 10, 40, 24, 6, 31, 29, 25, 19, 15	35b, 13d, 28a, 3c, 14b, 22a, 1d, 3d, 14c, 16a, 35c, 2b, 5b, 10a, 24c, 40a, 1a, 2e, 6b, 14a
(8) Altshuller contradiction matrix [5]	Reduction of energy consumption and losses	35, 10, 18, 3, 29, 28, 40, 31, 2, 15	
	Reduction of material consumption and losses	35, 19, 2, 18, 11, 15, 28, 7, 1, 38	

3.2 Sets of Recommended Inventive Principles and Sub-principles for PE

As presented in Table 5, the following sets of TRIZ Inventive Principles and sub-principles can be recommended for efficient ideation and systematic problem solving in specific domains of PE, such as intensification of processing technologies, equipment and methods in general (1), environmental problems (2), intensification of processes involving solids handling (3).

Table 5. Recommended sets of top 10 TRIZ Inventive Principles and sub-principles for ideation in process engineering

Set	Problem category	Inventive Principles and sub-principles
1	Intensification of processing technologies, equipment and methods	Top 10 Inventive Principles: 14. Sphericity and Rotation, 29. Pneumatic or hydraulic constructions, 35. Transform physical and chemical properties, 2. Leaving out/Trimming, 5. Combining, 36. Phase transitions, 6. Universality, 28. Replace mechanical working principle, 24. Mediator, 18. Mechanical vibration.
		Top 10 sub-principles: 36(a), 2(e), 14(c), 29(e), 6(b), 28(a), 14(b), 35(a), 35 (d), 5(a).
2	Environmental problems and eco-engineering contradictions	Top 10 Inventive Principles: 35. Transform physical and chemical properties, 2. Leaving out/ Trimming, 5. Combining, 25. Self-service/ Use of resources, 29. Pneumatic or hydraulic constructions, 28. Replace mechanical working principle, 15. Dynamism and adaptability, 22. Converting harm into benefit, 10. Prior useful action, 9. Prior Counteraction of harm.
		Top 10 sub-principles: 2(a), 29(e), 25(b), 2(e), 22(a), 35(d), 5(b), 10(a), 35 (a), 28(a).
3	Intensification of processes involving solids handling	Top 10 Inventive Principles: 35. Transform physical and chemical properties, 40. Composite materials, 14. Sphericity and rotation, 28. Replace mechanical working principle, 13. Inversion, 3. Local quality, 1. Segmentation, 5. Combining, 29. Pneumatic or hydraulic constructions, 24. Mediator.
		Top 10 sub-principles: 40(a), 35(b), 28(a), 13(d), 14(b), 22(a), 14(c), 29(a), 40(c), 16(a)

The authors also advocate the view that application of statistically strongest sub-principles is more efficient, less time-consuming and can be characterized by more precise ideation. For example, the top 15 inventive principles for solving environmental contradictions contain 61 sub-principles. Evidently, the use of the strongest 20…25 sub-principles with higher ranking significantly reduces time expenditures for idea generation.

3.3 Anticipated Variety of Ideation Based on 160 Inventive Sub-principles

In addition to the quantity and quality of ideas, the ideas breath or variety belongs to the major objective measures of ideation effectiveness [31]. One of the common approaches to assess the ideas variety stipulates that every idea must be assigned to the eight engineering MATCEM-IB fields known in TRIZ: Mechanical, Acoustic, Thermal, Chemical, Electric, Magnetic, Intermolecular, and Biological [4, 32]. A more uniform distribution of the ideas over the eight fields corresponds to a higher of breadth or variety. As the variety is strongly influenced by the ideation techniques [32], this section analyses how it can be affected by use of 160 inventive sub-principles. For this purpose, 160 sub-principles have been assigned to 11 categories, presented in Fig. 2. The category "Independent" includes sub-principles, which don't relate directly to any field or engineering domain, like for example (1e) *Segment process* or (2d) *Trim process steps*. The category "Universal" includes the sub-principles which can be assigned to any of fields, like (4b) *Enhance asymmetry*. To these categories belong respectively 36 and 29 sub-principles. The idea generation with the independent or universal sub-principles doesn't compulsorily lead to a change of the "field" in the working principle of a technical system. The remaining 95 sub-principles can be distributed with multiple selection between Mechanical (52 sub-principles), Acoustic (5), Thermal (19), Chemical (25), Electric and Magnetic (14), Intermolecular (13) and Biological (1) fields. Additionally, 6 sub-principles (23a, 23b, 23c, 23d, 26d, 26e) has been exclusively assigned to the introduced Data processing or Information field.

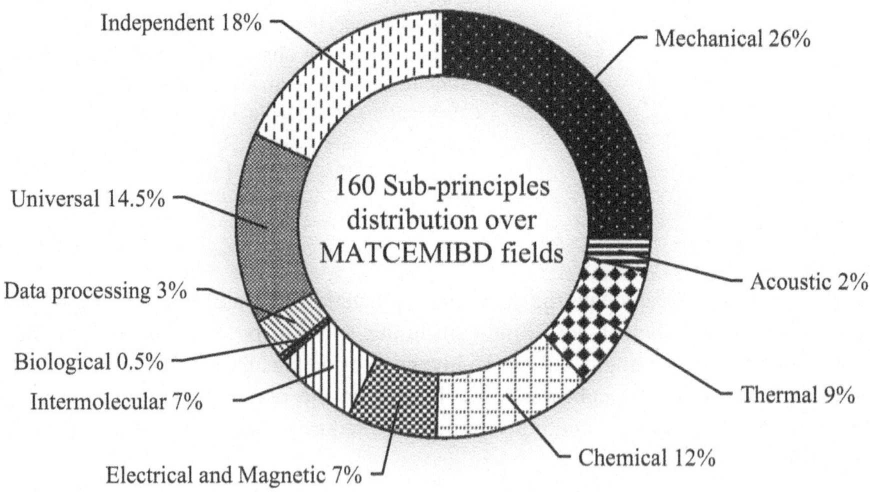

Fig. 2. Distribution of the 160 sub-principles over MATCEM-IBD fields, universal and independent categories (multiple selection for the MATCEM-IBD fields possible).

The performed analysis of sub-principles assignment to MATCEM-IBD fields depicts a rather unbalanced distribution with 26% of mechanical sub-principles on the one hand, and 3% data processing or 0,5% biological sub-principles on the other hand. This fact should be taken into consideration by the selection of the sub-principles for specific application sets in order to enable a higher ideation variety. At the same time the extension of classical 40 Inventive Principles with additional sub-principles helps to increase the shares of chemical (12%), thermal (9%) and intermolecular (7%) sub-principles relevant for process engineering.

4 Conclusions

The selection of strongest inventive principles for specific problems in process engineering remains more challenging due to the complexity of interdisciplinary problem situations. The presented research classifies 40 TRIZ Inventive Principles and sub-principles for their applications in different problem and innovation situations in process engineering with the objective to enable a fast selection of strongest ideation operators in the industrial practice. The proposed approach of multi-source identification of strongest inventive principles from complementary patent or technology databases and literature can be also applied in other engineering domains. The authors advocate that the idea generation with strongest sub-principles can significantly improve ideation efficiency in quantity, quality and variety in the early stage of innovation process. This statement can be the subject matter of a future research. The performed interdisciplinary and completeness analysis of 160 inventive sub-principles relating to the MATCEM-IBD fields attests balanced results for process engineering but reveals a necessity of taking into account additional informational and biological sub-principles.

Appendix: 40 Inventive Principles and 160 Sub-principles Without Description and Examples [3, 26]

1. **Segmentation**: 1(a) Segment object; 1(b) Dismountable design; 1(c) Segment to microlevel; 1(d) Segment function; 1(e) Segment process.
2. **Leaving out/Trimming**: 2(a) Take out disturbing parts; 2(b) Trim components; 2 (c) Trim functions; 2(d) Trim process steps; 2(e) Extract useful element.
3. **Local quality**: 3(a) Non-uniform object; 3(b) Non-uniform environment; 3(c) Different functions; 3(d) Optimal conditions; 3(e) Opposite properties.
4. **Asymmetry**: 4(a) Asymmetry; 4(b) Enhance asymmetry; 4(c) Back to symmetry.
5. **Combining**: 5(a) Combine similar objects; 5(b) Combine functions; 5(c) Combine different properties; 5(d) Combine complementary properties; 5(e) Combine opposing properties.
6. **Universality**: 6(a) Universal object; 6(b) Universal process.
7. **Nesting/Integration**: 7(a) Nested objects; 7(b) Passing through cavities; 7(c) Telescopic systems.

8. **Anti-weight**: 8(a) Use counterweight; 8(b) Buoyancy; 8(c) Aero- or hydrodynamics; 8(d) Use gravitational or centrifugal forces.
9. **Prior Counteraction of harm**: 9(a) Counter harm in advance; 9(b) Anti-stress; 9(c) Cooling in advance; 9(d) Rigid construction.
10. **Prior useful action**: 10(a) Prior useful function; 10(b) Pre-arrange objects; 10(c) Prior process step.
11. **Preventive measure/Cushion in advance**: 11(a) Safety cushion; 11(b) Preventive measures.
12. **Equipotentiality**: 12(a) Keep altitude; 12(b) Equipotentiality; 12(c) Avoid fluctuations.
13. **Inversion**: 13(a) Inversed action; 13(b) Make fixed parts to movable; 13(c) Upside down; 13(d) Reversed sequence; 13(e) Invert environment.
14. **Sphericity and Rotation**: 14(a) Ball-shaped forms; 14(b) Spheres and cylinders; 14(c) Rotary motion; 14(d) Swirling motion; 14(e) Centrifugal forces.
15. **Dynamism and adaptability**: 15(a) Optimal performance; 15(b) Adaptive object; 15(c) Adaptive process; 15(d) Flexible elements; 15(e) Change statics to dynamics.
16. **Partial or excessive action**: 16(a) One step back from ideal; 16(b) Optimal substance amount; 16(c) Optimal action.
17. **Shift to another dimension**: 17(a) Multi-dimensional form; 17(b) Miniaturization; 17(c) Multi-layered structure; 17(d) Tilt object; 17(e) 3D interaction.
18. **Mechanical vibration**: 18(a) Oscillate object; 18(b) Ultrasound; 18(c) Resonance; 18(d) Piezo-electric vibrators; 18(e) Ultrasound with other fields.
19. **Periodic action**: 19(a) Periodic action; 19(b) Change frequency; 19(c) Use pauses; 19(d) Match frequencies; 19(e) Separate in time.
20. **Continuity of useful action**: 20(a) Continuous process; 20(b) Operate at full load; 20(c) Eliminate idle work.
21. **Skipping/Rushing through**: 21(a) Skip hazardous operations; 21(b) Boost the process.
22. **Converting harm into benefit**: 22(a) Utilize harm; 22(b) Remove harm with harm; 22(c) Amplify harm to avoid it.
23. **Feedback and automation**: 23(a) Introduce feedback; 23(b) Enhance feedback; 23(c) Automation; 23(d) Data processing.
24. **Mediator**: 24(a) Intermediate object; 24(b) Temporary mediator; 24(c) Intermediary process.
25. **Self-service/Use of resources**: 25(a) Object serves itself; 25(b) Utilize waste resources; 25(c) Use environmental resources.
26. **Copying:** 26(a) Simple copies; 26(b) Optical copies; 26(c) Invisible copies; 26(d) Digital models; 26(e) Virtual reality.
27. **Disposability/cheap short-living objects**: 27(a) Short-living objects; 27(b) Multiple cheap objects; 27(c) One-way objects; 27(d) Create objects from resources.
28. **Replace mechanical working principle**: 28(a) Use electromagnetics; 28(b) Optical systems; 28(c) Acoustic system; 28(d) Chemical and biosystems; 28(e) Thermal Systems.
29. **Pneumatic or hydraulic constructions**: 29(a) Gaseous or liquid flows; 29(b) Gas or liquid under pressure; 29(c) Use vacuum; 29(d) Fluidization; 29(e) Heat transfer and exchange.

30. **Flexible shells or thin films**: 30(a) Flexible shells or films; 30(b) Flexible isolation; 30(c) Piezoelectric foils; 30(d) Use brushes; 30(e) Use membranes.
31. **Porous material**: 31(a) Add porous elements; 31(b) Fill pores with substance; 31 (c) Use capillary effects; 31(d) Physical effects and porosity; 31(e) Structured porosity.
32. **Change colour**: 32(a) Change colour; 32(b) Change transparency; 32(c) Coloured additives; 32(d) Use tracer.
33. **Homogeneity**: 33(a) Similar materials; 33(b) Similar properties; 33(c) Uniform properties.
34. **Rejecting and regenerating parts**: 34(a) Discard useless parts; 34(b) Restore parts; 34 (c) Create parts on time and on site.
35. **Transform physical and chemical properties**: 35(a) Change aggregate state; 35 (b) Change concentration; 35(c) Change physical properties; 35(d) Change temperature; 35(e) Change chemical properties.
36. **Phase transitions**: 36(a) Phase transitions; 36(b) 2nd order phase transitions
37. **Thermal expansion:** 37(a) Thermal expansion; 37(b) Bi-metals; 37(c) Heat shrinking; 37(d) Shape memory.
38. **Strong Oxidants**: 38(a) Oxygen-enriched air; 38(b) Use pure oxygen; 38(c) Use ionized oxygen; 38(d) Use ozone; 38(e) Strong oxidants.
39. **Inert environment**: 39(a) Inert environment; 39(b) Inert atmosphere process; 39(c) Process in vacuum; 39(d) Inert coatings or additives; 39(e) Use foams.
40. **Composite materials**: 40(a) Composite materials; 40(b) Use anisotropic properties; 40(c) Additives in composites; 40(d) Composite microstructure; 40(e) Combine different aggregate states.

References

1. Srinivasan, R., Kraslawski, A.: Application of the TRIZ creativity enhancement approach to design of inherently safer chemical processes. Chem. Eng. Process. Process Intensification **45**, 507–514 (2006)
2. Livotov, P., Mas'udah, Chandra Sekaran, A.P., Law, R., Reay, D.: Ecological advanced innovation design approach for efficient integrated upstream and downstream processes. In: Proceedings of the International Conference on Engineering Design ICED19 on 5–8 August, Delft, Cambridge University Press, vol. 1., Issue 1, pp. 3291–3300 (2019). https://doi.org/10.1017/dsi.2019.336
3. Livotov, P., Chandra Sekaran, A.P., Law, R., Mas'udah, Reay, D.: Systematic Innovation in Process Engineering: Linking TRIZ and Process Intensification. In: Chechurin, L., Collan, M. (eds.) Advances in Systematic Creativity, Palgrave Macmillan, pp. 27–44 (2019)
4. Livotov, P., Mas'udah, Chandra Sekaran, A.P.: On the Efficiency of TRIZ Application for Process Intensification in Process Engineering. In: Cavallucci, D., de Guio, R., Koziołek, S. (eds.) Automated Invention for Smart Industries. IFIP Advances in Information and Communication Technology, vol. 541, pp. 126–140. Springer, Cham (2018). https://doi.org/10.1007/978-3-030-02456-7_11
5. Altshuller, G.S.: Creativity as an Exact Science. The Theory of the Solution of Inventive Problems. Gordon & Breach Science Publishers, Amsterdam (1984)

6. Livotov, P., Petrov, V.: TRIZ Innovation Technology. Product Development and Inventive Problem Solving. Handbook. TriS Europe, Berlin (2015)
7. Abramov, O., Kogan, S., Mitnik-Gankin, L.: TRIZ-based approach for accelerating innovation in chemical engineering. Chem. Eng. Res. Des. **103**(2015), 25–31 (2015)
8. Rahim, Z.A., Sheng, I.L.S., Nooh, A.B.: TRIZ methodology for applied chemical engineering: a case study of new product development. Chem. Eng. Res. Des. **103**, 11–24 (2015)
9. Ferrer, B., Negny, S., Robles, G.C., Lann, J.M.L.: Eco-innovative design method for process engineering. Comput. Chem. Eng. **45**, 137–151 (2012)
10. Kim, J., Kim, J., Lee, Y., Lim, W., Moon, I.: Application of TRIZ creativity intensification approach to chemical process safety. J. Loss Prev. Process Ind. **22**(6), 1039–1043 (2009)
11. Kraslawski, A., Guang Rong, B., Nyström, L.: Creative design of distillation flowsheets based on theory of solving inventive problems. Comput. Aided Chem. Eng. **8**, 625–630 (2000)
12. Berdonosov, V.D., Kozlita, A.N., Zhivotova, A.A.: TRIZ evolution of black oil coker units. Chem. Eng. Res. Des. **103**(2015), 61–73 (2015)
13. Cascini, G., Rotini, F., Russo, D.: Functional modeling for TRIZ-based evolutionary analyses. In: DS 58-5: Proceedings of ICED 09, the 17th International Conference on Engineering Design, vol. 5, Design Methods and Tools (pt. 1), Palo Alto, CA, USA (2009)
14. Boodhoo, K.V.K., Harvey, A.: Process intensification: an overview of principles and practice. In: Boodhoo, K.V.K., Harvey, A. (eds.) Process Intensification for Green Chemistry: Engineering Solutions for Sustainable Chemical Processing, pp. 1–31. Wiley, Chichester (2013)
15. Wang, H., Mustaffar, A., Phan, A.N., et al.: A review of process intensification applied to solids handling. Chem. Eng. Process. Process Intensification **118**, 78–107 (2008)
16. Gerven, T.V., Stankiewicz, A.: Structure, energy, synergy, time - the fundamentals of process intensification. Ind. Eng. Chem. Res. **48**, 2465–2474 (2009)
17. Stankiewicz, A.I., Moulijn, J.A.: Process intensification: transforming chemical engineering. Chem. Eng. Prog. **96**, 22–34 (2000)
18. Lim, I.S.S.: The effectiveness of TRIZ tools for eco-efficient product design. In: Chechurin, L. (ed.) Research and Practice on the Theory of Inventive Problem Solving (TRIZ), pp. 35–53. Springer, Cham (2016). https://doi.org/10.1007/978-3-319-31782-3_3
19. Livotov, P.: The Undervalued Innovation Potential. Triz J. (2004). https://triz-journal.com/undervalued-innovation-potential/. Accessed 214 July 2018
20. Gazem, N., Rahman, A.A.: Improving TRIZ 40 Inventive Principles Grouping in Redesign Service Approaches. Asian Social Science vol. 10, No. 17. Can. Center of Science and Education (2014)
21. Russo, D., Spreafico, C.: TRIZ 40 Inventive principles classification through FBS ontology. Procedia Eng. **131**, 737–746 (2015)
22. Mann, D.: Evolving the Inventive Principles. TRIZ J. (2002). https://triz-journal.com/evolving-inventive-principles/. Accessed 02 July 2019
23. Grierson, B., Fraser, I., Morrison, A.: 40 Principles – Chemical Illustrations. Triz J. (2003). http://triz-journal.com/40-principles-chemical-illustrations. Accessed 11 Sept 2016
24. Hipple, J.: 40 inventive principles for Chemical Engineering. Triz J. (2005). http://triz-journal.com/40-inventive-principles-for-chemical-engineering. Accessed 11 Sept 2016
25. Petrov, V.: Universal Inventive Principles TRIZ, Inventive Principles for all fields (2018)
26. Livotov, P.: Eco-innovation in process engineering: contradictions, inventive principles and methods. Therm. Sci. Eng. Progress **9**, 52–65 (2019)
27. Commenge, J.-M., Falk, L.: Methodological framework for choice of intensified equipment and development of innovative technologies. Chem. Eng. Process. **84**, 109–127 (2014)

28. Asche, G.: 80% of technical information found only in patents – Is there proof of this? World Patent Inf. **48**, 16–28 (2017)
29. Cascini, G., Russo, D.: Computer-aided analysis of patents and search for TRIZ contradictions". Int. J. Product Dev. **4**(1/2), 52–67 (2007)
30. Spiral Flasch Dryer. INGETECSA Ingeniería y Técnica del Secado s.a. www.ingetecsa.com. Accessed 29 Mar 2019
31. Shah, J.J., Vargas-Hernandez, N., Smith, S.M.: Metrics for measuring ideation effectiveness. Des. Stud. **24**(2), 111–134 (2003)
32. Belski, I., Livotov, P., Mayer, O.: Eight fields of MATCEMIB help students to generate more ideas. Proc. CIRP **39**, 85–90 (2016)

Technological Landscape and Ideation in the Field of Waste Separation with Help of TRIZ

Luka Ivanovskis(✉), Timo Kärki, and Ville Lahtela

Fiber Composite Laboratory, LUT University, P.O. Box 20
53851 Lappeenranta, Finland
luka.ivanovskis@student.lut.fi

Abstract. Solid waste separation is an imperative part for closing material flow under principles of the circular economy. A multitude of technologies are at a different stage of development to perform this task and meet performance requirements at extracting valuable resources from waste streams. A thorough review of available options and possibilities for future development was required to pursue further progress. TRIZ (from Russian abbreviation: Theory of Inventive Problem Solving) methodology facilitated drawing a technological landscape for state of the art in solid waste separation for material recovery, as well as generating new directions of research. From the vast collection of TRIZ tools for systematic invention two approaches helped in the survey: effects databases and function-oriented search. Positive outcomes of their application include systematization of available knowledge, identification of potentially useful phenomena and getting ideas for the adoption of technologies from other domains. The case illustrates how rather loose (due to the broadness of the topic) application of TRIZ methods results in fruitful insights. A view at the effects databases as a collection of technological "genes" is given.

Keywords: Effects database · Function-oriented search · Material recovery · Waste separation

1 Introduction

Concerns about scarce natural resources and ever-increasing amount of waste promote the implementation of the circular economy principle. One of the key points of the circular economy is material recovery from waste for further reuse in new products. Material liberation and separation are the essential prerequisites for closing the loop of material flow, as materials recycled from waste should attain a certain level of purity to be used for new products of same quality [1]. Separation of materials from commingled waste streams poses technological challenges and addressing them requires an in-depth knowledge of state of the art in both industry and academia. Further development of technical means for waste separation cannot progress without novel ideas. Acquiring such knowledge together with insights into the future prospective is the task a research institution faces as it enters the field and seeks for its own path.

Published by Springer Nature Switzerland AG 2019
R. Benmoussa et al. (Eds.): TFC 2019, IFIP AICT 572, pp. 328–339, 2019.
https://doi.org/10.1007/978-3-030-32497-1_27

Various decision support tools were developed in the past for the recycling field. They suggested optimal waste treatment scenario [2], predicted achievable material recovery from complex products [3], maximized profit by rearranging waste separators in sequence [4]. Recent reviews of separation technologies discussed their pros and cons in a narrative manner [1, 5, 6], attempting to address one of the significant issues with technological roadmapping – capturing large sets of quantitative and qualitative data [7]. An idea generation tool for the treatment of a particular waste through structured web search queries of related terms was realized in [8]. Methods of technological roadmapping for manufacturing enterprises fall into four categories according to [9]:

- Causal models,
- Phenomenological models,
- Intuitive models,
- Monitoring and mapping.

When technological forecasting is taken more broadly (including research interests, for example), the analysis itself can be classified in nine dimensions (driver, locus etc.), whereas the methods fall into more than ten families of distinct purposes [10].

Review and comparison of technologies for mechanical separation of solid waste was done to determine their capabilities and limitations. The broadness of the topic and technological diversity required auxiliary tools to make the analysis systematic and facilitate the generation of feasible ideas. Tools applied in the study belong to the methods of modern TRIZ. TRIZ (from Russian abbreviation: Theory of Inventive Problem Solving) methodology provides a set of tools for systematic invention given the defined problems and goals [11]. Wide research question and limited experience in TRIZ narrowed the arsenal used in the study down to a couple of tools: databases of physical effects and the Function-Oriented Search (FOS) [12]. Presenting the outcomes of their fragmentary application is the subject of the present paper.

2 Methods

The study [13] consisted of two parts: a comparative review of technologies based on literature search and suggestion of new principles that could potentially improve waste separation. Although they have a different meaning, the latter stems from the former one, as it will become clear from the following description.

The use of effects databases had several goals in mind:

1. For every technology, there was found a set of effects that play the role in its operation. This could help to categorize technologies and draw boundaries between technologies of a similar kind.
2. Representation of technologies as the sets of effects allowed to see better the evolution path among technology families, especially for old separation technologies stemming from the centuries-long mining industry.
3. A list of effects (together with technologies) would suggest those that remain unused in modern recycling, some of which could find a real application.

As it can be seen already, the same database can have a positive effect on both review and idea generation parts of the study. The list of effects and technologies was taken from the online databases by Aulive [14] and Oxford Creativity [15]. Altogether they made about 600 entries (with repetitions). The idea of the effect lists was extended with a list of material properties that focused on the intrinsic properties by which materials were distinguished from each other. The list of material properties was taken from filter values of the material search database Matmatch [16].

For objective comparison of technology the diverse information found was stored in .json format text file in a nested form (see Fig. 1), namely a record of every technology constituted a tree, with the technology basic definition and associated properties (like target material properties, effects, affecting factors, maturity level) in the root and splitting into branches with instances of research or industrial devices and associated performance figures, both categorical (like materials sorted) and numerical (purity grade, recovery rate etc.). A custom piece of software was written in Julia language to parse the file and extract information about technologies meeting the search criteria in both tabular and graphical form (see example in Fig. 2). Information from 199 scientific publications, patents and commercial leaflets about more than 40 technologies was collected in the database.

```
"technologies" : {
        "active pulsing air classification": {
                "brief": "Intermittent airflow fed into a column with shredded waste particl
                "action": "sort",
                "continuity": "online",
                "medium": "air",
                "pressure": "normal",
                "temperature": "room",
                "property": "density",
                "factors": ["drag", "density", "size", "shape", "terminal velocity"],

                "effects": [
                        "drag",
                        "free fall",
                        "gravity",
                        "inertia",
                        "pump",
                        "valve",
                        "vibration"
                ],

                "instances": [
                        {
                                "reference": "Lee & Rahimifard 2012",
                                "maturity": "research",
                                "trials": [
                                        {
                                                "waste": "footwear",
                                                "size": [0, 5],
                                                "materials": ["rubber", "leather"],
                                                "shape": "flake",
                                                "parameter": [[0.9, 1.4], [0.7, 0.8]],
                                                "recovery": [0.96, 0.93, 0.87],
                                                "purity": [0.82, 0.91, 0.93]
                                        },
                                        .
                                        .
                                        .
}
```

Fig. 1. Excerpt from the .json text file, showing the nested structure of the database.

Finally, the FOS was used to recruit working principles and technologies used elsewhere outside recycling. A couple of striking similarities between waste sorting and other fields of technology will be shown.

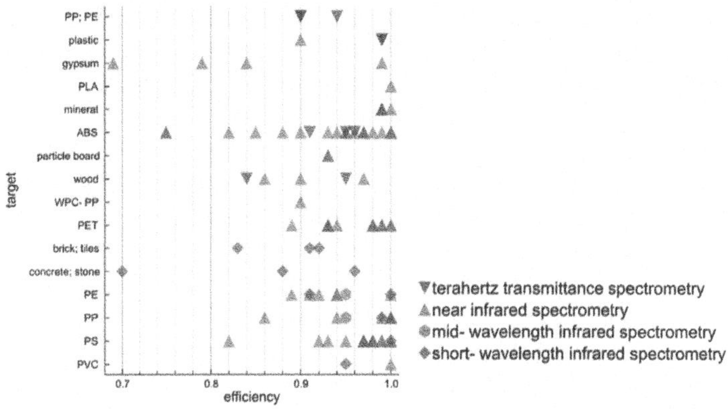

Fig. 2. The efficiency of several optical spectrometry methods for classifying different materials, plot generated straight from the database.

3 Useful Outcomes of TRIZ

In the following, some examples of the applied TRIZ procedures are given alongside with observations on their applicability.

3.1 Effects for Systematics

The organizing power of matching technologies with effects can be illustrated with the family of separation methods based on the difference in density. The very basic sink-float process lets waste fragments to segregate depending on their buoyancy in a liquid. The process is rather slow and obscured by material wettability and fluid viscosity. The gravity force can be replaced with centrifugal force produced either in hydrocyclone [17] or decanter centrifuge [18]. Another approach to diminish the unwanted secondary factors is replacement of hydrostatic (Archimedes') force with hydrodynamic forces acting intermittently in the wet shaking table [19], multidune [20], water jigging [21] or wet fluidized bed processes [22]. It can be further subdivided whether the alternating acceleration is excited with vibrations or zigzag flow of fluid. Practically for every aforementioned wet process, a complementary dry separation process can be found. Again, the underlying effects make the match rather explicit, like the use of zigzag flow pattern in multidune and zigzag air classifier [23].

Recently some new density-based methods emerged that introduced considerable adaptivity to the ordinary sink-float methods. The principle that attained the greatest success is manipulation of the Archimedes' force by placing the separation medium in the magnetic field. Options for the fluid are a solution of paramagnetic salt [24] or ferrofluid – the suspension of iron particles in water [25]. The interaction between the magnetic fluid and the field alters the apparent density of the fluid so that its layers attain different density. This enables separation of materials into multiple fractions in one separation volume (material particles float at the different depth), as well as adjustment of the density ranges without altering the fluid itself. One step further from that is the creation of a virtual inclined plane in the tank by inclining the external magnetic field. In this case, no propulsion for the floating items is needed, since they slide downhill along the layer of constant fluid density. This shows the broadness the effects can be treated with to build analogies between the processes. Also, the macroscale of material separation in waste processing allows utilization of effects not applicable for solid handling in conventional process engineering (compare with [26]): Magnus effect (eddy current separation [27]), stick-slip effect (air tabling [28]), triboelectricity (triboelectrostatic separation [28]).

Certain difficulties were faced in the description of sensor-based sorting, as the underlying interaction between matter and electromagnetic (EM) radiation is not so well covered by the list of effects and a significant amount of know-how is hidden behind the classification algorithms. Still, some systematization was possible as to which part of the EM spectrum is used, type of interaction, e.g. reflection, transmission or fluorescence etc.

3.2 Unused Effects and Material Properties

A large part of the effects remain unused in recycling for a good reason – they have limited applicability, for example, they concern a very narrow class of materials under special conditions (like piezoelectric or electrets). Consequently, there is not much to say about those effects that did not fall into approximately 100 that were used or tested in recycling. The same holds for material properties that are often challenging for continuous measurement (take stiffness, for example). However, a few effects and material properties have drawn attention and provided ideas for their application.

The first one is the Coandă effect – adherence of a fluid jet to a convex surface it flows along. An illustrative example of its use is the enhancement of lifting force of an airplane by deflecting the stream exhausted from the engines by utilizing its attachment to the upper surface of flaps pointed downwards (when being in the take-off or landing position). At this point, it becomes apparent that deflection of stream produces centrifugal action on the particles following the very same stream. There are commercial devices based on this principle, such as Coandă screen [29] and Coandă classifier [30], see Fig. 3. Coandă screen is a self-cleaning filter used to remove sediment from water stream without clogging and at high throughput. This device does not seem to be used in recycling, although it can help to recirculate the separation medium in the wet density-based separation methods without compromising their performance. Coandă (or elbow jet) classifier is laboratory equipment for separation of powders into fine, medium and coarse fractions by blowing them with the air around a rounded corner. Only the finest (and lightest) particles are able to follow the corner, while the heavier ones exit the stream and end up in other sectors. The size of powders classified (<200 μm) is below that typical for waste, but targeted development may result in separators for finely granulated printed circuited boards (PCB), for example.

A rather unexpected benefit of going through the effects list was finding separation technologies that did not appear in a targeted search. For example, supercritical fluids possess several properties highly desired for density separation medium, namely: liquid-like density, gas-like viscosity and compressibility, thus making adjustment of density rather straightforward. Indeed, the search about supercritical fluids revealed one

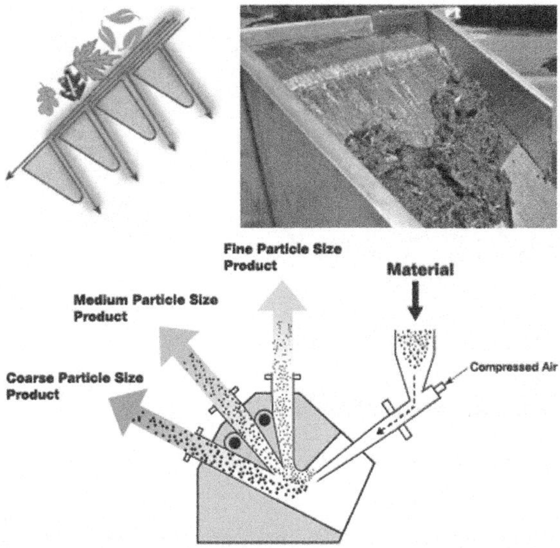

Fig. 3. Coandă effect applications: Coandă screen (above) [29], Coandă classifier (below) [30].

technology that was developed and patented back in the 1990s for separation of plastics by density [31]. The technology has not gained popularity, but without it, the technological landscape would be incomplete. Paramagnetism is yet another term that deserves attention as it leads to using gas for density-based separation. Oxygen possesses paramagnetic properties, which makes it possible to suspend solids in oxygen or even air in a high-gradient magnetic field with slight pressurization (tens of bars). The need for strong magnetic fields can be further reduced when using liquid oxygen-nitrogen mixture (which is essentially the product of air liquefaction) as separation medium [32]. The idea may benefit from the synergy with the other features of cryogenics:

- cryocomminution of waste allows to crush and liberate materials from certain kinds of waste more effectively [33];
- high-temperature superconducting magnets outperform permanent magnets and they work at the temperature of liquid nitrogen [34];
- liquid nitrogen enables dry, eco-friendly cleaning (already used in industry [35]), so it can be applied to the waste as well.

As cryogenic technology and superconductors are gaining widespread use, they may finally enter the field of waste processing.

It is quite challenging to find a new material property that is both sufficient for material discrimination and has adequate means for measurement. Still, two ideas got support for their feasibility. The first one should distinguish between thermoplastics with low and high softening temperatures. Among other test procedures, Vicat hardness test is used for plastics. Vicat softening temperature measures the point when the plastic softens enough to be penetrated by the steel test probe [36]. This test procedure could be approximated for continuous operation on a conveyor, analogue to the way the PaperSpike [37] mechanism separates cardboard items from paper, see Fig. 4.

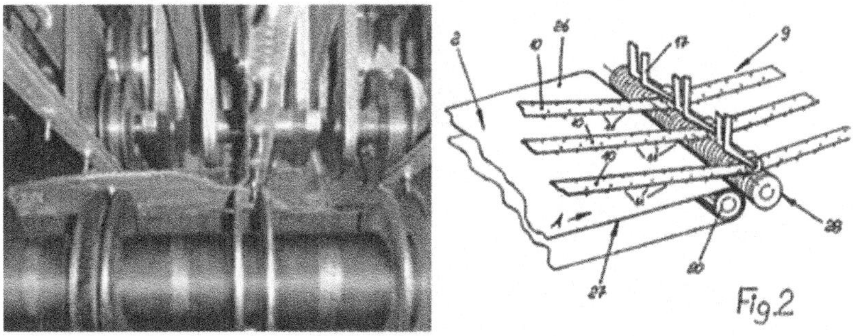

Fig. 4. PaperSpike pierce a piece of cardboard (left) [37], view of mechanism (right) [38].

Another material property that becomes attractive for discrimination between materials is the refractive index. Advances in the theory of light reflection resulted in computational algorithms for estimation of refractive index from several photos of an object [39]. It is worth mentioning that one of the key drivers for research here is photorealistic image rendering (for computer games as well). Given that the refractive index was successfully measured by this technique for objects like tomato and apple [40], it might help in sensor-based classification of materials in waste.

3.3 FOS: Security Scanners and Printers in Recycling

Two cases of the FOS have provided an insight into technologies that could be adapted for sensor-based material sorting. The general problem of extracting valuable materials from the commingled waste stream has a direct analogy to the security check for dangerous or forbidden objects, for example, in airports. Security scanners are at the cutting edge of technology, as they may use several kinds of radiation (X-ray, gamma and neutron) to classify materials in opaque containers [41]. With the recent trend for developing compact, portable, low-cost devices for threat detection (and related to that non-destructive testing) it becomes a fruitful source of inspiration for material recognition in recycling. For example, a technique that uses infrared stars of various wavelength to see through materials may become an affordable and safe replacement for X-ray scanners on sorting conveyors [42]. The technique is also remarkable for its use of mathematically-proven signal amplification method, which obviously cannot be found in physical effects databases.

Another FOS was run to address the existing gap between the ever-increasing resolution of sensors (such as hyperspectral cameras) and the dominant ejection method with an array of pneumatic valves, the so-called air jet blow bar. Although the nozzles can be placed as close as 3 mm from each other, their operation may lead to co-ejection of particles that belong to different fractions. Consequently, the waste is spread on the conveyor belt, so that it barely covers 5–10% of its area [43]. At the same time, air jets may divide the material flow into two, at the most three fractions, while sensors may classify several materials at once. From the viewpoint of energy consumption, the solution cannot be optimal either, as it is an inherent property of pneumatic circuitry to waste about 80% of energy [35]. The general problem statement, in this case, is how to deliver specific particles from a dense stream to the correct collection points. One of the ultimate leader in this respect is electrophotography that is used in laser printers. Indeed, a typical printer can deliver toner particles at the precision of several hundred dots per inch. The technology needs modification or even a completely different embodiment for adoption in the domain of recycling. Precisely activated electroadhesive devices should eventually outperform pneumatic ejectors in the waste sorting.

4 Discussion

The collected database of technologies has an advantage over paper reviews in that it is extendable with new information and can immediately show comparative infographics for the metrics chosen by the user (whose preferences may change over time). The tree-like storage of the data helps to cope with different level of details provided in publications, though some valuable information (such as price) remained in unstructured textual comments alongside with other categorical and numerical data. The developed software, however, lacks material modelling and simulation aids. The decision analysis is left outside and can be both algorithmic (e.g. Multi-Criteria Analysis) or merely judgmental. For example, in the case study [13] concerning the separation of plastics from construction and demolition waste the technologies were assessed as to which of them sort by the most divergent properties of the target materials and can sort them with associated impeding factors (dirt, moisture etc.). In the space of technological foresight, the conducted analysis leaned towards Monitoring and mapping class [9], as the study was conducted mainly through the literature search, enhanced by creativity approaches of TRIZ for ideation [45] and wider coverage of alternatives [10].

The effects-based approach takes the understanding of technologies and processes at another abstraction level that drives the search beyond the domain of the problem. A set of corresponding effects can be thought as a "genetic code" of the technology, which, in turn, allows to construct phylogenetic trees of technologies. Phylogenetic trees (see Fig. 4) are built using dedicated algorithms from bioinformatics for comparison of genomes and they visualize the genetic relationship between species, as well as the process of evolutionary development. Differences in genomes help to set borders between species, just as they facilitate classification of technologies (Fig. 5).

The idea of technological "genes" has already appeared in [46], where the morphological analysis of textual description in patents provided "chromosomes" of technologies that were fed into a genetic algorithm to get more versions of a particular technology. The quality of a "chromosome" was set proportional to the number of patents reflecting its structure. If a technological "genotype" (a set of genes for a particular mechanism) was explicit enough to reflect quantitatively the actual topology and physics of operation it could be used for the evolutionary optimization algorithm to search for a completely new solution and test in a multiphysics simulation environment.

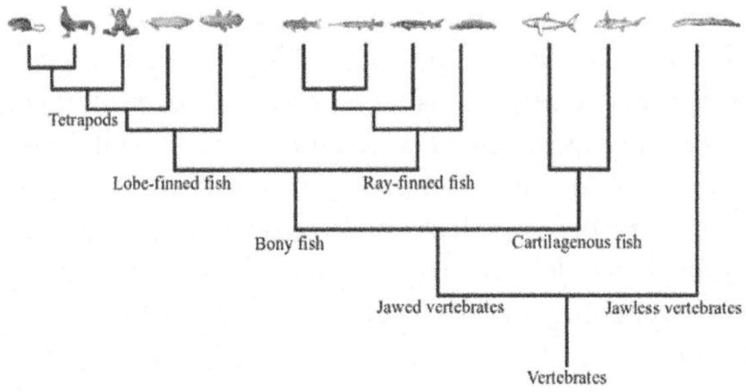

Fig. 5. Example of a phylogenetic tree, adapted from [44].

Evolutionary computing has shown in some cases enough creativity to outsmart researchers that set seemingly unsolvable problems to their algorithms [47].

A plain set of effects is a vague representation of technology, but it can be firmly concluded that the effects databases need enhancement with similar building blocks from information technology, the algorithms. There can be a true synergy between sensing hardware and data processing software that will result in qualitatively new detection capabilities, as was demonstrated in [30]. Awareness of such possibilities can become a competitive advantage in innovation.

The FOS seems to fall off from the paradigm of the strong problem-solving analytical tools of TRIZ, like the substance-field analysis, resource analysis, inventive principles and many more. Its application for innovation in process engineering stalled since the 2000s [11]. However, it is a ready-to-use heuristic to make a well-guessed jump into another industrial field and escape from a local optimum of domain-specific technologies towards the best globally available technique.

5 Concluding Remarks

The broad scope of the conducted technological survey impeded the use of many TRIZ tools aimed at defining inventive problems and resolving contradictions, however, even loose and fragmentary application of TRIZ principles promotes feasible search directions. New terms that are hardly associated with the domain under investigation lead to device concepts of considerable potential, as it was demonstrated in this work. The success of the conducted survey and ideation can only be proven by future implementation and testing of the concepts in practice, as the quantitative evaluation was hardly possible in such an early stage.

Acknowledgements. The authors thank Prof. Pavel Livotov for invaluable comments provided in preparation of the present paper, as well as anonymous reviewers for critical remarks.

References

1. Ragaert, K., Delva, L., Van Geem, K.: Mechanical and chemical recycling of solid plastic waste. Waste Manag. **69**, 24–58 (2017)
2. Mellor, W., Wright, E., Clift, R., Azapagic, A., Stevens, G.: A mathematical model and decision-support framework for material recovery, recycling and cascaded use. Chem. Eng. Sci. **57**(22), 4697–4713 (2002)
3. Van Schaik, A., Reuter, M.A.: Dynamic modelling of E-waste recycling system performance based on product design. Miner. Eng. **23**(3), 192–210 (2010)
4. Ip, K., Testa, M., Raymond, A., Graves, S., Gutowski, T.: Performance evaluation of material separation in a material recovery facility using a network flow model. Resour. Conserv. Recycl. **131**, 192–205 (2018)
5. Gundupalli, S.P., Hait, S., Thakur, A.: A review on automated sorting of source-separated municipal solid waste for recycling. Waste Manag. **60**(C), 56–74 (2017)
6. Singh, N., Hui, D., Singh, R., Ahuja, I.P.S., Feo, L., Fraternali, F.: Recycling of plastic solid waste: A state of art review and future applications. Compos. B **115**(C), 409–422 (2017)
7. Nabil, N.Z.G., Bülent, C., Hodgson, A.: Technology roadmapping for the next generation manufacturing enterprise. School of Mechanical, Materials and Manufacturing Engineering, University of Nottingham. J. Manufact. Technol. Manage. **17**(4), 404–416 (2006)
8. Dully, S.: Internetbasiertes Technologie-Scouting für Recyclingtechnologien; Internet-based technology scouting for recycling technologies. Doctoral dissertation. Jost-Jetter Verlag, Heimsheim, Germany (2011)
9. Słupiński, M.: Technology Forecasting – State of the Art Update. FORMAT Consortium Deliverable (2013)
10. Porter, A.L.: Technology foresight: types and methods. Int. J. Foresight Innovation Policy **6**(1–3), 36–45 (2010)
11. Livotov, P., Sekaran, A.P.C., Law, R., Reay, D., Sarsenova, A., Sayyareh, S.: Eco-innovation in process engineering: Contradictions, inventive principles and methods. Thermal Sci. Eng. Prog. **9**, 52–65 (2019)
12. Litvin, S.: New TRIZ-based tool—function-oriented search (FOS). The TRIZ Journal, August (2005)
13. Ivanovskis, L.: Systematic selection of perspective solid waste mechanical separation technologies for material recovery. Master Thesis. LUT University (2019). http://urn.fi/URN:NBN:fi-fe201903148916. Accessed 20 June 2019
14. Aulive Production Inspiration. http://www.productioninspiration.com. Accessed 20 June 2019
15. Oxford Creativity TRIZ Effects Database. https://www.triz.co.uk/how/triz-effects-database. Accessed 20 June 2019
16. Matmatch – Find Materials & Suppliers. https://matmatch.com/. Accessed 20 June 2019
17. Gent, M.R., Menéndez, M., Toraño, J., Torno, S.: Enhanced plastics recycling by cyclone media separation. In: ISWA APESB World Congress, Lisbon, Portugal (2009)
18. Andritz. https://www.andritz.com. Accessed 13 Feb 2019
19. Carvalho, M.T., Agante, E., Durão, F.: Recovery of PET from packaging plastics mixtures by wet shaking table. Waste Manag. **27**(12), 1747–1754 (2007)
20. Lupo, E., Moroni, M., La Marca, F., Fulco, S., Pinzi, V.: Investigation on an innovative technology for wet separation of plastic wastes. Waste Manag. **51**, 3–12 (2016)
21. Ito, M., et al.: Reverse jig separation of shredded floating plastics—separation of polypropylene and high density polyethylene. Int. J. Miner. Process. **97**(1–4), 96–99 (2010)

22. Kinoshita, T., Okamoto, K., Yamaguchi, K., Akita, S.: Separation of plastic mixtures using liquid-fluidized bed technology. Chemosphere **63**(6), 893–902 (2006)
23. Lee, M.J., Rahimifard, S.: A novel separation process for recycling of post-consumer products. CIRP Ann. **61**(1), 35–38 (2012)
24. EP2679310. European Patent Office (2014)
25. Bakker, E.J., Rem, P.C., Fraunholcz, N.: Upgrading mixed polyolefin waste with magnetic density separation. Waste Manag. **29**(5), 1712–1717 (2009)
26. Wang, H., et al.: A review of process intensification applied to solids handling. Chem. Eng. Process. **118**, 78–107 (2017)
27. Lungu, M., Neculae, A.: Eddy current separation of small nonferrous particles using a complementary air-water method. Sep. Sci. Technol. **53**(1), 126–135 (2018)
28. Dodbiba, G., Sadaki, J., Okaya, K., Shibayama, A., Fujita, T.: The use of air tabling and triboelectric separation for separating a mixture of three plastics. Miner. Eng. **18**(15), 1350–1360 (2005)
29. Coanda, Inc. Coanda Process Screen. http://www.coanda.com/products/processscreen.htm. Accessed 20 June 2019
30. Powder Systems Co. Small classifier. https://www.powder.co.jp/EN/products/01/. Accessed 20 June 2019
31. Super, M.S., Enick, R.M., Beckman, E.J.: Density-based separation of thermoplastics found in the post-consumer waste stream. Resour. Conserv. Recycl. **9**(1–2), 75–88 (1993)
32. Catherall, A.T., Lopez-Alcaraz, P., Benedict, K.A., King, P.J., Eaves, L.: Cryogenically enhanced magneto-Archimedes levitation. New J. Phys. **7**(1), art. no. 118 (2005)
33. Zhou, C., Pan, Y., Lu, M., Yang, C.: Liberation characteristics after cryogenic modification and air table separation of discarded printed circuit boards. J. Hazard. Mater. **311**, 203–209 (2016)
34. Bjørk, R., Nielsen, K.K., Bahl, C.R., Smith, A., Wulff, A.C.: Comparing superconducting and permanent magnets for magnetic refrigeration. AIP Adv. **6**(5), 056205 (2016)
35. Máša, V., Kuba, P.: Efficient use of compressed air for dry ice blasting. J. Clean. Prod. **111**, 76–84 (2016)
36. ASTM D1525-00 Standard Test Method for Vicat Softening Temperature of Plastics. West Conshohocken: ASTM International, West Conshohocken, 8 p. (2000)
37. Bollegraaf Recycling Solutions: Paper Spike. http://www.fissoreagency.com/pages/wp-content/uploads/2009/09/Paper-Spike.pdf. Accessed 20 June 2019
38. EP1291092. European Patent Office (2003)
39. Tominaga, S., Tanaka, N.: Refractive index estimation and color image rendering. Pattern Recogn. Lett. **24**(11), 1703–1713 (2003)
40. Saman, G., Hancock, E.: Refractive index estimation using photometric stereo. In: 2011 18th IEEE International Conference on Image Processing, pp. 1925–1928 (2011)
41. Sowerby, B., Tickner, J.: Scanner for the detection of contraband in air cargo containers. Physicist Aust. Inst. Phys. **42**(10) (2005)
42. Senni, L., Burrascano, P., Ricci, M.: Multispectral laser imaging for advanced food analysis. Infrared Phys. Technol. **77**, 179–192 (2016)
43. Yu, H.: Metal Recovery via Automated Sortation. Doctoral dissertation. Worcester Polytechnic Institute (2014). https://web.wpi.edu/Pubs/ETD/Available/etd-041714-211407/unrestricted/HaoYu.pdf. Accessed 20 June 2019
44. Yamamoto, K., Bloch, S., Vernier, P.: New perspective on the regionalization of the anterior forebrain in Osteichthyes. Dev. Growth Differ. **59**(4), 175–187 (2017)

45. Ilevbare, I., Phaal, R., Probert, D., Padilla, A.T.: Integration of TRIZ and roadmapping for innovation, strategy, and problem solving. Centre for Technology Management, University of Cambridge, UK, and Dux Diligens, Mexico (2011)
46. Yoon, B.G., Jin, S.Y.: Applications of genetic algorithm and text mining on technology innovation. Appl. Mech. Mater. **145**, 287–291 (2012)
47. Lehman, J., et al.: The surprising creativity of digital evolution: A collection of anecdotes from the evolutionary computation and artificial life research communities. arXiv preprint arXiv:1803.03453 (2018)

Technology Strategy by TRIZ Tools for Eco-Aircare Solution

Gukhyun Cho[1(✉)], Ahreum Lee[1], Jungin Kim[1], Wanseok Jeong[1], and Youshin Han[2]

[1] LG Electronics, Seoul 07336, South Korea
gukhyun.cho@lge.com
[2] CTL (Creative Tree Lab.), Seoul 06224, South Korea

Abstract. Recently, air pollution issues such as particular matter or atmospheric aerosol particles have been raised around the world, especially in China and Korea. To cope with these environmental issues, companies are providing a variety of air care solutions to consumers. With the addition of energy regulations such as the Montreal Protocol, the Kyoto Protocol and the Paris Agreement, there is a greater possibility that contradictions exist between alternatives in addressing air pollution as well as existing energy savings. In particular, the technology related to refrigerant is the core technology of air conditioning equipment, and when developing a system, it is one of the important processes to understand the relationship between refrigerant characteristics and the components inside and outside the system. In this paper, the TRIZ is used to establish a technology strategy by conducting a case study on GWP refrigerants (low and high) and air conditioning equipment.

Keywords: Air-care solution · Refrigerant · Low GWP · Technology evolution · Ideality · Resource

1 Introduction

There is a growing number of consumers who consider air quality as a means of evaluating quality of life. Year after year, the demand for air quality is increasing. In the past, the perception that was limited to temperature has changed to the type of pollutant such as particular matter or atmospheric aerosol particles, and recently, attention has been paid to the level of the pollutant. As a result, companies have provided a variety of air care solutions to meet changing requirements.

In addition, requirements beyond countries, such as climate and environmental regulations, are driving changes in relevant markets and technologies. Particularly, the goal of reducing consumption and emissions for refrigerants is severely influential throughout products using refrigerants. If the country does not have the relevant technology or infrastructure, the country will soon lose own competitive edge in the market. It is necessary to prepare according to the situation in each country before the reduction targets and schedules set through the Kigali Amendment to the Montreal protocol arrive. According to the amendment, the schedule is divided into four groups,

The original version of this chapter was revised: equations were corrected. The correction to this chapter is available at https://doi.org/10.1007/978-3-030-32497-1_42

Published by Springer Nature Switzerland AG 2019
R. Benmoussa et al. (Eds.): TFC 2019, IFIP AICT 572, pp. 340–349, 2019.
https://doi.org/10.1007/978-3-030-32497-1_28

starting from the non-A5 countries in Fig. 1. The countries have long been actively involved in research and institutional maintenance of refrigerants. The countries and schedules covered by the group are listed in Table 1.

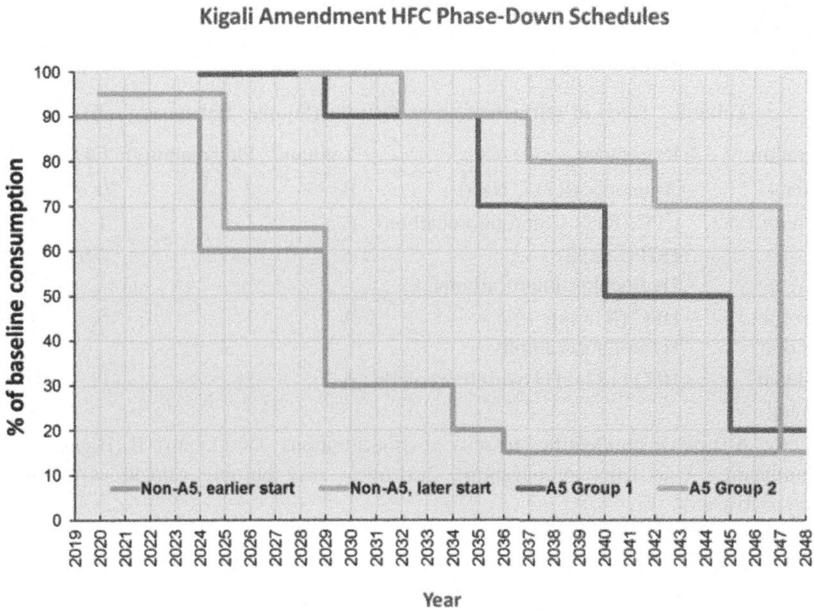

Fig. 1. Kigali Amendment HFC Phase-down for Classification of countries (Source: Reference [1, 2])

Table 1. Classification of parties and countries (Source: Reference [1, 2])

Classification of Parties	Year of HFCs Phase down Freeze	Countries
Non-A5, earlier start	Main group (2019)	45 Countries (included EU)
Non-A5, later start	Exceptions (2020)	Belarus, the Russian Federation, Kazakhstan, Tajikistan, Uzbekistan
Article 5 Group 1	2024	The 137 other Parties of the Montreal Protocol (included Republic of Korea, China)
Article 5 Group 2	2028	Bahrain, India, Iran, Iraq, Kuwait, Oman, Pakistan, Qatar, Saudi Arabia, and the United Arab Emirates

The EU has been implementing its own regulation since 2012, called the F-Gas Regulation. Air conditioners filled with 3 kg or less of refrigerant include only GWP750 (Global Warming Potential) since 2025. In addition, the refrigerant quota system has been registered since 2017. In United States of America, local government-led initiatives are being prepared, with guidelines similar to those in the EU. Japan is making all-out preparations under the initiative of the state, while China is conducting reduction activities according to the agreement schedule. Australia, the Middle East, South America and Southeast Asia are also preparing for regional cooperation [3].

Refrigerant use regulations have been an activity since the beginning of the development of refrigerants. As shown in Table 2, it has changed in the direction of reducing the harmful functions of refrigerants from initial refrigerants to alternative refrigerants.

Table 2. Trend of refrigerant characteristics (Source: Reference [4, 5])

Generation	Refrigerant	Toxicity[a]	Flammability[b]	ODP[c]	GWP[d]
1st Infant	Ammonia (R717, NH_3)	B	2	0	0
2nd Freon Era	CFC (R12) Chlorofluorocarbons	A	1	1	10900
	HCFC (R22) Hydrochlorofluorocarbons	A	1	0.055	1810
3rd Ozone protection	HFC (R134a) Hydrofluorocarbons	A	1	0	1430
4th Global Warming	HFO (1234yf) Hydrofluoroolefin	A	2L	0	<1

a Toxicity: A (Lower: no identified toxicity at concentrations $\leq$400 ppm), B (Higher)
b Flammability: 1(no flame propagation), 2L(Lower: max burning velocity <10 cm/s), 2L (Lower), 3(Higher)
c ODP: Ozone Depletion Potential, UNEP (2006). R11 = 1
d GWP: Global Warming Potential (100 year), IPCC 4th Assessment Report, (2007). CO_2 = 1,

The initial refrigerant was toxic and therefore high risk for the user. CFC (Freon) was developed in an effort to reduce the direct risks of toxicity, flammability, etc. And it has been used for a long time until fully phase-out in 2010. Since then, Cl (Chlorine) and F (Fluorine) components included in the CFC is known to adversely affect the environment, such as ozone depletion and greenhouse gas generation, has been developing a refrigerant in a direction to reduce this effect. Refrigerant-based systems have also been developed accordingly. Recently, the GWP has focused on finding a low (<750) or extreme low (<150) state.

Applicable alternative refrigerants appear in a pattern similar to the S-curve type in Fig. 2. Recently, HFO and HC refrigerants, which are emerging as alternatives, have excellent environmental performance, but there is a possibility that the risk is increased due to lower performance or flammability compared to existing refrigerants. Therefore, additional verification is needed to apply alternative refrigerants, and many companies are spurring related developments.

In order to maintain the performance of existing systems using alternative refrigerants, the costs of changing the system or investing in equipment must be considered. However, this is not an ideal solution from the idealistic view of TRIZ. Ideality, a key concept of TRIZ, can help you set goals so you can find the fundamental solutions to problems. In this paper, we will examine the direction of establishing technical solutions for related systems including refrigerants using TRIZ method. Through this, it was intended to be used in technology development strategy that secured sustainability.

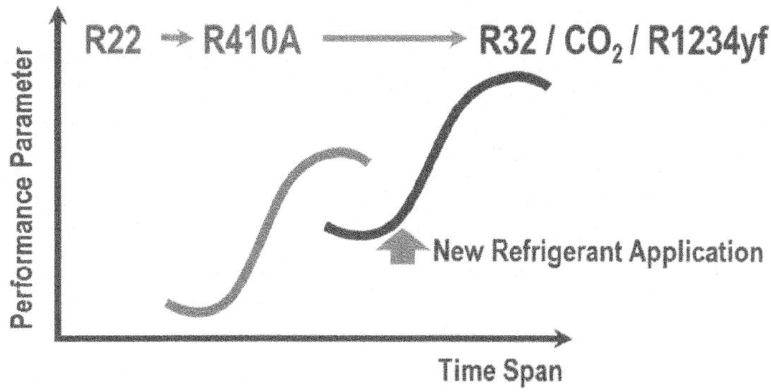

Fig. 2. S-curve of Refrigerant for air-conditioning system

2 Operating Time/Zone with Refrigerant Usage

In each country, we have established and implemented a policy to reduce the amount of used refrigerant and reduce the emission of existing refrigerants. Considering the lifetime cycle in which refrigerant is used, it is desirable to find the constraints and respond accordingly when a problem may occur.

In the case of existing refrigerants, six major greenhouse gases, CO_2, CH_4, N_2O, SF_6, PFCs, and HFCs, may be generated during the production or decomposition of the refrigerant, including Cl and F, which are ozone depleting substances.

From the standpoint of developing a product, there are three things about operating time of product. You can think about (1) products that have been on the market from the past to the present, (2) products that are in production, and (3) products that are under development or are in development. At each stage, specific measures are needed to reduce the use or reduce the emissions.

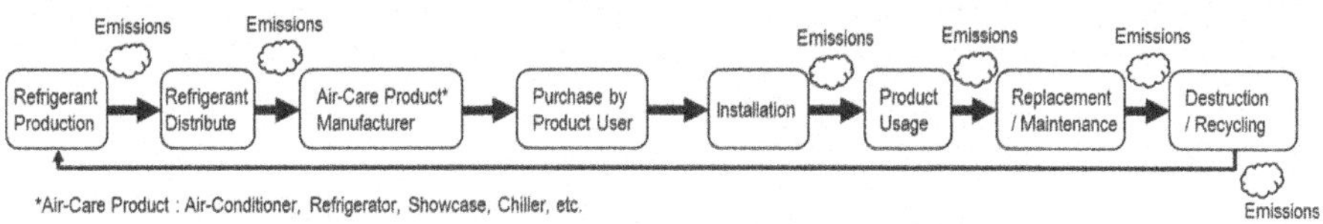

Fig. 3. Emission of refrigerant during air-conditioning system lifecycle

First, let's look at the emissions, that is, when the refrigerant is released into the air in Fig. 3.

From the point of view of a user using a product on the market, the product is purchased, installed, used, maintained, replaced or disposed of. The resolution direction may differ for each point of use. At the installation stage, a pipe joint structure without refrigerant leakage can be considered. Some products are used all year round, but some users use only one summer season. In this case, the refrigerant may be replaced during maintenance. It is important to consider whether there is a way to make it easier to replace the refrigerant or to prevent leakage. It is also necessary to consider how to reduce the period by checking the maintenance cycle. When disposing of the refrigerant or disposing of the product, it is necessary to check whether it can be recovered. In the case of waste water purifiers, some studies show that the remaining amount of refrigerant in the system is 40% [6].

After refrigerant was injected to the product, the refrigerant discharged to the atmosphere cannot be recovered. At the end of the product's lifecycle, recovery and treatment technologies are needed. Refrigerant may be released even when water is collected inside or mixed in the recovered refrigerant. Since the refrigerant is difficult to decompose, incineration may be performed using steam plasma. In this process, by-products such as CO_2, CO, and NO_X, which are other global warming materials, are generated, and the generated CF_4 is difficult to remove even by incineration. Therefore, it is necessary to secure a technology that suppresses the by-product generation itself and lowers power consumption. CF_4 is GWP 7390 and C_2F_6 is GWP 12200, which has 50,000 years and 10,000 years of atmospheric lifetime of refrigerant, respectively, causing secondary problems due to refrigerant disposal.

It can also be seen in terms of the space in which the refrigerant is present. It is possible to think of ways to prevent the leakage of indirect leakage between the coupling parts due to the two-phase refrigerant state connecting the pipelines through which the refrigerant flows. The atmospheric lifetime of the leaked refrigerant means the point at which the refrigerant components in the atmosphere naturally disappear. Therefore, it is conceivable to collect the refrigerant around the product before the refrigerant is discharged and after the discharge. In the case of flammable refrigerants, it is possible to consider how to spread rapidly in the space of use, so as not to form a cloud around the product. After being released into the atmosphere, one method may be to separate refrigerant gas from the earth's surface and the troposphere and between the troposphere and the stratosphere, using materials that react easily to the atmosphere.

3 Define Engineering System and Ideal System

It defines engineering system from the functional point of view and defines the fundamental reasons why the engineering system performs its functions. When the main function of the refrigerant is defined as absorbing or releasing heat, the refrigerant may also be defined as transferring heat from a heat source.

(1) Engineering System: Refrigerant (in Air-conditioning system)
(2) Main Function: Absorb Heat, Release Heat.

The ideal system for the above engineering system can be defined as a system that does not have refrigerant but absorbs or releases heat. Considering this ideal system, one can think break to psychological inertia. Making a refrigerant is not the desired result. What is your ideal goal? What is the desired result?

There is no refrigerant, but you need to think about whether absorbing heat is your ideal goal. We need to ask why absorbs the heat. For example, it can be considered to lower the temperature of the room or to maintain the temperature of the food. If your goal is to absorb heat constantly, you can think of ways to take advantage of other effects. The thermoelectric module using the Peltier effect is representative.

4 Ideality of Refrigerant

The definition of the equation of ideality that is commonly used by many people [7] is:

$$\text{Ideality} = \frac{All\ Useful\ effects}{All\ Harmful\ effects} \tag{1}$$

Among the methods of achieving the ideality of a technical system, defining an ideal component is one of the methods for achieving the ideal component while maintaining the whole system without change. This can be used to derive the ideality of the refrigerant [8]. Since the refrigerant exists as a component of the engineering system, such a air-conditioning system, if the ideal of the refrigerant is improved, the entire technical system can be closer to ideal system. Expressing the ideal of the refrigerant by the definition of the above equation is as follows.

$$\text{Ideality of Refrigerant} = \frac{Useful\ Function[Heat\ transfer\ efficiency + \ldots]}{Harmful\ Function[Environmental\ impact + Safety + \ldots] \times Cost[production + disposal + \ldots]} \tag{2}$$

- Safety: Toxicity, Flammability, stable, treatment, lubricant, etc.
- Environmental impact: Ozone Deplete Potential, Global Warming Potential, decomposition product.

By using the ideality equation of the defined refrigerant, we can compare the ideality when using the existing refrigerant and the alternative refrigerant.

(1) If using existing refrigerant, If use base refrigerant (ex. R410A)

$$\text{Ideality of Refrigerant} = \frac{UF(constant)}{HF(toxicity + nonflammable + GWP(>750)) \times constant\ cost} \tag{3}$$

(2) When using an alternative refrigerant, Alternative refrigerant (ex. HFC R32)

$$\text{Ideality of Refrigerant} = \frac{UF(constant)}{HF(taxicity + lower\ flammable + GWP(<750)) \times higher\ cost} \tag{4}$$

Refrigerant (R32 or R1234yf), which is considered as a strong alternative refrigerant, satisfies the existing thermodynamic characteristics and satisfies low GWP. However, it is flammable, which adds additional considerations in terms of user risk. Therefore, from an ideal point of view, the use of alternative refrigerants with low GWP is positive for the environment, and thus the Harmful function is reduced. Since additional costs for risk management, which were not present in existing systems, must be taken into account, it is necessary to prioritize in the short term and find the ideal refrigerant.

5 Multi-screen Thinking Approach for Refrigerant and Its Applicable System

In order to derive realistic goals from ideal system, it is necessary to examine the trends of related technologies and their surroundings. Use multi-screen thinking (MST), to identify applicable levels or resources to prepare in advance. Gather information to define how and where the engineering system absorbs or releases heat. The amount of heat absorption needed to keep a few bottles of beverage at the desired temperature is totally different from the amount of heat absorption required to maintain the temperature of a subway with dozens of people. These resources can then be used to step-by-step through the objectives of approaching ideality.

Resources can be found such as the time needed to maintain the temperature of the air during the day, the heat absorbed and emitted through the building's windows, the air density inside the building, the number of offices, and the size of the showcase. You can also find ways to reduce the cooling capacity load of an air-conditioning system inside a building by changing the size or number of windows in the building. There is also a case study to reduce the temperature inside the building by developing a polymer material that utilizes infrared heat radiation to absorb heat and reflects sunlight [9].

Information on climate change and seasons, such as temperature and humidity, in areas where the product is used, is also useful. In the Middle East, the sandy environment and temperature difference affect the operation characteristics of the compressor, which must consider both the oil and the refrigerant inside the compressor.

The stereotype of having to look for another refrigerant is an administrative contradiction because it cannot be used. The requirements need to be thoroughly reviewed, and whether the problem should be solved or not disappeared. If you look for the resources around you using multi-screen thinking, you can find where the refrigerant is used unnecessarily, or solve it by reusing the discarded refrigerant.

Therefore, the ideality of the air conditioning or refrigeration system, which is the supper-system, should be increased. Also, Technical development of refrigerant recovery and recycling systems should be carried out at the same time of maintenance or disposal. In addition, it is necessary to develop a technology for improving the compatibility with the compressor, heat exchanger, lubricant oil, etc., which are directly affected by the refrigerant. It is also necessary to review the compressor oil in anticipation of chemical changes with the refrigerant. It is also a way to reduce the CO_2 increase by minimizing the deterioration of efficiency due to the change in cooling capacity.

The ideality of the compressor, as the super-system of refrigerants, can be increased to improve the ideality of the whole system using refrigerants. For example, consider how to improve the insufficient function that can occur in a compressor. Low GWP (GWP 750 and below), which is currently considered as an alternative refrigerant, has a lower molecular weight compared to previous refrigerants, resulting in low suction density at the same compression volume [10]. Therefore, the lubrication is getting worse between the cylinders for compressing the refrigerant, the leakage may increase. If this is expressed as Su-field model, in Fig. 4. If solved using a 76-standard solution, an external environmental Su-field model that uses oil in the environment can be used. Consider increasing the oil supplied to the compression chamber.

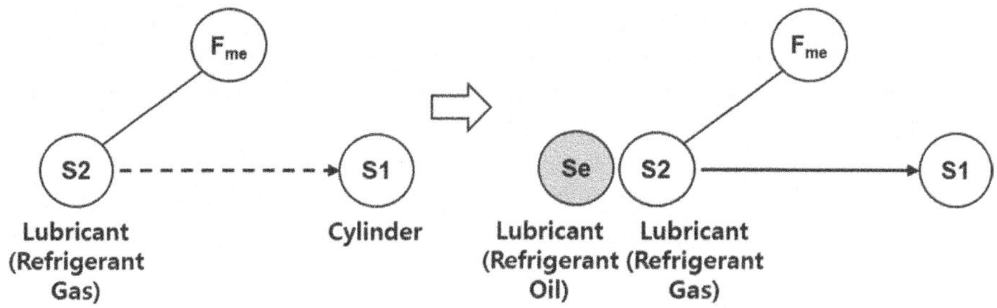

Fig. 4. Su-field Model of refrigerant gas and lubricant oil

6 Evolution of Materials (Refrigerant Composition)

It is possible to predict the core technology as a point of the evolutionary trend of the materials constituting the refrigerant. One of the evolutionary trends in technological engineering systems is the law of transition to higher-level systems [11]. This trend can be found in more detail in the materials and materials of technical systems. Most technical systems are made of the homogeneous material. This means they are used in combination with other materials or materials with opposite properties in order to perform better functions. It can be arranged as follows in Fig. 5.

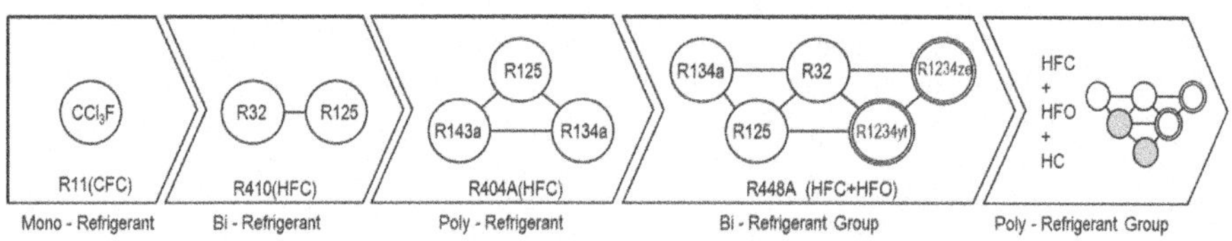

Fig. 5. Evolution of Refrigerant composition

In the case of ammonia, which is an early refrigerant, it is consisted of a single composition of molecular units, NH_3. The first CFC(R-11 or Freon), is also consisted of a single composition, CCl_3F. After phase-out the use of CFCs, HCFC or HFC refrigerants were developed and started to be used as single refrigerants. After that, two or three of composition were mixed with refrigerants having similar molecular composition (H, F, C). For example, in case of R-410 used in air conditioner, R-32 (CH_2F_2) and R-125 (CHF_2CF_3) are used in a mixture of 50:50. For R404A, a refrigerant used in a air-conditioner, is a refrigerant mixed with three refrigerants. Furthermore, it is possible to replace the existing refrigerant by developing a mixture of refrigerant groups having different molecular composition such as R448A [12]. According to this evolutionary trend, strategies for developing refrigerants that are suitable for product cooling capacity can be devised by diversifying the types of refrigerants mixed or optimizing the mixing ratio. In addition, depending on the ratio of refrigerants, it is change the cooling capacity (performance). So, conformity checks may be required between refrigerant and the product components (compressor oil, heat exchanger area, etc.) depending on the product's operating conditions. Considering the refrigerant usage scenario, it is also necessary to review the performance due to refrigerant filling, replacement or leakage from the equipment.

A list of Ideal status and technical strategy for refrigerant is below in Table 3. Considering the difference current with the target system, the actual technical approach direction was arranged by changing the target level through the step-back as shown in the table below.

Table 3. Ideal status and technical strategy for refrigerant

	Ideal status of refrigerant	Technical strategy goal
Ideal System	Refrigerant Free System	Improvement thermal capacity by thermoelectric effect (ex. Peltier effect)
Step Back 1	Using zero GWP, no concerned emission	Eco-friendly reusable nature
Step Back 2	Reuse or recycle whole refrigerant	Improvement of recycle equipment
Step Back 3	Allowed lower emission verified safety	Safety Risk assessment for flammable, high pressure refrigerant
Step Back 4	Only Using Low GWP Refrigerant using without System Change	Reduce refrigerant emission management and development devices
Step Back 5	Mixed Higher and Lower GWP Refrigerant with small system change	Find Specific Refrigerant for each application
Current	Gradually change usage rate of High GWP versus Low GWP refrigerant	Development of specific component for each application

7 Conclusion

In this study, in order to prepare a diversified solution to the tightening of refrigerant regulation, the technical approach to air-care solutions was derived using TRIZ. Instead of finding a solution in a situation where only requirements are given, an ideal system was defined in consideration of the internal and external components of the technical system from the TRIZ perspective. While the beneficial function of the thermodynamic performance is maintained, the direction in which the ideality of the refrigerant can be increased in the direction of eliminating the environmentally harmful function is examined. By multi-screen thinking approach, we examined not only the change trend of refrigerants but also the trends of the super-systems and sub-systems. Finally, the specific goal was found through step-back from the ideal system.

This study attempted to examine various alternatives beyond the solution focused on refrigerant development. Applying concepts of improving the ideality of components including refrigerant, the technical strategy was derived to improve the ideal of the whole system called Air-Care Solution. The results of this study can be used to construct roadmaps for future technologies in advanced and to prepare fundamental solutions.

References

1. UN environment Ozone Action. https://www.unenvironment.org/ozonaction/resources/factsheet/ozonaction-kigali-fact-sheet-1-introduction-kigali-amendment
2. International Institute of Refrigeration. http://www.iifiir.org/userfiles/file/webfiles/regulation_files/Synth%C3%A8se_Kigali_EN.pdf
3. Okada, T.: History of "Kobe Symposium and Global Issues of the HVAC Industry". In: The International Symposium on New Refrigerants and Environmental Technology (2018)
4. Linde Gases AG "Refrigerants Environmental Data". www.linde-gas.com/refrigerants
5. EPA (United States Environmental Protection Agency). https://www.epa.gov/snap/refrigerant-safety
6. Byun, S.H., et al.: Emission characteristics of HFC-134a from Water Purifier, Proceedings of Korean Society for Atmospheric Environment, 237 page (2013)
7. Terninko, J., Zusman, A., Zlotin, B.: Systematic Innovation. An Introduction to TRIZ, pp. 91–112. St. Lucie Press, Boca Raton (1998)
8. Han, Y.S.: The process of designing an ideal goal. In: Proceedings of The Korean Society of Creative Application Spring Conference (2018)
9. Stanford University News. https://news.stanford.edu/2017/09/04/sending-excess-heat-sky/
10. National Refrigerant Inc.: National Refrigerant Reference guide (2016).www.refrigerants.com/pdf/NRI-RefRefGuideINT-2016.pdf
11. Fey, V., Rivin, E.: Innovation on Demand. Cambridge University Press, NewYork (2005)
12. Honeywell, HCFC Retrofit Guidelines. https://www.fluorineproducts-honeywell.com/refrigerants/wp-content/uploads/2015/06/1667-Solstice-N40-Retrofit-Guideline-v1.pdf
13. Altshuller, G.S.: The Innovation Algorithm (In Korean Translation version) (2011)
14. Mann, D.: Hands-on Systematic Innovation for Technical Systems. IFR Press, Clevedon (2007)
15. Mann, D.: Design Without Compromise: A New Perspective on Refrigeration and Heat Pump Technologies. Systematic Innovation, Bristol (1999)

Enhancing Eco-Design Methods Using TRIZ Tools: the Case of ECOFAIRE

Fatima Zahra Ben Moussa[1(✉)], Fatima Ezzahra Essaber[1], Rachid Benmoussa[1], and Sébastien Dubois[2]

[1] SyLPRO/ENSA Marrakech, University of Cadi Ayyad, Marrakech, Morocco
benmoussafatimazahra@gmail.com
[2] LGECO/INSA Strasbourg, Strasbourg, France

Abstract. Green design is a relevant research topic because of the need of powerful and confirmed systematic methods that can support companies in their efforts to develop green products within acceptable time and costs.

TRIZ, as a theory of invention problem-solving has proven its effectiveness in stimulating designer's creativity in several areas. Therefore, the main research question we address in this research is the following: how can TRIZ tools enhance the ideality of green-design methods?

This paper presents an exploratory analysis of this question. First, our methodology aims to study the weakness of an open Eco-design method known as ECOFAIRE using a general problem solving methods characterization. Then, it attempts to enhance the ideality of ECOFAIRE through a reverse engineering process that has been applied to an eco-product known as Ecodistrib. As a result, ECOFAIRE's ideality improvement assumptions with TRIZ tools are derived. The conclusion presents some perspectives to validate these assumptions and move towards a systematic approach for Ecodesign based on ECOFAIRE.

1 Introduction

Fast industrial growth and technological advances have recently raised many environmental concerns. As a result, industrial companies are expected to become more environmentally responsible and reduce their negative environmental impact by applying new technologies and especially by delivering eco-friendly products. Additionally, environmental regulations developed recently by the European Union called energy using product have motivated engineers and designers to more heavily focus on how to create more environmentally friendly products.

Several methods exist for eco-design, to assess and improve environmental impacts [1]. The International Organization for Standardization ISO issued numerous norms, guidelines, and tools. For example, the ISO14040:2006 describes the principles and framework for life cycle assessment (LCA), ISO14044:2006 provides LCA guidelines, and ISO14006:2011 provides guidelines to implement Eco-Design as part of an environmental management system (EMS) within companies. A number of methods and tools have been developed to support the process of eco-innovation in the last two decades. To the best-known methods belong Eco-Compass, Life Cycle Design Strategy (LiDS Wheel), Sustainability Circle, EcoDesign PILOT, Eco-Ideation Tool, Value

Published by Springer Nature Switzerland AG 2019
R. Benmoussa et al. (Eds.): TFC 2019, IFIP AICT 572, pp. 350–367, 2019.
https://doi.org/10.1007/978-3-030-32497-1_29

Mapping Tool, Design for Environment (DfE) and Quality Function Deployment for Environment (QFDE), EcoASIT, Eco-ideation stimulation meso-mechanisms ESMs, Green Engineering with 12 Principles of Green Engineering, and other methods, presented in a comparative study of strategy and ideation-oriented eco-innovation tools [2]. In the field of process engineering should be mentioned in first place Green Process Engineering and Process Intensification (PI), Process Design for Sustainability (PDfS), and other approaches.

However, green design remains a relevant research topic because of the lack of powerful and confirmed systematic methods that can support companies in their efforts to develop green products within acceptable time and costs.

To overcome this lack, several works have addressed this issue. We focus in this paper on the ones that deal with TRIZ (a Russian acronym of "Theory of Inventive Problem Solving"). TRIZ, as a theory for inventive problem resolution has proven its effectiveness in stimulating designer's creativity in several areas. In green design, several TRIZ utilization attempts exist. The references [1–3] have largely addressed this issue.

With regard to eco-innovation, the authors in [1] defines primary and secondary eco-engineering contradictions and conceptualizes a correlation matrix between the eco-requirements for prediction of typical eco-contradictions in the field of processes involving solids handling. The implementation of eco-friendly solutions often causes secondary problems, and the application of the TRIZ-based approaches helps to identify these secondary problems, to predict and creatively solve eco-contradictions in advance, without efficiency losses. Additionally, a set of 20 TRIZ inventive principles most frequently used in environmental innovation was extracted from an analysis of a large number of patent and a process intensification technologies. The paper [2] focuses on the comparison of the ideation mechanisms during the eco-ideation phase, to help users generate relevant ideas with a strong potential of environmental impact reduction. In addition to that, some case studies are performed to compare the adapted creativity tool for eco-innovation, regarding its performance.

This research also validated the need to place greater emphasis on the ideation phase in the process of eco-innovation. Indeed, environmental knowledge, ideation mechanisms and the structuring of the session are interdependent factors to consider in order to optimize the eco-ideation session and to be closer to the industrial reality. The paper [3] presents a systemic literature review of TRIZ use in eco-design. Indeed, the paper provides information about what is currently performed in connection to creativity methods, when TRIZ is combined with LCA, LCE Eco-efficiency and other integrated methods for eco-design process.

Despite of all of the existing scientific contribution of TRIZ in eco-innovation summarized above, the literature doesn't show the existence of a powerful and systematic approach to green design. Therefore, the main research question we address is the following: "How can TRIZ tools enhance the ideality of green-design methods?".

To deal with this question, the paper aims to present a first exploratory analysis of the contribution of TRIZ tools to green design methods systematization based on a case study. In fact, the main goal of this study is to analyze ECOFAIRE in order to improve its ideality through TRIZ tools utilization. ECOFAIRE is a method proposed by the Ecodesign groups of the ECOFAIRE program. It has been proposed as a guide to promote and facilitate the integration of eco-design in small and medium-sized businesses in any sector of activity [4].

Our methodology is to study a green designed product known as Ecodistrib and to define how ECOFAIRE could have been used by anticipation in the ecological design process using TRIZ tools in the phases suffering from methodological lack. As a result, this study will lead to a first formulation of "TRIZ-ECOFAIRE", a systematic approach to ecological products design based on ECOFAIRE and TRIZ Tools.

The remainder of this paper is organized as follows. Section 2 introduces the background, including the TRIZ originality for problem solving, TRIZ in eco-design, Problem solving Methods characterization, and the ECOFAIRE method characterization. Section 3 presents a reverse engineering process applied to an eco-product known as Ecodistrib in order to enhance the ideality of ECOFAIRE. Section 4 presents the different hypotheses of the first formulation of Triz-ECOFAIRE methodology. A conclusion and perspectives are provided in Sect. 5

2 Background

2.1 TRIZ Originality for Problem Resolution

TRIZ (Theory of Inventive Problem Solving), developed by Genrich Altshuller, is a problem-solving, analysis and forecasting theory derived from the study of patterns of invention in the patent literature. TRIZ was developed to assist engineers to systematically solve product design problems and develop next-generation technologies and products with less risk. TRIZ is an organized theory for problem solving, which can be applied for eco-design. Altshuller stated that TRIZ can be aimed for minimizing energy requirements, as well as complexity of engineering products.

There are some key concepts which make TRIZ very valuable for innovative design:

- Ideality, describes the technical system development direction. The ideal final result (IFR) of eco-products is to perform desired functions without any environmental impacts. Therefore, looking at eco-innovative design problems of products from an ideal final result perspective is usually a very good first step towards success.
- Resources, are all the means used in a system or its environment, to improve its overall performance. Identifying and using resources in a TRIZ approach can bring new ideas and effectively solve the problem, so as to get closer to the final ideal result.
- Contradiction, helps to eliminate the contradiction and avoid the conventional tradeoffs. Their exist two levels of formulation of the contradiction: the contradiction known as the "technical contradiction" (TC), which expresses the opposition between two evaluation parameters (EP) of a system, and the "physical contradiction" (PC) that defines two states for the system's action parameter (AP), satisfying each of its conflicting objectives.
- Laws of evolution of technical systems, provides a means to reveal how systems evolve, predict the directions of evolve, and ultimately control the evolution.

In addition, The TRIZ theory includes methods for problem analysis and idea generation. These methods and tools can be classified according to three different categories:

- Tools for overcoming psychological inertia. The objective of these tools is to overcome the rigidity in the way of thought, and confinement of creativity in a certain pattern of thinking. Several tools for releasing psychological inertia are available in TRIZ, we can mention among them: (1) the nine-screen method (multi-screen vision), (2) Dimension-Time-Cost operators, and (3) smart little men method.
- Tools for solving technical and physical contradictions. Several methods and tools were created by Genrich Altshuller to solve the different types of contradictions, and to guide the designer towards generic solutions, as (1) the Matrix of solving technical contradictions, (2) the 40 inventive principles to solve technical contradictions, and (3) the 11 separation principles to solve physical contradictions.
- Standard solutions for solving system problems without the need of identifying contradictions. They are usually applied to correct the undesired interaction between two parts of a system.

2.2 TRIZ in Eco-Design

In the existing literature, a significant number of methods and proposals of integrating TRIZ with eco-design methods are proposed. As stated in the previous section, TRIZ is an organized method for problem solving, which is considered as supporting ideation and creativity component of eco-innovation and eco-design. TRIZ can be also used for minimizing energy requirements, as well as complexity of engineering environmentally friendly products [5, 6]. To comply with this purpose, several works are proposed in scientific literature dealing with the combination or the integration of TRIZ with other eco-design techniques, such as life Cycle Assessment (LCA), QFD (Quality Function Deployment) and CBR (Case Based Reasoning) to help designers achieve easily environmental design objectives. For example, in [7], an approach based on the integration of LCA, and eco-design guidelines converge in an integrated design for environment methodology. Rather new models have been developed to integrate the TRIZ theory and existing eco-design tools, with the aim of facilitating eco innovative product design. In [8], the author mentions an experiment within eco-design, and proposed a design methodology to support environmentally consciousness design of products by the integration of LCA, QFD, and TRIZ. The above- mentioned ideas are further developed in [9], which suggests the combination of QFD and TRIZ for an improved product life cycle management that supports knowledge codification and reuse. Another methodology is also presented in [10], that integrates the CBR and TRIZ methods is proposed. CBR can obtain the desired functional characteristics of a new design in an efficient way, and the TRIZ method ensures that designers can easily achieve design objectives due to the techniques provided by different technology fields. In [11], the authors elaborated an evolution of this approach and suggested integrating the TRIZ and CRB methods with Simplified LCA(s). In [12] the authors proposed an approach based on the integration of LCA and TRIZ eco guidelines, with the aim of supporting the implementation of the eco-design approach in small and medium European enterprises. The application of TRIZ eco guidelines help to develop alternatives or modifications to a given system to reduce its environmental impact. Finally, the last example of this application of TRIZ can be found in [13], where the authors developed an ARIZ based on the Life cycle engineering (LCE) model, to implement the eco-designs of products.

In addition to the synergetic application of TRIZ with eco-design tools, the scientific literature provides also papers that proposed an adaptation of TRIZ methods or tools to eco-design domain. For example, in [14] the authors formulated and linked the seven eco-friendly elements developed by the World Business Council for Sustainable Development (WBCSD) for green product design to the inventive principles to construct a new table for inventive principles. In [10, 11], two different methods for green product design are proposed. The first is based on the application of inventive principles with laws of evolution and the principle of Ideality to help designers focus on concepts that minimize energy requirements and the complexity of engineering products. The second one is based on the laws of evolution of TRIZ to develop innovative approaches to solve design problems. In a similar manner, [15] propose a step by step procedure based on the application of the Laws of evolution, substance field resources, ideality and the technical contradictions, to solve problems related to green product design. Another example which establishes the link between eco-efficiency and laws of evolution is presented in [16], where the authors present an innovative methodology to help designers to predict technological evolutions for more environmentally friendly products, by identifying the relationship between the strategies of the Eco-Design Strategy Wheel and the TRIZ evolution trends.

2.3 Problem Solving Methods Characterization

There are several standard techniques to search for a solution: non-systematic research techniques known as «Brainstorming»; Systematic research techniques also called "Systematic trials and errors" and systematic analysis of the problematic situation. Unlike the first two techniques, finding solutions in "Systematic analysis of the problematic situation" techniques are based on search space reducing. In this approach, the question that arises globally is "WHY does the problem exist?" and we try to develop or converge towards the solution by reducing the search space by answering this question. The model type of these techniques involves the following steps:

1. "Recognize the problem": consists of understanding the problem, knowing exactly where the problem lies, or measuring the problem, etc.
2. "Analyze the problem": tries to answer various questions to understand why the problem exists, what are the causes of the problem, what are the parameters and the factors that influence the problem, what is the desired result to eliminate the problem, etc.
3. "Synthesize Solution Concepts": formulates solution ideas called also conceptual solutions (to clearly distinguish from technical solutions).

4. "Concretize the solutions" seeks to transform the idea of solution or the conceptual solution into a concrete and applicable technical solution to solve the problem posed in the first step.
5. Logically the last step seeks to "evaluate the technical solutions" developed.

In general, each solution research method can be characterized by comparison of its flow logic with the model-type steps presented previously.

Indeed, the use of the Table 1 makes it possible to identify, for the considered method, the steps which correspond to the "recognition of the problem", "the analysis of the problem", "the identification of the conceptual solution", "the implementation of the solution" on the technical or application level as well as the evaluation of the solution. The tools used in each step are also identified. Also, by analyzing the tools used in each step of the considered method, we can deduce its nature and decide whether it is Unstructured, Semi Structured or Structured.

An unstructured step is performed randomly. His success depends heavily on analyst skill and know-how. The result obtained is uncertain and subjective.

A step described as semi structured one relies on reasoning and a precise logic to converge towards the desired result. It has a kind of roadmap to follow. However, the phases of this reasoning logic taken in isolation are unstructured. They do not operate the logic of reducing search space.

Conversely, a step described as Structured relies on a reasoning and a precise logic that makes it possible to converge towards the desired result in an algorithmic way. The reasoning could be based on a knowledge base, a set of good practices or any other type of expert systems. The result thus depends on the quality of the available knowledge and not only the analyst's know-how.

To conclude, if we analyze the nature of the steps of any problem solving method, we can deduce the standard technique to which it belongs and its capacity to provide original and quality solutions. Thus, a problem-solving method that has all the steps of the model-type (whether these steps are structured or not) is a "Systematic analysis of the problematic situation" method. A method that does not have the "Analyze the problem" step is either "non-systematic" method (brainstorming), or "systematic" (Trials and Errors) one. It depends on how the "Synthesize Solution Concepts" step unfolds. A method that has "unstructured" steps is of lower quality, it can be improved. The ideal method has all its stages structured. Thus, each method can evolve towards its ideality by improving the quality of its stages.

2.4 The ECOFAIRE Methodology

ECOFAIRE Presentation. The French ECOFAIRE program was organized and conducted by SEM Pays de Loire in collaboration with the environmental consulting firm EVEA between 2006 and 2008 [4]. This program aims to "promote and facilitate the development of environmentally friendly products". A collaborative study was conducted with companies, industrial designers and engineers. The methodological tool ECOFAIRE is part of this research work. It is composed of two introductory sheets followed by 18 others, to be used in five chronological stages: "Scope and stakes",

"Initial environmental assessment", "Solution search", "Evaluation of solutions", "Results and communication". Non-expert users are targeted here, whether they belong to industry or academia. On this paper, 9 analysis approaches are used. The E1 (3.1) approach proposes an analysis allowing a reference product to be assessed on six aspects combining life cycle thinking specially and environmental impacts to get a better review about it [2]. Concerning the E2 (3.1), this approach takes stock of the different phases raised during cycle E1 in a way to detect the environmental issues related to each stage with its risk of impact which depends of the stage and its stakes. E7/E8 approach (3.1) aims to identify and prioritize the aspects and impacts of each level of the end-of-life cycle of a reference product according to a ranking and motivations. About the ES1/ES2/ES3 (3.5), they allow to establish a comparison of solutions according to environmental indicators between a product and a reference product to get a view of the environmental consequences using ES2 wich is a DSI (Decision Support Instrument) while the ES2 is a visualization medium. R1 and R2 (3.3), allows to search for solutions by establishing an idea about different design choices that we can make by each level as well as the source of the solution. The operation of "Solution search" relies on "Synthesizing solution concepts" by the Eco design wheel (R1) and the checklist (R2).

ECOFAIRE Characterization. If we analyze the ECOFAIRE method, we notice that:

1. "Environmental Assessment of Product Reference" coincides well with the step "recognize the problem" using "R1, R2, E7/8" forms.
2. "Solution search" is consistent with "Synthesizing solution concepts" using the Eco design wheel (R1) and the checklist (R2).
3. "Evaluate the technical solution" coincides well with the step "recognize the problem" using the "ES1, ES2, ES3" forms
4. The steps "Analyze the problem" and "Realize the solutions" of the model-type are not covered by ECOFORM.

If we analyze the nature of the steps covered by the ECOFAIRE method, we notice that they are semi-structured because the analyst has a roadmap consisting of a multitude of forms and tools that guide him to identify solutions. But the answer provided in each form is subjective and strongly depends on the analyst's know-how.

The analysis of the Table 1 shows that the ECOFAIRE Model belongs to "Systematic Analysis of the Problematic Situation" techniques. The fact that some of its stages are not covered and that those covered are semi-structured, ECOFAIRE is not a complete method for Eco design problem solving that can insure original quality solutions (Table 1).

Table 1. Characterization of ECOFAIRE method

Model-Type steps	Recognize the problem	Analyze the problem	Synthesize Solution Concepts	Concretize the solutions	Evaluate the technical solutions
Ecofaire steps	Environmental Assessment of the RP	None	Search for solutions	None	Evaluation of the envisaged solutions
Ecofaire tools	***CE4:*** environmental expectations and requirements of the different actors ***E1:*** Life cycle description in first approach of the reference product ***E2:*** Environmental issues as a first step ***E7/E8:*** Identification and characterization of environmental aspects	No tool available	R1: Eco-design wheel R2: Check list	No tools	***ES1:*** comparison of solutions according to environmental indicators ***ES2:*** decision support ***ES3:*** visualization of the environmental consequences of design choices
Nature	Semi structured	–	Semi structured	–	Semi structured

3 Towards Triz-EcoFaire: A Case Study: «Ecodistrib»

Ecodistrib is a distributor of different types of liquid detergents installed in supermarkets to replace the act of purchasing cans of disposable detergents. This case is available on the following link: https://www.eco-conception.fr/exemples/h/eco2distrib-ecodistributeur.html.

Fig. 1. Ecodistrib

3.1 Recognize the Problem

This step consists of rolling out the CE4, E1, E2 and E7/E8 forms for the reference product: Detergent bottle (Fig. 2, 3, Tables 2, 3 and 4).

Table 2. Expectations and environmental requirements (CE4)

Chain of actors	Expectations and environmental requirements Specify whether explicit or implicit (=not formulated, or assumed)
Suppliers	
Transport and logistics subcontractors	Less packaging to ship
Top management of the company	Cost reduction
Departments of the company (marketing, BE, employees, ...)	Manufacturing: less packaging, gain energy
Clients, Specifiers, Other intermediaries	Super and hypermarkets: brand image, show implication in DD
End users	Eco-friendly products

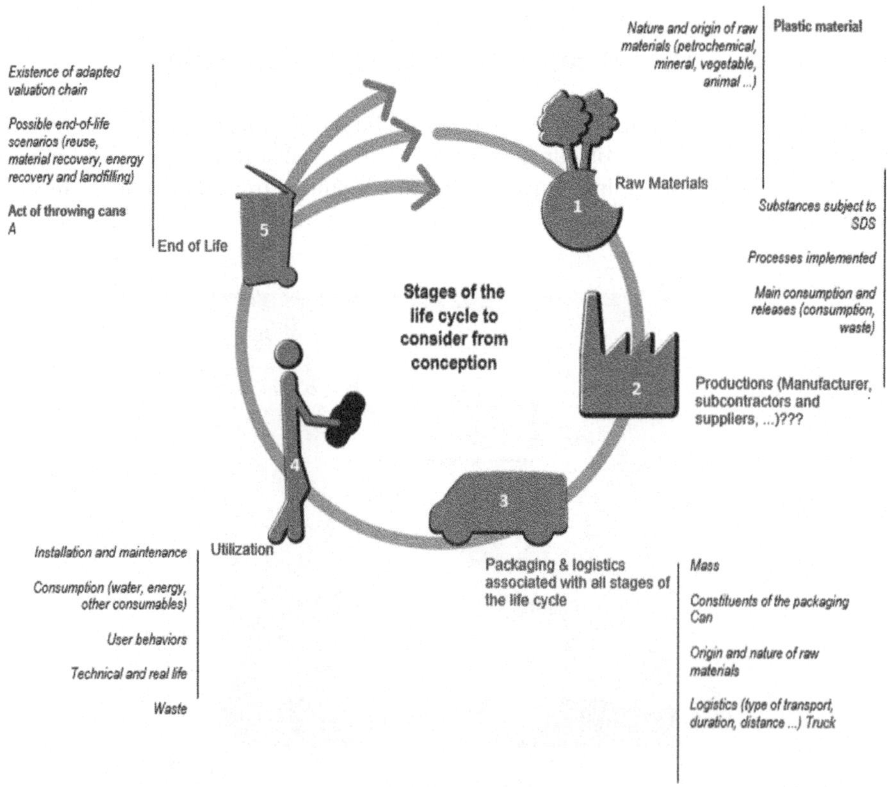

Fig. 2. Life cycle analysis of the reference product (E1)

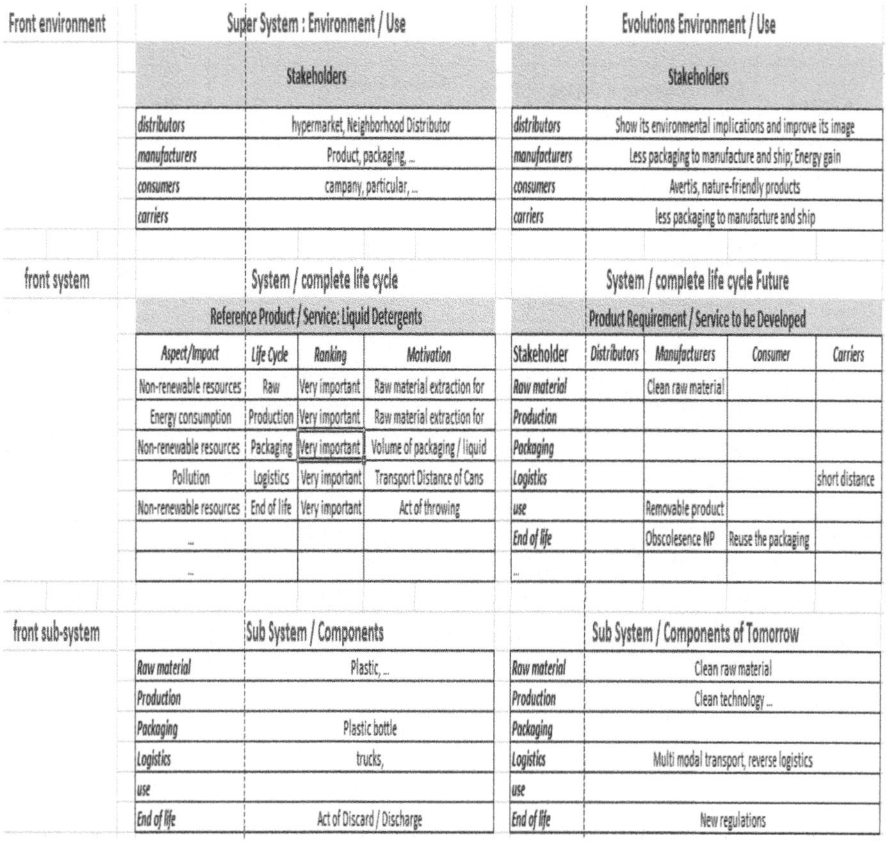

Fig. 3. 9 Screens tool

Table 4. Identification and prioritization of aspects and impacts (E7/E8)

	Aspects or impacts	Life cycle steps involved	Ranking Very important Important Secondary	Ranking motivations
A	Non-renewable resources	Raw materiel	Very important	Extraction raw material for packaging
B	Energy consumption	Production	Very important	Manufacturing packaging
C	Non-renewable resources	Packaging	Very important	Packing volume/liquid quantity
D	Pollution	Logistics	Very important	Transmission Distance of Cans
E	Non-renewable resources	End of life	Very important	Act of throwing
F				

Table 3. Environmental issues (E2)

Étapes	Environmental issues of the product	Risk of impacts				Your details, comments
		-- Bad	- Medium	+ Good	?	
1 – Raw Materials	Preservation of resources: Use of a threatened or limited resource (primary forests, oil ...)	--				
	Recycled source material					
	Origin of materials (distance and optimized means of transport)					
	...					
2 - Productions *- Subcontractons / suppliers* *- Maker*	Polluting processes					
	Hazardous construction waste, non-recyclable waste					
	Geographical situation (local, national ...) for subcontractors					
	...					
3a – Packaging	Optimized packaging in mass or volume					
	Reusable packaging	--				
	Shuttle packaging ...					
	Packaging integrating recovery channels for recovery					
	...					
3b - Logistics	Optimized logistics (distances, filling, full returns ...)					
	Types of transport (combined rail-road, fluvial, maritime, Euro V standard trucks ...)					
	Recovery during delivery: user products, packaging ...					
	...					
4 – Utilization	Consumption of energy, water ...					
	Using consumables					
	Features tailored to user needs					
	Waste production					
	User information and awareness					
	Life adapted to the reality of use and technological developments					
	Other (nuisances, emissions ...)					
	...					
5 – End of Life	Recyclable (existing channels AND possibility of dismantling the product for distribution in the sectors)	--				
	No "clean-up" of the product needed before recovery	--				
	...					

3.2 Analyze the Problem

ECOFAIRE doesn't present any tool for problematic analysis situation. We propose to use for this issue the TRIZ contradiction system. Thus, the main contradiction resolved by Ecodistrib is the following:

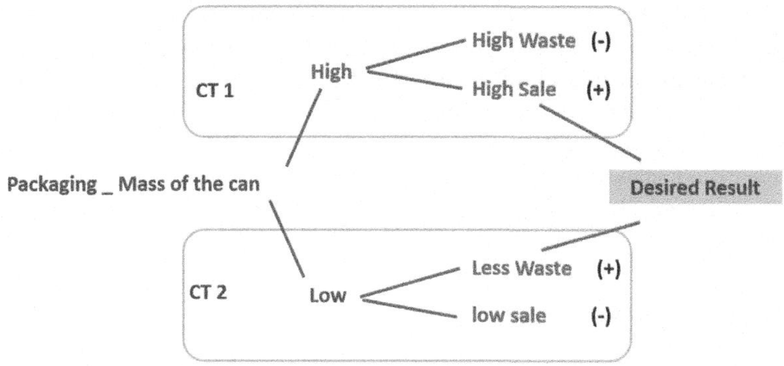

Fig. 4. The system of contradictions of EcoDistrib

3.3 Synthesize Solution Concepts

The search for solutions by ECOFAIRE's tools R1 and R2, allows drawing up the following table. This table presents the different design choices considered in Eco-Distrib by stage of the life cycle as well as the source of the solution (Table 5).

Table 5. Source of choices made in EcoDistrib

Design Choice	Production	Packaging logistics	End use	End of life
Demountable	None		R1: Lifespan/Adapted/Evolution/Modular	
Unplanned obsolescence			R1: lifetime/long since the start	
Close production place		R1: transport/Proximity		
Reusable packaging				
Close place of distribution		R1: transport/Proximity		
Distribution system			R1: consumption/standby mode	
Recoverable material				R1: Valorization/incineration/energy recovery
Local raw material source		R1: transport/Proximity		
Sealing			–	
Energy source			R1: Consumption/Energy/saved	

Two remarks emerge from the use of these two tools:

- The difficulty of using the R1 eco-design wheel. Indeed, this wheel doesn't give a procedure to choose the relevant principles. On the other hand, the list of solutions seems incomplete for the EcoDistrib case.
- The R2 checklist details the choices listed in R1. Its use is also difficult and does not aspire to trust, …

The search for solutions by the traditional tools of the TRIZ doesn't seem to find the choices made in the case EcoDistrib. Indeed, the solution adopted to solve the technical contradiction is to replace the act of buying the liquid in a disposable packaging by the act of buying the liquid in a reusable packaging through a distributor to resolve the contradiction presented in the Fig. 4.

The two parameters of the technical contradiction do not correspond to any parameter of the classical TRIZ matrix. This seems unsuitable for use in the field of eco-design. The analysis of the solution adopted in the case of EcoDistrib shows that none of the 40 principles invented, nor principles of separation could be exploited to achieve it.

3.4 Concretize the Solutions

According to a technical point of view, the purchase of the liquid is done by filling from a distributor. This solution could not have been generated by the use of traditional TRIZ tools such as effect pointers.

3.5 Evaluate the Technical Solutions

The comparison between Ecodistrib and the reference product "Can" as well as the visualization of the environmental consequences of Ecodistrib are presented in forms ES1, ES2 and ES3 of ECOFAIRE (Tables 6, 7 and 8).

Table 6. Comparison of solutions according to environmental indicators (ES1)

	Reference product **Can**	Proposition 1 **Ecodistrib**
Indicator 1 Name: **Waste Volume**	Important	Low
Indicator 2 Name: **Energy consumption**	Important	Low
Indicator 3 Name: **Pollution**	Important	Low

Table 7. Decision support (++very important; +important; - week; – very week) (ES2)

Solutions	Interests Customers/Users	Costs interest and Feasibility	Environment interests
Reference Product: **Can**			
Proposition 1 Description: **Ecodistrib**	++	++	++

Table 8. Visualization of the environmental consequences of design choices (ES3)

Conception choice	Production	Packaging Logistics	Use	End of life	Consequences for the environment
Disassembly	No final assembly (welds)		Repairable and evolutionary		Raw material economy, life extension
Unplanned obsolescence			Repairable and evolutionary		raw material economy, life extension
Close production area		Less transport			Energy saving, pollution
Reusable packaging					Raw material economy
Close production area		Less transport			Energy saving, pollution
Distribution system			Quantity bought at most fair		Raw material saving
Recoverable material				Energy recovery	Raw material saving
Local raw material source		Less transport			Energy saving, pollution
Sealing			No risk of liquid loss		Nuisance man: Cleanliness, raw material saving
Energy Source			Low Energy		Energy saving

The use of EcoForm forms also leads to several remarks:

- It is necessary to conduct LCA (life cycle analysis) to arrive to quantified indicators for the ES1 form
- The evaluation of different interests in ES2 is qualitative
- Overall, despite their sufficiency to evaluate and compare eco-design solutions, ECOFAIRE documents are not structured because their uses depend on the analyst's competence.

4 Hypotheses of First Formulation of Triz-ECOFAIRE

Conducting an inverse engineering analysis on the Ecodistrib case made it possible to identify a set of ECOFAIRE improvement hypotheses by the TRIZ tools. It also allowed to highlight a set of disadvantages compared to ECOFAIRE tools themselves.

The following table (Table 9) explains how can ECOFAIRE enhance its ideality by introducing TRIZ Tools in its incomplete or lower quality steps. However, Triz tools need to be updated to fit within Eco design and ECOFAIRE context. We describe in the following, how each tool introduced has to be adapted.

4.1 H1: Multiscreen Tool

The multiscreen tool can play its classic role in predicting the future eco-designed system. But for that it must be adapted to include the synthesis of the documents of ECOFAIRE of the analysis phase (See Fig. 3) in particular:

- The expectations and environmental requirements of the various actors
- The description of the life cycle
- Environmental issues
- Identification of environmental aspects and impacts.

4.2 H2: System of Contradiction

The contradiction system of TRIZ keeps all its importance to really understand the problem and to reveal the desired result. However, the terms of the EPV Model must be adapted to the context of eco-design, as follows (Fig. 5):

- Element: must reflect a stage of the life cycle (raw material, logistics packaging and transport, production, use, end of life), …
- Action Parameter: must reflect an environmental aspect from the context of the study. The environmental aspect is “an element of the activities, products or services of an organism likely to interact with the environment”.
- Evaluation Parameter 1: Must reflect an Environmental Impact. The environmental impact is “any modification of the environment, negative or beneficial, resulting totally or partially from the environmental aspects of an organism” (Exhaustion of resources, damage to biodiversity, air pollution, water pollution, soil pollution, waste,…).
- Evaluation parameter 2: must reflect an important outcome indicator in the context of the study to assess economic performance (use parameter).

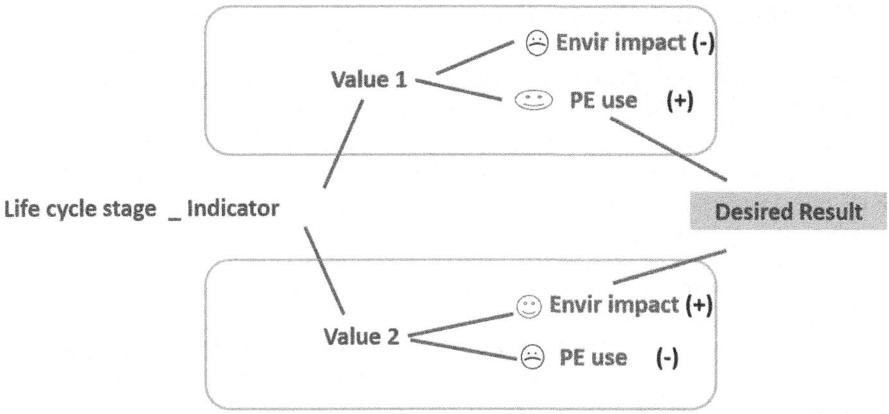

Fig. 5. Adaptation of the system of contradictions to the context of eco-design

4.3 H3: Principals

The principles of separation and the 40 inventive principles do not seem adaptable to the context. On the other hand, a new tool can be developed that links TRIZ's contradiction system to the principles stated in the R1 eco-design wheel and the R2 checklist.

4.4 H4: Effects Pointer

The base of the physical effect pointer of Triz also seems unsuitable for the case of EcoDistrib. It would also be wise to develop an effect base specific to the context of Eco-design.

Table 9. TRIZ-ECOFAIRE characterization

Model-Type steps	Recognize the problem	Analyze the problem	Synthesize Solution Concepts	Concretize the solutions	Evaluate the technical solutions
Ecofaire steps	Environmental Assessment of RP	None	Searching solutions	None	Assessment of the envisaged solutions
Existing Ecofaire tools	*CE4:* environmental expectations and requirements of the different actors *E1:* Life cycle description in first approach of the reference product *E2:* Environmental issues as a first step *E7/E8:* Identification and characterization of environmental aspects	None	*R1:* Eco-design wheel *R2:* Check list	None	*ES1:* comparison of solutions according to environmental indicators *ES2:* decision support *ES3:* visualization of the environmental consequences of design choices
Improvement by TRIZ	Adapt the 9 screens tool	Adapt the system of contradictions	To develop	To develop	Improve the formalization
Expected Nature	Semi Structured	Semi Structured	Structured	Structured	Semi structured

5 Conclusion and Perspectives

The literature has shown the existence of several attempts to adapt Eco-design methods through the TRIZ tools. However, this work presents ECOFAIRE's first adaptation attempt in this direction. This study aims first to characterize ECOFAIRE according to a model that we have developed by ourselves in this paper, then to state hypotheses of adaptation TRIZ tools to fill the limits of ECOFAIRE.

Several results emerge from this study. They can be summarized in the following:

- The adaptation of the 9 screens tool so that it can integrate the specificities of the design of ecological products.
- The adaptation of the EPV model of description of the TRIZ system of contradictions so that it can stand out in a structured way the conflicts to solve in the process of eco-design.
- The emergence, through the exploratory case study of EcoDistrib, of the inadequacy hypothesis of the classical tools of the TRIZ (40 principles, the principles of separation and the TRIZ matrix) with the context of eco-design.

In light of these results and the exploratory approach conducted through the Ecodistrib case, several perspectives emerge:

- Conduct other case studies to confirm the ECOFAIRE improvement assumptions made in this work.
- Make a comparison between the eco-design methods that attempt to adapt the TRIZ tools to eco-design.
- Develop, in the case of ECOFAIRE, a tool that links the new system of contradiction to the principles set out in the eco-design wheel R1 and the checklist R2.
- Develop a tool similar to the effect pointers for the Ecodesign context.

References

1. Pavel Livotova, T., et al.: Eco-innovation in process engineering: contradictions, inventive principles and methods. Thermal Sci. Eng. Prog. **9**, 52–65 (2019)
2. Tyl, B., Legardeur, J., Millet, D., Vallet, F.: A comparative study of ideation mechanisms used in eco-innovation tools. J. Eng. Des. **25**(10–12), 325–345 (2014)
3. Buzuku, S., Shnai, I.: A systematic literature review of TRIZ used in Eco-Design. J. Eur. TRIZ Assoc. **02-2017**}(04) (2017)
4. ECOFAIRE, https://www.ademe.fr/ecofaire-loutil
5. Altshuller, G.S.: Creativity As an Exact Science. CRC Press, New York (1984)
6. Altshuller, G.S.: Ariz, pp. 1956–1985 (1985)
7. Cappelli, F., Cappelli, F., Delogu, M., Pierini, M.: Integration of LCA and EcoDesign guideline in a virtual cad framework. Proc. LCE **2006**, 185–188 (2006)
8. Sakao, T.: A QFD-centred design methodology for environmentally conscious product design. Int. J. Prod. Res. **45**(18–19), 4143–4162 (2007)
9. Vezzetti, E., Moos, S., Kretli, S.: A product lifecycle management methodology for supporting knowledge reuse in the consumer packaged goods domain. Comput. Des. **43**(12), 1902–1911 (2011)

10. Yang, C.J., Chen, J.L.: Accelerating preliminary eco-innovation design for products that integrates case-based reasoning and TRIZ method. J. Clean. Prod. **19**(9–10), 998–1006 (2011)
11. Yang, C.J., Chen, J.L.: Forecasting the design of eco-products by integrating TRIZ evolution patterns with CBR and Simple LCA methods. Expert Syst. Appl. **39**(3), 2884–2892 (2012)
12. Russo, D., Bersano, G., Birolini, V., Uhl, R.: European testing of the efficiency of TRIZ in eco-innovation projects for manufacturing SMEs. Procedia Eng. **9**, 157–171 (2011)
13. Chou, J.-R.: An ARIZ-based life cycle engineering model for eco-design. J. Clean. Prod. **66**, 210–223 (2014)
14. Liu, C., Chen, J.L.: Development of product green innovation design method. In: Proceedings Second International Symposium on Environmentally Conscious Design and Inverse Manufacturing, pp. 168–173 (2001)
15. Russo, D., Regazzoni, D., Montecchi, T.: Eco-design with TRIZ laws of evolution. Procedia Eng. **9**, 311–322 (2011)
16. Vidal, R., Salmeron, J.L., Mena, A., Chulvi, V.: Fuzzy Cognitive Map-based selection of TRIZ (Theory of Inventive Problem Solving) trends for eco-innovation of ceramic industry products. J. Clean. Prod. **107**, 202–214 (2015)

TRIZ Applications in Software Engineering

TRIZ, a Systematic Approach to Create Quantum Activation Function for Deep Learning's Hidden Layers, in Order to Make AI Explainable with Quantum Computer

Adehi Guehika(✉)

HEC Montréal, 3000 Chemin de la Côte-Sainte-Catherine, Montréal, QC H3T2A7, Canada
Adehi.guehika@hec.ca

Abstract. Artificial Intelligence (AI)'s market is growing very fast all over the world, along with Deep Learning (DL) technologies requiring more and more data and speed to process them, in healthcare, agriculture, automotive, security, and in among several other industries. However, despite this AI rapid and increasing market expansion, there are numerous related challenges need to be tackled. In this paper, the purpose is to show through another structured approach derived from ARIZ algorithm and some principles coined by TrizStartup movement [1], some of the problems deep learning industries are trying to handle. This paper shows how TRIZ can be applied to fix one of those AI problems. In fact, due to DL neural networks (NN) hidden layers, their outputs are not reliable. If an error occurs, how could human reproduce the issue? Human are not able to identify activated neurons to analyse root causes of this malfunction. Therefore, reliability issue from hidden layers versus rapid AI market skyrocket, data and speed processing, generates innovation problems. In order to resolve this, principle 35-parameter changes with Althshuler Matrix, little people, Su-Field analysis, seventy-six standards solutions, have been used to generate quantum functions. The result described in this paper is a new function called QuantumReLU (QReLU), created with Quantum computer in order to extend classical activation function ReLU. It is then possible to fire neuron with activation function QReLU, and to use quantum states to identify activated neurons within hidden layers. Thus, Triz systematic approach led switching neural networks algorithms from classical to quantum computer, and therefore to build deep learning NN on quantum computer, based on the new QReLU activation function.

Keywords: TRIZ · Deep learning · Quantum computer · QuantumReLU

1 Introduction

This paper's purpose is not to discuss all deep learning and neural networks mathematical details and complexities. This was already well done by Goodfellow, Bengio and Courville [2]. Based on ARIZ algorithm and TrizStartup principles, this paper will be structured on nine main points, see Fig. 1 and Table 1, to have a big picture.

Published by Springer Nature Switzerland AG 2019
R. Benmoussa et al. (Eds.): TFC 2019, IFIP AICT 572, pp. 371–387, 2019.
https://doi.org/10.1007/978-3-030-32497-1_30

Brief Overview on the Method or Approach We Used

We first started by hearing deep learning market voice (P1) in order to understand what the market is, who is leading the market, and in which region it is most likely used. This shows us how far African regions and others are let behind this ongoing AI and deep learning revolution and market expansion. Secondly, we defined some specific problems (P2) this deep learning market is facing in terms of needs or improvement issues. We selected one of those issues and focus on it for the next steps. Then, in the third point, we took decision (P3) to generate typical problems based on this chosen specific problems, in order to generalize it. This brought us to the fourth point concerning the typical problem definition (P4). And then, in the fifth one, we got some insights from innovators, experts or experiences around the world, out of deep learning scope (P5), in terms of grabbing ideas on what else could have been done elsewhere, outside DL markets in order to fix this typical problem with innovative and typical solution (P6). Then in the seventh section, we went through training phases (P7) to master some deep learning tools, technics software from current trends, to transition from typical solutions to specific solution. Then, in the point height, we proposed a specific solution (P8) to apply and fix the initial specific problem we point out earlier. This proposal was tested and validated internally in a short scale. The section nine, was the last point. It covered how the proposed solution could transform deep learning market (P9). We opened discussions and concluded.

Fig. 1. Perpetual innovation's transformation wheel, adapted from TrizStartup principles

Table 1. High level organization of the steps used for analysis on this current paper.

Steps	Description	Flow used
P1	Hearing deep learning's market voices	Decision flow
P2	Define deep learning specific problem	Action flow (ARIZ)
P3	Take critical or management decisions	Decision flow
P4	Generate typical problem	Action flow (ARIZ)
P5	Get some insights by learning from innovators, experts, or from elsewhere out of DL scope and environment	Decision flow
P6	Define typical solution based on P5	Action flow (ARIZ)
P7	If necessary, train your team to master TRIZ, otherwise call TRIZ experts for assistance	Decision flow
P8	Find your specific solution based on P6 and P7	Action flow (ARIZ)
P9	Now, with your specific solution on P8, go and transform your DL market, and if possible, impact the World	Decision and action flow (P9) and (P2) to reinitiate the wheel

2 Analysis

2.1 P1 - Hearing Deep Learning Market Voices: The Rapid AI Market's Skyrocket Expansion and Processing Speed Increased

PricewaterhouseCoopers [3] shows that global World GDP could be increased to $15.7 trillion, by 2030, due to Artificial intelligence technologies. See Table 2 to notice how far Chinese AI GDP is, compare to the other countries, and even regions of the World. In this, $1.2 trillion would be added for Africa and others.

Table 2. Importance of Chinese AI GDP compare to Others, adapted from PwC.

Regions	GDP in Trillion $ US by 2030
China	7,0
North America	3,7
Northern Europe	1,8
Africa, Oceania and other Asian Market	1,2
Developed Asia (without China)	0,9
Southern Europe	0,7
Latin America	0,5

Inside AI demand growth, there are also some initiative which are led by deep learning Fig. 2. And concerning Deep Learning per say, some researches conducted by companies such as Markets and Markets (MM) [4], and Market Research Future (MRF) [5], expressed some projections. Deep learning's market was worth USD 2.28 Billion in 2017, then 3.18 Billion in 2018 and is expected to reach USD 18.16 Billion by 2023. For the MRF, the research was structured by component, application (Image recognition, signal recognition, data mining), End-User industry (automotive, health-care, manufacturing, retail, agriculture, security, marketing). And for MM: The research methodology was based on studying annual and financial reports, presentations, press releases related to DL top players. They also discussed with experts and analysed some specialized white papers such as The Zettabyte era regarding the trends and Analytics. They both came out with similar results. **Deep learning compound annual growth rate (CAGR) will jump quickly to reach 41.7% from 2018 to 2023.** According to the previous studies, there are three segments in deep learning market. The first segment is related to component industry, and is also sub-segmented into hardware, software and services. The second one is about application, and the last one concern end-user industry. From the component segment, the software sub-segment will hold the biggest share during the forecast period 2018-2023. But in the meantime, services sub-segment will be growing with highest rate. In the software sub-segment for example, emphasis will be made on software frameworks and platforms/APIs with algorithms and codes available for hardware to perform deep learning programs. The following non-ordered list shows some of the main open platforms to test deep learning algorithms, assertions, and codes: TensorFlow [6], PyTorch [7], Keras [8], Apache MxVet [9], Caffee [10], Caffee2 [11], DeepLearning4J [12], and so on. Figure 3 shows how DL market is shared in different regions trough the World:

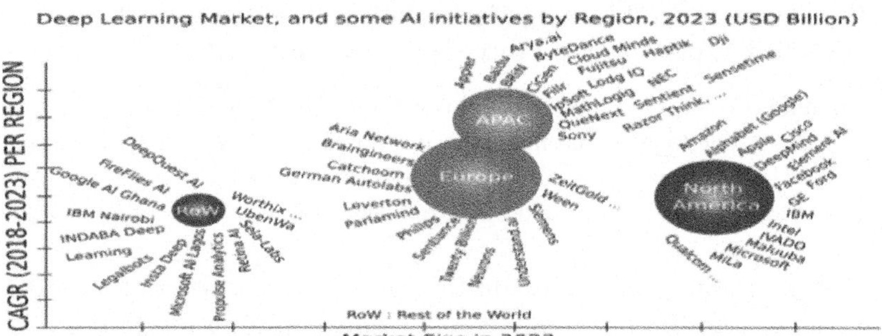

Fig. 2. DL market segments by region, based on MM

Figure 2 shows that deep learning initiatives are still so weak in rest of the World (RoW) region including Africa, and Latin America, even though, those regions could hugely work to generate their own DL applications based on biases adapted to cultural and local realities. Indeed, for emerging countries whose economies are based on agriculture, oil and gas exportations, for example, there are numerous possibilities to create deep learning applications to leverage their development. In agriculture, DL is widely used in several areas such as plant diseases early detections and diagnosed with image recognition, weed identification, plant classification, weather forecasting, yield prediction, fruit counting [13]. And DL could also be used for land and cover classification, soil moisture estimation, animal research and so on. In the next section we discussed some important challenges deep learning's market and industry are currently facing.

2.2 P2 - Defining Deep Learning Specific Problem

Quick Overview on Deep Learning Neural Networks Main Principle
Machine learning and Deep Learning are both branches of Artificial intelligence. Deep learning is a kind of crude imitation of how human brain works. It is also a kind of representation learning. And this one is also a sort of machine learning. See how Fig. 3 is showing the Venn diagram describing the relations between those concepts.

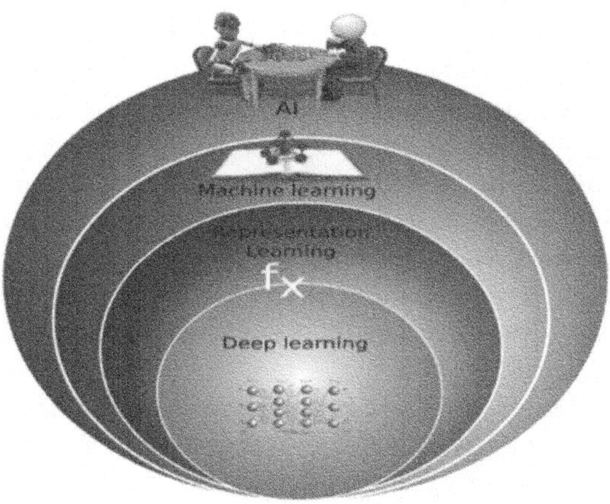

Fig. 3. AI to Deep Learning, adapted from Venn diagram, Goodfelow et al.

Difference Between Machine Learning (ML) and Deep Learning (DL)
The difference between them resides in the following. Machine learning uses algorithms to split data into significative parts and process them to take decision. Machine learning (ML) include supervise learning in which a human feed the machines and teach them with correct input-output. ML include also un-supervised learning through which a machine deduced its own output from recognized pattern, while given input were provided. ML use also reinforcing learning to observe gathered information while interacting with its environment and take actions in order to reduce risk and to optimise its rewards. DL is a subfield of ML. DL uses a layered structured algorithm so-called artificial neural network (NN), inspired by human brain's biological network, in order to analyse data with a kind of human logic, to draw its conclusions. But in case of inaccurate predictions, while ML need engineers or human operators to make some adjustments, DL can verify by it own if its prediction is accurate or not, by making intelligent human-like decisions. Basically, Deep learning classifies input information using layered neural networks. And those neural network (NN) are composed with multiple k-hidden layers of neurons fully connected between the input and output nodes.

Deep Learning, Speed versus Reliability Issues

There are numerous challenges discussed by AI experts on deep learning. But for the purpose of this paper, we will focus on some of them. In fact, details on deep learning limits and challenges were provided by Gary Marcus [14], professor at New York University and former AI head at Uber. There are also other issues such as the ones explained by professor Kunle Olukotun [15] from Stanford University whose explanation could be also benefitted to understand current Deep Learning limits.

- Deep Learning need data, thousands, billions, and now Zettabytes of data, in order to train their neural networks algorithms and to easily classify their outputs. (Problem 1)
- Speed of computation is now limited, according to Olukotun: "You've got these huge [computational] demands, but you have the slowing down of Moore's law," Olukotun said also: "The question is, how do you meet these demands while Moore's law slows" [16]. And for Greg Diamos [17] senior researcher at Baidu: "Today the job of training machine learning models is limited by compute, **if we had faster processors, we'd run bigger models**" (Problem 2)
- Deep learning lacks a mechanism to understand abstraction explicit verbal definition. It works better when there are thousands, millions or even billions of training examples, said Marcus (Problem 3).
- Deep learning is opaque, and **there is no transparency in the decision they make** based on patterns and correlations they generate through millions of data. This opacity can be critical in several scenario, and for example, medical treatment for patient, if any mistakes are made. **For Marcus, this lack of transparency is a potential liability** for financial trades, medical diagnosis, in which **human would like to understand how a given system made a given decision**. (Problem 4)

Our Selected Deep Learning Specific Problem

We reformulate all those issues as follow: As per Diamos, we want to run big models with neural networks, therefore we need to increase processors speeds. But in the meantime, we need to overcome this lack of transparency and any potential liability, as per Marcus, thus we need to preserve reliability. So, we want to improve the computing speed, but by doing so, the reliability of the neural network outputs becomes more and more worst, since this lack of transparency will be increased. How can we fix this innovative issue? Which decisions could we take in order to have this issue been resolved?

2.3 P3 - Tacking Decision: Where to Go? or Which Innovation Directions to Use so that We Can Fix This Specific Problem?

In this section we used innovation's 3 dimensional representations [18] shown in Fig. 4, in order to decide which direction was helpful to fix the specific problem defined in the previous section.

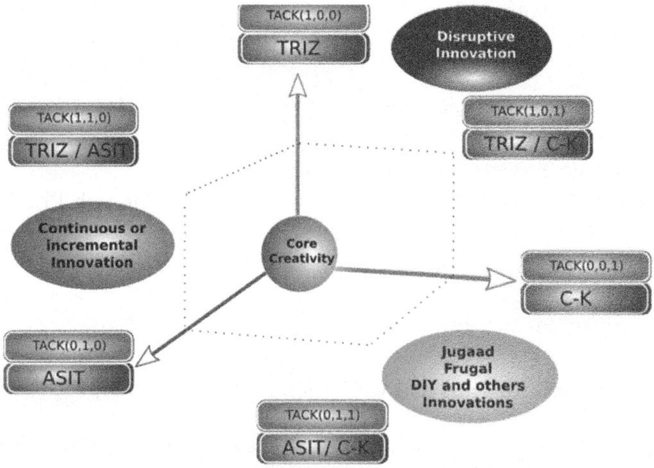

Fig. 4. Innovation directions, adapted from TrizStartup movement

Here:

- C-K [19] is defined as Concept – knowledge theory, a design theory to create the unknown,
- ASIT [20] is a method to help companies use their in-box creativity in order solve innovation problems. ASIT comes from TRIZ
- TRIZ 'Teoriya Resheniya Izobreatatelskikh Zadtch' is the (Russian) acronym for the "Theory of Inventive Problem Solving." Initiated by Altshuller [21].

The decision to use TRIZ, ASIT, or C-K, or any combination of those innovation and creativity theories, tools, and method depend of the following scenarios:

- Scenario 1: If the issue needs to be resolved by something based on completely unknown expression, then we use C-K to create that unknown by digging alternately from Concept to Knowledge, and vice-versa, until we reach knowledge or concept that can be used to fix the issue.
- Scenario 2: If the issue is formulated by a known expression, and if this issue required focusing on companies or organizations' internal resources to leverage their in-box creativity, by finding solutions from the problem's zone, then ASIT will be the direction to use to innovate.
- Scenario 3: If the formulated issue is with known expression, and if this time, we need to go out of the box, beyond our internal resources, and our engineering comfort zone, to grab some insights elsewhere in order to have the issue been resolved, then we will use TRIZ, as innovation direction.
- Between those extreme scenarios, we defined vector TACK (X, Y, Z), to position in 3 Dimensions, the decision regarding which innovation direction will be used to solve the issue. In fact, TACK stand for Triz Asit and C-K. From those TACK vectors we create 3 orthogonal innovation plans as following:

Breakthrough innovation plan:
Led by TRIZ: Tack (1, 0, 0) and C-K: Tack (0, 0, 1), through the following PLAN:

$$PLAN_{Breakthrough\ Innovation(TRIZ;C-K)} = P(Tack(1,0,0); Tack(0,0,1)) \quad (1)$$

Continuous or incremental innovation plan:
Led by ASIT: Tack (0, 1, 0) and TRIZ: Tack (1, 0, 0), through PLAN:

$$PLAN_{incremental\ Innovation(TRIZ;ASIT))} = P(Tack(1,0,0); Tack(0,1,0)) \quad (2)$$

Other innovation Jugaad, frugal innovation and others initiative such as DIY etc., pan:
Led by ASIT: Tack (0, 1, 0) and CK: Tack (0, 0, 1), through PLAN:

$$PLAN_{Jugaad;Frugal;Others(ASIT;C-K))} = P(Tack(0,1,0); Tack(0,0,1)) \quad (3)$$

As reminder, the specific issue was described as follow: *we want to improve the speed for computations for data processing. But, by doing so, the reliability of the neural network output becomes more and more worst, since this lack of transparency will be increased.* This issue in this case is about known expression with concepts such as «transparency» or «opacity» issue in neural networks due to hidden layers. So, we can use ASIT or TRIZ. In addition, this issue is a global issue, and it is not an issue that need to be dealt by a single company or organization, attempting to resolve it with their in-box creativity. Therefore, ASIT will not be used in priority. Instead, we will be starting with TRIZ to fix this issue. And if we want to generate a breakthrough innovation, we can use only TRIZ, or combine it with C-K, in the $PLAN_{Breakthrough\ Innovation(TRIZ;C-K)}$. And in this case any combination of TRIZ: Tack (1,0,0) vector and C-K: Tack (0,0,1) vector could be used. But for concision in this paper, we used, only TRIZ to fix this specific DL speed versus reliability issues.

2.4 P4 - Generating Typical Problem and Suggestions: Reliability Issue

In every single field where Deep Learning is used, it is making significant strides. This is true in speech recognition with deep recurrent neural network [22]. It is also true in image search without tag performed with deep convolution neural network. Todays, search ranking are made with deep neural network, email are smartly replied with feed-forward neural network combined with deep recurrent neural network. All those achievements made with deep learning, demonstrate how far and fast DL is expanding. We first used reinvention technics from Michael Orloff [23], to model and represent the specific issue. Secondly, we also used Su-Filed technique to represent another model of the same issue.

First Model of the Typical Problem Adapted from Reinvention Technics from Orloff [23]

Reinvention: eliminating neural network layers' opacity (Table 3)..

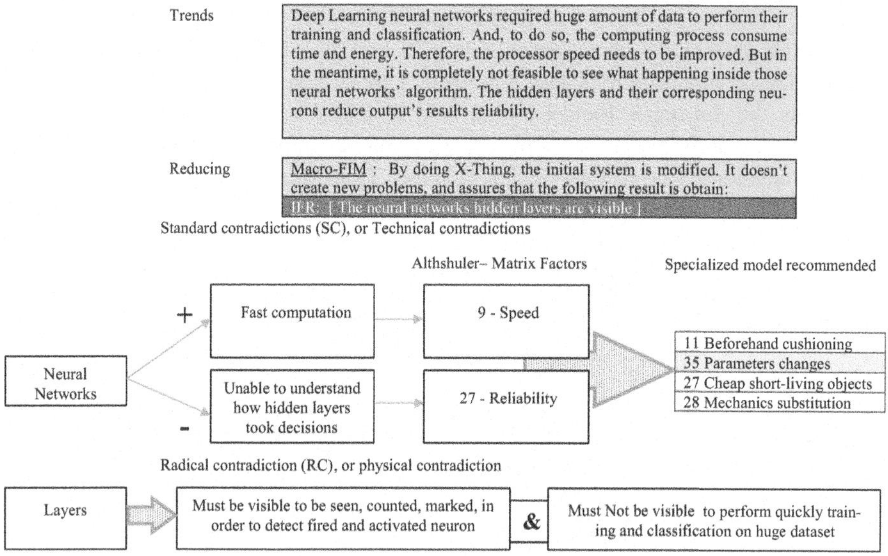

Table 3. Zooming expected for typical solution

Expected Zooming on the target typical solution	
Contradictions removed	Yes (this is a target decision we expected to get at the end)
Super-effects	The layers are visible, and now the outputs are reliable
Negative effects	The targeted typical solution will require digging on something hidden and invisible for human
Development trends	Possibility to create a path inside the neural network for any single output, from input feature to last output feature. And this could be done on all activated neurons inside the hidden layers. And any single neuron path will therefore make those layers become visible
Changes in the Ambient system	Activated neuron are visible, hidden layers are visible, and can be plot, extract, and interpretable
Extended uses	We can define new kind of jobs, for example, as Deep Learning Auditors, in case of trouble, they will be able to extract those paths, like working in a Plane Black-box after a crash, to analyze the reliable output, and at which point, on which layer, the issue emerged, and which neuron were involved in the issue, so that correctives actions could be taken for the current situation, but also to avoid them in the future
Beauty of the solution	Now the invisible world become visible in the deep learning universe

Second Model Used to Generate Typical Problem by Using Sub-field Analysis The current system needs to be improved. By digging in the 76 standard solutions, Class 2 and Class 3 are dominant classes to use to get a typical solution for this typical problem. In fact, as per Terninko, Domb, and Miller [24], Class 2 has some model to improve the system by changing it. Class 2, and its Class 2.2.2 gives us typical solution. This is also true for Class 3 as well. Typical solution from Class 2 is about: Developing the Substance-Field System. And its Class 2.2.2 is about: changing substance from a macro level to a micro level. Typical solution from Class 3 is about the System Transitions. And its Class 3.2.1. is about: Transition to the Micro-Level (Fig. 5 and Table 4).

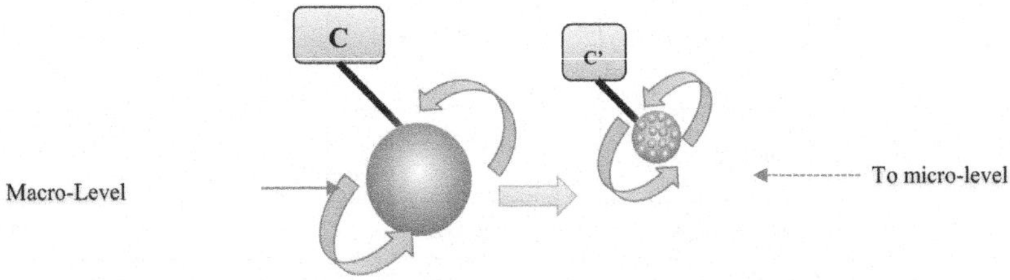

Fig. 5. Applying Class 3, Class 3.2.1

Table 4. Summary of suggested Typical Solution determination

Technic	Type	Suggested typical solution	Code
Contradiction	Standard (SC)	Change an object's physical state	Suggestion 1
	Radical (RC)	Move to the super-system or the sub-system	Suggestion 2
Su-field analysis	Class 2/2.2.2	Changing substance from a macro level to a micro level	Suggestion 3
	Class 3/3.2.1	Transition to the Micro-Level	Suggestion 4

2.5 P5 - Getting Some Insights by Learning from Innovators, Experts, or from Elsewhere Out of DL Scope and Environment and Grabbing Suggestions for Typical Solution

The idea behind getting those insights is to narrow the suggested Typical solutions in order to focus to the feasible one, based on what else have been done elsewhere, we selected the following suggestion: Selected suggestion: Change an object's physical state. Here we have: Neural Networks -> Layers -> Neurons, which are built on classical computer algorithm. Those ones are running programs based on bits 0 and 1 which are lowest information unit used in the system. So, changing the physical state of the Su-filed will be related to changing the physical state of this single unit of the system. So how can we change a physical state of something that is binary having states only equal to 0 or 1?

3 The Results

3.1 P6 - Talking About Typical Solution: Quantum Information and Qubits, the Solutions?

IBM lunch IBM Q [25], a free platform to test and write freely coded on quantum programming. Google asked, last year, for NASA's help to prove quantum supremacy within a matter [26]. The idea behind quantum supremacy is the challenge to prove quantum computer with sufficiently powerful should be able to perform easily where powerful classical machines failed to do so on certain mathematical calculation. At NASA, some benchmarking test on both quantum computer and on supercomputer, were conduct by Benjamin Villalonga [27] at the Quantum Artificial Intelligence Lab at NASA. In this way, they were able to compare performances and to conclude the supremacy of quantum computer. IBM provide also Qiskit, an open-source framework for quantum computing. Several other platforms exist to test quantum computer with ease. We emphasis on Qubit, because Today's computers are working on bits of information. Those bits have only two states: 0 or 1, as we mentioned before. But quantum computers possess more than two states; they use quantum bits so called Qubits, to encode information. Those Qubits can represent electrons, photons, atoms, ions. All those are working together to produce the computer processor and memory. Quantum computer can contain all these multiple states simultaneously. Thus, those quantum computers are fare and millions of times more powerful than most popular supercomputers.

3.2 P7 - Training the Team to Transition from Typical to Specific Solution

According to the previous explanation provided on this paper, related to suggested typical solution (suggestion 1, 2, 3, and 4), we decided to put our emphasis on trying to find a specific solution in quantum world. But to deal with quantum computing combined to deep learning, we used TRIZ nine's windows, DTC operators to break the psychological inertia [28]. Moreover, concerning deep learning and quantum computing programming, we used tools and software such as python 3.7 [29], pythorch [30]; and for Quantum computing, online resources such as Qiskit [31, 32].

3.3 P8 – Building the Specific Solution

The Solution: Inventing QReLU activation function, the ReLU equivalent for Quantum Computers.

We moved from micro level to quantum word. We used Qubits instead of bits to code in Qiskit, the information. Since qubits have more than two states, we parse a pointer as controller in the other available states. This parsed pointer is dynamically created each time a neuron is activated or fired. The pointer is located on the Bloch sphere [33] and we have several options to control those parses pointers with Ion traps, Optical traps, Quantum dots, Semiconductor impurities, Superconducting circuits, etc. (Fig. 6).

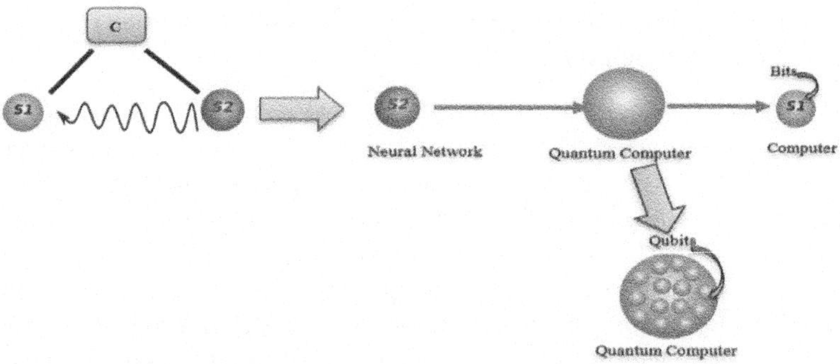

Fig. 6. Neural Network: from classical to quantum computer

How Do We Finally Come to the Solution?
We adapted artificial neural network structure combined with Bloch Sphere. We used Little people technic [34] to project ourselves inside the neuron, and in hidden layers (Fig 7):

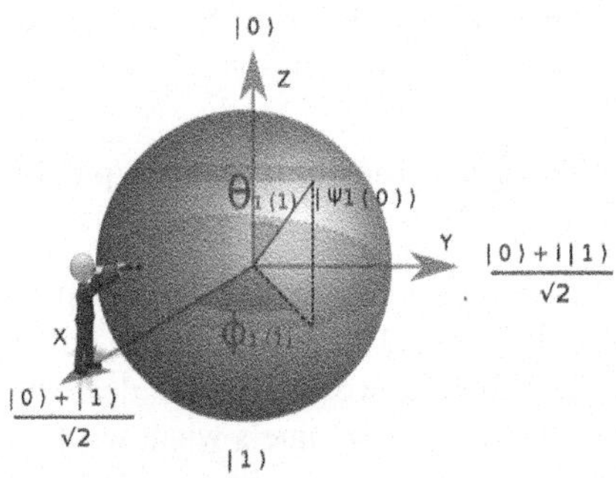

Fig. 7. Little people looking inside neuron as on a Bloch Sphere

We understood that little man, when inside the neuron, can see how this neuron structure is newly designed shaped with Bloch Sphere attributes. Same things inside the hidden layers (Fig. 8).

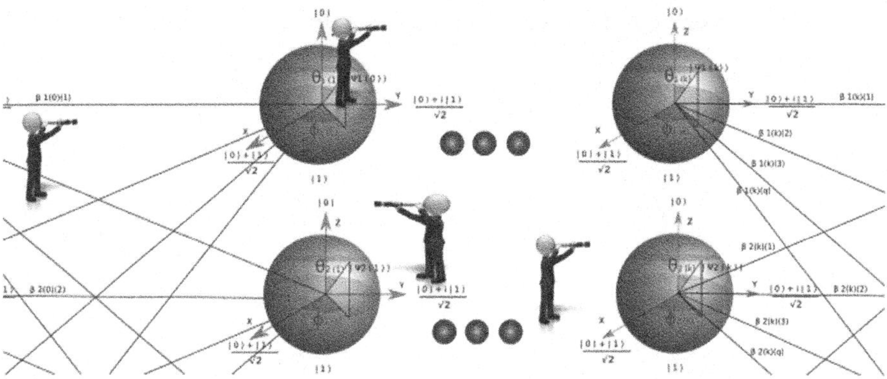

Fig. 8. Little people looking inside neural networks and hidden layers as in front of multiple Bloch spheres

Our New QReLU Function: The Mathematical Formula

The newly activated function will be call QReLU (Quantum ReLU or Quadratic ReLU), where:

$$|\Psi j(0)\rangle \text{ are input, for j} = 1 \text{ to n,} \quad (4)$$

$$|\Psi j(k)\rangle = \mathrm{QReLU}\left(\sum_{i=1}^{p} |\Psi j(k-1)\rangle.\,\beta\, i_{(k-1)(k)} + bjk\right),\ \mathrm{j} = 1 \text{ to q} \quad (5)$$

bjk are complexes biases added to activation function $|\Psi j(k)\rangle$ for j = 1 to q (Figs. 9 and 10)

$\beta\, i_{(k-1)(k)}$, are complexes numbers corresponding weight of previous activated neurons

$$\boldsymbol{QReLU}\left(|\boldsymbol{\Psi j}(\boldsymbol{k})\rangle_{(a_{jk},b_{jk},c_{jk})}\right) = \begin{cases} 0, & \left\| |\boldsymbol{\Psi j}(\boldsymbol{k})\rangle_{(a_{jk},b_{jk},c_{jk})} \right\| < 1 \\ |\boldsymbol{\Psi j}(\boldsymbol{k})\rangle_{(a_{jk},b_{jk},c_{jk})}, & \left\| |\boldsymbol{\Psi j}(\boldsymbol{k})\rangle_{(a_{jk},b_{jk},c_{jk})} \right\| \geq 1 \end{cases} \quad (6)$$

And,

$$|\Psi j(f)\rangle \text{ are output, for j} = 1 \text{ to w}$$

How We Created QReLU on a Quantum Computer, Using Qiskit and Python?

```
from numpy import linalg as LA
class QReLU():
    def _init_(self):
    pass
  # Let define a simple forward for our basic QReLU
  def forward(self,  input):
    #vect = np.vectorize(complex)(input)
    p = LA.norm(input)
    if p < 1 :
          QReLU_forward = 0
    else :
          QReLU_forward = input

          #QParse_pointer_f(QReLU_forward,QClassifier(QReL
          U_forward))

    return QReLU_forward

  # Now let define a simple backward function with basic
QReLU

  def backward(self, input, bwg_output):
    r = LA.norm(input)

    if  r > 1 :

        QReLU_bw = np.array(input)
        #QParse_pointer_bw(QReLU_bw,QClassifier(QReLU_bw))
    else :
         QReLU_bw = 0
    return QReLU_bw*bwg_output

# Testing the forward function
qrel1 = QReLU()
b=qrel1.forward([0,-0.25,4.5])
b
# QReLU's forward function Visualisation on a Bloch
sphere:
qiskit.tools.visualization.plot_bloch_vector(np.array(b))


                              #This previous neuron will be
                                  fired and activated.
```

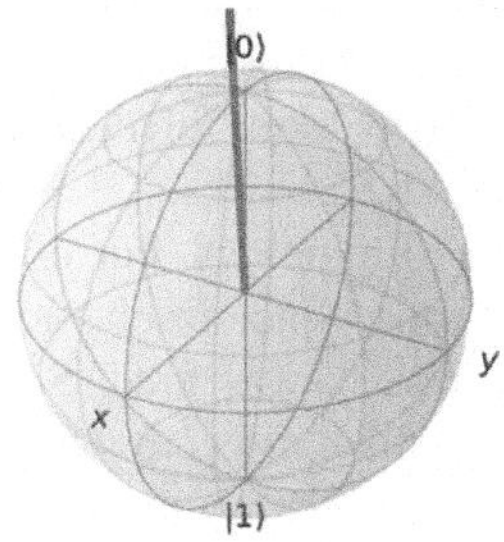

Fig. 9. Visualization of forward function on Bloch sphere

```
# But the following neuron will not be activated
qrel1 = QReLU()
b=qrel1.forward([0,-0.25,0.5])
b
>>>> 0
# Now, testing the backward function:
qrel2 = QReLU()
c=qrel2.backward([-3,0.25,5.05],0.2)
c
# QReLU's backward function Visualisation:
qiskit.tools.visualization.plot_bloch_vector(np.array(c))
```

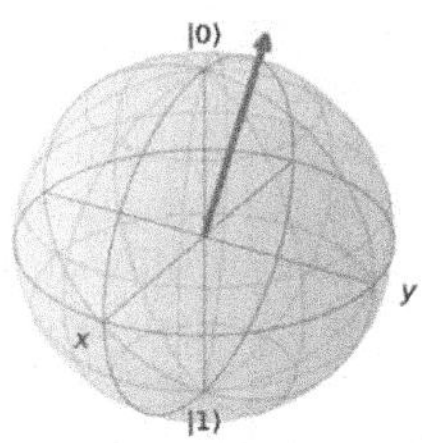

Fig. 10. Visualization of backward function on Bloch sphere

3.4 Discussion on the Method Contributions and Limitations

This method contributes to work on neural networks hidden layers, and therefore open the gates for new opportunities with new kind of jobs created. For example, Deep Learning Auditors, in case of NN malfunction or error in prediction, or any trouble with outputs, they will be able to extract significant paths. And, like working in a Plane Black-box after a crash, DL Auditors could analyze the reliable outputs, and activated neurons involved in the issue, so that correctives actions could be taken in the current situation, but also to avoid similar issues in the future. This reliability will give also opportunity to human to really have control or at least, will be able to investigate the root cause of any issue that will be made by machine. This method also extends ARIZ algorithms with intermediate steps in terms of decisions, directions, and actionable tools to take or to make between ARIZ blocks.

But this method presents some limitations. For example, to come to this QReLU function, we made some assumptions. Since in classical ReLU (x) = max (0, x) negative x were not fired. Only positive x was fired. So, we assumed that, in a Bloch sphere, with complex values, and qubits, inspecting negative values is useless. Instead, only neuron x with Frobenius [35], or others norm(x) >= 1 will be fired and activated. We used qubits to construct these neurons, and to evaluate their norms in order to activate or not the neuron. So how could we deal with neuron x inside the Bloch sphere near border where norm(x) = $1 - \varepsilon$, and $\varepsilon > 0$, and with ε, a float number close to 0?

4 Conclusion

In contrast to other researches on Deep Learning using trial and errors, we used TRIZ ARIZ algorithm, and TrizStartup methodology, to structure our thinking on this subject. This allows us to dig on Speed versus Reliability issues, and to come with a so-called QReLU, Quantum version of the classical ReLU function. TRIZ tools and technics could, therefore, be used for further systematic researches on deep learning and on AI development for helping open in systematic ways, new frontiers with Quantum computers. This will make Artificial Intelligence more and more explainable, to preserve human control over machines in the future of Humanity.

References

1. Trizstartup. http://trizstartup.com/index.php/en/home/. Accessed 8 Apr 2019
2. Goodfellow, I., Bengio, Y., Courville, A.: Deep Learning. MIT Press, Cambridge (2017)
3. Pwc.com: Sizing the prize: PwC's Global Artificial Intelligence Study. https://www.pwc.com/gx/en/issues/analytics/assets/pwc-ai-analysis-sizing-the-prize-report.pdf. Accessed 12 Apr 2019
4. MarketsandMarkets: Deep Learning Market: Analysis Size, Growth, Trend and Forecast to 2023. https://www.marketsandmarkets.com/Market-Reports/deep-learning-market-107369271.html. Accessed 11 Apr 2019
5. Marketresearchfuture: Deep Learning Market Research Report – Global Forecast to 2023. https://www.marketresearchfuture.com/reports/deep-learning-market-6058. Accessed 11 Apr 2019
6. TensorFlow: https://www.tensorflow.org/. Accessed 14 Apr 2019
7. Pytorch. https://pytorch.org/. Accessed 1 Apr 2019
8. Keras Home Documentation. https://keras.io/. Accessed 10 Apr 2019
9. MXNet. https://mxnet.apache.org/. Accessed 9 Apr 2019
10. Caffe: Deep Learning Framework. https://caffe.berkeleyvision.org. Accessed 12 Apr 2019
11. Caffe2. https://caffe2.ai/. Accessed 1 Apr 2019
12. Deeplearning4j. https://deeplearning4j.org/. Accessed 11 Apr 2019

13. Zhu, N., et al.: Deep learning for smart agriculture: concepts, tools, applications, and opportunities. https://ijabe.org/index.php/ijabe/article/view/4475. Accessed 14 Apr 2019
14. Marcus, G.: Deep Learning: A Critical Appraisal. solving. https://arxiv.org/abs/1801.00631. Accessed 11 Apr 2019
15. Stanford. https://engineering.stanford.edu/people/oyekunle-olukotun/. Accessed 11 Apr 2019
16. Lynley, M.: The red-hot AI hardware space gets even hotter with $56 M for a startup called SambaNova Systems. https://techcrunch.com/2018/03/15/the-red-hot-ai-chip-space-gets-even-hotter-with-56m-for-a-startup-called-sambanova/. Accessed 12 Apr 2019
17. EETimes: Baidu Releases. In: Intel, Nvidia post results training neural nets. https://www.eetimes.com/document.asp?doc_id=1330521. Accessed 14 Apr 2019
18. Guehika, A.: Cartographie des processus d'innovation (2014). https://www.amazon.com/Cartographie-processus-dinnovation-lInnovateur-French-ebook/dp/B00HVIC53Y. Accessed 13 Apr 2019
19. The C-K theory. https://www.ck-theory.org/c-k-theory/?lang=en. Accessed 15 Apr 2019
20. SolidCreativity: ASIT. http://www.asit.info/. Accessed 16 Apr 2019
21. Altshuller, G.: Creativity as an Exact Science. Gordon & Breach, New York (1984)
22. D2L: Deep recurrent neural network. https://d2l.ai/chapter_recurrent-neural-networks/deep-rnn.html. Accessed 12 Apr 2019
23. Modern Triz Academy. http://www.modern-triz-academy.com/. Accessed 11 Apr 2019
24. Terninko, J., Domb, E., Miller, J.: The Seventy-six Standard Solutions, with Examples—Class 2 (2000). http://www.metodolog.ru/triz-journal/archives/2000/03/d/index.htm. Accessed 19 Apr 2019
25. IBM Q. https://www.research.ibm.com/ibm-q/. Accessed 20 Apr 2019
26. arXiv, E.: The new benchmark quantum computers must beat to achieve quantum supremacy. In: MIT Technology Review. https://www.technologyreview.com/s/613507/the-new-benchmark-quantum-computers-must-beat-to-achieve-quantum-supremacy/. Accessed 19 Apr 2019
27. Villalonga, B., et al.: A flexible high-performance simulator for the verification and benchmarking of quantum circuits implemented on real hardware (2000). https://arxiv.org/pdf/1811.09599.pdf. Accessed 18 Apr 2019
28. Frenklach, G.: DTC operators. https://triz-journal.com/efficient-use-dtc-operator/. Accessed 19 Apr 2019
29. Python. https://www.python.org/. Accessed 22 Apr 2019
30. Pytorch. https://pytorch.org/. Accessed 01 May 2019
31. Boyer, J.: Using Quantum Operations to Achieve Computing Objectives (2018). https://medium.com/qiskit/using-quantum-operations-to-achieve-computing-objectives-868a7f1cfa09. Accessed 01 May 2019
32. QisKit: An open-source quantum computing framework for leveraging today's quantum processors in research, education, and business. https://qiskit.org/. Accessed 03 May 2019
33. Kyrillidis, A.: Introduction to quantum computing: bloch sphere. http://akyrillidis.github.io/notes/quant_post_7. Accessed 25 May 2019
34. Livotov, P.: Modelling 40 Innovation Principles with "Moving Little People" (2003). https://triz-journal.com/modelling-40-innovation-principles-moving-little-people/. Accessed 28 May 2019
35. Mathworld. http://mathworld.wolfram.com/FrobeniusNorm.html. Accessed 17 May 2019

Exploring State Machine CECA Model

Jerzy Chrząszcz[1,2(✉)]

[1] Institute of Computer Science, Warsaw University of Technology, 00-665 Warsaw, Poland
jch@ii.pw.edu.pl
[2] Pentacomp Systemy Informatyczne S.A., 02-222 Warsaw, Poland

Abstract. It was shown during TRIZ Future 2018 conference, that a diagram resulting from Cause-Effect Chains Analysis (CECA) might be transformed into a state machine model. Although the conversion was described with a set of rules, no specific benefits of switching to a state machine approach were presented then.

This paper focuses on enhancing the conversion and exploring the possibilities to simplify the output model without losing its information content. It briefly shows relations between the state machines and the formal grammars, proposes regular expressions as a compressed representation of the processes producing target disadvantages and provides SWOT-like analysis of the behavioral state machine CECA model with respect to the classic structural CECA model. It also shows the similarity of the state machine model to hardware-software approach.

Keywords: TRIZ · Cause-Effect Chains Analysis · State machine model · Formal grammar · Regular expression

1 CECA and Logical Model

Cause-Effect Chains Analysis method was developed by GEN3 in 1990s for building causality diagrams in a systematic way [1–3]. It is intended to be used after exploring structure and operation of the analyzed system with other TRIZ tools, such as Function Analysis or Flow Analysis. The procedure starts with selecting *target disadvantages* that should be eliminated and then their preceding causes (*intermediate disadvantages)* are investigated one by one until the *root causes* are found, which are recognized as remaining beyond control. The outcome of the analysis is a set of *key disadvantages* chosen amongst the revealed causes, considered to be the most appropriate to address in order to eliminate the target disadvantages.

The procedure is documented with a diagram composed of boxes with descriptions of disadvantages and arrows indicating the flow of causality. The linear chains of causes are usually connected on inputs (with common causes) or on outputs (with logical operators), indicating how the contributing causes trigger the effects. Similarity between the structure of a CECA diagram and a combinational logical circuit using AND/OR gates inspired the concept we have originally presented in [4] and expanded in [5, 6] later on. It relies on representing the structure of a CECA diagram with a set of

Published by Springer Nature Switzerland AG 2019
R. Benmoussa et al. (Eds.): TFC 2019, IFIP AICT 572, pp. 388–399, 2019.
https://doi.org/10.1007/978-3-030-32497-1_31

logical functions operating on root causes or intermediate disadvantages, perceived as Boolean variables, evaluating to 1/0 for an active/inactive cause, respectively.

Such a model allows the analysts to apply logical minimization and other techniques used for developing combinational logical circuits to support the selection of the key disadvantages. A drawback of this approach is the lack of time reference, inherited from the original CECA model, where the only notion of time comes from the arrows going from causes to effects, thus determining the sequence. In addition, the logical model only reflects the structure of the input diagram, ignoring the contents of the boxes, i.e. the specific disadvantages involved. To address these shortcomings, in [7] we have proposed modeling of CECA diagrams using Hierarchical Concurrent Finite State Machine paradigm [8] and the rules outlined in the next section.

2 Building State Machine CECA Model

The main assumption of the proposed state machine approach is that a CECA diagram describes interconnected *harmful processes*, i.e. sequences of operations performed within the system or super-system that jointly "produce" the target disadvantages. This seems to closely correspond with the concept of a *harmful machine* proposed in [9]. Each of these processes is modeled with a linear chain of causes and the connections between the chains (common causes and logical operators) indicate specific conditions, required for the "production" to progress. It is also assumed that the input CECA model is developed using the condition-action style devised in [10], i.e. it contains interleaved boxes representing interactions and conditions. A CECA model structured this way may be transformed into a state machine model, with nodes reflecting *states* and labelled edges reflecting conditional *transitions*, using the following guidelines [7]:

- nodes representing *actions* in the input diagram are converted into respective *states* in the state machine diagram,
- nodes representing *conditions* in the input diagram are converted into *transitions* with respective condition labels, positioned accordingly in locations of the incoming and outgoing edges of the original diagram,
- *common causes* being condition nodes, connected to several succeeding nodes in the input diagram, are reflected in the state machine diagram as *groups of edges* modeling transitions to respective states (labelled with the same condition inherited from the original cause),
- *OR operators* appearing in the input diagram are converted into *groups of edges* in the state machine diagram (one edge for each input), modeling *alternative* conditions required for transitions to the respective output states; in practice OR operators are often omitted and depicted as multiple edges, which do not need conversion,
- *AND operators* appearing in the input diagram are converted into *additional nodes and edges* in the state machine diagram, modeling *coincidence* of conditions required for transitions to the respective output states,
- a *loopback edge* is created for each of the nodes in the state machine diagram, with a condition complementary to conditions of all other outgoing edges of this node to model waiting in the same state; such a transition is default when none of the exit conditions are met and it is usually not shown in diagrams.

These instructions are illustrated in Fig. 1, together with two additional rules:

- *feedback paths* ("vicious circles") in the input diagram are converted into respective cyclic transitions in the state machine diagram, as for regular action-condition segments,
- *common causes* being action nodes, connected to several succeeding nodes in the input diagram, are reflected in the state machine diagram as *groups of edges* modeling transitions to respective states (labelled with the conditions inherited from the corresponding target nodes).

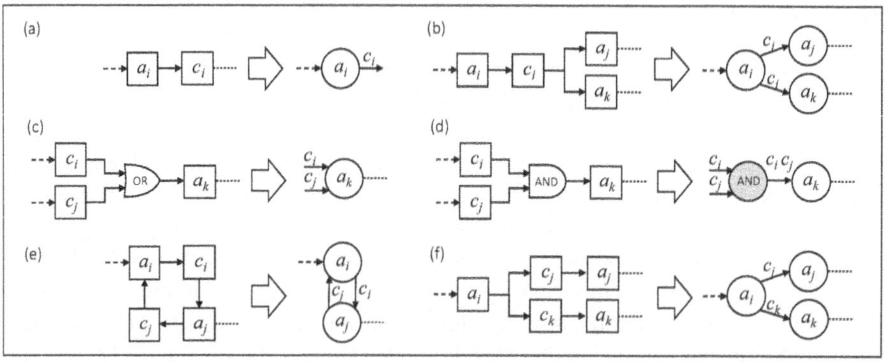

Fig. 1. Building blocks of a CECA diagram and their counterparts in a state machine model [7]: regular action-condition segment (a), action-condition segment with a common cause (b), OR operator (c) and AND operator (d). Additional building blocks: feedback connection (e) and branching to multiple next states with different conditions (f). Concatenation of symbols denotes logical AND. Loopback edges have been omitted for clarity.

3 Simplifying State Machine CECA Model

It was shown in [7] that above-mentioned conversion results in a decreased number of nodes in the diagram. This effect comes from changing the nodes reflecting conditions into edges representing conditional transitions. On the other hand, AND operators were also transformed into states, accordingly to the original method. It is worth noting, however, that an AND operator in a CECA diagram does not reflect any interaction and serve logical purposes solely, as it indicates that the output effect is triggered when all contributing causes are active.

Consequently, the state inherited by the state machine model from an AND operator does not reflect interaction either. It is only used to represent a stage where the process waits for a specific combination of conditions before progressing to the next stage. In terms of the synchronization scheme, it may be considered as deferring the transition until the last input cause becomes active. Such approach to AND conversion violates the clear differentiation among actions (represented by states) and logical conditions (represented by transitions), thus introducing a deficiency of the original method.

A solution to this problem is depicted in Fig. 2. An AND-state may be removed from the model if the transitions from all the input states are reconnected to the output state with conditions equal to logical AND (conjunction) of the original input conditions. In the example the AND-state inputs are c_i coming from a_i and c_j coming from a_j while the output transition to a_k requires $c_i\ c_j$ condition. After simplification both transitions from a_i and a_j to a_k require $c_i\ c_j$ condition and AND-state disappears.

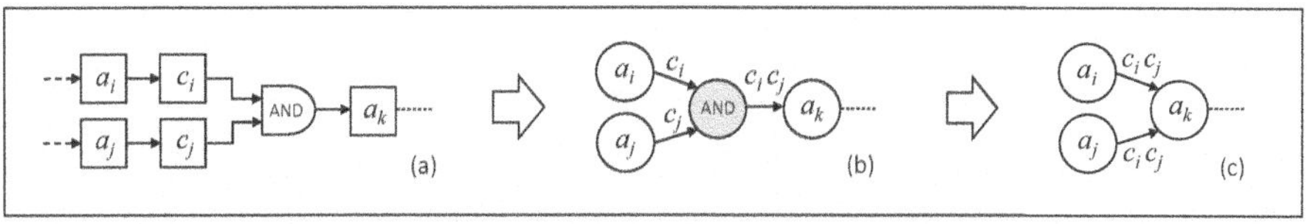

Fig. 2. Simplifying AND operator representation: original fragment of a CECA diagram (a), state machine model representation proposed in [7] (b) and minimized representation without artificial AND-state (c).

The basic rule for minimizing state machines indicates that two states may be unified (merged) if and only if their output functions are identical and their transition functions are compatible (identical or at least non-contradicting). Simply put, this requires that observed output behavior, as well as pattern of conditional transitions to the next states, are the same before and after the minimization. In the area of digital design this rule is used to decrease the number of states in order to simplify circuit construction and state encoding. Let us analyze if and how does this concept correspond to a state machine CECA model.

Identical output functions in an abstract state machine map onto identical actions in a sequential CECA model, i.e. pairs of interacting objects (tools and products) and the operations must be identical for both the candidate states. As for the output transitions, there are several generic variants possible. Identical conditions are conditions referring to same parameters, relations and threshold values, which is a special case of equivalent conditions, evaluating to equal logical values in all situations – even if they are formulated differently in the input model. This is illustrated with fully overlapped circles in Fig. 3c. Contradicting and non-overlapping conditions (Fig. 3a) never evaluate to true at the same time – e.g. $T < 25$ and $T > 30$. Partially overlapping conditions (Fig. 3b) only for some cases both evaluate to true – e.g. $T > 25$ and $T < 30$. For nesting (Fig. 3d) one condition is "stronger" than the other – e.g. $T < 25$ and $T < 30$, while complementary conditions (Fig. 3e) do not overlap and cover all situations – e.g. $T < 25$ and $T \geq 25$.

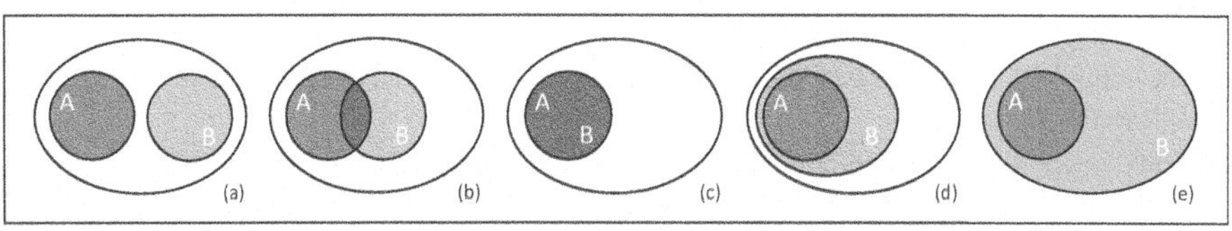

Fig. 3. Different combinations of conditions: contradicting/ non-complementary (a), partially overlapping (b), equivalent/ fully overlapping (c), nested (d), contradicting/complementary (e).

The simplest case of state merging is when the next states of both the candidates are the same. This situation is schematically depicted in Fig. 4a. In such a case the states a_i and a_j are merged into a single state, while the transitions c_i and c_j are merged into a single transition with condition $c_i + c_j$ describing an alternative (logical sum) of the conditions. If each of the merge candidates has a different next state, the states are merged like in the first variant described above and the conditions guarding particular transitions are preserved (Fig. 4b). As can be seen, the first scenario leads to combined conditions, while the second scenario leads to combined sets of the next states.

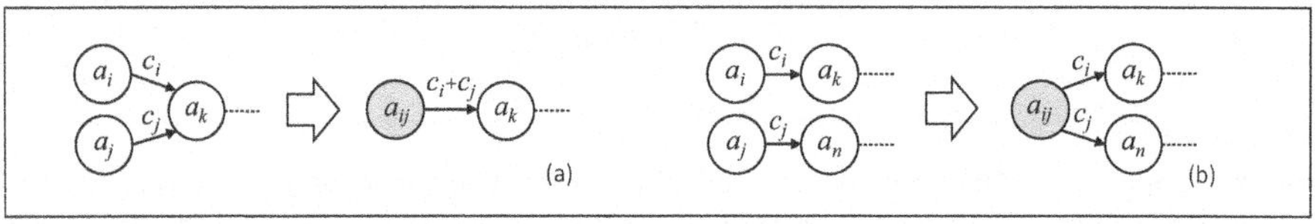

Fig. 4. Generic variants of state merging: for same next state (a), for different next states (b). Single next states are shown for simplicity; for multiple next states the rules apply respectively.

Depending on the relation between the conditions involved, these two scenarios may generate several specific cases, summarized in Table 1. As stated in [7], each linear chain of an input CECA model is represented by a separate state machine with an initial state reflecting respective root cause and all such state machines operate concurrently. An important consequence of this approach is the possibility of simultaneous triggering of several next states through separate transitions labelled with the same condition. This extended interpretation implies, that any two states representing same interaction may always be merged, because their transition functions are always compatible.

Table 1. Possible configurations of conditions and next states of the merge candidates.

Conditions	Identical next states	Different next states
(a) non-overlapping non-complementary	Conditional transition with sum of conditions	Conditional branch mutually exclusive (none, one or another next state)
(b) partially overlapping non-complementary	Conditional transition with sum of conditions	Conditional branch exclusive or concurrent (none, one, another or both states)
(c) fully overlapping non-complementary	Conditional transition with either of conditions	Conditional branch always concurrent (none or both next states)
(d) one nested in another non-complementary	Conditional transition with "weaker" condition	Conditional branch exclusive or concurrent (none, one or both next states)
(e) non-overlapping complementary	Unconditional transition (sum of conditions always evaluates to true)	Immediate conditional branch mutually exclusive, obligatory (one or another next state)

To conclude this section, it should be noted that a state machine model obtained from a converted CECA diagram may be simplified by removing the artificial AND-states as well as by merging the states reflecting the same interactions in the analyzed system.

4 State Machine Model vs. Formal Language

The concept of a formal language [11] comes from the field of Mathematical Linguistics and refers to a language generated (defined) by a formal grammar. There are several categories of formal languages, with different limitations regarding the generation rules. The most restricted are *regular languages*, generated by *regular grammars*, which are recognizable by Finite State Machines (FSM). A formal grammar is defined by indicating:

- set of *terminal symbols* (terminals),
- set of *non-terminal symbols* (non-terminals), containing a designated *start symbol*,
- set of *productions*, transforming sequences of symbols into sequences of symbols.

Non-terminals are symbols to be replaced with sequences of symbols determined by productions. The generation of an expression in a target language begins with a start symbol and uses particular productions to convert non-terminals in the successive output sequences, until the sequence contains terminal symbols solely.

An example of a simple grammar is given below. Using productions 1 and 3 we obtain expression "zm" and using the productions 1, 2, 2, 3 we obtain "zoom". As can be seen, this grammar defines a language containing all expressions starting with the "z" symbol, ending with the "m" symbol and containing zero or more "o" symbols in between – i.e. "zm", "zom", "zoom", etc.

```
terminals:      {z, o, m}
non-terminals: {S, T}, start symbol S
productions:    1. S→zT   2. T→oT 3. T→m
```

An alternative way of defining a set of expressions sharing common morphological characteristics uses notation called regular expressions [11]. Such expression describes a template of all target expressions and it may contain some terminal symbols and some special symbols indicating production rules implicitly. For instance, an asterisk denotes that preceding symbol may appear zero or more times, so that sample grammar defined above is represented by the regular expression: "zo*m".

As stated before, a state machine may be used to recognize particular grammar, i.e. to check if a sequence of symbols presented at the input constitutes a valid expression in this grammar. This requires that some states are designated "accepting states" and whenever any of such states is reached, the input sequence is considered valid. In other words, for each regular grammar an equivalent finite state machine may be created.

What we intend here, with regard to cause-effect analysis, is the opposite: we want to find a grammar or regular expression representing a given state machine CECA model. The target disadvantages are logical counterparts of the accept states in this case. And we are looking for a synthetic linguistic description of all paths existing in the model that lead from the root causes to the target disadvantages. Expected outcome of this approach is a compact specification (or a “prescription”), stating what exactly and in what order must happen in the analyzed system to generate all identified target disadvantages.

A definition of a state machine recognizing the sample grammar is presented below. It is described using the notation required by an online FSM simulator [12], with simplified formatting (originally, each entry should be put on a separate line). The diagram automatically generated by the application from this definition is shown in Fig. 5a.

```
#states         0    1    2    3
#initial        0
#accepting      3
#alphabet       z    o    m
#transitions    0:z>1    1:o>2    2:o>2    1:m>3    2:m>3
```

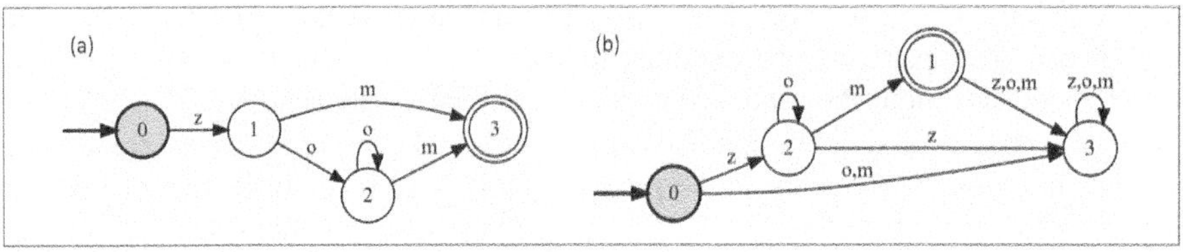

Fig. 5. State machine diagrams generated by application [12]: from the explicit definition of the state machine (a) and from the regular expression “zo*m”, as a grammar recognizer (b).

As can be seen, the accept state 3 may be reached from the initial state 0 through state 1 or through states 1 and 2, reflecting various production rules defined by the grammar. Such an automaton only describes the transitions expected for valid expressions and the diagram of a complete recognizer generated by the application for the regular expression “zo*m” is shown for reference in Fig. 5b. It introduces two important changes:

- an additional state is used for signaling invalid expressions violating the template,
- valid expressions are detected using smaller number of states than in grammar-based implementation (3 instead of 4), as the state 2 recognizes 0 or more “o” symbols.

5 Discussion

Let us begin the discussion with summarizing the main properties of the two modelling approaches. The classic (structural) CECA model features:

- three types of diagram components – boxes, logical operators and arrows,
- boxes represent disadvantages – whatever their nature is,
- logical operators indicate how do the causes combine to trigger the effects,
- arrows represent causality flow and do not have any attributes.

State machine (behavioral) CECA model features:

- two types of diagram components – boxes and arrows,
- boxes represent states reflecting the interactions within the system or super-system,
- arrows represent conditional transitions between the states, indicating causality flow, and they are labelled with the logical conditions.

Next, let us focus on the differences between the state machine approach and the classic CECA method using four perspectives of the SWOT analysis.

Strengths:

- states and conditional transitions represent behavior of the concurrent processes better than a structural diagram, which looks static in comparison,
- stages of the process and transitions between stages are clearly distinguished with dedicated types of diagram elements, which makes the model more comprehensible,
- logical operators are converted into states or transitions and disappear as a separate type of nodes, which makes the model simpler,
- state machine representation is more compact and therefore more expressive than a structural diagram with unlabeled arrows,
- state machine approach is much more disciplined than classic CECA, which uses guidelines rather than strict rules, leaving a lot of space for experience and style,
- condition-action duality is supported and enforced at the level of the state machine notation, while for structural diagrams it is only a modeling convention,
- state machine model may be minimized in a systematic way, with the states and logical conditions processed algorithmically,
- model correctness may be verified in a more orderly way than for structural model, by checking logical coherence of the conditions,
- transitions labelled with same conditions indicate synchronization points between concurrent processes reflected by particular state machines in the model,
- synthetic description of the harmful processes may be extracted from a state machine model in the form of a regular expression.

Weaknesses:

- state machine approach is more complicated and constrained than regular CECA, where anything considered a disadvantage may be included in the model,
- proposed theoretical model uses several unintuitive concepts, like many states being current and active at the same time [7] – structural CECA modeling is easier,
- the procedure for creating state machine CECA model from scratch has not been devised yet, so that for now the structural model has to be built first.

Opportunities:

- explicit references to transitions allows the analysts to focus on the configurations of conditions in time, possibly inspiring new solutions – e.g. desynchronizing events,
- state machine approach is well known in the IT and other engineering areas, which increases chances of successful communications with specialists in these areas,
- existing state machine notations and tools facilitate automatic processing of model descriptions (e.g. extraction of the regular expressions).

Threats:

- structural CECA method have been used and taught within TRIZ community for decades, hence the current demand for a new approach seems to be relatively low.

6 Example

We will use the sample CECA diagram discussed previously in [7]. As shown in Fig. 6, the original graph with 24 nodes and 24 edges is firstly converted into a state machine with 14 states and 14 transitions. Then the three AND-states are removed, as described in Sect. 3, yielding 11 states and 11 transitions. Finally, the conditions are mapped onto single symbols for obtaining state machine description in the linguistic form: $c_1 \rightarrow a$; $c_2 \rightarrow b$; $c_3 \rightarrow c$; $c_5 \rightarrow d$; $c_7 \rightarrow e$; $c_1c_6 \rightarrow p$; $c_3c_4 \rightarrow q$; $c_7c_8 \rightarrow r$.

The regular expression representing all scenarios leading to a given target disadvantage may be found by indicating the state reflecting this disadvantage as the accept state and checking the paths from all the initial states (reflecting the root causes). The regular expression representing all the harmful processes, obtained by aggregating the expressions found for all target disadvantages, reads as: "p + bp + cp + a + qe + qr + dr". This representation indicates 7 different scenarios generating the target disadvantages after encountering 1 or 2 specific combinations of conditions within each scenario.

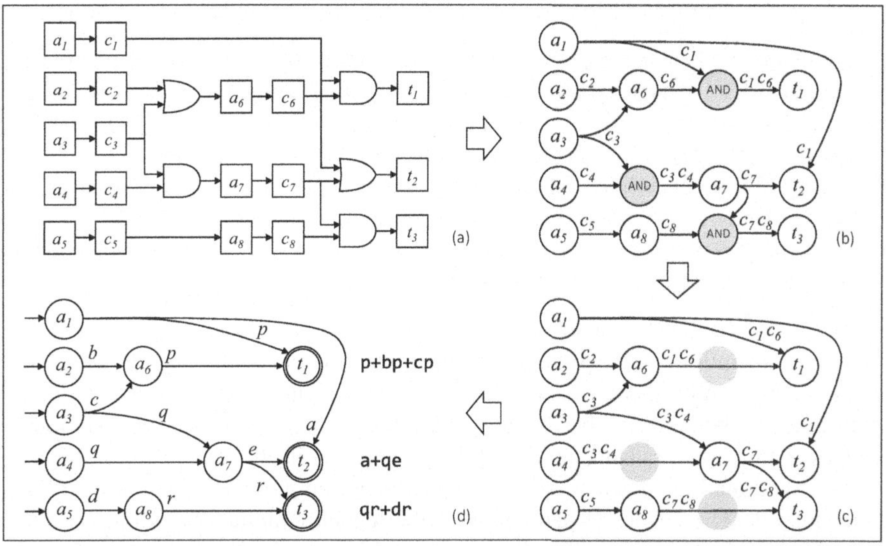

Fig. 6. Sample CECA diagram (a) and equivalent state machine diagram (b) as described in [7]. The same diagram with removed AND-states introduced during conversion (c) and transformed into form usable for linguistic approach (d). States representing target disadvantages are annotated with respective regular expressions.

7 Summary and Further Work

We have recalled the previous research on state machine CECA modeling and extended the results by indicating additional diagram conversion rules, as well as introducing and discussing two new topics: state model minimization and its linguistic representation. We have also compared the state machine model with the classic CECA diagram.

As can be seen in the example and the preceding sections, the linguistic approach focuses on the transitions and seems to neglect or ignore the intermediate disadvantages inherited from the original CECA diagram in the form of states reflecting interactions. This is an interesting intensification of distinguishing interactions and conditions in the model. To analyze it in a systematic manner, we will start with a short summary:

- the states in the state machine CECA model reflect actions and transitions reflect conditions required to progress the "harmful processes",
- the initial states reflect root causes (they are always active, such as gravity or law) and terminal (accept) states reflect "final products", i.e. target disadvantages,
- the states model how the things are going or may be going – i.e. existing or future harmful interactions between the components of the system or its super-system,
- the transitions indicate which operations, in what order and upon what conditions will produce particular target disadvantages.

Using this allegory of a production process, we may continue with the following:

- all the intermediate states jointly describe the "production means" or capabilities of the "factory" – which seems to fit in well with the harmful machine concept,
- the sequences of transitions form "prescriptions" or "instructions" for using these capabilities to develop respective target disadvantages,
- distinguishing capabilities (states) and instructions (transitions) looks very much like the hardware-software duality of the computer systems,
- regular expressions extracted from a state machine CECA model provide compact and complete representation of these instructions.

The success of the computer technology comes to a great extent from the ability to change the operation of the programmable hardware by changing the software solely. And therefore it presumably makes sense if we first focus on the "harmful program" controlling the behavior of the harmful machine, as it might be easier to introduce changes in this layer, rather than changing the machine itself.

The traditional approach to system improvement employs elimination of the key disadvantages. The enhanced perception of the logical conditions and time relations seems to open a wider perspective. Perhaps in addition to *removing* something from the model it is possible to get rid of the target disadvantages by *changing* some transitions as well? Maybe we could desynchronize some interactions in particular harmful processes or change their order of appearance or implement self-blocking or cross-blocking between the processes?

These questions indicate that the area for future research regarding the state machine approach and condition-action duality in cause-effect analysis is extensive. It would also be interesting to coordinate this work with other CECA-related activities [13, 14].

Acknowledgments. Author gratefully acknowledges Dr. Oleg Abramov for inspiring discussions regarding the CECA method and its extensions. Mr. Dariusz Burzyński should be credited for his linguistic support.

References

1. Litvin, S.S., Akselrod, B.M.: Cause-Effects Chains of Undesired Effects, Methodical Theses. CPB (1996). (in Russian)
2. Abramov, O., Kislov, A.: Cause-Effect Analysis of Engineering System's Disadvantages, Handbook on Methodology. Algorithm, Ltd. (2000). (in Russian)
3. Abramov, O.: TRIZ-based cause and effect chains analysis vs root cause analysis. In: Souchkov, V., Kässi, T. (eds.) Proceedings of the TRIZfest-2015 International Conference. Seoul, South Korea, pp. 288–295. MATRIZ (2015)
4. Chrząszcz, J., Salata, P.: Cause-effect chains analysis using boolean algebra. In: Koziołek, S., Chechurin, L., Collan, M. (eds.) Advances and Impacts of the Theory of Inventive Problem Solving. The TRIZ Methodology, Tools and Case Studies, 16th International TRIZ Future Conference TFC 2016, pp. 121–134 (2018). ISBN 978-3-319-96531-4

5. Chrząszcz, J.: Quantitative approach to Cause-Effect Chains Analysis. In: Souchkov, V. (ed.) Proceedings of the TRIZfest–2017 International Conference. Krakow, Poland, pp. 341-352. MATRIZ (2017)
6. Chrząszcz, J.: Indicating system vulnerabilities within CECA model. In: Mayer, O. (ed.) Proceedings of the TRIZfest-2018 International Conference, Lisbon, Portugal, pp. 31–37, MATRIZ 2018 (2018)
7. Chrząszcz, J.: Modelling CECA diagram as a state machine. In: Cavallucci, D., DeGuio, R., Koziołek, S. (eds.) Automated Invention for Smart Industries, 18th International TRIZ Future Conference TFC 2018 Proceedings, IFIP AICT, vol. 541, pp. 302–314 (2018). ISBN 978-3-030-02455-0
8. Girault, A., Lee, B., Lee, E.A.: Hierarchical finite state machines with multiple concurrency models. IEEE Trans. Comput. Aided Des. Integr. Circ. Syst. **18**(6), 742–760 (1999)
9. Lenyashin, V., Kim, H.J.: "Harmful System" – using this concept in modern TRIZ (2006). (in Russian). http://www.metodolog.ru/00859/00859.html. Accessed 30 June 2019
10. Yoon, H.: Occasion axis and parameter-function pair nexus for effective building of cause effect chains. In: Souchkov, V., Kässi, T. (eds.) Proceedings of the TRIZfest-2014 International Conference, Prague, Czech Republic, pp. 184-194. MATRIZ (2014)
11. Kandar, S.: Introduction to Automata Theory, Formal Languages and Computation. Pearson India (2013). ISBN: 9788131793510
12. Zuzak, I.: FSM simulator. http://ivanzuzak.info/noam/webapps/fsm_simulator/. Accessed 30 June 2019
13. Chrzaszcz, J.: Deriving quantitative characteristics from CECA model. In: Souchkov, V., Mayer, O. (eds.) Proceedings of the TRIZfest–2019 International Conference, pp. 89–99. MATRIZ, Heilbronn (2019)
14. Chrzaszcz, J.: Logical negation in CECA model. In: Souchkov, V., Mayer, O. (eds.) Proceedings of the TRIZfest–2019 International Conference, pp. 222–233. MATRIZ, Heilbronn (2019)

CALDET: A TRIZ-Driven Integrated Software Development Methodology

Stelian Brad[1(✉)], Emilia Brad[1], and Daniel Homorodean[2]

[1] Technical University of Cluj-Napoca, Memorandumului 28, 400441 Cluj-Napoca, Romania
stelian.brad@staff.utcluj.ro
[2] Arxia, Tipografiei 28, 400101 Cluj-Napoca, Romania

Abstract. Companies specialized in software development services and software outsourcing have adopted agile methodologies such as SCRUM and Kanban to drive the software development process. Along time, experts have introduced new methodologies that enhance agile roadmaps with lean patterns and design thinking tools. Despite the value added brought by aggregation of agile with lean and design thinking, the integrated methodology is still fuzzy at operational level. There is no scientific demonstration on the most appropriate way to alternate the steps of agile with those promoted by lean innovation and design thinking. This niche of opportunity is investigated by this paper. Conflicts and barriers generated by aggregation are treated with TRIZ. Inventive solutions are proposed to optimize the agile-lean-design thinking (ALDET) software development process considering a life-cycle perspective. Gaps identified in ALDET are additionally tackled with TRIZ and new tools of competitive engineering, including TRIZ contradiction matrix for software, are embedded within the optimized ALDET to enhance its potentiality. The methodology is called Competitive ALDET or CALDET. Its effectiveness was tested in a real project. Preliminary results demonstrate that CALDET provides a clearer and smoother path for project management, reduces ambiguities relative to traditional ALDET methodology, and increases the impact of outcomes to the user. By tackling conflicts in an iterative manner, CALDET avoids re-analysis and re-coding in software development, too. The presence of value engineering tools within the framework of CALDET reveals additional spaces of innovation, both technical and project management related.

Keywords: TRIZ · Conflict · Software development · Competitive engineering · Lean innovation · SCRUM · Agile · Design thinking · Qualitative optimization

1 Introduction

Software products and systems are characterized by complexity and invisibility [1]. These characteristics induce significant challenges for designers and especially for users to articulate how the system should look like from the early stages of conceptualization and development [1]; in contrast, for example, with a house project. Therefore, in software development, waterfall project management methodologies [2]

Published by Springer Nature Switzerland AG 2019
R. Benmoussa et al. (Eds.): TFC 2019, IFIP AICT 572, pp. 400–416, 2019.
https://doi.org/10.1007/978-3-030-32497-1_32

have been replaced in the last 15 years by more adaptive approaches, based on the paradigm "prototype-test-evaluate-learn-refine" (PTELR); the spiral model [2]. PTELR approach was actually encompassed into a new philosophy of software development some 20 years ago, under a set of 14 principles called "agile manifesto" [3]. These principles have been then deployed by experts into some practical project management methodologies, known as agile methodologies [1, 3, 4]. They incorporate frameworks such as SCRUM and Kanban [1, 4, 5] to assist developers in responding to uncertainty and unpredictability in building up new software systems.

In SCRUM, software systems are developed in small shippable increments that can be assessed by users very early in the development process, and all necessary adjustments, improvements and new ideas can be thus incorporated into the system in due time [6]. Every incrementing stage is called "sprint" and lasts about 2–4 weeks, with reviews at every 24 h, where both development team and system owner are engaged [6]. The schematics of this process is shown in Fig. 1. Kanban, another agile methodology, differs from SCRUM in several aspects such as: changes are accepted any time, working cycles follow the workflow, it does not use a backlog pool and it does not include roles, etc. [1].

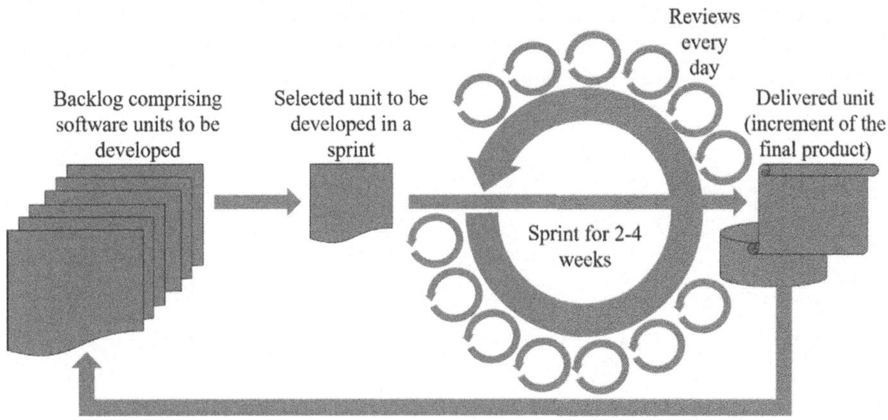

Fig. 1. SCRUM framework in agile software project management.

Based on the same principles as agile methodologies (i.e. uncertainty and fuzziness in defining solution in the early stages, continuous discovery by prototyping and testing, steering implication of users in co-creation and feedback), new technology driven innovation adopted a lean approach in the last decade [2]. In lean innovation, every phase of evolution involves a spiral model of gradual prototyping and pivoting of solutions by testing hypotheses and adjusting them from the feedback received from the end beneficiaries [7, 8]. Thus, the main phases of lean innovation - meaning insight, problem understanding, solution formulation, and business model design - are tackled in a progressive way, with gradual prototyping and pivoting, with rapid learning and refining of solution, such as to avoid perpetuation of non-value added issues. One might see that between agile development and lean innovation is a strong synchronism.

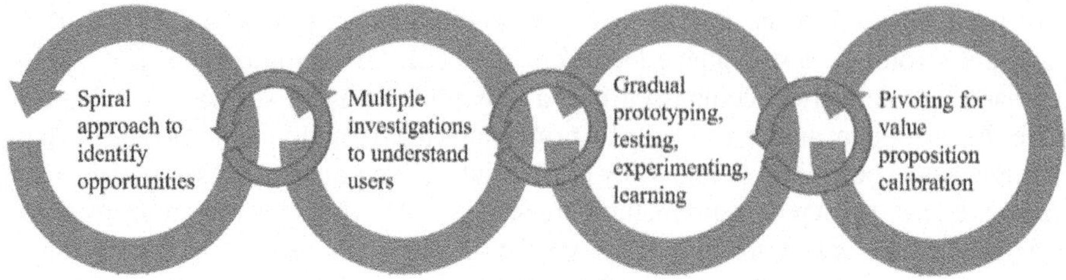

Fig. 2. Lean innovation methodology.

The graphical visualization of lean innovation is shown in Fig. 2. In addition, a third paradigm in new product development has gained in popularity in the last decade; that is, design thinking [9, 10]. This design model emphasizes on close collaboration with the end users during the development phases of a new product, starting with the process of need investigation, continuing with a deep understanding of users from multiple perspectives (roles), and then following an incremental process of solution formulation by looping ideas and prototypes in close collaboration with beneficiaries of solution [10, 11]. From the perspective of gradual prototyping and deep involvement of users in the design and development process, design thinking paradigm has many philosophical commonalities with agile development and lean innovation. An illustration of the main phases in design thinking model is shown in Fig. 3.

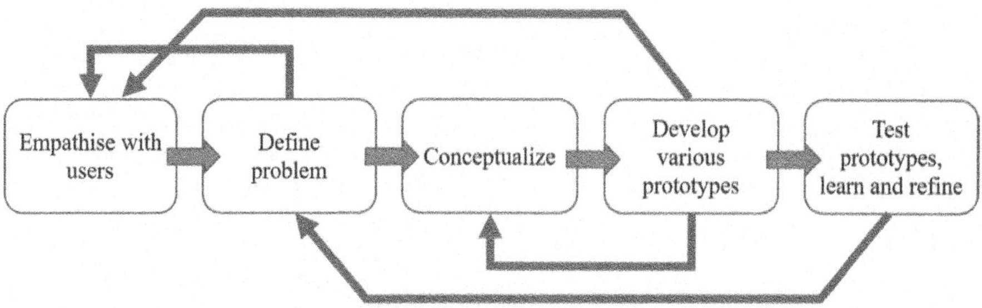

Fig. 3. Design thinking methodology.

Some researches have seen in the conceptual similarities of the three paradigms (agile development, lean innovation and design thinking) an opportunity to investigate the value added by combining them into an aggregated format. Hybridization of more frameworks is not a new approach in engineering. However, besides the benefits of bringing the strengths of each individual model, hybridization might come with some drawbacks, too, such as fuzziness of integration, more steps and higher complexity. Therefore, an important aspect of hybridization is to significantly incline the balance in the favor of benefits with respect to sacrifices. The second aspect is to refine the hybridized solution such as all conflicts brought by aggregation to be eliminated. The third aspect is to define a smooth framework from the combination of the individual concepts; otherwise, the adoption of the new model would not happen. The fourth aspect is to identify potential gaps or drawbacks in both the individual and the aggregated models and to complement them with new concepts (note: if they are available or possible to be discovered).

Thus, this paper continues with a synthesis of existent research contributions in combining the three concepts: agile, lean and design thinking. Value added and limitations of current results are highlighted in the background section. The third section of this paper introduces a roadmap for systematic analysis of the three concepts in order to discover areas with potential to set up an improved model of integration. Based on the conclusions obtained from roadmap application, a new model that integrates agile with lean and design thinking is formulated. Besides integration, the model is enriched with new tools for better handling product development, considering the necessity to tackle conflicts and to master value (i.e. the ration between impact and effort). The paper ends with findings from the application of the new model in a software project and with conclusions.

2 Background

In order to investigate the state-of-the-art on integrating lean, agile and design thinking methodologies in software development, several databases have been consulted: Web of Science, Scopus, Springer Link, IEEE Explorer, and Emerald. In addition, Google Scholar has been consulted. Searching process included combinations of "agile AND lean AND design thinking", as well as "TRIZ AND agile", "TRIZ AND lean AND agile", "TRIZ AND design thinking AND agile", as well as all these combinations with the additional keywords "software" and "project". After cleaning up information, the relevant papers selected for deeper investigation are introduced in the section "References". An important conclusion is that the majority of scientific papers on this topic are published in proceedings of international conferences or books with selected papers from international conferences. Another conclusion is that researches about combining lean and agile, or agile with design thinking are relative recent (not more than 8–9 years), whereas researches about the combination of the three concepts are quite recent published (in the last 2 years). Maybe, this is also the reason that only very few papers on this topic are present in the cited databases. Explicitly, only two research groups have published methodologies that integrate all three concepts [12–14].

Another important ascertainment in relation to the state-of-the-art is the fact that inventive problem solving and TRIZ are taken into account to improve the agile methodology in software development. Recent researches are reported in this respect, with representative results published in [15–17]. In closing the remarks on the searching process about the state-of-the-art relative to the subject under consideration in this paper, it makes sense to highlight the publication of researches that reflect integration of inventiveness in requirements engineering [18]. This element indicates that the early stages of either agile, lean or design thinking methodologies would benefit from structured innovation methods and tools.

Because various aspects of the combination between agile and lean, or lean and design thinking, or agile and design thinking have been analyzed also in relation with the integration of all three into a hybrid concept, it makes sense for the purpose of this paper to elaborate more on the findings currently obtained about the combination "agile-lean-design thinking" as a methodological approach to tackle software projects. The first group of findings comes up from the works [12] and [13], belonging to the same researchers who developed the methodology InnoDev that combines the three paradigms. Their analyses show that an integration of SCRUM practices with design thinking flow and lean innovation could be favorable. Their conclusions are actually based on perceptions of practitioners, as these have been extracted from a representative market survey. However, as the authors of this research highlight, the InnoDev model is only developed at the conceptual stage, with no validation in some projects. Thus, the current researches from papers [12, 13] cannot precisely articulate where and how the integration of agile, lean and design thinking should effectively happen at operational level, in which points methods, tactics and techniques are actually involved in the methodological flow. Nevertheless, besides the value added brought by these researches with the findings from market surveys, works from [12] and [13] indicate how the integration of agile, lean and design thinking would look like. It is a three-phase model, as indicated in Fig. 4. InnoDev introduces design thinking tools in an ad-hoc manner where blockers occur in relation to product development. Sprint and backlog concepts from agile/SCRUM are used in all project phases to plan and tackle activities, in order to provide transparency and to move forward while staying flexible to change requests.

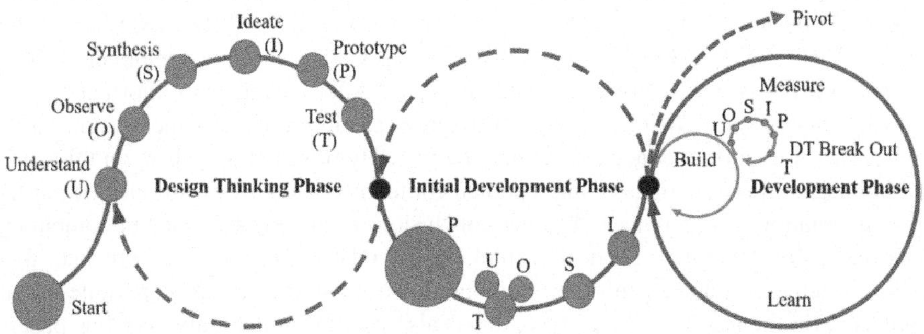

Fig. 4. InnoDev model for lean-agile-design thinking integration in software development (adapted from [12]).

According to InnoDev model, in the "Design Thinking Phase" only the vision to the problem is defined. The refined vision and the proof-of-concept (or minimum viable product (MVP)) realization are encompassed in the "Initial Development Phase" [12, 13]. In this second phase, concepts of user interfaces are designed and tested, technology stacks analysed and tested and the most important features are implemented in order to ensure a tangibility of the concept (e.g. viability, desirability and feasibility) [12]. In the "Development Phase" MVP is tested and continuously expanded towards the final solution, following the cycle "measure-learn-refine" or even pivoting [13]. By investigating the InnoDev model with over 60 SCRUM experts during 6 workshops, our conclusion is this model is still confusing, because in the vast majority of cases during the mentioned workshops, the impression was that the model can be reduced to the last circle from Fig. 4. This means that the first two phases of the model are seen only stages in the agile model, where design thinking tools might be considered within the sprints of the agile methodology. Moreover, the InnoDev model was compared by the consulted SCRUM masters with the model proposed by Gartner [19], which is illustrated in Fig. 5. Experts see the Gartner model and InnoDev model identical with respect to what it is called "customer problem definition" (phase I in InnoDev), but still, the lean startup phase is not well articulated in both InnoDev and Gartner models, as long as it simply looks like a depiction (for visualization purposes) of a sprint within the agile methodology.

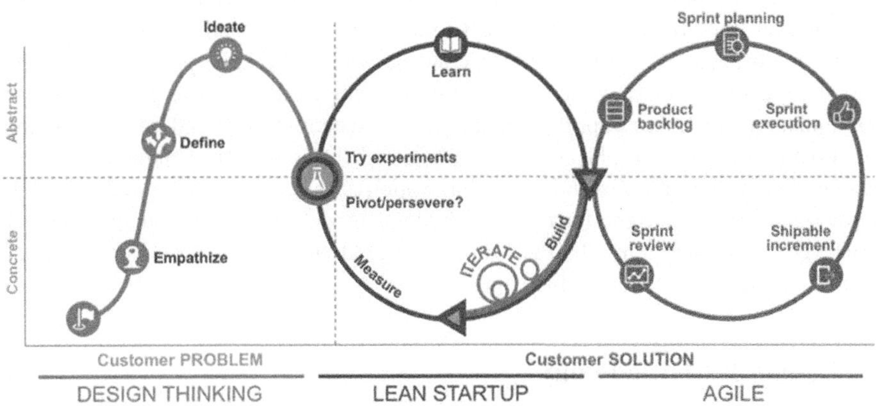

Fig. 5. The Gartner model of the combination agile-lean-design thinking paradigm (source [19]).

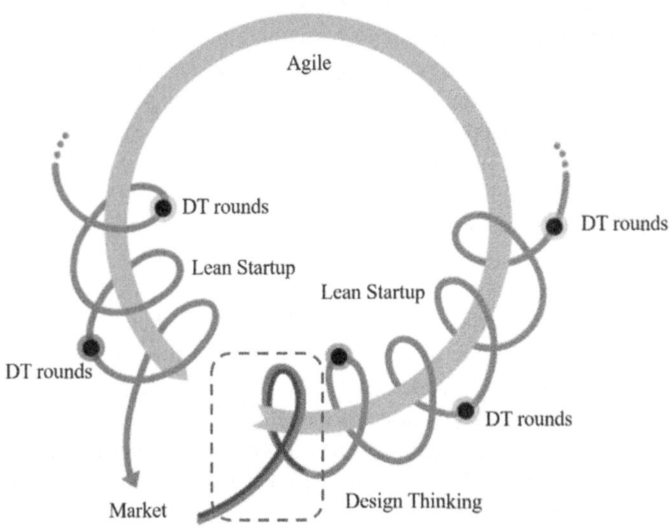

Fig. 6. The Converge model (adapted from [14]).

Another model that combines the three concepts (agile, lean, design thinking) is proposed in the work [14], under the name Converge. The authors indicate that this model is based only on empirical observations, and the combination of the three paradigms was experimented with a group of students over 8 weeks-project lab to develop a homonymous data storage app [14]. This research suggests that combination of the three concepts is productive in comparison with traditional software project management methods, but it cannot precisely indicate where, and why, this combination brings better results. The graphical representation of the Converge model is shown in Fig. 6. The quality of this model stands in the fact that it better visualizes the lean innovation as part of the sprints within the agile methodology. In terms of design thinking, the Converge model does not differ from InnoDev or Gartner models, because, as in those cases, design thinking is seen as the initial phase for project inception and included, where necessary, within the lean innovation loops.

However, the challenge with respect to all three models analyzed in this paper is around the capacity to master the lean concepts within the agile procedures. Lean is also about avoiding waste generation, not only about avoiding waste perpetuation and accumulation. Here, two important paradigms are seen important and not yet explored: (a) structured innovation (TRIZ and ideality), and (b) competitive engineering (value engineering, value analysis and value innovation). Researches of the authors of this paper on refining the agile-lean-design thinking model, as well as on improving its effectiveness by integrating the two additional paradigms in the model, are introduced in the subsequent sections of this paper.

3 Research Methodology

In order to improve the practical value of current models that combine agile with lean and design thinking, the first step in the research roadmap was to tackle the issue of fuzziness of the aggregated models proposed in the literature. In this respect, the first principle of the SAVE method was considered [20]; that is, the resonance principle. According to this principle, the goal is to harmonize the three concepts. To solve this problem, the following generic research approach was revealed: (a) do not consider combination of concepts, but rather creation of a new concept (model) that takes the best of the individual concepts and organize them into a value generation stream (b) depict all the three concepts (agile, lean, design thinking) along the whole life-cycle of a project in order to visualize them at operational level and see where they superpose (are similar), complement each other and where they are in conflict; (c) for the cases of superposition, keep only one of the three concepts, for the cases of complementarity add to the new model those practices, and for the cases of antagonism use inventive problem solving tools to fix the problem (e.g. TRIZ contradiction matrix [21]).

In order to best organize the modules generated from the first step of the research methodology, AIDA method is considered [22]. It can quantify the best arrangement from a set of possible (logical and viable) arrangements of modules. The next step is to investigate the selected arrangement (called ALDET: agile-lean-design thinking) for discovering gaps in terms of effectiveness and efficiency. The reference for gap identification is the paradigm of ideality from TRIZ [21]. In the case of software systems, ideality is related to complexity. The less complex the systems, the closer they are to ideality.

The ideal architecture for a software system is the one that includes completely independent elements (modules), where each element performs a single function. In such an ideal architecture/design the system complexity is minimized. Thus, from the ALDET perspective, the goal is to avoid generation and accumulation of complexity in both project life-cycle and product solution. To solve the conflict between dynamicity and complexity, TRIZ suggests application of asymmetry by more pivoting, concurrent development, fast-preplanning, and discard and recover resources.

To master value in system development from the perspective of lean philosophy, within the research methodology we opted for considering competitive engineering paradigm. This paradigm embraces things from concurrent engineering, lean six sigma, design for six sigma, and quality function deployment and it can be synthesized under the framework from Fig. 7.

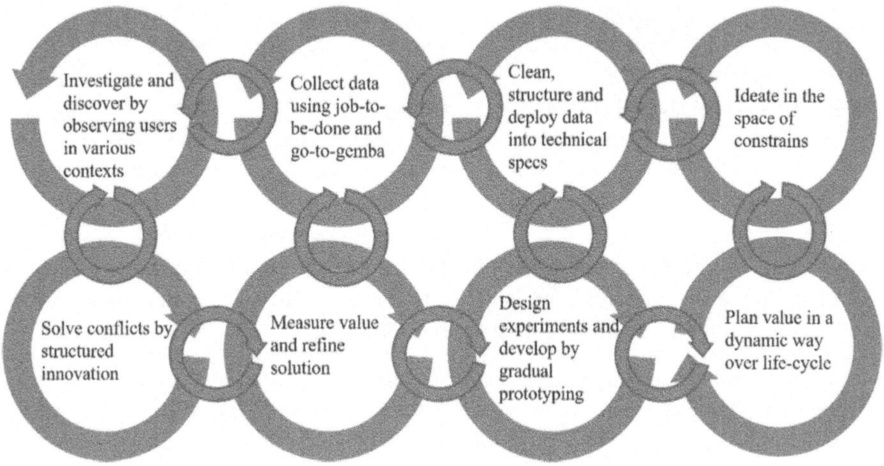

Fig. 7. Competitive engineering methodology (authors' synthesis).

By means of the same approach indicated in the first step of the methodology, competitive engineering can be captured in the ALDET model. The result is called in this paper CALDET (note: Competitive ALDET). The next section of this paper highlights the main findings from the application of the proposed research methodology.

4 ALDET and CALDET Models

The three methodologies have been depicted into smaller steps within the main phases, according to the recommendations of the proposed research roadmap. By analyzing similarities and differences, the key finding in this stage of investigation was that the three paradigms do not actually differ too much in practice and in philosophy, excepting the fact that each paradigm uses a different language because each of them has a different source of origin. Agile sprang from the world of software industry, lean has the source of inspiration in lean production and uncertain market management, whereas design thinking comes up from the world of designers and creative industry. Thus, this stage of the research led to a set of information that are summarized in the following Table 1.

Table 1. A view of agile, lean and design thinking by superposing their operational layers.

	Design thinking	Lean innovation	Agile management
Similarity	Iterative prototyping	Progressive prototyping	Sprint prototyping
	Periodic testing	Phase-gate testing	Sprint-framed testing
	Measure results	Measure results	Measure results
	Learn and refine	Learn and refine	Learn and refine
	Empathize with users	Identify opportunities	(No explicit step)
	Define problem	Understand users	Backlog initiation
	Co-creation	Co-creation	Product owner
	Ideation	Conceptualization	Brainstorming
	Feedback loops	(No explicit step)	Backlog updating
	Develop	Develop	Build
Complementarity	Jump-back loops	Pivoting	Sprint framework
Conflictuality	Deeper user planning	Early user mapping	Rapid solutions
	Choose and focus	Concurrent design	Late change requests

As Table 1 indicates, integration of the three paradigms requires either to select one path of the three in the conflicting areas or to solve conflicts in an inventive way. In essence, the following conflicting problems occur:

- start fast with what you have at the first glance and then adjust during sprints vs. spending a bit more time in the very early stage for mapping and planning users
- fix the solution at a certain stage of progress for consolidation and avoidance of complexity vs. accept change requests even in the very late stages of the project

With the support of TRIZ contradiction matrix, the problem above can be formulated as: speed versus reliability and adaptability versus complexity. For the first case, TRIZ suggests the following generic measures: moderation in advance, change the concentration of state and/or flexibility, dispose something expensive with several inexpensive elements, and introduce a softer approach. For the second case, TRIZ indicates the following generic actions: reconfigurable construction, interchangeability, expansion and contraction, as well as introduction of softer approaches.

Generic measures/actions have been translated into the following practical solutions: (a) any project will start with a time-boxing session where a task-force with representative of all stakeholders in the project will accelerate the formulation of a robust vision and a critical mass of specs; (b) besides the every morning session of 15 min. in the sprint framework, a mid-week ideation & co-creation session is included (including a platform for idea management, too); (c) technical development should consider in coding and architecting the core principles of reconfigurability for every sprint-related shippable prototype, i.e. modularity, convertibility, customizability, interoperability, scalability, portability, decoupling and avoidance of software asymmetry; (d) various tools and sessions can be added or eliminated in the context (e.g. application of various paths and means for problem formulation, ideation, etc.).

With these completions added to the elements from Table 1, and selecting only one perspective for those elements that are similar in the three models, the set of stage-gate elements of the ALDET model comprises: (e1) empathize with users, (e2) backlog initiation driven by user understanding, (e3) co-creation, (e4) sprint prototyping, (e5) sprint testing, (e6) measure results, (e7) learn, (e8) refine, (e9) ideation, (e10) backlog updating from multiple loops, (e11) build, (e12) sprint, (e13) pivoting, (e14) jump-back loops, (e15) time-boxing session, (e16) daily sprint session, (e17) mid-week ideation/co-creation session, (e18) reconfigurability-driven design and coding, (e19) flexible selection of tools. For every element from the set of 19 elements that can have more options, AIDA causality analysis was taken into account [22]. For exemplification, the selection of the best option for the element "co-creation" is shown in Fig. 8. The analysis criteria, also called constrains, are for this case the followings: (a) avoid complexity; (b) increase productivity; (c) reduce waste; (d) increase convergence. The options for "co-creation" are: (o1) application only at the early stage; (o2) application once in each sprint; (o3) application each mid-week session; (o4) application in each testing phase; (o5) inclusion of o1 and o2; (o6) inclusion of o1, o2, o3 and o4.

Step 1: influence of constrains on options [1 - low, 2 -medium, 3-high]

	o1	o2	o3	o4	o5	o6
a	3	2	3	2	3	1
b	3	2	2	1	2	1
c	3	2	1	1	2	1
d	3	2	1	1	2	1

Step 2: influence of options on constrains

	a	b	c	d
o1	3	1	1	1
o2	2	1	2	2
o3	1	1	3	3
o4	2	1	2	2
o5	2	1	2	2
o6	1	1	1	1

Step 3: products of coefficients from step 1 and step 2

	o1	o2	o3	o4	o5	o6	Σ C/6
a	9	4	3	4	6	1	4,5
b	3	2	2	1	2	1	1,8333
c	3	4	3	2	4	1	2,8333
d	3	4	3	2	4	1	2,8333
Σ O/4	4,5	3,5	2,8	2,3	4	1	

Fig. 8. Exemplification of AIDA to identify the best option for the element "co-creation".

According to the results from Fig. 8, option (o1) "application of co-creation only at the early stage" is selected. The result is counter intuitive. This indicates the usefulness of applying structured methods of analysis in the conceptualization process of new methodologies. The same approach has been applied for the rest of the 18 elements. At the end of this process, the necessary information to formulate the ALDET model was revealed. The result is shown in Fig. 9.

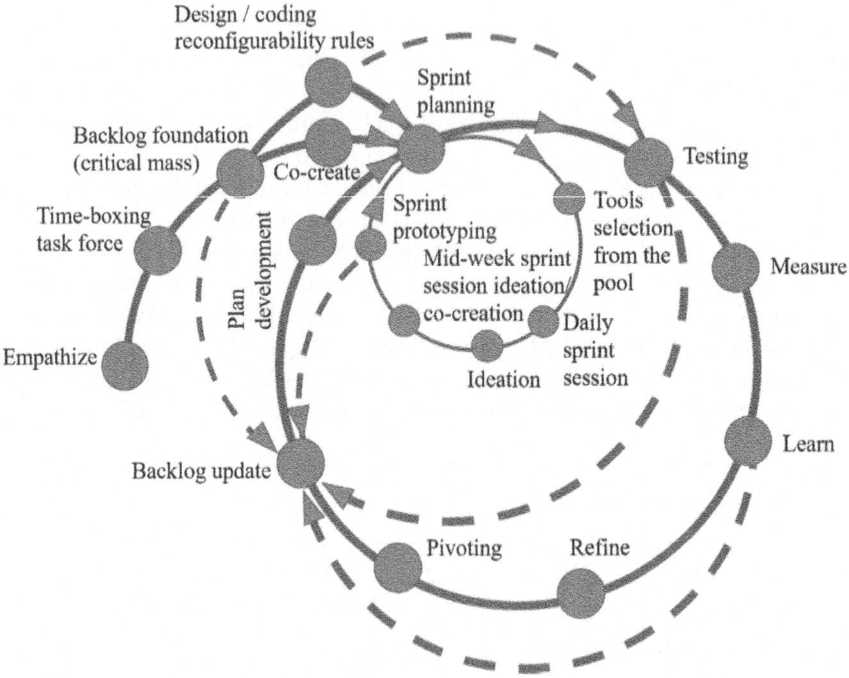

Fig. 9. The ALDET model.

ALDET model starts with the "empathize" phase in order to identify opportunities, and continues with a rapid development procedure (time-boxing session) to understand users and define a mature vision. Then, the backlog is fed with the critical mass of information. Before project starting, a co-creation hackathon is included. Simultaneously, the rules for reconfigurable design and coding is run. From this point, the first sprint is started. Each sprint comprises, besides the traditional elements, the continuous enhancement of the toolkit and selection of the most appropriate tools for the specific sprint, as well as the individual ideation and the mid-week session for collective ideation and co-creation. The iteration loop adds to the traditional agile process the stage of pivoting if lessons indicate this necessity. New to the model is the circuits of feedback loops (highlighted with dashed lines in Fig. 9).

The upgraded version of ALDET results at the intersection of ALDET with competitive engineering. The enhanced ALDET is called CALDET and its framework is illustrated in Fig. 10.

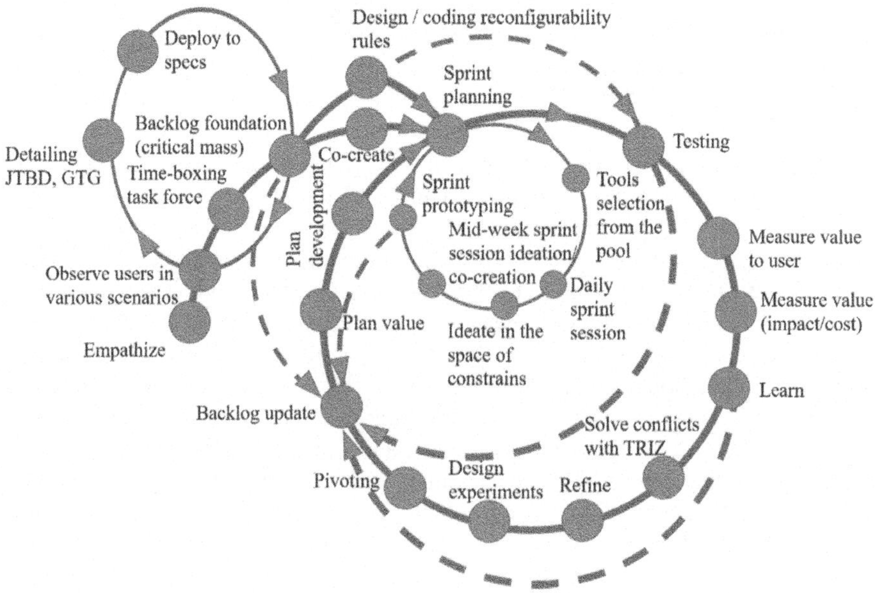

Fig. 10. The CALDET model.

CALDET goes deeper to master value quantification and management, and to speed up convergence to a mature solution by considering constrains and conflicts for innovating in a systematic way during spring progression and iterations. In addition, CALDET considers a loop for deeper investigation of users, which is simultaneously run with the main loop of ALDET. To handle value, this paper recommends the use of value analysis matrices (e.g. QFD, relationship matrices, etc.). This aspect is not treated here.

The next section introduces the feedback collected from a team which applied the CALDET model in a software project. The focus of the following section is on team's experiences and impact in using CALDET, rather than on illustrating the results of the project, which is less relevant for the purpose of this research.

5 Experimentation and Discussions

In this section we describe the experience of employing CALDET in a project called InnDrive, dealing with the development of a software tool dedicated to start-up entrepreneurs, in order to evaluate the innovative potential of their business ideas, execution maturity and capacity of the their teams.

The initial definition of the scope for the software tool was based on a systematic assessment of the challenges confronting the start-up team members involved in early stage innovations, with a particular focus on innovative projects having an IT component. Engaging with early stage entrepreneurs and start-up team members, conducting interviews and structured assessments on the knowledge and readiness levels of the subjects, the innDrive team concluded that there is a clear need for a tool that can assist the start-up founders to evaluate and refine their understanding on all dimensions of the new business, identify the weak points in their plan and the aspects where they should focus, gain knowledge or put more work.

The entire project was strictly confined in the calendar and in the budget determined by a grant. Thus, the innDrive team had to handle the project in the given time and cost and to make ready for the market a product that is both useful and competitive.

According to CALDET methodology, observation of entrepreneurs in various scenarios was the first challenge. This process was conducted with contextual inquiry interviews. One-day workshop can generate a significant amount of information, with clear advantage on calibrating the task-force team and the key subjects to be discussed during the time-boxing session. Time-boxing session was organized within two meetings, each meeting of 4 h, with several inter-disciplinary working teams (developers, researchers, consultants, mentors, entrepreneurs) operating in parallel to extract needs, functional specifications and candidate technologies. It was proved that, by calibrating the time-boxing in this way, sufficient information have been collected such as to feed the backlog to a critical mass of elements for starting the sprint processes. Co-creation in this project was directed towards getting suggestions for GUI, how the help module to be designed and what content to be included. Here experts, consultants and end users collaborated in a face-to-face session, continued by a collaborative work on a web platform dedicated for such purposes.

In parallel with the time-boxing session and co-creation session, innDrive team experts conduced a systematic analysis of the problem using the Job-To-Be-Done (JTBD) method in order to reveal processes in start-up evolution, outcomes, which outcomes are underserved by current means and tools, and to extract relevant specs for feeding the backlog. It is important to highlight the fact that, by simultaneously feeding the backlog with information generated from two different streams (JTBD and time-boxing), is essential in CALDET (both for reciprocal confirmation of the work performed and reciprocal support with sources of information).

The refinement process of data generated with JTBD actually continued even after the first sprint started. This is a powerful element of CALDET, because it allows to update the backlog anytime, with quality inputs, keeping no huge pressure on the pace to which data and info are generated. Another powerful element in CALDET is the package of rules to design and code based on reconfigurability rules. This input can be actually done outside the scope of a given project, as a good practice in the company. Once the know-how is present, it can be instantaneously deployed to any new project. Nevertheless, CALDET suggests to revisit these rules in the early stage of any new project, just to see if not new elements would be necessary for every particular project. This work is concurrently done with the co-creation process, it is run by the technical stuff, and it uses inputs from the backlog foundation stage.

In this particular project, sprints were calibrated at a two-week cadence. Another key strength of CALDET revealed in the project was the mid-week sprint session for ideation and co-creation, where various representatives of all stakeholders have been involved. The key finding in this process was the fact that, not the same representatives of the stakeholders have to be involved over the whole project duration. By introducing new representatives, the project gets new perspectives and proofs the capacity of fast understating and adoption by the new comers. Thus, in this project, entrepreneurs from both local ecosystem (i.e. Cluj-Napoca city) and international ecosystems (e.g. EU and non-EU countries) have been involved in various sprints. In the particular case of the InnDrive project, major contributions from the stakeholders during the mid-week sessions, with visible effects on the project's speed, were on clarity and relevancy of the content embedded in the developed tool, GUI's usability and intuitiveness, as well as functional details of the platform.

Another key elements of CALDET, which indicated its effectiveness in the project, were the value mapping step and problem solving step. Both are activated to treat the results of every completed sprint, in parallel with the run of the next sprint. For value mapping, a QFD-based matrix was used, but in a dynamic way (meaning that inputs and outputs in the relationship matrix can be changed any time). Value mapping created alarms for developers to handle sprints in a more innovative way, especially in relation with the ideation stage within the sprint. Value mapping creates a pressure on developers to achieve a certain level of performance in a given, justified, budget. This pressure was actually proved to be the engine for the TRIZ sessions within the incremental loops of CALDET. For example, one issue was in relation with the quantity and type of info to be included in the help module related to each assessment criteria. TRIZ was applied in this case such as: reduce the "amount of substance" without affecting "capacity". TRIZ indications are: reconfigurable construction, make the module more movable, design a heterogeneous construction such as to increase the local quality in a dynamic way, and/or dispose parts which are not anymore relevant. With these indications, the system was designed such as the "help module" to start with a info-graphic schematics and then to be continuously enriched with data, info, examples relative to each issue/assessment criteria by any contributor in the platform, anytime, under a control for uploading content in the system. Inputs can be added into modules that can be afterwards interlinked, added, enhanced or eliminated. It works like a living organism.

Pivoting stage of each iteration proved to be another strength of CALDET methodology. For the first rounds of sprints, the innDrive team used the pivoting stage only with start-up entrepreneurs and experts in mind. Once the innDrive system approached the minimal viable product (MVP) state, engagement was directed towards start-ups outside the focus group, including various organizations from various countries involved in the evaluation, mentorship or financing of start-ups, even incubators, accelerators, venture capital funds, innovation program management units at national level, management authorities of public financing programs, innovation management units in the private corporations, bank managers responsible with the evaluation of credit requests targeted to support new business projects, evaluators of calls for grants.

This massive engagement revealed new patterns that determined innDrive to pivot, both in how it supports various types of users and in the business approach. The major discovery was that start-ups that were approached with a more mature application and were not involved in the development process lacked the discipline to conduct the complex assessments by themselves, although invariably they expressed initial enthusiasm. The novelty and level of focus required by conducting a self-assessment based on the platform determined a staggering level of abandon, of 70–80% of the subjects. Off the other actors in the ecosystem that were engaged, the strongest positive reaction was obtained from the program managers who are facilitating or managing start-up funding and mentorship programs and they were very eager to implement the innDrive system into their programs, once it is optimized to support the mentorship and coaching interactions in the application itself.

As result, the innDrive team had to redesign the functional workflow, introducing the roles of program managers and mentors/coaches, and giving to those roles the possibility to initiate, assign, and evaluate project assessments in relation with the entrepreneurs and to develop and follow action plans resulting from the reports generated from the assessments. At this level, CALDET proved to show another strength, meaning reconfigurability-driven design and coding style. It was easy in the forthcoming sprints to make the necessary modifications without a big effort and in due time.

The entire development of innDrive was finished in time and in budget, preserving the initial scope of assisting start-ups and project teams in assessing their capacity to sustain the project, while introducing a strong emphasize on the assistance roles and focusing the commercial focus of the innDrive project towards the managers of venture programs.

6 Conclusions

This paper introduces researches conducted to understand the state of scientific progress on integrating sectorial models for managing innovative software projects (agile, lean, DT) into hybrids, with the purpose to bring the capacity of handling complex projects to an upper level. Three models (InnoDev, Gartner and Converge) have been analyzed in this respect, concluding that many empty spaces are present in doing integration and thus, opportunities for further researches are envisaged. The key findings about the state-of-the-art were the fuzziness of integration on one side, and the incapacity to demonstrate the effectiveness of the integrated model (e.g. why to follow the proposed stream of actions in that order and not differently) on the other side. However, from the three studied models, our researches conclude that Converge is better equipped, even if some drawbacks are signaled in this case, too, such as the justification of fully application of design thinking in every loop of lean innovation. Our investigation on this issue with SCRUM masters indicates a rejection in practice rather than adoption, because of time consumption that affects sprints and because it is not clear how to, for example, apply all steps of design thinking in a late loop of lean innovation.

Reflecting on the current state of developments with TRIZ tools, this paper introduces a model called CALDET that claims advantages with respect to previous models because it avoids redundancies between the integrated concepts, orders the steps in a justified way (due to the use of quantitative tools to prove this) and cleans the roadmap from fuzziness because the model not just integrates agile, lean and design thinking, but rather embeds them into a new flow that comprehends the best of the three sectorial approaches. Beyond these aspects, the novelty of CALDET comes also from the inclusion of the fourth concept; that is, competitive engineering, offering on this way tools to measure value in the lean approach and to reveal the relevance of structured innovation in any iteration of the agile flow. Even if up to this date CALDET was tested only in a single project, it proves to be very effective, encouraging the research team to continue investigating the model. In this respect, future researches will be conducted to enrich the model with refined templates at each stage, and especially to deepen investigation on the stage referring to reconfigurability of code, because this will bring a huge advantage in agility, especially when pivoting is involved.

References

1. Zapata-Roldan, F.: Design capabilities in software innovation settings. In: Portland International Conference on Management of Engineering and Technology, pp. 1236–1243. IEEE, Portland (2017)
2. Fraser, D., Abrahamsson, P., Davies, R., Kerievsky, J., Poppendieck, M., Succi, G.: The future of lean in an agile world. In: International Conference Agile Processes in Software Engineering and Extreme Programming, pp. 263–266. Pula (2009)
3. Staron, M., Meding, W.: Monitoring bottlenecks in agile and lean software development projects – a method and its industrial use. In: Caivano, D., Oivo, M., Baldassarre, M.T., Visaggio, G. (eds.) PROFES 2011. LNCS, vol. 6759, pp. 3–16. Springer, Heidelberg (2011). https://doi.org/10.1007/978-3-642-21843-9_3
4. Rodriquez, P., Markkula, J., Oivu, M., Garbajosa, J.: Analyzing the drivers of the combination of lean and agile in software development companies. In: International Conference on Product Focused Software Process Improvement, pp. 145–159. UPM, Madrid (2012)
5. Glomann, L.: Introducing 'Human-Centered Agile Workflow' (HCAW) – an agile conception and development process model. In: Ahram, T., Falcão, C. (eds.) AHFE 2017. AISC, vol. 607, pp. 646–655. Springer, Cham (2018). https://doi.org/10.1007/978-3-319-60492-3_61
6. Laanti, M.: Characteristics and principles of scaled agile. In: Dingsøyr, T., Moe, N.B., Tonelli, R., Counsell, S., Gencel, C., Petersen, K. (eds.) XP 2014. LNBIP, vol. 199, pp. 9–20. Springer, Cham (2014). https://doi.org/10.1007/978-3-319-14358-3_2
7. Halas, M.: Lessons for TRIZ from design thinking and lean 3P. In: Koziołek, S., Chechurin, L., Collan, M. (eds.) Advances and Impacts of the Theory of Inventive Problem Solving, pp. 159–168. Springer, Cham (2018). https://doi.org/10.1007/978-3-319-96532-1_15
8. Elberzhager, F., Holl, K., Karn, B., Immich, T.: Rapid lean UX development through user feedback revelation. In: Felderer, M., Méndez Fernández, D., Turhan, B., Kalinowski, M., Sarro, F., Winkler, D. (eds.) PROFES 2017. LNCS, vol. 10611, pp. 535–542. Springer, Cham (2017). https://doi.org/10.1007/978-3-319-69926-4_43
9. Canedo, E., Parente da Costa, R.: The use of design thinking in agile software requirements survey: a case study. In: International Conference of Design, User Experience, and Usability, pp. 642–657. UNB, Brasilia (2018)

10. Cockton, G.: Integrating both user-centered design and creative practices into agile development. In: Cockton, G., Lárusdóttir, M., Gregory, P., Cajander, Å. (eds.) Integrating User-Centred Design in Agile Development. HIS, pp. 249–276. Springer, Cham (2016). https://doi.org/10.1007/978-3-319-32165-3_11
11. Hildenbrand, T., Meyer, J.: Intertwining lean and design thinking: software product development from empathy to shipment. In: Maedche, A., Botzenhardt, A., Neer, L. (eds.) Software for People, pp. 217–237. Springer, Berlin (2012). https://doi.org/10.1007/978-3-642-31371-4_13
12. Dobrigkeit, F., Paula, D.: The best of three worlds - the creation of INNODEV a software development approach that integrates design thinking, SCRUM and lean startup. In: International Conference on Engineering Design, pp. 319–328. Design Soc., Vancouver (2017)
13. Dobrigkeit, F., Paula, D., Uflacker, M.: InnoDev: a software development methodology integrating design thinking, SCRUM and lean startup. In: Leifer, L., Meinel, C. (eds.) Design Thinking Research, pp. 199–227. Springer, Heidelberg (2019). https://doi.org/10.1007/978-3-319-97082-0_11
14. Ximenes, B., Alves, I., Araujo, C.: Software project management combining agile, lean startup and design thinking. In: International Conference of Design, User Experience, and Usability, pp. 356–367. UFPE, Recife (2015)
15. Casner, D., Souili, A., Houssin, R., Renaud, J.: Agile'TRIZ framework: towards the integration of TRIZ within the agile innovation methodology. In: Cavallucci, D., De Guio, R., Koziołek, S. (eds.) TFC 2018. IAICT, vol. 541, pp. 84–93. Springer, Cham (2018). https://doi.org/10.1007/978-3-030-02456-7_8
16. Ma, J., Zhang, Q., Wang, Y., Luo, T.: Construction of the dependence matrix based on the TRIZ contradiction matrix in OOD. In: Tan, R., Cao, G., León, N. (eds.) CAI 2009. IAICT, vol. 304, pp. 219–230. Springer, Heidelberg (2009). https://doi.org/10.1007/978-3-642-03346-9_24
17. Fulbright, R.: Incorporating innovation into iterative software development using the inventive problem solving methodology. Int. J. Innov. Sci. **5**(4), 203–212 (2013)
18. Sa'adah, H., Azrina, K., Novia, A., Marzanah, J.: Towards developing an approach to confluence innovative in requirements engineering. In: Fujita, H., Selamat, A., Omatu, S. (eds.) New Trends in Intelligent Software Methodologies, Tools and Techniques, pp. 164–175. IOS Press, Amsterdam (2017)
19. Mantini, N.: Design thinking, lean startup and agile: what is the difference? https://medium.com/xplor8/design-thinking-lean-startup-and-agile-what-is-the-difference-1eed3594b121. Accessed 03 Apr 2019
20. Brad, S.: Structured Activation of Vertex Entropy (SAVE): another way around creative problem solving for non-technical applications. INNOVATOR J. Eur. TRIZ Assoc. **01/2017** (03), 76–81 (2017)
21. Petrov, V.: TRIZ – Theory of Inventive Problem Solving – Level 1. Springer, Heidelbeeg (2019)
22. Brad, S.: Improving the use of AIDA method. Acta Technica Napocensis, Ser.: Appl. Math. Mech. **50**(1), 45–48 (2007)

Future Home 4.0 for People with Major Neurodegenerative Disorders, Finding the Contradictions

Jean Renaud[1,2(✉)], Rémy Houssin[1], Negar Armaghan[3], and Mickaël Gardoni[2]

[1] ICube UMR-7357, Strasbourg 67, France
jean.renaud@insa-strasbourg.fr
[2] ÉTS, 1100, Rue Notre-Dame Ouest, Montréal, QC, Canada
[3] Department of Technology Development Studies, Iranian Research Organization for Science and Technology, P.O. Box 33535-11, Tehran, Iran
armaghan@irost.org

Abstract. With the aging of the population, old people increasingly wish to stay at home before entering to a retirement home. There are several reasons such as: the cost of entry, the impersonal side and the lack of solicitation as well isolation and lack of identity are the elements that could delay the entry into the retirement home.

In this research, we would like to focus on persons with major neurodegenerative disorders who would like to stay at home as long as possible. These disorders are more and more present with aging of population, which lead us to reflect on the future home 4.0 by permitting residents to live their activities of daily living (ADL).

New technologies and connected objects could be the potential solutions for designing the future home. During this study, we will identify the contradictions that could be existed among different solution's concepts based on functional criteria. These criteria are proposed in parameters according to the TRIZ method in order to propose principles of solution's concepts.

Keywords: Usage · Multi-user · Contradiction · Design · Neurodegenerative disorders

1 Introduction

In the next ten years, the sociological face of French society will have changed because of ageing the population. People over 60 years old will represent a third of the population in 2040. People will live longer, but, with the emergence of new diseases, such as major neurodegenerative disorders, such as Alzheimer, Parkinson, Lewy bodies Corps, dementia vascular… [1], these pathologies differ from others as mobility difficulties or other physical disabilities.

The Neurological pathologies will have an effect on people staying at home, on their level of autonomy, as well, on their ability to continue the activities of daily living

Published by Springer Nature Switzerland AG 2019
R. Benmoussa et al. (Eds.): TFC 2019, IFIP AICT 572, pp. 417–426, 2019.
https://doi.org/10.1007/978-3-030-32497-1_33

[2]. People affected by this pathology have also an impact on the healthcare assistant, that make him/her exhausted, tired and depressed.

The aim of this research is how to care these fragile people at home by identifying the contradictions and complementarity between their needs and their hops. Hence, the interest of this research is to adapt the home to this new situation. We will focus in this research on the future home 4.0 [3], particularly on the needs and functional study.

2 Research Approach

Our approach in this research will be using a mix of the methods SWOT, User Experience and functional analysis. Each method will be satisfied and answered to the needs of our case.

The SWOT (Strengths, Weaknesses, Opportunities and Threats) method permit us to analyze and diagnostic the current situation of resident by Strengths, Weaknesses, Opportunities and Threats. The factors which are important role in her/his environment both interior and exterior of home. The objective of user experience is multiple. It can be user experience for a resident life style at home, healthcare assistance, nurses or other person who help the resident. We will discuss for all type of users in this paper. For example, the resident need to participate and to perform their daily activities.

She/he should use specific product, system, or services immediately in an easier way in our case. This products, system or service must be ergonomic and applicable immediately. The functional analysis method allows us to do study of needs for the new home 4.0. [4], that we used it based on TRIZ approaches. Figure 1 show the relations and needs in our methodological approach.

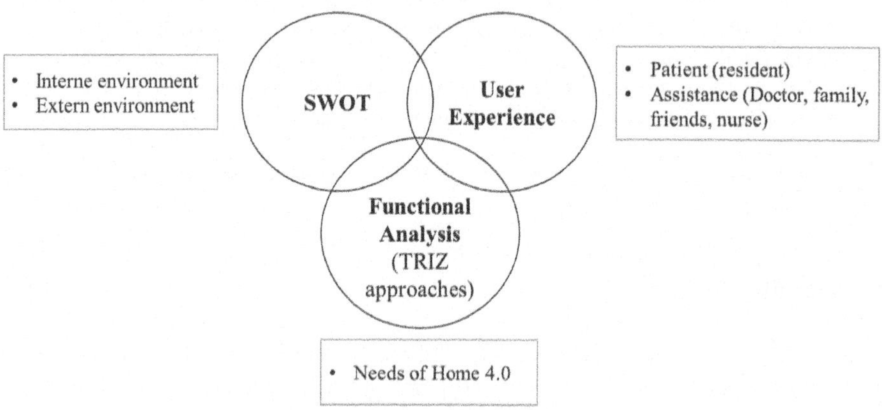

Fig. 1. Our methodological approach

3 Home 4.0

3.1 Current Situation

In these days, the old French people wish to stay at home as long as possible. They prefer to delay the time of moving to retirement home, whether alone or rally around. Therefore, their family at home tries to innovate or have a long-term planning. They start to modify their house or apartment, such as rearranging the bathroom (on a level) or removing the access of rooms on the floor and preparing house on a level. Sometimes, they sell their house and by another. Therefore, they try to change their house to have more functional and comfortable for their old person. That means they anticipate rearranging the house depending disabilities of their old person. In the framework of this work, it is necessary to demonstrate the way of preparing home for the old person in order that he/she could stay at home as long as possible. It is about replacing the user, the future resident, at home as part of his/her needs and imagine the future home to be functional [5]. The future resident of home 4.0 could be different kind of users at home and the user or resident in this paper is mainly the old person how will live in home 4.0. The other users could be presented at Home 4.0 such as: a healthcare assistant, nurse, family doctor or neighbors.

3.2 The Analyze of Current Home Based on SWOT Method

At first, we propose to perform analysis of strengths and weakness for the current home in order to reflect on the future home 4.0. These analyses are based on SWOT method. This assessment permits us to provide a better understanding of the resident's interests at home, about his/her strengths and limits and possibility to improve the house (Table 1).

Table 1. Study of the current home from the SWOT grid

Strengths	*Weaknesses*
- Continue to have her/his habits and activities at home - Social bond with friends and neighbors - The resident is not disoriented - The budget is lower regarding the place - Keep his mark on the surrounding, neighbors, friends. - Feel more comfortable in the apartment - The resident has self-confidence thanks to this autonomy - The resident could be always autonomous	- The resident is alone with an evolving pathology and with security risks - Less monitoring - Monitoring is not continuous - Isolation of the resident, anonymity - Non-regularity of needs - Any alerts in case of problems (fall down, slips, or movements…)
Opportunities	*Threats*
- Activities of daily living are not only stopped, but also are active by cognitive stimulation - The resident "EXIST" and has an identity - The effects of the disease could be delayed - Cost of retirement home could be still saved	- Retirements homes are growing… - There is no financial ways to renovate or update the home - The resident is ALONE at home - There is no more help, in case of natural disaster or technical problem in the building

In SWOT method, Strengths, Weaknesses are about intern factors, in our case it is about the situation of resident at home. The Opportunities and Threats are about extern factor, so in our case exterior of resident's home, means environment factors which could have an effect on the resident.

3.3 The Future Home 4.0

The connected and automated objects will have main place in this new future home 4.0. The objective is not setting up a hyper connected environment, but to assess the autonomy of the resident and evaluate her/his needs as an actor for his/her daily activities [6]. The renovated home will not only be a place to live her/his end of life in a way just "cared", but also, to be able as an actor to manage his/her handicaps and degree of autonomy. Hence, the home should not just be a place to live, but, a place where cognitive stimulation or other forms of stimulation are part of daily activities.

The type of home that we would like to design for the resident consist in being able to stimulate activities of daily living (ADL) safely, in a way that the social bond is as well safeguard.

Actually, in this case, there is the expertise of user instead of customer's needs. That means, the resident of the home is no more a customer who expects a service for a payment, but, an expert user who knows his/her pathology through the healthcare assistant. The healthcare assistant changes his role; she/he has to no more suffer the effects of disease, but must anticipate its effects. The medical body does not only provide the care or a specific service, but also, they must accompany the resident in his activities of daily life [7, 8].

4 User Experience UX

4.1 Definition of User Experience UX

In recent years, some authors have focused on the user experience, called "user experience (UX)" [9, 10]. This refers to the experience of a person using a specific product, system or service. It's about making a product, a system easy to use, understandable immediately, ergonomic, logical, by integrating user experience into product design [11, 12].

In this sense, design studies must be able to identify or consider different users according to the product's life cycle. It is not rare to note that the product in operation phase has several users. Designers must transform customer's/user's requirements into product performance. It should be noted that the requirements of the customer are not the same as those of user (it is the first level of contradiction). Subsequently, the designers will have to prioritize these users, in order to better understand the features of the product according to the type of user. The functional analysis makes it possible to answer it.

4.2 Different Users UX

Analyzing a need means translating the product into "Customer specifications" and/or "User's specifications". The "client as user" reasons in solutions rather than needs. When there are multiple users, we talk about multi-users. The functional analysis approach is a response to this search for users' needs. In our study for designing the future home, we are looking for different types of users as showed in Table 2.

Table 2. The different users at home.

User type	(UX_i)	User-Experience	Activities
Resident at home (different users)	UX_1	Cooker	Culinary activities, washings dishes, setting the table…
	UX_2	Gardener	Gardening, Planting, Watering…
	UX_3	Cleaning agent	Setting the table, clearing the table, washing dishes …
Healthcare assistant	UX_4	Nursing	Toilet, hygiene…
Nurse and/or doctor	UX_5	Medical follow-up, taking medicine	Manage medicine, perform care
Neighbors and/or Friends	UX_6	Conviviality, social bond,	Sharing moments, tea, outing…
Relationship, family	UX_7	Legal guardian, guardianship…	Guarantor against institutions
Care staff	UX_8	Speech therapist, Physiotherapist…	Bridging or stimulating the resident's lack of autonomy

5 Functional Analysis for Home 4.0

5.1 Study of Needs

A study of need is required in order to know exactly the needs for this new home 4.0. We propose to use the tools of study needs for functional analysis proposed by the firm APTE. There are some questions raise in order to define the goal or objective of this future home 4.0.

- Who does it help?
- What is used for?
- Who is it acting on?
- What does it work on?

At last, for what purpose or objective? We present in Table 3 a synthetic result of study of needs for future home 4.0 by using the tool of cabinet APTE.

Table 3. Study of the need for the future home4.0

Who does it help?	People with major neurodegenerative disorders (MND)
What is used for?	Make their life easy and safe
Who is it acting on?	Multi-user (patient, caregiver, etc.)
What does it work on?	Daily life activities' simulation
For what purpose or objective?	Allow people with MND to stay in their adapted home (future 4.0) to their pathology as long as possible
Why this need exists? (purpose, reason)	Many people will be getting old with this pathology and wish to stay at home as long as possible. The retirement homes are limited and do not completely respond to this new pathology
What could make it disappear? or evolve it?	A remedy, medicine… cure these pathologies of memory disorders
What is the risk of disappear?	Nowadays, there is no any positive sign that appears as a solution to fight against these pathologies

5.2 Functional Analysis

We made our analysis form two levels: outside environment search and Service and constraints functions. The results of our analysis from outside environment search is presented in Table 4.

Table 4. Outside environment search

Mi	Type of outside environment	Description of outside environment
M_1	Kitchen equipment	Set of utensils for cooking…
M_2	Gardening equipment	Bins, flowerpots, utensils, watering can,
M_3	Mobility system	seeds…
M_4	Home resident	Staircase, walker, wheelchair, cane
M_5	Help team and accompanied[a]	Person with MND, early stages (pathology) Healthcare assistant, Living Assistant Gerontology
M_6	Security ways	Alarm, keys, Digi code…
M_7	Nurse, doctor, parents…	Medical corps specialized in home care
M_8	Speech therapist, Kenseisha[b]	Specialists in effects of pathology
M_9	Hygiene equipment, maintenance	Sponge, broom, washing machine,
M_{10}	Entertainment system	brush, products
		TV, games, books, armchair

[a]*accompaniment (Healthcare assistant, Living Assistant...)*
[b]*physiotherapist*

In Service functions and constraints functions levels, the results are presented in the Table 5:

Table 5. Service functions' list or future home constraints

F_i	Description of functions	Criteria C_j	Level N_k	Flex. Fl..
F_1	The home 4.0 must allow resident to be mobile thanks to the mobility system	Mobility Type of material	100% Base	Fl.2
F_2	The home 4.0 must allow resident to dispose kitchen equipment for doing culinary activities safely	Type of material Type of activities	Autonomes	Fl.3
F_3	The home 4.0 must allow resident to welcome help team such as, doctor, nurse, physiotherapist, neighbors, parents… in good conditions.	Type of help Type of reception	Pathology Access Intervention	Fl.3
F_4	The home 4.0 must allow resident to practice gardening activities safely	Type of activity Type of security	Autonomous 100%	Fl.3
F_5	The home 4.0 must integrate home security systems of resident	systems Level	100%	Fl.1
F_6	Home 4.0 must be adapted to receive health personnel in order to provide personalized care to resident	Type of access Type of care	Free Autonomous	Fl.1
F_7	Home 4.0 must allow resident to continue the maintenance and hygiene activities of her/his home	Type of activities Maintenance level	Phase 1 to 5 (illness)	Fl.3
F_8	Home 4.0 must have an entertainment system for the resident based on his degree of independence	Type of autonomy Entertainment type	Phase 1 to 5 (according autonomous)	Fl.3

5.3 Interaction of Functional Criteria

In the Table 6, we privilege the functions and criteria related to safety according to the different users.

Table 6. Criteria's Functions and safety according to the type of user

Functions	Participant	Criteria	C_i
F_1 Mobility Assistance	Resident (without activity)	Degree of autonomy and Walking equipment	C_1
F_2 safety	Resident (without activity)	Fonct. degree of Autonomy	C_2

(continued)

Table 6. (*continued*)

Functions	Participant	Criteria	C_i
F_3 Reception of health staff, friends, healthcare assistants, parents	Healthcare assistant, helper	Resident Hygiene Access	C_3
	Physiotherapist, speech therapist	Adequate equipment, local,	C_4
	Doctor, Nurse	Access, secure medicine…	C_5
	Friends, parents	Access, service, conviviality	C_6
F_2 Cooking activities	Resident	Dexterity, security	C_7
	Assistant	Memory, procedure…	C_8
F_4 Garden activities	Resident	Dexterity, time…	C_9
		Products choice	C_{10}
F_7 Maintenance activities	Resident	Products safety	C_{11}
		handling	C_{12}
F_8 Relaxation activities	Resident	Comfort	C_{13}
	Resident	Freedom of movement	C_{14}
		Motivation of activity	C_{15}

6 Discussion

Based on different criteria, we will seek the opposition criteria or complementary criteria, in order to find a solution, as presented in Table 7. For examples, we present criteria that are complementary or in opposition one to another and we propose recommendations in terms of solutions. These recommendations can have a positive impact on the choice of solutions. For example:

From the criteria resulting from the functional analysis, the question is converting them into parameters in order to emerge contradictions among them, and find the principles of solutions' Concepts.

The criterion C2 (Function F2) is "Degree of autonomy". The degree of autonomy is specified: either total or less use of right hand or left hand (depends on the person is right-handed or left-handed). The criterion C7 is "level of dexterity" of resident to carry out certain cooking activities that require the use of both hands. A contradiction is:

- Either, to increase the degree of autonomy for criterion C2 by asking resident to work in groups of two people,
- Or, to decrease the C7 criterion by looking for an ergonomic device that comes to replace the deficient hand.

Table 7. The opposition criteria or complementary criteria

Opposition criteria	Comments
$C_2 - C_7$	Secure resident during cooking activities (knives, electrics…). Secure devices for people with MND Make the resident autonomous with a minimum of safety whereas the safety in the kitchen must be increased
$C_7 - C_{11}$	Safety systems for cooking as well, maintaining furniture, there are not the same level of protection on the floors or other parts of home The kitchen must be secured regarding the movement of residents, while, it is forbidden for maintenance
Complementary criteria	Comments
$C_9 - C_7$	About these two activities (garden and kitchen), we use cutting or slicing objects… in the same manipulations
	Only the base changes. Electrical tools are also dangerous and must be secured
$C_{11} - C_2$	In general, the resident must be safe in his basic daily activities such as arrangement and storage activities, maintenance… The use of dangerous products must be controlled, monitored… both in terms of arrangement and manipulation level
$C_2 - C_{13}$ et C_{14}	Safety depends on the disability of the resident and his pathology This security is done in agreement with the resident without risky activities (cooking, gardening, maintenance…)

7 Conclusion

In this paper, we wanted to discuss innovative research support such as the study of the future home in the medico-social sector. This support is topical because of the aging of the population and the response that society will have to provide.

In answer our research problem we used a mix of three methods SWOT, User experience and functional analysis. It is this framework we also used the functional analysis and the beginning of the TRIZ approach. This work is a beginning of reflection and deserves to be followed-up in subsequent studies. In the future work we work on how to transform the functional criteria into TRIZ parameters in order to look for principles of solutions.

References

1. Fior, S., Julien, M., Dorenlot, P., Lallemand, D.: L'aide aux aidants: approche internationale (Vivre avec la maladie d'Alzheimer). Fondation Médéric Alzheimer (Paris) Edition (2003)
2. Aguirre, E., Hoare, Z., Spector, A., Woods, R.T., Orrell, M.: The effects of cognitive stimulation therapy (CST) programme for people with dementia on family caregiver' health. BMC Geriatr **14**, 31 (2014)

3. Thomas, P., Ingrand, P., Lalloue, F., Hazif-Thomas, C., Billon, R., Vieban, F., et al.: Reasons of informal caregivers for institutionalizing dementia patients previously living at home: the Pixel study. Int. J. Geriatr. Psychiatry **19**, 127–135 (2004)
4. Tsai, T.-H., Zhang, K.-L.: Implementation of intelligent home appliances based on IOT. In: IEEE, APCCAS, pp. 146–148 (2016)
5. Abramiuc, B., et al.: Home video monitoring system for neurodegenerative diseases based on commercial HD cameras. In: IEEE 5th International Conference on Consumer Electronics Berlin (ICCE-Berlin), pp. 489–492 (2015)
6. Rossey, J., and all, Wi-Fi helping out Bluetooth Smart for an improved home automation user experience, IEEE, 2016
7. Darses, F., Wolff, M.: How do designers represent to themselves the users' needs? Appl. Ergon. **37**(6), 757–764 (2006)
8. Obradovich, J.H., Woods, D.D.: Users as designers: how people cope with poor HCI design in computer-based medical devices. Hum. Factors: J. Hum. Factors Ergon. Soc. **38**(4), 574–592 (1996)
9. Sun, X., Houssin, R., Renaud, J., Gardoni, M.: Integrating user information into design process to solve contradictions in product usage. Procedia CIRP **39**(2016), 166–172 (2016)
10. Sun, X., Houssin, R., Renaud, J., Gardoni, M.: Towards a use information integration framework in the early product design phase function-task-behaviour. Int. J. Prod. Res. (2018). ISSN: 1366-588X
11. Folcher, V.: Appropriating artifacts as instruments: when design-for-use meets design-in-use. Interact. Comput. **15**(5), 647–663 (2003)
12. Gero, J.S., Kannengiesser, U.: The situated function-behaviour-structure framework. Des. Stud. **25**, 373–391 (2004)

TRIZ Applications in Specific Disciplinary Fields

Using TRIZ in the Healthcare Environment: First Proposition of a New Design Method

Axel Degland(✉), Camille Jean, and Claude Gazo

Arts et Métiers ParisTech - Laboratoire Conception de Produits et Innovation, 151 boulevard de l'Hôpital, 75013 Paris, France
axel.degland@ensam.eu

Abstract. Design in the healthcare environment is challenging. More than in the other activity sectors, it requires to take the users (patients and medical staff) as experts in the loop. This article will describe the bases of a new design method integrating TRIZ concepts for the healthcare environment. A first case study will be presented on the design of an exoskeleton specialized in the assistance of hemiplegic patients during their re-education.

Keywords: Design thinking · TRIZ · Biomechanics · Robotic · Healthcare

1 Introduction

Designing a device that should be used in healthcare is a demanding process due to the standards in terms of quality, security and functionality. This involves that companies often interact lately with patients and doctors, working with them mainly during test phases. But this tendency to rely on the company's vision of the patients and doctors' need for the product can create a gap between the final product and the need. This problem becomes detrimental in public healthcare where funds and human resources are often limited. Those resources, may they be human or financial, end up being drained by products and projects that are not tuned to their need.

This paper will detail the design of an exoskeleton for post stroke hemiplegia rehabilitation. Stroke is sudden shortage of the brain's air supply leading to the death of cerebral cells [1]. Aftermaths of such an event can lead to psychological and neurological deficiencies [2]. One of the most frequent sequels is hemiplegia, the paralysis of one or more limb located on the same part of the body. This means that a hemiplegic patient will not be able to move the limbs on the right or left of his body but not both [3].

The lack of control of the limbs is due to the decay of the motor control centers of the brain which are frequently damaged during strokes. This means that the patients' muscles are healthy and that the problem lies inside the brain [4]. The control is damaged but not the limbs. But the brain can change its disposition, brain activity associated with a certain function can change location. This concept is called neuroplasticity and is the pivot around which all the hemiplegia rehabilitation revolves around. The therapy's goal is to stimulate the muscles in order to trigger the brain recovery process and heightened neuroplasticity [5, 6].

Published by Springer Nature Switzerland AG 2019
R. Benmoussa et al. (Eds.): TFC 2019, IFIP AICT 572, pp. 429–437, 2019.
https://doi.org/10.1007/978-3-030-32497-1_34

With the rise of computer sciences, robot assisted reeducation raised from a single paper theme to a full-on discipline and some companies have built themselves around the design of exoskeleton and other robotic devices for rehabilitation [7, 8]. Studies in laboratory suggest that robot assisted therapies have a real impact on the recovery of patients, helping them recover quicker than therapies that don't incorporate robotic means of exercise and papers about the design of similar exoskeleton have already emerged [9].

2 Goals

This paper investigates a new creativity and user centered design process using TRIZ allowing the integration of patients and medical personnel in the early design phase. Those future users of the device will be treated as experts in phases where technical experts are normally predominant. Concepts for the actuation of limbs will be generated and will be rated in term of creativity, feasibility and pertinence in order to qualify the pertinence of our proposition.

3 Methodology

3.1 Global Methodology of the Project

As we aim at integrating the patients and doctors in our design process, we chose to start from the basis of design thinking, a method that already integrates the users, and add elements in order to enhance the participation of users. The main addition to the process will be the addition of TRIZ elements, especially the notions of ideality and the contradictions networks. Papers suggest that the combination of the two process can lead to a better problem-solving process [10].

Design thinking is a method that includes the experience and knowledge of the user in the conception of the product [11–13]. It revolves around the concept of empathy, which is the understanding of what the user knows, want and need. But it also implies that the user should not be used solely for analyzing the problem but also during all the steps toward the final product. The user should be a full member of the team, placing all the steps in perspective. Another specificity of this process is the use of retroaction loops. The idea being that the process isn't linear but that steps should be interconnected, allowing the team to go back to previous parts of the project to quickly adjust what is needed before coming back to the current phase. This allows the team to adapt faster if a dissonance between the device and the expressed need is detected than more classic design method that are often reluctant on going backward.

Design thinking as defined by Stanford University can be resumed by 5 steps expressed as actions: empathize, define, ideate, prototype [12]. During the Empathize phase the team will discuss with the users in order to understand them, what they want, what they know, what they need. The idea is to create an empathic bond with the users in order to better understand the context. During the Define phase the team will define the problematic and the need. The user is still involved and validate the pertinence of the team's conclusions. It is also the phase where the team redact the specifications. The Ideate step is the problem solving one, the team will use the knowledge gained during the previous phases in order to solve the problems that they identified during the defined phase. The user should be involved in the process. The Prototype phase is used to prototype the solutions the team came up with during the previous step. Finally, the Test step is the one when users will be confronted to the prototypes and establish if the solutions are adequate to their problems. As the users have been heavily involved during all the previous phases, this phase is used in order to establish the ameliorations to the products rather than to test the adequacy to the need [14, 15].

TRIZ is a problem solving and analysis tool based on patterns of invention in patents literature. This tool is used to analyze a system in order to identify technical locks, establish contradictions and solve them [16]. Our goal being the integration of TRIZ inside the design thinking process, we changed the steps to integrate more TRIZ elements in the first three steps (empathize, define, ideate) where the impact of the patient experience could be the most significant (Fig. 1).

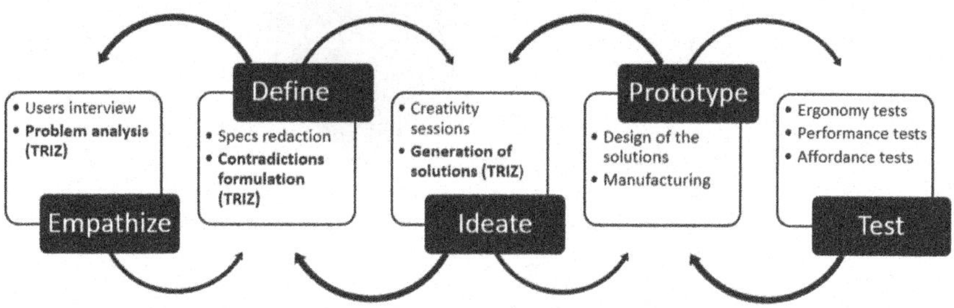

Fig. 1. Schematization of the new method

This new method keeps the basic structure of design thinking but integrate TRIZ elements in the different steps. The notion of feedback loops is still present as each step can impact the previous one. Each step is using different experts in its process: technical experts (engineers), field experts (doctors and patients) and TRIZ experts. Not all the experts are involved in each step. Empathize and define step involve the three types of expert but not the ideate step that only involve the TRIZ and technical experts (Fig. 2).

We will now explain the content of each step and how the TRIZ method is integrated inside each step. As said earlier we will focus on the first three steps (Empathize, Define, Ideate).

3.2 Empathize Phase

The Empathize step is the core of the Design Thinking method. As the problems that need to be solved are rarely the ones faced by the design team, it is important for them to understand who the users are, what they need and how they feel about it. During this phase, the goal is to link with the users in order to understand and integrate their needs and the problematics they encounter during the use of products similar to the one the

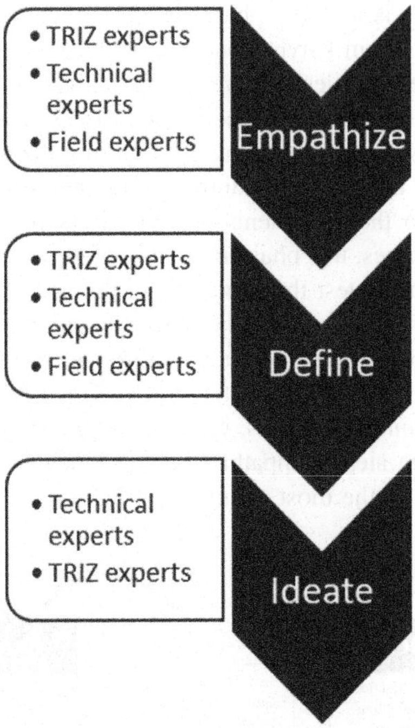

Fig. 2. Illustration of the experts involved in each phase

team is designing. In medical environment, this is important as recovery processes are difficult and put much stress on both patients and medical personnel, it is difficult for healthy person to grasp naturally the challenges that the users face daily.

The designer is supposed to observe the user in its environment in order to understand their behaviors and the situation. In our case study, during this step a rehabilitation center was visited in order to better understand the rehabilitation process and its challenges. This visit was also prepared extensively by a strong bibliographic study in order to understand the general process first. This allowed us to confront a more scholar approach and the reality of the process.

Then the designer should engage with the patient. They stop being observers and start involving themselves with their future users (medical personnel and patients). Typically, this is done by interviews that can be either by phone or in person. In our case study, two rehabilitation team managers, a physiotherapist and a patient were contacted for those interviews. Of all the interviewees, we only met one of the team managers in person, all the other were only met by phones due to busy schedules. The interviews were oriented toward the rehabilitation process, the user experience and the use of robotic means of recovery (like the upper limbs Armeo exoskeleton or the lower body Lokomat exoskeleton). The content of each interview wasn't fixed beforehand, and each interlocutor had the freedom to stir the conversation toward points they felt were important.

TRIZ was incorporated during this period by establishing a session of problem modeling soon after the end of the interviews. The idea is to analyze the problem with a user centered approach. 4 persons participated in the session: a TRIZ expert, an engineer that had conducted the interviews, an engineer acting as biomechanical expert and a designer outside of the project. The recovery process and the already existent exoskeleton were analyzed, focusing on the actuation of the limbs. But after discussing about the user experience, the session moved toward problems that were more in touch with the user's problems and we end up focusing on the hip articulation and the patient-exoskeleton interfaces. TRIZ allowed us to identify more easily the priorities and moving swiftly toward more primordial problems while keeping in mind the user experience.

3.3 Define Phase

The Define step is centered around the definition of the problems and the expressions of the goals. In engineering processes, it can be linked to the redaction of the specifications. The idea of this step was for us to use the knowledge and experience gathered during the previous step in order to structure our project and the idea of the product.

We wrote the specification for our product and while doing it we also established contradiction models for future TRIZ sessions. In order to keep the users (patients and doctors) in the loop we shared the specifications and contradiction models with the users that helped us during the Empathize phase. Doing this we established a link between the users and the technical team that allowed us to keep the user feedback and integrate it inside our work.

The idea being that we expressed to them our vision of the exoskeleton and the rehabilitation while translating the specifications in terms that people with no technical background could understand. Our contradiction problems evolved from the feedback as the medical personnel could establish parallels between their knowledge and the technical models. Certain problems that we expressed became irrelevant as the physiotherapists counterbalanced it during sessions while other things that we judged the responsibility of the medical team became specifications for the exoskeleton.

3.4 Ideate Phase

The Ideate phase is the time to generate ideas and solutions that respond to the problem defined during the earlier steps. In our case study, the participants consisted of 2 automations specialists, 3 biomechanics specialists, an ergonomist and a product design specialist. The team was gathered for a 3-h session. During this session, the results of the previous step were used in order to explain the problem to the participants. During the Empathize phase we used TRIZ to analyze the problem, the result of this was used during the Define phase to establish contradictions and problematics models. These models were presented and explained to the participants of the session as well as some notions of TRIZ (ideality, principle of final ideal result and contradiction principle). The participants used this in the ideation part of the session in order to generate concept.

The session consisted of a short recap of the project so far followed by a presentation of the technical contradiction identified during the define phase. After that the team chose on which contradiction to focus. The rest of the session was creativity oriented, consisting of a purge exercise, an inversion exercise and an ideation phase. The purge is a simple exercise, every participant notes key words on sticky notes and show them to the others. After that, the team gather and create poles of information, grouping the notes by categories they chose. The goal is to express everything they know and think about the subject in order to create a common pool of knowledge from where to gather later. The inversion is an exercise in which the team express the worst version of the product they can imagine and then use it to express an ideal version of the product. By doing so they identify functions that the product needs to fulfill and technical lock. Here it helped the team take in account the perception that patients would have of the product. After doing this, the team generated ideas for solutions. They focused on the actuation of the patient limbs. Rather than generating an important number of concepts and ideas, the team focused on generating solutions that were not already used and discuss on the technical locks identified during the inversion and the contradictions identified during the TRIZ session of the Define phase.

Elements that were identified during the previous phase of the project and that were presented to the participants were naturally used by them during the idea generation. They linked those elements with the results of the purge and inversion in order to build solutions based on the problem and their own knowledge.

Comparing this to classic creativity sessions, the integration of TRIZ components (the contradictions, the notion of ideality and sub/super systems) allowed the team to used creativity without losing touch with the technical aspect of the project. Solutions were detailed and the team laid the path for future TRIZ session on each sub systems. This will be detailed later in the results section of this article.

At the end of the session, it was decided to loop back to the empathize step in order to detail the exercises used during the rehabilitation. Doing so would allow us to start a new TRIZ process, focusing on sub systems rather than the complete exoskeleton.

4 Results

At the end of the session, we identify, for each solution, if TRIZ was used. The results in term of creativity, feasibility and pertinence of the ideas produced during the creativity session will be examined here.

During the session, the participants generated 14 ideas based on 5 axes of thinking. The axes correspond to principle of solutions from which they worked in order to construct their solutions (example: axis 2 regroup solution based on motors bound to the leg). In each of these axes, a certain number of solutions were generated by using the elements introduced with TRIZ (Table 1).

Table 1. Solutions per axis

Axis N°	1	2	3	4	5
Number of solutions	6	2	2	2	2
Number of solutions integrating TRIZ	6	1	0	1	1

When generating the solutions, participants could rely solely on creativity or TRIZ or even combine the two, taking an idea that was based on creativity and integrating TRIZ notions in order to make it evolve. In the figure below (Fig. 3), the solutions that used or were based solely on TRIZ are noted in red while ideas that came from creativity are noted in black.

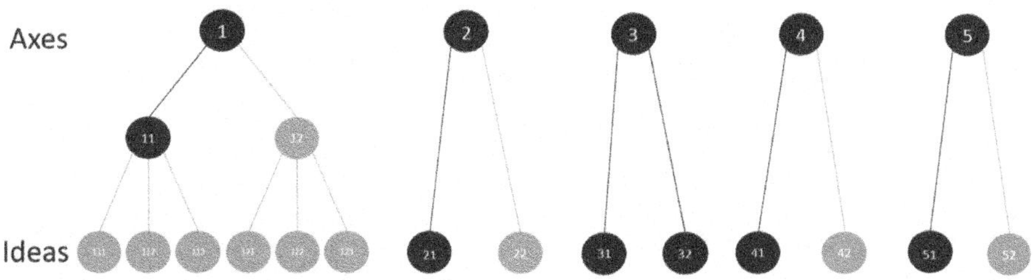

Fig. 3. Schematization of the generation of solutions (black: Classic creativity; red: TRIZ creativity) (Color figure online)

As seen in the figure, participants used TRIZ in order to improve ideas they came up with during creativity. This is visible in the first axis of solution where they generated ideas based solely on TRIZ but also used it to create new solutions based on one they imagined during the creativity. Ideas 111, 112 and 113 are based on creativity but integrated solutions that came from the use of TRIZ for the generation of ideas 121, 122 and 123. Without the use of TRIZ, the team would have imagined 1 solution for this axis, but by adding TRIZ notions and applying them to other axes of thinking, they came up with 6 solutions only for the axis 1. It can be suggested that the use of TRIZ improved their output of concepts.

An important fact to be noted is that solutions that came from the use of TRIZ tended to be used transversally, being applied to other axes. For example, idea 22 is based on TRIZ and the details of the solution were also used later in the session to create ideas 42 and 52. Without the use of TRIZ, only 3 solutions would have been created for the axes 2, 4 and 5. But with the addition of TRIZ, 6 solutions were generated in total.

After the session, all these solutions were graded on three criteria: creativity (whether the idea was original), feasibility (if the idea could be designed with the current knowledge at hand) and pertinence (whether the idea responded to the problematic). The grades were attributed by two members of the team based on their perception of the idea. Each idea are graded between 1 (the lowest grade) and 5 (the highest grade). Each idea would be graded between 1 (the lowest grade) and 5 (the highest grade).

For example, ideas based on the first axis of solution revolved around the use of cables to actuate the limbs. As few papers or products explore this kind of solutions, the ideas were considered more creative than ideas based around the second axis which revolves around the use of motors linked to a rigid exoskeleton that is widely represented in both papers and commercial products. But the ideas using motors were considered more feasible as there is a lot of papers explaining their implementation and control in exoskeleton.

Table 2 presents the mean and the standard deviation for ideas based on TRIZ and creativity in order to determinate the influence of TRIZ on the ideas.

Table 2. Mean and standard deviation of the solutions with Classical creativity and TRIZ creativity

Criteria	Creativity		Feasibility		Pertinence	
Use of TRIZ	No	Yes	No	Yes	No	Yes
Mean	3,80	3,20	3,00	4,11	3,40	3,78
Standard deviation	1,64	1,09	1,87	1,76	1,34	0,67
Min	1	1	1	1	2	3
Max	5	5	5	5	5	5

Ideas based on TRIZ tend to be less creatives but have a pertinence and a feasibility superior to ideas based on creativity. The standard deviation with TRIZ is also always inferior than without TRIZ.

5 Conclusion

During our case study, TRIZ was used to enhance the design thinking process by identifying technical difficulties that would need special care. Rather than using the problems solving elements of the methodology, the design process used the problem analysis elements (ideal results, sub and super systems analysis and contradictions generation) to create a pool of knowledge to use during the generation of solutions.

The TRIZ methodology also helped us focus the ideation process. Rather than imagining lots of solutions detached from reality, it helped the team understand the challenges and use the creativity to solve those difficulties. Integrating TRIZ notions in the methodology also helped separating the different levels of the project. Working with the notion of sub systems and their ideality, the participants easily identified the different challenges and used the flexible structure of design thinking to solve separately the problems.

Future work would consist to validate those results with other creativity session. Each idea would be graded as seen in the results part of the paper and compared to our preliminary results presented in this article in order to evaluate the pertinence of TRIZ in our methodology for the healthcare environment.

This methodology aims at perfecting the design process in the healthcare environment but is not limited to it. We believe it can be applied to other activity sectors where the human factor is highly relevant, as within the healthcare sector with the contribution of the doctors and the patients.

Acknowledgments. This research was carried out within the framework of the RehaByExo project supported by the Carnot Institute ARTS.

References

1. World Health Organization: Stroke, Cerebrovascular accident (2019). https://www.who.int/topics/cerebrovascular_accident/en/
2. Jørgensen, H.S., Nakayama, H.-L.: Outcome and time course of recovery in stroke. Arch. Phys. Med. Rehabil. **76**(5), 399–405 (1995)
3. Bourgeais, A.L., Guay, V., Laroudie, F., Marsal, C., Thevenin-Lemoine, E.: Informations et programme d'exercices dans les suites d'un AVC. Livret destiné aux patients, aux aidants et aux rééducateurs (2009). ISBN 978-2-7466-2220-3
4. Dobkin, B.H.: Rehabilitation after stroke. N. Engl. J. Med. **352**, 1677–1684 (2005)
5. Ferrucci, L., et al.: Recovery of functional status after stroke. A postrehabilitation follow-up study. Stroke **24**(2), 200–205 (1993)
6. Haute Autorité de Santé: Accident vasculaire cérébral: méthodes de rééducation de la fonction motrice chez l'adulte (2012)
7. Ali, H.: Bionic exoskeleton: history, development and the future. In: IOSR Journal of Mechanical and Civil Engineering (IOSR-JMCE), International Conference on Advances in Engineering & Technology (2014)
8. Anam, K., Al-Jumaily, A.A.: Active exoskeleton control systems: state of the art. Proc. Eng. **41**, 988–994 (2012)
9. Burgar, C.G., Lum, P.S., Shor, P.C., Van der Loos, H.M.: Development of robots for rehabilitation therapy: The Palo Alto VA/Stanford experience. J. Rehabil. Res. Dev. **37**(6), 663–674 (2000)
10. Rajesh, S.M.: Design of human exo-skeleton suit for rehabilitation of hemiplegic people. Proc. Eng. **51**, 544–553 (2013)
11. Lee, K.: Innovative Design Thinking Process with TRIZ (s.d.)
12. Faste, R., Roth, B., Wilde, D.: Integrating Creativity into the Mechanical Engineering Curriculum. ASME Resource Guide to Innovation in Engineering Design. American Society of Mechanical Engineers, New York (1993)
13. Doorley, S., Holcomb, S., Klebahn, P., Segovia, K., Utley, J.: Design thinking bootleg. Stanford (2018)
14. Dorst, K.: The core of 'design thinking' and its application. Des. Stud. **32**(6), 521–532 (2011)
15. Dym, C.L., Agogino, A.M., Eris, O., Frey, D.D., Leifer, L.J.: Engineering design thinking, teaching, and learning. J. Eng. Educ. **94**(1), 103–120 (2005)
16. Mann, D.: An introduction to TRIZ: the theory of inventive problem solving. Creat. Innov. Manag. **10**(2), 123–125 (2001)

The Concept of Contradiction Finding and Classification in the Field of Marketing Communication Quality Management

Joanna Majchrzak[1(✉)], Agnieszka Chuda[1], Arkadiusz Kalemba[1], and Gerhard Wilhelm Weber[1,2]

[1] Faculty of Engineering Management, Poznan University of Technology, 11 Strzelecka Street, 60-965 Poznań, Poland
joanna.majchrzak@put.poznan.pl

[2] METU Üniversiteler Mah., Dumlupınar Blv. No: 1, 06800 Çankaya Ankara, Turkey

Abstract. This article presents new concept of a systematic approach to quality management of marketing communication. The major research objective was to develop a method which facilitates efficient quality management of marketing communication in a holistic manner. The elements of marketing communication are defined, and the subsystem of marketing information is distinguished. A qualitative model of marketing communication was developed referring to the basics of Qualitology and the principles of qualitative modeling, valuation and systemic approach. Using the ENV and OTSM model of TRIZ contradiction, the problem of qualitative contradictions in the marketing communication system was indicated. Grey Incidence Analysis and Theory of Correlation and Regression are used to identify the structure of marketing communication and to find contradictions within its structure. The inventive principles for solving contradictions in the field of marketing are indicated. The innovative aspect of the research consists of an application of qualitative modeling, methods of Grey System Theory and Theory of Correlation and Regression, and methods of Theory of Inventive Problem Solving. The method introduced enables the recognition and classification of contradictions on its impact for marketing communication quality. In the last section, the direction for further research in the field of systematic thinking application for marketing communication quality management is indicated.

Keywords: Systematic thinking · Contradiction modeling · Qualitology · Grey relations · Marketing · Uncertain systems · Quality management

1 Introduction

The work considers the problem of contradictions in the area of quality management of marketing communication of industrial enterprises. The increasing complexity of production processes and the pursuit of enterprises for innovation (product, process, organizational or marketing) requires the creation of relationships with relevant market players (Pacholski et al. 2011). In the activities of industrial enterprises, several kinds

Published by Springer Nature Switzerland AG 2019
R. Benmoussa et al. (Eds.): TFC 2019, IFIP AICT 572, pp. 438–457, 2019.
https://doi.org/10.1007/978-3-030-32497-1_35

of relationships can be distinguished, among others (Mantura 2015; Morgan and Hunt 1994): relationships with the supply market (i.e., between the company and the suppliers and co-operators in the market supply), relationship with the sales market (i.e., between the company and the clients (agents and final customers) and co-operators in the distribution channel), relationships in the system of competition (i.e., between the company and competitors, current and potential, as well as industry and non-industry), relationships with the system of power (i.e., between the company and the institutions of power), relationships with the education system (i.e., between the company and the education institutions, relationships with research system (i.e., between the firm and research institutions), relationships with social system (i.e., inter alia, opinion-forming entities that affect the way in which the public perceives changes shaped by the company in diverse activities and situations). The management of the enterprise relationships in a complex and dynamically changing market structure requires from the management the so-called new generation competences (Duncan and Moriarty 1998) allowing for the creation of cross-functional knowledge (Korhonen-Sande and Sande 2014) and effective adaptation of the company to changing market environment conditions (Rajnoha et al. 2014). Shaping the relationships between the company and its market environment and the relationships between functionally diverse organizational units of the company is one of the basic functions of marketing (Gummesson 1994). The key roles here are the processes of information transfer as part of marketing communication. External Marketing Communication, i.e., communication between organizational units of the company and market environment entities, ensures the understanding the intentions, capabilities and potential of the company's partners (Andersen 2001). Internal Marketing Communication, i.e., communication between organizational units of the company, enables, among others, recognition of the surrounding market reality from different perspectives and contributes to the so-called synergy effect in shaping the targeted changes of the company and its environment (Lu et al. 2007). Internal Marketing Communication enables the integration of information shaped by functionally diversified employees of the company. Company employees are perceived as the so-called "part-time marketers" (Gummesson 1987). A comprehensive approach to marketing information of company employees is to improve the actions taken to adapt the company to the market environment and to impact this environment in order to achieve its own goals. The aim of this paper is to develop the concept of Contradiction Finding and Classification for improving the quality of Internal Marketing Communication of an industrial enterprise. When developing the concept of contradiction finding and classification, three different theories based on the principles of system thinking were referred to, namely:

1. basics of Qualitology (Kolman 2009; Mantura 2010), in order to develop a qualitative marketing communication model;
2. basic of Grey System Theory (Liu et al. 2016), to order the relations between particular features of elements belonging to the marketing communication system;
3. basics of Theory of Inventive Problem Solving (Altshuller 1996, 1999), in order to model and solve the problem of contradictions emerging during the improvement of the quality of marketing communication.

The studies also refer to the basis of Correlation and Regression Theories, by applying the method of correlations analysis using the Pearson's linear correlation coefficient to check whether there is a problem of contradictions between the elements of marketing communication. Firstly, the paper explains the essence of qualitology, Theory of Grey Systems and Theory of Inventive Problem Solving points out the principles, methods and tools used in this work. Secondly, a qualitative model of the marketing communication system was developed, defining the set of its elements and their structure. Attention was paid to the problem of contradictions between the various qualitative categories of the marketing communication system, emerging at the stage of designing desirable quality changes. A method for classifying qualitative contradictions was developed, due to their importance determined by the impact of certain contradictions on the changes in the state of marketing information quality (cf. Cavallucci et al. 2011). Fourthly, methods and tools derived from the basics of TRIZ that support the resolution of current and significant qualitative contradictions to improve marketing communication of the company have been distinguished.

2 Characteristics of the Applied Concepts of System Thinking

The use of methods, techniques and research tools of three different concepts that take the basis of a system approach, as well as methods of mathematical analysis of phenomena correlations, requires the indication of their essence and the relevance of applicability for solving specific problems in managing the quality of enterprise marketing communication. The subsequent subsections explain the essence, selected methods and tools of Qualitology, Theory of Grey Systems and Theory of Inventive Problem Solving.

2.1 Qualitology

Qualitology is an interdisciplinary field of knowledge dealing with all issues related to quality. Research referring to the fundamentals of Qualitology can be classified into two basic fields (Borys 1984), i.e., Qualitonomy, as the descriptive field of the quality theory (Kolman 2009; Mantura 2010) and Qualimetry as the formal field in the quality theory, dealing with the use of numeric (mathematical-statistical) methods in quality theory and their application (Borys 1984; Azgaldov et al. 2015). The general goal of qualitology is "to create a scientific basis for qualitative cognition and qualitative shaping of reality by man". The qualitative approach in researching and shaping objects is expressed in the application of the principles of a qualitative approach (Mantura 2010), i.e., Principles of Qualitative Mapping, Principles of Anthropocentrism (humanocentrism), Principles of Complexity, Principles of Systemicity, Principles of Synergy, Principles of Kinetics, Principles of Probability, Principles of Evaluation, Principles of Optimization, Principles of Normalization and Principles of Economics. In the literature on Qualitology, it is assumed that the qualitative principles can be applied to every object being recognized or created (Mantura 2010). In this paper, the Principle of Systemicity is applied, which consists in adopting the basics of general system theory and treating the object as a system. The system is a set of elements remaining in mutual relations. The principle of systemicity explains the "mysterious theorem" (von Bertalanffy 1968) that "the whole is more than the sum of parts" (Aristotle), which consists in the fact that "constitutive characteristics are not explainable from the characteristics of isolated parts" (von Bertalanffy 1968). It is assumed that the internal structure of the object is a set of relations between the qualitative categories (features and its states) belonging to the elements of this object (subsystem), and the external structure is a set of relations between qualitative categories belonging to the object and qualitative categories belonging to the objects in its surroundings (supersystem). For our conducted research, in order to identify the relations between the elements of marketing communication, the selected methods of Grey Systems Theory were used. This work also applies the Principle of Quality Evaluation, which consists in considering the need to transform the non-evaluated (absolute) quality of objects into evaluated quality. This is connected with the Principle of Anthropocentrism, i.e., axiological approach to reality and consideration of the quality of the object in relation to the system of human needs, values, goals and requirements. Quality evaluation is associated with the so-called phenomenon of Differentiation of Valued Quality. The reason for this phenomenon is the antinomy (contradiction) of the nature of the features evaluated on the basis of various criteria for assessing their value. This means that a feature belonging to an object can simultaneously take the form of:

1. maximizing, more-is-better (stimulant), i.e., a quantity that is beneficial for large values from the variability range of the feature;
2. minimizing, less-is-better (drawback, destimulant), i.e., a quantity favourable for small values from the variability range of the feature;
3. optimizing (mediment), i.e., the quantity used for intermediate values from the feature variability range (Kolman 2009, p. 66).

In the research conducted for the solution of the emerging problem of qualitative contradictions, reference was made to the fundamental postulate of classical TRIZ, postulate of contradictions and methods for modeling contradictions for business and management.

2.2 Grey System Theory

Theory of Grey Systems was introduced relatively recently in China, in 1982. It was created by a Chinese scholar, Professor Deng Julong, and presented in the publication entitled "The Control Problems of Grey Systems" (Liu and Lin 2006; Cempel 2014; Liu et al. 2016). It is assumed, like in control theory, that the darkness of colours is used to indicate the degree of clarity of information. The word "black" is employed to represent unknown information, "white" for completely known information, and "grey" for that information which is partially known and partially unknown (Liu and Lin 2006). Research methods and procedures developed within the framework of Grey Systems Theory entitle to inference based on incomplete, uncertain and few information about the systems being studied (Liu and Lin 2006). In the conducted research, the state of quality of particular elements in the marketing communication system is evaluated by the employees of a company's organizational units. Therefore, in the conducted research it is assumed that incomplete information means a limited, for pragmatic reasons, set of characteristics defining the individual elements in the marketing communication system. An uncertainty of information results from the human cognitive limitation and the experience of people who evaluated the state of the features belonging to the elements of the marketing communication system. Limited information refers to the research sample. Grey methods define the system mapping procedure based on the minimum sample $n \geq 4$ (Cempel 2014). On the basis of the concept of Contradiction Finding and Classification for improving the quality of marketing communication, Grey Incidence Analysis (GIA) method of Grey Relationship Analysis was applied. This methods refer to resolving problems such as which factors among the many are more important than others, have more effects on the future development of the systems than others, cause desirable changes in the systems so that these factors need to be strengthened or hinder a desirable development of the systems therefore they need to be controlled (Liu and Lin 2006). For such a future research objective, the basis of cooperative grey games, to capture the dynamics of interaction among individual assessment of the quality of marketing communication, can be applied (Fang et al. 2010; Palanci et al. 2017).

2.3 Theory of Inventive Problem Solving

Theory of Inventive Problem Solving was developed by Genrich Saulovich Altshuller in the period from 1946 to 1998, for the need of systematizing methods of solving creative issues (Skoryna and Cempel 2010). The essence of the developed concepts, in the most general terms, is to "help the inventor to use his current inventory of knowledge and experience most effectively" (Altshuller 1975) by adopting a systematic approach to solving complex problems. Theory of Inventive Problem Solving (TRIZ) has been greatly developed and has demonstrated great efficacy in solving difficult technical problems. The current stage of TRIZ evolution and its popularity has been illustrated by world interest in TRIZ, intensity of TRIZ usage in industry and what its recognized area of application is, and how aware the world is of TRIZ compared to other innovation methodologies (Abramov and Sobolev 2019). Initially, TRIZ was used only to solve technical problems, but over time its application has expanded into organizational, educational and social problems as well as the ones related to broadly understood business. For example, 40 Inventive Principles in Quality Management have been developed that include fields of quality standards, quality control, quality assurance, reliability, customer focus, supplier selection, project management, and improvement teams (Retseptor 2003), 12 innovation principles for business and management (Ruchti and Livotov 2001). It is pointed out that the application of TRIZ for business and management has worked in such areas of business operations as, e.g., increasing sales effectiveness, generating a new marketing concept, product or process, analysing customers behaviours and their preferences related with innovativeness of products, resolving a number of conflicts within a supply chain, discovering a new market for a service, predicting potential failures of a new business model, generating radically new advertising concepts, and risk management (Monnier 2004; Souchkov 2007; Regazzoni and Russo 2011; Pryda et al. 2018; Renaud et al. 2018, Koziołek 2019).

As part of the TRIZ, the principles of guiding thinking in solving inventive tasks have been defined (just principles and not specific formulas and rules) for organizing creative thinking independently of the area of human activity (Altshuller 1975). The classical TRIZ is based on three Fundamental Postulates, such as: first, postulate of objective laws, which means that engineering systems evolve not randomly but according to certain laws of evolution. Secondly, postulate of contradictions, which means that the inventive task is characterized by the fact that it requires the solution of the so-called technical, physical or administrative contradictions (Altshuller 1975). These contradictions emerge when the improvement of certain system properties comes into conflict with another of its properties (Andrzejewski and Jadkowski 2013). Altshuller states that the origin of any innovation problem is a contradiction: "Any problem, to be solved with TRIZ, must be formulated in such a way that it states a contradiction" (Hmina et al. 2019). Third, postulate of the specific situation, which means that each Inventive (non-typical, creative) problem arises within its own individual context (Khomenko and Ashtiani 2007). Classic TRIZ solutions include ARIZ (Algorithm for Inventive Problem Solving), Inventive Standards, Substance-Field. A set of complementary theories originated by TRIZ can also be distinguished, i.e., Theory of Technical System Evolution (TRTS in Russian) and Theory of the Development of Creative Personalities (TRTL), and he promoted the initiative to build a General Theory of Powerful Thinking (OTSM), which helps with the development of powerful thinking skills (Altshuller 1975 in: Cascini 2012). While developing the concept of contradiction finding and classification, in order to improve the quality of marketing communication, the contradiction toolkit (Gadd 2011) and the ENV model were adopted, taking into account the need to classify contradictions regarding their importance (Cavallucci et al. 2011) to positive qualitative changes in marketing communication. Contradiction modeling has been applied to identify or solve, e.g., engineering, education, managing, knowledge management, sociological problems (Messaoudene 2018; Nakagawa 2018; Slim et al. 2018; Livotov et al. 2019). As a result of the analysis of current research work, it can be concluded that selected TRIZ methods and tools are used to solve problems in the area of marketing (Semenova 2004), the need to consider the role of marketing in engineering creativity, especially relationship marketing, which supports integration of different sources of information (Belski et al. 2019) is indicated. Furthermore, attention is drawn to the diverse problems emerging in TRIZ application in marketing management and the need to conduct research that may lead to their solution (Zouaoua et al. 2010). Research is also being conducted in which TRIZ combines with uncertainty methods such as Grey Relation Analysis (Lin et al. 2011) or Fuzzy Logic (Su and Lin 2008) and indicates TRIZ application to deal with volatility, uncertainty, complexity, and ambiguity in the world (Kiesel and Hammer 2018). The innovative aspect of the concept of Contradiction Finding and Classification proposed in this paper is the application of the principles and fundamental operation of quality, methods of Grey System Theory and the Theory of Correlation and Tegression and the methods of the Theory of Inventive Problem Solving for improving the quality of marketing communication.

3 Marketing Communication System

In an etymological sense, the term "communication" derives from the Latin communicare (i.e., to be in a relationship with, participate in, associate with). Goban-Klas (2001, p. 43) indicates that for some authors communication denotes all forms of information transfer, both between people and between animals and machines. In this work, the approach used in social sciences, especially in sociology, is adopted, and the scope of marketing communication is limited to the transmission of information between people and market players. Marketing communication is the transmission of marketing information between entities on the market (Mantura 2012; Wiktor et al. 2013). In our research, the Internal Marketing Communication of the company is considered which, taken individually occurs under the name of the Marketing Communication Process. This process illustrates the transmission of marketing information between the organizational units of the company. The marketing communication process is mapped by a specific arrangement of elements such as (see Lasswell 1968; Westley and MacLean 1957; Mantura 2012): entering the marketing communication process (i.e., source of marketing information, reality components, market objects), the subject of action in the marketing communication process (i.e., organizational units of the enterprise, which are characterized by a specific semiotic system, a conceptual thesaurus and knowledge), tools of action in the marketing communication process (i.e., marketing communication channel and marketing communication tools, means of communication), object of action in the marketing communication process (i.e., marketing information, content, message), result of actions in the marketing communication process (i.e., the message of marketing information received), the exit from the marketing communication process (i.e., the recipient's reaction, and the qualitative change in the market situation). Internal Marketing Communication occurs in a specific organizational culture of the company. Specifying the term organizational culture, for research purposes of this work, the approach according to Schein (2004) is adopted. He indicates that the essence of organizational culture is a set of basic beliefs that have been established or adopted in order to solve the difficulties faced by the organization, adapting to external conditions and internal integration. Treating the organizational culture as a product of social interaction, Schein distinguishes its three levels: basic assumptions (which form the foundation for other cultural components, define the essence of existence, human nature, reality and the perception of truth), norms and values (which constitute a set of principles of everyday activities of group members, which are shaped by the impact of dominant values and thanks to them, the group members know how to cope in specific situations), and artefacts (which are manifestations of culture, but do not constitute its essence). The basic assumptions are defined, e.g., by the attitude to the environment, explanation of the nature of reality, beliefs about human nature, human activity, interpersonal relations. Standards and values are determined by, among others, values and norms declared, values and norms observed. Artefacts are determined by language artefacts, behavioural artefacts, and physical artefacts.

4 The Quality of the Marketing Communication System

According to the basics of Qualitology, the work adopts an epistemological (descriptive) definition of quality and the axiological criterion of the value of objects, defining the valued (relative) quality of objects. In this approach, the quality is expressed in a set of features, and the quality of an object is a set of features belonging to it (Mantura 2010, p. 49). Determining the quality of any object consists in recognizing, postulating and formulating a set of features belonging to it. The quality of the object is described by a finite set of features. The quality of the object is treated in a holistic approach, i.e., it is expressed by a set of features that belong to it and their structure. In fact, the features are identified on objects only in the form of specific own conditions/states. The state of quality of the object determines at least one state of each feature belonging to it. Conceptualization of features belonging to the object and their states in the Value Relation (*Rv*) with a defined system of human needs, goals and requirements is the basis for transforming the quality of the object into a valued (relative) state of the object's quality. The general and universal criterion of quality evaluation is the effectiveness of satisfying the set of needs, achieving goals and meeting human requirements (Mantura 2010). The overall marketing communication quality model is presented in Fig. 1.

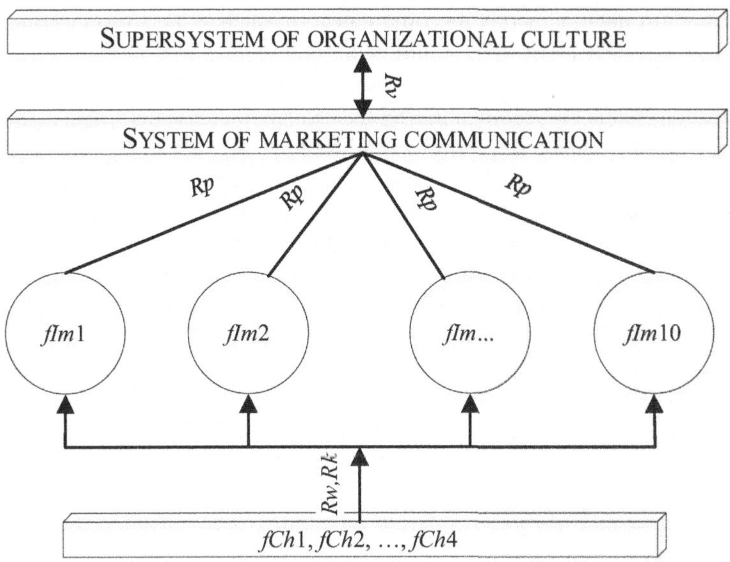

Here, *fIm*1, *fIm*2, ..., *fIm*10: the features belonging to marketing information; *fCh*1, *fCh*2, ..., *fCh*4: the features belonging to the marketing communication channel; *Rv*: Value Relation; *Rw*: Relation of Impact; *Rk*: Correlation between the states of individual features belonging to the communication channel and the states of features belonging to the marketing information.

Fig. 1. The qualitative model of marketing communication (Source: own elaboration).

Value Relation refers to the relationship between the state of marketing communication quality and usability in achieving the goals and functions of marketing in the company's organizational culture. According to the paradigm of systemic thinking adopted in the work, the goal of the existence of a given system (i.e., marketing communication of a company) is determined by the objective of its environment, the supersystem it belongs to (i.e., the supersystem of marketing in the organizational culture of the company). Relation of Impact expresses the so-called causality ratio (cf. Kotarbinski 1975) between elements occurring in the form of causes and elements occurring in the form of effects. In this paper, referring to the basics of information theory, it is assumed that the state of the quality of marketing information is influenced by features belonging to the marketing communication channel. The adequacy of these assumptions has been empirically verified in the authors' earlier research work, concerning the development of Integrated Marketing Communication Quality Management Method in the industrial company. The qualitative model of marketing information was tested by thirty industrial companies and the relation between the marketing communication channel (i.e., frequency of using a specific form of marketing communication channel, such as, advertising tools, public, sales activation, direct marketing, personal sales, personal promotion and partnership with market entities, or internal marketing communication tools) and the states marketing information quality was confirmed (Majchrzak 2018). In this paper, the marketing communication channel is defined only by the methods of internal marketing communication, such as, personal meetings, phone calls, e-mail messages, interactive multimedia communication. Correlation allows to recognize whether the change (increase/decrease) in the state of features belonging to the communication channel is accompanied by the change (increase/decrease) in the state of features belonging to marketing information. Recognizing the direction of correlation makes it possible to check whether a given feature belonging to organizational units or marketing communication channels is an feature of a minimizing nature (the smaller the value the better) or the maximizing (the higher the value the better) in relation to a given feature belonging to marketing information. In order to identify the problem of qualitative contradictions in the marketing communication system, the selected elements were determined in accordance with ENV model (Element, Name of the property, Value of the property), which is a universal model adopted in OTSM-TRIZ for representing any kind of problematic situation (Cascini 2012). The results of modeling the quality of marketing information and the marketing communication channel based on the ENV model are summarized in Table 1. The research assumes the interrelation between the specified elements of the marketing communication system. It is assumed that changing one part of the system has a negative effect on other parts of the system (Altshuller 2004). The problem of contradictions in the marketing communication system is determined using the model of a contradiction, consists in at least three parameters (Khomenko et al. 2007), where:

1. Evaluation Parameters (EP), constituting a measure of system satisfaction requirements, refer to the state of the at least two features of marketing information.
2. Control Parameter (CP) whose value impacts, with opposite results, both the Evaluation Parameters, refers to the state of features of the marketing communication channel.

Table 1. Qualitative modeling of marketing communication according to ENV model.

Element	Name	Values
Marketing Information (*Im*)	Features belonging to marketing information, such as: f_1^{Im}(amount), f_2^{Im} (understandability), f_3^{Im} (relevancy), f_4^{Im} (completeness), f_5^{Im} (free of error), f_6^{Im} (security), f_7^{Im} (timeliness), f_8^{Im} (accessibility), f_9^{Im} (believability), f_{10}^{Im} (ease of operation)	States of features values: 5 (very favorable), 4 (favorable), 3 (average), 2 (unfavorable), 1 (very unfavorable)
Marketing Communication Channel (*Ch*)	Features belonging to marketing communication channel, such as: f_1^{Ch} (personal meetings), f_2^{Ch} (phone calls), f_3^{Ch} (e-mail messages), f_4^{Ch} (interactive multimedia communication)	Frequency of use: 5 (very frequent) 4 (frequent), 3 (medium), 2 (rare), 1 (very rare)

Source: Own elaboration based on Lee et al. 2002.

Contradiction occurs when two Evaluation Parameters are coupled in such a way that the attempt of improving any of them determines the worsening of the other (Cascini 2012), which is shown in Fig. 2.

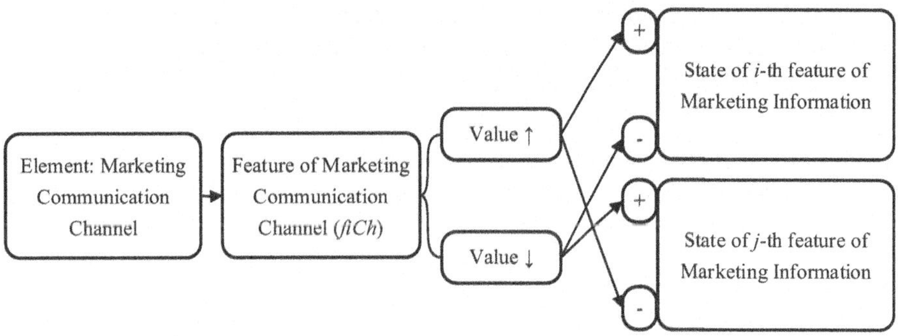

Fig. 2. OTSM model of TRIZ contradiction in the marketing communication system (Source: own elaboration).

When developing the concept of Contradiction Finding and Classification, the set of contradictions between the various features of the marketing communication channel and the features of marketing information is defined first. Then, the contradictions according to their importance are classified for positive changes in the quality of marketing information in a comprehensive approach.

5 Stages of Contradiction Finding and Classification

Contradictions between specific elements of marketing communication are identified by recognizing the Relation of Impact and Correlation between the various features of the marketing communication channel and marketing information. Another method of contradiction finding based on functional analysis was presented, e.g., in the problem product from the function of the product (Yang et al. 2018) and based on extended ad hoc method for the purpose of problem description (Koziołek and Słupiński 2018). In order to recognize the implementation of the influence, the method of studying Grey Relations of the Grey Systems Theory was used (Liu and Lin 2006). This method allows to check whether and what is the strength of the impact of particular system factors (*CP*: control parameters) on specific system characteristics (*EP*: evaluation parameters) (Liu and Lin 2006, p. 120). The level of impact of system factors on the nature of the system is identified by calculating the ratio of the absolute (total) impact ε_{ij}. The coefficient of impact ε_{ij} between the vectors of variable factors, X_i, and the characteristics, Y_j, of the system was chosen due to its following properties, significant in the study of the impact relationship between the specific elements of the marketing communication system (Liu and Lin 2006, p. 112; Cempel 2014, p. 15):

1. $0 < \varepsilon_{ij} \leq 1$;
   ε_{ji} is only related to the geometric shapes of X_i and Y_j, and has nothing to do with the spatial positions of X_i and Y_j or in other words, moving horizontally does not change the value of the absolute degree of grey incidences;
2. any two sequences are not absolutely unrelated, that is ε_{ji} never equals zero;
3. the more X_i and Y_j are geometrically similar, the greater ε_{ij};
   when X_i and Y_j are parallel, or Y_j^0 vibrating around X_i^0 with the area of the parts with Y_j^0 on the top of X_i^0 being equal to that of the parts with Y_j^0 beneath X_i^0, $\varepsilon_{ij} = 1$;
4. when any one of the data values in X_i or Y_j changes, ε_{ij} also changes accordingly;
5. when the lengths of X_i and Y_j change, ε_{ij} also changes accordingly;
6. $\varepsilon_{ii} = 1$, $\varepsilon_{jj} = 1$;
7. $\varepsilon_{ji} = \varepsilon_{ij}$.

In studies on grey relationship, different types of sequences of variable factors and system characteristics were specified, including: behavioural sequence (sequence of variables versus system observation conditions, e.g., evaluation of the same variable by different experts, in different conditions), behavioural time sequence (evaluation of the same variable determined at different times), behavioural criterion sequence (e.g., different system characteristics are evaluated by various experts), behavioural horizontal sequence (e.g., the value of a given characteristic is determined for different objects) (Liu and Lin 2006, p. 88). The individual calculation activities carried out in the method of testing grey relationships between control and evaluation parameters are explained below.

Operation 1. Determining the sequence of variable factors, X_i, and characteristics, Y_j, of the system:

$$
\begin{aligned}
X_1 &= [x_1(1), x_1(2), \ldots, x_1(n)],\\
X_2 &= [x_2(1), x_2(2), \ldots, x_2(n)],\\
X_3 &= [x_3(1), x_3(2), \ldots, x_3(n)],\\
X_4 &= [x_4(1), x_4(2), \ldots, x_4(n)].\\
Y_1 &= [y_1(1), y_1(2), \ldots, y_1(n)],\\
Y_2 &= [y_2(1), y_2(2), \ldots, y_2(n)],\\
&\cdot\\
&\cdot\\
&\cdot\\
Y_{10} &= [y_{10}(1), y_{10}(2), \ldots, y_{10}(n)].
\end{aligned}
$$

Here, X_1: vector of variable feature states, f_1^{Ch} (personal meetings), X_2: vector of variable feature states f_2^{Ch} (telephone conversations), X_3: vector of variable feature states f_3^{Ch} (e-mail messages), X_4: vector of variable feature states f_4^{Ch} (interactive multimedia communication). Furthermore, Y_1: vector of variable feature states f_1^{Im} (amount), Y_2: vector of variable feature states f_2^{Im} (understandability), Y_3: vector of variable feature f_3^{Im} statest (relevancy), Y_4: vector of variable feature states f_4^{Im} (completeness), Y_5: vector of variable feature states f_5^{Im} (free of error), Y_6: vector of variable feature states f_6^{Im} (security), Y_7: vector of variable feature states f_7^{Im} (timeliness), Y_8: vector of variable feature states f_8^{Im} (accessibility), Y_9: vector of variable feature states f_9^{Im} (believability), and Y_{10}: vector of variable feature states f_{10}^{Im} (ease of operation).

Operation 2. Transformation of the observation vectors against the zero starting point operator (Liu and Lin 2006, p. 102):

$$
\begin{aligned}
X_iD &= (x_i(1)d, x_i(2)d, \ldots, x_i(n)d),\\
Y_jD &= (y_j(1)d, y_j(2)d, \ldots, y_j(n)d),\\
x_i(k)d &= x_i(k) - x_i(1),\\
y_j(k)d &= y_j(k) - y_j(1).
\end{aligned}
$$

Here, X_iD: the image of the i-th observation vector of the system behavior transformed with respect to the operator of the zero starting point, Y_jD: image of the j-th observation vector of system behaviour transformed against the zero starting point operator, i - system factor (i.e., control factor), j: system characteristics (i.e., evaluation factors).

Operation 3. Calculation of behaviour measures of system observation vectors by adding, subtracting and the quotient of their values (Liu and Lin 2006, 104):

$$
\begin{aligned}
|s_i| &= \left|\sum_{k=2}^{n-1} x_i(k)d + \tfrac{1}{2}x_i(n)d\right|,\\
|s_j| &= \left|\sum_{k=2}^{n-1} y_j(k)d + \tfrac{1}{2}y_j(n)d\right|,\\
|s_j - s_i| &= \left|\sum_{k=2}^{n-1} [y_j(k)d - x_i(k)d] + \tfrac{1}{2}[y_j(n)d - x_i(n)d]\right|.
\end{aligned}
$$

Here, $|s_i|$: measure of the behaviour of the i-th factor of the system, $|s_j|$: a measure of the behaviour of the j-th system characteristic; $|s_j - s_i|$: measure of the behaviour of the i-th factor systems relative to the j-th characteristic of the system.

Operation 4. Calculation of the value of the impact coefficient ε_{ij} between specific factors and system characteristics (Liu and Lin 2006, 103):

$$\varepsilon_{ij} = \frac{1 + |s_i| + |s_j|}{1 + |s_i| + |s_j| + |s_j - s_i|}.$$

Here, ε_{ij}: coefficient of absolute level of impact between the i-th factor of the system, and j-th system characteristic. The coefficient of the absolute level of influence, ε_{ij}, takes values within the range of variability [0, 1]. The higher the value of the coefficient, the greater the impact of the i-th factor of the system on the j-th characteristic of the system.

Operation 5. Adding the values of impact coefficients ε_{ij} for each of the system's factors and ordering the system's factors in relation to the strength of their impact on the system's characteristics (cf. Liu and Lin 2006, 130). This leads to the ordering of features belonging to the communication channel in relation to the strength of their impact on the state of features belonging to marketing information.
Example:

$$f_1^{Ch} \succ f_4^{Ch} \succ f_3^{Ch} \succ f_2^{Ch}.$$

Thus, the feature f_1^{Ch} (personal meetings) has the greatest impact on changes in the quality state of marketing information.

The purpose of the next calculation activities is to recognize the direction of correlation between the states of marketing communication features and the states of marketing information features. To accomplish this goal, the method of analysis of phenomena correlations using the Pearson's linear correlation coefficient was used. The individual computational activities carried out in the method of analysing the phenomena correlations are explained below.

Operation 6. Calculation of the value of the Pearson correlation coefficient r according to the formula (Rutkowski 2004, p. 30 and p. 99):

$$r = \frac{\frac{1}{N}\sum_j (y_j - \bar{y})(x_i - \bar{x})}{S_y S_x},$$

for

$$S_y = \sqrt{\frac{1}{N}\sum_j (y_j - \bar{y})^2},$$

$$S_x = \sqrt{\frac{1}{N}\sum_i (x_i - \bar{x})^2}.$$

Here, x_i, y_j: particular variables of vectors X_i and Y_j, $\bar{x}, \bar{y}$: mean values of variables, S_x, S_y: standard deviation of independent variables x and dependent variables y, and N: population size.

The Pearson correlation coefficient r takes values in the range of variability from −1 to 1. The sign of the r Person correlation coefficient informs about the direction of correlation. Positive correlation means that the features of the marketing communication channel are the characteristics of the maximal character, and the negative correlation indicates the characteristics of a less-is-better nature in relation to the features of marketing information. The recognized character of features is put together in the so-called Contradiction Matrix.

Example:

$$CM = \begin{array}{c|cccc} & f_1^{Im} & f_2^{Im} & \cdots & f_{10}^{Im} \\ f_1^{Ch} & \uparrow & \uparrow & \uparrow & \uparrow \\ f_2^{Ch} & \downarrow & \downarrow & \downarrow & \uparrow \\ f_3^{Ch} & \downarrow & \downarrow & \downarrow & \downarrow \\ f_4^{Ch} & \uparrow & \uparrow & \downarrow & \downarrow \end{array}$$

Here, CM: contradiction matrix; $\uparrow$: the feature of the communication channel of a maximizing character; $\downarrow$: minimizing in relation to individual features of marketing information.

Thus, referring to the example presented it was recognized, that for features f_1^{Ch} and f_3^{Ch}, there is no opposite correlation with the features belonging to marketing information. Therefore, to improve the quality of marketing information, the value of the feature f_1^{Ch} should be increased and the value of the feature f_3^{Ch} belonging to the marketing communication channel should be reduced. The occurrence of contradictions for the feature f_2^{Ch} and feature f_4^{Ch} was identified:

1. increasing the value of the feature f_2^{Ch} positively affects the state of the feature f_{10}^{Im}, and negatively the state of the features f_1^{Im}, f_2^{Im};
2. increasing the value of the feature f_4^{Ch} positively affects the state of the feature f_1^{Im}, f_2^{Im}, and negatively the state of the features f_{10}^{Im}.

At this stage, the results of the Relation of Impact study are taken into account, and the set of ordered features of the marketing communication channel is checked against the strength of their impact on the state of marketing information features (Operation 5). Identified contradictions are classified in relation to the strength of the impact relation of Control Parameters on changes in the value of Evaluation Parameters (cf. Cavallucci et al. 2011; Becattini et al. 2011).

When designing qualitative changes, first of all it is considered what should be the state of those control parameters which have the strongest impact on the changes in the evaluation parameters. In accordance with the assumption that those elements of the system which have the greatest impact on changing the desired features of the system should be changed in the first place (cf. Gadd 2011, p. 104). The course of the proposed operations and the steps applied in concept of contradiction finding and classification in the field of marketing communication quality management is shown in Fig. 3.

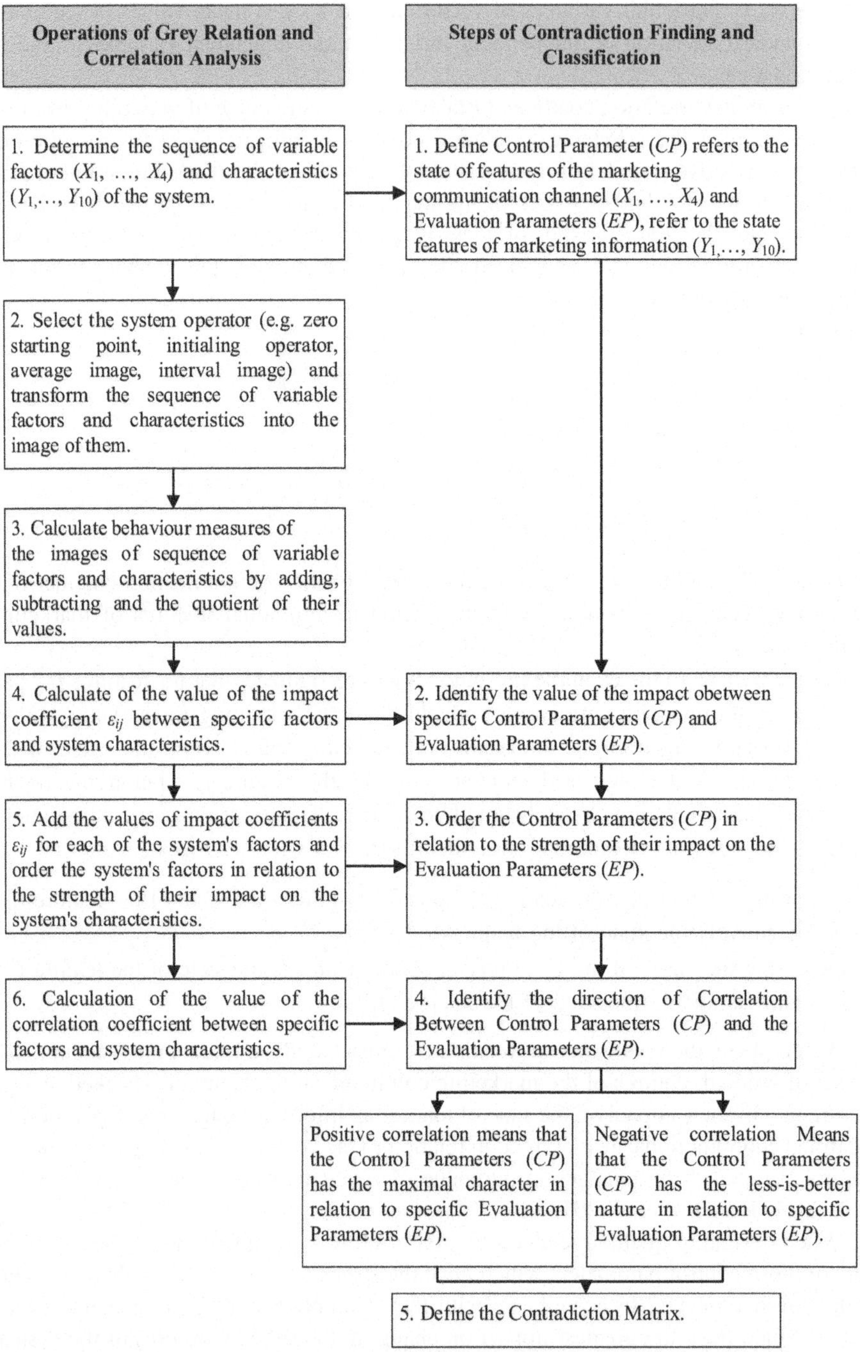

Fig. 3. The course of the operations and steps in contradiction finding and classification in the field of marketing (Source: own elaboration).

The operations refer to the specified methods of Grey Relation Analysis and Correlation Analysis. The results of specific operations are applied to achieve objectives of proposed steps in contradiction finding and classification. In solving the problem of contradictions, the problem of physical contradictions is first considered and a set of principles of separation applied, and then it refers to a set of appropriately selected inventive principles for solving problems of technical contradictions (cf. Gadd 2011, pp. 120–134). A specific set of inventive principles is of general nature and should be adapted and applied taking into account the specifics of the problem being resolved (Altshuler 1975). In solving the problem of qualitative contradictions in the marketing communication system, interpretations of standard inventive principles are used to solve problems in the area of marketing (Retseptor 2005).

6 Conclusion and Outlook

This paper deals with the problems of identifying and classifying contradictions for the purpose of managing the quality of marketing communication of an industrial enterprise. In our developed method, reference was made to the basic principles and operations of Qualitology, i.e., the Principle of Qualitative Mapping, Principle of Systematicity, and Principle of Quality Evaluation. At the stage of qualitative contradictions modeling, the ENV and OTSM models of TRIZ contradiction were used. The Evaluation Parameters (*EP*) in the conducted research refer to the state of the marketing information features, and the Control Parameter (*CP*) refers to the state of features of the marketing communication channel. In order to determine the impact relation between Control Parameter (*CP*) and Evaluation Parameters (*EP*), Grey Incidence Analysis method was used. In order to determine the direction of correlation between Control Parameter (*CP*) and Evaluation Parameters (*EP*), the method of analysis of phenomena correlations using the Pearson's linear correlation coefficient was applied. It has been assumed that when designing qualitative changes, the most important issues is to consider what should be the state of Control Parameters, which have the strongest impact on the changes in the Evaluation Parameters in the overall approach. It was pointed out that by solving the problem of qualitative contradictions, a set of separation principles is applied first, and then it refers to the interpretation of standard inventive principles developed for solving problems in the area of marketing. The course of this research process is shown in Fig. 4.

The aim of future research is, first, to verify the developed concept, including designing a questionnaire to assess the state of the quality of marketing communication in an industrial enterprise. Second, creating the computer software supporting computational activities at the stage of using Grey System Theory method and a statistical method of analysing the phenomena correlations. Third, integration of the developed method with other commercially available methods of computer-aided problem solving (e.g., Innovation WorkBench). Fourth, application of a mathematical model, such as system dynamics approach methodology of modern Operational Research (Pedamallu et al. 2012a) and methodology and computer simulation modeling technique (Pedamallu et al. 2012b) to improve the classification of the contradiction for its impact

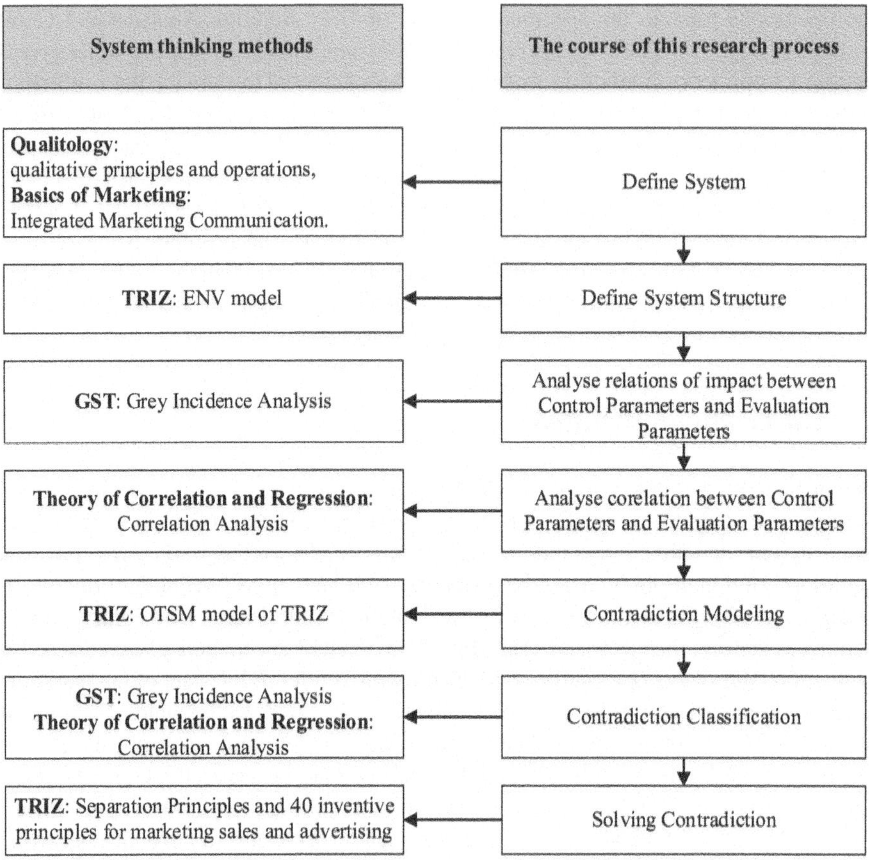

Fig. 4. The course of this research process in contradiction finding and classification in the field of marketing (Source: own elaboration).

on the marketing communication quality. Furthermore, application and verification of proposed concept of contradiction finding and classification in the other fields of industrial companies structure.

References

Abramov, O., Sobolev, S.: Current stage of TRIZ evolution and its popularity. In: Chechurin, L., Collan, M. (eds.) Advances in Systematic Creativity, pp. 3–15. Palgrave Macmillan, Cham (2019). https://doi.org/10.1007/978-3-319-78075-7_1

Altshuller, G.: Algorytm wynalazku. Wiedza Powszechna, Warszawa (1975)

Altshuller, G.: And Suddenly the Inventor Appeared: TRIZ, the Theory of Inventive Problem Solving. Technical Innovation Center Inc., Worchester (2004)

Altshuller, G.: The Innovation Algorithm: TRIZ. Systematic Innovation and Technical Creativity. Technical Innovation Center Inc, Worchester (1999)

Andersen, H.P.: Relationship development and marketing communication: an integrative model. J. Bus. Ind. Mark. **16**(3), 167–183 (2001)

Andrzejewski, G., Jadkowski, K.: TRIZ–metoda interdyscyplinarna. In: Materiały na II Konferencję Naukową KNWS (5), pp. 15–18 (2013)

Azgaldov, G.G., Kostin, A.V., Omiste, A.E.P.: The ABC of Qualimetry. Ridero (2015)

Belski, I., Skiadopoulos, A., Aranda-Mena, G., Cascini, G., Russo, D.: Engineering creativity: the impact of general knowledge and thinking heuristics. In: Chechurin, L., Collan, M. (eds.) Advances in Systematic Creativity, pp. 245–263. Palgrave Macmillan, Cham (2019). https://doi.org/10.1007/978-3-319-78075-7

Becattini, N., Cascini, G., Rotini, F.: Correlations between the evolution of contradictions and the law of identity increase. Proc. Eng. **9**, 236–250 (2011)

Borys, T.: Kategoria jakości w statystycznej analizie porównawczej. Wydawnictwo Uczelniane Akademii Ekonomicznej, Wrocław (1984)

Cascini, G.: TRIZ-based anticipatory design of future products and processes. J. Integr. Des. Process. Sci. **16**(3), 29–63 (2012)

Cavallucci, D., Rousselot, F., Zanni, C.: On contradiction clouds. Proc. Eng. **9**, 368–378 (2011)

Cempel, C.: Teoria szarych systemów–nowa metodologia analizy i oceny złożonych systemów. Przegląd możliwości, Zeszyty Naukowe Politechniki Poznańskiej. Organizacja i Zarządzanie, (63), pp. 9–20 (2014)

Duncan, T., Moriarty, S.E.: A communication-based marketing model for managing relationships. J. Mark. **62**(2), 1–13 (1998)

Fang, Z., Liu, S., Shi, S.: Grey Game Theory and Its Applications in Economic Decision-Making. Taylor&Francis Group, New York (2010)

Gadd, K.: TRIZ for Engineers: Enabling Inventive Problem Solving. Wiley, Hoboken (2011)

Goban-Klas T.: Media i komunikowanie masowe. Teorie i analizy prasy, radia, telewizji i Internetu, Wydawnictwo Naukowe PWN, Warszawa-Kraków (2001)

Gummesson, E.: Making relationship marketing operational. Int. J. Serv. Ind. Manag. **5**(5), 5–20 (1994)

Gummesson, E.: The new marketing—developing long-term interactive relationships. Long Range Plan. **20**(4), 10–20 (1987)

Yang, Z.H., Feng, Y.L., Wang, L.X.: Improvement of shaping paper rubber coating device based on TRIZ function and contradiction. DEStech Trans. Eng. Technol. Res. (ecar), 84–90 (2018)

Hmina, K., Sallaou, M., Abdelmajid, A.T., Larbi, L.: TRIZ The theory of Inventive Problem Solving State of the art. In: 2019 5th International Conference on Optimization and Applications (ICOA). IEEE, pp. 1–7, April 2019

Khomenko, N., Ashtiani, M.: Classical TRIZ and OTSM as a Scientific Theoretical Background for Non-Typical Problem Solving Instruments. ETRIA Future, Frankfurt (2007)

Khomenko, N., De Guio, R., Lelait, L., Kaikov, I.: A framework for OTSM TRIZ-based computer support to be used in complex problem management. Int. J. Comput. Appl. Technol. **30**(1/2), 88–104 (2007)

Kiesel, M., Hammer, J.: TRIZ–develop or die in a world driven by volatility, uncertainty, complexity and ambiguity. In: Cavallucci, D., De Guio, R., Koziołek, S. (eds.) TFC 2018, pp. 55–65. Springer, Cham (2018). https://doi.org/10.1007/978-3-030-02456-7_5

Kolman, R.: Kwalitologia: wiedza o różnych dziedzinach jakości. Wydawnictwo Placet, Warszawa (2009)

Korhonen-Sande, S., Sande, J.B.: Getting the most out of cross-functional cooperation: internal structural change as a trigger for customer information use. Ind. Mark. Manag. **43**(8), 1394–1406 (2014)

Kotarbiński, T.: Hasło Dobrej roboty. Państwowe Wydawnictwo "Wiedza Powszechna", Warszawa (1975)

Koziołek, S., Słupiński, M.: TRIZ based problem solving of tile manufacturing system. In: Koziołek, S., Chechurin, L., Collan, M. (eds.) Advances and Impacts of the Theory of Inventive Problem Solving, pp. 203–216. Springer, Cham (2018). https://doi.org/10.1007/978-3-319-96532-1

Koziołek, S.: Design for change: disaggregation of functions in system architecture by TRIZ-based design. In: Chechurin, L., Collan, M. (eds.) Advances in Systematic Creativity, pp. 17–26. Palgrave Macmillan, Cham (2019). https://doi.org/10.1007/978-3-319-78075-7

Lasswell, H.D.: The uses of content analysis data in studying social change. Soc. Sci. Inf. **7**(1), 57–70 (1968)

Lee, Y.W., Strong, D.M., Kahn, B.K., Wang, R.Y.: AIMQ: a methodology for information quality assessment. Inf. Manag. **40**, 133–146 (2002)

Lin, P.-Y., Lee, T.-R. (Jiun-Shen), Dadura, A.M.: Using grey relational analysis and TRIZ to identify KSFs and strategies for choosing importers and exporters: an example of the Taiwanese hand-tool industry. J. Manuf. Technol. Manag. **22**(4), 474–488 (2011)

Livotov, P., Sekaran, A.P.C., Law, R., Reay, D., Sarsenova, A., Sayyareh, S.: Eco-innovation in process engineering: contradictions, inventive principles and methods. Therm. Sci. Eng. Prog. **9**, 52–65 (2019)

Liu, S., Lin, Y.: Grey Information Theory and Practical Application. Springer, London (2006). https://doi.org/10.1007/1-84628-342-6

Liu, S., Yang, Y., Forrest, J.: Grey Data Analysis. Springer, Berlin (2016). https://doi.org/10.1007/978-981-10-1841-1

Lu, S.Y., ElMaraghy, W., Schuh, G., Wilhelm, R.A.: A scientific foundation of collaborative engineering. CIRP Ann. Manuf. Technol. **56**(2), 605–634 (2007)

Majchrzak, J.: The integrated marketing communication quality management method of an industrial company. Ph.D. thesis, Poznan University of Technology, Faculty of Engineering Management (2018)

Mantura, W.: Zarys kwalitologii. Wydawnictwo Politechniki Poznańskiej, Poznań (2010)

Mantura, W.: Comperative analysis of the category of quality information. In: Goliński, M., Szafrański, M. (eds.): Integrated Support System for Access to Information in Urban Space with use of GPS and GIS Systems, pp. 7–30. Publishing House of Poznan University of Technology (2012)

Mantura, W.: Reflections on contemporary problems of marketing. Stud. Work. Fac. Econ. Sci. Manag. **39**(2), 11–23 (2015). Scientific Publisher of the University of Szczecin

Messaoudene, Z.: Paradoxes and organizational learning in continuous improvement approaches: using the TRIZ principles for developing problem solving performance in a Michelin plant. In: Cavallucci, D., De Guio, R., Koziołek, S. (eds.) TFC 2018, pp. 40–51. Springer, Cham (2018). https://doi.org/10.1007/978-3-030-02456-7_4

Monnier, B.: 4. Innovation strategies: from SMEs to world wide corporates-4.5 application of TRIZ method to business management activities. In: TRIZ Future Conference, pp. 1000–1009. Firenze University Press (2004)

Morgan, R.M., Hunt, S.D.: The commitment-trust theory of relationship marketing. J. Mark. **58**(3), 20–38 (1994)

Nakagawa, T.: TRIZ/CrePS approach to the social problems of poverty: 'liberty vs. love' is found the principal contradiction of the human culture. In: Koziołek, S., Chechurin, L., Collan, M. (eds.) Advances and Impacts of the Theory of Inventive Problem Solving, pp. 179–188. Springer, Cham (2018). https://doi.org/10.1007/978-3-319-96532-1

Pacholski, L., Malinowski, B., Niedźwiedź, Sz.: Procesowe, strukturalne i kooperacyjne aspekty innowacyjności organizacyjnej przedsiębiorstw. Wydawnictwo Politechniki Poznańskiej (2011)

Palanci, O., Olgun, M.O., Ergun, S., Alparslan Gök, S.Z., Weber, G.W.: Cooperative grey game: grey solutions and an optimization algorithm. Int. J. Supply Oper. Manag. **4**(3), 202–214 (2017)

Pedamallu, C.S., Ozdamar, L., Akar, H., Weber, G.W., Özsoy, A.: Investigating academic performance of migrant students: a system dynamics perspective with an application to Turkey. Int. J. Prod. Econ. **139**(2), 422–430 (2012a)

Pedamallu, C.S., Ozdamar, L., Kropat, E., Weber, G.W.: A system dynamics model for intentional transmission of HIV/AIDS using cross impact analysis. Cent. Eur. J. Oper. Res. **20**(2), 319–336 (2012b)

Pryda, B., Mysior, M., Koziołek, S.: Method of innovation assessment of products and processes in the initial design phase. In: Cavallucci, D., De Guio, R., Koziołek, S. (eds.) TFC 2018, pp. 75–83. Springer, Cham (2018). https://doi.org/10.1007/978-3-030-02456-7_7

Regazzoni, D., Russo, D.: TRIZ tools to enhance risk management. Proc. Eng. **9**, 40–51 (2011)

Renaud, J., Houssin, R., Gardoni, M., Nour, M.: Multi-users of a product: emergence of contradictions. In: Cavallucci, D., De Guio, R., Koziołek, S. (eds.) TFC 2018, pp. 154–164. Springer, Cham (2018). https://doi.org/10.1007/978-3-030-02456-7_13

Rajnoha, R., Kádárová, J., Sujová, A., Kádár, G.: Business information systems: research study and methodological proposals for ERP implementation process improvement. Proc. Soc. Behav. Sci. **109**, 165–170 (2014)

Retseptor, G.: 40 inventive principles in quality management. TRIZ J. (2003). https://triz-journal.com/40-inventive-principles-quality-management/

Retseptor, G.: 40 inventive principles in marketing, sales and advertising. TRIZ J. (2005). https://triz-journal.com/40-inventive-principles-marketing-sales-advertising/

Ruchti, B., Livotov, P.: TRIZ-based innovation principles and a process for problem solving in business and management. TRIZ J. **1**(2001), 677–687 (2001)

Rutkowski, T.: Statystyka. Wyższa Szkoła Zarządzania i Przedsiębiorczości im.Bogdana Jasińskiego, Poznan (2004)

Semenova, L.N.: New opportunities and fields of application: TRIZ and marketing. In: TRIZ Future Conference, pp. 1000–1008. Firenze University Press (2004)

Schein, E.H.: Organizational Culture and Leadership. Jossay-Bass, San Francisco (2004)

Skoryna, A., Cempel, C.: Możliwości zastosowań metody TRIZ w diagnostyce maszyn. Diagnostyka, pp. 69–77 (2010)

Slim, R., Rémy, H., Amadou, C.: Convergence and contradiction between lean and Industry 4.0 for inventive design of smart production systems. In: Cavallucci, D., De Guio, R., Koziołek, S. (eds.) TFC 2018, pp. 141–153. Springer, Cham (2018). https://doi.org/10.1007/978-3-030-02456-7_12

Souchkov, V.: Breakthrough thinking with TRIZ for business and management: an overview. ICG Training & Consulting, pp. 3–12 (2007)

Su, C.T., Lin, C.S.: A case study on the application of Fuzzy QFD in TRIZ for service quality improvement. Qual. Quant. **42**(5), 563–578 (2008)

Von Bertalanffy, L.: General System Theory. New York, 41973 (1968)

Westley, B.H., MacLean, M.S.: A conceptual model for communications research. J. Mass Commun. Q. **34**, 31–38 (1957)

Wiktor, J.W.: Komunikacja marketingowa. Modele, struktury, formy przekazu, Wydawnictwo Naukowe PWN, Warszawa (2013)

Zouaoua, D., Crubleau, P., Mathieu, JP, Thiéblemont, R., Richir, S.: TRIZ and the difficulties in marketing management applications. In: PICMET 2010 Technology Management for Global Economic Growth, pp. 1–10. IEEE (2010)

Characteristics of Traditional Farm Equipment in Korea from the Viewpoint of TRIZ's Invention Principle

Sehoon Cho(✉)

Hanwha Precision Machinery, Seongnam-Si, Gyeong-Do, South Korea
sehoon.cho@hanwha.com, sh68.cho@gmail.com

Abstract. Agriculture is an industry based on human history, as anyone can easily recognize. There are various tools and cultivation methods for unique agriculture in many countries of the world. And such farming methods and tools used have evolved over time. It is accepted by the general public as an understanding of the uniqueness rather than an attempt to analyze which tools are relatively more efficient.

Today, a variety of traditional farm equipment in each country is being used in part. Where large-scale factory farming uses modernized equipment. In this study, I briefly analyzed how the characteristics of agricultural equipments used in rural villages are related to TRIZ's inventive principle and resource utilization.

The inventive principles of TRIZ are easily found in Korean farm equipment. Some tools are understood as aspects of modern science or sports science.

Over the past several hundred years, most farm equipment has been completed with materials and methods to create optimized structures, methods and tools. It has efficiency and environmental friendliness. Given the environmental conditions, the use of local materials and experience-based wisdom is dissolved.

Some tools also have semantic implications for environmental issues, cyclical economies, and sustainability that have emerged as problems in recent years.

Therefore, it is important to develop new complex systems or to study equipment with advanced functions. However, by using good examples already existing, I would like to get hints as another alternative to various problems arising from the recent industries of machinery, electronics, computers, petrochemicals, and so on.

Keywords: Cyclical economies · Sustainability · Korea · Traditional farm equipment · TRIZ · Invention principle · Resource analysis · Appropriate technology

S. Cho—Ph.D. student at Korea Polytechnic University.

Published by Springer Nature Switzerland AG 2019
R. Benmoussa et al. (Eds.): TFC 2019, IFIP AICT 572, pp. 458–471, 2019.
https://doi.org/10.1007/978-3-030-32497-1_36

1 Introduction

1.1 History and Agriculture in Korea

Korea usually has a history of 5000 years. It is presumed that many countries have historically developed into cultivated forms gradually as they settled around the river in nomadic life. Korea was estimated to have started full-scale farming since 3000 BC. However, ancient rice seeds found in Korean Shinbuk in 2003 were estimated to be about 15,000 years ago and recognized by the World Association. It is estimated that Korea has a very long agricultural culture all over the world.

Therefore, it is a nation that mainly engages in agriculture, and it has been various for a long time and various crops and food culture accordingly. It was in the early 1960s that the modernization of Korea's agricultural environment began to take full advantage of its power. Prior to that, agriculture was mainly farming with manpower, accumulation and natural environment. Nowadays, agriculture is applied to simple agricultural agriculture using advanced technology such as factory farming facility, hydroponics using LED, facility management using IoT technology, and spraying pesticide with drone. Mechanization Despite the computerized changes, farm tools that have been used for a long time are now being partially used. In this paper, we try to share some meaning of traditional agricultural equipments which are used now.

1.2 Korea's Natural Environment and Agriculture

Korea has four seasons of weather change in one year. This environment has played a very large role in agriculture. It can be divided into the farming season and the resting season depending on the weather. Farming season is a very busy time when the actual things necessary for farming take place in farmland. On the contrary, the rest period corresponds to a kind of preparatory period that takes place inside the house with little occurrence of farmland outside the house. There are traditions in which land is sown, sown and cultivated and harvesting work in cooperation with neighbors in a short period of time because the tasks to be carried out by the step of farming are decided. Some work alone, but many farmers are made to work as a group.

Most of the rest days are from the time when the harvest of late autumn ends, the temperature falls below freezing, the time when the cultivated area becomes frozen, and the beginning of the next spring, when the ice begins to melt. During this period, various preparations are made for practical farming. They will do follow-up work on harvested crops, and make consumable work tools that are often used in farming. It is the time when crafts and tools made of various straws are made using straws to make strings that are used as versatile strings. It is also the season for repairing the tools used in the farming season. To repair the farm equipment, we prepare and process the tree, or repair the necessary equipment in the blacksmith shop.

1.3 Challenges of Current Agriculture in Korea

Through a very short period of 20 to 30 years, Korea has changed from traditional farming to mechanized farming. After the Korean War, agricultural productivity was so low that it concentrated on increasing food production per unit area. As a result, food problems and productivity were solved, but the soil was acidified by massive use of chemical fertilizers, pesticides and chemicals, and many pollutants were generated in rivers and land.

Various efforts have been made to restore, but the recovery of nature is slower than expected. The rapid aging of the population is also recognized as a new problem. The relationship with neighbors is loosening by working with automated agricultural machinery without the help of neighbors. In front of these new challenges, we will learn the wisdom of the ancestors included in traditional farm equipment to gain wisdom in solving current problems.

2 Characteristics of Major Agricultural Equipment in Korea

We have extracted some features of Korean farm equipment from TRIZ's problem environment analysis aspect with characteristics of 130 different kinds of farm equipment in Korea, how to use it, and natural environment.

2.1 Village Cooperative Agriculture

In a situation where the changes in the four seasons of the year have to be met, farmers often cooperate in farming rather than individual farming. There are a lot of farm equipment that at least two people should join together in a variety of farm equipment, and the labor cost has developed much by region. There were a lot of cases where we worked together singing along with farming days that could be boring in wide fields. It is a sort of community structure, but it is a group that has a horizontal relationship and cooperates with each other. It is called 'Dure'. Similar to Kibbutz, a collective farming community in Israel, all of Korea has a different form of private property base. The workpieces transmitted by word of mouth were shared through festivals and various festivals. Several people have good structural characteristics to work together.

2.2 Agricultural Equipment Material and Circulation Economic Characteristics

Most of the farm equipment used very common materials that can be easily found around. As a result of rice farming, straw has been used for a variety of purposes (Fig. 1). They used various properties of the straw. Straw is also a by-product of producing food. The byproducts become the key material for tools to store and transport food.

Fig. 1. Straw cases

It is characterized by 100% circulation when the life span of the used farm equipment or the agricultural equipment is exhausted. Most are composted or become heating firewood. In addition, partial repair is easy for each component. Trees or straw are also used as additional fertilizer. On the contrary, today's petrochemical strings are mostly not recycled after use, and they cause soil and river pollution (Fig. 2).

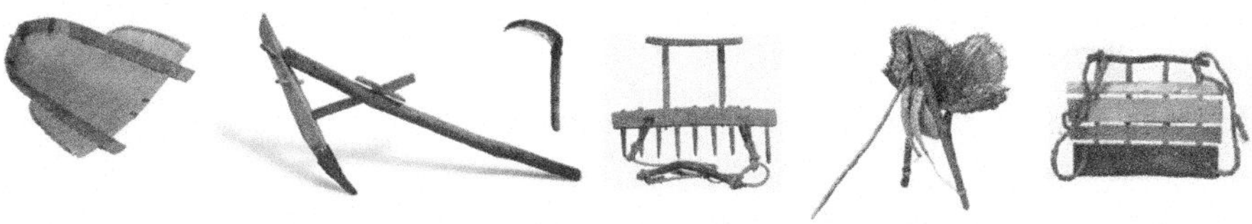

Fig. 2. A variety of farm equipment in Korea

All components are made of wood or straw except for the iron-made part made of blacksmith. This can be interpreted as a dimension that utilizes various derivative resources from the viewpoint of 'resource analysis'.

2.3 Systematic Classification and Various Kinds

There are more than 130 farm equipment in Korea. Table 1 below shows the types and types of farm equipment classified into 16 stages based on the timing and function of farming. It is estimated that more than 130 kinds of agricultural equipments did not appear at any particular time but gradually increased according to the working environment for a long time. Korea is known as an agricultural country, although the three sides are made up of sea. Historically, many kings have been noted for their success in agriculture, water management for agriculture, interest in rivers, reservoirs and so on. It can be considered that there is an attempt to improve the systematic farm equipment in the country if it is deduced that the national history document contains a lot of records about the farm equipment.

Table 1. Korea's farming season and farm equipment [2]

Procedure	Function	Name of farm equipment	Amount
1	Digging	따비, 쟁기, 극젱이, 괭이, 가래, 삽	6
2	Soil refinement	써레, 쇠스랑, 곰방메, 번지, 나래, 고무래, 발번지, 통번지, 발나래	9
3	Compost movement	장군, 새갓통, 귀때동이, 거름통, 삼태기, 거름대	6
4	Seeding	고써레, 드베, 파종기, 씨송곳, 씨망태, 씨삼태, 종다래끼, 꽁게, 실번지, 궁글대	10
5	Weed removal	호미, 밀낫, 칼자매, 매번지, 보토괭이, 제초기	6
6	Water supply	두레, 맞두레, 용두레, 무자위, 물풍구, 살포	6
7	Harvest	낫, 전지, 도리깨, 탯돌, 개상, 홀태, 그네, 탈곡기, 삼괭이	9
8	Dry	얼루기, 멍석, 도래방석, 발, 거적, 채반	6
9	Wheat extraction	부뚜, 듸림부채, 풍구, 바람개비, 키, 이남박, 체	7
10	Grain storage	독, 나락뒤주, 쌀뒤주, 통가리, 섬, 가마니, 중태, 멱서리, 뒤웅박, 씨주머니	10
11	Grain grinding	절구, 디딜방아, 물방아, 물레방아, 돌확, 맷돌, 매통, 토매, 연자매, 기름틀, 국수틀, 물절구, 안반	13
12	Carry	지게, 발채, 들 것, 망태기, 소쿠리, 광주리, 바구니, 다래끼, 멱둥구미, 길마, 거지게, 걸채, 옹구, 발구, 썰매, 수레, 달구지	17
13	Livestock tools	구유, 여물바가지, 쇠죽쇠스랑, 작두, 멱석, 부리망, 어리, 둥우리	8
14	Straw application	짚추리개, 자새, 돌물레, 섬틀, 가마니틀, 자리틀, 새끼틀	7
15	Fabric manufacturing	씨아, 물레, 돌꼇, 날틀, 베틀	5
16	Other	갈퀴, 넉가래, 함지, 메, 도끼, 까뀌, 톱, 반달낫, 도롱이, 태, 멎	11
		Total Amount	136

2.4 Breakdown of Structure and Name of Farm Equipment

Most of the farm equipment was improved and optimized according to the purpose of use. It can be seen that the structural features, functions and performance have become clear during the optimization process. As an example, a sickle cutting a tree or weed is a very simple tool, but its name is clearly distinguished as shown in the figure below (Fig. 3).

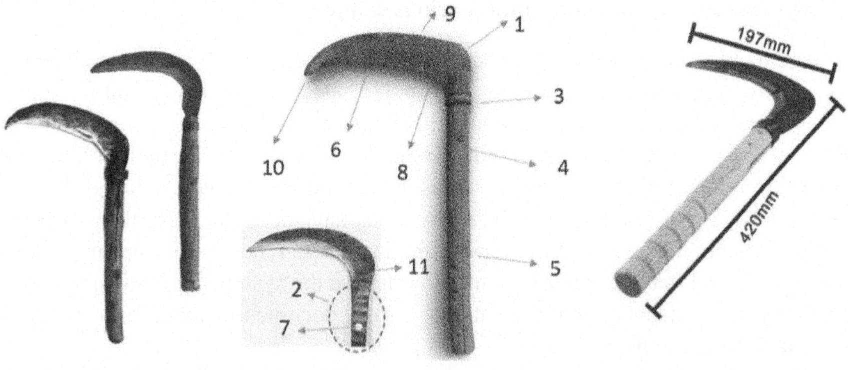

Fig. 3. Structure and name of Korean sickle [3]

It is a technical system that a simple tool has different names depending on structure, shape and function. In other words, it is a simple but seemingly simple technology system. It's as if each component of a complex mechanical system has its own manufacturing method and name. Each tool has its own name and the materials and manufacturing methods used in its manufacture. There is a whole name, but having a unique name for the parts that make up the whole means that there is a unique function.

2.5 Manufacturing Locally: Appropriate Technology

Most farm equipment is made in the local area, that is, the area where it is used. Strictly speaking, it was made in a home that needs it. It is a practical form of proper technique. Made with materials that are very easily available in your area. Most of the farmers at the time were able to make most of the farm equipment with only basic basic tools. It was made with tools that were readily available at village level. In the case of iron farming equipment, it is usually purchased through a market that is held regularly by city, or it is repaired in a blacksmith shop in winter. They have the same form, but they have made farm equipment with materials that are produced or naturally produced in the area.

2.6 Harmonization with Super Systems: Resource Analysis

It is in harmony with the operation of the human body, which is an upper system. The upper system has characteristics that are optimized to the characteristics of the upper system from the point of view of interaction with the human farm equipment. Farmers using livestock have also developed a variety of additional tools to keep the livestock constantly focused on their work, rather than simply using the power of livestock. Livestock, such as cattle, have the highest value of property in most households, and work has been done to take care of their health. In addition to farming equipment, it is also shown in the construction of trees along the shape of the surface of rocks and stones when pillars are erected on the foundation stone of Korean houses. The Ondol system, which exists only in Korea, is a heating system in which the properties of stone and soil and aerodynamics are studied in harmony (Fig. 4).

Fig. 4. Analyze and harmonize top system resources [4, 6]

In many cases, it is assumed that farm equipment has been improved in such a way as to study and use the properties of the natural state or the material before it is artificially processed.

3 Korea's Representative Traditional Farm Equipment

There are about 130 kinds of traditional farm equipment in Korea, but among them, only some of the farm equipment that have been used only in Korea until now and their characteristics are examined. Most of the farm equipment was visible in the museum. Most of the farmers have experience in using the farm, and this is the TRIZ theory. I will review why TRIZ has 40 generic inventions found in their farm equipment (technical systems), and why farming tools are virtually unchanged in form and usage for a long time.

3.1 Case: Homi

Homi was a traditional farming tool in Korea, but now it is known as a gardening tool sold by Amazon.

3.1.1 History and Uses of Homi

The shape of Homi varies slightly depending on the farming environment and region of Korea (Fig. 5). The shape of the work depends on the soil condition in each area. Depending on the type of weeds, the depth is different and the hardness of the soil varies depending on the soil. As a result, the shape of the body was slightly modified according to the problem, and the angle and length of the blade, the length of the handle, and the shape of the side were changed. Also, a customized order can be made in the blacksmith individually. This can determine the type of detail of the Homi by the user's experience.

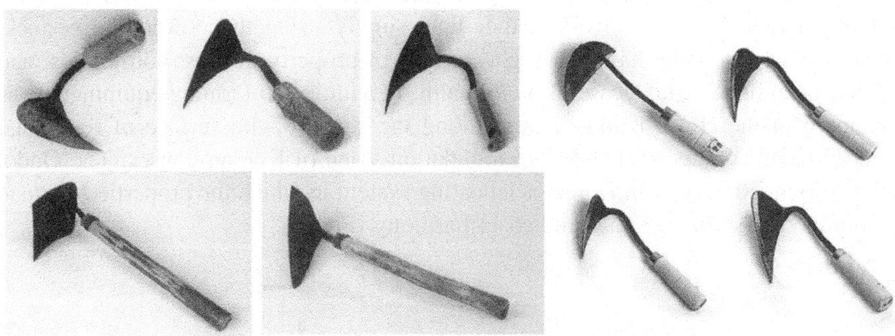

Fig. 5. Various aspects of Homi [5]

3.1.2 Structure and Function of Homi

Homi is mainly used by people to sit in a sitting position and to decorate their hands or garden. After sitting in the space to work, various tasks are possible. Depending on the proficiency level, the time and type of work will also vary.

Figure 6 shows the functional relationship when holding Homi by hand and pulling toward the body. Homi uses the power of the hands and arms of the human body to work with structures optimized for digging the soil or selectively removing or removing weeds. The pulling force will cause the lower part of the body to fall into the ground.

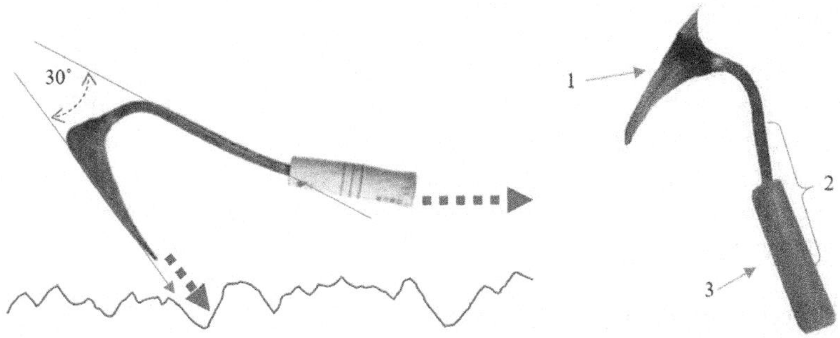

Fig. 6. Structure and function of Homi

Homi also has a versatile function in one shape. It can be used in a variety of times and places that usually do simple work in the field, such as the ability to scratch the earth or collect the soil, to move the soil, to cut off the roots of the weeds, to dig the ground. In some cases, the handle 3 may be wrapped with a cord so that the hand holding force is evident.

Though 1000 years later, the structure of Homi is still used. It is one sample of IFR of hand tool. It is still being sold as a best-selling product on Amazon (Fig. 7).

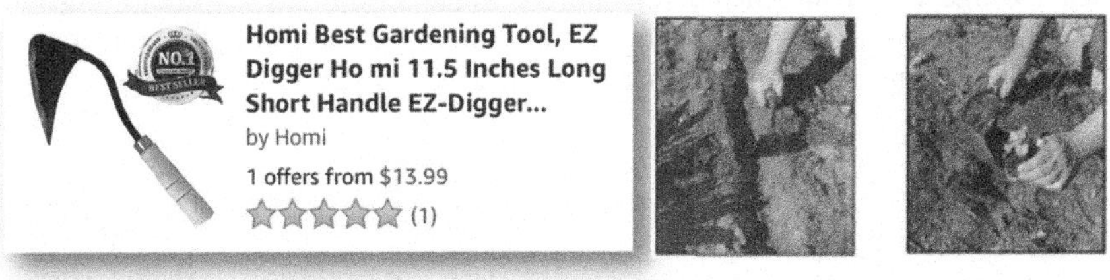

Fig. 7. Homi currently on the Internet [5]

There is a review of users who purchased Homi using Amazon, which expressed satisfaction with "I can not find a 30-degree curved day anywhere in the US" or "How did you make your garden before writing Homi?" [5].

3.1.3 Founding Principles of Invention

It can be found that at least five inventive principles are applied to Homi.

a. (3) Local quality - Different features are unique to each function.
b. (6) Universality - The body made of iron contains various functions.
c. (16) Partial or excessive action - When pushing in the handle, it burns quickly and pushes it in.
d. (25) Self-service - Bend the handle so that the handle does not come off the body.

e. (40) Composite materials - Handles are made of wood and wrapped around the surface with rope.

3.2 Case: Chige

There are several required functions and constraints to move things in the rural environment of Korea. A given situation can simply be set to Task. And the result of continuous improvement to solve such a problem situation can be interpreted as the current state. On the other hand, it is also possible that the current shape of the biceps has been created in a shorter period of time. It is structurally meaningful in interaction with components.

3.2.1 Necessity and Required Function

The necessity of the first Chige is not known, but based on actual experience, it can be demanded that the problem situation when Chige is not used is reverse estimated and summarized below.

a. Carry heavy objects or bulky luggage (carry as much luggage as possible)
b. Carrying baggage to limited places such as narrow roads and mountain roads (acceptance of upper system limit)
c. Shielding or minimizing the constraints of action on the move (not dangerous)
d. Easy to travel long distance

3.2.2 Chige's History and Change

Korea's Chige has maintained its shape for hundreds of years without substantial change. The figure below (Fig. 8) shows that Chige in the picture of a painter several hundred years ago is the same as that of the last 30–70 years ago.

Fig. 8. Past and recent Chige's appearance

Usually, it is difficult to use wheeled transport tools if you need to carry your luggage to a narrow, hilly or narrow place. In the same situation, Chige is still being used with its traditional structure. The form remains intact. During the Korean War, Chige was used to create a special unit to move military supplies to the mountains.

3.2.3 Structural Features of Chige

As mentioned above, the name of Chige can be divided into 15 kinds as well as the features of traditional Korean farming tools. And the location of each component is located where it interacts with the human body skeleton. Most houses in rural areas in Korea had Chige, which is the same shape but different in size. The reason is because the body size of the person using it is different. Patient height, shoulder width, and hip position are the main variables. Figure 9 compares the general structure of the body and the structure of Chige corresponding to the skeleton.

Chige has a form A so that the center of gravity is well caught when a heavy load or a bulky thing is carried. When hanging the Chige on the shoulder, the lower structure is arranged outward so that it is not caught on the legs. After the load is loaded on the Chige, it has a structure that supports it so that it does not move toward the head. In other words, it has been manufactured to fit well with the interaction position considering the structure and function of the body which uses the characteristics of human body well. There are a variety of things that you can carry on your Chige. You have additional options for when you need to move grain or small objects. 'Baroguri (15) can be temporarily connected to each structure (1, 6) while spreading to be well placed in the base structure of Chige.

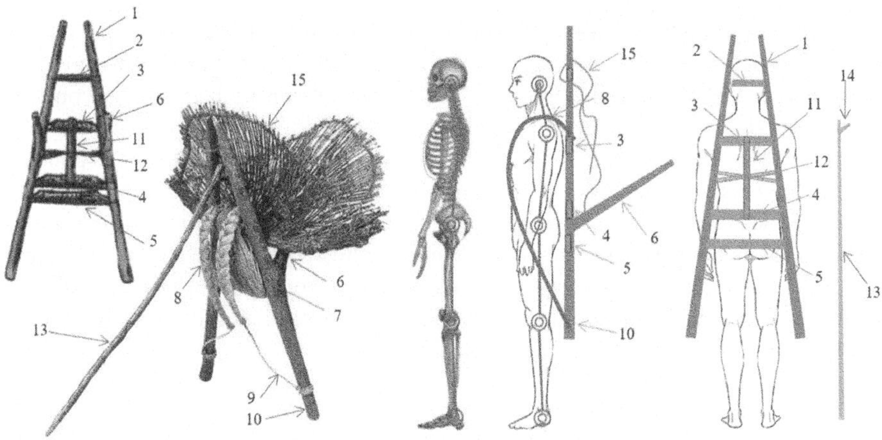

Fig. 9. Chige's structural features and human skeleton

3.2.4 Mechanism of Load Transport Using Chige

In Fig. 10, if the load is loaded on the Chige, it is fixed with the strap (15). It is possible to balance the erected Chige and stand it up with the support rod 13 slightly inclined. At this point, the user will remember the tilted level of Chige and (b) maintain the angle when he tries to stand up against Chige on his shoulder. If you shake a little, you will know how much strength it supports. These interactions are taught in principle and practice at the point of use of Chige. Therefore, parents should check whether they fit the body before making Chige for children or using Chige.

a. Chige depends on the size of the body, weight support position is different.
b. Depending on the weight of the body, the angle of the body and the angle of the Chige are different.
c. Structural features that maximize human body function.

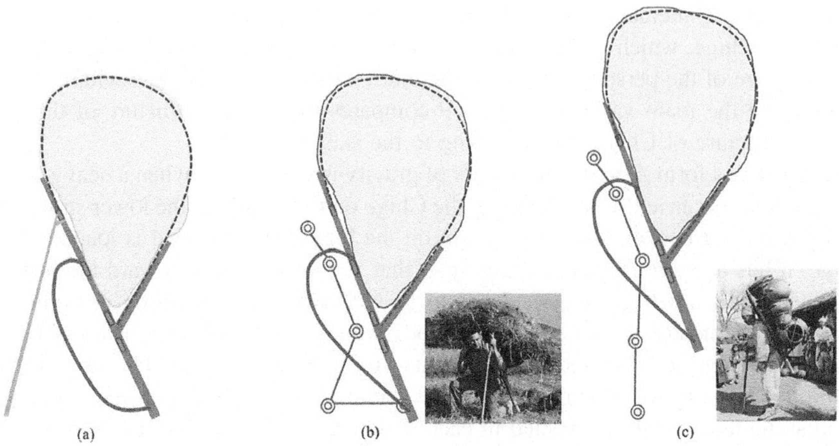

Fig. 10. Preparing for change and movement of the center of gravity

3.2.5 Problems and Solutions of Chige's Manufacturing Process

All the materials that make up Chige use local materials that are available to anyone in rural Korea. Most farmers directly manufacture. Manufacturing takes into account the physical condition of the person using it.

In the structure of Chige, the place where weight is most applied corresponds to branch (6). This weakness affects the bulk or weight of the load that can be loaded. Therefore, when choosing materials to support weight, we make a tree with branches that are angled about 60° from the main stem of the tree. Trees with bold branches have very rigid structural features when they are built. Cut the tree beforehand because the tree is distorted during the drying process. After the wood has been partially dried, it will become less warped after production (Fig. 11).

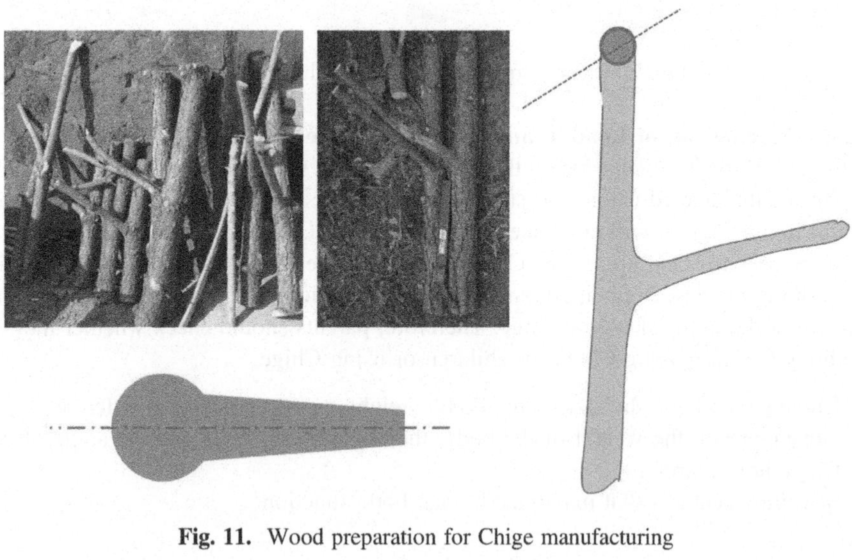

Fig. 11. Wood preparation for Chige manufacturing

Chige is an unbalanced structure from the side, but from the front, both sides need to be balanced in terms of structure, weight and stiffness. As shown above, it is difficult to obtain trees with the same structure and rigidity in nature. Most of the fixtures were somewhat imbalanced. In order to solve this problem, it is possible to make a tree by dividing the tree which is twice as thick as the tree which is necessary for making the final load. Especially in this case, the wood is cut and dried naturally because there is a possibility of distortion after production.

3.2.6 Founding Principles of Invention

It can be seen that at least five inventive principles apply.

a. (12) Equipotentiality - Raise a certain height from the ground to move heavy loads, and then make it easier to move.
b. (9) Preliminary anti-action - Check the center of gravity before carrying the baggage.
c. (2) Extraction - Cut out a part of the tree with branches.
d. (27) Cheap short-living objects - Use straw to easily replace major parts.
e. (24) Intermediary - Place a straw cushion on the frame of the frame and on the back of the person and directly touching the buttocks to make them hard.

In addition, the harmony with the upper system of the human body is outstanding.

3.3 Case: Treadmill

The basic principle of treadmill is known to come from China, but we do not know the exact time. However, the form and use of Treadmill in other countries have changed a lot. Since its introduction, it has been improved to Korean type according to the Korean environment.

3.3.1 Basic Structure of Treadmill

Figure 12 shows the general form of Korean Treadmill.

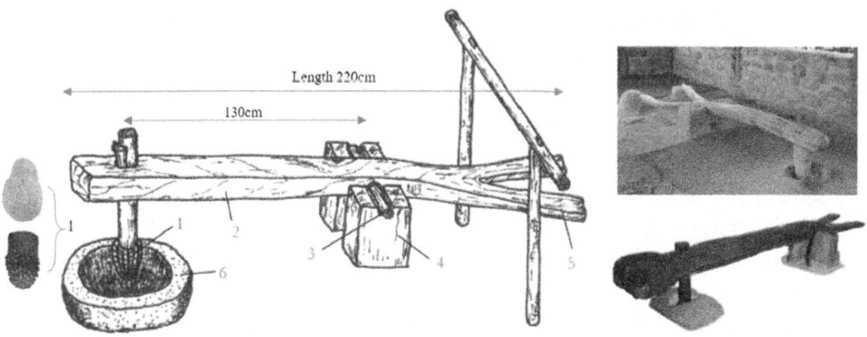

Fig. 12. Basic structure of treadmill [7, 9]

The biggest change is to use a tree with two branches so that both of them weigh the treadmill. The material is made of wood and stone. The end (1) of the armor is made of iron.

The end portion 1 may be replaced depending on the object to be ground. The container 6 containing the grain is mostly made of stone and the portion 4 receiving the rotation and the load of the body 2 is also formed by grooving the stone. Hang the strap from the transverse support or ceiling to support it, as the person may lose balance during operation. You can run the grain through your treadmill alone, but you can work faster if you have 2 or 3 people together. Of course, there is a song to sing while working with a treadmill.

3.3.2 Application and Change of Treadmill

Figure 13 shows the shape of the change in force that drives the treadmill. Currently, there is little threshing or crushing using these facilities. But it is an example of using water instead of manpower. Of course, in countries with windy winds, there is a structure connected to windmills.

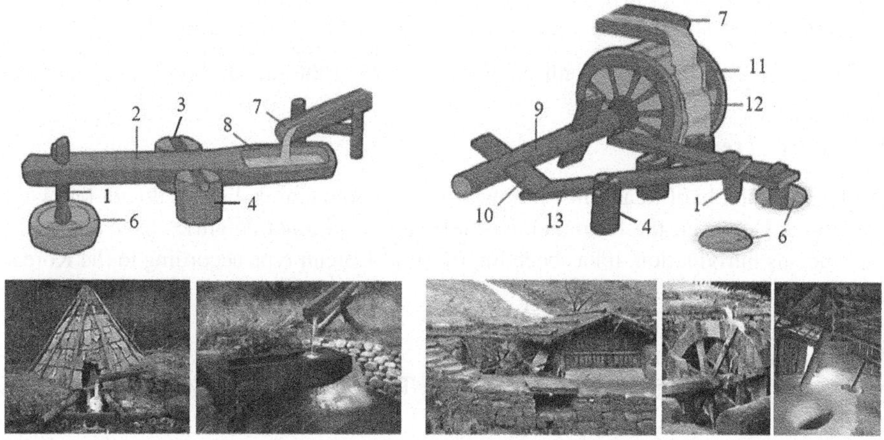

Fig. 13. Treadmill action by various hydraulic power [8]

3.3.3 Characteristics of Korean Treadmill and Principle of Invention

At least five inventive principles apply to treadmill.

a. (1) Segmentation - Allows two people to gain weight in the way a person applies weight.
b. (4) Asymmetry - Asymmetric structure.
c. (8) Counterweight - Counterweight - Counterweight is released after weight is applied.
d. (19) Periodic action - Periodic action to release and release weight.
e. (25) Self-service - The bottom of the container is narrowed so that the grain is lowered by self weight in the container.
f. (3) Local quality - The end of the arm that is easy to damage is made of stone or iron, so it is not easily worn.

4 Conclusions

Researching traditional farm tools and various life tools will solve various problems and see optimized results. The methodology of TRIZ [1] is a problem solving methodology which is learned from the examination of the patent literature. Especially, three kinds of agricultural equipments introduced are basically found that five or more inventive principles are found, and it can be seen that the life span of the technical system is long by applying various inventive principles.

This study is similar, but the other is to get a clue to solve present and future problems with real data. TRIZ has derived the methodology from a number of patents by Alschuller, which has been around for almost 50 years, but is still very useful. This is a small attempt, but if you study systematically more traditional farm equipment or systems, I think there is a possibility to find clues to new international issues such as cyclical economy and appropriate technology. It is similar to the fact that we are getting a clue to many technical principles and problem solving in nature.

Although some of the representative ones have been roughly reviewed, systematic research on more can lead to a more desirable solution in which one solution is used rather than a temporary one, rather than a longer one.

References

1. Altshuller, G.: The Innovation Algorithm: TRIZ, Systematic Innovation and Technical Creativity. Technical Innovation Center, Inc., Worchester (1999)
2. Korean Society of Agricultural Machinery (KSAM): Korean Farm Equipment Book (2001)
3. Kim, H.: Study on the form and principle of traditional sickle. Folklore Stud. **40**, 151–187 (2017). 6
4. https://ko.wikipedia.org/wiki/온돌
5. https://www.amazon.com/Hand-Ho-Mi-Digger-Inches-D9841-x/dp/B0091UPBDQ
6. https://m.blog.naver.com/12sungbok/40114513330
7. http://vsm.kisti.re.kr/agri/v-show/object/didil-1.htm
8. Yong Yong Yoon, National Science Museum
9. http://www.doopedia.co.kr

An Innovative Methodology to Design LCM Mold for Aeronautic and Automotive Industries

A. Ouezgan(✉), S. Adima, A. Maziri, E. Mallil, and J. Echaabi

Équipe de Recherche Appliquée sur les Polymères,
Département de Génie Mécanique, ENSEM, Université Hassan II de Casablanca,
Oasis, BP 8118 Casablanca, Morocco
Ahmedouezgan@gmail.com

Abstract. The liquid composite molding family (LCM) includes several processes like RTM ("Resin transfer molding") and VARI ("Vacuum assisted resin infusion"), to satisfy the requirements of each industry. The objectives of recent years in the automotive and aerospace industries tend towards better control of production costs by using of new materials, shorter manufacturing cycles, a higher level of performance and safety and better environmental respect. In the automotive sector, a short cycle time and a lower cost equipment are the most criteria to determine a suitable process, while the quality of the part is the primary parameter for aeronautical process selection. The main objective of this paper is to propose and discuss a new design of LCM mold, allowing at the same time to facilitate the manufacturing process, in particular to reduce the cycle time and to respect the material's health by obtaining a part with minimum defects. This innovation is achieved by using the TRIZ theory ("Theory of inventive problem solving"), in order to eliminate the contradictions that exist between the requirements of the two sectors.

Keywords: LCM · TRIZ · Automotive · Aeronautic

1 Introduction

Liquid composite molding (LCM) refers to composite manufacturing processes in which a fibrous preform material is placed into a mold cavity and a thermosetting resin with a relatively low viscosity is impregnated the preform until all empty spaces between the fibers are filled, and finally cured to create a polymeric composite structure [1]. Due to its capacity to significantly reduce the release of volatile organic compounds (VOCs) to the atmosphere, the LCM manufacturing processes has gained attention compared with current methods of open molding processes. They have also been created to overcome the intrinsic weaknesses of autoclave draping processes such as: their high tooling cost and their long cycle time. The LCM processes are distinguishable from each other by the nature of the mold used and the manner of the filling phase. The LCM mold is divided in two parts, the lower part of the mold is always rigid but the upper part is possibly be rigid, like in RTM, CRTM and flexible injection, semi-flexible (RTM-light) or flexible such as in VARTM, VARI and LRI, while the resin can

Published by Springer Nature Switzerland AG 2019
R. Benmoussa et al. (Eds.): TFC 2019, IFIP AICT 572, pp. 472–485, 2019.
https://doi.org/10.1007/978-3-030-32497-1_37

be introduced using a combination of a positive injection pressure (use of an injection machine), vacuum infusion (use of a vacuum pump), and possibly assisted by the compaction force.

The Resin transfer molding (RTM) is one of the most recognized LCM processes, it was adopted for composite manufacturing in the mid-1980s. RTM manufacturing includes several steps. It begins by placing a dry fibrous reinforcement inside a rigid mold, closing the mold, injecting a liquid resin, curing the resin and finally demolding the part. Due to its several advantages [2], RTM has received the most industrial attention [3, 4]. The most important objective of this process is to reduce the time it takes to fill the mold with resin. This will increase the production rate and reduce manufacturing costs and also ensure that the fabric preform is completely saturated before the resin starts to gel [5]. The conventional RTM processes usually have limitations in fabrication large parts due to the cost investments, pressure equipment, and the process time, that dramatically increasing proportional to the surface area of composite structures [6].

The vacuum assisted resin transfer molding (VARTM) process was introduced to overcome these challenges. In this process, a fibrous preform is placed into a mold cavity, and covers by a flexible polymer film, then a sealant tape is used to adhere it to the mold in order to avoid air-resin leakage. A vacuum pump is used to evacuate the air from the cavity, which leads to compact the preform. The inlet gate is opened and resin impregnates the preform under atmospheric pressure. The main disadvantages of the VARTM process are: First, the pressure gradient is limited to one atmospheric pressure so the mold filling is very slow and the filling time increasing proportional to the part's dimensions [1], along with the low permeability of typical fiber layers often leads the resin to not completely fill the mold cavity before the resin begins to gel. To solve these issues many authors and multinational companies have developed the new variants of VARTM, like as SCRIMP [7], FFC method [8] and VIPR [9]. However, as all these variants use only a single rigid side mold, the fabricated part has low dimensional tolerances due to the non-uniformity of part thickness, and low fiber volume fraction. These processes have still limited to non-aerospace applications.

The CRTM, compression resin transfer molding, also known as injection-compression molding (I/CM) [5, 6], is another variant of RTM. In this process, the upper part of the mold is rigid and moveable in order to increase the fiber volume fraction and to improve the surface quality of the part. Moreover, it minimizes the entrapment of air pockets, by applying a compression force that squeezes and displaces all air and volatiles bubbles out through the vent gate. Also, the CRTM reduces the injection pressure fill time and gives an answer to limitation of in-plane impregnation velocity as compared to RTM. The steps for fabricating the composite part by CRTM are described in details in [7]. Although its advantages, the CRTM needs a high force to displace the moveable upper mold and to better compress the preform, this leads to increase the cost equipment and to deform mold walls which influence the part quality.

Chang proposed another variant of VARTM called vacuum-assisted compression resin transfer molding. This process, has been developed to reduce the mold filling time, injection pressure and cleaning mold time compared with resin transfer molding. The vacuum-assisted compression resin transfer molding utilizes a flexible membrane placed between the upper mold and the mold cavity compared with RTM. Before the injection phase takes place, the air is evacuated from the upper mold by using a vacuum pump which forces the membrane to lift up and to relax the fibers. Thus, the resin can be easily entered into the cavity. Once enough amount of resin is introduced, a compression pressure is applied on the film that compacts the fibers and conducts the resin through the preform. Some shortcomings are inevitable including the edge effect and excess of injected resin. More resin leads to a longer injection and compression phase and more wastes [10].

The main objective of this paper is to propose and discuss a new design of LCM mold allowing at the same time to satisfy the requirements of aeronautic and automotive industries. This innovation is achieved by using the TRIZ theory (Theory of inventive problem solving), in order to solve the contradictions existed between these sectors.

2 TRIZ Theory

TRIZ is the Russian acronym for the inventive problem solving theory, created and developed by the Russian engineer G. Altshuller in 1946. Over the past years, TRIZ has used in different sectors, including electrical Engineering [11], chemical engineering [12], automotive sector [13], mechanical field [14], and environmental area [15]. Due to these large scope of applications, nowadays TRIZ has become as one of the most powerful, popular innovative method. Figure 1 illustrates TRIZ theory methodology.

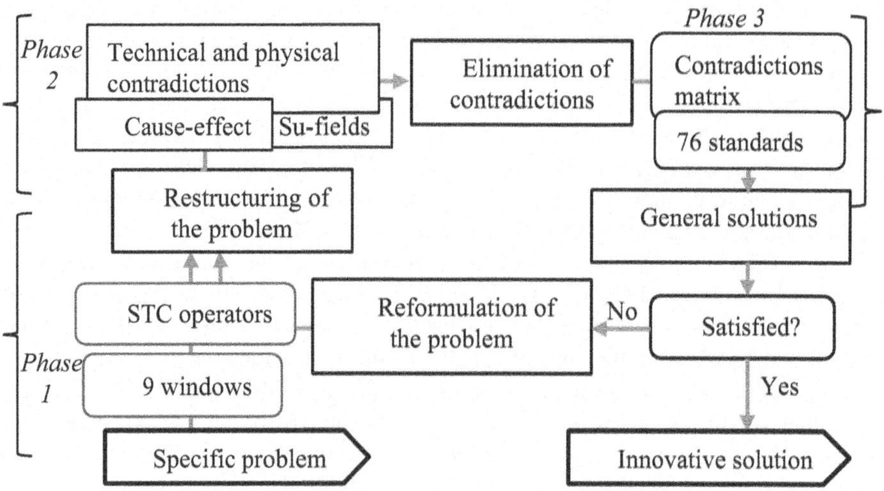

Fig. 1. TRIZ theory methodology.

This method is based on three main phases [16–19]:

Phase 1: Description and understanding of the specific problem
This phase is essential to better understand and formulate correctly the problem, it's applicable in four steps:

- The description of the project.
- The analysis of the system.
- The identification of the problems.
- Ideal final result formulation.

During this phase, it's recommended to use some rules and apply the TRIZ tools such as, miniature men's method, STC operators and the nine windows tool that allow us to avoid psychological inertia.

Phase 2: Formulation and modeling of the problem
It is used to find the contradictions between the parameters of the system by using the following tools.

- Cause-effect analysis.
- Technical and physical contradictions.
- Substances-field models (Su-field analysis).
- Laws of engineering systems evolutions.

Phase 3: generation of solutions
It allows to solve the previous contradictions and to generate models of solutions by using the following tools:

- Contradictions matrix.
- Separation principles.
- 76 standards.

3 Description and Understanding of the Specific Problem

3.1 External Functional Analysis

This tool is used to understand why the system exist, in addition to identify the principal functions (PF) and the constraints functions (CF) related to the system. Figure 2 shows external functional analysis of LCM processes [20].

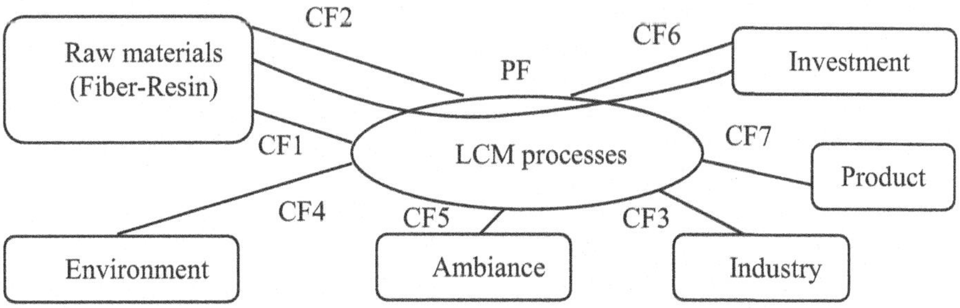

Fig. 2. External functional analysis.

PF: Transform the raw materials into the desired product.
CF1: Inject and quickly fill the mold without any resin leakage.
CF2: Compact uniformly the fibrous reinforcement.
CF3: Be profitable.
CF4: Resist to the aggressive environment (noise, dust, humidity and other industrial environments).
CF5: Do not pollute the environment (mechanical noise, Chemical emissions (styrene)).
CF6: Do not require a huge investment.
CF7: Give a good surface finish and close dimensional tolerances.

3.2 Structural Decomposition

This tool is used to identify all system and subsystems components and their functions. Figure 3 presents the structural decomposition of LCM mold.

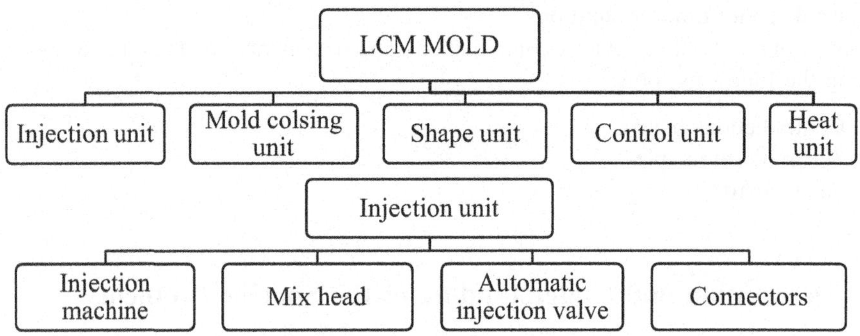

Fig. 3. Structural decomposition of LCM mold.

Mold closing unit: Allows to close the mold and ensure a better seal between the lower and the upper half mold, as well as to obtain a uniform fiber compaction.
Shape unit: Includes two sides of the mold, carved inside them the part shape, the inlet gates, the vent gates and the sealing tapes.
Control unit: Includes all tools used to measure and control process variables, as well as give information about system evolution.
Heat unit: Allows to control the temperature of the resin and the mold in order to govern the resin impregnation velocity during injection phase and polymerization reaction during consolidation phase.
Injection machine: Permits to store and to transfer the resin and additives from their separate tanks to the mold cavity.
Mix head: Allows to mix the resin with fillers and additives, and gives to operators a tool to control and change the velocity of polymerization reaction in the mold.
Automatic injection valves: Are mounted at the injection gates to connect the metering line. They protect against backflow and generate a defined back pressure.

3.3 Ideal Final Result Expression

In the automotive sector, a short cycle time and a lower cost equipment are the most criteria to determine a suitable process, while the quality of the part is the primary parameter for aeronautical process selection. These factors depend on the part dimension, fill time, cure time, surface quality, dimensional tolerances and fiber volume fraction. All these dictated conditions include the conflict links and contradictions that can't be solved by using only the compromises thinking. The use of TRIZ theory permits to achieve this goal by proposing a new process capable to satisfy the requirements of aeronautic and automotive industries.

4 Cause-Effect Analysis

The cause-effect diagram is a TRIZ tool, used to identify the useful and harmful resources of the LCM manufacturing processes and its environment, as well as to find the contradictions and conflict links between all parameters mentioned above. Figure 4 illustrates the process of generating creative solutions by using cause-effect analysis.

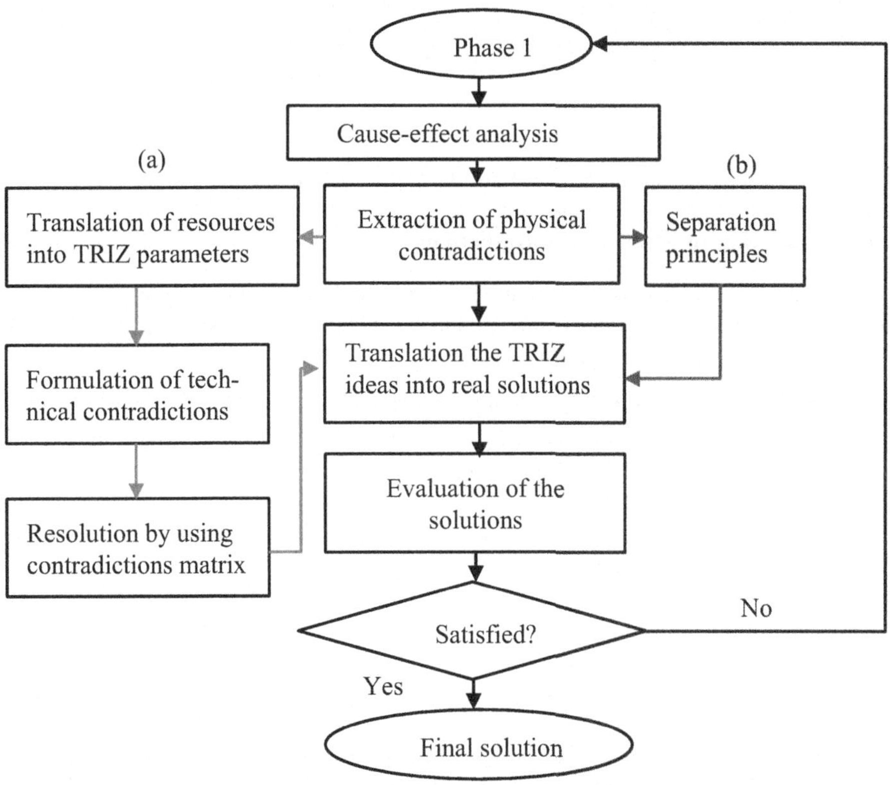

Fig. 4. Cause-effect analysis process (a) by using contradictions matrix (b) by using separation principles

In this article, we are interested to utilize cause-effect analysis methodology by using contradictions matrix (path a). The cause effect diagram of LCM manufacturing processes is presented in Fig. 5.

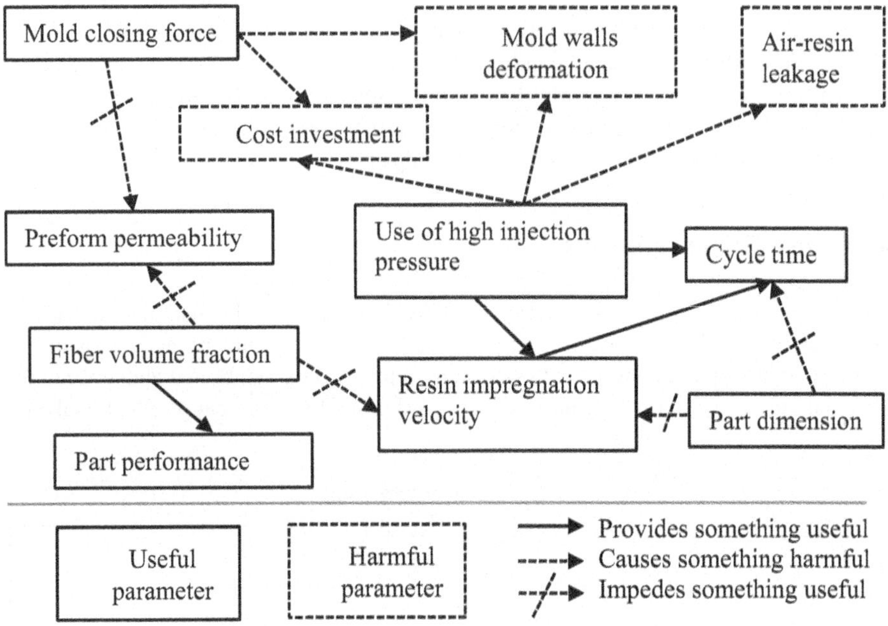

Fig. 5. Cause-effect analysis of LCM manufacturing processes.

4.1 Extraction of Physical Contradictions

A physical contradiction (PC) is a situation in which an engineering system require contradictory values from the same parameter [21]. In our problem, the physical contradictions are presented as follows:

PC1: The mold closing force should be high (should exist) to increase the fiber volume fraction and avoid air-resin leakage, and should not be high (should not exist) to avoid mold walls deformation and huge cost investment as well as because it impedes the preform permeability.
PC2: The useful factor (fiber volume fraction) should be high (should exist) to manufacture performance parts, and should not be high (should not exist) because it thwarts another useful factors (resin impregnation velocity) and (preform permeability).
PC3: The manufacture of large parts should exist to satisfy the requirements of industry and should not exist because it impedes the resin impregnation velocity and short cycle time.
PC4: The injection pressure should be high to reduce cycle time and increase the resin impregnation speed and should not be high in order to avoid mold walls deformation, air-resin leakage and huge cost investment.

4.2 Translation of Resources into TRIZ Parameters

In this step, we transform the specific expressions of LCM manufacturing processes to typical parameters in the engineering contradiction using the 39 universal technical parameters from TRIZ matrix.

Table 1. Translation of LCM parameters into TRIZ parameters.

Specific expression	TRIZ parameters
Mold closing force	Force
Mold deformation walls	Stability of object
Air-resin leakage	Waste of substance
Cost investment	Productivity
Preform permeability	Convenience of use
Use of high injection pressure	Tension/pressure
Cycle time	Waste of time
Fiber volume fraction	Amount of substance
Resin impregnation velocity	Speed
Part dimension	Manufacturability
Part performance	Reliability

4.3 Formulation of Technical Contradictions

A technical contradiction (TC) is a situation in which the improvement of a function or the elimination of a harmful effect leads to the unacceptable deterioration of another function [22]. A technical contradiction is formulated in the following form:

The improvement of (specific expression/*TRIZ parameter*) degrades (specific expression/*TRIZ parameter*).

From the physical contradiction 1 (PC1), we have obtained the following technical contradictions (TC):

TC1: The improvement of (Mold closing force/*Force*) degrades (Mold deformation walls/*Stability of object*).
TC2: The improvement of (Mold closing force/*Force*) degrades (Cost investment/*Productivity*).
TC3: The improvement of (Mold closing force/*Force*) degrades (Preform permeability/*Convenience of use*).
TC4: The improvement of (Fiber volume fraction/*Amount of substance*) degrades (Mold deformation walls/*Stability of object*).
TC5: The improvement of (Fiber volume fraction/*Amount of substance*) degrades (Cost investment/*Productivity*).
TC6: The improvement of (Fiber volume fraction/*Amount of substance*) degrades (Preform permeability/*Convenience of use*).

4.4 Resolution by Using the Contradiction Matrix

The contradiction matrix is the most recognized TRIZ tool because of its ease of use. In this matrix, the lines correspond to the parameters to be improved, while the columns include the parameters which are degraded. At the intersection, the matrix gives one to four inventive principles for guiding the user to solve this contradiction [23].

Figure 6 shows the distribution of the dominant inventive principles generated by the contradiction matrix, while Fig. 7 present the distribution of all the inventive principles generated by the contradiction matrix.

Table 2. The contradiction matrix.

Worsening parameter / Improving parameter	Force	Stability of object	Waste of substance	Productivity	Convenience of use	Tension/pressure	Waste of time	Amount of substance	Speed	Manufacturability	Reliability
Force		35,10 ,21	8,35, 40,5	3,28, 35,37	1,28, 3,25	18,21 4	10,37 36	14,29 18,36	13,28 15,12	15,37 18,1	3,35 13,21
Stability of object	10,35 21,16		2, 14, 30,40	23,35 40, 3	32,35 30	2, 35, 40	35,27	15,32 35	33,15 28,18	35,19	0
Waste of substance	14,15 18,40	2, 14, 30,40		28,35 10,23	32,28 2, 24	3, 36, 37,10	15,18 35,10	6, 3, 10,24	10,13 28,38	15,34 33	10,29 39,35
Productivity	10,37 14	35, 3, 22,39	28,10 35,23		1, 28, 7, 10	10,37 14	0	35,38	0	35,28 2, 24	1, 35, 10,38
Convenience of use	28,13 35	32,35 30	28,32 2, 24	15, 1, 28		2, 32, 12	4, 28, 10,34	12, 35	18,13 34	2, 5, 12	17,27 8, 40
Tension /pressure	36,35 21	35,33 2, 40	10,36 3, 37	10,14 35,37	11		37,36 4	10,14 36	6, 35, 36	1, 35, 16	10,13 19,35
Waste of time	10,37 36,5	35, 3, 22, 5	35,18 10,39	0	4, 28, 10,34	37, 36,4		35,38 18,16	0	35,28 34, 4	10,30 4
Amount of substance	35,14 3	15, 2, 17,40	6, 3, 10,24	13,29 3, 27	35,29 25,10	10,36 14, 3	35,38 18,16		35,29 34,28	29, 1, 35,27	18, 3, 28,40
Speed	13,28 15,19	28,33 1, 18	10,13 28,38	0	32,28 13,12	6, 18, 38,40	0	10,19 29,38		35,13 8, 1	11,35 27,28
Manufactur-ability	35,12	11,13 1	15,34 33	35, 1, 10,28	2, 5 13,16	35,19 1, 37	35,28 34, 4	35,23 1, 24	35,13 8, 1		0
Reliability	8, 28, 10, 3	0	10,35 29,39	1, 35, 29,38	27,17 40	10,24 35,19	10,30 4	21,28 40, 3	21,35 11,28	0	

From these graphs the inventive principles that should studied carefully are:

35: Parameter changes.
10: Preliminary action.
28: Mechanics substitution.
15: Dynamics.
3: Local quality
2: Taking out

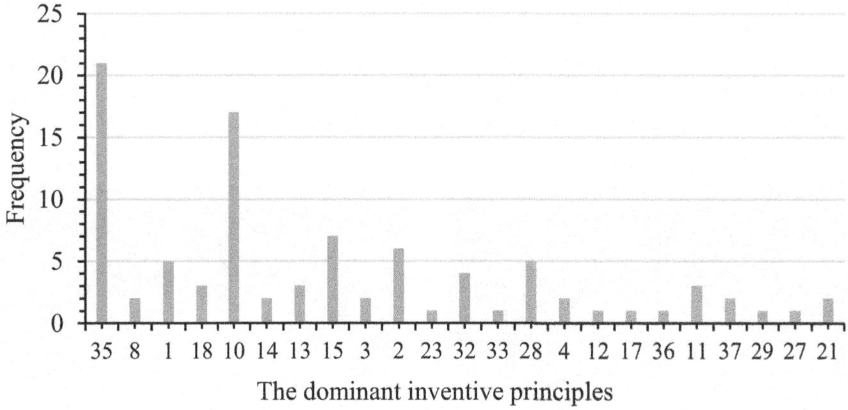

Fig. 6. The distribution of the dominant inventive principle.

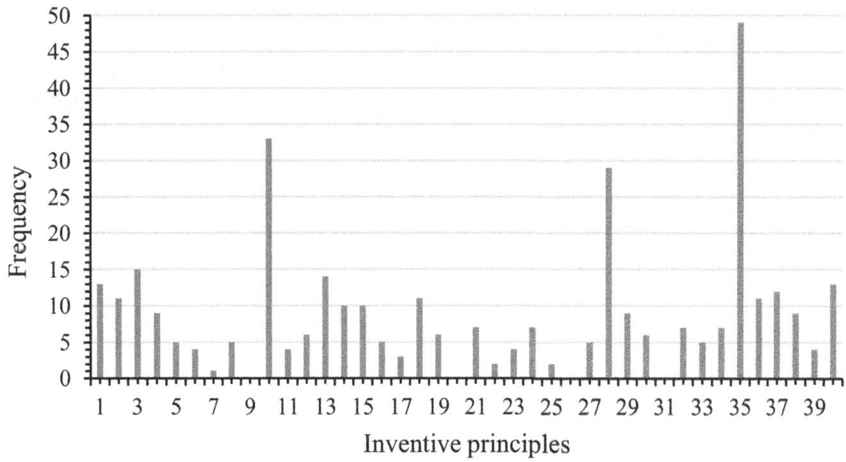

Fig. 7. The distribution of all inventive principles.

5 Concepts Generation

The application of these Inventive principles allow us to find the old LCM processes as well as to propose the new LCM mold. Details of the new LCM mold components and the main stage of the manufacturing cycle will be presented at the conference.

The use of the inventive principle: 35 "parameter changes" with the recommendation "change the degree of flexibility" permits to find the concept depicted in the Fig. 9.

In the CRTM process, the mold cover is always made of a single rigid part. Thereby the CRTM needs a high force to displace the moveable upper mold and to better compress the preform, this leads to increase cost equipment and deform mold walls which influence the part quality. However, these limitations can be minimized by using an upper mold made of several pieces that can be articulated separately. This variant called ACRTM ("articulated compression resin transfer molding") [24].

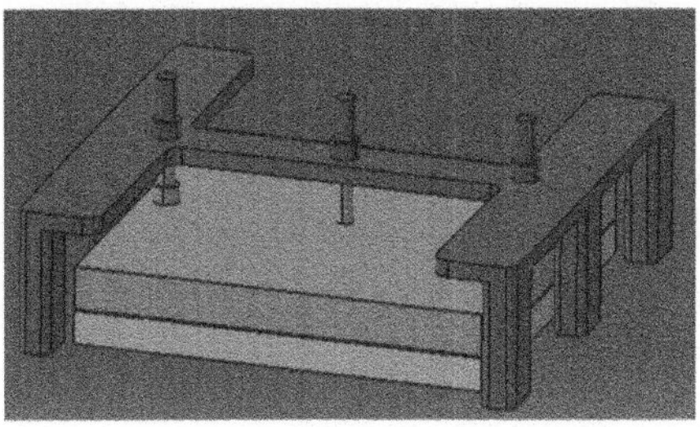

Fig. 8. The CRTM mold.

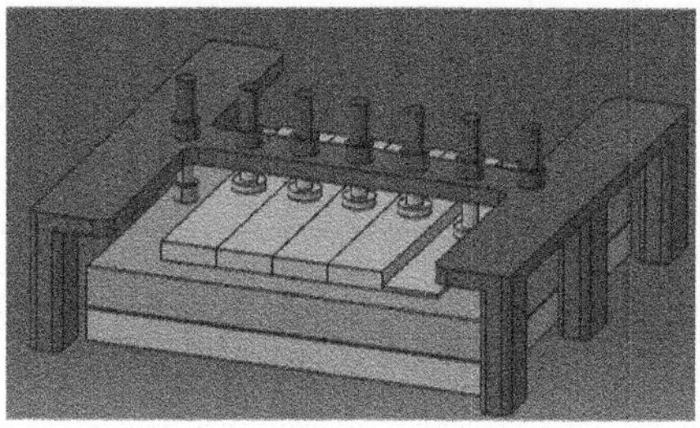

Fig. 9. The ACRTM mold.

The use of the inventive principle: 28 "Mechanics substitution" with recommendation "Use electric, magnetic and electromagnetic fields to interact with the object" allows us to propose a new variant of VARTM process called "Relaxation-compression resin transfer molding under magnetic field" as illustrated in the Fig. 10. In this process, we only use a single rigid side mold like as in the VARTM processes, that contains the fiber preform, and it covers by a flexible magnetic membrane, or by using a vacuum bag including a ferromagnetic sheet, gathered together by an effective glue. The magnetic field is controlled by the current intensity or by the separated gap between the coil and ferromagnetic membrane, so as to apply a magnetic force on the membrane and as a result, move it up to relax the preform or down in order to compress the fiber reinforcement. Which leads to speed up the impregnation velocity and increase the fiber volume fraction.

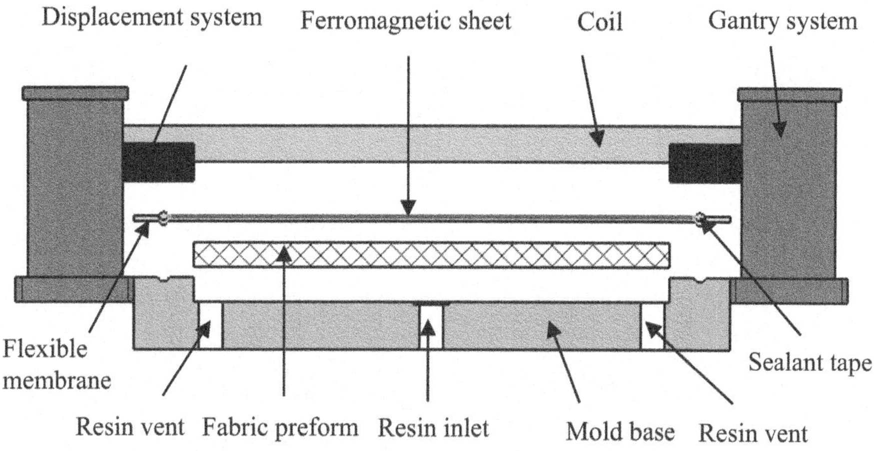

Fig. 10. Relaxation-compression resin transfer molding under magnetic field mold components

The use of the inventive principle: 15 "Dynamics" with recommendation "divide an object into parts capable to move relative to each other" permits to generate the process proposed by Chang, called "PCM: Progressive compression method" [25], as illustrated in the Fig. 12. This process belongs to the vacuum infusion processes (VIPs), as well as it's an evolution of the flexible injection process [26]. The PCM reduces the filling time compared to the vacuum infusion processes.

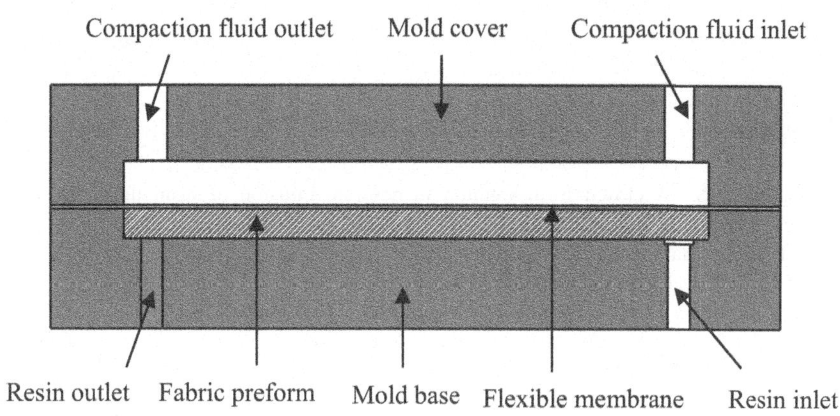

Fig. 11. Flexible injection mold components

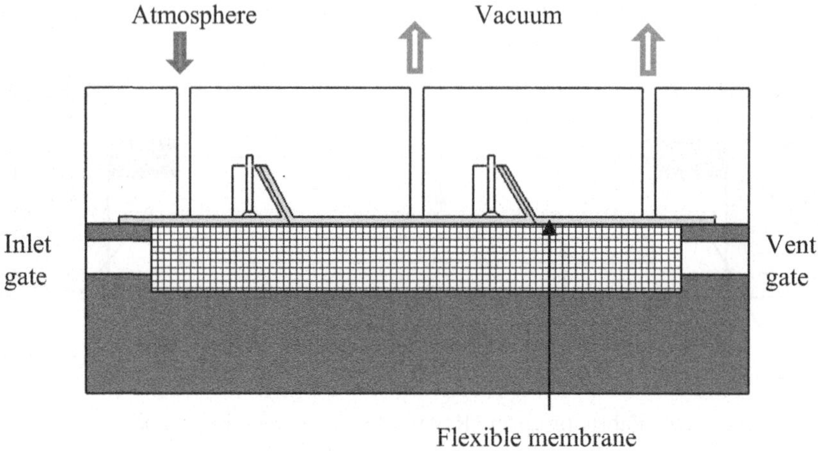

Fig. 12. The PCM mold [26]

6 Conclusion and Outlook

This paper emphasizes the capacity of TRIZ theory to solve the conflict links existed between the aeronautic and automotive requirements. Moreover, to propose the new solutions capable to maintain simultaneously the cadence of the automobile and the quality of the aerospace industries.

To evaluate the efficiency of each solution and its capacity to satisfy the aeronautic and the automotive conditions we suggest to use the analytical and the numerical approaches before fabricate the prototypes and going into the experimental approach.

References

1. Lopatnikov, S.: A closed form solution to describe infusion of resin under vacuum in deformable fibrous porous media. Model. Simul. Mater. Sci. Eng. **12**, S191–S204 (2004)
2. Sozer, E.M.: Manufacturing Techniques for Polymer Matrix Composites (PMCs). Woodhead Publishing Limited, Cambridge (2012)
3. Potter, K.: Resin Transfer Moulding. Chapman & Hall, London (1997)
4. Marsh, G.: Composites on the road to the big time? Reinf. Plast. **47**(2), 33–36 (2003)
5. Wang, J.: Use of medial axis to find optimal channel designs to reduce mold filling time in resin transfer molding. Compos. A Appl. Sci. Manuf. **95**(Supplement C), 161–172 (2017)
6. Song, H.: Study on high-speed RTM to reduce the impregnation time of carbon/epoxy composites. Compos. Struct. **119**, 50–58 (2015)
7. Seemann, WH.: Plastic transfer molding techniques for the production of fiber reinforced plastic structures. US Patent No. 4902,215 (1990)
8. Alms, J.B., Advani, S.G.: Simulation and experimental validation of flow flooding chamber method of resin delivery in liquid composite molding. Compos. Part A Appl. Sci. Manuf. **38**, 2131–2141 (2007)

9. Alms, J.B., Advani, S.G., Glancey, J.L.: Liquid composite molding control methodologies using vacuum induced preform relaxation. Compos. Part A Appl. Sci. Manuf. **42**, 57–65 (2011)
10. Chang, C.Y.: Experimental analysis of mold filling in vacuum assisted compression resin transfer molding. J. Reinf. Plast. Compos. **31**, 1630–1637 (2012)
11. Mansoor, M., Mariun, N., Toudeshki, A., Wahab, N.I.A., Mian, A.U., Hojabri, M.: Innovating problem solving in power quality devices: a survey based on dynamic voltage restorer case. Renew. Sustain. Energy Rev. **70**, 1207–1216 (2017)
12. Abramov, O., Kogan, S., Mitnik-Gankin, L., Sigalovsky, I., Smirnov, A.: TRIZ-based approach for accelerating innovation in chemical engineering. Chem. Eng. Res. Des. **103**, 25–31 (2015)
13. Azammi, A.M.N., Saquan, S.M., Ishak, M.R., Sultan, M.T.H.: Conceptual design of automobile engine rubber mounting composite using TRIZ-Morphological chart-analytic network process technique. Def. Technol. **14**(4), 268–277 (2018)
14. Cempel, C.: Application of TRIZ approach to machine vibration condition monitoring problems. Mech. Syst. Sig. Process. **41**, 328–334 (2013)
15. Zhang, J., Shang, J.: Research on developing environmental protection industry based on TRIZ theory. Procedia Environ. Sci. **2**, 1326–1334 (2010)
16. Zouaoua-ragab, D.: Lois d'evolution de TRiZ pour la conception des futures generations des produits: Proposition d'un modele. Ph. D. thesis Arts and Crafts ParisTech (2012)
17. Ilevbare, M., Probert, D., Phaal, R.: A review of TRIZ, and its benefits and challenges in practice. Technovation **33**, 30–37 (2013)
18. Fey, V.: Dilemma of a radical innovation - a new view on the law of transition to a micro-level. TRIZ J. (1999). https://triz-journal.com/dilemma-radical-innovation-new-view-law-transition-micro-level/
19. Domb, E., Miller, JA.: Applying the law of the completeness of a technological system to formulate a problem. TRIZ J. (2007). https://triz-journal.com/applying-the-law-of-the-completeness-of-a-technological-system-to-formulate-a-problem/
20. Belu, N., Rachieru, N., Militaru, E., Anghel, D.: Application of FMEA method in product development stage. Acad. J. Manuf. Eng. **10**(3), 12–19 (2012)
21. Ko, Y.T.: Modeling a hybrid-compact design matrix for new product innovation. Comput. Ind. Eng. **107**, 345–359 (2017)
22. Zhang, P., Essaid, A., Zanni-Merk, C., Cavallucci, D., Ghabri, S.: Experience capitalization to support decision making in inventive problem solving. Comput. Ind. **101**, 25–40 (2018)
23. Pokhrel, C., Cruz, C., Ramirez, Y., Kraslawski, A.: Adaptation of TRIZ contradiction matrix for solving problems in process engineering. Chem. Eng. Res. Des. **103**, 3–10 (2015)
24. Achim, V., Soukane, S., Gauvin, R., Trochu, F.: Simulation of articulated compression resin transfer molding. In: The 8th International Conference on Flow Processes in Composite Materials (FPCM8) Douai, France, 11–13 July 2006
25. Chang, C.Y.: Numerical study on filling process in progressive compression method. Adv. Compos. Mater **28**, 37–51 (2017). https://doi.org/10.1080/09243046.2017.1405598
26. Ruiz, E., Briones, LR., Allard, É., Trochu, F.: Flexible injection: a novel LCM technology for low cost manufacturing of high performance composites. Part I: experimental investigation. In: Proceedings FPCM9, p. 34 (2008)

Application of TRIZ and Innovation Management Theory on Decision Support for Transport Infrastructure

Giacomo Bersano[(✉)] and Pierre-Emmanuel Fayemi

IKOS Consulting, 155 rue Anatole France, 92300 Levallois Perret, France
gbersano@ikosconsulting.com

Abstract. Design Theory and Innovation management theory are commonly used in many industrial sectors, especially in highly competitive areas with also the presence of a high level of substitution. Nevertheless, these theories can be useful as well as a support to decision making in slower paced sectors, as railways. In this article the case study of various highly innovative projects in railways sector will be addressed, from the point of view of innovation management and design theory, using TRIZ and some derivatives as General Theory of Innovation (G. Yezersky). The systems under analysis are, respectively: High speed train TGV, 1st driverless metro VAL, tramway ground power supplying, intermodality solutions, Aerotrain, Personal Rapid Transit, Swiss Metro, Hyperloop.

Keywords: Disrupting innovation · Railways · Governmental role

1 Introduction

Since the origins, TRIZ theory has been used for solving technical problems [1]. Nevertheless, the application of this theory to other disciplines has been largely diffused, spacing from science, to business and even politics [2, 3]. The scope of this paper is then to see how TRIZ together with innovation management theory can be used for decision making and technology forecasting on a specific topic that is the potential development of disruptive transport systems. In this paper disruptive innovation theory will be introduced, then a general approach to technology forecasting will be provided, with application to case studies. Finally, comparisons will be done with some indication for future steps. The systems under analysis are, respectively: High speed train TGV, 1st driverless metro VAL, tramway ground power supplying, intermodality solutions, Aerotrain, Personal Rapid Transit, Swiss Metro, Hyperloop.

2 Disruptive Innovation Theory

The concept of disruptive innovation has been firstly created by Clayton C. Christensen from Harvard relating the model of innovation to the competitive position of the company on the market. According to [4] "Disruption describes a process whereby a

Published by Springer Nature Switzerland AG 2019
R. Benmoussa et al. (Eds.): TFC 2019, IFIP AICT 572, pp. 486–493, 2019.
https://doi.org/10.1007/978-3-030-32497-1_38

smaller company with fewer resources is able to successfully challenge established incumbent businesses. Specifically, as incumbents focus on improving their products and services for their most demanding….Entrants that prove disruptive begin by successfully targeting those overlooked segments, gaining a foothold by delivering more-suitable functionality—frequently at a lower price. Incumbents, chasing higher profitability in more-demanding segments, tend not to respond vigorously.."

This concept is very powerful and at the same time simple: the company has a limited choice about the kind of innovation to pursue, according to its position on the market as leader, or challenger. Amongst the case studies cited by Clayton C. Christensen, the hard disk, milling plants…

Today Disrupting innovation theory is used mostly for strategic planning, in small and large companies, as INTEL.

3 Design Theory Applied to Technology Forecasting and Decision Making; Its Coupling with Disruptive Innovation Theory

As described on a previous article from Bersano, Fayemi et al. [5], most used approach for forecasting is the classical prospective approach; this has various limitations (LCPx), that are overcome by the use of logistic curve and TRIZ theory, giving origin to a New Concept development Approach.

The following figure provides an overview on this approach, structured in various phases:

- Preparatory phase, in order to understand problem owner goals and expectation for the study, using Synectics theory [6];
- Phase A-B analysing the product and its surrounding systems, using typical TRIZ tools as Laws of Engineering System Evolution (LESE), System Operator Tool, Relevent analysis from GTI [7] and analysing future applications, using s-curves and expert interviews couples with statistical tool
- Phase C focused on inventive phase for new solutions, using TRIZ
- Phase D concerning the reinforcement of selected inventive ideas and development, both according to [6] and more in general to Project management best practise [8].

As described in Sect. 2, the disrupting innovation theory can be used to assist the marketing and strategic process of the forecasting approach. Basically, the alternatives from the point of view of the company are two:

If the company is leader on the market, an incremental innovation approach will be preferred; then, all inventive ideas too far from currently in house products and services will be delayed or suppressed; if the company is an outsider, breakthrough innovation will be preferred as an internal strategy in order to create a strong differentiation with incumbents. In the following chapter, an example around railways systems will be developed (Fig. 1).

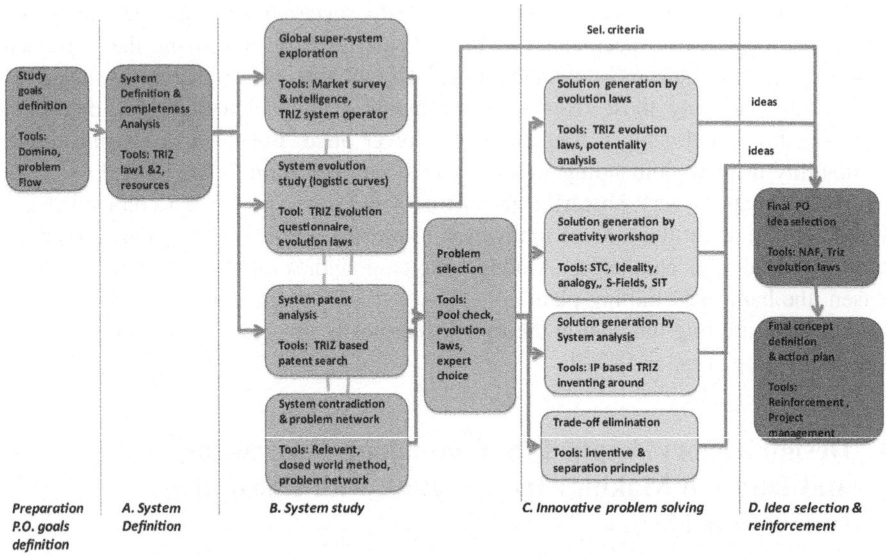

Fig. 1. Schematic process for technology forecasting

4 Case Study: Railways Transport Systems

Transport systems exist since 10000 years, with the development of first wooden boats (running on water). Then, from 3000 B.C, it started the development of first wheel chariots (running on ground). Since then, other transport systems were developed running over different means, respectively the trains on rails and airplanes on air. Most recently, a new transportation system has been imagined, the Hyperloop [9]. According to its inventors, it would be the 5th transportation system beside the existing ones. The research question posed is then the following: which are the probability of success of this radically new transport system in and existing and consolidated market? In order to answer to this question, technology forecasting based on TRIZ and the disruptive innovation theory will be here applied.

4.1 TRIZ Law 1 Application and Extension

According to TRIZ theory [1], the Laws of system evolution of systems (LESE) describes the conditions for the best development of systems. As an application example, the law n°1, describe the main components of a ground transport system. The following diagram describes the key elements of a transport system for a freight train and the evolution of systems (Fig. 2).

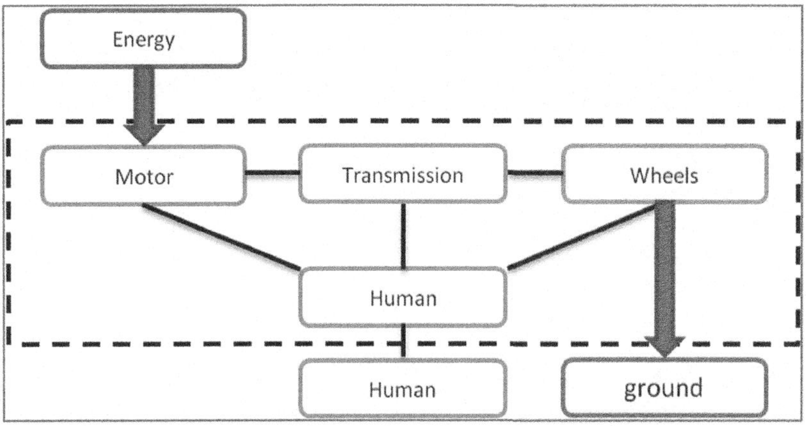

Fig. 2. Application of Law n°1 to transport system

In the following tables, the simplified evolution of system's elements is mapped in time (for cars and railways) (Table 1).

Table 1. Elements for Law 1 applied to cars.

System	Motor	Transmission	Tool	Control element	Decision element	Energy source	Road	Success
Chariot (3000 B.C.)	Horse (s)	…	Full wheel	Driver	Driver	Food	Earth	Y
(2000 B.C.)			Rays wheel	Driver	Driver			Y
Cugnot steam engine (1771)	Steam engine	Mechanical transmission	Rays wheel	Driver	Driver	Coal		N
Car	Gas engine	Mechanical transmission	Tires	Driver	Driver			Y

Analyzing the historically evolution of rail transportation, it is noted that:

- The evolution of the system is linked to the evolution of motor element
- The energy sources and running infrastructure, that are external elements in interface with the law 1 model of the system (i.e. the super system), are critical for the success of the new system

There is the need to add some external elements of the analysis, to help understand why some systems survive and other not, behind the technical aspects…this will be realized using innovation management theory later (Table 2).

Table 2. Elements for Law 1 applied to railways.

System	Motor	Transmission	Tool	Control element	Decision element	Energy source	Road	Success
Locomotive (1801)	Steam engine	Mechanical	Steel wheels	Driver	Driver	Coal	Steel rails	Y
	Electrical motor (1834)					Battery		N
						Catenary (1881)		Y
	Diesel engine (1931)					Oil tank		Y
Shinkansen (1964)						Catenary 25 kV		Y
TGV (1981)	SofA el motors							Y
Aerotrain (1971)	Gaz turbine	Mechanical	Air cushion	Driver	Driver	Gaz	Concrete elevated	N
VAL (1978)				Automatic Train Operation				Y
SwissMetro (2005)	El motors	Mechanical	Maglev			Electricity	Vacuum tube	N

4.2 System Operator Tool Application and Extension

System Operator Tool has been described in [1]. It is well adapted for this kind of analysis, identifying trends, advantages and disadvantages. The following table is an extraction of a larger table developed for locomotive for freight transportation.

4.3 General Theory of Innovation Application for Disrupting Value Chains

The history of innovation is full of failures, even for very promising systems; amongst most cited failed innovations, Segway, Google Glass, Sony Betamax [10, 11]. Various scholars analyzed the reason of failure, focusing on innovation value chain [12]. As an example, let's take the Betamax. A much better technical system than VHS, capable of high quality image and sound videotapes, the system was killed by Hollywood because of the risk of high quality copy of the movies, and by the retailers of video, that were already equipped with competing VHS system. Others have focused on the structure of the market and the potential impact on existing value chain, without unfortunately providing a methodological approach for evaluation. Amongst TRIZ theory and related developments, there is the Relevent analysis as developed par Yezersky [7]. According to this tool, the system to be improved is analyzed according to the following elements (Table 3):

- Identification of real customer and his extra value moment (behind expectations)
- Identification of application scenarios
- Identification of potential problems at different scenarios steps, partial solutions and secondary related problems
- Selection of innovative problems to be solved

Table 3. Elements for Law 1.

Super-system trends	System trends	Sub-systems trends
– Complete trains terminals – Simplicity/Performance/ Standardization – Rail sorting stations – modernization + reconversion – fast actions, high performances, competitiveness – Mega-hubs development – Rail terminal and sorting station – Multimodal (road) terminal station – Logistic platform – European networks interoperability	– Product used to meet very high capacity demand of freight market – Provide more safety and reliable operation. – Increase the travels frequency – Higher travel speed – Energy source change (more sustainable, renewable energy sources)	– Increase the autonomy (possibility of crossing sections without catenary) – Need to store more energy – Need to reduce the losses – Need to reduce the volume – Need to reduce the mass – Minimize the passive components – Lighten the transformers – Active filtration – Middle-frequency transformers – Integration technologies (converging to digital, full functional digital communication) – Better brake performance – Distributed traction power

Due to its clear sequential and logical approach, it is an easy way to represent a network of problems for a complex system. The following figure is an extraction of a representation of this analysis applied to the value chain as an example, of Amazon delivering some parcel to customers. In this example, problems concerning cost of expedition by rail and distance to loading-unloading are identified, nevertheless the analysis must include: final customer and all intermediate players and infrastructure providers (Fig. 3).

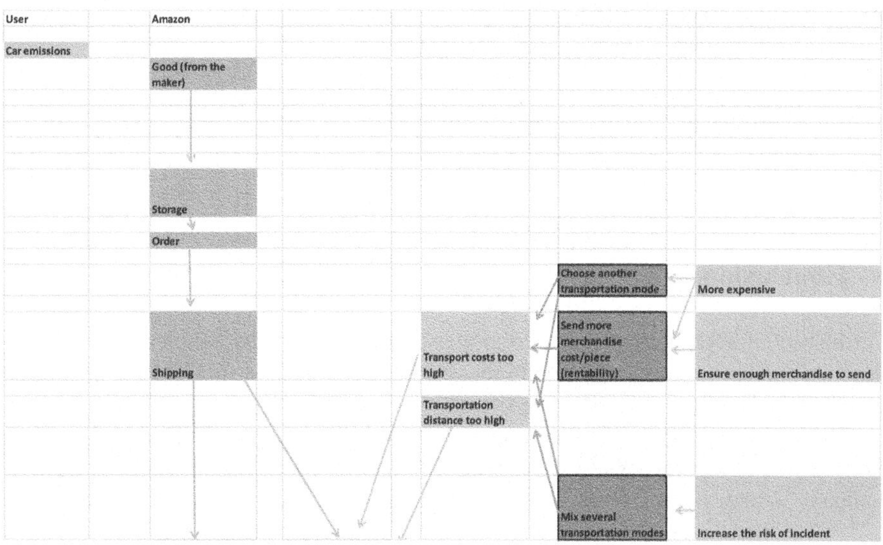

Fig. 3. Application of Relevent analysis on freight transportation (an extract)

4.4 Disrupting Innovation and the Role of Governments

Disrupting innovation is in general capital intensive; considering the transport sector, there are various certifications to be obtained before allowing the transportation of people, and huge validation tests. Therefore, innovators in this field are really crossing the valley of the death of innovation [13]. In this situation, if the value chain is against a disrupting innovation, what are the chances of success? A positive outcome to this kind of innovation can come from the government. According to Mazzucato [14], "government investment played a central role in developing nearly all of the technologies that make the iPhone a smart phone: the Internet, GPS, touch screens, and the advances in voice recognition underlying Siri". It is then possible to create a viability check-list in order to identify which innovation is more suitable to succeed in a complex and conservative market as the public transport sector.

The following table is a synthetic check-list for a transportation project, based on some major innovation in the last 50 years.

The system level involves large value chains to be impacted, then lower probability of success. The cost is high reduces as well the probability of success. If the innovation is pushed to an incumbent company, the company will try to disregard it. The state support is the necessary element for the development of the first transport system, that if successful it will reduce costs and will become a real competitor in mature transport world. Based on this analysis, for Hyperloop promoters it is necessary to focus the activity firstly on finalizing the design of the system (making it work) and in parallel on a strong lobbying action on regional and national governments (Table 4).

Table 4. Historical analysis on the check-list for success for a new transport system.

Innovation	System level	Cost	Company	State support	Success
TGV	SYS	High	Incumbent	Y	Y
VAL	SYS	High	Outsider	Y	Y
Ground Feed	SUB	Mid	Outsider	Y	Y
Intermodality	SUB	Low	Outsider	Y	Y
Areotrain	SYS	High	Outsider	N	N
ARAMIS PRT	SYS	High	Outsider	N	N
SwissMetro	SYS	High	Outsider	N	N
Hyperloop	SYS	High	Outsider	?	?

5 Conclusions

The history of TRIZ theory is related to the solution of technical problems, in a market free environment as former URSS. In this perspective, in classical TRIZ marketing and company strategy are not considered at all.

Various steps in this direction have been realized in modern TRIZ, and the current paper is exploring the synergy between different theories with a specific focus at company strategy for future developments. Specifically, a general approach for technology forecasting is presented, providing a lecture key for companies on the selection of innovation projects.

Then, a case study is given on railways, started by the questioning about the potential success of Hyperloop. For this specific point, the need of a governmental support seems mandatory for the development and penetration of this very innovative system.

As next steps, the previous table would be enlarged with more case studies, and would be also adapted to other sectors.

References

1. Savranksy, S.: Engineering of Creativity – Introduction to TRIZ Methodology of Inventive Problem Solving. CRC Press, New York (2000)
2. Zlotin, B, Zusman, A.: ARIZ on the Move. Triz J. (1999)
3. Souchkov, V.: TRIZ and Systematic Business Model Innovation TFC (2010)
4. Christensen, C.C., et al.: What is disruptive innovation? HBR **93**, 44–53 (2015)
5. Schöfer, M., Bersano, G., Fayemi, P, Calvez, J.: Methodological support for prospective studies in new concept development. In: Triz Future Conference (2014)
6. Nolan, V.: The Innovator's Handbook – The Skills of Innovative Management. Time Warner, New York (1989)
7. Yezerski, G.: General theory of innovation and its applications. In: Grundlach, C., Lindemann, U., Ried, H. (eds.) Proceedings of the TRIZ Future Conference, pp. 283–287 (2007)
8. Musk, E.: Hyperloop Alpha document (2013)
9. Chiocchio, F., Forgues, D., Paradis, D., Iordanova, I.: Teamwork in integrated design projects: understanding the effects of trust, conflict, and collaboration on performance. Proj. Manage. J. **42**(6), 78–91 (2011)
10. Mann, D.: On innovation timing. Triz J. (2007)
11. Bauer, R.: Failed Innovations: 5 decades of Failure? In: Symposia Anniversary Edition, vol. 20, no. 1, pp. 33–40 (2014)
12. McElheran, K.: Taking a Value-Chain Perspective on Innovation. MIT Sloan Blog (2016)
13. Ford, G.: A valley of death in the innovation sequence: an economic investigation. Res. Eval. **18**, 343–356 (2007)
14. Mazzucato, M.: What is government's role in sparking innovation? WEF (2015)

TRIZ in Teaching

Study on Finding Effective Measures in Education to Counter Googling Action Based on TRIZ

Yutaka Takafuji[1,2](✉)

[1] Tokyo City University, Setagaya, Tokyo 158-8557, Japan
ytakafuj@tcu.ac.jp

[2] 13-8, Jingu 3-chome, Nara-shi, Nara 631-0804, Japan
ytakafuji@me.com

Abstract. One of the recent issues in education at the university is that students tend to search to find directly specific solutions to the problems by Googling. As this behavior prevent students from acquiring expected educational effect, counter measure is necessary. However, this behavior is closely related to large change of environment provided by Information Technology (IT), finding counter measure is not easy. Therefore, a study is made on the above issue exploiting TRIZ. From the results a countermeasure to the above issue is proposed. As relevant conflicting features are unfamiliar to the teaching stuff, finding conflicting features and solutions for above problem with TRIZ is discussed in detail to enlighten teaching stuff, who are unfamiliar to the TRIZ. The problem introduced by Googling is taken as contradiction between "Saving time of busy students, and reducing energy consumption at the brain during thinking", and "Productivity, Adaptability or Versatility, Reliability, Manufacturing precision, and Loss of information". We found approach of "exchanging the role of teacher and student" which will encourage students to widen and deepen their thought, in addition to the ordinary well-known approaches from the study. Finally, additional study by matrix 2010 proposed by Mann is made and discussed. ...

Keywords: Conflicting features · Education · Googling · Matrix 2010 · TRIZ

1 Introduction

The important goal of university education is not only to develop wide and deep knowledge in the specialized field, but to develop student's creativity and ability of solving unprecedented problems, or acquiring implicit knowledge. Recently, students tend to look directly for the specific solution to the problem by Googling. As this behavior seems strongly related to the changed environment provided by Information Technology (IT), changing their mind is difficult.

R. Benmoussa et al. (Eds.): TFC 2019, IFIP AICT 572, pp. 497–507, 2019.
https://doi.org/10.1007/978-3-030-32497-1_39

They are too busy with part-time jobs, in communicating with their friends and class mates, gaming, and watching movies, etc. This behavior prevents them from deep and global thinking, acquiring ability of solving unprecedented problems, and to learn something to develop creativity and implicit knowledge. Therefore, establishing effective countermeasure is strongly demanded in the university education. To find effective solutions to the above issue, TRIZ(Russian acronym for "Theory of Inventive Problem Solving") [1] was exploited in the present work.

There may be a question, whether TRIZ framework can be applied to educational issues, since TRIZ was developed for technical problems based on the previous inventive ideas in the engineering or science fields. However, one of the basic ideas of TRIZ is that "someone, somewhere has most likely already solved something like present problem" [2] and based on the philosophy, that different disciplines don't communicate each other, and consequently much re-inventing is made. In addition, as strategies of TRIZ is highly abstracted, well-structured, and reduced to be only 40 principles, does help in contradiction elimination successfully. Considering above features, TRIZ seems also applicable to the non-technical fields.

Recently works on the business and management are reported [2,3], including an example of successful, win-win solutions in a business context [2]. Examples of using TRIZ in the educational field are also found [4,5]. Marsh et al. [4] has given excellent and helpful work, where 40 principles [1,6] are interpreted to the education related terms. However, as conflicting features are given as technical words unfamiliar to the teaching stuff, finding suitable conflicting features are still difficult for teaching stuff. Therefore, finding effective solutions and showing some examples of finding conflicting features and solutions for above problem with TRIZ seems to be valuable. Detailed process is discussed in the following section. Finally, additional study by using Matrix 2010 proposed by Mann [7], where parameters related to intangible things are added, on above problem is discussed.

2 Contradiction Matrix and Analysis

As mentioned above, one of important goal of education at the university is to achieve student's creativity and ability of solving unprecedented problems, and implicit knowledge, which are closely related with the intellectual ability discussed by Sternberg [8]. In his discussion, the investment theory for creativity is proposed. According to his theory, the confluence of six resources listed below, is required.

- Intellectual ability
- Knowledge
- Styles of thinking
- Personality
- Motivation
- Environment

As our problem seems to be closely related with 'Intellectual ability", "Knowledge", "Motivation", and "Environment" from above six resources, we will discuss these four resources. The intellectual ability consists of three skills, the synthetic skill, the analytic skill, and the practical-contextual skill. He discussed that synergy of these skills will improve creativity, but lack of any one will hinder creativity. To have correct and meaningful results based on the information by 'googling', intellectual ability above certain threshold is required, as shown in Fig. 1. However, acquiring or improving intellectual ability is not expected through 'googling' to find directly specific solution, where little intellectual activity is made. Students will develop and acquire their intellectual ability through hard brain activity and go through barriers where very hard brain activity is required. This is why 'googling' is the problem, and countermeasure is necessary. When a class project is given to the students, they tend to look for the specific solution directly in the cyber space (Googling). Reasons of this behavior are as follows: less time due to busy with part-time work, busy on the smartphone, cannot see how to approach due to lack of knowledge or background of the expected level, etc. This is the motivation to try to use TRIZ for solving above issue.

Intellectual ability	Required	Acquired
Synthetic Skill	Yes	No
Analytic Skill	Yes	No
Practical Contextual Skill	Yes	Yes (limited)

Fig. 1. Required intellectual skills to have meaningful results by 'Googling' and intellectual skills expected to be acquired.

Although there are approaches to develop creativity [8,9], and to develop creativity is even the most important in education, approaches to creativity is beyond current scope, and we will focus our discussions to the counter googling in the present paper.

To use TRIZ to solve above problem, at first two conflicting features have to be clarified. Then the features closest to the problem is selected out from the Altshuller's matrix (39 × 39 contradiction matrix) [1,6], where feature to be improved is given as the row, and feature that is getting worse is given as the column of the matrix. Several inventive principles are shown as specific numbers assigned to the inventive principles at the crossover of matrix. Then these principles have to be considered and analyzed to choose and focus on several promising candidates. The final step is finding the ideal final solution by analyzing and modifying these candidates until the useful practical solutions are obtained. As TRIZ is highly conceptual and abstracted framework, it is important to consider and analyze these candidates from various point. In this step, at least some experiences and knowledges of the relevant field are important. In the present approach, problem introduced by Googling is taken as contradiction between following features. From the teaching stuff point of view, features to be improved are, "24 Loss of Information", "27 Reliability", "29 Manufacturing Precision", and "35 Adaptability or Versatility". Features getting worse are, "22 Loss of Energy", "25 Loss of Time", and "28 Measurement Accuracy". "Loss of Information" is related to losing of various knowledges which is to be acquired, if they take an orthodox way as teachers expect, and expected to be improved. "Reliability" is related to the quality and reliability of acquired intellectual skill expected to be improved. "Manufacturing Precision" is related to the quality and correctness of acquired ability and knowledge, which is the products of education. "Adaptability and versatility" is related to the ability of applying acquired knowledge to solve various problems, including unprecedented problems. Generally, education to improve above knowledge and ability requires much time and hard brain activity. Therefore, these activities are considered to increase time and energy consumption, and let "Loss of Energy", and "Loss of Time" worse. "Measurement Accuracy" is related to the evaluation of acquired ability, which is considered to become more difficult to evaluate with improving ability, especially acquired implicit knowledge.

So far, study on the change of brain glucose metabolism with cognitive activity is mainly focused on understanding Alzheimer's disease using Positron Emission Tomography (PET). Reduction of brain glucose metabolism from normal cognition to Alzheimer's disease [10] is known. Increment in glucose metabolism (directly connected to energy consumption) by intellectual brain activity is

Features to be Improved	Features Getting Worse	Suggested Principles
24 Loss of Information	22 Loss of Energy	19, 10
	25 Loss of Time	24, 26, 28, 32
	28 Measurement Accuracy	N/A
27 Reliability	22 Loss of Energy	10, 11, 35
	25 Loss of Time	10. 30, 4
	28 Measurement Accuracy	32, 3, 11, 23
29 Manufacturing Precision	22 Loss of Energy	13, 32, 2
	25 Loss of Time	32, 26, 28, 18
	28 Measurement Accuracy	N/A
35 Adaptability or Versatility	22 Loss of Energy	18, 15, 1
	25 Loss of Time	35, 28
	28 Measurement Accuracy	35, 5, 1, 10
39 Productivity	22 Loss of Energy	28, 10, 29, 35
	25 Loss of Time	N/A
	28 Measurement Accuracy	1, 10, 34, 28

Fig. 2. Altshuller's contradiction matrix. Only part of interest is shown.

reported based on the study on the change of regional cerebral glucose consumption and regional cerebral blood flow [11], though the change is not large compared with basic brain glucose metabolism at rest. Therefore, assumption of increasing energy consumption by cognitive activity at the brain seems reasonable. From the selected conflicting features, candidates to be studied are picked out from the Altshuller's contradiction matrix. Relevant part of the matrix is shown in Fig. 2.

3 Analysis of Principles and Finding Solutions

From contradiction matrix of Altshuller, we can know candidate principles given at the crossover. From a part of matrix shown in Fig. 2, we can find candidate principles to be studied. All the candidate principles given in the matrix crossover of current relevant features are picked up and shown in Fig. 3. From Fig. 3, we can find several principles related to well known "Active Learning", and of course considered to be very effective and useful. However, we are looking for another more effective solution as countermeasure for "googling" problem.

3.1 Principles for Countermeasure to Googling

We have analyzed ideas of these principles for countermeasure to Googling through discussions and studies. The specific numbers for the principles are denoted by the prefixed #. Large part of the ideas was well-known and discussed among teachers, and thought to be useful. However, we have chosen several principles which are considered to be useful approach to improve especially "Googling" related problems. They are, #1, #13, #26, #28, #32, and #35. Ideas of countermeasure from these principles are explained below. The first one is to tear process of solving problems into flow chart to clarify algorithm (# 1), which will give students chances to recognize and clarify problem solving approach as algorithm. As this principle comes from contradiction between "adaptability or versatility" and "loss of energy", result seems reasonable. The second is to exchange role of teacher and students (# 13 and # 35), which is considered to drive students to deeper and wider ranged considerations and will help student to acquire higher level ability to solve unprecedented problems, as student has to prepare much more deeper and wider ranged thought and research and materials to teach, and will raise their motivation. In another word student can acquire or improve intellectual ability by these approaches. As these principles come from contradiction between "manufacturing precision" and "loss of time", and between "adaptability or versatility" and "loss of time", results also seem reasonable. The third is to use computer simulation as replaces of physical phenomena (# 26 and # 28). As these principles come from contradiction between "loss of information or manufacturing precision or adaptability or versatility" and "loss of time", and between "productivity" and "loss of energy", suggested principles also seem reasonable. Although experience on the authentic physical phenomena is better than simulation, condition settings may be changed easier and much

Principle	Possible Solution for Educational Case
#1 Segmentation	• Tears process of solving into flow chart to clarify algorithm.
#2 Taking Out	• Organizing multiple classes based on the experience, ability, etc. for efficient teaching. • Tear lecture contents shorter and insert discussions and practices.
#3 Local Quality	• Organize remedial class.
#4 Asymmetry	• Assign seating position of non-aggressive student close to teacher.
#5 Merging (Combining)	• Combine lecture with experience, practice, simulation and discussion.
#10 Preliminary Action	• Assignment question for the "Active Learning".
#11 Beforehand Cushioning	• Assignment question for the "Active Learning".
#13 The Other Way Round	• Make a flip question in the "Active Learning". (Add new point of view by changing stand point/environment) • Exchange role of teacher and student.
#15 Dynamics	• Change curriculum according to the relevant student's level. (Prepare plurality courses to adjust student's level)
#18 Mechanical Vibration	• Prepare plurality of class projects and decide next action according to the reaction of students. • Vibrate conditions under study to change view point for better understanding.
#19 Periodic Action	• Use periodic test and discussion.
#23 Feedback	• Introduction of PDCA cycle for lecture improvement. • Make feedback to the results of tests, reports, etc. • Use questionnaire to check understanding status etc.
#24 Intermediary	• Require student to include intermediate calculation or thought in the solution. • Use interim tests to give chances of feedback to students and teacher.
#26 Copying	• Use computer simulation as replaces of physical phenomena.
#28 Mechanics Substitution	• Replace physical phenomena by electrical data (simulation etc.).
#30 Flexible Shells and Thin Films	• Use one-on-one teaching (teaching aides).†
#32 Color Changes	• Use colored text for emphasis in the slide. • Make regulation to use colored texts to clarify cited part in the report.
#34 Discarding and Recovering	• Change instructional activities to maintain student's interes.† • Cencourage revising and sharing lesson plans.†
#35 Parameter Change	• Exchange role of teacher and student. (Parameter: Man, Function: Lecture)

Fig. 3. Suggested inventive principles on the Altshuller's matrix. Cited ideas from Marsh [5] is indicated by †.

more things could be learned in much shorter time. Through experiences students can acquire much better understandings, students can see more various phenomena and can compare with theory and their knowledge. And in addition, simulation meets preference of students. If simulation is combined with the lecture on the theory, it will become a very powerful tool for better understanding for students, and will improve their knowledge and motivation. The fourth is to use colored texts to clarify cited part in the report (# 32). As this principle comes from contradiction between "loss of information or manufacturing precision" and "loss of time", suggested principle again seems reasonable. This force student to include much more original thought and materials, which is impossible by 'Googling' only to find specific solution. This may improve their knowledge and intellectual ability. Thus, three of the six resources of Sternberg [8] seem satisfied.

3.2 Improving Evaluation Accuracy

For effective education, evaluation of student's progress is essential. To improve evaluation accuracy of the acquired ability of solving unprecedented problems and implicit knowledge, principles # 1, # 5, # 23, and # 35 are chosen. Ideas of improving evaluation accuracy from these principles are explained below. The first one is to tear process of solving into flow chart to clarify algorithm (# 1). This may help to see the level of student's understandings and knowledge level more correctly. The second is to combine lecture with experience, practice, simulation and discussion (# 5). By discussing with students, student's understandings and knowledge level could be seen more correctly. The third is to make questionnaire to check understanding status etc. (# 23). This may also be helpful to check student's understandings and knowledge level correctly. The final one is to exchange role of teacher and student (# 35). From the contents and way of teaching by students, their understandings and knowledge level could be evaluated more correctly.

3.3 Application of Simulation to the Oscillatory Phenomena

From above discussions, computer simulation can replace physical phenomena by electrical data. Although observing authentic physical phenomena is better than simulation, students can observe much more phenomena. Response of the system under various expected conditions could be learned easier and in much shorter time. As a teaching material, oscillatory phenomena, which is seen in various systems in dynamics, RLC circuits, electro-mechanical system, etc., are often taken. However, differential equation, necessary to understand these phenomena, sometimes becomes an obstacle for some students who don't like math. Therefore, following strategy is taken. First let student to have better understanding of phenomena through simulation, and then teach differential equation to understand the relationship between equations and phenomena. This approach will help students to have better understanding. As teaching materials, we have used well-known circuit simulator (Spice, developed at the University of California, and most widely used) to simulate response of RCL circuits and simple harmonic motion of mass point, as both systems are expressed by the same differential equation. Difference is only its constants and dimensions. Therefore, a circuit simulator can be used to simulate both systems. Followings are the examples of simulated response of RCL circuit, and simple harmonic motion of a mass point. Simulated current flow for various cases including critical damping, are shown in Fig. 4. Next example is simple harmonic motion of mass point. The results are shown in Fig. 5, which is exactly same as the results for RCL circuit, if $m = 1\,[\mathrm{kg}]$, $\gamma = 0 - 40\,[\mathrm{Pa}\cdot \mathrm{s/m}]$, $k = 100\,[\mathrm{N/m}]$.

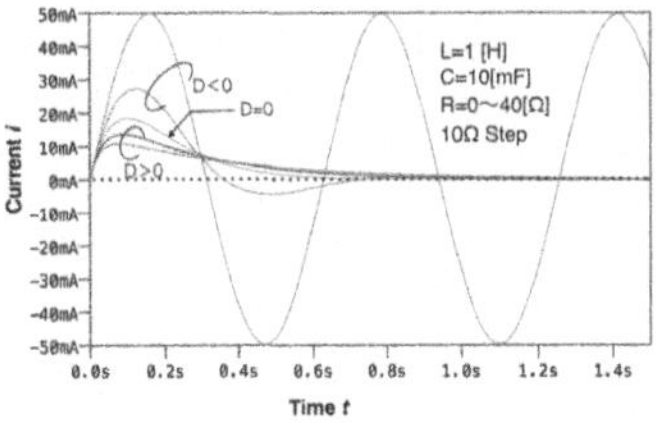

Fig. 4. Current response of RLC series circuit.

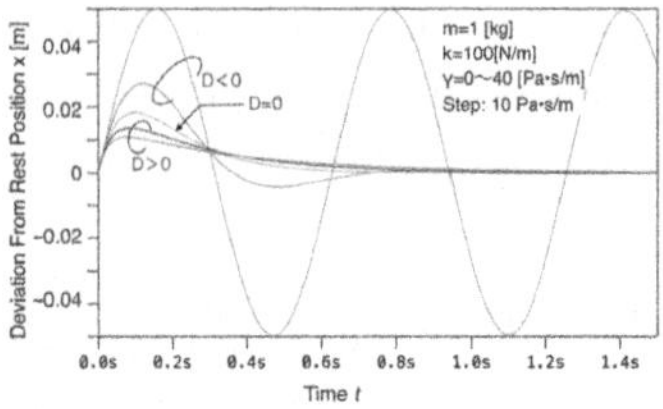

Fig. 5. Mechanical response of horizontal pendulum.

4 Additional Features and Principles from Matrix 2010

In the Matrix 2000 proposed by Mann, conflicting features are increased from 39 of classic TRIZ to 50, and inventive principles are increased from 40 to 82. Increased features and principles are mainly reflection of recent progress of nano- and bio-technologies. In addition, intangible parameters, which is related to motivation and discourage or idle feelings, are added. Therefore, as added part is considered to be strongly related to "Googling Problem", we have made additional study utilizing Matrix 2010.

4.1 Contradiction Analysis Using Matrix 2010

Again, from teacher's point of view, added features to the Matrix 2010 to be improved are, "11 Information Quantity", and "47 Positive Intangible Things". Added features getting worse is, "48 Negative Intangible Things". "Information Quantity" is related to the acquired amount of ability of solving unprecedented problems and amount of the implicit knowledge, and "Positive Intangible Things" is related to motivation, and "Negative Intangible Things" is related to

Features to be Improved	Features Getting Worse	Suggested Principles
11 Information Quantity	26 Loss of Time	2, 7, 3, 19, 28, 13, 17
	27 Loss of Energy	2, 10, 3, 6, 28, 13
	48 Intangible Negative Things	7, 1, 24, 13, 35, 25
	50 Measurement Accuracy	37, 3, 17, 28, 24, 4, 13
32 Adaptability or Versatility	48 Intangible Negative Things	13, 36, 40, 1, 24
35 Reliability	48 Intangible Negative Things	23, 3, 37, 17, 35, 28
42 Manufacturing Precision	48 Intangible Negative Things	2, 15, 24, 5, 19
44 Productivity	48 Intangible Negative Things	23, 15, 1, 19, 25
47 Intangible Positive Things	26 Loss of Time	5, 13, 10, 35, 24, 40
	27 Loss of Energy	2, 25, 18,13, 12, 28
	50 Measurement Accuracy	23, 25, 24, 4, 28, 12, 2

Fig. 6. Mann's Matrix 2010. Only a part of interest, newly introduced, is shown.

discouraging or lazy feelings. Other features are the same as those of classical Altshuller's matrix, discussed in the previous section, though the assigned numbers are modified.

Relevant part of the matrix is shown in Fig. 6. From a part of Matrix 2010 shown in Fig. 6, some of the candidate principles currently relevant features are picked up and shown in Fig. 7. From Fig. 7, we have had several new candidates of countermeasure for "googling problem". A part of assigned specific numbers for the principles are modified in Matrix 2010. Again, the specific numbers for the

Principle	Possible Solution for Educational Case
#1 Segmentation	• Tears process of solving into flow chart to clarify algorithm.
#2 Taking Out	• Organizing multiple classes based on the experience, ability, etc. for efficient teaching. • Tear lecture contents shorter and insert discussions and practices.
#3 Local Quality	• Organize remedial class.
#4 Asymmetry	• Assign seating position of non-aggressive student close to teacher.
#5 Merging (Combining)	• Combine lecture with experience, practice, simulation and discussion.
#6 Universality	• Use rubrics, checklists, and other scoring tools to standerdize expectations.†
#7 Nested Doll	• Create purpose for learning through communicating authentic real world experiences.†
#10 Preliminary Action	• Assignment question for the "Active Learning".
#12 Equipotentiality	• Use grouping of students whose grades and activities are similar, to promote discussions.
#13 The Other Way Round	• Make a flip question in the "Active Learning". (Add new point of view by changing stand point/environment) • Exchange role of teacher and student.
#15 Dynamics	• Change curriculum according to the relevant student's level. (Prepare plurality courses to adjust student's level)
#17 Another Dimension	• Prepare and use class room under jamming to prevent students from using web access.
#18 Mechanical Vibration	• Prepare plurality of class projects and decide next action according to the reaction of students. • Vibrate conditions under study to change view point for better understanding.
#19 Periodic Action	• Use periodic test and discussion.
#23 Feedback	• Introduction of PDCA cycle for lecture improvement. • Make feedback to the results of tests, reports, etc. • Use questionnaire to check understanding status etc.
#24 Intermediary	• Require student to include intermediate calculation or thought in the solution. • Use interim tests to give chances of feedback to students and teacher.
#25 Self Service	• Utilize rubrics quantifiable scoring systems.†
#28 Mechanics Substitution	• Replace physical phenomena by electrical data (simulation etc.).
#35 Parameter Change	• Exchange role of teacher and student. (Parameter: Man, Function: Lecture)
#37 Thermal Expansion	• Get synergy by mixing motivated students (mentors) with less motivated students.†
#40 Composite Materials	• Use composite teaching materials of visual, simulation, presentation, lecture, discussion, etc. • Introduce training/teaching with a combination of lecture, simulations, on-line learning, etc.†

Fig. 7. Suggested inventive principles on the Mann's Matrix 2010. Cited ideas from Marsh [5] is indicated by †

principles are denoted by the prefixed #. Large part of the ideas was overlapped with the principles obtained from classical Altshuller's matrix. However, we have found several new principles. They are, #6, #7, #12, #17, #25, #37, and #40. Ideas of countermeasure from these principles are explained below. The first one is to create purpose of the learning through communicating authentic, real world experiences (# 7), which will give students chances to recognize purpose clearly and improve motivation. The second is to use grouping of students whose grades and activities are similar, to promote discussions (# 12), which will encourage discussions and will improve motivation of students. The third is to utilize class room under jamming to prevent students from accessing internet (# 17), which will physically force to stop "Googling". The fourth is to get synergy by mixing motivated students (mentors) with less motivated students (# 37), which will also improve motivation of less motivated students. From above discussions, we have reached conclusion, "# 7, # 12, # 37" to improve motivation of students, and "# 17" to physically prohibit "Googling" as the Ideal Final Result (IFR), which corresponds to "Environment" of the six resources [8]. These results are mostly related with the emotional response of students, as expected, and two of the six resources of Sternberg [8] are realized,

5 Conclusion

From above discussions, exchanging role of teacher and students, and using simulation to help better understanding of phenomena were chosen as IFR for both countermeasure to "Googling Problem" and "Correct evaluation". And exchanging role of teacher and students was again chosen as IFR for "Correct evaluation". From these countermeasures, three (intellectual ability, knowledge, motivation) and as a countermeasure of environment four resources of the six resources of Sternberg will be satisfied. Remaining two are 'the styles of thinking' and 'the personality', and further works for these resources are necessary. Additional IFR is obtained by using Matrix 2010 of Mann, which is mainly related with emotional response of man. A complete solution of physically rejecting "Googling" is obtained also by using Matrix 2010. However, this principle comes from the feature related with emotion, relationship between them is unclear, and still further work and discussions are necessary.

Acknowledgements. The author gratefully acknowledges Dr. S. Ukon of Tokyo City University, and Dr. H. Yamazaki of Fukuoka Institute of Technology for useful discussions.

References

1. Altshuller, G.S.: Creativity as an Exact Science, Translated by Anthony Williams. Gordon & Breach, New York (1988)
2. Mann, D.L.: TRIZ J. (2002). Article no. 51
3. Ruchti, B., Livotov, P.: TRIZ J. (2001). Article no. 74

4. Marsh, D.G., Waters, F.H., Marsh, T.D.: TRIZ J. (2004). Article no. 34
5. Marsh, D.G., Waters, F.H., Mann, D.L.: TRIZ J. (2002). Article no. 98
6. Takagi, Y.: Inventive Principles of TRIZ (In Japanese), 1st edn. Discover 21, Tokyo (2014)
7. Mann, D.: Matrix 2010: Re-updating the TRIZ Contradiction Matrix. IFR Press, Devon (2009). [Japanese tranlation: by Nakagawa, T.: CrePS Institute, Chiba, Japan (2014)]
8. Sternberg, R.J.: Creative Res. J. **18**, 87–98 (2006)
9. Edmondson, A.C., Harvey, J.-F.: Hum. Resour. Manage. **28**, 347–360 (2018)
10. Mosconi, L., et al.: Eur. J. Nucl. Med. Mol. Imaging **35**, 811–822 (2009)
11. Roland, P.E., Eriksson, L., Stone-Elander, S., Widen, L.: J. Neurosci. **7**, 2373–2389 (1987)

World TRIZ Sites Project (WTSP) (2): To Build Catalogs of TRIZ-Related Web Sites in the World

Toru Nakagawa[1(✉)], Darrell Mann[2], Michael Orloff[3], Simon Dewulf[4], Simon Litvin[5], and Valeri Souchkov[6]

[1] Osaka Gakuin University, 3-1-13 Eirakudai, Kashiwa, Chiba 277-0086, Japan
nakagawa@ogu.ac.jp
[2] Systematic Innovation Network, Bideford, UK
[3] Academy of Instrumental Modern TRIZ, Berlin, Germany
[4] AULIVE, Glen Elgin, Australia
[5] GEN TRIZ, LLC, Newton, MA, USA
[6] ICG Training & Consulting, Enschede, The Netherlands

Abstract. We started the World TRIZ Sites Project (WTSP) in Dec. 2017 for the purpose of building catalogs of TRIZ-related Web sites in the World. Getting support by a number of TRZ colleagues, we started the project to achieve by voluntary cooperation of many (hopefully about 100) TRIZ colleagues coming from various countries. Our basic strategy was to build Country WTSP Catalogs in each country first and then build World WTSP Catalogs by using selected sites. Japan WTSP Catalog was made and posted in English in Apr. 2018 as an example. Internet surveys of TRIZ sites located in each country were shown for 33+ countries. Adding new members at TFC2018, we got over 70 voluntary members from 30+ countries. But the actual WTSP work in individual countries is proceeding only slowly till recently.

So we started Top-down approaches using Internet surveys in global scale, for TRIZ sites written in several major languages, and for sites around TRIZ by using different keywords in wider scopes. We also realized the importance of showing concrete images of our World WTSP Catalogs and practical processes for achieving it. Thus we proposed an 'Ideal image' in the form of WTSP Database System and turned it into a simple and feasible structure. Our World WTSP Catalogs is made as a small Web site, which has 'Table of sites' (or Index) page (s) and many 'Descriptions of sites' pages, where many hyperlinks flexibly connect individual sites from the Index to the Description. Japan WTSP Catalog (for people in Japan) was rebuilt into World WTSP Catalog (Japan Part) (for people in the world). Practical Guide for Teams to build the World WTSP Catalogs is shown with templates and easy processes based on a new strategy "to list up and describe highly recommendable sites only in each country and to build the World WTSP Catalogs as soon as possible".

We are going to report the draft version of World WTSP Catalogs at TFC2019. Getting Country Editors in every country is the crucial issue.

Keywords: World TRIZ Sites Project (WTSP) · Global collaboration · TRIZ information resources · Catalog of TRIZ-related Sites · World WTSP Catalogs

Published by Springer Nature Switzerland AG 2019
R. Benmoussa et al. (Eds.): TFC 2019, IFIP AICT 572, pp. 508–525, 2019.
https://doi.org/10.1007/978-3-030-32497-1_40

1 Introduction: Our Aims and Plans

This is the second report of the World TRIZ Sites Project (WTSP) [1] which was started in December 2017 [2]. The purpose of the project is to make the information sources on TRIZ and related methodologies viewable easily at the global scale.

For these three decades, TRIZ has been proliferated widely beyond ex-USSR across the world. A lot of activities, achievements, and knowledge of TRIZ have been accumulated, to the extent that their overview is not easily obtainable. There are many TRIZ-related Web sites in the world, but they are working separately and competing against one another. Ordinary Internet searches for TRIZ give messy/noisy outputs to hide valuable information. In this situation, interests in TRIZ in the world seems decreasing gradually even at the era when innovations are wanted everywhere.

As a solution to improve the situations, we have chosen to survey and build catalogs of TRIZ-related Web sites in the world. Web sites usually post various information publicly in the up-to-date form and are accessible freely from anywhere in the world.

The aims of the WTSP project are shown in Fig. 1 [3].

[2] Aims of WTSP

World TRIZ Sites Project
Together ! Connected !!

- **To build Catalogs of TRIZ-related Sites**
  - **of each country** (in their own language, then in English) and
  - **of the whole world** (in English, then in many languages)
  - with appropriate (brief but close) **introduction of individual sites**
  - with **appropriate selection** of (useful and important) sites
  - **for various people** (unfamiliar, beginners, users, and experts in TRIZ)
  - in the field of **TRIZ and relevant methodologies**
  - as **reliable sources of information** (on theories, applications, activities)
- **To keep the Catalogs up-to-date**
  - accepting new and revised information regularly
  - revising all the Catalogs every two years
- **For promoting TRIZ and relevant methodologies further in the world**
- **By voluntary collaboration of many TRIZ colleagues in the world**

Fig. 1. Aims of the WTSP project [3]

For achieving these aims, we set up our working plan as shown in Fig. 2.

As shown in these figures clearly, we take the bottom-up approach to build the Catalogs of TRIZ-related Web sites of individual countries first and then to build the

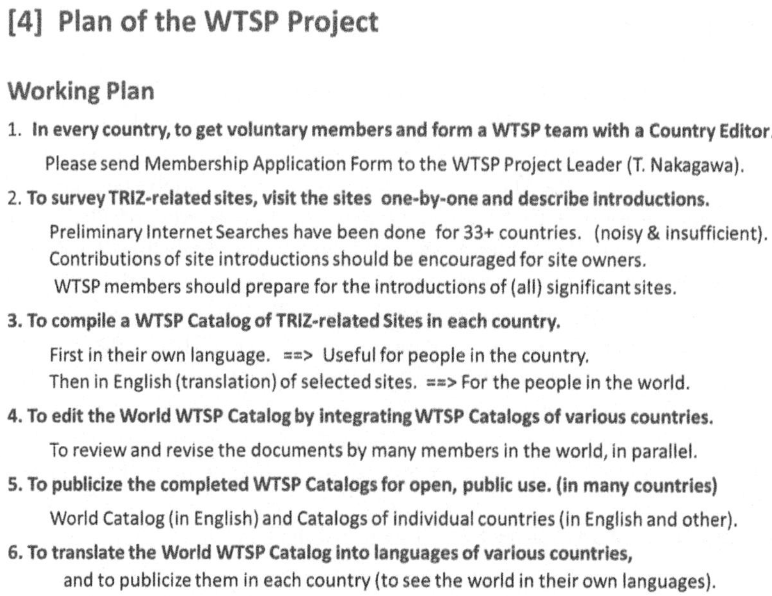

Fig. 2. Working plan for the WTSP project [3]

Catalog of the whole world. Various Web sites in different languages can be introduced best by the people in the country (i.e., not by foreigners nor by robots), so we need a number of people in each country. And we have chosen to carry out all the work on voluntary basis, as a symbol of collaboration of the global TRIZ community.

Many TRIZ colleagues supported the idea of WTSP. But the difficulty of the project is clear from the beginning. Talented, active TRIZ people are very busy to work in their own business, and hence they can spend only little time squeezed in their busy schedule. Thus our TRIZ solution was to divide various tasks into small ones which can be carried out by many people in parallel. This solution works well only with high motivation of people, clear instructions and proper coordination by some coordinators [1].

2 Activities and Achievements in the First Year (2018) [1]

2.1 Organizing the WTSP Project

The idea of WTSP was proposed by Nakagawa in Nov. 2017 in private communications and also in his several draft proposals to about 100 TRIZ leaders/colleagues in the world (on the basis of his networks of "TRIZ Home Page in Japan" readers). Having got support by a number of TRIZ colleagues, he started the project in Dec. 2017 and sent invitations to them showing basic policies, aims, plans, guidelines, etc. [2]. His Web site "TRIZ Home Page in Japan" (THPJ) [4] served as the hub for the WTSP project where all the relevant information, documents, communications, etc. are posted regularly and openly.

WTSP is open to anybody who volunteers to work for its aims in collaboration. And it expects to have Country Editors in every county and several Global Co-editors at the global level. About 30 people from various countries expressed their support but only 10 of them submitted the Membership Application Form. Having obtained 5 Global Co-editors, we sent the WTSP Appeal [5] in Jun. 2018.

2.2 Guidelines and Platform

Nakagawa's experiences of making "Extended 100 TRIZ Links (with annotation) in Japan" and "Extended 120 TRIZ Links (with annotation) in the World" (2008) [6] formed the basis of practical process. In order to handle a few hundred of Web sites, Guidelines and a Platform were prepared. A standard form in Excel sheet for describing an individual site, another form in Excel for a list of sites in each country, coding rules of file names, a standard process of documentation and reviewing in the project, etc. were set.

For allowing parallel and cooperative work by a number of project members, a platform was prepared using the Bitrix24.com Standard Plan. It is an In-Cloud groupware system, accepting unlimited number of users (without per-user charge), providing documentation facilities with freely customizable folder system and version control, allowing easy communication among the members, having nice user interfaces and various support of instructions. So it looks very useful and powerful for cooperative work by many members.

2.3 Pilot Project to Build Japan WTSP Catalog

It is most important to perform a pilot project and show a good example as a model. Thus Nakagawa started to survey TRIZ-related sites in Japan and to make a Catalog. Since all the TRIZ-related Web sites in Japan are written in Japanese (and only a few of them have English pages as well), the survey and description were started in Japanese in mid Jan. 2018.

The Yahoo!.Japan search engine (instead of Google) was selected, because its option "displaying only one representative page for each site, and forming URL for the internal search of the site" is very useful. The search was made with the Keyword TRIZ, giving 400 sites displayed. The output on the browser was Copy & Pasted onto an MS Word file keeping the hyperlinks active. The sites were visited one by one, to see the output page, the top page, the 'About us' page, and some more main pages. The site name, site domain URL, owner of the site, the role, special features, etc. were detected. With these information (together with background knowledge), introduction of the site was described in 3 to 10 lines and evaluated roughly (either important, worthy of listing, or irrelevant/no listing). In this manner about 70 sites were selected from the outputs. By use of his background knowledge he selected about 20 more sites of relevant methodologies and functions around TRIZ.

Finally a Catalog of 92 TRIZ-related sites in Japan was built in Japanese for Japanese users in mid Mar. 2018, where the sites are categorized with their roles (including 24 selected sites as the role of (a) TRIZ information sending sites). The Japan Catalog was then translated into English with full introduction for the 24 selected sites and brief introduction for other 68 sites [7]. It was found that about half of the sites listed in 2008 have gone or inactive and about 2/3 of the 92 sites have emerged after 2008.

Through this pilot project, it was recommended for the practice of surveying and site description at the early stages that we should better use free format in MS Word rather than the formal formats in Excel. The experiences, knowhow, and results of this pilot project were reported in detail in THPJ [8].

2.4 Preliminary Internet Searches in Various (33+) Countries

Despite showing the results of Pilot project in Japan (Jan.–May, 2018) [8] and the WTSP Appeal [5] (Jun. 2018), the WTSP project did not start smoothly in various countries. There were communications from individual persons from time to time mentioning their own sites or some trials of surveys. Team activities did not start at any country. In such a situation we prepared for the paper presentations by the 6 Global Co-editors at Japan TRIZ Symposium (Sept. 2018) and at ETRIA TFC2018 [1].

For the purpose of initializing the survey activities in various countries, Nakagawa started the Preliminary Internet Searches of TRIZ-related sites in various countries. The searches were carried out by specifying the (target) site location to be individual country (intending to make a Catalog of each country). Keyword is TRIZ or ТРИЗ. The site language is taken various ways such as any language, English, Russian, French, German, etc. depending on the countries. Yahoo!.Japan search engine was used as before for using advantage of the special option. The outputs on the browser were Copy & Pasted onto MS Word with active hyperlinks. Many sites, ranging 20 to 100 in number, are listed in the outputs (sometimes including apparently irrelevant sites, mostly due to a female singer's name Triz). Such results in Word, with the note of search conditions, were sent to the relevant people in each country and posted publicly in THPJ [9]. Table 1 summarizes the search results for the 33+ countries.

Table 1. Results of Preliminary Internet Searches for individual countries [9]

Region	Country (outputs sites - irrelevant sites)
A. Europe	Austria (55 - 5), Belgium (51 - 14), Switzerland (48 - 12), Czechoslovakia (67 - 8), Germany (95), Denmark (33 - 11), Spain (79 - 37), Finland (33 - 3), France (76), Italy (76), Netherlands (67 - 9), Norway (32 - 25), Poland (76 - 11), Portugal (82 - 62), Sweden (33 - 6), UK (68)
B. Russia	Russia (100)
C. Mid-East	Any in Arabic language (55), Iran (72 - 1), Turkey (80 - 1)
D. Asia	China (82)(62 - 6), Taiwan (28), Indonesia (40 - 13), Japan (finished), Korea (72 - 4), Thailand (37 - 7)
E. Oceania	Australia (42 - 11)
F. North America	Canada (59 - 19), USA (English 86 - 11; Russian 61; Ger. Fr. It. Sp. 65 - 20)
G. Central & South America	Argentina (52 - 33), Brazil (96 - 59)
H. Africa	Any in Arabic language (55)

2.5 Presentation and Appeals at ETRIA TFC2018

The ETRIA TRIZ Future Conference 2018 at Strasbourg on Oct. 29–31, 2018 was a nice chance for promoting WTSP. We, in the name of the 6 Global Co-editors, presented a full paper [1]. And we prepared a Summary edition of 8 slides printed on both sides of an A4 paper [3]. Getting a desk at a corner of the hall, Nakagawa talked with many participants one by one to invite them to join WTSP. About 40 participants signed in the sheet stating to join WTSP as a Member. This pushed the WTSP project to a new stage with about 70 Members (including Members to be).

3 Activities and Achievements in the Second Year (Till May 2019)

3.1 Setting Up a Concrete Goal and Bottom-Up Activities

Just after the TFC2018, we set up a concrete goal "To report the completion of the World WTSP Catalogs (2019) at ETRIA TFC2019 (in Oct. 2019)". For achieving the goal, we set up the time schedule as follows:

- Dec. 31, 2018: Formation of WTSP Teams in every country
- Mar. 31, 2019: Completion of Country WTSP Catalogs in every country, for open reviewing inside the project; First draft of Categorized World WTSP Catalog
- Jun. 30, 2019: Completion of revised Country WTSP Catalogs and Completion of World WTSP Catalog for open reviewing inside the project
- Sept. 20, 2019: Completion of revised World WTSP Catalogs and revised Categorized World WTSP Catalog for open public reviewing

WTSP Letters were sent from time to time to Members, Members to be, and Invitees of WTSP to inform about the TFC presentations, welcoming new Members (to be), plans and time lines, results of Preliminary Internet Searches, Invitation to WTSP, Practical ways to form WTSP Teams in each country, Tasks for surveying Sites, etc. We expected that the WTSP project was starting their activities in various individual countries, along the bottom-up process for building the Country Catalogs and then the World Catalogs.

Actually, however, the process of forming the WTSP Teams in individual countries did not start smoothly. Many of the people who stated to join WTSP at TFC2018 did not submit the Membership Application Form. In mid Jan. 2019, WTSP posted in THPJ its List of Members having 78 Members (including about 40 Members to be) from 29 countries/areas. Country Editors were assigned in 10 countries, i.e., Austria, Czech Rep., Spain, France, Portugal, Iran, China P.R., Japan, Malaysia, and Brazil. Some preliminary activities were reported in France and Germany. Team formation was especially difficult in the two important countries, Russia and USA, because of their big activities in TRIZ.

3.2 Top-Down Surveys of TRIZ-Related Sites in the World

The bottom-up activities in various countries seemed to be very weak even in late Mar. 2019, near the scheduled date for the completion of Country WTSP Catalogs. For supporting the activities from a different side, Nakagawa started Internet Surveys in the top-down direction [10]. TRIZ-related sites in the world were surveyed without specifying the site location, but specifying the site languages. The results are summarized in Table 2.

Table 2. Results of Internet Surveys in the global scale [10]

Case	Site location	Site language	Keywords	Sites found (with evaluation)
(2A)	World	English	TRIZ	◎ 6, ○ 13, □ 29, Δ 33, – 25
(2B1)	World	Russia	ТРИЗ	106 sites
(2B2)				26 selected professional sites +49 user pages
(2B3)				35 selected professional sites +73 user pages
(2C)	World	German	TRIZ	107 sites, – 7 sites
(2D)	World	French	TRIZ	90 sites, – 8 sites
(2E)	World	Spanish/Portuguese	TRIZ	50 sites, – 73 sites
(2F)	USA	English	TRIZ	◎ 6, ○ 11, □ 27, Δ 24, – 22

For these Internet Surveys, the Yahoo!.Japan search engine was used as before. The output sites were visited quickly to find Site name, Site domain URL. The internal site search was carried out for all the sites, and the number of pages hit with the keyword TRIZ in the site was shown for each site. In the cases of survey of sites written in English, the sites were visited more closely and were evaluated tentatively in 5 grades; i.e., ◎ Most important in the World Catalog (i.e., about top 30), ○ Important in the World Catalog (i.e., about top 100), □ Worthy in the World Catalog, Δ Worthy in Country Catalog, – Irrelevant/negligible. As you see in cases (2A) and (2F), the output sites are (almost random) mixtures of very high to very low grades in their quality/relevance.

These results were posted in detail in THPJ [10] and sent to relevant people asking for their further work. Michael Orloff's reaction may be typical and important. He found the results for the Russian language sites (2B1) messy, and took a different approach as shown in (2B2). He listed up 26 Web sites of TRIZ professionals using his background knowledge, and also listed 49 users' sites/pages he recognized in various searches. Later, Nikolay Shpakovsky reviewed (2B1) and (2B2) and showed a revised list as in (3B3). Cases in other languages are under examination by the people in the relevant countries.

In May 2019, Nakagawa started the 3rd round Internet Surveys for extending the scope of methodologies wider around TRIZ. For such a purpose the choice of keywords is delicate and important. Results of initial trials are shown in Table 3 [11].

Table 3. Results of Internet Surveys in wider scopes of methodologies [11]

Case	Keywords	Sites found (with evaluation)
(3A)	Creat* Think* Method*	◎ 1, ○ 4, □ 15, Δ 3, – 84
(3A2)	Creative Think Method	◎ 1, ○ 15, □ 65, Δ 31, – 56, **L** (Listed already elsewhere) 15
(3B)	(Creative OR innovative OR Systematic) Problem Solve (Method OR Process OR Technique)	◎ 10 (L 8), ○ 26 (L 7), □ 64 (L 7), Δ 32 (L 1), – 39
(3C)	Innovation (Process OR Strategy OR Method OR management OR Technology)	◎ 3 (L 3), ○ 36 (L 11), □ 76 (L 8), Δ 70 (L 0), – 19
(3D)	(Quality OR Value OR Cost OR Productivity) (Deploy OR Engineering OR Management OR Control OR Analysis) (Method OR Technique OR Theory OR Process OR "Case Study")	223 (under examination)
(3E)	(Patent OR IP OR "Intellectual Property") (Analysis OR Protect OR Circumvent OR Mapping OR Strategy)	186 (under examination)

When a wild card * is used in the keywords (3A), the search engine interpreted it very widely, including the words: make, build, believe, way, etc. The keywords in cases (3A2) (3B) and (3C) seem to be productive. We have two more cases (3D) and (3E) of surveys, which seem useful but taking much time and efforts for examination.

3.3 Proposal of WTSP Database System for Generating Categorized World WTSP Catalogs

At the stage of late Mar. 2019, a few hundred of Web sites were expected to be shown in our World WTSP Catalogs. How should we categorize and arrange them in the Catalogs? Alphabetical order of the site names? Arranging by countries? In which ways users want to use the WTSP Catalogs? – Considering these issues, we have found that users want to see the contents of WTSP Catalogs from multiple views of aspects. As such aspects we listed up Site location, Site language, Roles of the site (or site owner), Application phases, Application fields, Methodologies, and Evaluation. Thus it is desirable for us to be able to categorize and arrange hundreds of sites in these multiple views of aspects as requested by the users.

In late May 2019, Nakagawa proposed a conceptual design of WTSP Database System as illustrated in Fig. 3 [12].

The system installs multiple sets of Indexing Schemes [13], or aspects of views, as shown at the top. It is important to set and define these schemes systematically yet practically. The data of individual sites should contain the information as shown at the bottom. All the sites registered in the database should have records in the Flat Table of all the sites, with the attributes of basic information, Answers to the multiple sets of indexing schemes, and hyperlink to the site description.

The system may be used as the WTSP Catalog Generator, where a user (or Catalog Editor) inputs the control specifying a hierarchical indexing scheme for extraction, categorization, and arrangement of sites. Then the Database Indexing System inside the

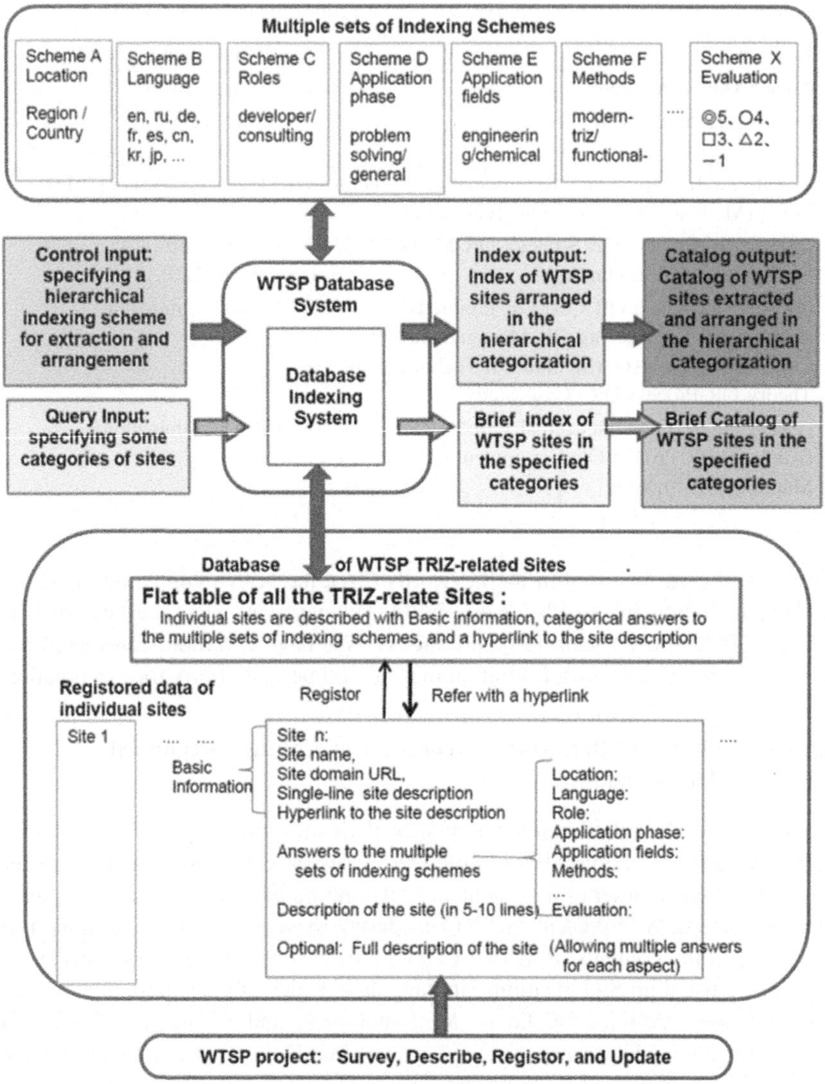

Fig. 3. Conceptual Design of WTSP Database System [12]

WTSP Database system operates on the temporary copy of the Flat Table to select, categorize, and arrange the sites as specified, by using the function just like Excel's sorting algorithm. Thus the Index form of WTSP Catalog is output, and then the WTSP Catalog may be output by inserting the Description of the sites.

We should note that the WTSP Database System can also be used as an On-line Query System. Users request some categories of sites, and the System outputs Brief Index of WTSP sites in the specified categories, and Brief WTSP Catalogs of specified categories further.

Once this System is installed, the WTSP project can concentrate their efforts to survey, describe, register, and update the TRIZ-related sites in the world, because the system can generate World WTSP Catalogs semi-automatically with the registered data of sites.

4 Practical Approaches for Completing the World WTSP Catalogs (Since June 2019)

4.1 Reconsidering the Difficulties

As described so far, the WTSP project have developed the visions, guidelines, project teams, processes, methods, etc. step by step for building the Country and World WTSP Catalogs. However, our project is much behind the time schedule for completing the World WTSP Catalogs before TFC2019, to be held on Oct. 9–11, 2019. The weak point of our project is the fact that in many countries the WTSP Teams are not formed well and not working actively.

The problem situation is "Many people support the aims of the WTSP project, but very few actually join to work together". And the main reason for it is "Talented, active persons in TRIZ are always too busy", as known from the beginning. Considering the reasons further, we have found the following points.

(a) The WTSP Database System is a proposal of an 'Ideal form', which is not feasible in a few months. We need to find some structure of the WTSP Catalogs, which is clear, practical, easy to build and update, and allowing integration of parallel works by many Teams of various countries.
(b) We need a prototype of World WTSP Catalogs. Japan WTSP Catalog [7] is for people in Japan and not appealing to people in the world. We need "World WTSP Catalog (Japan Part)" containing sites selected for the people in the world.
(c) Trying to make Country WTSP Catalogs with thorough survey is a heavy task in each country. At the stage of June 2019, we should change our basic strategy to focus our efforts on the World WTSP Catalogs, containing selected, smaller number of sites from various countries.
(d) We have not seen actual image of the World WSP Catalogs yet. What kinds of sites are actually arranged in the ◎ and ○ levels. People want to see them, even in a rough draft. Thus, we should better apply the "20–80 Principle", i.e., "Do the rough but essential 20% efforts and get the 80% results".
(e) On the basis of (a) to (d), we need to have a Practice Guide for the WTSP Teams in various countries to contribute actively to achieve the World WTSP Catalogs together. It should have step by step instructions to prepare for the manuscripts of their own parts of the World WTSP Catalogs.
(f) We should have two-step plan. A preliminary version of World WTSP Catalogs we should make first as a draft containing smaller number but important sites. Then we will make revised and enhanced versions of World WTSP Catalogs.

(g) Many TRZ colleagues, when they look at these visions and strategies, will be able to see their own tasks and feasibilities to achieve the WTSP goals meaningful for themselves as well as for the world.

All these new tasks and strategies have been pursued since June 2019, as described in the following sections.

4.2 Structure of the World WTSP Catalogs, Practical and Useful

Considering to make the 'ideal' WTSP System (Fig. 3) more practical and feasible without assuming a new automating system, we reached the structure shown in Fig. 4 [14].

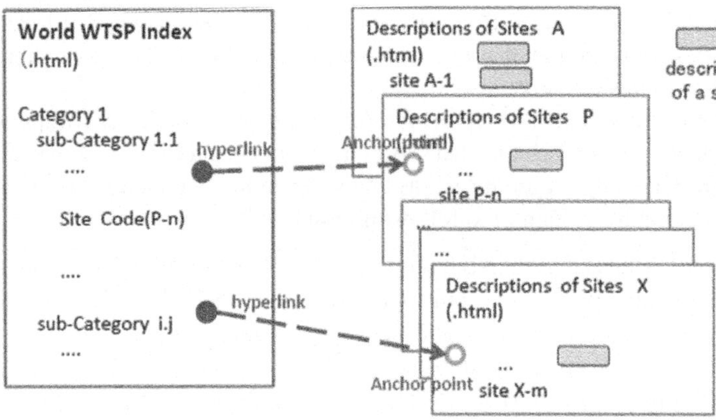

Fig. 4. Structure of the World WTSP Catalogs [14]

The right part of Fig. 4 is a simple collection of files of 'Descriptions of sites' submitted by various Teams. Each Team makes a Word file, where various sites may be written in the standardized tabular form or in more relaxed ways, and convert it into an HTML file.

The left part of Fig. 4 is the Index of the WTSP Catalog, which corresponds essentially to the 'Flat Table of all the sites' in Fig. 3. Individual WTSP Teams submit 'Flat Table of sites' in Excel, and all the tables are merged into one Flat Table. Then the Table is sorted and rearranged manually in Excel in various hierarchical ways, and is converted into an HTML page.

Each Team, before submission, should set hyperlinks from individual site in the 'Flat Table' to actual description of sites in the 'Descriptions of sites' file. Hyperlinks have a big advantage that their links are flexibly connected even though the sites are rearranged in any manner in the Flat Table (or the Index) or the site descriptions are rearranged in the 'Descriptions of sites' files. This structure also allows to revise and add site descriptions afterwards and to make multiple Catalog Indexes by rearranging the sites in the Flat Table in different ways.

The completed World WTSP Catalogs may be posted as a small Web site (and even delivered easily in a folder) containing one (or multiple) Index page(s) and many pages of site descriptions. Users may read the Index page of many sites arranged in some systematic manner, and may click any site to read some more details of the site. Users may also read the 'Descriptions of sites' pages, where sites are arranged in a manner the Team of a country or the editor of a top-down survey supposed best.

4.3 World WTSP Catalogs (Japan Part) Instead of Japan WTSP Catalogs

All the 92 sites in Japan WTSP Catalog (i.e., WTSP Catalogs of TRIZ-related sites in Japan for the people in Japan) have been re-evaluated in the criteria of World WTSP Catalogs. The results [15] are summarized in Table 4.

Table 4. Sites to be included in World WTSP Catalog (Japan Part)

Sites in TRIZ	Sites around TRIZ
◎ TRIZ Home Page in Japan (Toru Nakagawa) ○ Japan TRIZ Society (NPO) ○ IDEA Co. (Mamoru Zenko) ○ MOST LLC (Kazuya Yamaguchi) ○ Ideation Japan Ltd. (Teruyuki Kamimura) ○ TRIZ Study (Shinsuke Kurosawa) ○ Monodukuri.com (Osamu Kumasaka) □ (Former) Japan TRIZ CB □ Cybernet System Co. Ltd. □ Pro-Engineers (Shigeru Kasuya) □ Idea Plant (Rikie Ishii) □* MEMODAS (Kimihiko Hasegawa)	○* Idea Marathon Institute (Takeo Higuchi) □ J-STAGE (JST) □ Daiichi Kousha (Akihiro Katahira) □* Netman (Ken-ichi Nagaya) □* JST (Japan Science & Technology Agency) □* NEDO (New Energy and Industrial Technology Development Organization) □* Japan Creativity Society □* JUSE (Union of Japanese Scientists & Engineers) □* JSQC (Japanese Society for Quality Control) □* SJVE (Society of Japan Value Engineering) □* JIII (Japan Institute of Invention and Innovation) □* JAIST (Japan Advanced Institute of Science & Technology) □* i.school, The University of Tokyo □* Keio SDM, Keio University Graduate School

The sites in the left column are more or less specialized in TRIZ. They include 1 ◎ site, 6 ○ sites, and 5 □. They are mostly TRIZ promotors and consultants. The sites in the right column are related to the methodologies around TRIZ, in the sense that they share nearly the same interests and goals with TRIZ. Most of them are national governmental organizations, academic or professional associations of methodologies close to TRIZ, and universities with special research/teaching activities in the field of creative thinking.

The * marks mean that they are not selected in the 24 sites in the Japan WTSP Catalogs. Among the 24 selected sites in the Japan WTSP Catalog, 11 sites will not be shown in the World WTSP Catalogs. Many of them were active in '90s and '00s but not much in '10s. And 3 knowledge-sharing sites. i.e., Wikipedia, YouTube, and Slides Share, are also dropped because they are certainly shown as ◎ sites in the World WTSP Catalogs principally based in USA.

4.4 Practice Guide for Preparing WTSP Catalogs in Various Countries

The new Practice Guide was first written in early June and revised little by little until mid-July [14]. It describes how to form WTSP Teams and how to prepare the manuscripts of the World WTSP Catalogs. The basic points are described below along the process.

(1) To get people as voluntary WTSP Members and form WTSP Team with a coordinator

This is the initial step of our process. Even though we meet much difficulty at this step in many countries, we need to keep trying various activities, as discussed so far. They include:

You are invited to understand the aims, visions, significance, importance, etc. of the WTSP project, by referring to our Appeal [5] and Summary slides [3].

You may look at the prototype examples of WTSP Catalogs, such as World WTSP Catalog (Japan Part) [15] and some others coming soon, and compare them with some simple lists of TRIZ links and also with messy/noisy outputs of internet surveys. You may learn many interesting examples of sites in the WTSP Catalogs which were not known much so far. Then you might realize the importance of introducing good TRIZ-related sites in your own country to the people in the world.

You may study the structure of WTSP Catalogs and the basic process for listing up the sites and describing the site introductions [14]. Then you might understand that the tasks for you (and your TRIZ colleagues in your country) is to make the manuscripts of your Country Part of World WTSP Catalogs and that such tasks can be achieved in cooperation with your TRIZ colleagues in your country without so much burdens.

Then you would eventually find that the merits and significance of contributing to the World WTSP Catalogs by making manuscripts of your Country Part is certainly greater than the efforts and time you need to spend for making the manuscripts. At such a stage you are welcome to join WTSP together with your colleagues and form a WTSP Team for your country.

You would naturally agree that a group of several people need a coordinator for working effectively in cooperation. In WTSP, Country Editor plays the role of a coordinator. The coordinator must understand the vision, tasks, processes, etc., and coordinate the members in their work, i.e., dispatch various tasks to the members and integrate the results by the members, etc. Since WTSP is operated entirely on a volunteer basis, getting a Country Editor is most important for the activities in each country.

(2) List up candidate sites, by recommendations and by Internet surveys

An easy and best way to list up candidate sites is getting recommendations from many TRIZ colleagues in your country. Using a template in our Practice Guide [14], list up a number of candidate sites by the Team members and send the list to other keypersons as widely as possible, asking them to list up some more. This process is usually good enough for listing up candidate sites to be included in the World WTSP Catalogs.

If you want to find useful TRIZ-related sites thoroughly, e.g., to make a complete Country WTSP Catalogs, you need to make Internet surveys. When you make a survey, using the keyword TRIZ for example, you will find that the search engines produce a flood of information, which is messy and noisy and hiding useful information. A lot of experiences and obtained knowhow are described in Nakagawa's reports [8–11]. Because of so much noise in the Internet searches, WTSP members in many countries were discouraged so much and quitted/postponed their WTSP activities. This is the biggest reason for our failure in the initial Bottom-up Approaches, i.e., to make thorough Country Catalogs and then go to (Country part of) World Catalog with selected sites. Thus we recently shifted our strategy to make efforts for building the World WTSP Catalogs first, with the manuscripts from countries containing the sites recommended highly as explained above.

(3) Describe individual sites, either by the site owners or by other surveyors

Now we should describe individual sites one by one as the manuscripts to be shown in the WTSP Catalogs. We may use the template of Site Description posted in the Practice Guide [14].

It is best to get the site owner fill in the template. The mandatory information is Site name, Site domain URL, Site location, Site language, Roles of site, Evaluation, and (most desirably) Description of introduction. Sometimes an organization/company operates their sites in multiple countries, in multiple languages, and hence with different URLs and different site names; in such cases we may show the representative one(s) as the site in the World WTSP Catalog, with information of subsidiary sites attached. Roles of site should be expressed according to the codes specified in the 'Multiple sets of Indexing Schemes' shown in [13]. Typical roles may be: (a1) Dedicated for information sending, (e1) Method developers, (e4) Consultants, (g3) Knowledge sharing, etc. Description of introduction may be written in free format in about 3 to 10 lines.

In cases when we need to describe any site, it takes much time for us to visit the site to understand it and describe it concerning to the items in the standard format. You may learn Nakagawa's experiences and know how [8–11, 14]. Typically, we visit a page of the site (with the key of Internet search output), then go to the top pages, 'About us' pages, and a number of principal pages. Carrying out a site search (i.e., Internet search of relevant pages inside a specified site) is useful. Excerpts from top pages and 'About us' pages may be useful as a quick alternative of the site introduction. Evaluation of the site is a delicate job, but necessary even as a tentative one for us to proceed to build WTSP Catalogs. For only the sites with evaluation ◎○□, we should describe the site closely.

(4) Making 'Flat Table of sites' as the manuscript of World WTSP Catalogs

You gather the descriptions of sites of high evaluation (◎○□) in a Word file. And you make a 'Flat Table of sites', using the template in Excel shown in [14]. Basic information of site in the standard format can be used to fill in. Site code is a numbering given to the sites in some proper way for managing the sites, and a hyperlink is set with it for referring to the site description. (Note that numbering itself is not so important because the sites are rearranged in the WTSP Catalogs in various ways by use of other items in the Flat Table.)

(5) Build and check Your Part of World WTSP Catalog as a small Web site

You now convert your 'Flat Table of sites' file and 'Descriptions of sites' file into HTML (i.e., Web pages). Then at the beginning of each site description, set an anchor point having the ID of the Site code. Put the two pages in a folder and test that every hyperlink in the Flat Table (i.e., Index) page jumps to the proper description of sites. In this manner, you now have a small Web site of Your Part of World WTSP Catalog.

(6) With your manuscripts the World WTSP Catalogs are now completed

You should submit your Flat Table file in Excel and Descriptions of Sites file in HTML to the WTSP Project. Integrating many such parts, World WTSP Catalogs can be built as shown in Fig. 4. The results of top-down Internet surveys will also be important parts of the World WTSP Catalogs. Handling duplications of sites in many manuscripts of parts may be a tedious issue. It is possible to make multiple sets of Index of World WTSP Catalogs by simply using different sorting of sites in the Flat Table.

4.5 Plans of Preliminary and Completed World WTSP Catalogs

On the basis of our new strategy (especially based on the "20–80% principle") described so far, we have just announced our concrete 2-step plans as follows:

(A) First Preliminary version of World WTSP Catalog:
Containing sites evaluated as ◎○ only.
Manuscripts due: Jul. 28, 2019; Completion/Posting: Aug. 4, 2019;

(B) Second (and last) Preliminary version of World WTSP Catalog:
Containing sites evaluated as ◎○□.
Manuscripts due: Sept. 15, 2019; Completion/Posting: Sept. 30, 2019

In the current situations of WTSP Teams in many countries, we expect not so high quality in (A), but after people see it they will contribute to make (B) much improved.

After the presentation and discussions at ETRIA TFC2019 and reviewing (B) closely, we should better complete the World WTSP Catalogs:

(C). First Edition of the World WTSP Catalogs (2019):
Containing sites evaluated as ◎○□.
Manuscripts due: Nov. 15, 2019; Completion/Posting: Dec. 10, 2019

5 Concluding Remarks

5.1 Necessity of Collaboration of Human Work

As described so far, the WTSP project has been working to show the visions and their significance, the structure and its building process, prototypes and actual processing, etc. and to convince TRIZ colleagues to work together. It is clear we still needs some more time for getting voluntary contributions by many people.

We would like to mention again the basic points of needing collaboration.

Because of language barriers and necessity of handling a huge amount of information, any person can survey only some limited range of Web sites for durable spending of time and efforts. It is the first responsibility for the site owners and then the people in the same country to introduce their sites. Even they did so, editors and writers of the World WTSP Catalogs can visit, understand, and evaluate only some portions of sites in the Catalogs. Thus, it is very delicate to be fair in selecting, introducing, and evaluating all the sites in the World WTSP Catalogs. Cooperative work by many people in the preparation is of course necessary. Reviews by many people and suggestions/recommendations by them need to be reflected in the revision process. This implies that the quality and usefulness of World WTSP Catalogs can be improved only by keeping update with global cooperation.

For avoiding the hard tasks in surveying, describing, and evaluating many sites, some people suggest to use AI or software robots. But we should realize that the current difficulty of surveying significant sites comes from the poor quality in the Internet surveys. Unfortunately, the current software technology (including AI) can't make introduction of a site with satisfactory quality and can't select good sites in a topic. The flood of messy/noisy outputs of internet surveys shows us we can't use AI at moment. We should better rely on our colleagues' professional ability for describing site introduction and selecting good sites.

Thus it is clear that getting good voluntary members and especially good Country Editors is most crucial for the success of our WTSP Project.

5.2 TRIZ Spirits in the WTSP Project

We believe that our WTSP Project has its basis on the TRIZ Spirits. Namely,

(a) To have a vision, to overcome difficulties one by one, and to achieve the goal.
(b) To divide the tasks appropriately and to divide the systems appropriately as well, in order to build the overall system functioning effectively, and consequently to make the work by all the cooperating people fruitful.
(c) To build the Catalogs of Web sites in the whole world in the areas of TRIZ and related methodologies, to connect the activities, accumulated knowledge, and results by the huge number of people working in such areas, and to form a basis for developing and proliferating such methodologies further in mutually cooperating ways.
(d) To promote the project by relying on the passion of those people in the world who are inspired with TRIZ and holding TRIZ as their important guiding principle.

References

1. Nakagawa, T., Mann, D., Orloff, M., Dewulf, S., Litvin, S., Souchkov, V.: World TRIZ Sites Project (WTSP) for Building and Maintaining Global Catalogs of TRIZ-related Web Sites, Presented at ETRIA TRIZ Future Conference 2018, held on Oct. 29–31, 2018, at Strasbourg, France; posted in THPJ. http://www.osaka-gu.ac.jp/php/nakagawa/TRIZ/eTRIZ/epapers/e2018Papers/eNaka-WTSP-TFC2018/eNaka-WTSP-TFC2018-181108.html. Posted 11 Nov 2018, Accessed 20 Sept 2019
2. Nakagawa, T.: World TRIZ Sites Project: Its Plan and Invitation: Volunteer Project for Connecting TRIZ Sites in the World, THPJ. http://www.osaka-gu.ac.jp/php/nakagawa/TRIZ/eTRIZ/eforum/e2017Forum/eNaka-WorldTRIZSitesProject2017/eNaka-WTSP-Invitation-171207.html. Posted 9 Dec 2017, Accessed 20 Sept 2019
3. Nakagawa, T., Mann, D., Orloff, M., Dewulf, S., Litvin, S., Souchkov, V.: World TRIZ Sites Project (WTSP) for Building and Maintaining Global Catalogs of TRIZ-related Web Sites, Summary slides of ETRIA TFC2018 presentation, Oct. 31, 2018; THPJ. https://www.osaka-gu.ac.jp/php/nakagawa/TRIZ/eTRIZ/epapers/e2018Papers/eNaka-WTSP-TFC2018/eNaka-WTSP-TFC2018-Summary-4P-181023.pdf. Posted 11 Nov 2018, Accessed 20 Sept 2019
4. Nakagawa, T. (ed.) TRIZ Home Page in Japan. https://www.osaka-gu.ac.jp/php/nakagawa/TRIZ/eTRIZ/. Posted 1 Nov 1998, Accessed 20 Sept 2019
5. Nakagawa, T., Mann, D., Orloff, M., Dewulf, S., Litvin, S., Souchkov, V.: WTSP Appeal: An Appeal for Building Catalogs of TRIZ-related Sites in the World, THPJ. http://www.osaka-gu.ac.jp/php/nakagawa/TRIZ/eTRIZ/eWTSP/eWTSP-B2-News2018/eWTSP-News2018-Appeal-180625.html. Posted 25 June 2018, Accessed 20 Sept 2019
6. Nakagawa, T.: Extended 120 TRIZ Links in the World, THPJ. http://www.osaka-gu.ac.jp/php/nakagawa/TRIZ/eTRIZ/elinksref/eWorldLinks.html. Posted 4 May 2008, Accessed 20 Sept 2019
7. Nakagawa, T.: Catalog of TRIZ-related Sites in Japan, THPJ. http://www.osaka-gu.ac.jp/php/nakagawa/TRIZ/eTRIZ/eWTSP/eWTSP-Outputs/eWTSP-D-jp-Japan/eWTSP-D-jp-Japan.html. Posted 24 Apr 2018, Accessed 20 Sept 2019
8. Nakagawa, T.: Starting the preparation of 'A Catalogue of TRIZ-related Sites in the World', (1) Findings through Practices in Japan, (2) For more practical ways of preparation, THPJ. https://www.osaka-gu.ac.jp/php/nakagawa/TRIZ/eTRIZ/eWTSP/eWTSP-B2-News2018/eWTSP-News2018-Trial-Japan1-180127.html. Posted 30 Jan 2018, 7 Feb 2018, Accessed 20 Sept 2019
9. Nakagawa, T.: Preliminary Internet Searches of TRIZ-related Sites in Various (33+) Countries, THPJ. https://www.osaka-gu.ac.jp/php/nakagawa/TRIZ/eTRIZ/eWTSP/eWTSP-B2-News2018/eWTSP-News2018-PreliminarySearch-180919.html. Posted 21 Sept 2018, 27 Sept 2018, Accessed 20 Sept 2019
10. Nakagawa, T.: Preliminary Internet Searches (2) of TRIZ-related Sites in the world, THPJ. https://www.osaka-gu.ac.jp/php/nakagawa/TRIZ/eTRIZ/eWTSP/eWTSP-B3-News2019/eWTSP-News2019-PreliminarySearch-2nd-190328.html. Posted 18 Mar 2018, 31 Mar 2018, Accessed 20 Sept 2019
11. Nakagawa, T.: Preliminary Internet Searches (3) of TRIZ-related Sites in wider scopes in the world, THPJ. https://www.osaka-gu.ac.jp/php/nakagawa/TRIZ/eTRIZ/eWTSP/eWTSP-B3-News2019/eWTSP-News2019-PreliminarySearch-3rd-190516.html. Posted 18 May 2019, Accessed 20 Sept 2019
12. Nakagawa, T.: Proposal of the WTSP Database System for the World TRIZ-related Sites Project (WTSP), THPJ. https://www.osaka-gu.ac.jp/php/nakagawa/TRIZ/eTRIZ/eWTSP/eWTSP-DatabaseSystem/eWTSP-DBSystem-Proposal-190522.html. Posted 24 May 2019, Accessed 20 Sept 2019

13. Nakagawa, T.: Multiple Sets of Indexing Schemes for the WTSP DB System, THPJ. https://www.osaka-gu.ac.jp/php/nakagawa/TRIZ/eTRIZ/eWTSP/eWTSP-DatabaseSystem/eWTSP-DBSystem-IndexSchemes-190522.html. Posted 24 May 2019, Accessed 20 Sept 2019
14. Nakagawa, T.: Practice Guide to Complete the World WTSP Catalogs and to Report It at ETRIA TFC2019, THPJ. https://www.osaka-gu.ac.jp/php/nakagawa/TRIZ/eTRIZ/eWTSP/eWTSP-B3-News2019/eWTSP-News2019-PracticeGuide-Jun2019-190607.html. Posted 14 June 2019, Accessed 20 Sept 2019
15. Nakagawa, T.: World WTSP Catalogs (Japan Part): WTSP Catalog of TRIZ-related Sites in Japan for the people in the whole world, THPJ. https://www.osaka-gu.ac.jp/php/nakagawa/TRIZ/eTRIZ/eWTSP/eWTSP-Outputs/eWTSP-D-jp-Japan/eWTSP-World-D-jp-Japan.html. Posted 14 July 2019, Accessed 20 Sept 2019

World TRIZ Sites Project

Together ! Connected !!

Lower Abstraction Level of TRIZ Inventive Principles Improves Ideation Productivity of Engineering Students

Pavel Livotov(✉), Arun Prasad Chandra Sekaran, and Mas'udah

Offenburg University of Applied Sciences,
Badstr. 24, 77652 Offenburg, Germany
pavel.livotov@hs-offenburg.de

Abstract. The 40 Altshuller Inventive Principles with numerous sub-principles remain over decades the most frequently applied tool of the Theory of Inventive Problem Solving TRIZ for systematic idea generation. However, their application often requires a concentrated, creative and abstract way of thinking that can be fairly challenging for the newcomers to TRIZ. This paper describes an approach to reduce the abstraction level of inventive sub-principles and presents the results of the idea generation experiment conducted with three groups of undergraduate and graduate students from different years of study in mechanical and process engineering. The students were asked to generate and to record their individual ideas for three design problems using a pre-defined set of classical and modified sub-principles within 10 min. The overall outcomes of the experiment support the assumption that the less abstract wording of the modified sub-principles leads to higher number of ideas. The distribution of ideas between the fields of MATCHEM-IBD (Mechanical, Acoustic, Thermal, Chemical, Electrical, Magnetic, Intermolecular, Biological and Data processing) differs significantly between groups using modified and abstract sub-principles.

Keywords: TRIZ Inventive Principles · Engineering creativity · Ideation performance · Automated invention

1 Introduction

The theory of inventive problem solving TRIZ developed by Altshuller and his co-workers [1] is considered as one of the most organized and comprehensive methodologies for invention knowledge and creative thinking [2], as confirmed by the analysis of the top cited scientific publications on innovative design [3]. The engineering educators have gathered considerable experience in different education approaches in the systematic innovation with TRIZ [4]. As engineering curricula are tightly packed with subjects and offer little room to TRIZ, it is necessary to successfully embed the TRIZ tools into existing engineering subjects. Recent experiments indicate that effective idea generation with simple TRIZ heuristics of the eight MATCEM-IB fields (Mechanical, Acoustic, Thermal, Chemical, Electric, Magnetic, Intermolecular and Biological) can be successfully taught in just one or two hours [5]. The fast-to-learn ideation technique based on five cross-industry analogies, corresponding to TRIZ

Published by Springer Nature Switzerland AG 2019
R. Benmoussa et al. (Eds.): TFC 2019, IFIP AICT 572, pp. 526–538, 2019.
https://doi.org/10.1007/978-3-030-32497-1_41

feature transfer, function-oriented search, scaling and biomimetics, significantly improves idea generation outcomes both in the quantity and variety [6]. Among other TRIZ tools, the 40 Inventive Principles are most frequently used in practice. Inventive Principles are simple to modify for a specific technical domain and can be easily integrated in brainstorming. There are also many proposals of examples illustrating the breadth of application of Altschullers' original 40 Inventive Principles [1] in specific engineering domains, such as electronics, chemical engineering, food processing, ergonomics, maintenance, software engineering etc. 40 Inventive Principles have been updated or extended with new sub-principles in the recent years, as shown for example in [7]. One of the latest updates [8] contains 160 sub-principles with nearly 70 additional sub-principles relevant for process engineering.

However, the application of Inventive Principles often requires simultaneously a concentrated, creative and abstract way of thinking that can be challenging for engineering students or newcomers to TRIZ. For example, the abstract term "object" used in sub-principles may be understood as a system, system component, substance, process or process step, or any other material or virtual object. Also, the abstract definition of "action" can be understood as function, positive or negative effect or any interaction between the objects. Therefore, the outcomes of ideation work with the TRIZ Inventive Principles may depend on a certain interpretation of the abstract terms. Thus, the research goal of the presented study is to analyze how the level of abstractness in formulation of inventive sub-principles can influence the ideation productivity and variety.

The sub-principles can be understood as inventive operators for transformation of technical systems or heuristics for idea generation. In this context, some of the inventive operators are more specific and can be clearly assigned to at least one of the MATCHE-IBD fields, where D – is the abbreviature of Data processing or Information field. There is also a group of generally formulated sub-principles, which are independent of any field and hence may have a higher level of abstraction. Thus, the application of field-oriented (specific) sub-principles and of field-independent (general) sub-principles can have different impact on ideation outcomes. The distribution of the 160 sub-principles [8] over the nine MATCEM-IBD fields is presented in Fig. 1.

It can be assumed, that the difficulties in the interpretation of the abstract recommendations in sub-principles can be higher by the application of more abstract field-independent sub-principles. In Fig. 1 the 160 sub-principles are assigned to 11 categories. The category "Independent" includes 36 sub-principles, which don't relate directly to any field or engineering domain, like for example *(1a) Segment object.* The idea generation with these field-independent sub-principles doesn't compulsorily lead to a change of the "field" in the working principle of a technical system. The category "Universal" includes 29 field-universal sub-principles which can be assigned to any of the MATCEM-IBD fields. The remaining 95 sub-principles are distributed with multiple selection between MATCEM-IBD fields.

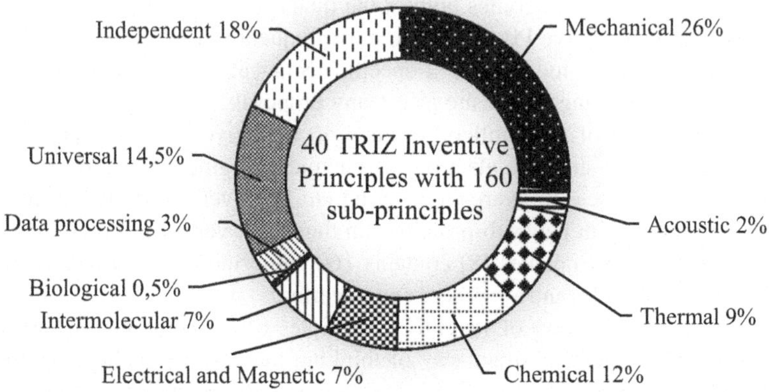

Fig. 1. Distribution of the 160 sub-principles over specific MATCEM-IBD fields, field-universal and field-independent categories.

This paper presents and discusses the results of the experiments that were conducted with the undergraduate and graduate students in mechanical and process engineering in 2019. In total 194 single experiments engaged students from different years of study in order to establish the correlation of a number and the breadth of ideas proposed with applied ideation techniques. The students were asked to generate solution ideas for three pre-defined problems using in total 15 different sub-principles, i.e. with 5 sub-principles for each problem. The original abstract formulation of sub-principles was offered in 97 experiments, whilst other 97 experiments were carried out with the modified "less abstract", version of the sub-principles. In the modified sub-principles, the abstract terms "object", "action" or "function" were replaced with a context-specific name of a real system component, real function or action in order to reduce the level of abstractness as proposed in [9]. The authors wanted to prove the hypothesis, whether the use of modified inventive principles with less abstract wording helps students in generating more ideas with higher breaths in comparison with application of originally formulated TRIZ Inventive Principles.

2 Experimental Methodology

Three groups of students from the Offenburg University participated in the experiments. Forty undergraduate students from the group 1 were in their 4th or 5th semester of the Bachelor of Mechanical or Process Engineering Degree. The group 2 contained 23 students enrolled into the Master Degree in Mechanical Engineering (8th and 9th study semesters). The group 3 consisted of 34 undergraduate students that were in their 4th semester in the Bachelor of Mechanical Engineering Degree. All the groups were involved in the experiments at the beginning of the scheduled tutorial classes and were not get acquainted with the TRIZ Inventive Principles beforehand. Experiment participation was voluntary, and the number of participants deviated slightly from one problem to another, as shown in the Table 1. The groups were supervised by the same tutor.

The groups 1 and 2 participated in idea generation for all three problems within 3 consecutive weeks with one experiment per week. The idea generation forms with the predefined abstract and modified sub-principles were distributed randomly in proportion 50:50. Each student from the groups 1 and 2 has used at least once the idea-generation form with abstract and once with modified sub-principles during the experiments. The 34 students of the group 3 were involved in the experiment dealing with last problem only and had no experience in applying TRIZ Inventive Principles before. This control group 3 should help to estimate a possible influence of previous TRIZ experience of groups 1 and 2 on ideation outcomes.

Three problems selected for the experiments are presented in the Table 2. They represent three typical cases of the initial problem situation which can be defined as *insufficient positive function* (problem 1), *elimination of harmful effect* (problem 2), and *engineering contradiction* (problem 3). All problems were introduced to all groups for 3 min using one Power Point slide as exemplarily shown in Fig. 2. The slides contained the problem statement and a photo or drawing. All students were given 10 min to record as many individual ideas as possible by using recommendations of the five inventive sub-principles, printed on the idea-generation forms. No special explanation of TRIZ Inventive Principles or any introduction how to apply them has been offered to the students. The filled idea-generation forms were evaluated by the authors.

Table 1. Number of students participated in experiments.

Students group	Inventive principles	Number of participants			Total number of experiments
		Problem 1	Problem 2	Problem 3	
1. Undergraduate students	Abstract	18	15	14	47
	Modified	22	16	9	47
2. Graduate students	Abstract	12	11	10	33
	Modified	11	12	10	33
3. Control group (undergraduate students)	Abstract	–	–	17	17
	Modified	–	–	17	17
All groups	Abstract	30	26	41	97
	Modified	33	28	36	97

For each problem the idea generation was supported by five inventive sub-principles corresponding to 7 statistically strongest TRIZ Inventive Principles as shown in the Table 3. All sub-principles pre-defined for idea generation in the problems 1 and 2 can be assigned to the engineering fields MATCEM-IBD, as well as the sub-principle *(15d) Flexible Elements* in the Problem 3. On the contrary, the four selected sub-principles in the problem 3, such as *(1a) Segment object*, *(3c) Different functions*, *(10a) Prior useful function* and *(19a) Periodic action*, are field-independent, i.e. don't relate directly to any field or engineering domain.

Table 2. Problems used in the experiments.

Problem	Description	Initial problem field	Problem type
1. Ship hull cleaning	How to intensify the hull cleaning of big ships from maritime organisms (alga and shell layers) with high-pressure water jetting without paint layer damage?	Biological, Intermolecular, Mechanical	Insufficient positive function
2. Removing lime build-up in pipes	Calcium carbonate, or lime, is a hard deposit found in the inner surface of pipes and other surfaces. How to remove the lime build up in pipes?	Chemical, Intermolecular, Mechanical	Elimination of harmful effect
3. Roadway condition monitoring	A camera (sensor) for detection of roadway condition is placed in a vehicle close to the road surface to detect its properties: dry, wet, dirty, icy etc. How to protect the sensor from getting dirty or damages without impairment of road monitoring?	Electromagnetic (optical), Mechanical, Data processing	Engineering contradiction

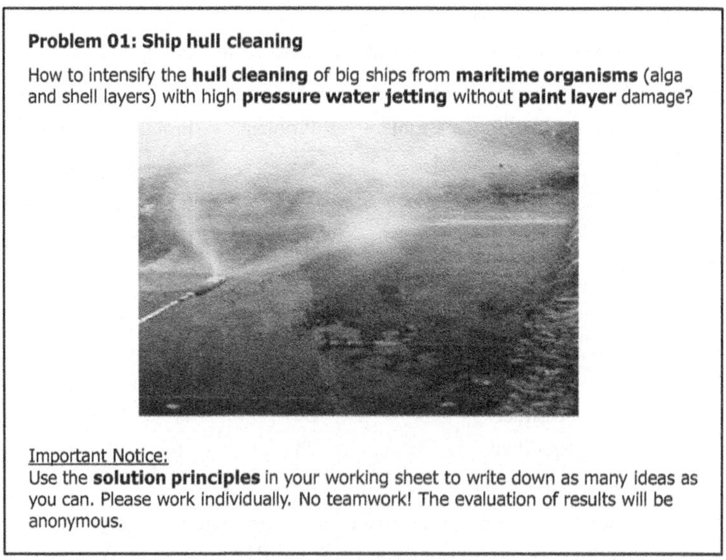

Fig. 2. The Power Point slide of the problem statement 1 presented to the students.

Table 3. TRIZ Inventive Principles and sub-principles used in the experiments.

Problem	Recommended TRIZ Inventive Principles (IP) and sub-principles	Corresponding fields MATCEM-IBD
1. Ship hull cleaning	IP35. Transformation of the physical and chemical properties: sub-principles 35a, 35b, 35c, 35d, 35e	M-T-C-E-M-I
2. Removing lime build-up in pipes	IP28. Replacement of mechanical working principle: sub-principles 28a, 28b, 28e, 28d, 28e	A-T-C-E-M-B
3. Roadway condition monitoring	IP1. Segmentation: sub-principle 1a IP3. Local Quality: sub-principle 3c IP10. Prior useful action: sub-principle 10a IP15. Dynamism: sub-principle 15d IP19. Periodic action: sub-principle 19a	Field-independent Field-independent Field-independent M (mechanical) Field-independent

The examples of the abstract and modified sub-principles in the idea-generation forms are presented in the Table 4. The exact wording of all abstract and modified sub-principles for the problems 1, 2 and 3 is enclosed in the Appendix.

Table 4. Examples of the abstract and modified sub-principles in the idea-generation forms.

Abstract inventive sub-principle	Modified inventive sub-principle
Example of sub-principle 35a applied for problem 1	
(35a) Change an object's aggregate state: e.g. solid to liquid or liquid to gas - or vice versa	(35a) Change the aggregate state of the *water jet* or *maritime organism* e.g. solid to liquid or liquid to gas - or vice versa
Example of sub-principle 28c applied for problem 2	
(28c) Use an acoustic working principle, for example, sound, ultrasonic or infrasonic oscillations, cavitation	(28c) Use an acoustic working principle *to remove lime build up*. For example, sound, ultrasonic or infrasonic oscillations, cavitation
Example of sub-principle 1a applied for problem 3	
(1a) Segment object: divide the objects into independent objects or parts	(1a) Segment object: divide the *sensor* into *independent sensors* or parts

Among the major metrics for objective assessment of ideation effectiveness, such as ideas quantity, variety, and quality [10], the quantity and variety of independent ideas proposed with abstract and modified inventive sub-principles were evaluated in the experiments. The assessment of the ideas quality and novelty was not a part of this study. It was also difficult to judge about the quality of ideas developed by the students as the ideation time of 10 min in total was too short for detailed design or feasibility check.

3 Results and Discussion

3.1 Quantity of Generated Ideas

The quantitative analysis of 902 ideas generated by students in 194 experiments is summarized in the Table 5. It undoubtedly shows that the number of ideas generated with modified sub-principles exceeded the number of ideas generated with abstract sub-principles in all groups and for all problems. On average students proposed 1.53 times more ideas with the less abstract sub-principles (5.63 versus 3.67 ideas per person).

Table 5. Quantity of ideas generated by different students' groups.

Students' group	Inventive principles	Number of ideas/mean number of ideas per person					
		Problem 1	Problem 2	Problem 3	Total number	Total Mean	Total SD
1. Under graduate	Modified	131	89	46	266	5.66	2.06
	Abstract	59	54	62	175	3.72	1.78
2. Graduate	Modified	77	71	49	197	5.97	2.42
	Abstract	52	44	31	127	3.85	1.44
3. Control	Modified	–	–	83	83	4.88	2.81
	Abstract	–	–	54	54	3.18	1.34
All groups	Modified	208	160	178	546	5.63	2.36
	Abstract	111	98	147	356	3.67	1.62

Although, the average number of ideas generated by a graduate student in the group 2 exceeded the number of ideas generated by an undergraduate student in the group 1 (5.97 versus 5.66 for modified sub-principles and 3.85 versus 3.72 for abstract principles), this difference was not statistically significant. Nevertheless, the graduate students were able to describe their ideas more precisely and as a rule on a higher qualitative level.

The gain in ideation productivity by using modified sub-principles can be defined as a quotient of number of ideas generated with modified and abstract sub-principles:

$$g = \frac{N_{mod}}{N_{abst}} \quad (1)$$

where:

N_{mod}: number of ideas per person generated with modified inventive principles

N_{abst}: number of ideas per person generated with abstract inventive principles.

As documented in the Table 5, the gain in ideation productivity remains almost constant over all student groups with $g = 1.52$ (group 1), $g = 1.55$ (group 2) and $g = 1.53$ (group 3). At the same time, Fig. 3 shows uneven ideation performance over the problems, both in number of ideas per person and in gain of ideation productivity with modified inventive sub-principles. Interestingly, that the average number of ideas per person, generated with abstract sub-principles remains almost constant and varies between 3.59 and 3.77 within the range of ±2.4%. Consequently, one cannot explain these results simply with different complexity level of the problems, even if it's thinkable that the problem 3 "Roadway condition monitoring", formulated in form of engineering contradiction, could appear to be more difficult for the students.

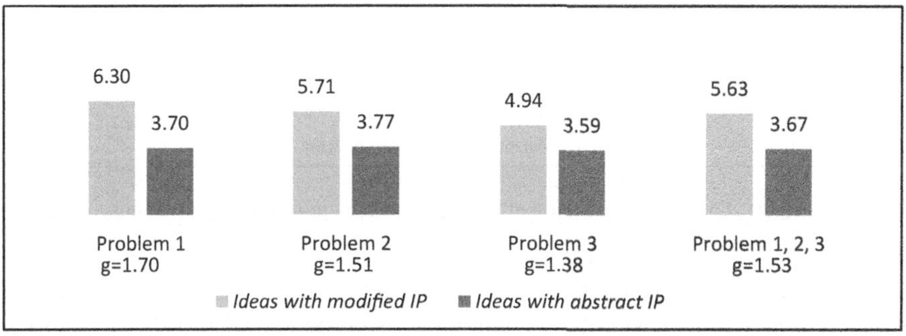

Fig. 3. Ideas generated by students for different problems (ideas per person, mean values).

Another reason for a relative lower number of ideas per person generated with modified inventive principles for the problem 3 could be the fact that 4 from 5 proposed sub-principles (1a, 3c, 10a, 19a; see Table 3) belong to the category of more abstract *field-independent* sub-principles. With the help of these four sub-principles the students proposed on average 0.81 ideas per person with modified wording and 0.54 ideas per person with abstract formulation. The average number of ideas per person generated with other 11 field-oriented sub-principles (35a, 35b, 35c, 35d, 35e, 28a, 28b, 28c, 28d, 28e, 15d) in all experiments was 1.21 for modified and 0.83 for abstract sub-principles respectively.

Moreover, it is worth to note that the application of inventive sub-principles as separate heuristics both in abstract and modified form allowed to reach a higher discipline of idea generation as the directions of thinking were clearly pre-defined by the sub-principles. Thus, from 546 ideas formulated with modified sub-principles only 29 ideas (5.3%) could not be assigned to the recommended sub-principles. From 356 ideas formulated with abstract sub-principles solely 18 ideas (5.1%) are not related to any recommended sub-principle.

The distribution of ideas per person over the number of all experiments is shown in Fig. 4. It illustrates that the application of modified sub-principles increases the number of students with higher personal ideation output. For example, using modified sub-principles the students could generate between 7 and 8 ideas per person in 25 experiments from 97. On the contrary, the students working with the abstract sub-principles proposed 7…8 ideas per person in only 4 experiments from 97.

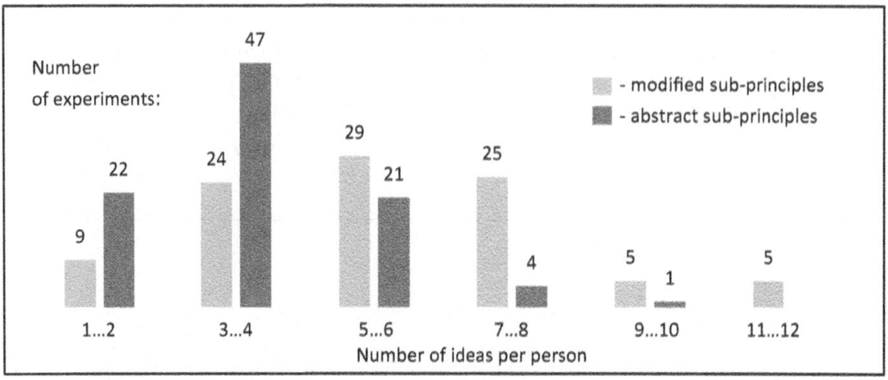

Fig. 4. Distribution of number of ideas per person over all experiments.

Finally, the comparison of the ideation outcomes of all student groups 1, 2 and 3 for the problem 3 "Roadway condition monitoring" is presented in the Table 6. Although the 34 undergraduate students of the control group 3 participated in the idea generation for the problem 3 only, their ideation productivity does not significantly differ from the outcomes of the undergraduate students (group 1) and graduate students (group 2), who have already gained some experience in applying TRIZ Inventive Principles for the problems 1 and 2.

Table 6. Quantity of ideas generated by different students' groups for the problem 3.

Students' group	Inventive sub-principles	Problem 3. Roadway condition monitoring		
		Number of ideas per person	SD	$g = N_{mog}/N_{abst}$
1. Undergraduate	Modified	5.11	1.91	$g = 1.15$
	Abstract	4.43	1.93	
2. Graduate	Modified	4.90	1.92	$g = 1.58$
	Abstract	3.10	1.64	
3. Undergraduate (Control group)	Modified	4.88	2.81	$g = 1.54$
	Abstract	3.18	1.34	

The following are some outcomes of the Mann-Whitney test that was used for the statistical comparison of responses in the experiments. With $Z = -4.38$ and $p < 0.01$ the 47 undergraduate students from the group 1 generated for the problems 1, 2 and 3 on average significantly more ideas with the modified inventive sub-principles than with the classical more abstract sub-principles. With $Z = -3.62$ and $p < 0.01$ the 33 graduate students from the group 2 generated more ideas with the modified sub-principles for all three problems as well. And finally, 17 undergraduate students from the control group 3 proposed for the problem 3 with $Z = -1.98$ and $p < 0.05$ significantly more ideas with the modified sub-principles as well.

3.2 Breadth or Variety of Generated Ideas

In order to assess the variety of the ideas proposed in the experiments, the ideas generated in each group were assigned to the most appropriate knowledge domains or fields, using the MATCEMIBD classification. The distribution of different ideas over the nine MATCEMIBD categories in all groups is illustrated in Fig. 5. The students from all groups proposed significantly broader ideas using the modified inventive sub-principles. Substantial differences of the gain in ideation productivity $g > 1{,}5$ are observed for Acoustic, Thermal, Biological fields and especially for Data processing with $g = 3{,}56$.

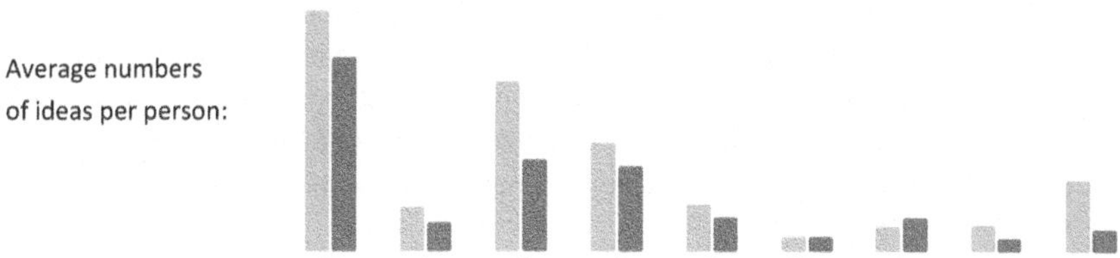

	M	A	T	C	E	Mg	I	B	D
Ideas with modified IP	1.91	0.33	1.34	0.85	0.35	0.09	0.18	0.19	0.55
Ideas with abstract IP	1.54	0.21	0.71	0.66	0.25	0.09	0.25	0.08	0.15
$g = N_{mod}/N_{abst}$	**1,24**	**1,57**	**1,89**	**1,29**	**1,40**	**1,00**	**0,72**	**2,38**	**3,67**

Fig. 5. Variety of different ideas and their distribution over MATCEMIBD categories.

The students from the groups 1, 2 and 3 while using the modified sub-principles, proposed 67% of non-mechanical ideas which can be assigned to the fields ATCE-MIBD. On the contrary, only 58% of ideas generated by all students using the classical abstract sub-principles, can be assigned to these non-mechanical fields.

4 Concluding Remarks

The overall results of the study support the assumption that the less abstract and problem specific formulation of TRIZ Inventive Principles can visibly improve idea generation outcomes of engineering students and newcomers to TRIZ both in the quantity and variety of proposed ideas. In 194 experiments conducted at the Offenburg University the students generated nearly 1.5 more ideas with the modified inventive sub-principles. Also, the breadth of the proposed ideas over the nine MATCEMIBD fields has been essentially enhanced. However, it wasn't found that the differences in the knowledge level of the students from different years of study have a significant effect on their ideation performance with the modified or abstract inventive principles. This statement can be the subject matter of a future research. Based on the outcomes of the study, the authors recommend the proposed approach to be taken into consideration by the educators and practitioners in creativity and innovation with TRIZ methodology. The authors advocate the idea that the adaptation of Inventive Principles for specific tasks will make it considerably easier for newcomers and companies to apply TRIZ in engineering work. Most modifications in inventive sub-principles can be made automatically and the development such algorithms is the subject of the current research.

Appendix

Abstract and modified inventive sub-principles applied in experiments.

N	Abstract sub-principles [8]	Modified sub-principles
Problem 1: Ship hull cleaning		
35a	Change an object's aggregate state: e.g. solid to liquid or liquid to gas - or vice versa	Change the aggregate state of the *water jet* or *maritime organism* e.g. solid to liquid or liquid to gas - or vice versa
35b	Change the object's concentration or consistency	Change the concentration or consistency of the *water jet* or *maritime organisms*
35c	Change the object's physical properties: pressure, density, hardness, viscosity, conductivity, magnetism etc.	Change physical properties of the *water jet* or *maritime organisms* e.g. pressure, density, hardness, viscosity, conductivity, magnetism etc.
35d	Change the object's temperature	Change the temperature of the *water jet* or *maritime organisms*
35e	Change other chemical properties: formulation, pH, solubility etc. Change process chemistry	Change other chemical properties of the *water jet* or *maritime organism* formulation, pH, solubility etc. Change process chemistry

(*continued*)

(*continued*)

N	Abstract sub-principles [8]	Modified sub-principles
Problem 2: Removing lime build-up in pipes		
28a	Replace the mechanical working principle by electric, magnetic, or electromagnetic one. Use electric, magnetic or electromagnetic effect on the object	Replace the mechanical working principle by electric, magnetic or electromagnetic one. Use electric, magnetic or electromagnetic effect on *lime build up or pipe*
28b	Use optical working principle. For example, infrared, ultraviolet light, laser, LED	Use optical working principle to *remove lime build up*. For example, infrared, ultraviolet light, laser, LED
28c	Use an acoustic working principle. For example, sound, ultrasonic or infrasonic oscillations, cavitation	Use an acoustic working principle to *remove lime build up*. For example, sound, ultrasonic or infrasonic oscillations, cavitation
28d	Use thermal effect on the object. For example, heating, cooling, thermal expansion/shrinking	Use thermal effect on *the lime build up or pipe*. For example, heating, cooling, thermal expansion or shrinking
28e	Use chemical or biological working principle. For example, chemical reactions (dissolution synthesis) or bio-organisms (microbes, enzymes)	Use chemical or biological working principle to *remove lime build up*. For example, chemical reactions (dissolution, synthesis) or bio-organisms (microbes, enzymes)
Problem 3: Roadway condition monitoring		
1a	Segment object: divide the objects into independent objects or parts	Segment object: divide the *sensor* into *independent sensors or parts*
3c	Different functions: the various parts of the object should fulfill different functions	Different functions: the various parts of the *sensors* should fulfill *different monitoring functions*
10a	Prior useful function: perform the required action or useful function in advance, either fully or partially	Prior useful function: perform the *road monitoring in advance*, either fully or partially
15d	Flexible elements: use adaptive and flexible elements like joints, springs, elastomers, fluids, gases	Flexible elements: protect the *sensor by using adaptive and flexible elements* like joints, springs, elastomers, fluids, gases
19a	Periodic action: replace a continuous action with a periodic or pulsed one	Periodic action: replace a continuous *road monitoring with a periodic or pulsed one*

References

1. Altshuller, G.S.: Creativity as an Exact Science. The Theory of the Solution of Inventive Problems. Gordon & Breach Science Publishers, London (1984). ISSN 0275-5807

2. Cavallucci, D., Cascini, G., Duflou, J., et al.: TRIZ and knowledge-based innovation in science and industry. Proc. Eng. **131**, 1–2 (2015). https://doi.org/10.1016/j.proeng.2015.12.341
3. Chechurin, L., Borgianni, Y.: Understanding TRIZ through the review of top cited publications. Comput. Ind. **82**, 119–134 (2016). https://doi.org/10.1016/j.compind.2016.06.002
4. Belski, I., Cavallucci, D., Hentschel, C., et al.: Sustainable education in inventive problem solving with TRIZ and knowledge-based innovation at universities. In: Cavallucci, D., de Guio, R., Koziołek, S. (eds.) Automated Invention for Smart Industries. IFIP Advances in Information and Communication Technology, vol. 541, pp. 51–74. Springer, Cham (2018). https://doi.org/10.1007/978-3-030-02456-7
5. Belski, I., Livotov, P., Mayer, O.: Eight fields of MATCEMIB help students to generate more ideas. Proc. CIRP **39**, 85–90 (2016)
6. Livotov, P.: Enhancing innovation and entrepreneurial competences of engineering students through a systematic cross-industry innovation learning course. In: Proceedings of the 29th Annual Conference of the Australasian Association for Engineering Education (AAEE), 9.-12.12.2018, Hamilton, New Zealand (2018)
7. Petrov, V.: Universal Inventive Principles TRIZ: Inventive Principles for All Fields. Kindle Edition, ASIN: B07CRRY99N, 226 p. (2018)
8. Livotov, P., Chandra Sekaran, A.P., Law, R., Mas'udah, Reay, D.: Systematic innovation in process engineering: linking TRIZ and process intensification. In: Chechurin, L., Collan, M. (eds.) Advances in Systematic Creativity, pp. 27–44. Palgrave Macmillan, Cham (2019). https://doi.org/10.1007/978-3-319-78075-7_3
9. TRIZ Trainingsbuch: Systematische Produktentwicklung und erfinderische Problemlösung mit TRIZ Methodik (Selbstlernkurs). TriS Europe Berlin, 88 p. (2012)
10. Shah, J.J., Vargas-Hernandez, N., Smith, S.M.: Metrics for measuring ideation effectiveness. Des. Stud. **24**(2), 111–134 (2003). https://doi.org/10.1016/S0142-694X(02)00034-0

Correction to: Technology Strategy by TRIZ Tools for Eco-Aircare Solution

Gukhyun Cho, Ahreum Lee, Jungin Kim, Wanseok Jeong, and Youshin Han

Correction to: Chapter "Technology Strategy by TRIZ Tools for Eco-Aircare Solution" in: R. Benmoussa et al. (Eds.): *New Opportunities for Innovation Breakthroughs for Developing Countries and Emerging Economies*, IFIP AICT 572, https://doi.org/10.1007/978-3-030-32497-1_28

The original version of this chapter was revised. Equations 1–4 in section 4 were corrected.

The updated version of this chapter can be found at
https://doi.org/10.1007/978-3-030-32497-1_28

Published by Springer Nature Switzerland AG 2019
R. Benmoussa et al. (Eds.): TFC 2019, IFIP AICT 572, p. C1, 2019.
https://doi.org/10.1007/978-3-030-32497-1_42

Author Index

The manufacturer's authorised representative in the EU is Springer Nature Customer Service Centre GmbH, Europaplatz 3, 69115 Heidelberg, Germany. If you have any concerns regarding our products, please contact ProductSafety@springernature.com

Printed and bound by CPI Group (UK) Ltd, Croydon, CR0 4YY
23/07/2026
02175016-0015